Reconsidering the Renaissance

MEDIEVAL & RENAISSANCE
TEXTS & STUDIES

VOLUME 93

Reconsidering the Renaissance

*Papers from the
Twenty-First Annual Conference*

Edited by

MARIO A. DI CESARE

ᗰEᗪIEVAL & ᖇEᑎAISSAᑎCE TEXTS & STᑌᗪIES
Binghamton, New York
1992

© Copyright 1992
Center for Medieval and Early Renaissance Studies
State University of New York at Binghamton

Library of Congress Cataloging-in-Publication Data

State University of New York at Binghamton. Center for Medieval and Early
  Renaissance Studies. Conference (21st : 1987)
    Reconsidering the Renaissance : papers of the Twenty-first Annual
  Conference of the Center for Medieval and Early Renaissance Studies /
  edited by Mario A. Di Cesare.
      p. cm. — (Medieval & Renaissance texts & studies : v. 93)
    Includes index.
    ISBN 0-86698-107-1 (cloth)
    1. Renaissance—Congresses. I. Di Cesare, Mario A. II. Title.
III. Series.
CB361.S68 1987
940.2—dc20   92-17281
                                                                  CIP

This book is made to last.
It is set in Palatino, smythe-sewn
and printed on acid-free paper
to library specifications

Printed in the United States of America

Donatello, *Judith and Holofernes* (bronze), Palazzo Vecchio, Florence.

Table of Contents

List of Illustrations	viii
Acknowledgements	ix
Introduction	xi
D. S. CHAMBERS: Spas in the Italian Renaissance	3
PAUL OSKAR KRISTELLER: Renaissance Humanism and Its Significance	29
JOHN MONFASANI: Platonic Paganism in the Fifteenth Century	45
M. J. B. ALLEN: Summoning Plotinus: Ficino, Smoke, and the Strangled Chickens	63
RAYMOND ADOLPH PRIER: Neapolitan *Imitationes Propertianae*: Ancient Sound in the Verses of Pontano and Chariteo	89
JANE TYLUS: Silencing Partenope: The Origins of Culture in Sannazaro's *Arcadia*	109
LINDA L. CARROLL: Giorgione's *Tempest*: Astrology Is in the Eyes of the Beholder	125
WENDY STEDMAN SHEARD: Giorgione's Portrait Inventions c. 1500: Transfixing the Viewer (With Observations on Some Florentine Antecedents)	141
JAMES V. MIROLLO: "Where'er you walk": My Lady's Beautiful Foot and Generative Footsteps: The Literary Context of Parmigianino's *Madonna del Bel Piede*	177
THOMAS S. FREEMAN: From Catiline to Richard III: The Influence of Classical Historians on Polydore Vergil's *Anglica historia*	191
KENNETH LLOYD-JONES: From Sewers to Triumphal Arches: Dolet's Ideal of Civic Oratory	215
PATRICIA FRANCIS CHOLAKIAN: Signs of the "Feminine": The Unshaping of Narrative in Marguerite de Navarre's *Heptaméron*, Novellas 2, 4, and 10	229
SHEILA FFOLLIOTT: A Queen's Garden of Power: Catherine de' Medici and the Locus of Female Rule	245

DORA E. POLACHEK: Imagination, Idleness and Self-Discovery: Montaigne's Early Voyage Inward — 257
LAWRENCE F. RHU: Young Tasso's Reckoning with the *Orlando furioso* — 271
BARBARA ODABASHIAN: Thomas Wyatt and the Rhetoric of Change — 287
NITA KREVANS: Print and the Tudor Poets — 301
DONALD FRIEDMAN: Bottom, Burbage, and the Birth of Tragedy — 315
DOUGLAS E. GREEN: Shakespeare's Violation: "One face, one voice, one habit, and two persons" — 327
REBECCA BUSHNELL: Tyranny and Effeminacy in Early Modern England — 339
DYMPNA CALLAHAN: Wicked Women in *Macbeth*: A Study of Power, Ideology, and the Production of Motherhood — 355
AMY LECHTER-SIEGEL: Isabella's Silence: The Consolidation of Power in *Measure for Measure* — 371
JYOTSNA SINGH: The Influence of Feminist Criticism / Theory on Shakespeare Studies, 1976–1986 — 381
ALBERT H. TRICOMI: Shakespeare, Chapman, and the Julius Caesar Play in Renaissance Humanist Drama — 395
ROBERT WILTENBURG: Donne's Dialogue of One: The Self and the Soul — 413
DEBORAH RUBIN: "Let your death be my Iliad": Classical Allusion and Latin in George Herbert's *Memoriae Matris Sacrum* — 429
LEE A. JACOBUS: Milton Hero: The Rhetorical Gesture of Monody — 447
R. A. SHOAF: "Our Names are Debts": Messiah's Account of Himself — 461
LARS ENGLE: Milton, Bakhtin, and the Unit of Analysis — 475
RONALD J. CORTHELL: Milton and the Possibilities of Theory — 489
GORDON CAMPBELL: Popular Traditions of God in the Renaissance — 501

Index — 521

Illustrations

Donatello, *Judith and Holofernes* (bronze), Palazzo Vecchio,
    Florence   *Frontispiece*
Map of Italian spas   5
Pliny, *Natural History* (Rome, 1513), fol. clxxx^v 7
Jacopo da Montagnana, Miraculous recovery of Pietro Falco
    (Santuario di Monteortone, Padua)   17
Inscription recording Colleoni's founding of the baths at
    Trescore (Bagni di Trescore, Bergamo)   19
Inscription recording Federico Gonzaga's visit to Caldiero, 1524
    (Bagni di Caldiero, Verona)   21
Illustration to G. A. Panteo, *De thermis Calderianis* (Verona,
    Biblioteca Comunale, MS. 278 [2072])   21
Giorgione, *Tempesta*, Venice, Accademia   132
Giorgione, *Tempesta*, detail of towers   133
Anonymous, *Sign of Leo*, fol. K1r, Johan[n]e Angelis [but Pietro
    d'Abano], *Astrolabum planum* . . . , Venice, 1502   134
School of Niccolò Miretto [?], *Cart* (astrological degree),
    Padua, Palazzo della Ragione   135
Giusto de' Menabuoi [?], *St. Justina*, Padua, Palazzo
    della Ragione   135
Venetian Painter, *Portrait of a Man*, Munich, Alte Pinakothek   144
Giorgione, *Portrait of Girolamo Marcello*, Vienna, Kunst-
    historisches Museum   145
Titian, *Il Bravo*, Vienna, Kunsthistorisches Museum   145
Giorgione, *Self-portrait as David*, Braunschweig, Herzog Anton
    Ulrich-Museum   154
Wenzel Hollar, *Giorgione's Self-portrait as David*, engraving   154
Giorgione, *Self-portrait*, Budapest, Szépmüvészeti Múzeum   155
Andrea Mantegna, *Self-portrait* bust, Mantua, Sant'Andrea   155
Caravaggio, *David with the Head of Goliath*, Rome, Galleria
    Borghese   156

Lorenzo Ghiberti, *Self-portrait*, Florence, Baptistry, Gates of Paradise   162
Leon Battista Alberti, *Self-portrait*, National Gallery of Art, Samuel H. Kress Collection, A–278.1B   162
Andrea del Castagno, *Portrait of a Man*, National Gallery of Art, Andrew W. Mellon Collection, 17   163
Pietro Perugino, *Francesco delle Opere*, Florence, Uffizi   172
Giorgione, *Portrait of a Young Man of the Giustiniani Family*, Berlin, Staatliche Museen Preussischer Kulturbesitz   173
Parmigianino, *Madonna of the Long Neck*, c. 1535. Panel, 7'1" x 4'4". The Uffizi, Florence   179
Antoine Caron, *Les Placets / The Petitions*, c. 1560s, pen and ink and wash, 41 x 56 cm. Paris, Bibliothèque Nationale, Estampes (Réserves) Ad 105, f. 37   250
Detail from John Bunyan, *The Mapp of Salvation* (c. 1664)   506
J. A. Comenius, *Orbis Sensualium Pictus*, trans. Charles Hoole (London, 1659), 6   506

Introduction: Reconsiderations

HERE ARE THIRTY-ONE ESSAYS IN VARIOUS MODES AND ON various subjects important to any discourse of early modern Europe. I use the more familiar term *Renaissance* in my title, at the risk, of course, that the title will raise the question of the very existence of the phenomenon here considered and reconsidered. Was there a Renaissance? In the sense of a period of rebirth, of easy rejection of the past, of a coherent "period" dominated by certain kinds of world-view and ideological consistency, no there certainly wasn't.

Perhaps, in fact, the concept *Renaissance* makes sense only as a concept to be reconsidered. None of our papers quarrels with the basic notion that the term *describes* a phenomenon with certain recognizable features, a definable outline, a generally congruous, even acceptable shape. But an important part of that shape is, in fact, the suppleness of the boundaries, even the assortment of ways in which boundaries recede or dissolve. Thus, Milton — and Milton in modern theoretical terms — has as well-defined a place here as does Shakespeare (who surely escapes all boundaries even as his work defines them) or as does the persistence of classical harmonies and disharmonies. But what of George Herbert? what of Parmigianino? Like Donne, are these species of chronological disruption? The Renaissance is a generously accommodating term, hardly limiting or defining but rather constantly being (and needing to be) redefined, rethought, like the canon of art or literature.

Intending to group these essays into some identifiable order, I resisted the easy temptation to adopt or adapt current forms of ancients-vs.-moderns polarities — e.g., to divide some groups into camps which espouse or exemplify feminism or social history or deconstruction or other recent forms of theory, or philology or new criticism, or traditional approaches to historical analysis. The divisions do of course exist, the polarities incline towards further intensity, as polarization always does, a phenomenon increasingly discernible in recent years, but one which only a few, perhaps of a more radical (fanatical?) turn of mind or spirit, can observe with any kind of complacency.

In organizing the original conference and in creating this book, I adhered to no particular agenda.[1] My sense of the conference originally and of the papers selected (after rigorous review at several levels) for this volume remains the sense I had when I founded the publishing house which defines another part of my professional life — a sense that the ephemeral and the polemical, and particularly the ephemerally polemical, threaten to obscure the perennial values of humanistic study, particularly study of the period which gave birth to certain fundamental notions of the humanities — notions which persist despite attempts to banish them, attempts which are often ill-conceived, sometimes ill-mannered, and always intellectually coercive. But intellectual coercion is not only a property of those, whether committed altruists, flaming radicals, or merely pragmatic self-promoters, who would displace what they regard as the hegemony of the traditional. It persists also in those who, through inertia and complacency, have betrayed their calling and become impervious to any new ideas.

I prefer to see the Renaissance as generously accommodating, and so to call for large and wide-ranging discourse, unhampered by the certainties which comfort some scholars, fixed only in the certainty that scholarship and critical discourse are perennial; that we engage in a noble pursuit when we engage in the search for substance and understanding through sound scholarship; that texts are more substantial than theories divorced from texts; that facts can be reported honestly and without the partisan distortion required by contemporary fancies or careerist ambitions or narrow positivism; and that sound scholarship must eventually prevail even if it is sometimes rudely shoved aside in the name of networking, careerist values, the fun of rhetorical pyrotechnics, or the exigencies of political apocalypticism.

Relevant to the making both of the conference and of this book are some phrases and clauses from the charter of our journal, *Exemplaria: A Journal of Theory in Medieval and Renaissance Studies*. The principle which the editors made theirs — and which, as publisher, I unreservedly endorsed and supported when *Exemplaria* was founded[2] — is a principle of intellectual generosity. We are opposed to the "frequent tendency

---

[1] No doubt this is to say, in the terms some of my colleagues might prefer, that I subscribe to a conservative ideology. Might it be more charitably and accurately called conservationist?

[2] The brain child of one of the authors in this volume, who began planning it in 1987, as *A Journal of Theory in Medieval and Renaissance Studies*; publication began in 1989.

to premature closure in favor of some familiar terminology." Our aim is to provide a forum where diverse methods, diverse terminologies, diverse approaches are welcomed and given the freedom to "communicate without sacrificing any of their distinctiveness," without invading in any way the "multiple, often random, voices of modern ... Renaissance scholars."

This book aims to be a multi-voiced conversation by responsible scholars, whose views and academic work span most of the intellectual and critical spectrum. To allow those voices their distinctive timbre, the organization of the volume is generally chronological. Dates remain pretty well in the realm of acceptable fact. Virtually every sort of concept, theory, category, or approach has become subject to some kind of radical skepticism or been declared indeterminable, but we generally agree that, whatever the Renaissance may have been, it "happened" during various periods (subject to geographical location) between the middle of the fourteenth century in Italy (not coincidentally the middle of Petrarch's life) and the latter part of the seventeenth century in England. The latter English experience and its claim to a place in Renaissance seems very late; so much has already happened in Italy, France, the Iberian peninsula, as well as in other parts of northern Europe. The early modern era had modulated into the modern world a half-century before, when Galileo sighted troubling wonders in the lens of his telescope. But while fully aware of all this, Milton remained, towering as always, an unrelenting rebel against the tradition which he inherited, absorbed, and finally vanquished. Milton ends decisively an era, one which had its distinctive ways of seeing the ancient world and its glories, ways nurtured by the Italian quattrocento and cinquecento and not defeated by the Protestant Reformation.

The first papers address wide areas of the first two centuries, the early and high Italian Renaissance, studying subjects new and old, beginning with David Chambers' discussion and documentation of Italian spas in a social-historical context and Paul Kristeller's discussion of the overarching feature of traditional history of ideas, Italian Humanism. These are followed by papers on early Italian philosophy, culture, literature, and art; only when we are well into the sixteenth century does the venue shift, first briefly to England in the too-little-known figure of Polydore Vergil and then for a time to France. Like Milton, however, Tasso prolongs the Renaissance in Italy in his own way, reckoning (in Lawrence Rhu's term) with the *Orlando furioso*. Beginning slow and late, English concerns — rhetoric, poetry, print — move swiftly to Shakespeare and an exciting group of papers on acting, power, feminism, gender, and ideology. Following the papers on Donne, Herbert, and Milton, the final paper in the volume, Gordon Campbell's skeptical inquiry into popular notions of the concept of deity, ranges as widely as do the first papers, though its main concern is with specifically English creative artists of the seventeenth century, Milton and John Bunyan, the latter as a post-Renaissance figure articulating popular views which had persisted for many decades. It is a fitting close to a series of successive approximations of *reconsidering*.

Acknowledgements

A lot of people helped make this book. I want to acknowledge here the generous help and counsel of many colleagues (leaving unspecified those who shared the trials of decision), both in preparing for the conference itself and then, later, sorting out and reading and discussing the many papers from which these were finally selected. Many friends and colleagues advised in one way or another: Charles Burroughs, Gayle Whittier, Arthur Kinney, Richard Trexler, Norman Burns, Paul Szarmach, William Kennedy, Diane McColley, Albert Ascoli, Albert Rabil, Alvin Vos. I want particularly to recognize the MRTS staffers who exercised such scrupulous care in making this book — Judith Sumner, Michael Pavese, Lee Hoskins, Lori Vandermark, Stefaan Heyvaert, Karen Guest, Kristen Lippert, Laurie Litchford, Michael Horan, Lisa Lovell, and Jennifer Glennon. They manifested yet again their usual sense of urgency and responsibility.

MDC

The frontispiece — Donatello's bronze *Judith and Holofernes* — forces anyone who looks at it with care to reconsider. It is as splendid and surprising a piece of sculpture as were, for me, other of Donatello's works, particularly the Magdalene, which I first saw after the flood of 1966 stimulated its restoration, and the *Lo Zuccone*, that inexorable angry prophet, allegedly Habakkuk.

Reconsidering
the Renaissance

D. S. CHAMBERS

Spas in the Italian Renaissance

TAKING THE WATERS WAS NOT ONE OF THE MOST VOLUPTUOUS OR intellectually charged features of the Renaissance. From Jakob Burckhardt onwards, cultural historians have generally overlooked the subject. Nevertheless, in the northern half of Italy, hot springs and mineral waters were among those common elements of civilization which transcended political division, like Roman remains, language, religion, civil law, and good wines. Since the thirteenth century, spas developed as profitable and fashionable institutions, combining elements of antique tradition with clinical observation, providing a setting for relaxed human contact and a subject for medical literature, even, to a limited extent, for other forms of literature and art.

Therapeutic baths were not, of course, confined in Europe to northern Italy. There were many, some also with a Roman past, beyond the Alps. Montaigne, whose travel diary of 1580–1581 is informative about his experiences in numerous spas,[1] including those in Italy, found none so diverting as Plombières in Lorraine, with its mixed bathing, singing, and music (notwithstanding severe rules against sexual license); none so comfortably equipped, with even a reading room set out with little tables, as Baden, near Schaffhausen, the spa which in 1416 the Florentine humanist Poggio Bracciolini had also found a haven of innocent sensual delights.[2] Nor, in talking of Italy, should one forget that the most celebrated of all its spas was in the south, at the ancient site of Pozzuoli near Naples.[3] The volcanic baths of Pozzuoli—with about

---

[1] Montaigne, *Journal de Voyage en Italie par la Suisse et l'Allemagne en 1580 et 1581*, ed. M. Rat (Paris, 1955), passim. For Plombières and Baden see 7–11, 20–25.

[2] Poggio Bracciolini to Niccolò Niccoli, 18 May 1416, translated in P.W.G. Gordan, *Two Renaissance Book Hunters*. Records of Civilization. Sources and Studies, 91 (New York: Columbia Univ. Press, 1974), 24–31.

[3] See C. M. Kauffmann, *The Baths of Pozzuoli. A Study of the Medieval Illuminations of Peter of Eboli's Poem* (Oxford, 1959). Since this paper was written there have been two important contributions in English: Victoria Boyarsky, "Medicinal Baths and

thirty-five different springs—had perhaps never been wholly abandoned and were in full working order by the late twelfth century; the verse description of them by Peter of Eboli, probably dedicated to the Hohenstaufen Emperor Frederick II, long continued to spread their fame. Even after the earthquake of 1538, usually taken to date their demise, the baths of Pozzuoli were still visited; that Italianate Englishman, Thomas Hoby, for instance, mentions them in 1550.[4]

The northern half of Italy, however, where the associations of the word "Renaissance" are most resonant, will have to suffice for this paper.[5] The map [fig. 1] gives an idea of the large number of places involved; the biggest clusters of baths being—by coincidence—in just those areas most related to Renaissance learning; in Tuscany, indeed all along the main routes to Rome from the north, and in the vicinity of Padua and Verona. Only a few were relatively more isolated, such as Acqui in Piedmont, Bagno di Romagna high in the Appenines, or the most distant (and probably least visited) of all, Bormio, at the far end of the Valtellina in the Alps.[6] Most of the places shown on the map will be mentioned below. Rather than travel around it, I shall try to synthesize the subject under a number of general headings: the scientific basis in literature and clinical procedure; the popular element of hydrotherapeutics, including religious faith in miraculous cures; promotional and patronal aspects of spa management; and finally, some reflections on the wider cultural functions of the baths.

There is no doubt that the great revival of ancient medical science in the schools of Padua and Bologna in the thirteenth century had much to do with the concurrent revival of hydrotherapy. But as well as scattered precepts of ancient Greek and Arabic physicians (newly available in

---

Bathing in the Renaissance with special reference to Tuscany" (M. Phil. dissertation, Warburg Institute, Univ. of London, 1989); Richard Palmer, " 'In this our lightye and learned tyme,' Italian baths at the end of the Renaissance," in *The Medical History of Waters and Spas*, ed. Roy Porter, *Medical History* supplement 10 (London: Wellcome Institute, 1990), 14–22.

[4] *The Travels and Life of Sir Thomas Hoby . . . Written by Himself*, ed. E. Powell. Camden Miscellany 10 (London, 1902), 31.

[5] There is no comprehensive modern work on the Italian spas, but particularly useful are the *Atti* of the *Primo Congresso Europeo di Storia della Medicina*, Montecatini, 1962, hereafter *Congresso* (Montecatini, 1962); and of the *Primo Congresso Italiano di Studi Storici Termali*, Salsomaggiore, 1963, hereafter *Congresso* (Salsomaggiore, 1963); among the best monographs on particular spas is Coturri, cited below n. 19.

[6] On Bormio and a cancelled visit there by the duke of Milan, see C. Canetta, "I Bagni di Bormio," *Archivio storico lombardo* 9 (1882): 722–26; E. Motta, "Francesco Sforza ed i bagni di Bormio," *Archivio storico lombardo* 8 (1881): 651–67; idem, "Francesco Sforza non fu ai Bagni di Bormio in 1462," *Archivio storico lombardo* 13 (1886): 673–75.

Fig. 1
ITALIAN SPAS

Latin), various passages in the elder Pliny's *Natural History*—that famous and never lost work of the first century AD—discuss the medicinal properties of waters,[7] and some of the springs of which Pliny wrote could still be located. Though the *Natural History* was not a text taught in universities, its wide diffusion[8] probably had something to do with the vogue for medical baths among the literate elite of Italy: even a pictorial representation of therapeutic bathing is found in one late manuscript.[9] The first printed version came out in 1469 and many followed, including an Italian translation; the edition printed by Melchior Sessa in Rome in 1513 has woodcut illustrations, including (fol. clxxx v) a depiction of water drinking as well as bathing [fig. 2]. What with Pliny's evaluations, lines written in praise of spring waters by other Roman authors, particularly the poets Horace, Martial, and Claudian, and descriptions by the younger Pliny, those blessed with some learning but not with good health could feel they were following the right tradition by resorting to the waters.

Meanwhile, the medical literature was also growing in the fourteenth century. It consisted of comparative assessments of different waters and their mineral properties (depending in part on the discussion of minerals in the great compendium attributed to Albertus Magnus) or learned opinions about particular procedures to be followed in treatment. The principal early authors in this field were Gentile da Foligno, who taught medicine in Bologna, Padua, and Perugia (where he died in 1348), and Ugolino da Montecatini, who taught in Pisa, Florence, and Perugia (he died in 1429).[10] How widely these early treatises circulated is hard to estimate, but their continuing weight of authority is shown by the fact that Gentile's work was printed in Venice in 1503, a century and a half after he had written it; and Ugolino's, although not printed until 1553, had been rewritten in classical Latin by Pier Candido Decembrio for presentation to Borso d'Este of Ferrara.[11] They had been joined, if not

---

[7] Loeb ed., trans. W. H. S. Jones (Cambridge: Harvard Univ. Press, 1975), bk. 31, ii–xvii, xxxii.

[8] See G. C. Nauert Jr., "Humanists, Scientists and Pliny. Changing Approaches to a Classical Author," *American Historical Review* 84 (1979): 72–85.

[9] Biblioteca Nazionale, Turin, MS. 1.1.22–23, copied for Marquis Ludovico Gonzaga in the 1460s, illuminated later by Pietro Guindaleri, badly damaged by fire in 1904. See U. Meroni, *Mostra dei Codici Gonzagheschi* (Mantua, 1966), 27, 56–58, 67, 80–81; tav. 105–8. Cf. in general, Lilian Armstrong, "The Illustration of Pliny's *Historia naturalis* in Venetian Manuscripts and Early Printed Books," in *Manuscripts in the Fifty Years after the Invention of Printing*, ed. J. B. Trapp (London: Warburg Institute, 1983), 97–107.

[10] Ugolino da Montecatini, *Tractatus de balneis*, ed. M. G. Nardi (Florence, 1950) includes Latin text and Italian translation. References below are to the latter.

[11] The 1553 *De balneis* (see below), 47r–57v, gives Decembrio's text, including his

Fig. 2. Pliny, *Natural History* (Rome, 1513), fol. clxxx^v

superseded, in 1440 by the even more comprehensive book on the baths (not only Italian) by Michele Savonarola, professor of medicine at Padua and Ferrara, where he was also the principal court physician. Savonarola's treatise was in print by 1485; over the next century the literature continued to grow, and in 1553 much of it (including, as the first item, Savonarola's treatise) was incorporated into the volume entitled *De balneis* printed with woodcut illustrations by the Giunta press in Venice.[12] This anthology did not stop the flow—indeed it probably stimulated more—partly because much of its content was out of date. Medical opinion could change, and, either for this or other reasons, some baths declined in fame while others continued to flourish. For instance, the Sienese spa of Petriolo, so celebrated in the fifteenth century, was virtually abandoned in the sixteenth; the baths of Lucca (Corsena and

---

preface addressed to Borso. No manuscript of this version appears to have survived.

[12] See the essays by U. Stefanutti, "Un capolavoro dell'idrologia medica e della balneoterapia: la collezione *De balneis*...," in *Congresso* (Montecatini, 1962), 457–66; G. Bellagarda, "Il trattato cinquecentesco *De balneis*," in *Congresso* (Salsomaggiore, 1963), 92–102.

Villa), however, became ever more fashionable. The medical literature went on incessantly; among the most authoritative books published was the *De thermis* of Andrea Bacci, printed in Venice in 1571.

Essentially, the medical treatises are very similar, though there were differences of opinion or prejudice between one expert and another, supposedly based on their clinical observations. There were differing views, for example, about the waters of Porretta, a spa conveniently situated on one of the main routes from Bologna to Tuscany. Tura di Castello had pronounced his opinion in *circa* 1350 (printed at Padua as early as 1473) that to drink Porretta water every day for three years would ensure a life without anxiety. Ugolino of Montecatini thought otherwise; it could cause cramps and pain, although he conceded it was good for gastric disorders and was beneficial to horses.[13] Porretta water remained fashionable, but its sometimes drastic side-effects continued to be noted as a warning, or even turned to advantage, as in the recommendation that it would provoke vomiting.[14] Medical opinion often insisted upon caution; thus Ugolino both praised the waters at Ascoli and criticized them for causing harm to the eyes.[15]

Ugolino da Montecatini and Michele Savonarola pioneered for fifteenth-century invalids and hypochondriacs a sort of topography of the waters, relating them to most ailments short of plague and other infectious diseases. Thus Ugolino particularly recommended various waters of Viterbo for the digestion, muscular pains, and irregular menstruation; Petriolo was also good for arthritic disorders, though Ugolino confessed to not having firsthand experience of the Sienese baths and to relying on what Gentile da Foligno had written. Of the Lucchese baths, Corsena was good for nervous and rheumatic complaints; Villa he considered

---

[13] Ugolino, ed. Nardi, 116; cf. Savonarola (1553 edn.), 20v–21v. A serious inquiry was made from Mantua about these equine benefits; "Nicholaus Paduanus camerarius" wrote to Barbara of Brandenburg from Porretta, 16 July 1461: "per la commissione havuta da la Illustrissima Signoria Vostra che intendesse se l'aqua de' questi bagni fosse apropriata a cavalli bolsi, gli notifico come da l'hoste dove son allozato, chi è homo del paese, me ha dechiarato che dicta aqua è molto apropriata a simeli cavalli, e che bisognaria la bevesse per spacio de uno mese, et che per quello tempo manzasse paglia in loco de feno" (Archivio di Stato, Mantua, Archivio Gonzaga b. 1141 c. 91—hereafter ASMn AG).

[14] Giovanni Arrivabene to Marquis Ludovico Gonzaga, Rome, 13 November 1475, reported that Cardinal Francesco Gonzaga "dice havere trovato giovarli molto per la provocatione del vomito" (ASMn AG b. 845 c. 416). Further professional pronouncements about Porretta water were made by the Sienese doctor Ugo Benzi (printed five times, 1482–1523, and included in the 1553 collection): see L. Lockwood, *Ugo Benzi* (Chicago, 1951), 336–37; and by the papal physician "Maestro Baverio": see A. Nitto, "Le terme di Porretta e l'uso terapeutico di esse nel 'Consilia' di Baverio Bonetti," in *Congresso* (Montecatini, 1962), 318–29.

[15] Ugolino, ed. Nardi, 65.

better for digestive troubles. Of the Paduan baths, Abano was specially advised for gout and muscular pains, or indeed any malady arising from an excess of moist humor. Among other qualities of the waters of Corsena and of Caldiero (near Verona) was the cure of sterility. For this condition, Ugolino also praised a cold spring at the Pisan baths of San Giuliano, to which he had sent his own wife with success; a success which he confessed he did not quite understand, but suggested that the intensely cold water had invigorated the natural heat of the body to expel overmoist humor from the uterus.[16] Maybe Ugolino was invoking science as a cover; spa cures for infertility were a longstanding source of jokes among the laity, and Montaigne in 1581 recorded a saying at Lucca which can be roughly translated as "Who wants a son, leaves his wife at the baths, where she'll have fun."[17] Readers of Machiavelli's play *Mandragola* will remember that the original scheme for cuckolding Messer Nicia was to persuade him to send his wife to a spa, though this had to be abandoned for various reasons, including his confusion by the doctors' differing advice as to which baths were more suitable.[18] Indeed, no spa confined its claims to curing only one complaint; most had a number of springs to which different cures were attributed. The major locations, in the vicinities of Padua, Viterbo, and Lucca, boasted such wide benefits that they sound almost like polyclinics. The manager of the Corsena baths near Lucca, Domenico Bertini, erected in 1471 an inscription which makes the nearby baths of Villa sound an even better choice (disregarding medical opinion, which had reservations about the water's coldness).[19]

Treatment procedures were meticulously prescribed by the medical writers, and professional supervision was declared essential. No doubt some patients were exploited by this, not only by the doctors, but by the apothecaries too, in cases where it was thought necessary to supplement water with pharmaceutical concoctions.[20] Among the main rules laid down were those concerning time. Spring and early or late summer

---

[16] Ugolino, ed. Nardi, 29, 43–44.

[17] "Chi vuol che la sua donna impregni, Mandila al bagno e non ci vegni": *Voyage en Italie,* 179.

[18] Machiavelli, *Mandragola,* ed. F. Gaeta, *Il teatro e gli scritti letterari* (Milan, 1965), 64: [Nicia] "io parlai iersera a parecchi medici. L'uno dice che io vadia a San Filippo, l'altro alla Porretta, l'altro alla Villa; e' mi parvono parecchi uccellacci, e a dirti il vero questi dottori di medicina non sanno quello che si pescono"; cf. also 67, 71.

[19] E. Coturri, "Le acque dei Bagni di Lucca negli scritti pseudomedici e medici fino ai primi del '600," *Minerva Medica* 40 (1958): 739. Bertini, formerly a papal functionary (see *Dizionario Biografico degli Italiani*) had been made commissary of the baths in 1469.

[20] It was pointed out to Montaigne at the bath of Villa that apothecaries were the main inhabitants there; *Journal de Voyage,* 212.

were the usual seasons most recommended, though some baths, such as Petriolo, were visitable as late as November or December. After sunrise and early evening were the appropriate times to bathe or drink. About appropriate times, however, another professional group, the astrologers, might also be asked for an opinion. Ludovico Gonzaga's court astrologer, consulted in July 1477 about when he should go to Corsena, said that he could not change his advice in view of the nature of the illness, but he could provide a choice of good or bad days and times of day.[21]

As for the treatments, beyond immersion of the whole body in straightforward bathing, copious drinking of waters, intended to purge ill-assorted humors, was the most common process. Nine glasses or beakerfuls, weighed in pounds, was a quite common daily dose, though enthusiastic patients sometimes exceeded it. At Caldiero in July 1524, Federico II Gonzaga, whose dose was nine, on one day drank eleven, vomited the equivalent of more than three, and then took another four to make up the loss.[22] Drinking could also be done away from the springs; although it was held that the waters' properties diminished if not fresh,[23] quantities were transported great distances. Cardinal Gonzaga had Porretta water sent to Bologna, to be drunk within the space of fifteen days;[24] Bianca Maria Sforza had it sent to Milan in 1461,[25] and Lorenzo de' Medici was drinking it in Florence for his stomach trouble in 1485.[26] The poet Ariosto was ordered to bring water from the Villa spring all the way from Lucca to Ferrara for Duke Alfonso d'Este in 1525.[27] Another treatment was the douche, which, according

---

[21] Protonotary Ludovico Gonzaga to Marquis Ludovico Gonzaga, Mantua, 1 August 1477: "Ho parlato al astrologo de Vostra Illustrissima Signoria per haver altro ponto de l'andata sua a li bagni, secundo Quella me commise. Me ha risposto, per la infirmità in che hè, non esser possibile iterum dar altro ponto; ma che de la nota ha datto a Vostra Illustrissima Signoria de li dì e hore (cioè quali boni e quali cativi) Quella po ellezere il meglio" (ASMn AG b. 2418).

[22] Stazio Gadio to Isabella d'Este, Caldiero, 26 July 1524, cited by D. S. Chambers, "Federico Gonzaga ai Bagni di Caldiero," *Civiltà Mantovana* n.s. 4 (1984): 49.

[23] E.g., Giovantonio Zaita to Barbara of Brandenburg, Abano, 23 May 1475, advising her against drinking Abano water at home: "me dubito che, dovendose portare ditta aqua a Mantua o de novo scaldarse al foco, se resolverebe tanto de sua virtù che, ritrovando le vene vostre strette et opilate, non ve rimanesse una gran parte de ditta aqua longo tempo nel corpo" (ASMn AG b. 1591).

[24] Antonio Donato to Marquis Ludovico Gonzaga, Bologna, 3 August 1472 (ASMn AG b. 2413 c. 764).

[25] Motta (1886), as above n. 6, 67.

[26] G. P. Arrivabene to Marquis Francesco Gonzaga, Florence, 3 March 1485 (ASMn AG b. 1102), quoted in D. S. Chambers, "Giovan Pietro Arrivabene (1439–1504), Humanistic Secretary and Bishop," *Aevum* 58 (1984): 428 n. 167.

[27] Coturri, as above n. 19, 735, n. 6. Montaigne notes that water from one of the Lucchese springs was transported in barrels to Reggio Emilia; *Journal de Voyage*, 163.

to Montaigne, was peculiar to Italy.[28] This was administered through pipes, under which the patient had to sit for a prescribed period, so that the hot jet or trickle would strike the appropriate part of the body, usually the head or shoulders. Ugolino wrote that at Petriolo the jet was directed onto the bare head, first at the front and then the back;[29] a device like a wooden helmet with holes might be fitted over the head, or else a sort of cape upon the shoulders.[30] At the Corsena bath the practice was similar, though Ugolino considered that the water of one of the springs there was too cold for the head and needed to be artificially heated.[31] The douche must have been unpleasant; Federico Gonzaga had only a daily half-hour of it prescribed at Abano in August 1524, but complained that the period seemed a thousand times longer.[32] Another method of treatment used steam, either by means of the hot steam bath and inhalation, or by special, localized methods, as, for instance, the curious pipe entering the ears devised for Ludovico Gonzaga by his doctor at Acqui in 1458.[33] Finally, there was the hot mud treatment, particularly esteemed at Acqui and at the Paduan baths. According to letters describing the visits of two Gonzaga daughters to one of the latter—the baths of Sant' Elena—in May 1475, structures formed by wooden beams were prepared containing the mud, and the patient lay or placed within them the afflicted parts. Paola Gonzaga, whose morale remained high despite the experience, was encased from the waist upwards for an hour twice daily; her sister Cecilia shared the same mud bath for her feet and had another small one for her arms.[34]

---

[28] *Essais*, vol. 2, chap. 37, ed. A. Thibaudet (Bruges, 1950), 871.
[29] Ugolino, ed. Nardi, 51.
[30] G. V. Pesciolini, "I Bagni senesi di Petriolo nel Medioevo," *La Diana* 6 (1931): 120.
[31] Ugolino, ed. Nardi, 40.
[32] Stazio Gadio to Isabella d'Este, Abano, 11 August 1524, quoted in Chambers, as above n. 22, 53.
[33] Arrivabene Benedusio to Barbara of Brandenburg, Acqui, 8 September 1458: "ho li concegnato a una stufa stasera che è li a lo usso. Li ho fato uno buso, dove ho fato meter uno cano, e luy tole el vapore caldo, che insi a tute due le orechie per una meza hora, che dice la Sua Excellentia farli uno singular zovamento" (ASMn AG b. 745).
[34] Giovanni Santi to Barbara of Brandenburg, Sant' Elena, 9 May 1475: "Questa mattina cominciò la Illustre Madona Paula a tore el fango in una mesa de asse, dove stagando comodissimamente cum la scena tutta nel fango per spatio de una hora, el tolse benissimamente, senza uno affanno al mondo, et el simile ha fatto questa sera cercha le xxii hore." Stefanino Guidotti wrote more specifically (probably the same day: the letter is damaged): "La Illustre Madonna Paula era acolegata dal mezo in su in una di quelle casse dal fango e in quella medesima dal'altro capo era la Illustre Madonna Cecilia cum li piedi e in un'altra picola cum li brazi dentro . . . se sentano bene e gaiarde"; Paola herself on 10 May assured her mother of her obedience "di

Mud, like water, was sometimes transported for home treatment; Duke Ercole d'Este of Ferrara required both to be sent from Abano.[35]

Patients might be prescribed a combination of all the treatments, preceded by a purgative and blood-letting. Surviving letters of the Gonzagas and their doctors continue to be instructive, for theirs was one of the most disease-prone and spa-frequenting of prominent Italian families. Tainted with a disease inherited from his Malatesta mother, Ludovico Gonzaga tried almost everywhere in turn, often taking some of his sons with him. In September 1458, his course of therapy at Acqui, already mentioned, began with a half-hour of the hot bath in the morning, with application of the douche to his shoulder; after he had dressed he had the steam treatment in his ears and another half-hour with his head beneath the douche; in the evening he had a mud bath.[36] Not content with this, he once insisted on extending the sessions under the douche until, his doctor reported, his face took on a strange appearance.[37] Ludovico Gonzaga was generally very obedient to his doctors' orders and invariably optimistic. At Corsena in 1464, on a prescription of nine and a half beakers of water daily, he reported a great easing of the pain to his feet and back, and declared that he felt twenty-five years old again.[38]

Not all patients, however, were so sure of the benefits. Ludovico's crippled brother Alessandro Gonzaga was at Petriolo in May 1461. Each morning, he wrote, he entered the bath, and in the evening he stood

---

tuore alegramente questi bagni." Stefanino wrote on 12 May that Paola was having the mud treatment both morning and evening, but Cecilia "lasando il fango piglia la stufa" (ASMn AG b. 1591).

[35] Ercole d'Este to Eleonora d'Aragona, Reggio, 27 June 1493, in L. Chiappini, *Eleonora d'Aragona, prima Duchessa di Ferrara* (Rovigo, 1956), 88.

[36] Bartolomeo Bonatto to Barbara of Brandenburg, Acqui, 3 September 1458. (ASMn AG b. 745; cf. L. Gualino, "Le terme acquesi all'epoca del Rinascimento Italiano," *Minerva Medica* 23 (1932): 800–801, where Ludovico's visit is described). For a visit to Acqui by Alessandro Gonzaga, accompanied by Vittorino da Feltre, in 1441, see D.S. Chambers, "An unknown letter by Vittorino da Feltre," *Journal of the Warburg and Courtauld Institutes* 52 (1989): 219–21.

[37] Arrivabene Benedusio to Barbara of Brandenburg, Acqui, 4 September 1458: "sabbato matina che tolse el bagno tanto caldo li fece recressimento, in tanto che haveva uno stranio volto" (ibid).

[38] Bartolomeo Bonatto to Barbara of Brandenburg, Corsena, 10 September 1464: "ogni hora più se loda de questo bagno et pone magiore speranza portarne gran fructo di pedi. Dice sentirsene bene come facea de xxv anni per le fine. Heri bevi nove tace e meza d'aqua de bagno" (ASMn AG b. 1100 c. 215). Cf. the reports of Giovanni Suardi, 10 September 1464, "molto gli giova a li piedi e la schena, e solicita etiam la dozza a la testa" (c. 224), and of the doctor Giovanni da Grignano (ibid cc. 206–9).

beneath the hot douche for a half-hour.[39] After a week or two he developed a cold on the chest. Strange to say, this was taken as a good sign, meaning that the bad humor had left his head and descended to the chest, from where it could be expelled more easily.[40] But when he left Petriolo, Alessandro complained of great lassitude, made worse by the summer heat and the purgative he had taken for his stomach.[41] Another rather unsuccessful case history was that of Margaret of Bavaria, the young wife of Ludovico's eldest son, Federico Gonzaga. In July 1467 she had been packed off to Porretta with an eminent doctor in attendance. He prescribed an hour in the bath twice daily on every third day, with two beakerfuls of water to drink on the bath days, and six on the other days.[42] She followed this for some time, but complained of exhaustion and heaviness in the head, and another doctor who took over the case recommended that she go to Petriolo instead.[43] Once there, Margaret had to submit to two-hourly sessions of the warm douche every day for another three weeks, not to mention bathing and drinking. By early October, her new doctor could report that at least she was no longer suffering from headache, but he could hardly claim a complete cure. Perhaps she was one of those patients who felt better only after leaving, as Roberto Sanseverino hoped to do, having expressed the view that neither the waters of Porretta nor those of Vignoni had helped him much.[44]

Doctors certainly warned that there were risks of fevers or even more serious side-effects, hence they insisted on keeping strictly to the rules. Vigorous exercise, sexual activity, and eating of red meat or food

---

[39] Alessandro Gonzaga to Barbara of Brandenburg, Petriolo, 6 May 1461 in A. Portioli, *I Gonzaga ai bagni di Petriolo di Siena nel 1460 e 1461* (Mantua, 1869), 30.

[40] Letter dated 17 May, in Portioli, 33.

[41] Letter dated 24 May, in Portioli, 37.

[42] Polycletus de Ferrariis to Barbara of Brandenburg, Porretta, 30 July 1467 (ASMn AG b. 1100 c. 383).

[43] Margaret of Bavaria to Barbara of Brandenburg, Porretta, 7 August 1467: "sto in continuo exercicio e faticha, che mal mi lassia conoscere lo giovamento del bagno" (ASMn AG b. 2099); Johannes Cusatrus to Barbara, Porretta, 18 August 1467: "questa benedecta aqua . . . ha educti tanti humori dal corpo de la prefata illustrissima vostra figliola che non so pensare dove se fossero, ne haveria poduto pensare li fosse stata tanta inextimale quantità, per la qual cosa essa. . . . da la testa in giù dice sentrse linzerissima, pur la testa li pesa e se sente la solita frigidità vel quasi. La qual dispositione spero mediante la divina gratia el bagnio de Pedriolo doverli levare" (b. 1100 c. 382).

[44] Roberto Sanseverino to Duke Francesco Sforza, Porretta, 29 August 1453, in Motta, article cited above n. 6, (1881), 665; and from Vignoni, 7 October 1455: "io son ancora qui a questi bagni, li quali non sento però me habieno giovato, benché secondo comunemente se dice, giovano più de poy la partita che in residentia" (ibid. 655 n. 5).

flavored with strong spices were generally forbidden; most dangerous of all was sleeping in the afternoon. No doubt the rules were often breached with impunity; but there were some fatalities. The Mantuan court painter Francesco Buonsignori, for example, died at Caldiero in 1519, supposedly from sleeping in the afternoon;[45] other victims claimed by the waters included Cardinal Giordano Orsini at Petriolo in 1438,[46] and Giovanni de' Medici, Caterina Sforza's second husband, at Bagno di Romagna in 1498.[47] Such instances do not, however, seem to have been notably bad for business or to have lessened confidence in the curative power of the waters.

As well as this clinical, even empirical medical science and practise of hydrotherapy, there were other currents, relating more to belief in divine providence and faith healing, which sustained enthusiasm for the baths. Moreover, one must not suppose that taking the waters was only something for the elite; it had a much wider popularity, as suggested in a letter which Francesco Datini, the famous merchant of Prato, received from Petriolo in 1405: there were so many people there, he was told, that it was difficut to move.[48] The doctors disapproved, of course; Ugolino complained about the crowds of arthritic peasants and artisans taking the waters at his native Montecatini without any medical supervision or use of the proper facilities; many, he declared, just came and dug a ditch and lay down in an oozey mixture of mud and water, though local pride forced him to note that they seemed to derive great relief from it.[49] Religious superstition might also be involved; the Corsena baths had such a reputation for curing cases of paralysis that the local people believed the water came from Jerusalem, and on the first Friday of March many came to bathe there believing that an angel had blessed the spring the previous evening.[50] On the other hand, a century later Montaigne was told[51] by an inhabitant there that local people did not go to their baths, but that taking the waters was like the attraction of pilgrimages: the further you went, the greater the benefit. The resort of the simple-minded to the baths made another good subject

---

[45] G. Vasari, *Le vite de' più eccellenti pittori etc.*, ed. G. Milanesi (1880), 5.305, cited by Chambers, as above n. 22, 46, n. 12.

[46] Piscolini, as above n. 30, 121.

[47] P. D. Pasolini, *Caterina Sforza* (Rome, 1893), 1: 27–28, doc. no. 844, pp. 305–6, for Giovanni's last letter to Caterina from the baths, 31 August 1498.

[48] F. Melis, "La frequenza alle terme nel basso medioevo," *Congresso* (Salsomaggiore, 1963), 42: "qui ci sono assai fiorentini e c'è tanta gente che non ci si vive."

[49] Ugolino, ed. Nardi, 36.

[50] Matteo Bendinelli, *Tractatus de balneis Lucensis* (c. 1483, first printed in Pescia, 1489) quoted by Coturri, as above n. 19, 742).

[51] *Journal de Voyage*, 212.

for literary anecdote; Sercambi of Lucca tells the story of Ser Ganfo, a furrier, who was afraid of losing his identity when he found himself in the bath with so many naked people.[52]

The remark in a letter of Alessandro Gonzaga, that the sulphurous smell of the steam at Petriolo was like the Inferno, was also meant to be funny,[53] but the religious authorities faced some problems with the popularity of the baths throughout Italian society. Many of the sites had ancient pagan associations: at Viterbo and Abano, or Montegrotto, for instance, there were even some fragments of Roman buildings still extant.[54] How could such places become respectable equivalents of the Pool of Bethesda or other scriptural healing resorts? The celebration of the natural properties of a spring by Christian medical opinion was surely not enough. It is true that in correspondence about their patients, doctors sometimes used pious phrases concerning the need for divine grace to assist the water to take effect,[55] but the right spiritual forces needed to be credited more securely with the benefits.

Some effort was made to provide oratories or churches near to the baths, though the lack of regular parishioners in such places might present a difficulty. At Corsena a church had been established by 1294 for the use of bathers;[56] at Petriolo in 1341 measures were taken to try and ensure that there was a priest in residence, or at least a couple of friars;[57] at Porretta a church was founded in 1429, and permission to hold funerals there was granted, rather inauspiciously.[58] Clergy, from the highest dignitaries of the Church down to vagrant friars, certainly frequented spas as patients like everyone else. Friars, indeed, seem to have haunted the baths; there were so many of them at Petriolo in May 1461, wrote Alessandro Gonzaga,[59] that they could have filled ten monasteries; but their secondary motive in being there was probably

---

[52] Giovanni Sercambi, *Novelle*, ed. G. Sinicropi (Bari, 1972), nov. 3, 1.20–22. Another anecdote about baths is in Franco Sachetti, *Trecentonovelle*, ed. V. Pernicone (Florence, 1946), nov. 26, 59–60. Cf. also above nn. 17, 18.

[53] Letter of 6 May 1461, cited above n. 39, Portioli, 32: " che de odore trapassa lo moscato, e fame redure a memoria lo fetore sulfureo ho inteso più volte essere in lo inferno."

[54] C. Zei, "Le Terme romane di Viterbo," *Bollettino d'Arte* 11 (1917): 155–57; V. Gloria, *Il Territorio padovano illustrato* (Padua, 1862; repr. Bologna, 1983), 1: 179–83.

[55] E.g., in letter of 18 August 1467 cited above n. 43.

[56] Coturri, as above n. 19, 735.

[57] D. Barduzzi, *Provvedimenti per le stagioni termali senesi nei secoli xiii e xiv* (Siena, 1899), 21.

[58] G. Zarri, "Il carteggio tra don Leone Bartolini e un gruppo di gentildonne bolognesi negli anni del Concilio di Trento," *Archivio italiano per la storia della pietà* 7 (1976): 351 n. 5. This article contains much useful bibliography.

[59] Letter of 17 May 1461 in Portioli, as above n. 39, 35.

more to beg than to preach or to provide pastoral care. At Acqui a community of Franciscans was granted some special rights as hostel keepers,[60] but this seems to have been exceptional, as was the evangelical activity of a certain priest at Porretta in the mid-sixteenth century, specializing in the spiritual needs of fashionable Bolognese ladies taking the waters.[61] While there was little ecclesiastical control of the spas, Christian miracles were sometimes associated with them. With newly discovered waters this was perhaps inevitable; thus the spring of San Filippo in southern Tuscany was supposedly discovered by a beatified (later canonized) Servite friar, Filippo Benizzi (1253–1285), who had struck a rock with his rod and caused the water to gush out.[62] Not far from there another therapeutic spring was miraculously discovered as late a 1577, when a local woman of Sarteano claimed the water had cured her bad eyesight.[63] Efforts to establish a spa there were not very successful, as the Grand Duke of Tuscany was unimpressed and unwilling to encourage competition with longer established resorts nearby. But in the early seventeenth century, the so-called Holy Bath of Sarteano was in use, and its ophthalmic merits caused a church there to be dedicated to St. Lucy.

Some of the Roman sites had Christian sanctity imposed on them. Bagno di Romagna was also known as Mary's Bath, for example; the Roman bath near Ascoli was simply known as Acquasancta, and one of the Paduan baths had acquired a particular association with St. Bartholomew.[64] But it was an event near Abano in 1428 which provides perhaps the most striking example of a Christian miracle being superimposed upon an antique site.[65] In that year a wounded soldier called Pietro Falco, who had received no benefit hitherto from the famous waters, was resting in the woods at the foot of the nearby hill called Monte Ortone, when allegedly he had a vision of the Madonna, who

---

[60] Gualino, as above n. 36, 797. Ercole d'Este wrote to his wife Eleonora of Aragon from Acqui on 30 May 1485 that he had arranged with the *guardiano* to bathe in "un suo bagno che hanno nel monastero dove non practicano tanta gente come fano a questo altro." Chiappini, as above n. 35, 58.

[61] Zarri, as above n. 58, 335–865 passim.

[62] A. M. Serra in *Bibliotheca sanctorum* (Rome, 1964), 5.742.

[63] D. Bandini, "Memorie del Bagno Santo di Sarteano," *Bollettino senese di storia patria* n.s. 10 (1939): 132–39.

[64] Michele Savonarola recorded that there was a hospice there dedicated to the saint; "coniunctum est hospitale ad pauperos recipiendos: ut sic commoditate ampliori ab eorum languoribus precibus sancti intervenientibus curarentur." *De balneis* (1553), 19v–20r.

[65] G. Ambrosini, *Il santuario di Monteortone* (Padua, 1968; repr. 1977), based mainly on G. F. Tomasini, *Historia della B. Vergine di Monte Ortone* (Padua, 1644); cf. also M. Savonarola, 1553 ed., 20v.

Fig. 3. Jacopo da Montagnana, Miraculous recovery of Pietro Falco
(Santuario di Monteortone, Padua)

told him to drink from a stream there. After so doing, he felt his strength suddenly restored, and then, looking down, found a picture of the Virgin and Child. This image, and the site of the miracle, were inspected and approved by both secular and church authorities, and an oratory, and later an imposing monastic church, were built there. The interior of the church was decorated (c. 1494–1497) with frescoes by Jacopo da Montagnana,[66] and one of them has the story of Falco, twice depicted, kneeling beside the new bath with other worshippers with the icon in his hand, and also kneeling devoutly before the Madonna [fig. 3].

In spite of such claims of the Church over the healing power of waters, it is a fact that the management of baths and the provision of facilities were almost entirely a secular business. Where civic governments had territorial rights, they asserted them; the authorities of Bologna, Lucca, Padua, Siena, and Viterbo each legislated in the thirteenth century concerning the baths in their vicinity.[67] Provision was

---

[66] See the exhibition catalogue *Dopo Mantegna. Arte a Padova e nel territorio nei secoli XV e XVI* (Padua, 1976), 35, 46.

[67] For Bologna see L. Frati, *Statuti di Bologna* (Bologna, 1869), 2:370; G. B. Comelli, "Di Nicolo Sanuti, Primo Conte della Porretta," *Atti e memorie per la Provincia di Romagna* 3rd ser. 17 (1899): 101–2, 145. For Lucca, Coturri, as above n. 19, 735. For

made for bathhouses, shelters, and hostels, and norms laid down about charges for admission, cleaning of the baths and the non-admittance of undesirable persons. In a statute of 1331 the Sienese established a magistracy of three officials responsible for the baths and a military guard. Petriolo was particularly in need of protection; it was sacked by military companies at least eight times in the fourteenth century, and the Sienese built new, stronger walls between 1404 and 1419.[68]

The republic of Florence came rather later on this scene than did its neighbors, Siena and Lucca, but when the Florentines expanded their Tuscan dominion in the fourteenth century, they likewise became interested in exploiting the water resources. At Montecatini, for instance, they built a bathhouse in 1379 in order to develop a new spring, although the native expert, Ugolino, was sceptical about it.[69] Volterra had come under Florentine control in 1388, and a doctor was ordered to prepare a report on the nearby baths known as Bagno a Morba; both the chancellor of the republic, Coluccio Salutati, and the acknowledged expert, Ugolino of Montecatini, gave their support to the development of this spa.[70] Florentine enterprise continued with the take-over of Bagno di Romagna in 1404 and the Pisan baths in 1406.[71] The Medici, another chronically sick family, were regular patients at the baths—and not only those in Florentine territory—during their political ascendancy in Florence. In the 1470s they even gained a proprietorial interest in the baths near Volterra. Lucrezia Tornabuoni, the wife of the gouty Piero de' Medici, had been for many years a regular visitor there with her children, and in 1477 this energetic widow decided to buy the whole estabishment, which was becoming dilapidated and bug-infested.[72]

Padua, A. Gloria, as above n. 54, 184–85. G. Beda *Ubertino da Carrara* (Città di Castello, 1906) pp. 73, 188–89. For Siena, D. Barduzzi, as above n. 57, includes statutes of 1310 relating to Macareto, Petriolo, and Vignoni, and of 1331 relating to Rapolano; see also Pesciolini, as above n. 30, 129–35, and W. Bowsky, *The Finances of the Comune of Siena, 1287–1355* (Oxford, 1970), 18, 116–23, 244. For passages in the statutes of 1251 of Viterbo see I. Ciampi, *Cronache e statuti della città di Viterbo* (Florence, 1872), 576–77, 588, 592–93. It is likely in the case of Verona, too, that the fifteenth-century provisions concerning Caldiero, mentioned in Chambers, as above in n. 22, 5–6, refer back to much earlier legislation.

[68] Pesciolini, as above n. 30, 118.
[69] Ugolino, ed. Nardi, 36–37.
[70] Idem, 49.
[71] Idem, 41, 56.
[72] Y. Maguire, *Women of the Medici* (London, 1927), 82–87 for Lucrezia's earlier visits to Bagno a Morba, 100–9 concerning its purchase and redevelopment, especially Lucrezia's letters to Lorenzo de' Medici, 16 May 1477 (text 105–6), and the letter of Piero Malagonelle to Lucrezia, 16 September 1477 (106–7 n. 60, text 211–12). The letter from a doctor dated 28 April 1480 (text 108–9) should be dated 1478; the sender signs as "Oliverus medicus" (Archivio di Stato, Florence, MAP, 34.no. 314).

Fig. 4. Inscription recording Colleoni's founding of the baths at Trescore
(Bagni di Trescore, Bergamo)

Works there included the building of new cisterns, a bathhouse, and twelve showerbaths, for which a method was devised of bringing the waters in two different pipes to ensure that the showers were more evenly warm. An inn was built and was already receiving guests in April 1478.[73] How profitable the project was is not clear, but since Lorenzo de'Medici chose to build a villa nearby at Spedaletto, the family's faith in the Volterra waters was evidently undiminished.

Signorial governments were also interested in exploiting baths. Pietro Gambacorta, lord of Pisa in the late fourteenth century, invested in the waters of San Giuliano, advised by Ugolino of Montecatini, and built a so-called palace there for bathers.[74] Similarly, the Guidi da Bagno family, as their name suggests, controlled Bagno di Romagna in the fourteenth century,[75] and the Paleologo counts of Savoy took a keen interest as the patrons of Acqui.[76] One of the last signorial initiatives in establishing a spa was that of Bartolomeo Colleoni, the famous condottiere from Bergamo [fig. 4]. In 1470 he undertook to restore the nearby baths of Trescore, which, if not Roman, were believed to have been founded by Charlemagne. The waters were highly praised by a local doctor, and Colleoni did not hesitate to evict a convent of nuns in order to develop his spa at Trescore.[77] Some remains of his buildings

---

[73] The letter concerning this from Piero Malegonelle to Lucrezia, quoted by Maguire 107–8, should be dated 5 April 1478, and is now to be found in MAP 34 no. 306.

[74] Ugolino, ed. Nardi, 41.

[75] See F. Aulizio, "Le antichissime terme di Bagno di Romagna," *Congresso* (Montecatini, 1962), 54–64.

[76] Gualino, as above n. 36, 797–99.

[77] *De balneis transcherii opidi Bergomatis* (Bergamo, 1582), includes the texts of the

can be seen there, with an inscription and sculpted capitals including his coat of arms.

Facilities for visitors to these north Italian spas varied. There would usually be a combination of a larger public bath with smaller ones affording greater privacy; the former, uncovered, survive recognizably in some places, such as Caldiero or Vignoni. A public lodging house was sometimes available; at Acqui there was one since 1480, and a century later the duke of Monferrato was insisting that it must be filled before local inhabitants could let rooms.[78] However, there was certainly a flourishing private sector providing services. Some authorities leased out rights over particular springs, as happened at Viterbo; one Viterbese with a franchise was so enthusiastic a promoter of the local waters that he composed a poem in praise of them.[79] But the most comprehensive and long-lasting act of privatization occurred at Porretta, which Pope Nicholas V in 1447 granted as a fief to a Bolognese nobleman, Niccolò Sanuti; after his death without heirs in 1471, Porretta was regranted to another Bolognese, Girolamo Ranuzzi, whose family retained it until 1797.[80]

What determined the fame of particular spas? Patronage of the famous must have had much to do with it. Ugolino da Montecatini and Michele Savonarola readily named their more famous patients in testifying to the merits of a particular spa. But, whether or not they were named in a medical treatise of limited circulation, the famous would have conferred reputation upon a spa just by their conspicuous manner of travel and residence there, sometimes visually recorded by an inscribed plaque, as was Federico Gonzaga's visit to Caldiero [fig. 5].[81] Federico was given his military title, as commander for both the

---

Descriptio balneorum vallis transcheriis Ludovici Zimalie Bergomensis Medici (1470), and Bartholomeii Albani Bergomensis, *De balneis vallis transcherii libellus per Bartholomeum Coleonum* (1474–75). Cf. B. Belotti, *La vita di Bartolomeo Colleoni* (Bergamo, 1923), 426–27, where the text of the inscription is given. Various later sixteenth-century inscriptions also survive at Trescore.

[78] Gualino, as above n. 36, 798–99.

[79] Agostino Almadiani, noted in E. Celani, *Johannis Burckardi, Liber notarum*, R.I.S. 32(i), vol. 2 (Città di Castello, 1911–13), 373 n. 2. His *Delle virtuti et bagni di Viterbo con alcuni sonetti et canzoni da piacere* (Rome, 1510; for a photocopy of this rare work I am grateful to Dr. Peter Denley) begins: "Io vo dell'aque Viterbesi scrivere / perché calor che vengano ad li bagni / sappian la lor virtù & possan vivere. / O Biondo Appollo te prego che bagni / le labra mie nel fonte.... /" He cites the younger Pliny and proceeds to praise each in turn of the Viterbo springs and their therapeutic properties.

[80] Comelli, as above, n. 67, 106, 115; Zarri, as above n. 58, 348.

[81] Chambers, as above n. 22, 45, reproduced on 61. The practice of erecting such commemorative plaques was long-established: Montaigne (*Journal de Voyage*, 201) mentions one dated 1300 which he had seen at the Casciana baths near Pisa.

Fig. 5. Inscription recording Federico Gonzaga's visit to Caldiero, 1524
(Bagni di Caldiero, Verona)

Fig. 6. Illustration to G. A. Panteo, *De thermis Calderianis*
(Verona, Biblioteca Comunale, MS. 278 [2072])

Church and for Florence, on the inscription—he had recently returned from a heroic defence of Pavia against the French—and it is a point worth making that war (so long as it kept its distance) was just as profitable for the spas as peace. Hosts of distinguished soldiers with rheumatic and other complaints frequented them; nearly all the big military names in the Milanese-Venetian wars of the earlier fifteenth century, seem, for example, to have sought relief from the waters of Petriolo. Jacopo Piccinino came there three times with enormous retinues; Gianfrancesco Gonzaga and Gattamelata also came to be cured there;[82] so did Carmagnola, who was suspected by his hosts, the Sienese, of wanting secretly to inspect their defense arrangements,[83] though Carmagnola probably did have a genuine health problem: he also tried the water or mud at Sant'Elena, near Padua, in the territory of his Venetian employers.[84] This military tradition of bathgoing or bath promoting was carried on, as we have seen, by Ludovico Gonzaga and by Bartolomeo Colleoni; Federico da Montefeltro, duke of Urbino, was another patient at Petriolo in 1478.[85] Of course it was not only the military aristocracy who set the fashion in bathgoing; so did many other wealthy people. The revival of the Caldiero baths in the fifteenth century owed much to the patronage of a local Veronese patrician, Antonio Banda, who had a villa there, and to the learned Venetian bishop of Verona, Ermolao Barbaro. The latter's humanist secretary, Gianantonio Panteo, turned the treatise of a Veronese doctor, Aleardo Pindemonti, into a dialogue in praise of the Caldiero baths, the manuscript of which includes an illustration meant to represent two of them: the circular *Brentella* and the larger, half-moon shaped *Cavalla* [fig. 6].[86]

However, two popes were probably the most distinguished of all patrons of hydrotherapy in fifteenth-century Italy. Nicholas V (1447–1455) appointed as his doctor one of the leading authorities, Baverio Bonetti,[87] a champion in particular of Petriolo; though it was to Viterbo that Nicholas most resorted, coming there in May 1448 with his mother and sister in the hope of curing his chronic gout.[88] Pius II (1457–1464),

---

[82] Pesciolini, as above n. 30, 121–22.

[83] *Cronache Senesi*, ed. G. Carducci, V. Fiorini, P. Fedele, R.I.S. 15, 6 (Bologna, 1936): 811–12.

[84] Savonarola, *De balneis* (1553), 20r.

[85] Pesciolini, as above n. 30, 123.

[86] Chambers, as n. 22, 45–46 nn. 7–8. The MS of Banda's copy of Panteo's *Annotationes . . . de thermis calderianis* is in Bib. Comunale, Verona, MS. 278 (2072). Its four watercolor illustrations are reproduced in G. P. Marchi, *Cultura e vita civile a Verona* (Verona, 1979), 46.

[87] See *Dizionario Biografico degli Italiani*, also above n. 14.

[88] Niccola della Tuccia, in Ciampi, as above n. 67, 56, 209. — On baths appropri-

a fellow sufferer, also frequented Viterbo, but more habitually favored the baths in the territory of his native Siena. It is not impossible that part of his motive in founding the new town of Pienza at his birthplace in southern Tuscany was on account of the numerous mineral waters and baths in the vicinity. From the spas' point of view, it was obviously a great boon to enjoy the patronage of the papal court. When Pius descended upon Macereto, Vignoni, or Petriolo, these tiny water holes became, for a few days, the capital of the Universal Church, where the pope carried on business as usual, hearing petitions, signing letters,and receiving ambassadors.[89] It was not only the pope, of course, who brought fame to the waters, but also the cardinals and numerous other dignitaries in his entourage, many of them also sufferers from diverse diseases. Among notable benefactors of Viterbo, the spa principally frequented by members of the papal court, were the Greek Cardinal Bessarion, and his secretary Niccolò Perotti, later governor of the Patrimony, both of whom sponsored buildings there.[90]

In view of all this bathgoing by the good and the great, it is surprising perhaps that more was not attempted in the way of magnificent building projects to improve the look and the facilities of favored spas, especially since there were ruins of Roman baths to provide an eloquent precedent, if not model. The main problems, inevitably, were time and money; eminent invalids did not have an excess of either to spend in distant hill villages. There were also problems concerning the supply of labor and building materials. Ludovico Gonzaga abandoned plans to endow Petriolo with some better accommodation in 1460 because of these difficulties.[91] Borso d'Este of Ferrara found another solution, taking along with him to Abano in 1458 two canvas pavilions joined by

---

ate to cardinals, and a particular recommendation for Viterbo ('aut salubritate utilius aut urbis propinquitate commodius'), see Paolo Cortese, *De cardinalatu* (Casa Cortese, 1510), LXXX–LXXXXIIIv.

[89] See Pius II, *Commentarii*, ed. A. van Heck (Vatican City, 1984), 260–61; trans. F. A. Gragg and L. C. Gabel, Smith College Studies in History 30 (Northampton, Mass., 1947), 311–12.

[90] Niccola della Tuccia in Ciampi, as above n. 67, 90–91, notes that in 1466 Perotti, by then rector or governor of the Patrimony, had built "certi bagni belli con camere belle, e casamenti d'una casata chiamata la casa de'Perotti," and the arms of Bessarion were placed above the entrance to another bath. Cf. E. Lee, *Sixtus IV and Men of Letters* (Rome, 1978), 140, 233 noting transference to the hospital of Santo Spirito, Rome, of the *hospitium* of Bessarion and the *balnea Perotta*, setting aside a clause of Perotti's will, according to which his heirs had claimed possession.

[91] Zaccaria Saggi to Barbara of Brandenburg, Petriolo, 14 May 1460: "El dissegnio de la camera e saletta che voleria fare Sua Signoria qui a bagni è rimaso, perché non basta el tempo, e anchora male si trovano qui le cose necessarie a tal bisogni" (Portioli, as above n. 39, 15).

a covered way.⁹² However, there was some initiative taken by Nicholas V, who had a so-called palace built adjacent to two of the Viterbo springs. According to a local chronicler, it had halls and smaller rooms on two floors, all with windows and fireplaces, and a crenellated roof with towers at either end.⁹³ Nevertheless, this building may not have been very well maintained; when Pius II came to Viterbo in 1462 he did not mention it in his memoirs, but stayed in the citadel and had water brought to him there.⁹⁴ Probably Nicholas V's building did not survive at all the military invasions of the next century; just as Pietro Gambacorta's so-called palace at the Pisan baths had been destroyed by military action.⁹⁵ The sheer insecurity of spa sites may well have been another deterrent to prestigious building there; springs of warm water in under-inhabited places were simply not worth a heavy defense expenditure. This is not to say that the baths were totally without interest for architects; Alberti made a sketch for a therapeutic bathhouse, while Filarete described imaginary building plans, digressing from his main theme to list some Italian spas,⁹⁶ and there are drawings by Giuliano da Sangallo of one of the bathhouses near Viterbo.⁹⁷

Even if the Italian spas were, then, rather deficient in on-site monumental building and related very little to other visual forms of art, the gatherings they attracted of ailing members of the elite from all over the peninsula had other cultural implications. The acquaintances they promoted, the meetings of minds, hardly need to be emphasized; when Ludovico Gonzaga encountered Pius II and the members of their respective retinues also mingled at the baths of Macereto and Petriolo in May 1460, the occasion must surely have assisted the exchange of ideas and knowledge, not to mention employment opportunities.⁹⁸

---

⁹² T. J. Tuohy, "Studies in Domestic Expenditure at the Court of Ferrara, 1451–1505" (Ph.D. thesis, Warburg Institute, University of London, 1982), 148.

⁹³ Niccola della Tuccia in Ciampi, as above n. 67, 235.

⁹⁴ G. P. Arrivabene to Barbara of Brandenburg, Viterbo, 14 May 1462: "Havendosi Nostro Signore lunedì passato fatto portare a li bagni, et havendo ritrovato li muri de la casa dove prima terminava habitare lì suso li bagni essere aperti et menaciare a ruina, deliberoe farsi portare l'aqua in roccha, e cussì li continua el bagnarsi" (ASMn AG b. 841 c. 729).

⁹⁵ Zei, as above n. 54, 170; Ugolino, ed. Nardi, 42.

⁹⁶ Howard Burns, "A drawing by L. B. Alberti,"*Architectural Design* 49 (1978): 49–56; *Filarete's Treatise on Architecture*, ed. J. R. Spencer (New Haven and London, 1965), 2: 294–95. Though Filarete provides no information about buildings at the spas, his work is of interest concerning the cavernous Bagno di Romagna.

⁹⁷ L. Zdekauer, in R. Falb, *Il taccuino senese de Giuliano da Sangallo* (Siena, 1902), tav. 8: "un tempio che serve per bagnio"; Zei, as above n. 54, 166, 170. Zei also reproduces drawings improbably ascribed to Michelangelo.

⁹⁸ E.g., the suggestive letters in Portioli, as above n. 39, 4–22; Rolandino Soardi

Meanwhile, the medical rules which insisted on rest but not sleep, encouraged diversions like story-telling and the playing of music. There is a well-known letter from Cardinal Francesco Gonzaga, who when planning his first visit to Porretta in 1472, asked his father to send the court painter Andrea Mantegna to entertain him there and discuss his collection of cameos and other antiquities, and to send also Malagise, a Florentine lute player and singer.[99] It is less well known that almost certainly they did not come, because the cardinal was advised by his doctors not to go to Porretta after all.[100] But the letter still makes the point that this sort of diversion was ideally desirable during the boring, sleep-forbidden afternoons. The cardinal's uncle, Alessandro Gonzaga, had despaired until he found a witty Sienese to entertain him in May 1461;[101] others were less fortunate: two Mantuan courtiers at Porretta in 1463 complained it was a tedious place with only friars and people of no importance for company.[102] The Bolognese writer Sabadino degli Arienti did his best for Porretta's reputation by borrowing from it the title and setting for a collection of Boccaccian short stories.[103] Sickness and sulphurous fumes are not even mentioned in his *Porretane* (c. 1471); the spa simply becomes, unrealistically, a radiant hillside where jolly picnic parties are graced by Antonio Bentivoglio and the cream of Bolognese society. Literature was, of all the arts, the one best served by the baths. Pius II, when still a cardinal, began writing his *Historia Bohemica* during a visit to the waters of Viterbo,[104] and there was no

---

records the meeting with Pius II who was receiving the douche at Macereto (19; cf. Pius II's account, above n. 89). Ludovico was anxious to read Vergil while taking his cure (Portioli, 11–12).

[99] P. Kristeller, *Andrea Mantegna* (Berlin, 1902), doc. 45: 527; cf. letters of the Marquis of 25 July, ibid., nos. 46–47, 527–28.

[100] G. P. Arrivabene to Barbara of Brandenburg, Bologna, 3 August 1472, wrote that "mastro Bavero dissuade il bagno" (ASMn AG b. 1141 c. 243); cf. letters of Antonio Donato, Bologna, 3, 8 August 1472 (b. 1141 cc. 241, 243; also letter of Bartolomeo de Cusatris b. 2413 c. 764).

[101] Letter of 6 May 1461 in Portioli, as above n. 39, 31–32: "la prima regula e ordine che se debe servare è de stare continuo in piaceri e bandire ogni melanconia, e maxime ge conviene dicto Guizardo in questo bagno dove bisogna havere uno forte diversivo a farse domenticare la grande puzo ge è."

[102] Gianfrancesco Uberti and Antonio da Gonzaga to Barbara of Brandenburg, Porretta, 17 July 1463 (ASMn AG b. 1100 c. 162): "questa è una tediosa stantia et *presertim* ch'el c'è, secondo intendiamo, pochissima zente a rispecto di quello è usitato esser li anni passati, et *presertim* homini da bene; la più parte sonno frati et zente di pocha condicione. Pur ce inzegnamo, e sforzamo de vivere più lietamente possiamo, et senza uno pensiero al mondo" (ASMn AG b. 1100 c. 162).

[103] Sabadino degli Arienti, *Le Porretane*, ed. B. Basile (Rome, 1981), especially 4–7 (Lettera Dedicatoria).

[104] *Commentarii*, ed. Van Heck, 1: 96.

lack of poems written about different baths. Bartolomeo Scala, Chancellor of Florence, wrote one about the nymph Amorba, whom he imagined presiding over the baths of that name near Volterra, and one of his *Apologues*—on the theme of immortality—was also an invocation of the healing waters.[105] A Mantuan courtier and diplomat, Annibale Litolfi, in 1554 wrote Latin verses in praise of those at Lucca; this was in part, he wrote, a way of passing the time, but also because he felt so much better after six days of drinking eleven or twelve beakerfuls, that he considered it was a way of expressing his gratitude.[106]

It should not be suggested, however, that all diversions were elevated or literary. Gambling was common at spas; the Sienese had in the fourteenth century tried to suppress this and approved chessplaying as an alternative,[107] but there is no doubt that in practise gambling continued to be a principal amusement. When Federico II Gonzaga was at Caldiero in 1524, elegantly escorted to the bath each morning by a company of flute players, drummers, and pipers, it was in fact on gambling and other entertainments that most of his money was spent.[108] On the last day in July, a Sunday when the moon was in a conveniently unpropitious phase, he interrupted his cure altogether and entertained a large crowd of local notabilities and dancing girls; wine flowed in abundance.[109]

This raises the question to what extent the spas did indeed become scenes of license and debauchery. A letter about Porretta in 1494 claims that it did; the writer, Floriano Dolfo, a canon law professor of Bologna with a somewhat caustic wit, no doubt exaggerated in order to titillate and entertain the young Marquis Francesco Gonzaga, whom he was addressing; what he wrote, after a reference to current opinion which compared Porretta to the biblical Pool of Siloam, was formerly considered too indecent to publish even in extract,[110] but his ideas are not uninteresting. He suggested that Porretta represented something be-

---

[105] Alison Brown, *Bartolomeo Scala 1430–1497, Chancellor of Florence* (Princeton, 1979), 199. I am grateful to Alison Brown for this information.

[106] The ode accompanying Litolfi's letter of 20 May 1554, in ASMn AG b. 1138 cc. 221–24 (as signified by A. Luzio, *L'Archivio Gonzaga* [Verona, 1922], 2:192) is published in E. H. Gombrich with David Chambers, "Annibale Litolfi, A Sixteenth-Century Nature Lover: *spoglie* from the Gonzaga Archives," *Renaissance Studies*, 2, 2 (*A Tribute to Denys Hay*, ed. D. S. Chambers and J. E. Law) (1988): 321–26. See also Almadiani's vernacular verses cited above n. 79.

[107] Barduzzi, as above n. 57, 11.

[108] Chambers, as above n. 22, 47–49, 53.

[109] Idem, 50–52.

[110] The letter is mentioned in A. Luzio and R. Renier, "La Coltura e le relazioni letterarie di Isabella d'Este," *Giornale storico della letteratura italiana* 38 (1901): 43 n. 1. On Dolfo, see the same article, 42–48. On the Pool of Siloam, see John 9.7.

tween the Golden Age of natural liberty before class distinction existed and a sink of lewdness where every sort of taboo might be violated.[111]

Within certain guidelines, a play element was then, as now, admitted to be a beneficial part of balneotherapy; and where benefit was manifest, quite a lot of it may, one suspects, have been owing not only to recreation, but also simply to fresh air (at least outside the bathhouses) and a quiet environment. The contemplation of landscape may itself have been fostered at the spas, particularly those in Tuscany; Montaigne's delight in the baths near Lucca had something to do with the beautiful view from his window.[112] Taking the waters was, however, a serious business—not exactly a "patrician fad" as a recent writer has declared[113]—and it surely has wide relativity as a phenomenon in cultural history, as well as being a subject which helps to establish continuity with the past. Aches and pains, after all, bothered intelligent people in the Renaissance no less than ideas about form and order and the uses of speech; and they hoped that nature could provide the answer to their corporeal, as well as to some of their more cerebral problems.

The Warburg Institute, University of London

---

[111] "L'aqua del bagno da la Porreta ... mi pare esser simile a quella piscina probatica narrata da Santo Ioanne nel suo evangelio, ma questa suole curare tute le infirmitate ... veramente, Illustrissimo principe, in questo solo loco fra tuti li loci de' cristiani se adora et mantene la vera libertade che mi resembla quella prima etade aurea, che senza alcuna discretione et cognitione de pronomi ogni soa cosa era in comune. Qui le donne quantunque nobile et gentile non si cognoscono da le plebe, si nele loro habitatione como nel vivere, che ad ogni homo è equale. A la doza dove del saxo la beata aqua deriva, cossì si serve il povereto como lo richo uno pane, uno vino, una carne, uno lecto ad ogni persona parimente, e dato le camere de li hosti tute aperte, non si trova chi entro per furare li vada. Ogni reverentia et pudore è alieno da li bagnaroli, che non si vergognano pedere, cacare, rutare et pissare in publico, monstrando spessissime volte senza rubore li culli, cazi et pete ... et perché il coito dicono esser nocivo a le done che beno l'aqua per amore de la matrice, si contentano et consentono queste damiselle esser fotute nel buso del cullo.... insieme maschi et femine vanno al bagno et entrano nel'aqua ignudi, et qui cum piedi et mano et parolete amorose se piglianno grandissimo piacere; il marito non ha gielosia de la moglie, il patre di la figlia, el fratello de la sorella, sapendo che la morte qui custodisse la corruptione.... tute consumano il loro tempo in giochi, balli, canti et feste senza pensiero de alcuna mercantia o arte, et le boteghe non meno se apreno et vendesse le roba la domenica ..." (ASMn AG b. 1143).

[112] *Journal de Voyage*, 159–61.

[113] K. Park, *Doctors and Medicine in Early Renaissance Florence* (Princeton, 1985), 213.

PAUL OSKAR KRISTELLER

Renaissance Humanism and Its Significance

HUMANISM WAS ONE OF THE MOST PERVASIVE TRAITS OF THE Renaissance period, and it affected more or less deeply all aspects of Renaissance culture, including its thought and philosophy.

Humanism has been described and interpreted in many different ways, and its meaning has been the subject of much controversy, as has that of the Renaissance itself. Whereas the term *humanism* in current discourse often denotes an emphasis on human values unrelated to any intellectual or cultural tradition, Renaissance humanism was understood and studied by most historians of the nineteenth and early twentieth centuries as that broad concern with the study and imitation of classical antiquity which was characteristic of the period and found its expression in scholarship, education, and many other areas including the arts and sciences. The modern term *humanism* has been used in this sense since the early nineteenth century. It was derived from the term *humanist* coined in the late fifteenth century to designate a teacher or student of the "humanities" or *Studia humanitatis*. The word *humanity* and its derivatives were associated with a "liberal" education by several Roman writers, especially Cicero and Gellius. The term was revived by Petrarch, Salutati, and others in the fourteenth century, and by the middle of the fifteenth century it came to stand for a well-defined cycle of studies called *Studia humanitatis*, which included grammar, rhetoric, poetry, history, and moral philosophy (as those terms were then understood). Unlike the liberal arts of the earlier Middle Ages, the humanities did not include logic, arithmetic, geometry, astronomy, or music, and unlike the fine arts of the eighteenth century they did not include the visual arts, music, dancing, or gardening. The humanities also failed to include the disciplines that were the chief subjects of instruction at the universities during the later Middle Ages and throughout the Renaissance, such as theology, jurisprudence, and medicine, and the philosophical disciplines other than ethics, such as logic, natural philosophy, and metaphysics. In other words, humanism does not represent, as is often believed, the sum total of Renaissance thought and learning, but only a well-defined sector of it. Humanism has its proper domain or home territory in the humanities, whereas all other areas of learning, including philosophy (apart from moral philosophy), followed their own course that was largely determined by their medieval tradition and by their steady transformation through new observations, problems, or theories. They were affected by humanism mainly from the outside and in an indirect way, though often quite strongly.

If we want to understand the role of the humanists and of humanism during the Renaissance and their impact on learning and philosophy, we must consider not only the place of their subject matter, the humanities, in the classifications of the arts and sciences and among the subjects taught in the schools and universities, but also their professional activities and their literary production. The humanists are best known for their role as educators, and they played an important part as theorists, teachers, and tutors in reforming secondary education, first in Italy and then in the rest of Europe. The core of their instruction was the careful study of the classical Latin language (its vocabulary, grammar, metrics, and prose style), the study of classical Greek to a lesser extent, and the attentive reading and interpretation of the major ancient writers, both Latin and Greek, in prose and in verse. The schools of Guarino in Ferrara and of Vittorino da Feltre in Mantua attracted students from all over Europe, and their curriculum and methods were followed everywhere and served as a model for the Protestant reformers as well as for the Jesuits. The humanistic school, animated by the idea that the study of the classical languages and literatures provided valuable information and intellectual discipline as well as moral standards and a civilized taste to the future rulers, leaders, and professionals of its society, flourished without interruption, though with some significant changes, down to our own century. It survived many religious, political, and social revolutions and has but recently been replaced, though not yet completely, by other more practical and often less demanding forms of education.

The role of the humanists at the universities of the Renaissance was not as powerful as in the secondary schools which they came to dominate completely, but it was not as insignificant as is often believed. The view expressed quite recently that humanism played no role at the universities of the Renaissance is certainly wrong. In the curriculum of the universities, grammar played a minor but persistent role as an elementary and preliminary subject, and rhetoric and poetry, which involved the reading of the major classical Latin poets and prose writers (including the historians and moralists), was a regular subject of teaching at the Italian universities from the early fourteenth century on. The teaching of the Greek language and literature was added with increasing frequency during the fifteenth century. By the late fifteenth and early sixteenth centuries, the chairs of Latin and Greek oratory and poetry had greatly increased in number, prestige, and even in salary, and sometimes they were given the more ambitious and fashionable title of the Humanities. Moreover, if we study the career of individual humanists, we find that many of them, great or small, were professors at the various universities (including Florence, whose *Studio* was of course a regular university) or provided advanced instruction (for a public salary) in cities which had no regular or complete university, such as Lucca, Venice, or Milan.

Another professional activity frequently practiced by the humanists was that of chancellors or secretaries. Popes, cardinals, and bishops, emperors, kings, princes, and republics, as well as many prominent noblemen, patricians, and businessmen, needed and employed a large staff of trained people capable of composing and copying the numerous documents and papers, letters, and speeches, that constituted an essential part of the daily routine of politics and administration. As trained masters of Latin prose composition, the humanists were eminently equipped to perform these functions, and it is well known that numerous humanists, great and small, had their careers not as teachers or professors, but as chancellors and secretaries. Even Petrarch occasionally served the princes of Milan or Padua who were his patrons as an informal secretary or orator, and there is a long line of distinguished humanists who served the papal curia, the Florentine republic, the kings of Naples, the dukes of Milan, or other princes or republics. Humanist chancellors appear also at the court of foreign kings and princes in France and Germany, England, Spain, Hungary, and Poland, and they were often Italian humanists who pursued a career abroad. Many of the humanist chancellors, both in Italy and elsewhere, were also commissioned to write an official history of the kingdom or republic which they served, for history was a part of their training, and as secretaries they also had easy access to the archives that contained the source material for their undertaking. Machiavelli received a stipend from the university of Pisa for his history of Florence, and the Venetian republic employed a whole series of official historiographers, some of them quite distinguished.

Although the chanceries were important centers of humanist activities, they were not the only ones, as is often assumed. Apart from the humanist teachers of whom we spoke before, we must also keep in mind that many of the students trained in humanist schools were princes or patricians who in later life were not obliged to earn a living on the basis of their humanist training (as did the teachers and secretaries), but were active as churchmen or statesmen, bankers or merchants. Many of them were active patrons of humanist scholarship and literature, and some of them were distinguished and productive scholars and writers in their leisure time. Pius II continued to write and speak when he was a cardinal and pope, and many humanists happened to be bishops, clerics, monks, or members of the ruling circles in Florence or Venice. Moreover, after the middle of the fifteenth century we encounter many professionals, lawyers, and physicians, as well as theologians, who had received a more or less thorough humanist education in school or at the university and who became humanist scholars or writers in their leisure time or applied the standards of humanist scholarship to their professional work and thus helped to transform their traditional and medieval subjects through their humanist style, method, and outlook.

Finally, we should not forget another more modest activity which provided a living for a large number of humanist scholars, that is, the book trade. The manuscript book had traditionally served the needs of monastic and cathedral libraries, of ecclesiastic, princely, and noble collectors, and later of school and university teachers and students. During the fourteenth and fifteenth centuries there was a new demand for classical Latin texts and for the writings of contemporary scholars. We find many humanists who in their youth or in periods of unemployment worked as copyists or calligraphers employed by princely or patrician patrons who started or increased their private libraries. They were also employed by successful scholars, such as Petrarch, who could afford to have their own secretaries, or by professional booksellers, such as Vespasiano da Bisticci, who sold their manuscripts to princes and scholars alike. The products of these humanist scribes were written in one of two new styles of handwriting that were both different from the earlier "Gothic" script and were invented and propagated by the humanists: the so-called Roman script, invented by Poggio after the model of the Carolingian minuscule which he mistook for an ancient Roman script; and the humanist cursive, presumably invented by Niccoli, which was a favored book hand during the second half of the fifteenth century and became the model of the Italic type. These two scripts—and especially the first—are the kind of scripts which are used both in our longhand and in our printed characters; our use of the humanist rather than of the Gothic script is the direct consequence of the reform of the script brought about by the Italian humanists of the fifteenth century. It is perhaps the most lasting effect of Renaissance humanism on our modern world. The palaeographical study of the Renaissance period and of humanist script has but recently become a subject of serious study, and the identification of individual humanist hands, which is making rapid progress right now, is often an important instrument when it comes to establishing the date and authorship, as well as the diffusion, of Renaissance texts.

The printing press was invented by Gutenberg in Mainz in 1450, but it took some time before the new technique reached other countries, and even after that time, the manuscript book continued for many decades to compete and to coexist with the printed book. The contribution of the humanists to the production and diffusion of the printed book was no less important than their role during the period of the manuscript book. The printing press was introduced to Italy in 1465, and from that time on, an ever increasing number of printed books was published, first in Subiaco and Rome, and soon afterwards in many other cities, including Florence, Milan, and Venice. Many of the early printed books contained classical Latin texts and the writings of contemporary humanists, and they were usually printed in the same Roman and Italic characters that had been used in the humanist manuscript books of the same or immediately preceding period, whereas many of the university text books and religious and popular writings were printed in Gothic characters. The humanists soon became involved with the printing press in several ways. They saw their own writings through the press, as we know in a number of cases, and they acted from the beginning as advisers for some of the texts to be printed and as responsible editors for the classical Latin texts published by the presses. The same is true of the first editions of Greek classical authors which appeared rather sparingly during the first decades of printing and became more frequent only during the sixteenth century. Among the early printers, we encounter a few humanist scholars of distinction, although they probably acted as publishers rather than as typesetters, such as Aldus Manutius and his successors in Venice and the Estienne family in Paris and Geneva. By the sixteenth century, countless printing presses were active all over Europe and in numerous towns, but the leading international centers of publishing and of the book trade were Venice, Lyons, and Basel, especially for the books of classical or humanist content. Humanist scholars continued to be active as editors of classical texts and of their own writings, and often served as proofreaders for their publishers. Erasmus worked for years as an editor and proofreader for Aldus in Venice and for Froben in Basel. Without his close relations with these and other publishing houses, his enormous scholarly production would not have been possible, and we have reason to believe that a part of his income derived from the work he did for his printers and publishers.

Having discussed the intellectual interests and the professional activities of the humanists, we must now briefly describe their scholarly and other achievements, and above all, the form and content of their literary work and some of the basic attitudes that underlie and pervade its production. Needless to say, much of it is closely related to their professional activities, although the tastes and preferences of individual humanists also played an important role.

The deep interest in classical literature and history which was common to all humanists was not only expressed in their activity as copyists and editors. Before a text could be copied or edited, it had to be located or discovered, and it was essential to find old and correct manuscripts that deserved to be copied or edited, since late and inaccurate manuscripts were likely to offer a corrupt text. The search for old manuscripts of the Latin classics all over Europe was a favorite concern of many leading humanists. They and their companions and successors found not only older, better, or more complete manuscripts of known classical writers, but they also discovered additional authors or writings that had not been well known or widely read during the preceding medieval centuries. It has been argued that we should not speak of real humanist discoveries since the manuscripts they found were copied in Carolingian times and hence not unknown to the copyists or to their contemporaries. Yet the fact remains that these texts survived in only one or two copies and that they had not been known or read for centuries, until the humanists introduced them into the mainstream of western scholarship and helped to bring about their wide diffusion in manuscripts and in printed editions. The newly discovered texts included Manilius and Celsus, a complete Quintilian, many works of Cicero, and, above all, Tacitus and Lucretius. As to the Greek classics, prior to 1350 the number of Greek and especially of classical Greek manuscripts in western libraries was very small. It was during the period from 1350 to 1600 that most of the classical Greek manuscripts that are now in western libraries and that have been the basis of all modern editions were brought over from the east (both before and after the Turkish conquest of Constantinople) by Western scholars visiting the east and by Byzantine scholars who fled to the West.

Once the classical Latin (and Greek) texts were available in manuscript and later in print, the humanists carefully annotated their texts, recording variant readings from other manuscripts and their own emendations, and adding explanatory notes and glosses. We also have a large body of full-fledged commentaries by humanist scholars on practically all ancient Latin texts then available, some in manuscript and some in print, which are usually the result of class lectures given on these authors at various schools or universities and copied by a student and sometimes by the teacher himself. Also, the classical Greek authors were copied and edited by the humanists, Byzantine or western, and frequently annotated and glossed in Latin. From the sixteenth century we have a number of Latin commentaries on classical Greek texts.

However, the knowledge of Greek, even among humanist scholars, was never as thorough or as widespread as was their knowledge of Latin because the study of Greek was a new and purely scholarly pursuit that lacked the indigenous tradition and the practical usefulness which the study of Latin had inherited from the Middle Ages. As a result, a large amount of effort was dedicated by the humanists to the task of translating ancient Greek texts into Latin in order to make them available to a larger number of their contemporaries, even among the humanists. Between the fifteenth and sixteenth centuries, the humanists translated into Latin practically all classical Greek authors then available—some of them more than once and many for the first time—and they also made new translations of those texts that had been available in medieval Latin translations. These translations introduced for the first time practically all of Greek poetry, oratory, and historiography, as well as a sizable proportion of Greek writings on mathematics, geography, medicine, botany, and a great deal of early Christian literature and of philosophical literature. Also, the scholarly study of Hebrew and Arabic made progress among Western scholars, some of them humanists, during the Renaissance period and benefited the study of the Old Testament, of Rabbinical and Cabalistic literature, of the Coran, and of Arabic philosophy and science.

The reading public of the Renaissance consisted not only of people who had received a humanist or university education and hence were able to read Latin, but also included many intelligent and curious persons, especially merchants, craftsmen, and ladies who knew no Latin but were eager to read not only poems and narratives but also works of varied instruction in their native vernacular. Many humanists catered to this audience, which included many princes and noblemen, and made vernacular translations of both classical and humanist writings or even composed some of their own works in the vernacular. This happened in Italy, especially in Tuscany, as early as the fifteenth century, and during the sixteenth century, if not before, a large body of classical and humanist literature was translated into French, Spanish, German, and English. An increasing number of writings that were humanist in form and content came to be composed in those languages.

In order to facilitate the reading and understanding of the classical authors, the humanists wrote commentaries on Donatus, Priscian, and other ancient grammarians and also produced a number of textbooks of Latin grammar and a few of Greek grammar.

Whereas the study of Greek was mainly aimed at the reading of the classics, that of Latin served the additional purpose of mastering it as a written and even as a spoken language. The humanists were keenly aware of the great difference that separated medieval and, above all, scholastic Latin from the Latin of the ancient Roman writers and especially of Cicero. The humanists made it their avowed goal to imitate in their own writings the Latin of the classical writers, and to avoid all those "barbarous" features that separated medieval from classical Latin. They attempted with some success to imitate and restore classical Latin as a living language and to bring about a kind of linguistic and literary revolution that discredited and gradually abolished many, if not all, features of medieval Latin. This reform affected spelling, prosody, punctuation, vocabulary, phraseology, inflection, syntax, and the whole structure and rhythm of sentences. Although some scholars allowed new words for objects and concepts unknown to the ancient Romans, others would ban any words not sanctioned by the usage of ancient Roman writers, especially Cicero. The result was a Neo-Latin language and literature that was much closer to that of the ancient Romans than anything written in that language after the end of antiquity. In the learned disciplines, including philosophy, this humanist reform tended to abandon the technical terminology that had become refined and precise through the usage and discussion of several centuries and had often served to render in Latin some philosophical terms of ancient Greek origin that had not been adopted or rendered by Cicero or other ancient Roman writers. This humanist habit led in some instances to an emphasis on a smooth literary style and a vague phraseology at the expense of the conceptual precision needed for an adequate philosophical discourse.

All the activities and writings which we have described so far may be roughly subsumed under *grammatica* (as this term was understood at the time). It remains to mention briefly the literary contribution of the humanists to the other *Studia humanitatis*. Rhetoric, which was the second of the humanities and in many ways the core of them all, consisted primarily in the theory and practice of prose composition, but also in the theory of plausible or probable arguments and in the theory of persuasion. The humanists produced a large number of commentaries on the rhetorical works of Cicero, Quintilian, and later of Aristotle, and they analyzed Cicero's orations for their rhetorical qualities. They also produced a number of rhetorical textbooks that tended to multiply during the sixteenth century and many treatises on more specific subjects as the figures of speech or imitation. Like their medieval predecessors, they used some of their own compositions as models of style to be imitated by their students or composed formularies of fictitious letters or of their parts, such as *Exordia* or *Salutationes*.

More important was the claim advanced by most humanists that the pursuit of eloquence (*eloquentia*) is a major task for the humanist scholar and writer, and that it is inseparable from the pursuit of wisdom (*sapientia*). This means that philosophy should always be combined with rhetoric, an ideal for which Cicero served as teacher and example. In the name of this ideal, many humanists, beginning with Petrarch, criticized scholastic philosophy. Some of them even tended to subordinate philosophy to rhetoric, and at least one leading humanist, Lorenzo Valla, came close to replacing philosophy with rhetoric, or at least with a kind of philosophy which he chose to call rhetoric.

The rhetorical practice of the humanists was much more extensive than their rhetorical theory. The genres most frequently cultivated by them were the oration and the letter, both of them closely connected with their professional activity as chancellors and secretaries. The speeches composed by them and often delivered by others were seldom of the judiciary or deliberative type prevalent in classical theory and practice, but usually epideictic and linked to the social and institutional practice of their time: funeral and wedding speeches; speeches by ambassadors in the name of their government; speeches of congratulation to newly elected popes or prelates, princes or magistrates; speeches of welcome to distinguished visitors; speeches at the beginning of a school year or a particular university course; speeches given at the graduation of students; speeches for the opening of lay or religious gatherings or of a disputation; speeches given in praise of saints or other illustrious persons; and many more. In fifteenth-century Italy, the sermons preached on holidays or on special occasions were often delivered by priests or friars who had received a humanist education, and these sermons were influenced in their form and content, if not in their religious doctrine, by the secular oratory of the humanists. The large literature of humanist speeches was widely copied and printed, but it has not been frequently studied by modern scholars, although it contains a large amount of biographical, historical, and scholarly information, and although some of it expresses the thought of their authors and touches on problems and themes often discussed in other writings of the same period.

Even larger and probably more interesting is the literature of humanist letters. The ancient models for the letter were less numerous than for the speech or other genres, and ancient rhetorical theory provided but scanty guidance for its composition. Yet the state letter was the most important assignment for humanist chancellors and secretaries. Although they were bound to follow in the content and legal terminology of their letters and documents the example of their predecessors, the medieval notaries and *dictatores*, they did their best to improve upon the script, the vocabulary, and the style of their products.

For their private letters, the humanists were not limited by any constraints except by their own taste and by the example of such ancient writers as Seneca, Pliny the Younger, and especially Cicero. They maintained an extensive correspondence with their patrons, friends, and colleagues, often preserved, collected, and edited their own letters, and considered and treated them as an important part of their literary production. Actually, the letters of the humanists have enjoyed more favor with modern scholars and readers than most of their other writings. This is due to their elegant style and to their interesting content which often reflects the life of the author and of his friends, the events of his day, and his thought and opinion on a variety of subjects. For reconstructing the thought of a humanist, his letters are as important as any of his other writings.

Although the skill of the humanists as orators and practicing rhetoricians found its most direct expression in their speeches and letters, it also shaped the form and style, if not the content, of all their other prose compositions, including their historical and philosophical writings. As authors of histories and biographies dealing with ancient, medieval, and contemporary subjects, and of antiquarian works dealing with ancient topography and mythology, the humanists cultivated a fluent and elegant style, and the fictitious speeches which they inserted in their histories after the example of their ancient and medieval predecessors gave them a special opportunity for showing their rhetorical expertise. On the other hand—and for this they have not always received due credit—they used their critical judgment and their knowledge of older sources and documents to expose forgeries and conventional errors and to reconstruct the events of the past in a rational and plausible fashion; thus they often attained a high degree of accuracy and credibility. The humanist concern with history led them to reflections on the method, sources, and theory of history which appeared first in the prologues to their courses and commentaries on ancient historians and later found their expression in special treatises on the art of history.

Among the numerous prose works composed by the humanists on a great variety of topics, we find a considerable number of treatises dedicated to moral and other philosophical problems These show the same concern for style and elegance that characterized their other prose works, and they also pay their tribute to the ancient authors by frequent quotations, examples, and allusions. Aside form the plain treatise, the humanists show a marked preference for the invective and the dialogue. The invective had its models in some of Cicero's speeches and in the apocryphal invectives attributed to Cicero and Sallust that enjoyed a wide circulation and popularity. It enabled authors to give a more personal tone to their discourse and to exaggerate their points beyond the limits of plausibility, something they evidently enjoyed. The dialogue, usually patterned after the model of Cicero rather than that of Plato, offered the advantage of presenting more than one opinion or viewpoint on the same subject without seeming to take a definitive stand (although the author's true opinion may often be inferred from his preface, from the composition of the dialogue itself, or from his other writings). The dialogue also gives a personal and almost dramatic vivacity to the problems discussed. On the other hand, it provides a literary excuse for avoiding the tight argument and precise terminology that had characterized the philosophical literature of the ancient Greeks and of the medieval scholastics.

The narrative prose of the humanists, apart from their historical works, is limited to a few short stories in Latin, some of them translations from Boccaccio's *Decameron*, and a few descriptions and eulogies of cities, countries, and public festivities. Much more extensive is the humanist contribution to Latin poetry. It has, with few exceptions, not received much applause from modern critics, though it has been more widely studied in recent decades. Apart from isolated pieces, there are many collections of epigrams and elegies composed after the model of the ancient Roman poets. Odes and other Horatian strophes are much rarer because of their greater metrical difficulty and the limited knowledge of ancient prosody. There are quite a few long poems in epic hexametres which are historical, mythological, religious or didactic in content. Some of the didactic poems deal with philosophical or scientific topics and hence are interesting for their doctrinal content as well as for their literary form. There are a certain number of hymns, and pastoral poetry patterned after Virgil's eclogues enjoyed great popularity from the early fourteenth century. More limited, though not without interest, is the humanist contribution to dramatic literature. There exist a few Latin tragedies, but a somewhat larger number of Latin comedies, most of which were written and performed at the universities of northern

Italy. In the sixteenth and seventeenth centuries, the genres of Latin comedy and tragedy were much cultivated by the Jesuits, who in this sector, as in some others, followed the humanist tradition. Humanist influence came to be felt also in the vernacular literatures. Many of the genres of classical and humanist poetry were imitated and adopted in the vernacular literatures.

The humanists also played an important role in the development of poetical theory and of literary criticism. The defense of poetry against the theologians led to the formulation of some interesting principles. The humanist commentaries on the ancient poets, and especially their introductions, contained some pertinent reflections. Horace's *Ars poetica* was commented upon and occasionally imitated in separate treatises on poetics, and in the sixteenth century, Aristotle's *Poetics*, which had been practically unknown during the preceding centuries, was extensively discussed in commentaries. There were also a number of independent treatises on poetics that culminated in the work of Julius Caesar Scaliger.

In concluding my survey of the literary production of the humanists, I should like to emphasize that it was characterized throughout by a desire to imitate the ancient authors and to emulate them in the elegance of their style, vocabulary, and literary composition, but that the humanists added a new dimension that is not typical of ancient literature and that is largely new: the tendency to take seriously their own personal feelings and experiences, opinions, and preferences. An air of subjectivity pervades all humanist literature that is absent from most classical literature and also from much modern literature prior to Romanticism or to our own age. It accounts for the often uninhibited gossip, flattery, and polemics present in much humanist literature, and it also helps to explain the Renaissance preference for such literary genres as the invective, the dialogue, the speech, the letter, and the essay. I should like to think that this is what Jacob Burckhardt meant when he spoke of the individualism of the Renaissance, a concept that has been more often criticized than understood. In the sense in which I understand it, it is perfectly valid, if not for the Renaissance in all of its aspects, then at least for that large sector of its thought, learning, and literature that is dominated by the humanists.

I hope this sketchy survey has shown how rich, varied, and pervasive Renaissance humanism was. It was essentially a scholarly, educational, and literary movement, and among its many concerns, philosophical thought was not the only or even the dominating one. On the other hand, Renaissance philosophy as a whole owed no less to the traditions of medieval scholasticism and to the original ideas of contemporary thinkers than it did to humanism and to the ancient ideas transmitted by the humanists. Much of the work of leading humanists, and all of the work of many minor humanists, has significance not for philosophy in any sense of the term, but only for scholarship or literature. Vice versa, much of the philosophical literature of the Renaissance was due not to the humanists but to Aristotelian philosophers with a scholastic training, to Platonist metaphysicians influenced by humanism and scholasticism, and above all by Plato and the Neoplatonists such as Ficino and his followers, or to original thinkers marginally influenced by humanism, from Cusanus down to Telesio, Bruno, and Francis Bacon.

The influence of humanism on Renaissance philosophy was very great indeed, but the importance we attribute to it will depend on our conception and definition of philosophy. If we limit philosophy to the systematic and technical discussion of the subjects and problems defined by ancient, medieval, and modern traditions, the humanist contribution is still significant, especially in ethics and political thought, and to a lesser extent in logic. It is even greater if we take philosophy in a broader sense to include the wide areas of less systematic and more popular thought and discussion and the philosophical implications of other disciplines such as theology, jurisprudence, the arts, the humanities, and especially rhetoric and poetics, which occupied a place even in the Aristotelian *corpus*.

If we want to assess this contribution, we must distinguish between the direct and the indirect contributions of Renaissance humanism to philosophy and between the contributions due to the movement as a whole and those due to individual humanists whose ideas and intellectual interests were not necessarily shared by other humanists.

The direct contribution of Renaissance humanism to the philosophy of the period was concentrated in the area of moral philosophy and its ramifications, including political thought. Moral philosophy was the only branch of philosophy which was recognized as a part of the humanities and was hence of professional concern to the humanists. Even the university chairs of moral philosophy were at times, though not consistently, assigned to humanists, and it is the only area of philosophy where the humanists found themselves in direct conflict and competition with their scholastic contemporaries. As we have seen, the humanists actually produced a large body of moral treatises and dialogues which express their ideas on a variety of traditional or new problems. It is this part of their work which has always (and understandably) attracted and even monopolized the attention of historians of philosophy, such as Garin, Trinkaus, Rice, Tateo, and others. We might add that the humanists offered not only traditional or new thoughts on conventional problems, but also formulated or emphasized problems that were either new or had not occupied the center of attention in earlier thought. They wrote extensively on such themes as fate and free will, the highest good, the various virtues and vices, the active and contemplative life, will and intellect, the immortality of the soul, and the dignity of man. Moreover, the ideas of the humanists on a variety of moral and other philosophical questions were not only expressed in the treatises they dedicated to the respective themes, but also hidden away in their letters, orations, and other writings.

Of equal and perhaps greater importance was the indirect contribution of humanism to Renaissance thought. The humanists were actively involved in making the sources of ancient philosophy and science available to their contemporaries by discovering, copying, and editing classical Latin texts; by translating Greek texts into Latin (and later into the vernaculars), and by discussing and interpreting them in their commentaries. Many important works of ancient, and especially of Greek, philosophy and science were made available for the first time, whereas others that had been previously known were more widely discussed and better understood. Many of the new texts contributed to the advance of mathematics, medicine, botany, and other sciences. The direct knowledge of the Greek commentators of Aristotle influenced the interpretation of the philosopher by Renaissance Aristotelians, and the new knowledge of ancient philosophers who were outside the Aristotelian tradition led to increasing doubts about the exclusive validity and authority of that tradition, a widespread eclecticism, and a renewed interest in, and adherence to, other ancient schools of philosophy, especially Neoplatonism, Stoicism, Epicureanism, and Scepticism (Academic and Pyrrhonian). The libraries and the minds of Renaissance readers and thinkers were stocked with many texts and ideas unknown to their predecessors. Even if we were to deny any lasting validity to the doctrines of most Renaissance philosophers, the intellectual fermentation brought about by the addition of new sources and of new ideas to the medieval heritage was an important factor in preparing the intellectual climate for the new science and the new philosophy of the seventeenth century. The great role played during the Renaissance by astrology, alchemy, magic, and other occult sciences has few links with humanism or for that matter with Aristotelianism, but came to be associated with Platonism. This area of thought was also cultivated by at least some humanists and was influenced by some ancient sources made available by the humanists.

The indirect influence of the humanists on Renaissance thought and philosophy was not limited to the diffusion of ancient texts or of ancient and new ideas. It also affected, and perhaps in a more pervasive and lasting way, the style and pattern of philosophical literature. The philosophical dialogue continued to flourish to the early nineteenth century, though it has since practically disappeared. However, if most philosophical literature in recent centuries, even the most technical, has followed the form of the short essay or of the neatly composed treatise rather than that of the commentary or of the *Quaestio*, this fact is clearly due to humanism rather than to scholasticism, as is the practice of arguing precisely and also plausibly instead of accumulating arguments regardless of their relative strength, as had been the medieval scholastic practice. Philosophical literature has also followed the rules of Latin vocabulary, syntax, and composition as defined by the humanists—rules that were later transferred to the modern vernacular languages after Latin ceased to be used for academic or scholarly discourse (which happened much later and much more gradually than is usually believed). In view of the fact that terminology has always played a vital part in philosophical discourse, the impact of humanism on the development of philosophical terminology seems to be in need of much further exploration. The subjective and individualistic attitude that characterizes and pervades humanist discourse from Petrarch to Montaigne and that explains to some extent the humanist preference for the letter, the dialogue, and the essay, also tends to penetrate much philosophical and scientific literature during the fifteenth and sixteenth centuries and appear even in authors where we might least expect it, such as Pomponazzi. This tendency seems to recede in later philosophical literature, but it is not entirely absent in Descartes, Spinoza, or Leibniz.

Finally, if we view Renaissance philosophy and Renaissance thought in the broader context of the history of Western philosophy, we may assert that for a long time philosophy was linked, though not identified, with religion and theology, as in the Middle Ages, and with the mathematical and natural sciences, as during much of the last four centuries. We should not be surprised if Renaissance philosophy was to some extent allied with the humanities, that is, with rhetoric, poetry, historical and classical scholarship. We might even wonder whether this may provide a lesson for the present and for the future. If philosophers were to pay greater attention to the humanities, as a few have done in our century, this might be beneficial not only for the humanities and humanist scholarship, but also for philosophy and for a more complete and more balanced understanding of our world and experience.[1]

Columbia University

---

[1] A longer annotated version of this paper appeared in the *Cambridge History of Renaissance Philosophy* (Cambridge: Cambridge Univ. Press, 1988).

JOHN MONFASANI

Platonic Paganism in the Fifteenth Century

THE PAGAN RENAISSANCE IS A HISTORIOGRAPHICAL CLICHÉ WHOSE classical formulation we owe to the nineteenth century, but whose roots extend as far back as the seventeenth.[1] Like their Enlightenment predecessors, nineteenth-century historians found in the authors of the Italian Renaissance the free-thinking neo-pagans who were, in Jacob Burckhardt's memorable phrase, "the first-born among the sons of modern Europe." No matter that Burckhardt discovered this neo-paganism amongst the Italian humanists while Ernest Renan found it amongst the intellectual rivals of the humanists, the Paduan scholastics.[2] When Charles Alexandre proved that the contemporary Greek philosopher and visitor to Italy, George Gemistus Pletho, was also a neo-pagan,[3] a nineteenth-century student might well have wondered if there were any serious thinkers left in Renaissance Italy who were not neo-pagans. Indeed, far from refuting the cliché, pious historians conceded it and merely regretted its truth.[4] Readers today

---

[1] See W. K. Ferguson, *The Renaissance in Historical Thought: Five Centuries of Interpretation* (Cambridge: Houghton Mifflin, 1948), 93, 97, and "paganism" in the index; P. O. Kristeller, "The Myth of Renaissance Atheism and the French Tradition of Free Thought," *Journal of the History of Philosophy* 6 (1968): 233–43.

[2] J. Burckhardt, *The Civilization of the Renaissance in Italy*, tr. S. G. C. Middlemore (Vienna: Phaidon [1937?]), 264–67 (*Die Cultur der Renaissance in Italien: Ein Versuch* first appeared at Basel in 1860); E. Renan, *Averroès et l'averroïsme*. The first edition was Paris, 1852; I consulted the eighth edition of Paris: Calmann Levy, 1925. See 353 ff., 414–14.

[3] George Gemistus Pletho, *Traité des lois*, ed. C. Alexandre, tr. A. Pellissier (Paris, 1858; repr. Amsterdam: Hakkert, 1966). See, for instance, Alexandre's introduction, p. L ff. Alexandre was rebutting the older view of Leo Allatius and Ignatius Hardt, who argued for Pletho's Christianity.

[4] In addition to the examples provided by Ferguson (n. 1 above), even the editor of Pletho, Charles Alexandre, who was himself a devout Catholic (see the *Dictionnaire de biographie française* 1 [1933]: 1455–57), was unsympathetic to what he perceived to be Italian attitudes in Pletho's day (p. LXXXV): "Toutefois, l'esprit philosophique se développa moins vite dans cette société fort peu sérieuse que l'élément

may smirk at Ludwig von Pastor's distinction between a bad pagan humanism and a good Christian humanism in the Renaissance, first enunciated in 1886.[5] But, in fact, Pastor's thesis was one of the first successful attempts to shrink substantially the domain of Renaissance neo-paganism.

Recent scholarship has shrunk that domain even further. If we understand a Renaissance neo-pagan to have been someone who no longer considered himself a Christian and who embraced instead what he believed to be a specifically pagan world view, then I know of no Italian humanist whom present-day scholarship would confidently label a neo-pagan, not even Pomponio Leto, the founder of the supposedly pagan Roman Academy.[6] Indeed, the most recent trend is to find religious purposes and sources for much of what was once considered distinctly pagan manifestations of Renaissance culture. Francis Petrarch and Lorenzo Valla, former prize examples of the pagan spirit of the Renaissance, are now increasingly viewed as serious Christian thinkers.[7] Following the lead of Paul Oskar Kristeller, few today would consider Marsilio Ficino a neo-pagan,[8] nor, for that matter, Giovanni Pico della Mirandola, the other major philosopher with close ties to

---

païen favorisé par les études de la renaissance et par la corruption des moeurs."

[5] See L. von Pastor, *Geschichte der Päpste seit dem Ausgang des Mittelalters* 1 (Freiburg im B., 1886; I used the ninth edition, ibid.: Herder, 1926), 1–63, 271, 313–17, 379, 513–70.

[6] See A. J. Dunston, "Pope Paul II and the Humanists," *The Journal of Religious History* 7 (1973): 287–306; and R. J. Palermino, "The Roman Academy, the Catacombs and the Conspiracy of 1468," *Archivium Historiae Pontificiae* 18 (1980): 117–55. A piece of evidence generally overlooked is the notice on Leto in the necrology composed c. 1525 by an anonymous scholar who was demonstrably knowledgeable and a rigidly orthodox member of the Roman curia (see my "Platina, Capranica and Perotti: Bessarion's Latin Eulogists and His Date of Birth," in A. Campana and P. Medioli Masotti, *Bartolomeo Sacchi detto il Platina . . . Atti del convegno internazionale di studi per il V centenario (Cremona 14–15 nov. 1981)* [Padua: Antenore, 1987], 97–136, at p. 112). The anonymous necrologist gives the impression that he knew Leto quite well when he affectionately refers to him as "homo totus simplex."

[7] An early extreme formulation of this position concerning Petrarch is G. Toffanin, *L'Umanesimo italiano (dal XIV al XVI secolo)*, which first appeared in 1933 (I used the English translation by E. Gianturco, titled *History of Humanism* [New York: Las Americas, 1954]), which reflects ideas expressed in his *Che cosa fu l'Umanesimo* of 1919 (see Ferguson, 349–51). For Valla see M. Fois, *Il pensiero cristiano di Lorenzo Valla* (Rome: Università Gregoriana, 1969); G. Di Napoli, *Lorenzo Valla: Filosofia e religione nell'Umanesimo italiano* (Rome: Storia e Letteratura, 1971); and S. Camporeale, *Lorenzo Valla: Umanesimo e teologia* (Florence: Istituto Nazionale, 1972).

[8] For recent literature see in *Marsilio Ficino e il ritorno di Platone. Studi e documenti*, ed. G. C. Garfagnini (Florence: Olschki, 1986), especially P. O. Kristeller, "Marsilio Ficino and His Work after Five Hundred Years," 15–196, which is now available in revised form as a separate publication with the same title (Florence: Olschki, 1987).

Renaissance humanism.⁹ The Renan thesis concerning Paduan scholasticism is today accepted as even plausible only in the case of a very small number of figures.¹⁰ Lucien Febvre has dissipated the pagan aura surrounding sixteenth-century French humanists.¹¹ And on a Europeanwide scale, Richard Popkin and Charles Schmitt have effectively dashed any hopes of finding pagan revivalism in the growth of Renaissance scepticism.¹² Finally, some scholars have raised doubts about the evidence for Pletho's paganism, since most of it seems to have been selected by Pletho's chief accuser, George Scholarius.¹³

In short, we have come full circle. Are there any pagans left in the Renaissance? Was paganism ever a viable option within Renaissance culture? Before constructing a model of the cultural impossibility of neo-paganism in the Renaissance, one should be sure that there were no pagans. I shall try to answer that question apropos Renaissance Platonism; and, since I find compelling the evidence for the orthodox intent of the Florentine circle about Marsilio Ficino, I shall concentrate on George Gemistus Pletho and his influence.

In their books on Pletho, François Masai and C. M. Woodhouse

---

⁹ This is clear from the proceedings of the congress on Pico: *L'opera e il pensiero di Giovanni Pico della Mirandola nella storia dell'Umanesimo*, 2 vols. (Florence: Istituto Nazionale di Studi sul Rinascimento, 1965).

¹⁰ In his two fundamental surveys, *A Critical Survey and Bibliography of Studies on Renaissance Aristotelianism 1958–1969* (Padua: Antenore, 1971) and *Aristotle and the Renaissance* (Cambridge: Harvard Univ. Press, 1983), C. Schmitt felt that Renan's paganism thesis was no longer a serious issue, and referred to it only incidentally as "the extreme position of Renan" (*A Critical Survey*, 83). Even M. L. Pine, *Pietro Pomponazzi: Radical Philosopher of the Renaissance* (Padua: Antenore, 1986), who supports Renan's thesis as it appertains to Pomponazzi, flatly denies that "the medieval Averroist tradition, with which Pomponazzi was certainly associated, was fundamentally irreligious" (354).

¹¹ L. Febvre, *Le problème de l'incroyance au XVIe siècle, la religion de Rabelais* (Paris: A. Michel, 1942).

¹² R. H. Popkin, *The History of Scepticism from Erasmus to Descartes* (Assen: Van Gorcum, 1960; rev. ed. New York: Humanities Press, 1964); idem, "Scepticism and the Counter Reformation in France," *Archiv für Reformationsgeschichte* 51 (1965): 58–88; C. B. Schmitt, *Gianfrancesco Pico della Mirandola (1469–1533) and His Critique of Aristotle* (The Hague: Martinus Nijhoff, 1967); and idem, *Cicero Scepticus: A Study of the Influence of the "Academia" in the Renaissance* (The Hague: Martinus Nijhoff, 1972).

¹³ See E. Wind, *Pagan Mysteries of the Renaissance*, rev. ed. (Oxford: Oxford Univ. Press, 1980), 244–47, 256; P. O. Kristeller, "Byzantine and Western Platonism in the Fifteenth Century," in his *Renaissance Concepts of Man and Other Essays* (New York: Harper & Row, 1972), 86–109, at 97; and N. G. Wilson, *Scholars of Byzantium* (London: Duckworth, 1983), 270. Undecided on Pletho's paganism was W. Gass (*Gennadius und Pletho: Aristotelismus und Platonismus in der griechischen Kirche*, 2 vols. in 1 [Breslau, 1844], 1:36–37), who wrote before the appearance of Alexandre's edition of the *Laws*.

have assumed that Pletho was a neo-pagan philosopher.[14] In fact, the vast majority of modern scholars who have written on Pletho share this assumption.[15] However, if one looks at the works Pletho published in his own lifetime, one finds that Pletho never explicitly embraced paganism nor pretended to do any more than explain the ideas of Plato, Zoroaster, and other ancient sages.[16] Furthermore, in his eulogy of the

---

[14] F. Masai *Pléthon et le platonisme de Mistra* (Paris: Les Belles Lettres, 1956); C. M. Woodhouse, *Gemistos Plethon: The Last of the Hellenes* (Oxford: Oxford Univ. Press, 1986).

[15] After Alexandre, the most influential nineteenth-century expositor of Pletho's paganism was F. Schultze, *Georgios Gemistos Plethon und seine reformatorischen Bestrebungen* (Jena, 1874; repr. Leipzig: Zentralantiquariat der Deutschen Demokratischen Republik, 1975). In our century, both M. Mamalakis, *Georgios Gemistos Plethon* (in Greek) (Athens: Byzantinisch-neugriechischen Jahrbücher, 1939), 176, and B. Knös, ("Gémiste Pléthon et son souvenir," *Bulletin de l'Association Guillaume Budé* 9 [1959]: 97–184, at 128) believed that Pletho turned from Christianity to paganism only about the time of his trip to Italy. Quite convinced of Pletho's paganism are John Wilson Taylor, *Georgius Gemistus Pletho's Criticism of Plato and Aristotle* (Menasha, WI: George Banta, 1921), 87 ff.; M. Anastos, "Pletho's Calendar and Liturgy," *Dumbarton Oaks Papers* 4 (1948): 183–305, at 189; B. Tatakis, *La philosophie byzantine* (Paris: Presses universitaires de France, 1949), 282–93; D. Zakythinos, *Le Despotat grec de Morée*, 2 vols. (Paris: Les Belles Lettres, 1932–53; rev. ed. London: Variorum, 1975), 2:365 ff.; and D. Dedes, "Theskeia kai politike kata ton Georgio Gemisto Plethona," *Philosophia* (in Greek) 5–6 (1975–76): 424–41.

[16] For instance, the opuscule that is frequently described as a summary of Pletho's views is by its very title and Pletho's own statement at the start, a summary of the teachings of Plato and Zoroaster; it is edited in Alexandre, 262–69 (with a French translation). It is commonly assumed that Pletho himself released for publication as a separate treatise under the title *De fato* what was actually book 2, chap. 6 of the *Treatise on the Laws*, and which clearly presumes his belief in the gods (see Alexandre, pp. XC–XCI, and Masai, p. 396, n. 1). However, Scholarius never referred to it in anything he wrote while Pletho was alive, and our earliest evidence for its circulation is the attack Matthew Camariotes launched against it in the 1450s shortly before or after Pletho's death (for the commonly accepted date and my disagreement, see my *George of Trebizond: A Biography and a Study of His Rhetoric and Logic* [Leiden: Brill, 1976], 170, n. 176). I suspect that the *De fato* was an unauthorized publication, similar to the release of the opening section of the *Laws* which Scholarius maliciously quoted from without attribution in a letter to Pletho of 1450 (first pointed out by Alexandre, p. XLVI, n. 1; for the date of the letter see George Scholarius, *Oeuvres complètes*, eds. L. Petit, X. A. Sidéridès, and M. Jugie, 8 vols. [Paris: Maison de la bonne presse, 1928–35], 4:V–VI, XXVI–XXVII; cf. Masai, *Pléthon*, 390). In book 3, chap. 20 of his *Comparatio Platonis et Aristotelis*, George of Trebizond refers to hymns of Pletho to the sun, which he had read, but he also mentions that he is writing three years after Pletho's death. In any event, nothing like a hymn to the sun survives among Pletho's *oeuvres*. Some scholars have suggested that what George really read were Proclus's hymn to the sun and/or the Orphic hymn to the same, both copied by Pletho himself, but without attribution, in MS. Marc., Zan. gr. 406, which contains autograph writings of Pletho and which once belonged to Cardinal Bessarion. See Alexandre, p. LXXVI, n. 2; Anastos, "Pletho's Calendar," 211; and I. P. Medvedev, "Solar Cult in Plethon's Philosophy?" *Byzantina* 13 (1985): 737–49.

princess Cleopa, he spoke of her taking the "bread of the most holy of *our* mysteries," in an obvious reference to the Eucharist;[17] in his treatise on the *Filioque* Pletho defended the Byzantine position as the one which *we* hold;[18] and at the Council of Ferrara-Florence he clearly argued for the maintenance of traditional Greek positions against the Latins.[19] Consequently, any belief in Pletho's paganism must depend on his posthumously published *Treatise on the Laws*. There, and only there, did Pletho prescribe in his own person a polytheistic creed and religious practices based on a Neoplatonic hierarchy of gods.[20]

The scholars who assume Pletho was a pagan also convey the impression that we have only a small portion of what was once an enormous work, i.e., that we have only those parts of the *Laws* which George Scholarius did not consign to the flames and which Scholarius preserved for the sole purpose of proving that Pletho was a pagan.[21] They therefore vitiate their own assumption by tacitly admitting that we do not have the context of the extant sections of the *Laws*. After all, by selective quotation a determined inquisitor could even make Thomas Aquinas into a neo-pagan.

Their mistake, however, lies not in believing Pletho a pagan, but in supposing that his *Laws* was a massive work, of which only a small fraction survives. The truth is otherwise, and consists in taking Scholarius at his word. In his well-known letter to the Exarch Joseph explaining how and why he burned Pletho's autograph copy of the *Laws*, which apparently was the only extant complete copy, Scholarius states that he read the whole work in four hours.[22] Scholarius explicitly distinguishes this four-hour reading from two other readings where he did no more than read the chapter headings and the introduction.[23] Moreover, the book was short enough that he later could give it still a second complete reading. He tells us that when making preparations to burn it, he tried in a second reading to find sections untainted by polytheism so that he might at least save these parts of the book for the sake of the

---

[17] J. Migne, *Patrologiae cursus completus. Series Graeca*, 160 (Paris, 1866): 945A: "arti tou hagiotatou ton hemeteron ... mysterion."

[18] Edited in Alexandre, 300–11. For "we" see p. 300, line 3 from the bottom. See also 309–11.

[19] See n. 36 below.

[20] The surviving fragments are edited by Alexandre (n. 3 above). See Masai, *Pléthon*, 303–404, for a discussion of the present state of the text.

[21] Cf. Alexandre, LXXXVIII ("grand ouvrage"), XCI–XCVII; Schultze, 116–121; Masai, *Pléthon*, 13; Woodhouse, 320–21.

[22] Scholarius, *Oeuvres* 4:160.4–5; Alexandre, 420.2–4.

[23] Scholarius, *Oeuvres* 4:159.18–19, and 160.25–26; Alexandre, 419.4; and 420, last line—421.1

philosophical and scientific learning they contained.[24] This I very much doubt he would have done if the *Treatise on the Laws* was an exceptionally large book. Pletho cultivated a dense style of prose.[25] Furthermore, Scholarius was reading a manuscript, where one invariably encounters ambiguities of script, abbreviations, and not always helpful punctuation. It is hard to believe that Scholarius read the *Laws* at a rate faster than 60 pages an hour in Alexandre's edition. But assuming that Scholarius read at a rate of 60 pages an hour, we arrive at a figure of approximately 240 pages for the whole *Treatise on the Laws*. The surviving Greek text in Alexandre's edition comprises 130 pages. I do not contend *tout court* that we possess half of the *Treatise on the Laws*. Perhaps Scholarius did skim over parts of the book when he read it. Perhaps he did read faster than I have estimated. Perhaps we should not take him literally when he estimated his reading time (though in that case, given his desire to stress the care he took with the work, we ought to suppose that he exaggerated rather than minimized the length of time). Nonetheless, if Scholarius's statement on the time it took him to read Pletho's work has any truth to it, then we have much more than a small fraction of the book, certainly a quarter, and perhaps even a third or more. Furthermore, the parts we do possess consist mainly of long continuous texts rather than isolated quotations, which would be the preferred method of a tendentious excerpter.

It is true that in Alexandre's edition we can read whole or in part only 21 of the 101 chapters recorded in Pletho's table of contents. But this organization of the chapters must be taken with a grain of salt. Masai has shown that what Alexandre treated as book 1, chapter 21 is, in fact, part of book 3, chapter 36, and that the text Alexandre called book 2, chapter 27 really belongs to chapter 26 of the same book.[26] More to our purposes, over a hundred years ago Schultze showed that most of what Alexandre took to be part of book 1, chapter 5 was most probably the text of chapters 5, 6, 7, 8, 9, and 10 of book 1, with several of these chapters being quite short.[27] If my earlier argument about the size of the *Laws* is correct, then we have to assume that many of the lost chapters were equally brief.

The very organization of the three books of the *Laws* suggests this. Masai has plausibly argued that the way to explain the helter-skelter

---

[24] Scholarius, *Oeuvres* 4:171.13–14; Alexandre, 438, last two lines from the bottom.
[25] See the remarks of Alexandre, p. LXXV.
[26] Masai, *Pléthon*, 395, n. 2, and 397, n. 2.
[27] Schultze, 121–22. Masai, (*Pléthon*, 395, n. 1) called this hypothesis "ingénieuse," but did not himself endorse it because the MSS do not have this division. However, he recognized that the MSS combined other chapters which are really separate.

and repetitious pattern of the chapters is to suppose that book 1 was initially meant to be a self-standing work and that at a later time Pletho embarked upon a further elaboration of his law code which resulted in books 2 and 3.[28] In respect to the organization of the work I would also call attention to a numerological aspect. The number of chapters in the *Treatise on the Laws* is really a hundred with the hundred-and-first being, as Pletho specifically called it, an *Epinomis*, an appendix to the law code, in imitation of the pseudo-Platonic *Epinomis*, a separate work appended to Plato's book of *Laws*. But if this is so, then the number of precisely a hundred chapters was probably not an organic development, but an artificial contrivance which Pletho decided upon part way through the writing of the *Laws*. This explains why book 1 has 31 chapters; book 2, 27; and book 3, the inflated number of 42 chapters plus the *Epinomis*. Pletho eventually sliced up the contents of book 3 so that he would come out with exactly 100 chapters and an *Epinomis*, just as he also made sure that his hymns to the gods in book 3 were twenty-seven in number consisting of nine lines each composed of three sets of tercets.

We have in a fairly complete state the beginning and the end of the *Laws*, where Pletho summarized his main positions. In the extant middle sections he frequently reiterated these same points. Therefore, according to Pletho's own assertion, we have in essence the main contours of what he had to say in the *Laws*. Moreover, on the supposition that much less of the *Laws* is lost than previously thought and in light of the consistency between the extant parts of the *Laws* and Pletho's other writings, we can reasonably expect that some of these other writings, such as his treatise on the virtues and his memoranda on reforming the Byzantine state in the Peloponnesus, reflect at least partially the sixteen chapters or so in the *Laws* on morals and political organization[29] Lastly, it should be pointed out that the titles of the remaining missing chapters give not the slightest hint that Pletho viewed any part of his doctrine as allegorical in nature. Quite the contrary, if anything, the titles of the missing chapters suggest that he repeated and reinforced what we know from the extant sections of the *Laws*.

The upshot of all this is that we seem to possess in the fragments of the *Laws* and in his other extant writings the essence of what Pletho thought. There is no new Christian Pletho yet to be discovered. The Pletho we have is the Pletho that was. And that Pletho was not an

---

[28] Ibid., 402–3.
[29] The lost chapters which seem to duplicate these extant works are book 1, chaps. 14 and 20, and 3, chaps. 3–4, 6–10, 12, and 14–19.

orthodox or, for that matter, an unorthodox Christian; nor was he an overly enthusiastic antiquarian. Rather he was an unequivocal neo-pagan.

In the *Treatise on the Laws*, Pletho claimed that he was restoring authentic pagan religious creed and ritual (the *theologia prisca*, Ficino would say) taught by true philosophers and lawgivers from Zoroaster through Plato and the Platonists. I see no reason not to believe that Pletho meant what he said; that he believed not only in the one supreme god, but also in the supercelestial gods, the subcelestial gods, and the demons, which fill his chain of being between the supreme god and man, and which he talked about time and time again. I take him at his word that he wished his prayers and hymns to these gods to be sung in accordance with the calendar he had devised; that he affirmed the eternity of the world, the unchangeable determinism of divine fate, and the transmigration of souls from body to body; and that he rejected as ridiculous the Christian notions of intercessory prayer, resurrection, and paradise.[30]

The decisive issue, it seems to me, is not the reality of Pletho's paganism, but rather the extent to which he influenced others in that direction. Here again I think the recent studies by Masai and Woodhouse have gone wrong in a basic assumption. Masai was convinced that Pletho established a pagan brotherhood in Greece and then exported it to Italy when he visited the peninsula as a member of the Greek delegation to the Council of Ferrara-Florence in 1438–1439.[31] Woodhouse is more cautious as to the Italian context, not denying, however, that Pletho inspired Italian followers, but merely recognizing that the evidence does not permit us to demonstrate these links.[32] He also accepts the idea of a pagan coterie about Pletho at Mistra, where Pletho lived and taught in the later part of his life.[33] Yet, the supposition that Pletho proselytized for the pagan brotherhood seems to me to distort what Pletho was all about.

To begin with the Italians, I have long believed that Arnaldo Della Torre enunciated the correct view *grosso modo* in 1902.[34] Far from being indefinite on whether Italians accepted Pletho's brand of Platonic pa-

---

[30] These specific criticisms of Christianity (which are also applicable to Mohammedanism) are found in the *Epinomis*, 256, last line ff. in Alexandre's edition.

[31] 300 ff., 337 ff. The term "brotherhood" comes from a letter of Scholarius concerning the apostate Juvenal (see n. 71 below).

[32] See chap. 9, p. 154 ff. Concerning Woodhouse's recitation of possible Latin contacts, see my review in *Renaissance Quarterly* 41 (1988): 116–20.

[33] Woodhouse, 42, 223–25, 228, 363.

[34] A. Della Torre, *Storia della Accademia platonica di Firenze* (Florence: G. Carnesecchi, 1902), 438 ff.

Platonic Paganism in the Fifteenth Century 53

ganism, the evidence is quite clear that the Italians were positively unreceptive towards it.

Both Scholarius and Pletho allude to Pletho's discussions with Latins at the time of the Council.[35] We have no reason to doubt that Pletho held such talks directly and through the aid of interpreters. The question is, "to what effect?" The Greek memoirist of the Council, Sylvester Syropoulos, refers to a dinner party attended by Pletho where the Greeks bested the Latins in philosophical debate.[36] However, we have several Latin reports of the same dinner party, and none mention Pletho.[37] Worse, the Latins have the story the other way around, i.e., that the Italian doctor Ugo Benzi singlehandedly defeated the assembled Greeks. Indeed, the only Latin source cited by the biographers of Pletho that actually speaks of Pletho's activities at the Council is Marsilio Ficino's preface to Lorenzo the Magnificent for the translation of Plotinus, published in 1492, fifty years after the Council. Ficino says that the talks Pletho gave in Florence inspired Cosimo de' Medici to found the Platonic Academy.[38] Kristeller comments, "knowing Ficino's manner of speaking, I hesitate to accept this story in as literal a sense as has been by many historians."[39] Another Latin source is Iacopo Zeno's

---

[35] These passages are well known; e.g., see the English translations in Monfasani, *George of Trebizond*, 202; Woodhouse, 156 and 166; in French in Masai, *Pléthon*, 331–34. The credit for identifying as Pietro Vitali and not Pomponio Leto the "Peter of Calabria" whom Pletho mentions as an interlocutor in Italy, belongs to Della Torre, *Storia della Accademia platonica*, 440–41.

[36] V. Laurent, ed., *Les "Mémoires" du Grand Ecclésiarque de l'Eglise de Constantinople Sylvestre Syropoulos sur le concile de Florence (1438–1439)*. Concilium Florentinum, 9 (Rome: Pontificium Institutum Orientalium Studiorum, 1971), 258. Syropoulos is our major source for Pletho's activities at the Council. Therefore his references bear on the question of Pletho's paganism. I count fifteen separate incidents mentioned by Syropoulos where Pletho is mentioned (see Laurent's index). All but one are neutral or not inconsistent with his paganism. The exception is on 366, where Syropoulos reports a meeting which Pletho and the patriarch had by themselves and in which Pletho is quoted as speaking of holding "our faith" from "our Lord Jesus Christ," "the Apostle," and "our doctors." Though Pletho would, and did, argue that the Greeks should hold to their traditional principles, I suspect that the wording of this private conversation as reported by Syropoulos (if it did in fact take place) is more Syropoulos's than Pletho's. On the reliability of Syropoulos see Laurent's introduction, 27–30, and J. Gill, *Personalities of the Council of Florence* (Oxford: Blackwell, 1964), 144–85.

[37] They are conveniently collected in D. P. Lockwood, *Ugo Benzi: Medieval Philosopher and Physician 1376–1439* (Chicago: Univ. of Chicago Press, 1951), 31, 155 (Socino Benzi, *Ugonis vita*), 157 (Pope Pius II).

[38] M. Ficino, *Opera omnia* (Basel, 1576), 1537.

[39] "Byzantine and Western Platonism" (see n. 13 above), 105. The sentence continues: "but there is a nucleus of truth in it, and Ficino surely intended to establish a historical link between his own work and that of Plethon."

panegyric letter to Ciriaco d'Ancona written in Florence about 1441, only two years after the Council.[40] Twice in the letter, Zeno refers to the "doctissimus Gemistus," who, Zeno says, is Ciriaco's dear friend and whom Ciriaco had persuaded to come to the Council. Because of this last assertion and because of the fact that Zeno seems not to have been at the Council, Zeno's references probably reflect Ciriaco's own enthusiasm for his friend rather than a more generalized Italian interest in Pletho. From Zeno's references, one would not even know that Pletho was a philosopher, let alone a Platonist.

If we look at those Italian humanists at Ferrara and Florence with command of Greek who could conceivably have talked with Pletho in private, we shall quickly arrive at a dead end. The pious Camaldulesian monk Ambrogio Traversari was obviously no candidate for the heathen brotherhood, nor certainly was the leading humanist of Ferrara, the conservative and devout Guarino da Verona. Leonardo Bruni, the chancellor of Florence, might superficially appear promising, especially since he wrote his *Constitution of Florence* in Greek during the Council and because we have a copy of the work corrected by Pletho himself.[41] However, by the late 1430s Bruni was a staunch Aristotelian, and, pointedly, he addressed the *Constitution of Florence* not to Pletho, but to the Greek Aristotelian George Amiroutzes.[42] The only scholar knowledgeable in Greek whom Pletho actually mentions speaking to is Pietro Vitali, who was abbot of Grottaferrata and about as pagan as Ambrogio Traversari.[43]

Woodhouse several times refers to Gregorio Tifernate hearing Pletho in Florence.[44] But his source, Antonius Antimachus, never mentions Florence, and was writing, in any case, in 1540, more than a hundred years after the Council. Tifernate himself, on the other hand, speaks of learning Greek only at Mistra. He also never felt the need to mention Pletho, though it made little sense to go to Mistra except to study with

---

[40] L. Bertalot and A. Campana, "Gli scritti di Iacopo Zeno e il suo elogio di Ciriaco d'Ancona," *La Bibliofilia* 41 (1939–40): 356–76; repr. in L. Bertalot, *Studien zum italienischen und deutschen Humanismus*, ed. P. O. Kristeller, 2 vols. (Rome: Storia e Letteratura, 1975), 2: 311–32. The references to Pletho are on 329 in Kristeller's edition.

[41] See A. Moulakis, "Leonardo Bruni's Constitution of Florence," *Rinascimento* ser. 2, 26 (1986): 141–92.

[42] Ibid., 145 ff. for the Aristotelian influence; see also G. Griffiths, J. Hankins, and D. Thompson, *The Humanism of Leonardo Bruni*, Medieval & Renaissance Texts & Studies, vol. 46 (Binghamton, NY, 1987), 261 (Hankins).

[43] Pletho called him Peter of Calabria; see Della Torre, cited in n. 35 above, for the identification.

[44] Woodhouse, 161–62, 217, and 376.

him.[45] True, Tifernate translated the Platonic author Timaeus Locris for Pope Nicholas V, but soon after he may have also translated some sermons of St. John Chrysostom.[46] In any event, there is nothing in his *curriculum vitae* to suggest contamination by the virus of paganism.

The much travelled antiquarian Ciriaco d'Ancona is an interesting case. Woodhouse calls him a "true pagan spirit,"[47] I suppose because Ciriaco considered Mercury his special *genius*, and liked to address a prayer of thanksgiving to Mercury after a voyage.[48] But Mercury held a relatively modest place in Pletho's polytheistic system,[49] nor would anyone argue that Ciriaco, for all his archaeological enthusiasm and admiration of Pletho, had any grasp of Pletho's Neoplatonic philosophy.[50] But most importantly, Ciriaco was a Christian, if we are to give credence to his reverent references to the Resurrection,[51] the Virgin, the saints, and relics.[52] He practiced Christian piety,[53] wished to save Christianity from the Turks, and was good friends with many clerics.

---

[45] See G. Mancini, "Gregorio Tifernate," *Archivio storico italiano* 81 (1923): 65–112, at 71.

[46] Ibid., 75–77; the preponderance of manuscript evidence points to Lilio Tifernate as being the translator.

[47] Woodhouse, 165 and 228.

[48] See E. Bodnar and C. Mitchell, *Cyriacus of Ancona's Journeys in the Propontis and the Northern Aegean 1444–1445*. Memoirs of the American Philosophical Society, vol. 112 (Philadelphia, 1976), 33–34, 59; O. Jahn, "Intorno alcune notizie archeologiche conservateci da Ciriaco di Ancona. Lettera del prof. O. Jahn al cav. G. B. de Rossi," *Bullettino dell'Instituto* [sic] *di corrispondenza archeologica* (= Deutsches archäologisches Institut), an. 1861, pp. 180–92, at p. 183; see also Ciriaco d'Ancona, *Itinerarium*, ed. L. Mehus (Florence, 1742), pp. LXV and 8; I. D. Mansi, *Addenda* in I. A. Fabricius, *Bibliotheca Latina Mediae et Infimae Aetatis*, 6, ed. I. D. Mansi (Padua, 1754), 13; G. B. de Rossi, *Inscriptiones Christianae Urbis Romae septimo saeculo antiquiores*, 2 vols. (Rome, 1857–88), 2:367, col. 1, n. 1; from whom is extracted the criticism of Mommsen in E. W. Bodnar, *Cyriacus of Ancona and Athens* (Brussels: Latomus, 1960), 51, n. 5 (continued from the previous page). De Rossi remarks apropos Mercury: "cuius cultum Cyriacus poetice affectabat."

[49] Pletho mentions Mercury's planet twice (Alexandre, 166.5 and 210.5), and Mercury himself only once (Alexandre, 160.8), where he is described as having authority over the demons.

[50] Woodhouse, 228, admits as much.

[51] See R. Sabbadini, "Ciriaco d'Ancona e la sua descrizione autografa del Peloponneso trasmessa da Leonardo Botta," in *Miscellanea Ceriani: Raccolta di scritti originali per onorare la memoria di M. Antonio Maria Ceriani* (Milan: Hoepli, 1910), 181–243, at 228 (repr. in R. Sabbadini, *Classici e umanisti da codici ambrosiani* [Florence: Olschki, 1933], 1–52).

[52] Ciriaco, *Itinerarium*, 57, 66–67.

[53] Ibid., 57. Cf. also the travel report published by H. Graeven, "Cyriacus von Ancona auf dem Athos," *Centralblatt für Bibliothekswesen*, 16.5 (1899): 209–15, at 213–14, in a passage where it was not necessary to praise Christianity: "sed in his potissimum e sacris almae religionis nostrae auctoribus nomina legi."

That his religious views may have been in some respects unconventional does not gainsay the fact of his Christianity.

Grasping at straws, Pletho's biographers invariably suggest some sort of link, at least in spirit, between him and Lorenzo Valla. But Valla was not even at the Council. Moreover, it has been obvious to scholars for a long time that Valla was especially hostile to philosophic threats to Christianity.[54] He tried to Christianize Epicureanism; and he attacked Aristotelianism and Stoicism as subversive of Christianity. I have little doubt that had he known about it, Valla would have excoriated Pletho's polytheism.

Nor are Greeks in Italy any help. One of them, George of Trebizond, detested Pletho, and was matched in the violence of his opposition to Pletho only by George Scholarius and Scholarius's pupil Matthew Camariotes.[55] To be sure, the great Cardinal Bessarion was Pletho's student, but Bessarion's life and writings give the lie to any suggestions of heathenism. True, at Pletho's death, Bessarion wrote to his teacher's sons a letter of consolation which sounded surprising themes for a cardinal of the Roman Church. Bessarion said that Pletho had passed on to the Olympian gods and that if one were to believe in metempsychosis, then one would have to say that the soul of Plato had inhabited Pletho's body.[56] But Bessarion was not revealing his own views here, but delicately acknowledging those of his departed mentor. It is no accident that in his massive *In calumniatorem Platonis* where he meticulously refuted George of Trebizond's criticisms of Plato point-by-point, Bessarion never took up George's culminating attack on Pletho's neo-paganism. George's whole prior discussion of Platonism built up to this finale, and to have stopped short of answering it was tantamount to admitting its truth.

The proponents of the pagan brotherhood thesis put forward as star exhibits three letters of Michael Apostolis.[57] In the first, addressed to Pletho, Apostolis expresses his admiration and begs to be accepted as a disciple. The other two, addressed to John Argyropoulos, are marked by enthusiastic references to the pagan gods, show some inkling of Pletho's polytheistic scheme, and refer to Pletho as "pious." We may also add that Apostolis hotly defended Pletho and the Platonists in the contemporary Plato-Aristotle controversy. Were Apostolis and Argyropoulos

---

[54] See n. 7 above.

[55] Monfasani, *George of Trebizond*, passim.

[56] For a discussion of this letter see Wind, *Pagan Mysteries*, 256–58.

[57] The letters are edited together by Alexandre, 370–75, and most extensively discussed in Masai, *Pléthon*, 312–13. On Apostolis see D. J. Geanakoplos, *Greek Scholars in Venice* (Cambridge: Harvard Univ. Press, 1962), 73–110.

members of the pagan brotherhood? I think not. It is always dangerous to assume that letters express the views of those to whom they are addressed; and in the case of Agyropoulos, we do not have to depend upon what Apostolis wrote him since we can consult Argyropoulos's own words. In a number of texts, Argyropoulos explicitly avowed his Christianity.[58] Consciously or not, proponents of the pagan brotherhood theory follow a sort of perverse law of hermeneutics, to wit, that no one ever means what he says unless he says what you want him to mean. As for Apostolis, he was an ambitious, flighty man of rapid changes of mood.[59] Pletho was a famous teacher who had trained some of the most important men in Byzantine society. So why not some mythological effusions if they helped to make you a disciple of the master? I simply point out, first, that in an address to Emperor Constantine XI, Apostolis strenuously affirmed his Christian faith against those who misunderstood his literary references to the pagan gods;[60] second, that the honor Apostolis gave Mercury in his mythological letter is quite at variance with Pletho's own scheme of the gods;[61] and, third, that it is easy to find references to his Christian beliefs in Apostolis's correspondence.[62] *Pace* the perverse law of hermeneutics, the preponderance of evidence strongly points to Apostolis being Christian.

Of all the Byzantine émigrés to Italy, perhaps the most devoted to Pletho's memory was the aristocrat Demetrius Raoul Kavakes. Kavakes diligently collected and copied Pletho's writings. More importantly, he praised the Sun god in various marginal notes with a fervor that amounted to heliolatry.[63] In Kavakes we would seem to have a dyed-in-the-wool pagan, a true member of the Plethonian heathen brotherhood. Yet Kavakes's worship of the sun is destructive of Pletho's polytheistic scheme, where the sun has an important, but nonetheless quite

---

[58] See S. P. Lampros, *Argyropouleia* (in Greek) (Athens: P. D. Sakellarios, 1910), 66.5, 107–41 passim, and 194.

[59] See the comments of H. Noiret, *Lettres inédites de Michel Apostolis* (Paris: E. Thorin, 1889), 24–26.

[60] S. P. Lampros, *Palaiologeia kai Peloponnesiaka* (in Greek), 4 vols. (Athens: Epitros ekdoseos ton kataloipon Sp. Lamprou, 1912–30), 4:83–87. Masai and Woodhouse ignore this opuscule; Geanakoplos, *Greek Scholars*, 78, n. 16, is in error when he refers to Masai.

[61] See n. 49 above.

[62] See, e.g., letters 64, 80, 89, 93, 105, and 125 (the date) in Noiret; and letter 6 in E. Legrand, *Bibliographie hellénique des XVe et XVIe siècles*, 4 vols. (Paris, 1885–1906; reprint Paris: G.-P. Maisonneuve & Larose, 1962), 2:236.

[63] A. Keller, "Two Byzantine Scholars and Their Reception in Italy," *Journal of the Warburg and Courtauld Institutes*, 20 (1957): 363–70, at 366 ff., surveys the prior literature.

circumscribed place.⁶⁴ Kavakes's heliolatry and Pletho's brand of polytheism are mutually exclusive. Furthermore, Kavakes asserts that he became a devotee of the sun when he was seventeen. But it is hard to imagine Pletho initiating a teenager into his supposedly secret brotherhood. The price of exposure could be an absolutely ghastly death. Moreover, even as a mature man Kavakes's literary culture remained rather mediocre.⁶⁵ Why should we presume that Pletho found him to be an especially promising pupil as a teenager? We also have some evidence that Kavakes had a devotion to the Virgin.⁶⁶ Kavakes may have been merely a Christian with some bizarre paganizing ideas. But whatever the extent of his paganism, it was *sui generis*, and to a substantial degree independent of Pletho.

As for Greeks in Greece, unless we assume that anyone who was friendly with Pletho or who praised him was a crypto-pagan, there is no one associated with Pletho for whom there is any evidence of paganism. Of Pletho's two eulogists at his death, one, Jerome Charitonymus, admits that he never was a pupil of Pletho.⁶⁷ The other, the monk Gregory, was a pupil of Pletho, but also, as his name indicates, a monk who invoked not only St. Paul and David in praise of Pletho,⁶⁸ but also Saints Basil the Great, John Chrysostom, and Gregory of Nazianzus.⁶⁹ Gregory's discussion of the virtues, immortality, and the one supercelestial god show some familiarity with Pletho's doctrines, but these particular doctrines were quite consistent with Christianity.

---

⁶⁴ In Pletho's scheme the Sun was hardly the grand, isolated figure he was in Kavakes's imagination. For Pletho the sun was the head of the third order of the gods, the first order consisting of Zeus alone, the second of the supracelestial gods, and the third of the intracelestial gods, who are joined to matter. Pletho addressed the sun in only one of the hymns in the *Laws* (Alexandre, 210). The supracelestial gods, especially Neptune, had far more power and honor in Pletho's hierarchy. The pairs Sun-Moon and Saturn-Venus in conjunction with the Titans and the gods of Tartarus generate the mortal creatures in the hierarchy (Alexandre, 106 ff.; Schultze, 180–81; Medvedev, "Solar Cult," 741). Another indication of the standing of the sun in Pletho's scheme of things is the fact that he demonstrably knew Proclus's hymn to the sun as well as the Orphic hymn *Eis helion*, and yet chose not to duplicate them in any of the prayers in the *Laws*; see n. 16 above.

⁶⁵ Virtually every scholar who has dealt with Kavakes has remarked on his barbarous orthography; e.g., J. Bidez, *La tradition manuscrite des éditions des discours de l'empereur Julien* (Ghent: Van Rysselberghe & Rombart-Paris: Champion, 1929), 76, speaks of his "orthographe fantaisiste"; and G. Mercati, *Opere minori*, vol. 4 (Vatican City: Biblioteca Apostolica Vaticana, 1937), 173, n. 2, says concerning a passage: "Demetrio ha scritto colla solita sua scorrettezza [the Greek which follows]."

⁶⁶ Keller, 367.

⁶⁷ Alexandre, 385.1 ff.; Migne (n. 17 above), 160:811B–C.

⁶⁸ Alexandre, 390.11 ff.; Migne, 160:814B–C.

⁶⁹ Alexandre, 392.21–22; Migne, 160:815C.

Pletho would have had no fear talking about them.[70]

There was one contemporary Greek who apparently was a pagan. This is Juvenal, who about 1450 was burned at the stake after having suffered horrible tortures.[71] A letter of Scholarius of about 1451–1452 is our only source of information concerning Juvenal. The significant point for our purposes is that even though Scholarius had kept close eye on Juvenal's activities for years, even though he had intercepted Juvenal's letters to those whom Scholarius called other members of the pagan brotherhood, even though Juvenal did circulate for a time in the Peloponnesus, even though Juvenal was tortured after capture, and even though in the letter Scholarius makes it clear that the ultimate objective of his investigations had been Pletho, nonetheless, in the end Scholarius had not a shred of evidence linking Juvenal to Pletho. Juvenal may have been a pagan; but if Scholarius could not find any real proof connecting Juvenal to Pletho, I do not think modern historians should blithely assume a link.[72]

In sum, scholarship has yet to discover anyone whom we can describe as a pagan follower of Pletho in the sense of adhering to Pletho's specific pagan creed. But that is a disturbing conclusion only if we assume that Pletho actively sought converts to his polytheistic vision. For in spite of all his admirers, friends, and pupils, I doubt that Pletho ever initiated anyone fully into his polytheistic teaching or that he ever gave more than a small number of adherents even a glimpse of it. Contemporary circumstances would have made it very dangerous to proceed otherwise. The times called for circumspection and preparation, not proselytizing and open conversion.

In this regard, we should consider one of the most famous texts concerning Pletho, i.e., George of Trebizond's report of his conversation with Pletho in 1439. It runs as follows:

> I myself heard him at Florence (for he had come with the Greeks to the Council) asserting that in a few more years the whole world would accept one and the same religion with one heart, one mind, and one proclamation. And when I asked him whether

---

[70] The efforts which Schultze, 51–54, and Woodhouse, 9–11, have made to extract some sort of cultist code in Gregory's words are patently strained. E.g., I see no reason why Gregory's use of the usual word for writings, *syggrammata*, must be understood as a cryptic reference to the *Treatise on the Law* (*Nomon syggraphe*). Again, it is true that he refers to Pletho as a mystagogue, but such language was normal in Byzantine tradition, e.g., Gregory himself in speaking of St. Paul (see n. 68 above).

[71] Scholarius, *Oeuvres* 4:476–89; Lampros, *Palaiologeia* 2:247–65.

[72] Masai, *Pléthon*, 300 ff., accepts Juvenal as part of Pletho's brotherhood; Woodhouse, on 35 and 225, is cautious about making the link; but then on pp. 271–72 and 315–18, he reports Scholarius's letter without criticism.

it would be Christ's or Mohammed's, he said, "Neither; rather, it will not differ much from heathenism."[73]

George goes on to claim confirmation from what Greek refugees told him in the 1450s. In George's words, "[Pletho] openly said before he died ... that not many years after his death Mohammed and Christ would collapse and the true truth[74] would shine through every region of the globe." George reasserts elsewhere that he indeed spoke with Pletho in Florence.[75] Since I have never caught George in an outright lie, I have no reason to think that he is lying here.

The scholars who have believed George have taken his statements as evidence for Pletho's paganism. But in point of fact George's reports are quite neutral as to Pletho's own religious views. Rather, what they show is not Pletho's creed, but his confidence in predicting the future. In his eulogy of Pletho, Jerome Charitonymus confirms that Pletho enjoyed a certain reputation as a prophet.[76] From the *Treatise on the Laws*, it is clear that Pletho held that the future is utterly foreordained and that lives and periods repeat themselves in some sort of pattern.[77] Pletho was a student not only of philosophy, but also of astronomy, chronology, and history. Among other items, we have from his pen a brief summary of the sequence of world empires[78] and also an account of the Greek world from the death of the Theban general Epaminondas in 362 BC to the eve of Alexander the Great's ascension to the Macedonian throne in 336 BC.[79] We also have strong indications from Bessarion and Kavakes that Pletho believed himself to be the reincarnated soul of Plato.[80] I therefore offer the following hypothesis as Pletho's thinking: just as after the death of Plato, Alexander the Great made the Greeks supreme throughout the ancient world, so too after the death of Pletho,

---

[73] *Comparatio Platonis et Aristotelis* (Venice, 1523), fol. V6r (I have collated the passage with the manuscripts).

[74] Both the manuscripts and the 1523 edition have *vera veritas*.

[75] Ibid., fol. B8v.

[76] Alexandre, 379.20 sq.; Migne, 160:808D.

[77] See Alexandre, 64 sq. (chapter on fate), and 256.4 ff.

[78] See A. Diller, "The Autographs of Georgius Gemistus Pletho," *Scriptorium* 10 (1956): 27–41, at 31; and, for the text, I. Hardt, *Catalogus codicum manuscriptorum Graecorum Bibliothecae Regiae Bavaricae*, 5 vols. (Munich, 1806–1812), 5:125–27.

[79] The latest edition is *Georgii Gemisti Plethonis Opuscula de historia Graeca* (Leipzig, 1989), ed. E. V. Maltese. On this work see J. Dräseke, "Zu Platon und Plethon," *Archiv für Geschichte der Philosophie* 27 (1914): 288–94; Woodhouse, 221–22; E. V. Maltese, "Una storia della Grecia dopo Mantinea in età umanistica," *Respublica Litterarum* 10 (1987): 201–7.

[80] See Masai, *Pléthon*, 384–86; Woodhouse, 187–88; and Wind, *Pagan Mysteries*, 256–58.

a new Alexander would arise and once again raise the victorious banner of Hellenism over the whole earth. Pletho wrote the *Treatise on the Laws* not to make converts amongst his contemporaries, but to provide a written model for the future world Hellenic state. His life's task was not to create a brotherhood of pagans—contemporary society would not permit that—but to prepare the intellectual foundations of the coming new world order.

In the last analysis, Pletho's prophesy gave meaning and purpose to his paganism.[81] That is why in the 1440s he chided those Greeks who had despaired of divine Providence and, out of expediency, had accepted Latin theology.[82] No longer trusting in Providence, they had surrendered their Greek identity. But Pletho was convinced of the imminent Greek revival. That is also why in the first decades of the century, in a memorandum on the reforming of the government and society of the Peloponnesus to the Despot Theodore, he cited the examples of the defeated Trojans who survived to found Rome and of the Persians who restored their empire after being conquered by Alexander and the Romans.[83] The Greeks, he said,[84] first achieved greatness when Hercules gave them a constitution, just as the Spartans first became powerful after they accepted Lycurgus's laws, and the Thebans after they heeded Epaminondas, a student of the Pythagoreans. Before conquering Asia, Alexander the Great absorbed not only what his father Philip had learned from Epaminondas, but also the tuition of Aristotle. Pletho obviously failed to find in the last Byzantine rulers a new Epaminondas or Alexander who would implement his plans for social and political reform. But true to his own advice, he did not despair of Providence. By the time he spoke with George of Trebizond in Florence he had transferred his hopes to a coming age and probably had already written at least book 1 of the *Treatise on the Laws*.[85] He wrote for the future, for the *Restitutio rerum Graecarum* which would come after his death and which would have as its spiritual core a *Restitutio Hellenismi*.

State University of New York at Albany

---

[81] As if anticipating my thesis, Knös, "Gémiste Pléthon," 128, specifically denied that "[Pléthon] n'était un prophète, il était un savant et érudit." But he agreed that Pletho did not establish an "academy" of pagan followers at Mistra (129).

[82] Alexandre, 309–10.

[83] Migne, 160:844C.

[84] Ibid., 845B–C.

[85] Scholarius had heard of the *Laws* before leaving Greece for the Council of Ferrara-Florence; see his *Oeuvres* 4:155.30 ff.

M. J. B. ALLEN

Summoning Plotinus: Ficino, Smoke, and the Strangled Chickens

TWO EXTRAORDINARY BUT RELATED EVENTS IN THE LIFE OF PLOTInus are described by Porphyry in chapter 10 of his biography. He tells of the several abortive attempts by a jealous Alexandrian magician, Olympius, to cast star spells on—to put a hex on—the austerely benign and ascetic founder of Neoplatonism. These spells apparently recoiled on their author and he was racked with convulsions, his body "shrivelling like a money-bag pulled tight," until he wisely desisted. Porphyry next recounts the tale of how an Egyptian priest, newly arrived in Rome and anxious to impress Plotinus with his hieratic powers, offered to evoke Plotinus's presiding genius or spirit. The sage readily consented and the evocation took place in the temple of Isis, the only location in Rome pure enough for the event. Upon the summons of the priest, the spirit momentarily appeared; whereupon, the priest declared that Plotinus was singularly graced, not with a spirit from the ordinary ranks of daemons, but with a higher kind of divinity, one that was truly a god. Porphyry is led to observe that "Thus Plotinus had for an indwelling spirit a being of the more divine degree, and he kept his own divine spirit unceasingly intent upon that inner presence."[1] It was this preoccupation that led him to write his treatise enti-

---

[1] Ficino translated Porphyry's *Vita Plotini* into Latin for his monumental Plotinus translation and accompanying commentary, *Plotini Enneades* (Florence, 1492): see Paul Oskar Kristeller, *Supplementum Ficinianum*, 2 vols. (Florence, 1937; repr. 1973), I:cxxvi–cxxviii, clvii–clix. Future references will be to the signatures of the copy in the Elmer Belt library at UCLA. In the second and standard edition of Ficino's *Opera omnia* (Basel, 1576; repr. Turin, 1959, 1983), the life appears on 1538 [misnumbered 1528] to 1547 (with chapter 10 on 1541–42), and the commentary on 1548–1800; the important proem addressed to Lorenzo de' Medici appears on 1537–38. Ficino also refers to Porphyry's account of the attempted planet-striking of Plotinus in his *De vita* 3.18 (ed. and tran. Carol V. Kaske and John R. Clark as *Marsilio Ficino: Three Books on Life*, Medieval & Renaissance Texts & Studies, vol. 57 [Binghamton, 1989], 340.122–26); see also his *Letters* 10 (*Opera* 911.1). — All translations from Ficino are my own. Citations from Ficino's *Opera* and his *Plotini Enneades* have been repunc-

tled "Our Tutelary Spirit" (the *Enneads* 3.4), an essay explaining the differences among our spirit guides.[2]

The theory of our attendant daemon has deep roots in ancient religion, folklore and mythology, but for a Platonist it stems directly from the enigmatic and often ironic references in a number of Plato's dialogues to Socrates' "warning voice," the prohibitory, apotropaic impulse that we would call the voice of conscience.[3] Xenophon too bears witness in his *Apology* 12 to the phenomenon, referring to it as "the voice of god." The "warning voice" was soon identified as an attendant spirit or daemon in the morally neutral sense, and such eminent Middle Platonists as Plutarch of Chaeronea and Apuleius of Madaura wrote exceedingly influential treatises on Platonic daemonology, with Socrates' daemon as their point of departure or ostensible theme.[4] Other important Platonic texts were the great myths of the

---

tuated, with contractions and diacritics expanded and the *u/v* and the *ae/e* distinctions observed.

[2] Interestingly, Plotinus insists that our tutelary demon is an inner psychological principle, not an exterior anthropomorphic daemon; this principle is within us and yet transcendent (see especially 3.4.3.3–8 and 3.4.5.19–24). Ficino refers to it in the introduction to his commentary on the *Enneads* 3.4 as *potestas praestantior animae*: it is "the intellect in each person which, like the reason's daemon, is always watching over (*speculans*) all things" (*Plotini Enneades*, sig. u vii verso, i.e. *Opera*, 1707.2). The notion that man's soul, or its highest part, *nous*, is a daemon derives from the *Timaeus* 90C, as Ficino recognized; cf. *summa* 12 of his *Timaeus* Commentary—"rationis autem apex, id est, mens nobis est pro daemone" (*Opera*, 1484.1). Cf. Heraclitus, *êthos anthrôpôi daimôn* (Diels-Kranz 119), cited in Plutarch's *Quaestiones Platonicae* 999E, etc.—a reference suggested to me by Professor Paul Oskar Kristeller. — In addition to the daemon who was "a part of the soul" (*pars animae*), however, both Plotinus and Ficino acknowledged what Ficino calls *extranei* or *externi* personal daemons. See Ficino's *Timaeus* Commentary, chapters 27 and 45 [misnumbered 42]—"Ait intellectum homini pro daemone datum, scilicet intimo; alterum enim daemonem habet externum" (*Opera*, 1451, 1465); and also *summae* 23 and 24 (*Opera*, 1469.2,3). See too his epitome for the *Laws* IX—"Ac memento nostrum daemonem geniumque non solum, ut quidam putant, nostrum intellectum esse sed numen" (*Opera*, 1515). — For Iamblichus's views, see *De mysteriis* 9.6–10 (ed. Des Places, 206–9), with Ficino's paraphrase in his *Opera*, 1906.2–3. Iamblichus remarks in 9.6 that the daemon guides us "until, having atoned with sacred works, we yield to the god instead of the daemon as our guide; and thereafter the daemon so yields to the god that either he is idle when the god is present or he serves him in some matter" ("quousque sacris operibus expiati deum subeamus pro daemone ducem, cui post hac daemon ita cedit ut vel vacet eo praesente vel conducat ad idem"). In 9.7 Iamblichus declares optimistically that evil daemons are never alloted as guardians. Ficino's debts to Iamblichus's daemonology await exploration.

[3] See the *Euthydemus* 273A, *Alcibiades I* 103A, 105E, 124C, *Euthyphro* 3B, *Apology* 31C, 40A, *Republic* 6. 496C, *Theaetetus* 151A, *Phaedrus* 242C, and for Ficino (see below) also the *Theages* 128D.

[4] Plutarch, *De genio Socratis* 591D ff., 593D ff.; Apuleius, *De deo Socratis*. See John Dillon, *The Middle Platonists 80 B.C. to A.D. 220* (Ithaca, 1977), 219–23, 317–20.

guardian daemons in the *Phaedo* 107DE and at the end of the *Republic* 617DE and 620DE; the definition in the *Symposium* at 202DE that "every *daimonion* is midway between a god and a mortal being"; and the rejection of the notion that gods or daemons could be influenced by spells or rituals in the *Laws* 905D–907D, a rejection also voiced in the *Republic* at 364B–E, with the provision of severe penalties for anyone who practiced necromancy.

The attendant divinities of Socrates and Plotinus, however, and presumably those of other great sages such as Pythagoras, were not ordinary daemons but rather gods. For the ancient Greeks, the demarcation line between daemon and god was necessarily blurred given their complex notion of divine immanence in the world of nature and of men, and from the beginning poets such as Hesiod had posited an ascending hierarchy of divine beings that went from the souls of the heroes at one end to the primordial pre-Olympian deities at the other. Within this framework, Porphyry was stressing an important distinction: Plotinus belonged to a higher spiritual order than most men, and his daemon was divine. Continually dedicated to the purgation of earthly affections and perturbations, he had almost managed to slough off his earthly body—that compounded from the four elements—in order to dwell wholly in his daemonic body, the body that is rightfully ours, but that only the purest, the most philosophical souls can repossess.

For a Platonist, however, this daemonic body was itself usually thought of as twofold or even threefold. Since the daemons are by nature airy beings and are distributed in the main through the three zones of the air—the upper, middle, and lower—it follows that the daemonic body can be characterized in terms generally of upper or lower, or specifically in terms of the three zones.[5] In its most rarefied form it will partake of the nature of the upper fiery or aethereal air. And we should note that the Neoplatonists were careful not to adopt the Aristotelian definition of aether as the fifth and highest element. Swayed by the authority of the *Timaeus* and the *Epinomis*, and then by Plotinus's own speculations, they thought of it as intermediate between the air and the pure celestial fire, and thus as the fieriest form of air or the airiest form of celestial fire.[6] In a less rarefied form the daemonic

---

[5] *Plotini Enneades*, sig. u vii verso, i.e., *Opera*, 1708. See M.J.B. Allen, *The Platonism of Marsilio Ficino* (Los Angeles, 1984), 11 ff. In the *De civitate Dei* 8.14–16,21, Augustine insisted on the fact that the daemons dwelt in the air, the gods in the aether.

[6] Plato, *Timaeus* 58D, *Epinomis* 981C, 984B–E; Plotinus, *Enneads* 2.1.2,4,6,7; 6.7.11. Ficino was also influenced by Calcidius's *Timaeus* Commentary 178. See his *Epinomis* epitome and his *Timaeus* Commentary, *Opera*, 1445, 1451, 1463, 1527.

body will partake of the unaethereal air, air in its sovereign purity, uncontaminated by the presence of cloud or water vapor or smoke. In its least rarefied form it will partake of vapor-laden air, like the bodies of naiads, nereids, and other water daemons, or even of smoky air, like the bodies of the subterranean, plutonian daemons. The theory requires that all daemons are, almost by definition, airy beings, however contaminated by the lower elements in a vaporous form on the one hand, or aetherealised to the point of being almost fiery gods on the other, though those dwelling with the gods in the celestial spheres presumably possess bodies of pure or virtually pure fire.

The eminent and influential fifteenth-century Florentine Platonist, Marsilio Ficino, some of whose views I shall explore in this paper, followed Proclus, the last great ancient Neoplatonist, in his daemonological speculations, at least for the most part. He thus inherited the most systematic version of Platonic daemonology with its host of intricate scholastic distinctions. Some of these distinctions he rejected as unnecessary, and he was obviously uncertain whether to go along with the notion of an airy but vapor-laden body.[7] He certainly toyed with it, however, as he did with the Pythagorean notion that philosophers who remain true to philosophy through three millennia can reassume their airy bodies after they have purged themselves of earthly affections and taint.[8] These bodies he seems to have equated with the body we shall occupy in the Christian scheme in purgatory.[9] In them philosophers in effect become daemons (though the reverse corollary that all daemons should be philosophers does not apparently follow!). Porphyry does not affirm exactly that Plotinus had transcended this airy stage, still less that he had entered into the daemonic body in its most rarefied form, as the celestial or aethereal body, the glorified body we shall occupy in the Christian scheme at the Resurrection.[10] Indeed, since he is still alive, Plotinus is accompanied rather by his attendant spirit, a companion that leaves us once we dwell exclusively in our own spiritual body after death. Nevertheless, Porphyry does affirm that his attendant genius occupied an aethereal rather than a merely aerial body; and we may

---

[7] See Allen, *Platonism*, 12–13. The distinction between the two airs derives ultimately from the *Timaeus* 66DE (cf. 58D).

[8] *Phaedrus* Commentary, *summae* 25 and 33 (ed. and tran. M.J.B. Allen, as *Marsilio Ficino and the Phaedran Charioteer* [Berkeley and Los Angeles, 1981], 168–71. 190–91).

[9] See Ficino's epitome for the *Phaedo* (*Opera*, 1392 [misnumbered 1390]); also Allen, *Platonism*, 12–13, 97–103.

[10] *Opera*, 1392; also Paul Oskar Kristeller, *The Philosophy of Marsilio Ficino* (New York, 1943; repr. Gloucester, Mass., 1964), 195–96, 371.

presume that Plotinus would immediately assume a similarly aethereal body upon his death.

This daemonological lore also had consequences for psychology and epistemology. In the case of personal daemons, Ficino writes in his Plotinus Commentary, in the introduction or *summa* to the *Enneads* 3.4, that the daemons who inhabit the water-laden, cloudy air are able to work upon our imaginations by means of their own imaginations, if our lives are given over to the imagination. But, if we live the life of reason, then the daemons who inhabit the pure air will be able to work upon our reasons by means of their own discursive intellects. If we live the intellectual life, then the purely fiery daemons—either those living in the pure fire and thus accompanying the celestial gods from whom they are hardly distinguished, or those living in the uppermost reaches of the air in the fiery aether—will be able to work on our intuitive understandings by way of their own intuitive intellects.[11] In other words, theoretically each order of daemon constantly strikes upon (*pulsant*) each of our major faculties; but "the order of higher daemons works much more secretly and more tranquilly than the lower ones in recalling us constantly to intuitive understanding."[12] Consequently, writes Ficino, since "Plotinus lived governed not so much by his reason as by his intellect [let alone his imagination], and since he strove to understand intuitively rather than by way of discursive reasoning, uprooting all passions utterly and not merely pruning them," then it must follow that his attendant daemon came from the upper end, as it were, of the scale: "It was this kind of higher daemon who seems to have led Plotinus, and that is why the daemon was called a god; Socrates' daemon was of the same kind."[13] We certainly cannot suppose Plotinus was attended by one of the cloud loving daemons, the lords of perturbation and passion, but rather, like Socrates, he must have been

---

[11] *Plotini Enneades*, sig. u vii verso (i.e., *Opera*, 1708): "Ubi enim secundum imaginationem vita disponitur, externus daemon noster est aerius in aere videlicet infimo, ac per imaginationem nostram imaginatione sua nos agitans; ubi vero secundum rationem vivimus [*Opera* ratio-non viv?ur], daemon foris ex aere medio ratione sua rationem versat humanam; ubi denique intellectualis est vita, daemon ex aere summo per intelligentiam aspirat intelligentiae; atque id non tam electione faciunt quam more naturae."

[12] Ibid.: "daemones viribus suis nostras assidue pulsant; sed excellentior ordo daemonum agit occultius admodum atque tranquillius ad intelligentiam assidue revocans."

[13] Ibid., sig. u vii verso (i.e., *Opera*, 1707–8): "quippe cum Plotinus non tam ratione quam intelligentia viveret, nitens videlicet intuitu plurimum potius quam discursu, neque perturbationes amputans sed extirpans ... qualis utique daemon videtur duxisse Plotinum, ideoque appellatus est deus, qualis et daemon ipse Socraticus."

accompanied by the "most preeminent among the airy daemons, a daemon who is led by one of the most preeminent of the aethereal daemons, who in turn is led by the best among the celestial daemons."[14] Moreover, Ficino observes, we can speak Platonically of this attendant spirit as a god, since the higher daemons are customarily called gods just as the lowest gods are customarily called daemons.[15]

Nevertheless, how was it possible for the Egyptian magician to summon Plotinus's attendant spirit? And how did it actually appear? It is here that Ficino enters into interesting speculative territory involving more than folklore and ghostlore, but examining problems intrinsic to the Platonic system and its development. In a long passage on the airy daemons—and we recall that all daemons are in essence airy even if they habitually dwell in other elemental realms—Ficino describes them as unlike the animals dwelling on the earth in that they are "greater" and "more eminent." "Rotund" or spherical in form like the air (which is more closely akin to the reason than the water or the earth), they possess a swift circular motion as the reason does. Their sensation is "most acute" (again because of the air) and is present throughout their whole body—that is, they are not confined to differentiated and localized perception as we are.[16] Perhaps we can think of them in contemporary terms as resembling that extraordinary but authentic phenomenon, ball-lightning, rather than the ghouls of the popular imagination. Such daemons, Ficino continues, are effectively the "stars" of the sphere of air, their sphericity of shape and circularity of motion reinforcing the resemblance. In their motions "they imitate the circuits of the heavenly stars" in the translunar spheres, and thus they rise and set. Like the planets, moreover, these daemons, and especially those above the turbulent lower air, "progress and regress at the appointed times, now inclining toward the north, now toward the south, now ascending, as it

---

[14] Ibid., sig. u viii recto (i.e., *Opera*, 1708): "Plotinum igitur atque Socratem praestantissimus inter aerios ducit daemon, ductus videlicet a quodam inter aethereos praestantissimo ducto similiter ab aliquo inter caelestes daemones optimo. Socrates igitur atque Plotinus continuata serie moventur a summo."

[15] Ibid. sig. u vii verso (i.e., *Opera*, 1708): "Solent enim praestantissimi quique daemones deorum nomine nuncupari, quemadmodum et infimi dii appellatione daemonum designari." Cf. Augustine, *De civitate Dei* 9.1–2, 6–13.

[16] Ibid.: "aeris ipse globus est amplior atque praestantior et vitae praesertim rationali cognatior.... Ingentia igitur rationaliaque [*Opera* rationalique] in aere animalia degunt, figura quoque rotunda, qualem figura haec aeris exigit. Sensus et in toto corpore totus et pro natura aeris acutissimus; motus ratione simili velocissimus; motionis ordo ferme qualis in stellis." — In the *Timaeus* 44D (cf. 73C–D) Plato had argued that the gods imitated the spherical shape of the universe in making the human head spherical and therefore capable of mind; cf. Calcidius, *In Timaeum* 231, Macrobius, *Somnium Scipionis* 1.14.9.

were, to the apogee and now descending again in a determined order."[17] It follows from this correspondence with the motions of the celestial bodies that the daemons influence us in the literal sense that they too rain down their "hidden but efficacious" powers upon us. Indeed, astrological lore supposed that the daemons aided or directed the celestial influences or variously interacted with them, not only by their choice but by their nature—and we can see why their orbital paths, interweaving with those of the stars and planets, would produce an awesomely intricate mesh of influences.[18]

We might note that it would follow from this analysis that the heavenly bodies, ruled by celestial gods, should affect our intuitive understandings rather than, as traditionally held, our temperaments, humors, and bodies; and that the airy star-like daemons should influence our discursive reasons, and lower daemons our lower faculties. But the Ptolemaic astrological tradition, along with daemonological problems raised by the Middle Platonists and the Neoplatonists, generally militated against such a simple if logical delimitation of zones of influence. At times, moreover, Ficino seems anxious to reject the notion that our higher faculties can be influenced by the daemons lest he open himself up to the charge of being a radical determinist. Even so, he was prepared to expatiate on occasions, with his customary prolixity and learning, as to how the stars and daemons alike can and do influence our imaginations as well as the lower faculties governing health, growth, and reproduction; and as to how they might signify if not influence intellectual events, as we shall see.

Accordingly, we have to bear in mind the constant presence and influence of the airy daemons who circle over us as lesser stars and who are in the train of the higher stars as their instruments. Whereas the astrologer, however, can only compute the motions of the planets and their spheres and offer predictions as to the nature of their influ-

---

[17] *Plotini Enneades*, sig. u vii verso–u viii recto (i.e. *Opera*, 1708): "Daemones igitur stellae sunt aerei caeli, circuitus stellarum caelestium pro viribus imitantes ab ortu ad occasum, atque vicissim statutis ubique temporibus progredientes quoque regredientesque ac tum ad septentrionem vergentes, tum ad meridiem, tum etiam velut in augem ascendentes, tum iterum descendentes ordine certo, praesertim daemones super aerem turbulentum." A planet inclines (*vergit*) toward the north as it grazes the Tropic of Capricorn and starts uphill towards the Tropic of Cancer, and the reverse when it "verges" toward the south. "Auge" means here the point at which a planet is at its greatest distance from the earth; cf. Ficino's *De vita* 3.2 (ed. Kaske and Clark, 252.41). I am greatly indebted to Carol Kaske for clarifying this passage for me and for this and another *De vita* reference.

[18] Ibid. sig. u viii recto (i.e., *Opera*, 1708): "Neque electione dumtaxat in nos agunt, ut diximus, sed plurimum stellarum instar ipsa natura radiisque suis quamvis occultis tamen admodum efficacibus."

ence, a magician can exercise much greater powers over the airy daemons than mere prediction. Ficino at this point adduces some arcane possibilities, though ones familiar to him from his extensive reading of the Platonists. The airy daemons, like the higher stars, emit rays. A ray or beam theory tends to use light as its paradigm (though the image of a wave governs our notions of the flow of other less focused kinds of energy). It is possible, he writes, that a knowledgeable magician could possess the power to "gather together" the invisible rays emitted by the daemons, and in so doing make them visible to himself, and then to others. As an analogy Ficino first adduces the image of the sun: "Immediately after the sun sets, one cannot discern the sun's rays unless occasionally they are gathered together on certain vapors or clouds. At that point they can immediately be seen in the guise of red and white."[19] Obviously, by "gathered together" he means the same as "reflected": the clouds serve almost as mirrors to catch and reflect the rays of the sun and to make them visible to the naked eye in the spectrum of sunset colors. His second, less effective analogy adduces a flame in the brightness of noon that cannot be seen unless silhouetted against a burning log. Both analogies require the notion of an invisible ray of pure light and of some kind of reflector that catches or even in a way concenters or focusses the rays in order to render them visible.

It is instructive at this point to turn to a rather striking passage in Ficino's treatise on the Magi's star, in actuality one of his more influential sermons.[20] Having declared that this star was a comet, citing the authority of Origen and others, Ficino had then argued that it was a comet created by, and then illuminated by, the archangel Gabriel. Gabriel had created the comet by standing in the middle air and congregating a thousand *stadia* from roundabout, confining it into a narrower space. Then "he had bound it all up to himself as the soul has bound the body, and separated it from the rest of the air. Similarly milk, when subjected to the power of a coagulant, is often contracted into a narrower space and separated from the water."[21] Ficino then poses the ques-

---

[19] Ibid.: "quos [radios] quidem magus, qui congregare sciverit, poterit et videre caeterisque monstrare, sicut et solis radii evestigio post occasum, qui per se minime discernuntur, aliquando certis vaporibus congregati, statim sub ruboris vel palloris forma videntur, et flamma nonnunquam in meridie accensa procul in ligno [*Opera* lino] non cernitur, adhibitis vero lignis apparet."

[20] *Opera*, 489–91; see Kristeller, *Supplementum*, I:lxxxii–lxxxiii; also Stephen M. Buhler, "Marsilio Ficino's *De Stella Magorum* and Renaissance Views of the Magi," *Renaissance Quarterly* 43 (1990): 348–71.

[21] *Opera*, 490–91: "Quo autem modo angelus cometam accumulavit? Stans protinus in aere medio, mille aeris stadia circumfusa sibi in spatium aliquantum angustius congregavit, idque totum velut anima corpus sibi mira potestate devinxit [*Opera*

tion: "Why did the archangel condense the air?" The answer is that the air, when condensed, would be able to make the light, which the archangel himself has imparted to it, visible to men's eyes: for "things that are exceedingly rarefied or thin escape even the acutest eye."[22] But whence did Gabriel derive the light he imparts to this body of contracted reflecting air? For Ficino unequivocally it came from "the light of his own understanding"; "for what in the understanding is invisible or intellectual light," Ficino reasons, "becomes visible once it is transmitted to the air." If transmitted only to the most rarefied and subtlest air, then it can only be seen by the blessed—meaning I take it those already occupying the glorified aethereal body, or those few who perhaps can temporally escape from their earthy habitations to occupy such a body. But if the light is subsequently transmitted to thicker or denser air, then, Ficino affirms, it can be witnessed by others also.[23] In other words, the light of the understanding has to be reflected in order to be made visible. Like the rays of the sun after sunset, it has to be caught on the clouds before it can be seen by the many as red and white.

But what corresponds exactly to the intermediate stage, when the blessed see the light of angelic understanding, not upon the banners of the evening clouds, but upon the rarest most purified regions of the upper air? Does Ficino have in mind merely the blue of the noonday heaven? Or some kind of intensely white light or dazzling scintillation? For he was familiar with ancient, particularly Iamblichian, and no doubt with contemporary, accounts of *autopsia*, of the divine manifestation in

---

devixit] et a reliquo elemento secrevit; proinde ac virtute coaguli lac plurimum cogitur in angustius et ab aqua secernitur."

[22] *Opera*, 491: "Et cur angelus aerem condensavit? Ut lumen quod huic aeri exhibiturus erat hominum oculis appareret, quae enim rarissima sunt subterfugiunt acies oculorum." Cf. Ficino's *Timaeus* Commentary, s. 24 (*Opera*, 1469): "Dii daemonesque, sub luna si apparent quando volunt, corpora quidem semper habere sed tenuissima. Apparent vero quando vel corpus suum lumenque condensant, vel radios oculorum nostrorum aut virtute terminant aut non densitate sed potestate reflectunt, vel imaginatione naturam intus sibi conformant, vel aerem circumfusum illustrant atque figurant."

[23] *Opera*, 491: "At unde lumen corpori huic adhibuit angelus? Ab ipso videlicet suae intelligentiae lumine. Quod enim in ea est intellectuale et invisibile lumen, si quomodo traducatur in aerem, fit visibile: in aerem quidem subtiliorem conspicuum fit [*Opera* sit] beatis, in aerem denique densiorem ab aliis quoque videtur." — This raises the intriguing question whether all comets and meteors are the bodies of sublunar daemons in momentary or temporary condensation. Though Ficino conceives of the daemons, at least those above the "turbulent air," as having the same regular motions as the planets and stars (see n. 17 above), his Nativity comet account suggests other, if occasional, possibilities, even for the higher daemons.

light at the climax of certain sacred rites.[24] Clearly he is attempting to find an intermediate stage between invisibility and visibility, between light with color and form and light that is radiance. But it does raise the possibility that the purest air is full of many forms that are invisible to our clouded intelligences but which can be seen by the blessed; forms which, like invisible, intellectual comets, stream their tails across the azure heavens as the signs and symbols of the gods, and are the artifacts, the condensations of angels and of daemons. Nevertheless, the general principle stands, namely, that it is by increasing the vaporous content of the air that such shapes and signs can be rendered fully manifest to ordinary eyes. Such a notion lends another grim irony perhaps to Dr. Faustus's despairing prayer in Marlowe's masterpiece that, in order to hide from the heavy wrath of God, he might "be changed into little water drops, And fall into the ocean, ne'er be found" (5.2.183–84).

However, whereas it took the archangel Gabriel to congregate the extensive vapors of the Nativity comet and to render it visible to the wise men of the east, how was it possible that an ordinary wizard could summon, or appear to summon, the ghost or deity of Plotinus to materialize, if only momentarily, before the company in the Iseum? Ficino surmises that the wizard was able to "congregate," to bring into focus, the rays emitted by Plotinus's tutelary deity.[25] Such a feat, we can now appreciate, must have involved somehow the vaporizing or beclouding of the air, on the analogy of the clouds that catch the rays of the setting sun. And this in turn must have depended on one of two conditions pertaining, or possibly both.

First, writes Ficino, it occurred in all likelihood as a gift from the higher daemons or the gods to those who were worshipping them in a sanctuary. The daemon of Plotinus appeared, in other words, because it wanted to appear and it did so in order to reward those, including Plotinus himself, who had already assembled there in a proper spirit of devotion and of reverence. This alternative would circumvent any suggestion that the gods could be summoned under compulsion. Again, we might recall Mephostophilis's rejoinder to Faustus that his speeches of conjuration were only an accidental cause of Mephostophilis's ap-

---

[24] Cf. Iamblichus, *De mysteriis* 2.4, 7 (ed. and tran. Edouard Des Places [Paris, 1966], 83.76.16 ff., 87.83.10); see Georg Luck, *Arcana Mundi: Magic and the Occult in the Greek and Roman Worlds* (Baltimore, 1985), 23. Predictably, Ficino was struck by Iamblichus's sections on various epiphanies of the divine in the *De mysteriis* 2.3–8, as his rather full summary demonstrates, *Opera*, 1879.3–1882.1.

[25] *Plotini Enneades*, sig. u viii recto (i.e., *Opera*, 1708): "Videtur itaque sacerdos Aegyptius daemonis Plotinici radios congregasse, atque (ut Porphyrius testis est) praesentium oculis ostendisse."

pearance; for he had come thither of his own accord, choosing to do so at the time Faustus had chosen to perform the invocatory formulas (1.344–46). This is a subtle, not to say equivocatory, denial of the autonomous efficacy of daemonic magic.

Ficino's second condition is more interesting. In order to render the air more vaporous, and thus potentially imprintable by a daemonic form, the priest did have one recourse (given the absence of a humidifier or a dry-ice machine): he could shake or pour into the air "a certain vapor" as long as it was "cognate with the daemons." At that point, it would be possible apparently to congregate or focus the rays of their aethereal or airy bodies and make them appear.[26] We are principally concerned in this Plotinian context with such higher daemonic bodies, since the cloudy bodies of water and earthy daemons are sometimes visible, Ficino writes in his *Epinomis* epitome, to "the inner sight" of mortal eyes anyway, at least on those occasions when the soul passes out of the body, though it might be dangerous to provide them with a special medium in which to materialize.[27] But what does Ficino mean by "a certain vapor," and how can it be "cognate" to the daemons or to a group of daemons?

For some light on this problem, it is instructive to turn, I believe, to the ancient Orphic hymns that Ficino had studied and translated into Latin in 1462 at the time he had first achieved mastery of Greek, and before he had embarked on his great translations of Plato and Plotinus. These translations have not survived as a body.[28] Nonetheless, we do have

---

[26] Ibid.: "sive colens daemones hoc eorum munere tunc impetravit, sive vaporem certum daemonibusque cognatum infuderit aeri, quo certo modo radii daemonis congregati patuerint."

[27] *Opera*, 1528, "significat ... aethereos quidem aereosque [esse] invisibiles. Aqueos vero, quos nominat semideos, videri ait nonnunquam et vix, visu scilicet intimo potius quam externo. Addit admoveri animos a daemonibus per somnia, voces, va[ti]cinia, ostenta, maxime vero quo tempore animus migrat e corpore."

[28] An anonymous Latin translation of the *Hymns*—apparently in the hand of Fra Giovanni Giocondo da Verona—appears in the Laurenziana's MS 36.35, fols. 1–23v (and Kristeller has discovered another, and probably later, copy of the same translation in the Vatican's MS. Ottob. lat 2966, fols. 67–103). It is followed on fols. 23v–26v by translations in the same hand of Proclus's four Hymns and of the *magica dicta magorum ex Zoroastre*. Until recently scholars were inclined to attribute these translations to Ficino. Dr. Ilana Klutstein has now proved this impossible on palaeographical and textual grounds in her recent edition and study, *Marsilio Ficino et la théologie ancienne: Oracles Chaldaïques, Hymnes Orphiques, Hymnes de Proclus* (Florence, 1987), 21–52. And Sebastiano Gentile has attributed the translations to Janus Lascaris, in *Marsilio Ficino e il ritorno di Platone: Mostra di manoscritti, stampe e documenti, 17 maggio–16 giugno 1984*, ed. S. Gentile, S. Niccoli, and P. Viti (Florence, 1984), 25–27 (20)—hereafter *Mostra*. — Another anonymous and different translation of the

versions of two Orphic hymns that Ficino apparently felt safe enough to include in a letter of June 1492 to his close friend, Martinus Uranius (alias Prenninger). Perhaps this is because he had found them in Trapezuntius's version of Eusebius's *Praeparatio evangelica*, a manuscript of which is in the Laurenziana bearing the Medici arms and dated 1462. The first of these is an extremely free or incompetent Latinizing of the opening "Palinode," with the recantatory warning to Musaeus omitted. The second is addressed to universal Jove and is followed by Porphyry's "expositio."[29] Clearly, Ficino deemed them monotheistic enough to be acceptable, or at least not dangerous. Even so, he presents them to Prenninger as if they were merely curiosities or learned relics rather than genuinely important texts of Platonic theology worthy of the attention he had lavished on the profundities of Plato or Plotinus. Versions of the "Hymn to the Cosmos" (properly entitled "Hymn to Heaven") and the "Hymn to Nature" have been identified by Paul Oskar Kristeller in other Ficino letters.[30]

Orphic hymns—one apparently based on a different Greek text—appears in the Vatican's MS. lat. 6891, fols. 1–19v, but is definitely not by Ficino. See Kristeller, *Supplementum*, I:cxliv–cxlv; idem, *Marsilio Ficino and His Work After Five Hundred Years* (Florence, 1987), 72, 106, 108, 135–36; and Klutstein, *Ficino et la théologie ancienne*, 24 ff., 28.

[29] *Opera*, 934–35: they were taken respectively from the *Prae. Evang.* 13.12 and 3.9 (ed. Karl Mras, 2 vols. [Berlin, 1954–56], 2:191–94 and 1:126–27). In Otto Kern's *Orphicorum Fragmenta* (Berlin, 1922), the Eusebian version of the "Palinode" is numbered frag. 247, and that of the "Hymn to Jove" frag. 168—*disiecta membra* of this are also found in Proclus's *In Timaeum* 1.313.20–30. There is a shorter version of the "Hymn to Jove" (Kern's frag. 21a) in Pseudo-Aristotle's *De mundo* 7.401a ff., a text Ficino knew from his youth and assumed canonical. He had quoted from this shorter version of the hymn in a letter on the divine madnesses he had written to Peregrino Agli as long ago as 1457 (*Opera*, 614). See D. P. Walker, *The Ancient Theology: Studies in Christian Platonism from the Fifteenth to the Eighteenth Century* (London, 1972), 27–29, 36–37; also Kristeller, *Ficino and His Work*, 135 (where the references to Eusebius should read, however, XIII.12 and III.9). — Ficino frequently refers to the opening lines from the shorter version of the "Hymn to Jove" (Kern's frag. 21), "Jupiter is the first, Jupiter the last, high-thunderer: Jupiter the head, Jupiter the middle; from Jupiter all things spring." See, for instance, his *Philebus* Commentary 1.11 (*Opera*, 1216), and his epitome for the *Laws* 4: "Item ubi ait Deum rerum principia, et fines et media continere, intellige Deum esse causam rerum efficientem atque finalem, servare omnia, omnibusque adesse" (*Opera*, 1499). Ficino assumed Plato himself was referring to these lines at 715E. — For the numbering of the Orphic *Hymns*, I shall refer throughout to the edition by Wilhelm [Guilelmus] Quandt, *Orphei hymni* (Berlin, 1955). The "Palinode" is unnumbered and the "Hymn to Jove" is numbered 15.

[30] For the "Hymn to Heaven (Uranus)" (4), see Ficino's letter to Cosimo de' Medici dated 4 September 1462 (and drawing attention, predictably, to the pun on "cosmos"). This has been edited by Kristeller, *Supplementum*, II:87–88; see also Klutstein, *Ficino et la théologie ancienne*, 35–37. The letter survives in only one manuscript, the Laurenziana's codex 54.10, fol. 81r-v, which contains the *Collectiones*

This guarded reticence with regard to the Orphic hymns is both interesting and problematic given the prestige accorded Orpheus by the later Neoplatonists of antiquity, and preeminently by Proclus, and accorded him subsequently in the Renaissance by Ficino and by his contemporaries. Ficino assigned Orpheus the third position after Zoroaster and Hermes Trismegistus in his chain of six sages. This chain culminated with Plato himself, and constituted the *prisci theologi*, the line of non-Hebrew seers and prophets that had prepared the gentile world for Christianity as the Prophets had prepared the Jews.[31] Ficino's reticence is also strange in light of his deliberate and successful attempt to model himself on Orpheus, particularly at the onset of his Platonic career. This attempt was centered, predictably, on his activities as a musician, and specifically on his hymn-singing to a Orphic lyre, an instrument he played with considerable skill by all accounts and often in a state or pose of rapture, of divine frenzy.[32] The lyre bore a picture of Orpheus taming the beasts of the forest, and his friends complimented, or flattered, Ficino by addressing him in verse and letter as another Orpheus.[33] The recitals, if that is what we may call them, impressed contemporaries as spiritual and not just as artistic events; and D. P. Walker has suggested that they probably resembled enraptured psalm-singing—David being the Hebrew Orpheus—or a religious rite.[34] Given his pro-

---

Cosmianae assembled by Bartolomeo Scala after the death of Cosimo to celebrate his memory. See the discussion by August Buck, *Der Orpheus-Mythos in der italienischen Renaissance* (Krefeld, 1961), 22 ff.; also Arnaldo Della Torre, *Storia dell'Accademia Platonica di Firenze* (Florence, 1902), 537–38; Gentile in *Mostra*, 27–28 (21); and Kristeller, *Ficino and His Work*, 72. — For a paraphrase of, and commentary on, the "Hymn to Nature" (10), see Ficino's letter to Germain de Ganay. This has been edited by Kristeller and dated to sometime before 1498 but after 1494; see his *Studies in Renaissance Thought and Letters* (Rome, 1956; repr. 1969), 50–54 (commentary), 96–97 (text); also *Ficino and His Work*, 135.

[31] Walker, *Ancient Theology*, intro. and chap. 1.

[32] See D. P. Walker, *Spiritual and Demonic Magic: from Ficino to Campanella* (London, 1958), chap. 1; idem, *Ancient Theology*, 22–29, 36–37; and John Warden, "Orpheus and Ficino," in *Orpheus: The Metamorphoses of a Myth*, ed. John Warden (Toronto, 1982), 85–110.

[33] The most notable of the many references are: in Corsi's *Vita Marsilii Ficini* 6 and Lorenzo de' Medici's "L'Altercazione" (2.2–4); in two poems to Ficino by Naldo Naldi, "Panthoidem priscum" and "Orpheus hic ego sum" (in Kristeller, *Supplementum*, II:262–63); in Poliziano's acknowledgement of his debt to Ficino and to Argyropoulos at the end of his *Opera* (Basel, 1553), 310 (also in Kristeller, *Supplementem*, II:281): and in a letter to Ficino from Johannes Pannonius (in Ficino's *Opera*, 871). Naldo's epigram "Orpheus hic ego sum" is entitled: "Ad Marsilium Ficinum de Orpheo in eius cythara picto."

[34] *Spiritual and Demonic Magic*, 20: "[H]is astrological singing came near to being a religious rite... [A]ll that can be said about the purely musical side of Ficino's singing is that it was monodic and he was aiming at the same ideal of expressive,

clamation, following Plato, of four divine frenzies, Ficino probably considered the goal of such Orphic music to be hieratic rapture: if not theurgy or god-making, then certainly the transformation of oneself into a perfect instrument or medium for the divine presence.[35]

Why then did he think twice about presenting, or even perhaps preserving, his translations of the Orphic hymns, particularly given what he saw as their endorsement by Plato himself? Admittedly, he attributed more texts to Orpheus than modern scholarship allows. For we now realize that the *fragmenta* quoted by Plato should be distinguished from other post-Platonic *fragmenta* quoted by Proclus and the Greek Fathers; that the apocryphal *Hymni* probably date from the second or third century AD and are not quoted by any ancient writer before that time; and that the *Argonautica* is a late fourth century AD poem based on the work by Apollonius of Rhodes.[36] Even so, why conceal the translations of the *Hymns* when he was eager to cite individual lines from them and from the other *Orphica* throughout his works (they far exceed the sum of references to scholastic authors, as Kristeller has observed); and when, even more remarkably, he considered Orphic hymn-singing to the lyre to be one of the glories of his revival of ancient Platonism? This he makes strikingly clear in his famous letter of 13 September 1492 to Paul of Middelburg, a physician and astronomer. Florence's new golden age has brought the "liberal disciplines" back from virtual extinction, namely, "grammar, poesy, oratory, painting, sculpture, architecture, music, and the ancient singing of songs to the Orphic lyre."[37] It cannot have been the music of the Orphic lyre, therefore, with its mysterious symbolic stringing,[38] nor the intonation or

---

effect-producing music as the later musical humanists."

[35] For Ficino's theory of *furor divinus*, see his letter to Agli of 1457 (cf. n. 29 above); his *Platonic Theology* 13.2 (ed. Raymond Marcel, *Marsile Ficin: Théologie Platonicienne de l'immortalité des âmes*, 3 vols. [Paris, 1964, 1970], 2:201–22); and his *Phaedrus* Commentary 4 (ed. Allen, 82–87). — See André Chastel, *Ficin et l'art* (Geneva and Lille, 1954), 129–35; Sebastiano Gentile, "In margine all'epistola 'De divino furore' di Marsilio Ficino," *Rinascimento* 23 (1983): 33–77; also my *Platonism*, chap. 2.

[36] See Walker, *Ancient Theology*, 14–16. Ficino also apparently translated the *Argonautica* in 1462; see Kristeller, *Supplementum*, I:clxiv. It has been edited and translated by G. Dottin as *Les Argonautiques d'Orphée* (Paris, 1930).

[37] *Opera*, 944.3: "Hoc enim seculum tanquam aureum liberales disciplinas ferme iam extinctas reduxit in lucem, grammaticam, poesim, oratoriam, picturam, sculpturam, architecturam, musicam, antiquum ad Orphicam lyram carminum cantum. Idque Florentiae." Joannes Pannonius's letter to Ficino underscores Ficino's responsibility for reviving Orphic singing: "antiquum cytharae sonum et cantum et carmina Orphica oblivioni prius tradita luci restituisses" (*Opera*, 871.2). See Della Torre, *Storia dell'Accademia Platonica*, 589.

[38] In the *Philebus* Commentary 1.28 (ed. and tran. Allen, 266–67), Ficino claims

perhaps incantation of selected hymns, that made Ficino cautious, but some other dimension of the hymns entirely.

In dispatching the two "safer" hymns Ficino observes in his prefatory letter to Prenninger that he had suppressed his youthful renderings of the other hymns—and indeed of the hymns of Homer and Proclus and of Hesiod's *Theogony*—because he feared that people might think he were encouraging the revival, not of a Davidic psalm-singing, nor even of a declaredly Platonic hymn-singing, but rather of "the ancient cult or worship of the gods and daemons so long and deservedly condemned."[39] Now why should this be so?

It is true that the hymns themselves are polytheistic: each hymn is addressed to a separate deity, though several hymns are addressed to the same deity. Not all the hymns address the familiar Olympian gods, however—predictably so, given the peculiarities of the Orphic pantheon (with which, incidentally, Ficino was acquainted as his epitome of book 4 of the *Republic* demonstrates); and some invoke pure abstractions like Justice. The collection as a whole is prefaced by the palinodal hymn to the universe that is monotheistic and had been accorded pride of place since antiquity. Polytheistic statements and images in themselves could hardly have deterred Ficino, given the armory of interpretive techniques

---

that Orpheus introduced the tetrachord on the grounds that in the "Hymn to Apollo" (34, lines 21–23) he had given Phoebus a lyre with four strings, the top one invoking summer, the bottom one winter, and the two in between autumn and spring. Cf. his *Platonic Theology* 2.9 (ed. Marcel, 1:102–3) where he again cites the hymn: "Tu habes mundi terminos universi. Tibi curae est principium atque finis. Per te virescunt omnia. Tu sphaeram totam, cithara resonante, contemperas" (lines 14–17). This may suggest a similar stringing for Ficino's own Orphic lyre. On the other hand, the lyre is usually seven-stringed, the seven strings representing the planets and producing a universal harmony. See Ficino's *De divino furore* (*Opera*, 614), and *Timaeus* Commentary chaps. 30 and 32 (*Opera*, 1453 [misnumbered 1417] ff., 1457); also Warden, "Orpheus and Ficino," 93–94.

[39] *Opera*, 933.2: "Argonautica et hymnos Orphei et Homeri et Proculi, Theologiamque Hesiodi, quae adolescens (nescio quomodo) ad verbum mihi soli transtuli, quemadmodum tu nuper hospes apud me vidisti, edere nunquam placuit, ne forte lectores ad priscum deorum daemonumque cultum iamdiu merito reprobatum revocare viderer." In his *Vita Marsilii Ficini* 8, Corsi attributes Ficino's earlier reluctance to publish these translations to an "animi dolor": "cogitavit hoc tempore ... Orphei hymnos ac sacrificia invulgare, sed divino prorsus miraculo, id quo minus efficeret, in dies magis impediebatur, quadam, ut aiebat, spiritus amaritudine distractus." Apart from the many problems with Corsi's account of this "distracted" period of spiritual "bitterness" (see, for instance, Kristeller, *Studies*, 202–5, contra Della Torre, *Storia*, 587 ff.), it does not explain the grounds for the decision of 1492. In his *De vita* 1.7, 1.10 (ed. Kaske and Clark, 128.116–18, 134.49–54), moreover, Ficino recalls that David rose at dawn to sing and to play the lyre as the best remedy against melancholy, and that Hermes, Pythagoras and Plato command us to cheer "our sorrowing and dissonant" souls with the harmonies of lyre and song; David too had freed Saul from madness with psaltery and song.

he had inherited from within the Platonic, or what we might properly call the Proclian, tradition for extracting monotheistic or monistic profundities out of the most recalcitrantly polytheistic myths. In particular he was accustomed to interpreting the many gods as aspects of one Jove, despite the strictures of Augustine in the *De civitate Dei* 4.11 against this procedure. For Homer's pantheon was fully compatible with the Neoplatonic doctrine of the One; it was simply a matter of peeling away the rind, to use the timeworn metaphor, or of unveiling the hidden beauty by brushing aside the clouds of the many with the caducean staff of mercurial interpretation. Moreover, Ficino was never reluctant, given Orpheus's authority and primacy in Greek theology, to follow in the footsteps of Plato and the Platonists in citing individual lines from the Orphic fragments and the Orphic hymns in support of, or in some instances as the source of, various philosophical or theological arguments.[40] Indeed, we might even go so far as to say that it was precisely Orpheus's monism or monotheism, his understanding, that is, of the One and the many, and of the One, Mind, and Soul as the three primary hypostases, that entitled him to his privileged position in the hexad of ancient theologians. For this monism was virtually the sole criterion for selection to the hexad, the sole test of whether a theologian had been the guardian of the "ancient theology."

It must have been something more than, if not other than, the polytheism of the hymns viewed collectively or individually that deterred Ficino from presenting them to his Florentine contemporaries, even to the enlightened members of his own Platonic circle, who, we must presume, would have been mithridatically prepared already by his instruction to recognize the interpretive dangers and the pitfalls of an

---

[40] That Orpheus was the father of Greek poetry and philosophy was a commonplace among the Platonists and was of ancient origin; see the texts assembled by Kern in his *Orphicorum fragmenta*, frags. 244–52, and also the study by Martin L. West, *The Orphic Poems* (Oxford, 1983). Porphyry, as cited by Eusebius, claims, for instance, that Orpheus is "the oldest and most eminent of the theologians" (Kern, frag. 17); Olympiodorus maintains in his *In Platonis Phaedonem commentaria* (ed. W. Norvin [Leipzig, 1913], 58) that "in every respect Plato is imitating Orpheus's teaching"; and Proclus argues that "all Greek theology is the offspring of the mystical doctrine of Orpheus" in his *Platonic Theology* 1.5 (ed. and tran. H. D. Saffrey and L. G. Westerink as *Proclus: Théologie Platonicienne*, 5 vols. to date (Paris, 1968–), 1:25.26–27, with a note on 138–39. — The role of Pletho in orchestrating the Renaissance response to Orpheus and the *Orphica* has yet to be fully documented, but we know that he prized hymn-singing, that he wrote chapters in his lost *Laws* on "Hymns to the Gods" and their arrangement, and that he copied out fourteen of the Orphic hymns; see Milton Anastos, "Pletho's Calendar and Liturgy," *Dumbarton Oaks Papers* 4 (1948): 183–305. Nevertheless, we should note that Orpheus was already the *theologus poeta* for Petrarch and Boccaccio; see Buck, *Der Orpheus-Mythos*, 18; and Warden, "Orpheus and Ficino," 91.

overly literal reading. Thus, if it was not primarily the words of the hymns that Ficino was afraid would revive daemonic cult rather than the worship of the one God, what then?

Accompanying all but nine of the 87 hymns are little-noticed fumigatory instructions.[41] For example, the "Hymn to Justice" (63) has the instruction "Use the fumigation from frankincense"; the "Hymn to the Graces" (60), "Use the fumigation from styrax"; the "Hymn to Adonis" (56), "Use the fumigation from aromatics"; the "Hymn to Poseidon" (17), "Use the fumigation from myrrh"; and the "Hymn to Bacchus Licnitus" (46), "Use the fumigation from manna." The fumigations are referred to either generally as aromatics, or specifically as styrax, frankincense, manna, or myrrh, or as some combination of these. For instance, the "Hymn to the Sea or Tethys" (22) reads "Use the fumigation from frankincense and from manna" and the same goes for the "Hymn to Jove Author of Lightning" (20). There are several unusual instructions. For instance, the "Hymn to the Earth" (26) reads "Use the fumigation from every kind of seed, except from beans and aromatics"; the "Hymn to the Mother of the Gods" (27) reads "Use the fumigation from a variety of odiferous substances"; the "Hymn to Aether" (5) reads "Use the fumigation from saffron"; and the "Hymn to Sleep" (85) enjoins us, appropriately enough, to use the fumigation from poppies.

Fumigation has a long and complex history in cult practices all over the world, and a number of the fumigants enjoined in the hymns are rich in medical, magical, and religious associations, none more so perhaps than frankincense and myrrh. What these various aromatics meant to Ficino in the context of Orphic worship, however, we may best discover if we turn to an odd series of annotations in his commentary on Plotinus's *Enneads* 4.4.38, where he provides the following scheme: frankincense is burnt to the Heavens, saffron to the Aether, aromas to the Stars, to the Moon and also to Nature, frankincense and manna to the Sun, styrax to Saturn and to Jupiter, myrrh to Neptune, and frankincense again to Mercury.[42] We might note that nothing is assigned to

---

[41] It is noteworthy that the Latin translation of the *Hymns* in the Laurenziana's MS. 36.35, fols. 1–23v, once attributed to Ficino (see n. 28 above), retains the fumigatory instructions with the formula *thymiama*.

[42] *Plotini Enneades*, sig. dd viii verso (i.e., *Opera*, 1747.1): "Item Caelo incensi thuris odorem, Aetheri ferventem crocum, Stellis aromata, Soli thus et manna, Lunae et Naturae aromata, Saturno et Iovi styracem, Neptuno myrrham, Mercurio thus. Spiritus enim per affectum, cantum, odorem, lumen cognatior effectus [*Opera* affectus] numini uberiorem haurit illinc influxum." — Of course, another purpose for aromatic smokes might have been to inspire a *furor nasi*! As such they would be higher than the merely pleasant or therapeutic smells, those from flowers and fruits, for instance, some of which Ficino lists in his *De vita* 1.10 (ed. Kaske and Clark, 134.35–47). Later in the *De vita* 3.20 (ed. Kaske and Clark, 350.30–33) Ficino notes

Venus or to Mars, and that the scheme, given its astronomical cast, rather oddly includes Neptune.

However, I believe we must also entertain another dimension to, another use for, these fumigations in Ficino's eyes. As holy or sacred smokes of various kinds they would affect not only our senses of smell and taste—and the lower daemons we recall especially relish the richness of certain sacrificial smokes—but would serve also to function as vapors, making the air less rare and more cloudy and dense. Yet they are particularly refined and subtle smokes: they are, to adopt a Proclian formula familiar to Ficino, earth under the form or species of fire and air.[43] In any event, they would serve like mists or clouds upon which light could play as the sunbeams play across the insubstantial pageants of the evening. Consequently, they would serve to make the air sufficiently dense for it to become, at least temporally, the medium for the manifestation of daemonic light, for rendering visible the spherical bodies not only of the watery or earthy daemons, but, if they so willed themselves, of the airy or fiery daemons; or alternatively, of the lowest ranks of the daemons in any planetary train.[44] The daemonic bodies must necessarily appear to us, therefore, like other circular optical phenomena, those we associate with rainbows, sundogs, lunar and solar nimbuses, and other prismatic splayings of light. Pertinent here is the analogy between the daemon who may choose to reveal his presence and the rays of the fire which cannot be seen at noonday until they are silhouetted against the burning log.

Thus the Orphic hymns came down to Ficino with their accompany-

---

that the Arabs argue that odorous fumigations "accommodated" to the stars directly affect the air, the rays of the stars and the spirit itself of the fumigator and thus enable him to capture the gifts of the planet reigning at the time. The odors of plants and flowers and medicinal ointments and the finest powders and their vapors are all apparently under the general patronage of Venus; see *De vita* 3.21 (ed. Kaske and Clark, 356.30–32). These curiosa await further exploration.

[43] Ficino enunciates this principle that "omnia in omnibus esse sed pro natura suscipientium ubique singula suscipi" for instance in his *Timaeus* Commentary, chap. 24 (*Opera*, 1449); see Allen, *Platonism*, 97n. He almost certainly derived it directly from proposition 103 of Proclus's *Elements of Theology* (ed. and tran. E. R. Dodds, 2d rev. ed. [Oxford, 1963], 93, with commentary on 254): "panta en pasin, oikeiôs de en hekastôi." Dodds notes that the principle was ascribed by the Neoplatonists to the Pythagoreans.

[44] We should note that Pico also recognized the magical potential of the *Hymns*. His fourth Orphic conclusion reads: "Sicut hymni David operi Cabalae mirabiliter deserviunt, ita hymni Orphei operi vere licitae et naturalis Magiae." However, he eschewed the notion that the *Hymns* might summon demons, for his third conclusion reads: "Nomina deorum, quos Orpheus canit, non decipientium demonum, a quibus malum et non bonum provenit, sed naturalium virtutum divinarumque sunt nomina a vero Deo in utilitatem maxime hominis, si eis uti sciverit, mundo distributarum."

ing instructions for burning various sacred smokes. While the hymns were being sung, intoned or chanted Ficino would see in his mind's eye the aromatic wisps arising from the ritual lamps and censers and serving tantalizingly and hauntingly as the ever-changing medium for rendering visible daemonic forms which might grace the worshipper with their presence, if the daemons were so inclined and the aromas were to their particular liking. This is not to restrict such daemonic manifestation to aromatic smokes, since Ficino was demonstrably familiar with vapors, hazes, sprays, sacred dusts, and powders of various kinds, all of which could function in essentially the same way;[45] but it is to underscore an ancillary role, perhaps even the primary role, of the fumigation instructions accompanying the Orphic hymns.

Orpheus's hymns are addressed, however, not to daemons, but to Olympian and other deities and to divine abstractions like Justice. Would these gods have been expected to appear as seems highly unlikely? And is this another reason why Ficino was reluctant to broadcast the hymns even in a Latin translation? We must recall at this juncture an important aspect of Ficino's Neoplatonic daemonology, namely, that accompanying each major god in the sense of the twelve Olympian deities who presided over the eight celestial and the four sublunary spheres—and possibly, given the oddities of the Orphic pantheon, this might include other deities like Phanes or Nature—were hosts of lesser gods and of daemons who shared to varying degrees the powers and attributes of that god and who were committed to doing his or her bidding and to serving as ministrants and as intermediaries between the god and men. These hosts, furthermore, were composed of all the ranks of daemons, from the fiery to the earthy, from those dwelling as far away as Saturn's sphere or as close as the Moon's or down in the darkest subterranean caverns, though particular kinds of daemons preferred particular kinds of places and preeminently the sphere directly under the patronage of their own sovereign deity. Thus it was customary, for instance, to find neptunian daemons by or in the sea and plutonian daemons in the caves, mines, and grottoes under the

---

[45] We should recall that in the Galenic tradition the animal spirit itself was conceived of as a kind of fiery haze or corporeal vapor that after combustion produced a kind of smoke, the cause of depression and lethargy; see Walker, *Spiritual and Demonic Magic*, 3–11. This might have well served to reinforce for Ficino the pregnant notion that a magician can use his own *spiritus* as a smoky medium for, or a reflector of, demonic presence; see my *Icastes: Marsilio Ficino's Interpretation of Plato's "Sophist"* (Berkeley and Los Angeles, 1989), chap. 5.

earth, though it was possible, in rare circumstances, to encounter a neptunian or plutonian daemon in some other realm on some special mission. Each one of these daemons, whether mighty or lowly, translunar or sublunar, could on occasion be referred to by the name of its sovereign deity, following a principle laid down by Proclus.[46] Thus the mention of Mercury in an ancient "theological" text could signify an order or "chain"[47] of possible Mercuries from Mercury himself (or even possibly from the Idea of Mercury, as it were, in the head of Zeus or the head of Cronos) down to a minor terrene daemon presiding over a mercurial bird like the ibis, or to a local daemon presiding over a mercurial place such as an artisan's shop in Naucratis in Egypt, or to a subterranean daemon presiding over a ladle of quicksilver in an alchemist's hand, even though the subterranean realm in its entirety was the domain of Pluto and the plutonian daemons.[48]

Thus the dedication of an Orphic hymn to Mercury was primarily intended to draw the worshipper's mind in singing that hymn to the contemplation of Mercury in his highest intellectual form as an aspect of Mind. Still, at the same time it would also serve to attract, necessarily, any one or more of a number of lesser mercurial daemons. Since the hymn-singing was accompanied by fumigations, it was possible, furthermore, for such a lower daemon to become visible at any time, reflected or haloed on swirling clouds or even on fading wisps of frankincense. Thus the Orphic hymns might indeed serve as a means of reviving, however unintentionally or inadvertently, the cult of the lower daemons. For Ficino certainly believed in the daemons, as did the majority of his contemporaries, since their philosophical assumptions about the world's plenitude and continuity required a category of

---

[46] *Platonic Theology* 1.26 (ed. Saffrey and Westerink, 1:115.7–12); *In Alcibiadem* 72.12–74.10, 78.10–79.14, 158.3–159.5 (ed. L. G. Westerink as *Proclus: Commentary on the First Alcibiades* [Amsterdam, 1954]); *In rempublicam* 6 (ed. G. Kroll, *Procli in Platonis rem publicam commentarii*, 2 vols. [Leipzig, 1899–1901], 1:91.11–19); *In Timaeum* 5 (ed. E. Diehl, *Procli Diadochi in Platonis Timaeum commentaria*, 3 vols. [Leipzig, 1903–1906; repr. Amsterdam, 1965], 3:204.23–32).

[47] *Plotini Enneades*, sig. u viii recto (i.e., *Opera*, 1708): "Memento tamen a summis ad infima passim extendi catenas. Itaque a singulis stellis certos daemonum ordines stellarum pedissequos certis affici modis, atque similiter animas a daemonibus, a suis ubique suas. Sunt ergo plures in qualibet sphaera tam infra lunam quam super lunam daemones Saturnii sub Saturno, Ioviique sub Iove, caeterique similiter." The "chains" here are the *seirai* of Neoplatonism; see Brian Copenhaver, "Scholastic Philosophy and Renaissance Magic in the 'De Vita' of Marsilio Ficino," *Renaissance Quarterly* 37 (1984): 551, who cites a "Phoebean" chain from the *De vita* 3.14 (ed. Kaske and Clark, 310.11 ff.).

[48] *Phaedrus* Commentary, *summa* 49 (ed. and tran. Allen, 208–11); see Allen, *Platonism*, 35–37.

daemonic beings between the earth and the Moon. Therefore, it was not so much the fear of reviving a moribund or atavistic superstition about the existence of such beings, as it was the fear rather of reviving their cult; of strengthening, as it were, the demons' hand.[49] Revealing in this regard is a passage in chapter 4 of his Commentary on St. Paul, where Ficino recalls Iamblichus's condemnation of the Egyptians for their daemonolatry and in particular for their worship of the airy daemons: they had rested content with prayer and worship at the level of fumigations and vapors, lights and songs, instead of turning to higher rites involving the understanding and the will.[50] This is not to say, incidentally, that Ficino denied that there was a legitimate use for sacred smokes, vapors, mists, hazes, or powders. To the contrary, we know from the *De vita* that he recommended attar of roses and other efficacious and attractive perfumes as part of a holistic medical regimen for ensuring mental and physical health. And one even suspects he was attracted to the daemonological uses to which a magus could put them as long as he was doing so in the right Platonic spirit and with properly benevolent intentions.

The Orphic hymn was intended to function on several levels. Even as the vaporous and smoky fumigations would serve to attract the lower daemons, so the accompanying music and lights would serve to attract higher daemons, and the words and prayers themselves would serve to attract the highest daemons of all. As such the hymn would work upon the imagination, the reason, and the intuitive understanding alike of the worshipper. It was thus a powerful instrument of meditation, and due care had to be exercised by a singer in its recitation in order that only the best daemonic presences might be witnessed, however fleetingly, in the clouds of frankincense around the festal tapers, be heard in the waves of song and sound, be visualized in the aura of

---

[49] See, for example, Augustine, *De civitate dei*, 8.14-22, 26; 9.1-3, 6-13, 16, 18-23; 10.9-11, 21, 27. In 10.11 he writes that, while it was difficult for so distinguished a philosopher as Porphyry to acknowledge the society of demons or to censure them, "any Christian old woman would have no hesitation about the fact of their existence, and no reserve about denouncing them."

[50] *Opera*, 432-33: "Iamblichus Porphyriusque Platonici species quinque cultus esse disputant pro quinque speciebus spirituum qui coluntur. Spiritus enim infimos crassum aerem habitantes sacrificiis ex frugibus animalibusque coli solitos. Spiritus autem purum aerem incolentes vaporibus sonisque et cantibus atque luminibus. Aetherea vero numina orationibus luminibusque simul. Sed intellectus a corporibus separatos intelligentiae viribus atque motibus. Horum denique patrem excessu quodam mentis et ineffabili voluntatis affectu. Iamblichus inter haec damnat Aegyptios quod materiali cultu prae caeteris uterentur, aeriorumque daemonum cultores essent. Anteponit autem iis Chaldaeos qui spiritalem cultum potius sequerentur, utpote qui separatas a materia mentes patremque earum praecipue colerent."

thoughts that arose in a worshipper's mind. No wonder that Ficino's own Orphic recitals were such rapturous but also, I believe, carefully planned and premeditated affairs; for they were the rituals of a Platonic priest who had inwardly purged his spirit, and was not to be caught by a daemonic presence unawares.

In considering the Porphyrian account of the summoning of Plotinus's tutelary spirit, Ficino writes, "But in what form did Plotinus's god appear in order for the Egyptian magus to be able to suppose that it belonged to the highest order of daemons?" The answer is that "it did not appear with a misshapen (*deformis*) splendor like the rainbow and in the way that the lowest kinds of daemons customarily appear in the cloudy air. Nor again did it appear just in paleness and redness, in the manner sometimes of the middle ranks of daemons. But it appeared instead in a pure and completely clear light, in the manner proper to the aethereal and celestial daemons alone."[51] Ficino is suggesting that the lowest daemons must always appear in colors and in a shape that is only partially circular like the rainbow's arc; that the middle appear with a radiance that has only a suggestion of color, particularly redness, though in a shape, presumably, that is wholly circular; and that the highest appear in pure white radiance. And yet the three kinds of tutelary daemons certainly affect, in the sense of move, our imaginations, reasons, and understandings respectively, even though they can sometimes also be seen.

Thus we must assume that the Egyptian magus and the attendant worshippers indeed saw an intense white radiance when Plotinus's deity appeared. But the conviction that this numinous presence was a god and not a daemon was not the result in itself of seeing such a pure light, but rather a matter of intuition, of intelligential certainty. Since the daemons move in circles like the circling celestial spheres, the daemons can be said to circle through our imaginations, reasons, and intuitive understandings, although we must think of such circling figuratively. Just as the air is all around us, so the daemons, essentially airy beings, are circumambient and ceaselessly circling over and within us, the tutelary daemons circling within our faculties, as the stars and the celestial spheres circle above us. Such circling inspires in us the deep

---

[51] *Plotini Enneades*, sig. u viii recto (i.e., *Opera*, 1708): "Sed quanam forma coniecit magus Plotini daemonem esse supremum? quia videlicet non difformi quodam [*Opera* quoniam] instar iridis fulgore venit, sicut infimi solent daemones in aere mixto; non pallore iterum vel rubore, sicut medii nonnunquam consueverunt; sed lumine puro penitus atque clarissimo, quod aetheriorum caelestiumque daemonum dumtaxat est proprium."

conviction of the truly godlike nature of the spirit, while the pure radiance of its momentary manifestation in the eyes of those privileged to behold it serves as further confirmation. While luminosity is the principal, it is not a necessary accompaniment, however, of such deep conviction.

Interestingly, it was not possible, Porphyry says, to interrogate Plotinus's tutelary deity, because the priest's assistant, whether through jealousy or terror, strangled the birds he was holding—presumably the usual apotropaic, solar cocks—and the deity disappeared.[52] In the Ficinian analysis this would imply the fading of the white radiance from the smoke or vapor which the magician had created for the seance, and the corresponding loss of the conviction of its extrasensory presence in the highest faculty of understanding in the devotees.

We might be permitted to wonder to what extent Ficino himself was the orchestrator of similar seances. We do know that he was a trained and successful exorcist.[53] We must now entertain the probability, I believe, given his sustained interest in, and demonstrable knowledge of, the occult, of his also having taken up the role on particular occasions of summoning the ghosts and tutelary daemons of both the living and the dead in "Platonic" seances. We may speculate that the famous Orphic lyre, which Cosimo urged Ficino to bring with him from Careggi as long ago as 1464,[54] would have had a critical role to play in such seances, particularly if their aim was to bring the living into inspirational contact with a Platonic past, with the spirits of Plato and Plotinus, and not to summon up some hapless, Blavatskian wraith still haunting the banks of the Styx. For Ficino there must have also been an occult

---

[52] For these birds, see E. R. Dodds, *The Greeks and the Irrational* (Berkeley and Los Angeles, 1966), 289–91. Ficino was of course familiar with the notion that the cock, along with the hawk, was a solar bird; see his *De vita* 3.13, 14 (ed. Kaske and Clark 308.67, 310.11–13, 24–28—where it even daunts the lion). Diogenes Laertius, in his *Lives of the Philosophers* 8.34–35, reports Aristotle as observing in his treatise *On the Pythagoreans* (no longer extant) that Pythagoras had enjoined us not to touch a white cock because the bird was sacred to the Month, since it announces the hours and is a suppliant; cf. Iamblichus, *De vita Pythagorica* 18.84 and *Protrepticus* 21, symbol 18.

[53] His *Timaeus* Commentary, *summa* 24 (*Opera*, 1469–70) gives an account of two exorcisms he conducted, with accompanying fumigations, one in October 1493, the other in December 1494. The account includes a reference, incidentally, to the contentions of "Orpheus and the poets" that there are "water divinities" (*numina aquatica*) and that the "mixed" or vaporous air is probably the home of brutish demons as well as rational ones. Whereas the latter use their reasons, the former most often use "a prepotent imagination" to work upon our imaginations. The object of such brutish demons is to make us forget our homeland by drugging us, like Circe or the Sirens, with earthly delights and beguiling songs; see Ficino's letter to Cavalcanti of 12 December 1494 (*Opera*, 961.2).

[54] *Opera*, 608.1: "Vale et veni non absque Orphica lyra."

and specifically a daemonological dimension to the burning of aromatics at his Orphic hymn-singing. And these occult dimensions may well account, at least in part, for his singular success as a mediumistic performer on the lyre in the porticos and halls, and conceivably in the private chapels themselves, of the Medici; and before an enraptured audience that often included priests and monks and consisted unquestionably of pious believers. Certainly, it is a mediumistic stance which the sculptor Andrea di Piero Ferrucci opted for in his notable and noticeable bust of Ficino, erected in 1521 and now one of the few remaining monuments in Santa Maria del Fiore.[55] It would be fanciful and erroneous to suggest that the book Ficino is cradling there, as if it were a lyre, is a book of the Orphic hymns; for the volume is far too weighty. It is almost certainly intended to be his translation of the collected works of Plato published in Florence in 1484.[56] Plato was the ultimate source, however, of the authority invested in Orpheus in the Platonic tradition, and it was the revival of Plato and of Orphic music together which lay at the heart of Ficino's whole revivalist program. The success of this program eventually inspired in him an intense conviction that he personally had been divinely elected to summon into Florence a truly Plotinian spirit to inaugurate its golden age. In the *exhortatio* to his 1492 Plotinus translation and commentary, Ficino boldly imagines Plato looking down upon Plotinus and declaring in the words of the Father in the synoptic gospels, "This is my beloved son in whom I am well pleased. Hear him."[57] As Plato *redivivus*, as Plotinus *redivivus*, Ficino had himself called upon and felt himself to be the recipient of divine grace, if not as a beloved son, then as a priest who had offered up the *vapor* of his great learning to catch the radiant light of Platonic theology. This might suggest a curiously personal dimension to his reading of Porphyry's account of the summoning of Plotinus's attendant spirit-guide, one underscored by his concluding remarks in his introduction to Plotinus's singular treatise on personal and other daemons, the *Enneads* 3.4.

---

[55] For convenient reproductions, see the frontispiece of *The Letters of Marsilio Ficino, Volume I,* tran. Members of the Language Department of the School of Economic Science (London, 1975); and Kristeller, *Ficino and His Work*, plate 18. For an account of its commission, see Raymond Marcel, *Marsile Ficin (1433–1499)* (Paris, 1958), 580–82; also Chastel, *Ficin et l'art*, 48, and Viti in *Mostra*, 198 (174).

[56] For the correct date of publication see Kristeller, "The First Printed Edition of Plato's Works and the Date of Its Publication (1484)," in *Science and History, Studies in Honor of Edward Rosen*, Studia Copernicana 16, ed. Erna Hilfstein, Pawel Czartoryski, and Frank D. Grande (Wroclaw, 1978), 25–35.

[57] *Plotini Enneades* sig. b ii (i.e., *Opera*, 1548.1). See Edgar Wind, *Pagan Mysteries in the Renaissance*, rev. ed. (New York, 1968), 23–24.

He has just outlined the problems associated with "chains" of daemons and the power of particular chains over particular men, and is led to the speculative problem of why it is that extraordinary accomplishments are achieved by men without teachers and the other customary aids to learning. The answer must be that we are born to achieve a work where our personal daemon alone is our principal instructor and where he is most powerful and effective: "Exceeding their own expectations and the opinions of others, men opportunely light upon the occasions, the regions, the persons, the materials, the instruments, and the faculties that they rightly need in order to perfect the work they are destined for by nature. Indeed, a natural cause does not channel the confluence of these mutually diverse factors to one end, but rather a daemonic cause; it is this which directs all individual things to an end already known to itself."[58] "Certainly," he continues, "the cause assists the heavens by always providing the means to effect the end already known to the heavenly understanding, and also its own power to effect the end, which the motion of the heavens often does not make happen, but merely signifies." Accordingly, "from a certain disposition of the heavens, as from a sign," sometimes an astrologer will "preannounce what things a certain daemon who is linked with such a disposition is doing."[59] However, Ficino again affirms, it is for ourselves and to the extent that we are able, that we later perfect our work, long after many years have passed and the "aspect of the heavens" has completely vanished away, and indeed will never return in our lifetime. "From this it appears," he concludes, "that the aspect signified our achievements rather, not that it is their author."[60]

---

[58] *Plotini Enneades*, sig. u viii verso (i.e., *Opera*, 1709): "Tum vero praeter spem suam et aliorum opinionem opportune incidant in tempora, in regiones, in personas, in materias, in instrumenta, in facultates quibus rite suppeditantibus opus ipsum expleant naturaliter destinatum. Quorum sane inter se diversorum confluxum non naturalis causa sed daemonica ad unum connectit eventum, ad praecognitum sibi finem singula dirigens." Cf. *De vita* 3.23.

[59] "Interea caelo ministrans pariter atque suppeditans, ministrans inquam media semper ad finem intelligentiae caelesti praecognitum, suppeditans insuper propriam efficaciam ad id peragendum, quod saepe non facit caelestis motio, sed significat. Unde nonnunquam astrologus ex certa dispositione caelestium velut ex signo praenuntiabit quae certus daemon dispositioni accommodatus eiusmodi agit." See Eugenio Garin, "Le 'elezioni' e il problema dell'astrologia," in his *L'età nuova: Ricerche di storia della cultura dal XII al XVI secolo* (Naples, 1969), 421–47; idem, *Lo zodiaco della vita: la polemica sull'astrologia da Trecento al Cinquecento* (Rome, 1976), chap. 2.

[60] *Plotini Enneades*, sig. u viii verso (i.e., *Opera*, 1709): "Utcunque potest [om. *Opera*] in [*Opera* id] nobis et utcunque possumus nos efficimus, postquam videlicet e multis annis ille caelestium aspectus evanuit, etiam si non revertatur ad idem; ex quo apparet illum nostra potius significasse quam facere." This was of course a problem of ancient standing; see A. Bouché-Leclercq, *L'Astrologie grecque* (1889),

Ultimately the supreme summoning of Plotinus had been not, of course, in any Orphic seance, but in the completion in 1492, after years of labor, of the great translation of the *Enneads*, along with extensive and accomplished commentary. This labor had itself been the result, Ficino fancifully surmised, of a Socratic or Platonic or Plotinian daemon presiding over him, and instructing him to a work which he had been destined to perfect by the preconceived design of a heavenly providence, all occasions uniting miraculously to further this design. As an intellectual event such a labor could have been earlier deciphered perhaps by the astrologers from the aspect of the stars, but the aspect had not been its cause. The night sky over Medicean Florence had been an Iseum where learned men might indeed have read the signs of Marsilio's own impendingly daemonic achievements as a scholar, magus, and philosopher. Even so, the introduction had concluded, the perfected work is our own, not that of our attendant daemon. Similarly, for all the occult allure of the summoning of Plotinus's external daemon by the Egyptian medium, and for all the luminous radiance of its momentary appearance, the supreme achievement had remained Plotinus's own, namely, the cultivation of the inner daemon of spiritual understanding. Despite an abiding fascination with daemonology and the occult, Ficino's controlling interest was unquestionably the cultivation of a like spiritual understanding; and the supreme means to that end were neither the aromatics nor the tapers of Iamblichian and Proclian theurgy, but rather the revival of Platonic "theology," or what for us is Plotinian metaphysics, in all its complexity and austerity. In this, as in most Platonic matters, Ficino remained faithful to the deity of Plotinus and not to the daemons, however alluringly powerful, of his later disciples.

University of California—Los Angeles

600–4. Of particular significance for Ficino was Plotinus's *Enneads* 2.3, which begins, "That the course of the stars indicates what is going to happen in particular cases, but does not itself cause everything, as most people think, has been said before elsewhere [a reference to 3.1.5.33 ff.]" (tran. Armstrong).

RAYMOND ADOLPH PRIER

Neapolitan Imitationes Propertianae: *Ancient Sound in the Verses of Pontano and Chariteo*

A TEXT IS NO LONGER KNOWN MERELY FROM ITS ARCHETYPE OR from its relative position in the history of literature. Intertextual "spaces" or "interstices" have, at least since Petrarch, concerned poets and critics alike, whose mutual interest rests in language and more recently in its "resonance." What I shall suggest in this paper is that the Latin language underwent a poetic agglutination under the pen and linguistic instinct of Propertius.[1] There a lexis of love (the *paroles d'amour*) sustained itself in the physical text[2] to be resuscitated in Pontano's Neo-Latin and translated into fainter echoes over the traumatic shift from referential to relational semantics[3] and into the Italian of Chariteo.

---

[1] The specific type of linguistic generation I refer to in this paper was probably first grasped by Ferdinand de Saussure in his *Les Anagrammes* (J. Starobinski, *Les anagrammes de Ferdinand de Saussure: textes inédits* [Paris: Paulet, 1964]) and made a proper issue by Roman Jakobson's review of Saussure's linguistics outside of the text of the *Cours de linguistique générale*. (See my *Thauma Idesthai: The Phenomenology of Sight and Appearance in Archaic Greek* [Tallahassee: The Florida State Univ. Press, 1989], 246–49.) Jakobson argued that Saussure was extremely interested in a "forme anagrammatique du phonisme" or "polyphones anagrammatique" in which the question is always of "signifiers doubling their signifieds" (R. Jakobson, "La première lettre de Ferdinand de Saussure à Antoine Meillet," *Selected Writings*, 8 vols. [Berlin: Mouton, 1971–], 7:242, 246–47). What I shall introduce here is an extension of this essentially temporal insight into a lexis of love poetry, the significance of which is imitated in a multiple doubling of signifieds both in Pontano and in Chariteo. I view such a linguistic agglutination as a direct variation upon quantitative linguistic principles first practiced in Homeric verse (again, see *Thauma Idesthai*).

[2] N is dated from around 1200. See H. E. Butler and E. A. Barber, *The Elegies of Propertius* (Oxford: Clarendon Press, 1933), lxx–lxxiii; *Sexti Properti quae supersunt opera*, ed. O. L. Richmond (Cambridge: Cambridge Univ. Press, 1928), 9.

[3] See Richard Waswo, *Language and Meaning in the Renaissance* (Princeton: Princeton Univ. Press, 1987), 3–82.

1. The Propertian Text

To ask of any text some full revelation of its author as a man[4] is autobiographically naive. Although the genre of Roman Love Elegy might well be "subjective," it is a mistake to obviate the critical disjunction between Propertius and his narrator, and one must welcome even Teutonic oppositions that advertise the ontology inherent in this important distinction.[5] No structural analysis of the text succeeds without it,[6] for this ultimately ironic and, yet, profound "area of hide and seek" allows Propertius and his imitators the "distance" from the immediate identity with language that otherwise would hinder the act of composition. The critics have sensed, somewhat vaguely to be sure, an unusual character to Propertius's *process of thought* and, hence, *his use of language*.[7] Without a doubt, he is a poet of journey and isolation,[8] but, perhaps more importantly, his use of language is arguably "self-conscious."[9] The "subjectivity" inherent in his chosen genre, his "emotion," as Pound would have it, is undoubtedly "an intellectual instigation" and "logo-poetic."[10] It is my purpose, however, to establish a "general linguistics" of the Propertian text that must underlie and provide some partial validity for such critical observations, that must also represent a source and re-source for Pontano and Chariteo. I shall develop the textual presence of this "general linguistics" through a specific analysis of *Monobiblos* I.1.

---

[4] See Butler and Barber, *Elegies*, xviii–xxv; Richmond ed., 63–70. For a criticism of such missteps, see H. Cherniss, "Biographical Fashion in Literary Criticism," *University of California Publications in Classical Philology* 12 (1943): 279 ff. and D. R. Shackleton Bailey, *Propertiana* (Cambridge: Cambridge Univ. Press, 1956), 1–2.

[5] Erich Reitzenstein, *Wirklichkeit und Gefühlsentwicklung bei Properz* (Leipzig: Dieterich, 1936).

[6] Observe the limitations inherent, for instance, in: W. A. Camps, *Propertius Elegies: Book I* (Cambridge: Cambridge Univ. Press, 1961), 10–11; O. Skutsch, "The Structure of the Propertian Monobiblos," *Classical Philology* 58 (1963): 238–39; Brooks Otis, "Propertius' Single Book," *Harvard Studies in Classical Philology* 70 (1965): 1–44.

[7] F. E. Plessis, *Études critiques sur Properce* (Paris: Hachette, 1884), 283–84 (although the book is primarily autobiographical in its critical nature); Richmond ed., 64–65; A. W. Allen, "Elegy and the Classical Attitude Towards Love: Propertius I, 1," *Yale Classical Studies* 11 (1950): 258–77.

[8] F. Solmsen, "Three Elegies of Propertius' First Book," *Classical Philology* 57, 2 (1962): 73–88; E. W. Leach, "Propertius 1.17: The Experimental Voyage," *Yale Classical Studies* 19 (1966): 211–32.

[9] J. P. Sullivan, *Propertius: A Critical Introduction* (Cambridge: Cambridge Univ. Press, 1976), 149–51.

[10] Ezra Pound, *Literary Essays of Ezra Pound*, ed. T. S. Eliot (London: Faber and Faber, 1954), 25. See also J. P. Sullivan, *Ezra Pound and Sextus Propertius: A Study in Creative Translation* (Austin: Univ. of Texas Press, 1964).

Propertius's self-conscious use of language, a kind of *distentio* of returning moments, is first discerned by reading his poetry aloud. A controlling sound of "r" soon forms a matrix of lexical choices that, with the exception of a handful of examples that encompass the "r" of other words, e.g., *miser, verba, carmen, lacrimae, rarus, durus, cura,* etc., one might lodge in two grammatical categories: *abstract* nouns ending in "r" (originally "s") and a small group of deponent verbs. Propertius's language of love consists of at least the following, in the various possibilities of their declensions or conjugations: *amor, dolor, error, furor, horror, livor, timor, candor, pallor, ardor, calor, liquor, labor, rumor, conor, queror,* and *cogor.* In addition, through grammatical extension, sonant identities, or a false sense of etymology, one may also note *cogo, quaero, querelae, patior, memor,* and *tempus,* a noun that appears *only* in the oblique cases (*tempor-*) in the *Monobiblos.*

This is clearly at least the partial vocabulary of a love poet. I think it was, originally, in the lexical reaffirmation of sound, Propertian.[11] Moreover, insofar as it partakes of the "r-abstract," it indicates a peculiar combination of "frames of mind" (*amor, dolor, error, furor, horror, livor,* and *timor*) and "external characteristics" (*candor, pallor, ardor, calor, liquor,* even *labor*).[12] Propertius is very much taken with an abstract representation of human emotions as they appear physically in a specific human experience. For the poet, and, hence, for his imitator, this is a decidedly "distancing" use of language. This point is, of course, revealed even more exactly in the use of the three deponents, *conor* ("I strive"), *queror* ("I lament"), and *patior* ("I suffer, experience").

---

[11] *Amor, furor, querela,* and *lacrimae* have been argued to entail a particular Propertian usage for Roman Love Elegy: F. M. Ahl, "Propertius 1, 1," *Wiener Studien* N.F. 8 (1974): 82; P. J. Connor, " 'Saevitia Amoris': Propertius 1.1," *Classical Philology* 67, 1 (1972): 53; Charles F. Saylor, "Querelae: Propertius' Distinctive Technical Name for his Elegy," *Agon* 1 (1967): 142–49. With the exception of *tempus* for reasons of its nominal form, the interesting statistic about Propertius's lexical choices I have cited in this essay is that if one compares the incidence per line between any one of them in the *Monobiblos* and any one of them in either *all* of the Propertian text *or* any of the other three books, only *labor* and *quaero* appear more frequently outside the *Monobiblos*. In no instance does any of the vocabulary arise more frequently per line in the four books as a whole. Moreover, if one compares the same lexical choices by incidence per line in Plautus, Terence, Lucretius, Catullus as a whole and Catullus in his elegiacs, Vergil in the *Aeneid* and Vergil in the *Aeneid, Georgics,* and *Eclogues,* Tibullus, Ovid in *Amores* 1 and Ovid in the *Amores* as a whole, one discovers several instances when the concentration per line is higher than in Propertius as a whole; but only in four cases, of which two are expected for reason of specific context (*labor* in Tibullus and *calor* in Lucretius), is there a concentration higher than in the Monobiblos.

[12] F. Stolz, *Lateinische Grammatik,* 5th ed., vol. 2 (Munich: C. H. Beck, 1926–1928), 128.

Propertius's *paroles d'amour* create an idiosyncratic language that establishes *Amor* as a major linguistic control, within and without, words conscious yet semiotically and symbolically of sufficient ambiguity not to create of consciousness a graveyard of separated, nominalizing, all-pervasive *eidea*. *Amor*, acting for itself and the pitiable, miserable (*miser*) poet, forces (*cogor*) him in his complaints (*querela*) to strive after (*conor*) an *almost* concrete perception of some *object* that is hard, rare, and slow (*durus, rarus, tardus*), a "thing" that lies at the base not only of the "cares," "tears," and "complaints," but also of his song (*carmen*) and "words" (*verba*) themselves, his *paroles*. These *paroles d'amour* refer, moreover, to one another within their idiosyncratic, "mutually resonanting," generative matrix, which in itself is a continual questioning (*quaero*) and hence a "road towards a kind of self-knowledge." It is here in the crux between what we and Propertius *hear* and consequently *feel* as the poetic "objective" experience and the ever-abstracting knowledge, not of a "philosophy" of love, but of a "philology" thereof (the objectifying verbalization of that experience)[13] that the unusual semiotics of the poet-narrator's "psychological" condition bares itself to us in its utmost complexity. "Emotion" indeed becomes an "intellectual instigation."

Propertius carries his general linguistics throughout the *Monobiblos*. One notes how *dolor* and *lacrimae* set his poet-narrator apart from Ponticus at 9.7 and the Mimnerman song which "love seeks" in the same poem (*quaerit Amor* [9.12]). Nor can one dismiss the insane force of *furor* in 13 ("tantus erat demens inter utrosque furor"; "such was the mad fury between [you] both [13.20]") and its clear links with *flagrans amor* (13.23), *ardor* (13.28), and *novus . . . error* (13.35). No listener forgets the *insolitos . . . timores* ("unaccustomed terrors") of 3.29 and the phantom lover who might constrain (*cogeret* [3.30]) the sleeping Cynthia against her will as the poet-narrator approaches her under the aegis of *Amor* and *Liber*, hard gods with double *ardor*:

> hanc ego, nondum etiam sensus deperditus omnis,
>   molliter impresso *conor* adire toro;
> et quamvis duplici correptum *ardore* iuberent
>   hac *Amor* hac *Liber, durus* uterque deus.[14]

---

[13] I make use of "philology" in August Boeckh's sense of a science both presupposing the philosophical concept and at the same time seeking to produce it (*Encyclopedie und Methodologie der philologischen Wissenschaften* [Berlin: B. G. Teubner, 2. Auf., 1886], Einleitung, passim).

[14] I use these editions: Propertius, *Carmina*, ed. E. A. Barber (Oxford: Oxford Univ. Press, 1960); Pontano, *Carmina*, ed. J. Oeschger (Bari: Laterza, 1948); Chariteo, *Rime*, ed. Erasmo Pèrcopo, 2 vols. (Naples: Academia della Scienza, 1892).

> With sense not yet abandoned to my cups, her
> on soft-impressed couch I sought to near,
> And though twain holocausts enslaved and mastered me—
> Now Love, now Wine, two gods most obdurate.   (3.11–14)

It is no difficult matter, moreover, to establish the significance of complaint in both its nominal and verbal forms (*querelae, queror*) throughout the book,[15] e.g., the lamenting of abandonment placed in the mouth of Cynthia (*deserta querebar* [3.43]) which anticipates the poet-narrator's own in 16, 17, and 18. He longs in vain for an absence of such a condition ("nec quicquam ex illa quod *querar* inveniam!"; "may I come upon no source from which I might lament" [4.28]). He speaks of an absence in the past of sorrowful complaints (*dolore queri* [18.26]). Yet, *querelae* eventually bring the lovers together, for the poet-narrator cannot endure them (*non ... possum durare querelis* [6.11]). They are, in the end, equivalent to the *carmina* or "song" itself by which he contends, "I was able [to make her mine] by submission to my alluring song" ("sed potui blandi *carminis* obsequio" [8B.40]). Here lies, I believe, a clear proof of a disjunction between Propertius, the poet, and the poet-narrator: the former regards the *Monobiblos*, as a whole, a set of blandishments—as must the uncritical listener; the latter, perforce of his narrative position *within* the text, may be allowed to pick and choose.

In any case, Propertian complaint is joined with "sadness," "forcing," and "harsh time" to such an obvious extent in the *Monobiblos* that one senses that it generates the poetry itself. Note how the vocabulary occupies, "formulaically," the strong points and spaces of the line:

> nec tantum ingenio quantum servire *dolori*
>   *cogor* et aetatis ‖ *tempora dura queri*.
> To serve much less my native genius than my sorrow,
>   I am forced, of life's harsh time to moan.   (7.7–8)

Propertius fills the *Monobiblos* with unwilling complaints (*cogor ... querelis* [16.13]); the eighteenth poem will make use of a panoply of language generated from the general linguistics: *amor* (8,19), *carmina* (9), *cogor* (30), *color* (17), *cura* (23), *dolor* (3,13,26), *dura* (28), *furor* (15), *lacrimae* (16), and *querelae* or *queror* (29,1,26). The lonely woods (*silvae*), hence, only resonate (*resonent*) "Cynthia" (31), Propertius's self-consciously linguistic, ontological construct. Yet, this linguistic "program" does not issue from 18, but from the incipit to the *Monobiblos* as a whole. It begins:

---

[15] Again see Saylor, "Querelae."

> Cynthia prima suis miserum me cepit ocellis,
>   contactum nullis ante cupidinibus
> tum mihi constantis deiecit lumina fastus
>   et caput impositis pressit Amor pedibus,
> donec me docuit castas odisse puellas
>   improbus, et nullo vivere consilio.
>
> Cynthia whose lovely eyes first captured me in misery,
>   A sick desire contracted ne'er before,
> Crushed my arrogance, the glowing power of the proud,
>   And love begrooved my head with adamantine stride
> Until, perverted fiend, he tutored me too well
>   To hate the chaste and live a senseless life.   (1.1–6)

Cynthia might indeed begin Propertius's misery as she literally does his poetry. The gutteral, consonantal, unvoiced stop wreaks havoc with the life of the lover. "She snatches me, the wretch (*miserum me*—post-caesural)," he declares in direct first person subjective narration, "with her eyes" (*cepit ocellis*—post-bucolic diaeresis), "me touched before by no desires" (*contactum . . . cupidinibus*—beginning and endline), but *Amor* "hurled down" (*deiecit*—post-caesural) "my glance of steadfast" (*constantis*—pre-caesural) (*constantis* ‖ *diecit*) "pride and suppressed (*pressit*) my head (*caput*) with his imposed feet, whereby he taught" (*docuit*—pre-caesural) "me to hate virtuous" (*castas*—pre-caesural) (*docuit* ‖ *castas*) "girls, perverse *Amor*" (*improbus*—beginning line), "and to behave in no rational way" (*nullo . . . consilio*—endline). Cynthia's harsh sounds, made all the more palpable by their metrical positioning in the strong areas of the hexameter and pentameter lines, drive the poet-narrator away from his rational self, while also—and this is phonemically most interesting in these opening lines, although somewhat paradoxical for the listener—throwing him under the *ratio absurda* that is one with and yet underlying all Propertius's *paroles d'amour*: *Amor improbus*, the perverted Love that presses hard upon his head and makes him rave.

It is here, at the transference of his experience from the girl to the general, yet humanly palpable force of Love (an *Amor* whose sonant mark, "r," gains metrical priority in placement as the poem continues and obscures Cynthia's "c" as her own specific mark) that Propertius allows the first indications of the cerebral nature of his wretched passion.[16] The experience is immediate, the *topos*, the reality it expresses, however, is abstracting. Love throws the poet-narrator from rationality into *furor* (7); he is forced (*cogor*) into misfortune (*adversos* ‖ *cogor habere*

---

[16] See Ahl, "Propertius 1.1," 82 for a discussion of the interplay of gutturals, labials, mutes, and sibilants.

deos [8]). Instantly the passion elicits a mythological reflection upon the *labores* of Milanion. But regard the metrical impression of "word placement": *furor* appears immediately after the caesure of 7; *cogor* begins the second half of its pentameter in 8; *labores* ends line 9. This placement is conscious, yet also traditional. Only within a purely written metrics do words arise simply *causa metrica*. In a Propertian line, strong verse areas and points are *syntactically* and *semiotically linguistic*, phenomenologically so in the sense of *paroles spoken* to appear, and one *must* expect generally that the poet's language to be there, unless, of course, it finds itself "dislocated" because of dissonant forces from other sonant nexus, e.g., the *Amor* of line 4 as it "struggles" with the more concrete, but ultimately less important nature of the "Cynthia" of line 1.

Much might be said of Propertius's use of myth, including the presence of Milanion and the daughter of Iasus in the *incipit*. Here the poet achieves a striking reversal of plot[17] (*mythos* in the Aristotelian sense) in order not only to make more immediate his narrative of love, but also to portray the poet-narrator's ever more evident isolation. Yet the essential phonemic and psychological nature of love remains the same. Atalanta is *dura* (10). The mythical hero in love, we are told, was wont to wander madly in caves (*amens errabat in antris* [11]),[18] and once again we perceive Love's affect upon the mind. Yet in love (*in amore*—pre-caesural) Milanion's prayers (*preces*—post-caesural) bode well (16). But for Propertius's narrator?

> In me tardus Amor non ullas cogitat artis,
>   nec meminit notas, ut prius, ire vias
>
> Yet within my heart Love knows no arts
>   Nor minds those ways he was once wont to tread.
>   (17–18)

Propertius turns abruptly now to the Colchian witches (19–24) whose magic, whose *labor* (20) is devoted to love. He addresses his friends (25 ff.). They are to ask or to seek (*quaerite* [26]) aid for an unclean breast. "Bravely I shall suffer" (*patiemur* [27]). "Bear me through lands and seas," he begs, "by which no woman shall have known my way" (*iter*) (29–30). The poet-narrator becomes ever more remote in the resonances marking his idiosyncratic ways of love. "May your way be *facilis*, not *durus*," he pleads (31); "may you be *in tuto amore*"—"in a full, safe love" (32). "Against me Venus works bitter nights" (*noctes amaras* [33]), "and there is no moment which Love does not fill" ("et nullo vacuus

---

[17] See Allen, "Elegy," 269; Leach, "Propertius 1.17," 220.
[18] For *amens* as a pun on *amans*, see Ahl, "Propertius 1.1," 87.

tempore defit Amor" [34]). Time flies not for Propertius, but remains sodden with the wretched, heavy presence of Love. Here, as it is in the nexus of his *paroles d'amours*, *tempus* in its oblique cases indicates no measured, Aristotelian or even Platonic sense, but only *Amor*, the "transcendental signified" pointed to by a multitude of metrically generated and/or phonemic signifiers.

In the last four verses of this program poem, Propertius solidifies the role of the poet-narrator by creating of him a *vates* or priest. Here lies the narrative *presence* of the elegiac first-person subjective voice that incorporates the reader into the text through its generic and grammatical status. It also permits a commonality of experience: "Avoid ill; let *cura* tarry with whomever; never change your place (*assueto . . . amore*) when love is tried and true" (35–36). "But if anyone will have turned *tardas auris* to my warning, alas, by what *dolor* will he recall my *paroles* (*verba*)."

The significant "r-phoneme" escalates in the last couplet of the poem:

> quod si quis monitus tardas adverterit auris,
> heu referet quanto verba dolore mea!

> For if a lover takes his heed with tardy ears,
> How he'll bemoan my fate he could avoid!
>
> (37–38)

The aural echo of *tardas auris* returns us to the couplet at 17:

> in me *tardas Amor* non ullas cogitat artis,
> nec meminit notas, ut prius, ire vias.

The "*tardas auris*" recall semantically the "*tardus Amor*," one leading to great sorrow in *remembered paroles*, the other to the ignorance of *ars*, the loss of memory in the conventional ways of love. Some have mistakenly translated "*tardus*" as "late in life"; another, more suggestively, assumes it concerns Propertius's so-called "literary career,"[19] but they have neglected the all-important cognitive value created by the poet himself. *Amor* as a subjective experience is "slow." It is also "late" (*serus*) as one gleans from the linkage of "*serus Amor*" and "*tardus Amor*" between 7.20 and 7.26. Through "slow ears," Love assumes not the knowledge of skills, nor the memory of conventional love, but the knowledge and understanding of *paroles* (*verba*). Hence in lines 17 and 37 of the *incipit*, the quantitative metrical resonances, both caesurally and semantically,

---

[19] C. F. Saylor, "The Meaning of *Tardus Amor* in Propertius," *Latomus* 36 (1977): 785.

create a most unusual, barely concealed line:

> *in me tardus Amor ‖ tardas adverterit [auris/artis].
> In me tardy Love has turned tardy [ears/convention].

1.1 is most certainly a program piece devoted consciously to the isolated *paroles d'amour*.

The profundity of our poet lies in this stark and personal ontology of a sensual, self-contained and containing language and the knowledge it implies. His loneliness is grounded in this precise alienation that his position towards language entails and that much of his poetry, especially the *Monobiblos* as a whole, reflects. In short, in seemingly concrete terms that force palpability to reveal what is in fact a "philosophical-philological and psychological insight," the poet's language resonates through, by, and in the poet-narrator's *caput* on which *pressit Amor*.

2. The Pontanian Text

Pontano appropriated his elegiac, narrative stance primarily from the texture of Propertian poetry. Clearly he perused the N manuscript carefully and acknowledged the full extent of its attraction in the first book of his early *Parthenopei sive amorum*. There in 1.18, entitled "Ludit Poetice" ("He Plays in a Poetic Vein"), he speaks fully of his debt.

Pontano's initial play or al-lusion is to a specific, well-known Propertian text: 3.3.1 ("I Had Seemed to Be Lying in the Soft Shadow of Helicon"). Herein Propertius attempts to define himself not as a poet of epic and hence of the political grandeur of Rome, but as a poet of elegiac love (see also 2.10 and 3.1). *This is not a political statement, but a generic and, hence, narrational one.* Pontano's poet-narrator, like his classical "father's," finds the encampments of war too harsh (*dura* [67]). Yet, it is not the presence of mood or even genre that has attracted Pontano, but an extended language-play. Regard the *linguistic* similarities between the first line of 1.18 and that of the Propertian model-text:

> Iam satis est *molli* ‖ residem lusisse sub *umbra*....
> Visus eram *molli* ‖ recubans Heliconis in *umbra*....
>
> Now 'tis enough that sitting I have played 'neath soft shadow.
> I'd seemed to be lying in Helicon's soft shade....

Pontano's key addition is *"lusisse"* ("to have played"), an acknowledgment not only of the playful relationships *within* the two texts but also of the *linguistic* playfulness *between* both. The same playful mastery appears again at line 48:

> Ut reor a calamis, ‖ Pan Tegeaeus erat.
>
> As I deem from the pipes, 'twas Tegeaen Pan.

This line is a close composite of two in Propertius 3.3: "ut reor a facie, ‖ Calliopea fuit" ("As I deem from the face, 'twas Calliope" [38]); "fictilis et calami, ‖ Pan Tegeaee, tui" ("clay [image] and your pipe, Tegeaen Pan" [30]). I think that what Pontano wishes to draw our attention to here is not only an identity of lexical choices, but especially the *quantitative metrical* identities that bind the model to its imitation. The opening-line positions of *ut reor a* (-˘˘-) are identical, and from it Pontano generates the rest of his line, not lexically but *metrically*. The generation is subtle, for Pontano provides the second Propertian material not after the caesura—that would be an overly simplistic linkage of two blank hemiepesbut with the noun that holds the strong point *before* the caesura: "*calami[s]*." The "play" here is metrical, but is purpose is surely to emphasize Pontano's *dependence* upon the quantitative meter of the ancient, Propertian text. The al-lusion is more than merely thematic; it is *linguistic*.

In this manner, Pontano urges his listener to sense beyond the more superficial parallels that might suggest themselves: a "weak" nature of elegiac poetry over epic (Pro. 3.3.17–18; Pon. 1.18.3 ff.) or the general concern with "great deeds" as the prerequisite for glory (Pro. 3.3.3; Pon. 1.18.13–14). The justification of poetry in political terms was no doubt prevalent in both ancient Rome and the Renaissance, but the elegiac justification in both indicates a "subjective perception" that is personal and "alienated by locus":

> quod si forte animis respondent carmina nostris
>   vel Croesi fuerint vilia regna mihi.
>
> If perhaps, however, my songs respond to my *animi* even
> Croesus's realms would be things of naught to me.
>   (1.18.15–16)

Elegiac poets, claims Pontano (17), transgress the epic genre as *priests* (*vatibus* [20]), and here lies the *narrational* stance that identifies the elegy of both model and imitation. Propertius 1.1.35 ff. provides the familiar al-lusion (see also 2.10.19, 2.17.3, 4.6.1,10). It is in the elegiac stance of a priest that the poet creates his poet-narrator. Pontano signifies the total elegiac milieu *objectively* by claiming for *himself as poet* a common geographic source with Propertius: Umbria.

> *Umbria carminibus* non *inhonora* meis,
> Umbria Pieridum cultrix, patria alta Properti.

Umbria who does not dishonor my songs, Umbria, she who
tends the Pierian Muses, high fatherland of Propertius
(24–25, see Pro. 1.22.9–10)

Umbria generates the elegiac *vates*, but it also generates, it would appear, something with which we have become familiar: lexical choices with the "r-phoneme." From this land (*loci* [30]) arises the voice of the Coerulian Nymph who endeavors to seduce Pontano into writing her poetry:

"tu mea *cura*, puer, tu meus *ardor* eris;
hanc tibi nos dabimus, ne sis modo *durus* amanti
quam dederat nobis Delius ante lyram."

"You, boy, will be my care; you, my ardor. We'll give you this lyre which Apollo has given us before." (34–36)

Yet, granted the poetic power, Pontano's wild play leaps beyond the bounds the nymph suggests, and the poem takes a drastic turn (37–64). The nymph in *horror* immerses her head in her own founts (37–38). *Liber* (Bacchus) lurches upon the scene and about him whirl satyrs [Flushed Inebriation and Unwholesome Love (*malsanus Amor*)], Silenus on an ass, and Priapus (39–44). Tegeaen Pan appears with his pipes and recites the travels and powers of Bacchus, especially his place in the making of love, his play (*lusus*), his quietude, and his *terror* (48–58).

The carnival is out of hand. Little wonder the nymph hides her head. Then, just as suddenly as the poet-narrator had wildly transgressed and extended the nymph's poetic bounds, he breaks his poem with a joke: Pan's *urceus* ("wine-pitcher") breaks, and he grieves in his thirst and is silent in front of shame ("Ille dolet sitiens praeque *pudore* tacet" [62]). Laughter shakes Bacchus and his crowd—only Silenus and Priapus grieve (64), and the poet-narrator, the elegiac *vates*, ends his words with his model's rejection of martial, epic poetry in which the camps are much too harsh (*dura*) for him (65–68). In short the joke is rather much on the muse herself:

Scilicet in nobis est consuetudo magistra;
haec studia, haec *artes* ingeniosa facit.
Quod si censuesces paulum sudare sub *armis*,
mox tibi fidenti Martius *ardor* erit.

Evidently in us habit rules. This learned study, skillful convention she [the muse] creates with her genius. But if you become accustomed to sweat a little under arms, soon the ardor of Mars will be yours in your courage. (69–72)

The poet-narrator has "cleared his space of play," established his poetic program through a direct al-lusion to the Propertian elegiac stance, not only generically, but especially linguistically. He directs us to the *metrical* content of his creation and reinforces his parameters with direct lexical or generative choices from the Propertian *paroles d'amour*: Glory must be sought (*quaerenda est* [13]), *labor* (19), *ardor* (34,72), *cura* (34), *Amor* (42), *liquor* (51), *horror* (37), and his additions of *in-honorus* (24) and *terror* (57). The poet casts this language in context with *durus*: *durus* in love (35) and the *dura castra* of the war god whom the *vates* cannot endure celebrating (67). Then appears *pudor* (62). In the end these are all characteristics of the Propertian-Pontanian sense of song (*carmen* [15,24]).

Pontano's poetic choices are clearly conscious, and they may be traced throughout much of his poetry,[20] which is, of course, not entirely Propertian in allusion.[21] Perhaps the most revealing of his poetic declarations lies in the incipit to the second book of the *Eridanus*, the last book of elegiac poetry.

Ariadna, his wife, has long been dead, and Pontano ostensibly turns to another woman, Stella. Yet, this situation is neither as brutal nor as simple as it might seem. One must, once again, keep an eye on the difference between the poet and the poet-narrator. The *latter* begins in a *harsh* tone:

> Quid *querere*, a Ariadna? Tuae non iusta *querelae*
>   causa subest; solvit *mors* sua *iura tori*.
> *Liber* ago; si nulla cavet lex, desinit esse
>   peccatum; *quare* desine et ipsa *queri*.
>
> Why complain, Ariadna? No just cause underlies your complaints; death has dissolved your bedrights. I move free—a Bacchus. If no law prohibits, no longer is it a sin. Wherefore, desist, even you, from complaint. (2.1.1-4)

---

[20] E.g., see *Hendecasyllabi* 1.21.1–11, *Partheneopei* 2.3.77–82, *De amore coniugali* 1.5.24–30, 1.7, and especially 3.2, *Eridanus* 2.26.1–22; *Iambics* 2.14–20; *De tumulis* 1.50, 2.29, 60, 62.

[21] What scholarly criticism that exists on the elegies of Pontano tends to regard Catullus as his primary classical model: U. Renda, *Giovanni Pontano* (Turin: G. B. Paravia, 1939), 85; E. Paratore, *La poesia di Giovanni Pontano* (Rome: Ateneo, 1967), passim. Specific studies addressing his elegiac poetry are linguistically and philologically marginal: G. R. Orsini, *L'espressione del dolore nella lirica di G. Pontano* (Lodi: C. Dell'Avo, 1915); G. Sentore, "Giovanni Pontano poeta della famiglia," *Arch. stor. per la prov. Napol.*, n.s., 25 (1939): 5–24; P. Nespoulous, "L'expression des sentiments familiaux dans la poésie de Giovanni Pontano," *Pallas* 19, n.s., 8, fas. 4 (1972): 97–117 and "La poésie élégiaque de Giovanni Pontano," *Pallas* 21, n.s., 10, fas. 5 (1974): 77–98. For a more sophisticated analysis, however, see A. Mazzoni, *Giovanni Gioviano Pontano* (Milan: Cantelli, 1967).

This is an extremely revealing opening to a book of elegiac love. Propertian complaint, both in terms of Ariadna and the poet-narrator, is surely Pontano's internal textual source, but he immediately underscores the generic stance of the poet-narrator, in contradistinction to what might be his own, with a play on the word *"liber."* The poet-narrator is generically drunk, but he, the objective poet, is the character *his* society regards as "free." Pontano underscores his distinction with a multitude of *objective*, legal lexical choices: *causa, solvit, cavet lex, peccatum, ius* (5). This is the vocabulary of a Ciceronian oration, not of some hypothetically simple love elegy. Its non-elegiac nature is, however, immediately revealed by a characteristic Pontanian shift:

> Quid *loquor*; ah, *demens*? Stant et mea foedera tecum;
> iunxit *Amor* dextras, foederis *auctor Amor*
> *auctor Amor* fidei, sistendi et pignoris *auctor*.

Insane? Of what do I speak: My pacts with you remain. Love joined our right hands; Love is the author of the pact. Love is the author of fidelity, author of the firm-standing pledge of love. (9–11).

"Demens"? "Amens"? "Amans"? We return to the labors of Milanion, to the incipit of the *Monobiblos* (Pro. 1.11 ff.), and to the elegiac "subjectivity" that in the end upholds marriage, the pact (*foedus*), fidelity (*fides*), and the pledge (*pignus*). The poet-narrator can focus only upon Ariadna's beauty, one that instills new envy (*livor*) in the blessed themselves(!) (twice stated: 15 and 16).

What poetic, compositional shift does Pontano now elicit from the "locus of Love"? He demands that Ariadna spread out the marriage couch (17–24) in the name of play and elegy:

> Hinc patiare licet tantisper ‖ *ludere* nostram
> canitiem; fas sit ‖ *ficto in amore queri*....

Thence, meanwhile, let my grey old age play; let it be right to complain in "fictioned" love. (17–18)

Pontano's present and living *querelae* are, like his wife's, *fictionalized*, sustained, in other words, in the play of the poet-narrator, that is, in his elegiac stance. Here he, unlike, I suspect, the Christian poet himself, may deal *directly* with the classical tradition of an Elysian Wedding-God (*Elysiusque* [beginning line] ... *Hymen* [endline][20]). We are now within a poetically created realm in which the poet-narrator, the *vates*, communicates beyond the grave and ushers both Pontano and the listener into a common "subjective intimacy." Yet, this intimacy is signified by an old friend:

> *durat amor*, cuicumque diu *suspiria durant*,
>   gliscit et in vero semper *amore timor*.
> Quisque amat, timet ipse quidem; *timor* auget *amorem*,
>   auctus in immensum gaudia tollit *amor*.
>
> Love endures; long too, the sighs of any man,
>   Always in a true love, fear does grow.
> He who loves does fear; fear does love engender—
>   Augmented love bears out joys to their full. (27–30)

So the first half of this elegiac poem ends in play upon a repetitive lexical "note" of the "r-linguistics," the interwoven presences of *amor* and *timor* set within the poet-narrator's enduring sighs (*dura/durant* and *suspiria*). Pontano appears fully conscious of his Propertian linguistics.

In the following lines (31–46), Pontano turns to material somewhat more general and historical: allusions to his "play" (*ludere*—beginning line [32, 33]) in some previous poetic works; the first book of the *Eridanus*; his didactic poem, *De hortis hesperidum*; and *De amore conjugali*. He expands his last al-lusion into a specific praise of Ariadna when he identifies her with the classical heroines, Evadne (39), Penelope (39), and Laodomia, the beloved of Zeus(!) (40, 46). Unmindful (*im-memor* [41]) of war, the poet-narrator—in this case rather closely identified with Pontano who *himself* had been separated from his wife in the Barons' War during the eighties of the quatrocento (see *De amore conjugali* 3.2)—speaks of an Ariadna "mindful of grief, mindful of her husband carried off" ("illa *memor* luctus: *memor* et consortis adempti" [43]) Yet, although these specific al-lusions focus upon Pontano, the poet, they, in the end, define the condition of the poet-narrator, and the poem ends in a formal reaffirmation of the elegiac stance (47–60). In it the poet-narrator sports with the fictionalized "decorous Stella" ("Stella decora" [48]). There swim the swans on the Eridanus (Po) (49). There "let Stella sing, following the swans' quantitative metrical feet" ("Cantet olorinos Stella secuta modos" [50]). The Graces attend her, as does *Amor* (55), and the Eridanus (elegiac poetry) provides "now flame, now waters" (56). The poet is, however, well aware of the fictionalized nature of his "elegiac space," and he wishes Ariadna and us to know it too:

> huic quoque tantisper *spatium* concede *iocandi*,
>   Elysius dum nos conciliarit Hymen.
> Haec mora parva quidem; mortem post cuncta perennant
>   atque sub aeterna condicione manent.

To her [Stella] concede, [Ariadna], a space of elegiac playfulness until the Elysian Hymen unites us. This delay is indeed small. All things last after death and remain in an eternal condition. (57–60).

So ends the *incipit* of Pontano's last elegiac book. Therein he has affirmed *in the mouth of his poet-narrator and himself* that "space of elegy" which he has developed from the time of his *Parthenopei sive amorum* and his primary identification with the narrative peculiarities of the ancient text. Moreover, it is possible now that his "narrative space" has claimed not only his poet-narrator and his listener, but also Pontano himself, the husband who may speak through and by "elegiac subjectivity" to a character *located* beyond the living in death. As the "poetic imitator" of the Propertian text, Pontano evinces a clear consciousness of the linguistic and elegiac texture of poetry that establishes for himself and his Neo-Latin listener a convincing poetic, both sensual and intellectual, in which the poet-narrator moves.

3. The Charitean Text

Chariteo was some twenty years Pontano's junior. Spanish by birth, he composed in Italian but also made use of the Propertian model. His major text is the *Endimione*, which is comprehensively Petrarchan and heavily political.[22] Yet, Propertius (see 4.10) was not always "elegiacally pure," and surely Chariteo found in the ancient text support for his seemingly contradictory position. What, however, are the distinguishing Propertian, traditionally elegiac characteristics in the Neapolitan text?

> Volete saper come e da qual parte
> Mi vengon gli amorosi e dolci versi ... ?
> Le Muse o Phebo non m'han fatta parte
> Di lor canti soavi, ornati e tersi;
> Ma poi che a mirar voi le luci apersi,
> Donna, mi venne il molle ingegno e l'arte.

Do you want to know how and from what part the amorous and sweet verses might come to me...? Neither the Muses nor Phoebus has made me part of their delightful songs, embellished and

---

[22] W. J. Kennedy, "Chariteo's Petrarchan Classicism" (Paper delivered at the Twenty-first Annual Conference, Center for Medieval and Early Renaissance Studies, Binghamton, NY, 17 October 1987). For an introductory, philological study of the poetry, see G. Getto, "Sulla poesia del Cariteo," *Giornale storico della letteratura italiana*, 123 (1946): 53–68. For Chariteo's emergence from the linguistic traditions of Naples, see Marco Santagata, *La Lirica aragonese: studi sulla poesia napoletana del secondo quattrocento* (Podova: Antenore, 1979). Generally speaking Pèrcopo's introduction to his two volume edition is still very useful.

polished; but after I opened my eyes to wonder at you, lady, soft
genius came to me, and art. (Sonetto 25.1–8)

This simple sonnet is a clear, almost reconstituted, imitation of Propertius 2.1.1–16. The first four lines are especially key:

> *Quaeritis,* unde mihi totiens scribantur *amores,*
> unde meus veniat mollis in ora liber.
> non haec Calliope, non haec mihi cantat Apollo.
> ingenium nobis ipsa puella facit.

You ask whence my love songs often might be written, whence might come my soft book in my mouth. Neither Calliope nor Apollo sing these things to me; my mistress herself makes my genius. (2.1.1–4)

By recalling this particular text Chariteo is unequivocally identifying with the elegiac stance, and, although the last half of the sonnet deals with a decidedly "Petrarchan donna," he is careful to oppose his poetry, once again, to the Latin Muses and sacred Apollo (12–14), hence reaffirming elegy over epic. Unlike Pontano, Chariteo does not mention Propertius directly here, but the Latin poet's name, linked with that of Callimachus in the closing canzone of the book (20.19), can leave little doubt that the poet turns to Propertius throughout the *Endimione* as his major elegiac text.

Sonnet 70 provides a more subtle understanding of his model. The piece clearly recalls Propertius 2.30a:

> quo fugis a demens? nulla est fuga: tu licet usque
> ad Tanain fugias, usque sequetur *Amor.*...
> instat semper *Amor* supra caput, instat amanti,
> et gravis ipse super libera colla sedet.

> Whither in madness do you flee? There is no flight:
> 'Though to Tanais, there will follow Love....
> Always Love bestrides the lover's hard-pressed head
> And sits heavy on a once-free neck. (2.30a. 1–2, 7–8)

This text, of course, recalls the first four lines of the *incipit* to the *Monobiblos* and also the wanderings of Milanion in the same poem. But Chariteo develops more than merely a thematic or generic al-lusion as he did in sonnet 25, for in 70, in an address to his "Soul" (*Alma*), he asks some "spatial" questions in familiar tones.

"Which is better," his poet-narrator queries, "to run to the West or drink the fertile surge of the Nile, or seek the deep in order not to sense such ardent sadness?" ("per non *sentir dolor* si *ardente?*" [4]). He follows his rhetorical question with a reversal reminiscent of Pontano: "What do

I speak? What furor spins my mind?" ("Che parli?, o qual *furor* gira la mente?" [5]). Where can he flee or hide? "Where does love not come with you and is all about?" ("Ch'*amor* teco non venga e ti circonde" [7]). He is haunted by his love's beautiful visage. "Then, weary, unhappy (*misera*) Soul, will you not flee this prison. . . ? Search out the location of the sleeping sun or where it wakes—from first the Indies to as far as Britain. What Love will you not see always right on your head!" ("Ch-e'*amor* ti vedrai *sempre* in su la testa" [9–14]). Two distinctly Propertian poetic traits begin to emerge here: one, the lexical choices of the "r-linguistics," and two, a cerebral, in this case spiritual, "space" of the poet-narrator's lament on which *pressit Amor*. The language might well be Italian, but the stance and linguistics are of Latin elegy. These details become ever more evident in Chariteo's first canzone.

Canzone 1 at first glance seems to be unabashedly Petrarchan, perhaps at some points even a copy of sonnet 35 of the *Rime* ("Solo e Pensoso i Piú Deserti Campi"; "Alone and Deep in Thought [I Walk] the Most Deserted Fields"), the one Petrarchan poem that is arguably composed on a Propertian model.[23] In both the *canzone* and the sonnet, the lover, isolated from his beloved, despairs his loneliness, tears, and insatiate pain. Much about both poems sounds and appears rough:

> Ma pur sí *aspre* vie né si selvagge

Yet there are no ways so rough and wild. (Pet. *Rime* 35.12)

> Tra *questi boschi agresti*,
> Selvaggi, *aspri* e incolti.

Among these harsh woods, wild, rough, and uncultivated.
(Char. *Canzone* 1.1–2)

> Sol che *constante* fede
> Si *trove* un *questi sassi*

Alone what constant faith is found on these rocks? (7–8)

Chariteo is clearly developing a sonant harshness that one just barely discerns in the Petrarchan model. Particularly harsh, moreover, is a mythological insertion under the banner of war, blood, and human limbs ("nel sangue e membra humane" [36]) that terminates with Medea's killing of her brother and children (34–38). The severity is especially evident, however, when the poet introduces the main and certainly the most interesting element of the poem: reflections upon the writing *and* singing of the canzone itself: "Nè vuol ch'io cante o *scriva*,

---

[23] E. H. Williams, "Notes on Petrarch," *MLN* 32, 4 (1917): 193–96.

/ Et di parlarne meco *anchor* mi *priva"* (She does not will I sing or write, and because I speak not with myself I am deprived: 25-26).

> Però quest'*aspre* pene
> Con rime *acerbe* e *dure*
> Conformi assai con *questo horribil foco.*
>
> Whenever these rough pains with bitter and harsh rhymes,
> overly consonant with that horrible fire. (40-42)

Chariteo's transformed elegiac stance applies, expectedly, to poesis itself, and the Italian, as does the Latin and Neo-Latin, maintains that observation in familiar lexical choices.

Yet, this is but a part of the sonant texture of this poem of eighty-one verses, for Chariteo also exhibits a sense of "sonant amelioration" that results in oxymoron. He introduces a phonemic softness with unbridled authority at the beginning of the fifth stanza:

> Talhor quand'io *cantava*
> In piú *soavi accenti*
> Col cor pien d'ardentissima *dolcezza.*
>
> At times when I sang in more gentle intonations
> with a heart full of the most ardent sweetness. (53-55)

This sonant opposition provides a linguistic rationale to the last line of the last stanza, a much-used and routinely-expected Petrarchan oxymoron of the icy fire: "Ond'un *gelat o ardore* al cor mi nacque" (Whence an icy ardor is born in my heart: 78). In the midst of silent rocks and woods, the poet-narrator laments in words—but he cannot speak—and experiences a "superbissima tacque," an "incredibly proud silence" (77) in the self-conscious composition of his song, one that must never stray from the lonely forest or the curb of the poet-narrator's will as long as a heavenly mercy promises release:

> Canzon mia, no uscir fuor da la selva,
> Pon freno a la tua voglia
> Finché mercé del cielo indi ti scoglia.
>
> My song, do not leave outside the wood; put a curb on your will.
> As long as mercy from Heaven then releases you. (79-81, compare Petrarch, *Rime* 125.79-81 and 126.66-68)

On the surface, therefore, the poem appears Petrarchan to a fault. Like its Italian model, it is much more subjectively psychological than the general run of either Pontanian or Propertian texts. Yet it is bound to its Propertian model much more clearly than is Petrarch's thirty-fifth sonnet, and the tie is a linguistic one. Although both Petrarch and

Chariteo make clear allusions to *Monobiblos* 18.1-4 ("Haec Certe Deserta Loca et Taciturna Querenti"; "Full Sure This Lies a Dumb, Deserted Place, As I Lament"), the latter's are, even from a point of simple thematic al-lusion, more developed. The Propertian lines 1 through 8 and 14 through 19, which form the opening verses of the first and second stanzas of the *canzone* respectively, allude to *Monobiblos* 18.1-6, to be sure, but there is a more profound sense of linguistic transformation than that.

The listener notices this transforming bond first, perhaps, in a certain Latinate sound in some of the lexical choices: "tormenti occolti" (5), "murmurar lo sento" (10), "membra humane" (36), "morte indegna" (37), "in altro loco" (45), "ardentissima dolcezza" (55), "volto minace" (75), and, by far the most startling to my ear, "superbissima tacque" (77). Then too one might regard eliptical choices such as "sol" (7), "empion" (16), "horribil" (42), or "cagion" (47) as both Latinate and characteristically Neapolitan. The point I wish to stress here is that one hears *through the Italian* the language's Latin base and some highly familiar Propertian *sounds*. Note, for instance, how the "poetic" dropping of an "e" from an infinitive can only stress the "r":"murmurar" (10), "parlar" (13), "satiar" (32), "macular" (35). Listen to such phrases and words as "il mio *dolore*" (24), "*Amore* ingrato" (31), "rime *acerbe* e *dure*" (41), "*horribil* foco" (42), "folle *ardire*" (66), "tacitamente il *dolor mio*" (71), "*ardo*" (73), "*ardore*" (78).

Suddenly we see that the linguistic texture of this poem reveals not only the general closeness of Latin to Italian or even, perhaps, a veiled Latinicity of lexical choice,[24] but especially our familiar Propertian "r-linguistic" in *parallel lexical choices*. What cements this "Propertian textuality" is, however, what might seem an almost forlorn attempt to *reproduce Latin quantitative verse* in the Italian qualitative variety: the endline positions of "errore" (21), "dolore" (24), "dolor mio" (71), "acerbe e dure" (41), and, perhaps, "morte" (47) and "sorte" (50). In short it is, once again, in the developed resonance of Propertian sound and meter that Chariteo appears able to establish his classical model in ways familiar to us in Pontano's Neo-Latin text, a linguistic usage that again maintains the ontology of elegiac space for the poet-narrator who composes in a vulgate incapable of a full quantitative metrical force. The subjective poesis retains its constitutive elegiac linguistic sense.

If indeed, as I have endeavored to show, there is a particular linguistic-elegiac textuality retained in both Neo-Latin and Italian texts *because of*

---

[24] On Chariteo's Latinisms, see Getto, "Sulla poesia," 60.

an ancient poetic model, certain interesting answers to questions posed about imitation and the culturally disruptive shift from Latin to the vernacular begin to emerge. Yes, Petrarch's insight into the metaphors of imitation in his *Familiares* 23.19 is valid and reveals silent and isolating "investigations of the mind," just as Greene has so elegantly explained.[25] Moreover, an ontology is definitely established in the interstices between the model and its imitation. Yet, where Greene might emphasize an "ontology of the self,"[26] it becomes evident that the spatial and local characteristics established similarly in the three poets I have here discussed suggest a generically reserved realm, an interaction between the poet and his poet-narrator of considerable ontological importance, one that assumes a Propertian idiosyncratic phonemic usage and links it to a similar proto-morphology of metrical construct that in turn dictates lexical choices in all three poets. Moreover, the attempts at "imitative conservation" in both Pontano and Chariteo broaden the understanding of the parameters of the Renaissance culture's shift from Latin to the vernacular, one important later to the Pléiade, the Areopagus, and even the nineteenth-century Lanier. All fought to retain quantitative measures in vernacular verse.

Durham, North Carolina

---

[25] T. Greene, "Petrarch and the Humanist Hermeneutic," in *The Light in Troy* (New Haven and London: Yale Univ. Press, 1982), 81–103.
[26] Ibid., "Petrarch: The Ontology of the Self," 104–26.

JANE TYLUS

Silencing Partenope: The Origins of Culture in Sannazaro's Arcadia

> The epic tradition has in a very real sense been built upon female silence.
> — Christine Froula[1]

IN THE MIDST OF *CIVILIZATION AND ITS DISCONTENTS*, A CITY RISES UP solidly and profoundly terrestrial: Freud's vision of eternal Rome, in all its varied historical shapes: "Where the Coliseum now stands we could at the same time admire Nero's vanished Golden House. On the Piazza of the Pantheon we should find not only the Pantheon of today, as it was bequeathed to us by Hadrian, but, on the same site, the original edifice erected by Agrippa."[2] Freud invokes this dazzling image of totality as a picturesque demonstration of his thesis that "in mental life nothing which has once been formed can perish." Yet halfway through the analogy, he abandons it—not because the archaeologist's dream fails to illustrate the theory of psychic conservation, but because the theory itself is doomed to failure. Had not Freud admitted earlier that he was completely unable to recover in himself the "oceanic feeling" which his essay exposes as uncivilized, that dangerous pre-oedipal fantasy of infants who imagine that their own boundaries extend to the borders of the world? It would be out of place here to suggest that the Roman empire may have suffered from the *same* fantasy. More relevant is the point that Freud must abandon the analogy because, like his infantile narcissism, threatening traces of the past *must* be lost for psychic life and civilization alike to function.

Nonetheless, Freud leaves his incomplete fantasy looming in his text, a ruin in the very place where he had wanted to deny the existence of ruins. Like the Freudian text, Jacopo Sannazaro's *Arcadia*, that great and enigmatic work of the early sixteenth century, suffers as do so many

---

[1] Christine Froula, "When Eve Reads Milton," *Critical Inquiry* 9 (1983): 338.
[2] Sigmund Freud, *Civilization and its Discontents*, trans. James Strachey (New York: Norton, 1961), 17.

other humanist writings of the period from the Freudian desire for totality.[3] Yet while the humanists, like Freud, envisioned a version of human history that militates against erasure and fragmentation, they interpreted "civilization" as providing a fortress not against a regressive narcissism, but against the overwhelming loss of the self in something uncontrollable beyond it. This is perhaps nowhere as clear in Sannazaro's corpus as in his "Elegy on the Ruins of Cumae," in which the speaker laments, "Here, where the famous walls of Cumae once rose, the chief glory of the Mediterranean ... now a deep forest hides wild beasts. And where the prophesying Sibyls kept their secrets, now the shepherd confines his well-fed sheep at night."[4] The extinction of the city becomes the moment of barbarism—a barbarism briefly equated with pastoral, as a shepherd wanders oblivious to the historical forces that have conspired to bring about the circumstances of his marginalized existence. A similar moment occurs in the *Arcadia* when the young narrator of that work, Sincero, abruptly departs from his usual stance as unengaged observer of the customs and pastimes of Arcadians and embarks on an account of his own life, punctuated with this surprisingly trenchant value judgment:

> massimamente ricordandomi in questa fervida adolescenzia de' piaceri de la deliciosa patria, tra queste solitudini di Arcadia, ove ... non che i giovani ne le nobili città nodriti, ma appena mi si lascia credere che le selvatiche bestie vi possano con diletto dimorare.[5]
>
> in this fervent youthfulness, I recall the pleasures of my delicious homeland among these solitary places of Arcadia, where ... I can hardly believe that savage beasts can find it delightful to dwell, not to mention young men nurtured in noble cities.

Sincero's "deliciosa patria" is, of course, Naples, which he left because of unrequited love:

---

[3] On the nostalgic desire for totality in the work of early humanists such as Petrarch, see Thomas Greene's important *The Light in Troy* (New Haven: Yale Univ. Press, 1982).

[4] "Hic, ubi Cumeae surgebant inclyta famae / moenia, Tyrrheni gloria prima maris / ... Atque ubi fatidicae latuere arcana Sibyllae, / nunc claudit saturas vespere pastor oves." In *Il Quattrocento*, ed. G. Ponte (Bologna: Zanichelli, 1966), 1316. For a reading which emphasizes the pastoral dimension of the elegy, see William Kennedy, *Jacopo Sannazaro and the Uses of Pastoral* (Hanover: Univ. Press of New England, 1983), 74–79.

[5] In *Opere di Iacopo Sannazaro*, ed. Enrico Carrara (Turin: Torinese, 1952), 111. All further references will be to this edition.

famosa e nobilissima città, e di arme e di lettere felice, forse quanto alcuna altra, che al mondo ne sia; la quale da' popoli di Calcidia venuti, sovra le vetuste ceneri de la Sirena Partenope edificata, prese et ancora ritiene il venerando nome de la sepolta giovene.[6]

famous and noblest of cities, perhaps more fortunate in its arms and letters than any other in the world. A city built by people from Chalcis above the ashes of the Siren Partenope, which took and yet retains the reverent name of that entombed maiden.

This paean to the city, which initiates the *Arcadia*'s seventh chapter and constitutes the midpoint of the text, will culminate in Sincero's return to Naples in the work's final (1504) edition. At least since the late sixteenth century when Giuseppe Massarengo offered to "peregrini" his services as a guide to Sannazaro's "nuovo paese," such nostalgia for the city and Arcadia's failure to console Sincero's melancholy has tended to produce a criticism that sharply distinguishes the world of primitivism from civilization.[7] Thus Ellen Zetzel Lambert derides Sannazaro for his unconvincing gestures of sorrow, Francesco Tateo speaks of the "morte della poesia bucolica" which accompanies the *Arcadia*'s closing moments, and David Quint characterizes Arcadia's fictive autonomy as insufficient for the man who would go on to write an epic of Christ's birth.[8] For Quint, as for Maria Corti, this very different world of epic is partly anticipated in the work's final two chapters, which Sannazaro added following the *Arcadia*'s premature publication in 1502. Chapter 11, the funeral games and song for the shepherd Ergasto's mother, clearly echoes the memorial games for Anchises in book 5 of the *Aeneid*; and Sincero's underwater return to Naples in chapter 12, during which he learns of the death of his love and, as many critics believe, the fall of the Aragonese house in Naples, recalls Aristaeus's descent in the fourth *Georgic* to learn the cause of his bees' sickness.[9]

---

[6] Ibid., 107-8.

[7] Massarengo's copious annotations can be found in *Le Opere volgari di M. Jacopo Sannazaro . . . da Persona Anonima novellamente postillata* (Venice, 1752); quote, p. 207.

[8] Ellen Zetzel Lambert, *Placing Sorrow: A Study of the Pastoral Elegy Convention from Theocritus to Milton* (Chapel Hill: Univ. of North Carolina Press, 1976), 100; Francesco Tateo, *Tradizione e realtà nell'Umanesimo italiano* (Bari: Laterza, 1967), 38; David Quint, *Origin and Originality in Renaissance Literature: Versions of the Source* (New Haven: Yale Univ. Press, 1983), esp. 43-48. Against these readings, see Marco Santagata's hesitant claim that "even after the turn taken in chapter 7 . . . the text does not always respect the rule regarding the distinction between places." *La lirica aragonese* (Padua: Antenore, 1979), 372.

[9] See Maria Corti's comment in *Metodi e fantasmi* (Milan, 1969) that in the final two chapters Sannazaro "is already packing his bags, preparing more or less

Yet this opposition of pastoral and epic, of a pristine but barbarous simplicity and the complex world of historical change, may depend too much on Sincero's own, ultimately limited, interpretation of Arcadia, an interpretation that can be challenged by focusing on the figure with whom Sincero begins his unexpected midnight confession to an Arcadian shepherd: the siren Partenope. Particularly in the two chapters added to the 1504 text, the siren becomes, if not an omnipresent figure, at least a far from peripheral one. First invoked by Sincero as the tragic maiden whose tomb gave rise to a city, she next appears as a bitterly weeping figure whose lament almost causes Sincero to drown in a nightmarish vision strikingly similar to Dante's dream of Beatrice's death in *La Vita Nuova*.[10] She is finally reincarnated in two Neapolitan singers whom Sincero encounters when he returns to Naples and whose song beguiles him into believing that the sirens had indeed lived there, "and with the sweetness of their song detained those who were going that way." Sincero too is detained, charmed into spending "questo breve spazio, questa picciola dimoranza" with his former friends who no longer recognize him, transfigured as he is by his own "soverchio dolore."[11]

Sannazaro's engagement with the myth of Partenope and the mythic lore of his city of Naples should come as no surprise. Like other humanists of a circle that included Giovanni Pontano, Sannazaro was intent upon asserting Naples' cultural importance in the late fifteenth century, and thereby upon celebrating the Greek and Roman origins of their city and of nearby Cuma.[12] But Sannazaro's interest in ruins —revealed not only in his Cumaean elegy and Piscatorial eclogues but

---

consciously to head toward the shoreline of his future works" (303). William Kennedy also maintains that chapters 11 and 12 create a radical break with the preceding material, amounting to a "deconstruction" of the work's earlier values; see 135–48.

[10] "Poi pareva che stando ad ascoltare una Sirena, le quale sovra uno scoglio amaramente piangeva, una onda grande del mare mi attuffasse et mi porgesse tanta fatica nel respirare, che di poco mancava che io non morisse" ("Then it seemed that while I stood to listen to a siren bitterly weeping upon a rock, an immense wave from the sea struck me, and made it so difficult to breathe that little was lacking to cause my death"); *Opere di Iacopo Sannazaro*, 194.

[11] *Opere di Iacopo Sannazaro*, 202–3. One of the few critics to note the possible importance of Partenope is Vittorio Gajetti, who in a Jungian reading of the *Arcadia* discusses the maternal aspects of the siren; see his *Edipo in Arcadia. Miti e simboli nell' Arcadia del Sannazaro* (Naples: Guida, 1977), 98–99.

[12] In his lengthy history of the Neapolitan war, Giovanni Pontano alludes to Partenope's sepulcher and the siren's status as the city's "matron" (*De bello neapolitano*, in *Opera omnia* [Basel, 1566], 2:1949). Pontano also wrote a elegies entitled *Parthenopei*. His famous epithalamion *Lepidina*, moreover, celebrates the marriage of the nymph Parthenope to Sebeto, the god of the small river that runs to Naples from the bay. See lines 41–82, for an account of the siren's compelling beauty and music.

in the *Arcadia*'s twelfth chapter when Sincero encounters the "torri et le case et i theatri e i templi" (the towers and homes and theatres and temples) of Italy's ancient cities—produces neither the exhilaration of a Petrarch nor the sad reflections of a medieval moralist obsessed with the cycle of decay.[13] Rather, Sannazaro's *resurrection* of Partenope reveals an engagement in reversing and thereby exposing the process through which a city—and ultimately civilization itself—is formed. Raising Partenope from the dead takes Sincero beyond Naples' origins, to the threatening powers of the singer which the city suppresses and appropriates. This pattern of appropriation, moreover, is revealed not in the Naples for which Sincero yearns, but in its mirror image, Arcadia. As will become apparent in the following pages, the "nuovo paese" which Massarengo's reader, like Sincero, encounters, is not at all new; rather, it becomes the locus in which the civilizing process is staged, with all its concomitant discontents. These discontents in turn can only be understood by first discussing the legend of the sirens themselves.

These legendary half-birds, half-women with whom Sincero opens his autobiography make their first literary appearance in the *Odyssey*, when they attempt to lure the epic hero to their shores: "Come here, come to us, Odysseus Odysseus, the pride of the Achaeans.... For we know all things; we know what was suffered on the fields of Troy by the will of the gods, both by the Trojans and the Danaans, and all else that happens upon the nourishing earth."[14] In characterizing themselves as omniscient, the sirens offer a haunting and, as the bleached white bones on their island attest, an alluring vision of total knowledge. But this totality paradoxically has limits. As Jean-Pierre Vernant writes, the sirens sing not about Odysseus as he is, but as he was, and more importantly, as he "will be when he is dead, as death will make him, forever magnified in the memory of the living, transmuted from the suffering and misfortune of his actual, miserable existence to the glorious brilliance of his fame and of the story of his exploits."[15] The si-

---

[13] In all five of the *Piscatorial Eclogues*, Sannazaro refers to the siren's relationship to Naples, most explicitly in Eclogue 4: "Tum canit antiquas sedes opulentaque regna / Auricomae Sirenis et altum in monte sepulcrum, / Sacraque Chalcidicosque deos magnisque per aequor / Auspiciis vectas haec ipsa ad litora classes" ("Then he sings the ancient seats and opulent kingdoms of the golden-haired Siren, and the lofty tomb on the mountain, and the rituals and the Chalcidean gods, and the fleet drawn on through the deep sea under great auspices to these very shores"; trans. Ralph Nash, in *Arcadia and Piscatorial Eclogues* [Detroit: Wayne State Univ. Press, 1966], 181).

[14] *Odyssey* 12.47–50, trans. Robert Fitzgerald (Garden City, NY: Anchor Books, 1963).

[15] "Feminine Figures of Death in Greece," *Diacritics* 16:2 (1986): 61.

rens' song functions as the vehicle of this transmutation, of a purging, like an obituary, of unwholesome or unpleasant details, an alluring fragment masquerading as totality. It is readily apparent why the world of the *Odyssey* in all its squalor and detailed misery cannot coexist with the sirens' song, why Odysseus must sail past the enchanting women: Greek, more specifically, Homeric civilization depends on silencing their formidable demand that one must die before he can survive in "imperishable glory with the status of a dead hero."[16]

This temptation to foreclose epic existence and the offer of complete absorption in a dangerously alluring fragment are both present in the most memorable account of the siren in Italian literature preceding Sannazaro. This is the passage in the *Purgatorio*, when Dante, asleep on the terrace of sloth, encounters an ugly, crippled hag whom his loving gaze transforms into a beautiful singer:

> Io volsi Ulisse del suo cammin vago
> al canto mio; e qual meco s'ausa,
> rado sen parte; si tutto l'appago![17]

> I turned Ulysses from his wandering path to my song; and he
> who rests with me seldom departs: so completely do I satisfy!

Dante's initial absorption transforms the siren as readily as she turned Odysseus from his wandering path; and she offers, like the sirens of Homer and the song of Casella earlier on the banks of purgatory, total fulfillment. Into this realm of Saturn, both an angel and a bewildered Virgil must step to avert what has largely been the threat posed by Dante's generative powers: for Dante's transformation of hag into beauty through his *fantasia* is a creative act, albeit negative in light of God's *positive* mimetic capabilities. The sign of Saturn becomes the sign of a dark and dangerous parody from which Dante must be rescued by heavenly light.

Dante's negative portrait of the siren is typical of the period, as Renaissance commentators bear out, thereby furnishing a convenient backdrop for Sannazaro's own, more sympathetic portrayal of Naples' *genius loci*.[18] More importantly, it establishes a connection between the

---

[16] Ibid., 61.

[17] *Purgatorio* 19.22–24, ed. C. H. Grandgent (Cambridge: Harvard Univ. Press, 1972), 476. See Barbara Bono's discussion of this passage and the Siren's "threat" in *Literary Transvaluation: From Vergilian Epic to Shakespearean Tragicomedy* (Berkeley: Univ. of California Press, 1984), esp. 55–56. Sara Sturm-Maddox also considers the *Purgatorio* episode in her fascinating exploration of "Petrarch's Siren: 'Dolce Parlar' and 'Dolce Canto' in the *Rime Sparse*," *Italian Quarterly* 103 (1986): 5–19.

[18] One example of "negative" mythography includes Vincenzo Cartari's *The*

invocation of the siren and the condition of *acedia* or sloth, that largely monastic vice characterized by such symptoms as torpor, pusillanimity, despair, and the *evagatio mentis* or wandering mind, the "cammin vago" of Ulysses.[19] It is precisely this wandering mind, forgetful of past and future, which transforms the crippled and stammering old woman into the bewitching siren. Dante's release from the compelling song as well as from the "pensier" which burden him shortly upon awakening must be procured by heavenly intervention; his burden which threatens to confine him in an interminable present is dissolved when he is miraculously granted upward flight through a passage between two hard walls of rock. To return to the *Arcadia*, Sincero is denied this Dantesque, upward movement, as well as any comparable relief from the burden of melancholy thoughts. Yet like Dante's lady, "santa e presta," and the guiding angel who speaks "in modo soave e benigno, / qual non si sente in questa mortal marca"[20] ("in sweet and benign tones that are not heard in mortal bounds"), the Arcadian community seems prepared to rescue Sincero from Partenope's melancholy "threat." But what is striking about this community is that rather than demystify and expose the melancholy siren, they transform her. Like the dreaming Dante, the Arcadian shepherds and, by extension, the Neapolitan community, change "una femmina balba" into a beautiful woman, although one now entombed, enclosed, and bracketed off from the civilization which the community purports to create.

For this transformation, Sannazaro looked neither to Homer nor Dante but to a Homeric epilogue on which Sannazaro and other Neapolitans such as Pontano insisted, in which the Sirens *themselves* eventually attain the role of an Odyssean hero who is immortalized when dead—and only when dead. As of the fifth century BC, a third siren plummeting from the bare reef into the ocean below begins to appear on funerary artifacts, and various commentators will eventually identify her as Partenope, who, despairing over the failure of her song to woo

---

Fountaine of Ancient Fiction, trans. R. Linche (1599) (New York: Da Capo Press, 1973), f. Oiv–r: the sirens "sing so melodiously, and with such a sence-besotting sweetnesse, that the suspectlessly inchaunted sea-travellers are infinitely beguiled and lulled asleepe with the harmony and pleasing blandishment thereof." See also the commentaries of Sansovino (for whom the siren represents "false and imperfect happiness") and Landino (who discusses the sirens' cannibalism and the worldliness of those attracted to them) on Dante; *Dante con l'espositione di Christoforo Landino et di Alessandro Vellutello* (Venice, 1564), 227–28.

[19] For a stunning characterization of the medieval "disease" of *acedia*, see Giorgio Agamben, *Stanze. La parola e il fantasma nella cultura occidentale* (Turin: Einaudi, 1977), 5–35.

[20] *Purgatorio* 19.44–45; Grandgent, 477.

Odysseus, threw herself into the sea and drowned.[21] Her body was washed up along the western coast of Italy and, as Sincero notes, buried in what is now Naples. And it is with this burial that the story of Neapolitan civilization and the siren's own fame as a tragic and beautiful suicide begins. For as Strabo, Pliny, Statius, and Lutatius Catullus recount, her tomb became the site for annual funeral games which featured gymnastic and poetic competitions among the Chalcideans and Cumaeans alike, who promised—out of piety or, as one commentator ominously suggests, because the siren threatens vengeance from beyond the grave—to honor the anniversary of her death for all time.[22] Thus did a story of powerful song that leads to death initiate a second story about the failure of such power and the singer's death, a singer whose burial site will become the center of cultural and religious life for a burgeoning Greek colony that would one day take the name of Neapolis. In her aftermath, the siren continues to be associated with elegy, although not one which she sings, but which others sing *for* her, as her powers are both silenced and appropriated in the name of a new myth: civilization.[23]

It is just this process which constitutes the focus of the first half of

---

[21] See Emily Vermeule, *Aspects of Death in Early Greek Art and Poetry* (Berkeley: Univ. of California Press, 1979); and J. R. Pollard, "Muses and Sirens," *Classical Review* 66 (1952): 60–64.

[22] Strabo in *Geography* 1.2.12–13, provides the earliest and most complete account of the siren's death and transformation among the Chalcideans; 5.4.7 elaborates on the games celebrated around Partenope's tomb. See Giovanni Carratelli, "Napoli antica," and Mario Napoli, "Realtà storica di Partenope," both in *La parola del passato* 7 (1952): 243–68; 269–85, for an excellent summary of the mythical and historical origins of Naples. Various mythographers who refer to this postscript to the Homeric account include Pontano; Natalis Comes, *Mythologiae sive explicationis fabularum libri decem* (Padova, 1616), 397; Alexander Ross, *Mystagogus Poeticus or the Muses Interpreter* (London, 1648); and Antoine Banier, *Mythologies and Fables of the Ancients explain'd from History* (London, 1740).

[23] Even in the accounts of Ovid (*Metamophoses* 6) and Claudian (*De raptu Proserpinae* 3) of the sirens' life *before* Odysseus, there is the suggestion that loss itself generated their compelling song in the first place. According to Claudian, the three singers were once young virgins who lived on the coast of Naples as friends of Proserpina. Only after Proserpina's rape by Pluto did they use their gift of song for destruction; "And now they did not hesitate to turn their lyres toward evil" (3.254–58; trans. Maurice Platnauer [London: Heinemann, 1922], p. 365). In this sentimentalized version of the sirens' past—a far cry from Plato's (and Dante's) insistence that the women were "dark beings of the Underworld"—the singers become vengeful agents of their sex, much like Demeter, another deity worshipped in the area of archaic Naples, who forces sterility upon the world for the six months during which her daughter must live with her infernal abductor. — On the "project" of Renaissance elegy, see most recently G. W. Pigmann III, *Grief and English Renaissance Elegy* (Cambridge: Cambridge Univ. Press, 1985) and Peter Sacks, *The English Elegy: Studies in the Genre from Spenser to Yeats* (Baltimore: Johns Hopkins Univ. Press, 1985).

the *Arcadia*. Beginning with the encounter in chapter 1 between the disconsolate shepherd Ergasto and a sympathetic Selvaggio who asks him the nature of his apparent despair, the Arcadian community consistently transforms private, melancholic lament into a public and benign performance. After relating his woes in supposed confidence to Selvaggio, Ergasto glances up in surprise (as does the reader) to discover an entire community of appreciative listeners gathered about him. Similarly, Eclogue 2, a seemingly private contest between Montano and Uranio, becomes a performance as shepherds, who speak afterward of the "tanto diletto" they have found through listening, silently coalesce about the two singers. Initially, Sannazaro portrays Arcadia as a realm where private song is turned suddenly into a performance which disowns and ignores the *content* of song—a disjunction that grows only more apparent as one approaches Sincero's autobiographical account in chapter 7. On the one hand, the *Arcadia*'s prose chapters focus not only on the pleasurable reactions of the shepherds, but on the delights of the Arcadian landscape, the ornate doors which open onto the temple of Pales, the shepherdesses who gather shyly before the contemplative shepherds. Yet on the other hand, the eclogues become increasingly elegiac in tone as they express a rupture between a wretched present and a radiant past. For the sorrowing Ergasto, "Primavera e soi dì per me non riedono" ("Spring and her days no longer return for me"); upon one shepherd's death, another asks, "Chi vedrà mai nel mondo / pastor tanto giocondo / che cantando fra noi sì dolci rime / sparga il bosco di fronde" ("When will we again see in this world such a happy shepherd, who sang among us such sweet rhymes while he spread foliage through the forest"); and in the bleakest eclogue of all, the sixth, Opico sings of a lost golden age when the fields had no boundaries and the earth was full of herbs which brought one health.[24] Until Sincero's surprising acknowledgment of his "fiera malinconia" however, these elegiac sentiments are rigorously contained within the metrics of the eclogues, primarily because the listening Arcadian community responds to them not with lament or consolation but with a "grandissima ammirazione" that is focused on the songs' harmony, novelty, and style rather than their content.

Such formal closure or *en*closure of the eclogues brackets off the elegiac sentiments of the shepherds from a setting which offers no room for the acknowledgment of any disparity between present and past. This resolute insistence on the *present* is more generally felt in the *Arcadia*'s prose chapters as an insistence on boundaries, temporal as

---

[24] *Opere di Iacopo Sannazaro*, 54–55; 94–95; 103–4.

well as spatial, as in the third chapter where the "priest" Enareto, virtually translating a passage from Ovid's *Fasti*, asks the goddess Pales that she pardon the shepherds from any transgressions they have unwittingly committed:

> se non sapendo avesse seduto, o pasciuto sotto alcuno albero, che sacrato fusse; o se entrando per li inviolabili boschi avesse con la sua venuta turbate le sante Driade e i semicapri Dii dai solacci loro.[25]

> if one of them has unknowingly sat or fed his sheep beneath a sacred tree; or if entering the forbidden woods one has disturbed with his coming the Driads and the satyrs in their rest.

The fear of violating sacred centers is most pronounced in the closing words of the prayer, where Sannazaro has made a telling addition to the Ovidian text:

> Tu, Dea pietosissima ... nè consentire, che gli occhi nostri non degni veggiano mai per le selve le vendicatrici Nimfe, nè la ignuda Diana bagniarse per le fredde acque, nè di mezzo giorno il silvestre Fauno, quando da caccia tornando stanco.[26]

> You compassionate goddess ... do not permit our unworthy eyes ever to see in these woods the vindictive Nymphs, or nude Diana bathing in her cold waters, or the woodland Faunus at noon when he returns tired from his hunt.

Ovid does not include the adjective "vendicatrici";[27] in the *Arcadia*, the supplemental description ominously suggests that the nymphs must be avoided, not because they are too dignified to be gazed at by base shepherds, but because they are dangerous. More importantly, the prayer to Pales occurs between two considerably mediated confrontations with potentially "vindictive" women. In the first, Sincero and the other shepherds are examining the paintings above the entrance to the temple of Pales, on which are depicted "certain naked Nymphs," who are fleeing from satyrs; in the second, the group stands gazing at a number of shepherdesses who are dancing about wearing garlands "sì come Naiade o Napee state fusseno, e con la diversità de' portamenti oltra misura le naturali bellezze augmentavano"[28] ("as if they had been Naiads or Napaeans, and whose diverse dresses enhanced their

---

[25] Ibid., 71.
[26] Ibid., 72.
[27] The relevant passage in the *Fasti* is 4.747–67.
[28] *Opere di Iacopo Sannazaro*, 79.

natural beauty"). As Giuseppe Velli has rightly suggested, "the very power of contemplation neutralizes the implications of threat. It is not accidental that feminine beauty is consigned to the unreal staticness of the *descriptio*, as in a gothic portrait."

Velli goes on to point out that time—historical time—is the enemy in this stylized world of boundaries and mediated threats. Only the inexhaustible cycle of "alba, meriggio, e sera" dominates the text:[29] in short, an infinite and changeless present within which the elegiac that yearns for a lost, happy presence must either be silenced or tactfully "enclosed." Perhaps more correctly, the elegiac as an expression of radical dissatisfaction with the present must be transformed into an expression of aesthetic fullness; the community achieves its identity only by interpreting personal loss as communal gain. As long as Sincero's own identity remains submerged within this communal persona, the inexhaustible cycle remains seemingly inexhaustible, as presence and present coincide. Similarly, as long as the dangerous female is confined and enclosed through the shepherds' powers of contemplation, her powers as seductress are severely curtailed. But once Sincero is asked by a sympathetic Carino to tell the story of his *origins*, and once Sincero delivers that tale free from the aesthetic restrictions of the poem and unheard by the other members of the community, this ritual of benevolent suppression comes to an end. For with Sincero's account, the threat which the eclogues pose to Arcadian plenitude can no longer be contained by the admiring and aestheticizing stance of the audience. Moreover, Sincero's confession, which intrudes into what had been static and descriptive prose about the happy *present*, acts as the catalyst for the remainder of the text. Immediately following Sincero's account, Carino tells (in prose) of his thwarted love and near-suicide, and another shepherd recounts the story of his lingering love malady and seeks a "cure" which consists largely of reciting the infuriated *carmina* of Medea and a desperate Dido. Sincero's disruptive word thus acts as a catalyst for the rest of the *Arcadia*, in which the contemplative powers of the present fail to contain and properly "aestheticize" the melancholic burden which began in the past.

The original 1502 *Arcadia* ends not with Sincero's return to Naples but with the disclosure of Arcadia's origins in an account of a communal history which corresponds surprisingly to that of Naples, Sincero's beloved city. Arcadia's history begins in loss—a loss for which no song can compensate. In chapter 10, the priest Enareto recounts the grief of the solitary god Pan as he lamented a transformed Syrinx:

---

[29] *Tra Lettura e Creazione: Sannazaro, Alfieri, Foscolo* (Padua: Antenore, 1983), 48, 49.

poi che per la subita transformazione di lei si vide schernito, sospirando egli sovente per rimembranza de le antiche fiamme.... E così solo in questa sola grotta, assiso presso a le pascenti capre, cominciò a congiungere con nova cera sette canne ... con la qual poi gran tempo pianse in questi monti le sue sventure.³⁰

Mocked with her sudden metamorphosis, he sighed often, recollecting the ancient flames.... And thus alone, in this lonely grotto, seated near the grazing goats, he began to join together with new wax seven reeds ... with which for a long time he cried in lament into these hills.

"Solo, in questa sola grotta": Sannazaro emphasizes, as Ovid does not in his account in the *Metamorphoses*, Pan's solitude. No Arcadian community intervenes to deflect Pan's elegiac excess onto the *arte nova* that is made. Such deflection can take place only when the instrument with which Pan lamented passes mysteriously into the hands of the first "official" pastoral poet, Theocritus: "Indi [la siringa] venne, e non so come, ne le mani d'un pastore siracusano"³¹ ("Whence the pipes came, nor do I know how, into the hands of a shepherd from Syracuse"). Between Pan's symbolic suicide, and Theocritus's pleasing songs to pines, oaks, nymphs, and fauns, there is an unexplained and unexplored discontinuity which Theocritus will not perpetuate because he will give the "siringa" to the "mantuana Titiro" (Virgil) with the words, "Tu sarai ora di questa il secondo signore con la quale potrai a tua posta riconciliare li discordevoli tauri, tenendo graziosissimo suono a li selvatichi Idii"³² ("Now you will be the second master [of this pipe] with which you will be able to reconcile the combative bulls and bring the most graceful of sounds to the savage gods"). Pan's lonely, suicidal lament becomes a song that civilizes in the hands of his Arcadian descendants. Moreover, once his reedpipes come into human hands, Pan is permanently relegated to the lonely grotto which now serves as both his altar and his tomb, having become, like Partenope, a god more docile in death than in life.

The origins of the Arcadian community, like the origins of Naples, thus appear to consist in the necessary silencing of its savage god, in avoiding potentially disruptive centers: the noonday heat, the "vendicatrici nimfe," the "demone meridionale" which was, by some, equated with the sirens.³³ That these aestheticizing strategies are shared by

---

³⁰ *Opere di Iacopo Sannazaro*, 153.
³¹ Ibid.
³² Ibid., 154.
³³ See Nicolas Perella's fascinating *Midday in Italian Literature* (Princeton: Prince-

Arcadia and Naples alike becomes particularly clear in the first of *Arcadia*'s two "epic" chapters added to the 1504 text, where the Arcadian community gathers around the tomb of Ergasto's mother to compete in various games and to hear Ergasto's elegy.[34] It is here where the annual rituals for Partenope, long ago instituted by the Chalcideans, are again invoked as Ergasto sings not only of his mother but of the siren. But in solemnly pronouncing Partenope dead—speaking to the Neapolitan river the Sebeto, Ergasto sings, "Tu la bella Sirena in tutto il mondo / facesti nota con sì altera tomba: / quel fu 'l primo dolor, quest'è 'l secondo"[35] ("You have made renowned throughout the world / The beautiful Siren, with so proud a tomb: / That was your first sorrrow, this is your second")—the elegiac singer implicitly assumes that a living Partenope, a singing siren, and the community that honors her cannot possibly coexist. She must first die so that she can be cleansed and transformed, through elegy, into Naples' "second sorrow": the mother Ergasto and the community weep for, whom Statius addressed in his *Silvae* ("As for you, lady, at thy birth my own Partenope took you to her embrace") and of whom Virgil wrote at the close of the fourth *Georgic*, "In those times, I, Virgil, was nourished by sweet Partenope."[36] The silencing of Partenope's elegy, with its claims to a totality that is false, gives rise to "civilization" and, as Virgil, Statius, and finally Sannazaro attest, to poetry and elegies that are equally revisionist. The elusive totality that is civilization, whether it is envisioned as Virgil's and Freud's Rome or Sincero's Naples, is founded on an even more elusive myth of totality represented by the sirens' song, which civilization must both silence and appropriate.[37] Such an appropriation is enacted as Partenope becomes, like the once-threatening Furies of

---

ton Univ. Press, 1979) for a discussion of the "noonday demon" and its numerous analogues in Italian literature.

[34] For an understanding of the parallels and virtual interchangeability between Arcadia and Naples, see Eduardo Saccone's chapter on Sannazaro in *Il soggetto del Furioso* (Naples: Ligouri, 1974). Such interchangeability, in turn, suggests that Sannazaro may not be contrasting a pastoral aesthetic which remains on the level of aesthetics, and the world of the city which takes for its model the rigorous and realistic epic—a world which is gradually disclosed in the last two chapters as Sincero returns to Naples—but highlighting their continuity.

[35] *Opere di Iacopo Sannazaro*, 189.

[36] Statius, *Silvae* 1.2, trans. J. H. Mozley (Cambridge: Harvard Univ. Press, 1955); Virgil, *Georgics* 4.563–64, in *Works*, ed. H. R. Fairclough (Cambridge: Harvard Univ. Press, 1924), 1:237.

[37] For a comparable account of such silencing and appropriation in Renaissance poetics, see Nancy Vickers's stimulating comments on Petrarch's "fragmentation and reification" of Laura's Medusa-like powers in " 'The blazon of sweet beauty's best': Shakespeare's *Lucrece*," *Shakespeare and the Question of Theory*, ed. Patricia Parker and Geoffrey Hartman (New York: Methuen, 1985), esp. 110–12.

Aeschylus's play, a "eumenide," a blessed one. Curse becomes blessing, a threat to civilization becomes the cornerstone of civilization, as the siren's binding voice is silenced and other voices—the poets who participate in the annual competitions held around Partenope's tomb—prevail.

To this wishful revisionism, through which civilization produces its own cultural artifacts and thereby legitimates itself, epic—and more specifically, the *Aeneid*'s fifth book—furnishes an especially striking subtext. For it is finally Virgilian epic to which Sannazaro turns, not as contrast to the Arcadian community but as its analogue. Anchises' funeral games are situated uneasily between Dido's siren-like plummet from her funeral effigy for Aeneas, and the haunting and beautiful allusion to the navigator Palinurus's savage death near the cliffs of the sirens, "perilous of old and white with the bones of many men," where Aeneas's ship, like so many ships of old, begins to go astray.[38] An even more immediate threat to the games and the Roman enterprise arises from the central events of book 5. The competitions are brutally interrupted when the Trojan women set fire to Aeneas's ships, provoked to such wrath by the "raging" Juno but also by their own yearnings, as the terse phrase suggests, for a city: "urbem orant." They are *given* a city on the site of Anchises' tomb, although it is only a poor substitute for the Rome Aeneas is destined to found. On the surface, the contrast between this pale simulacrum of Rome, full of "old men and sea-worn matrons," and the *real* Rome might argue for a similar contrast between the Arcadian "city" where the community mourns Ergasto's mother and Sincero's Naples.[39] But thanks to Dido's dying curses (which Sannazaro has just rehearsed by including them in the "magic rite" through which a shepherd may be cured of love), the city Aeneas eventually founds is *also* a necessary compromise, a substitute for the real thing envisioned in dreams. Aeneas's navigator Palinurus, inexplicably dead in the region of Partenope, is himself a token of this compromise, "amissum...gurgite," lost in the abyss. Like his navigator and the men who sailed precariously close to the sirens to hear their elegy before their time, Aeneas too, because of Dido, will die before his time and lie unburied on the sand. Book 5 stands as solemn testimony to the fact that interpreting Rome as a pinnacle of civilization depends on the suppression and appropriation of the female powers of a Dido or Partenope—a suppression and appropriation which can only be partial at best.

Like Aeneas, Sannazaro was also forced to compromise; writing

---

[38] *Aeneid* 5.865; in *Works*, 1:503.
[39] *Aeneid* 5.715 ("senes ac fessas aequore matres"); *Works*, 1:493.

these final chapters in exile in France, following the fall of the Aragonese kingdom in Naples, he may have been led to re-examine his earlier hopes and dreams for his city, now shattered by political realities. What the *Aeneid* so profoundly articulates—as do the closing chapters of the *Arcadia* where the siren, symbol of an elusive totality which civilization embraces as its own, is subtly resurrected in the figure of two Neapolitan elegists—is the Freudian dream (or perhaps nightmare) of a plenitude that is eventually revealed as ruin: the *reverse* of the elegiac impulse, the reality of the sirens' reef: scattered bones on a flowering meadow. But to be aware of the ruins at all, one must, like Freud, indulge in the myth of totality in the first place, as did humanists from Petrarch to DuBellay and Spenser, with their fantasies of Rome—or in Sannazaro's case, of Arcadia and Naples. To *perpetuate* that myth, and thus to retain the illusion, requires a sympathetic community which will supplant loss with aesthetic fullness, restoring past plenitude to the present. But Sannazaro finally rejects such a strategy, choosing to locate the *Arcadia*'s last song on the margins between Naples and Arcadia. Here he instructs his *sampogna* to pray that anyone of kindly nature who wanders to hear its song "be preserved in his felicity and kept far from our miseries." Following Petrarch's footsteps to a solitary locale which is neither "savage" nor "civilized," Sannazaro's final elegy to a Naples which is no more ("Le nostre Muse sono estinte: secchi sono i nostri lauri: ruinato è il nostro Parnaso"[40] ["Our muses are dead, our laurels are dry, our Parnassus is ruined"]) acknowledges that the plenitude into which Sincero had hoped to escape is no more. But that it ever *was*, given the text's own elegant deconstruction of the elegiac process, is unconvincing, as it was meant to be. And it is in the face of such failed conviction, in the realization that all versions of plenitude are inevitably false ones, that the symptom known as Renaissance melancholy is born: in the *failure* of elegy's aestheticizing powers, as the siren herself well knows, and not, as Erwin Panofsky and other students of Arcadia have claimed, in their triumph.[41]

University of Wisconsin—Madison

---

[40] *Opere di Iacopo Sannazaro*, 218.
[41] See Panofsky's influential claim that Sannazaro restored the elegiac by reviving "after fifteen hundred years, that enchanting vision, Arcady," in *Renaissance and Renascences in Western Art* (New York: Harper and Row, 1969), 111.

LINDA L. CARROLL*

Giorgione's Tempest:
Astrology Is in the Eyes of the Beholder

THE IMPORTANCE OF ASTROLOGY IN RENAISSANCE ITALY, PARTICUlarly after the middle of the fifteenth century, is well known. But few scholars have attempted to recapture the role it played in cultural and political interpretations of contemporary life. An awareness of Renaissance astrological practice and its application to events in sixteenth-century Venice aids in reconstructing the significance of Giorgione's enigmatic *Tempest*.

In March of 1509, Venice faced the massed forces of the League of Cambrai and pondered an uncertain future.[1] The count of Sogliano, seeing an opportunity to cultivate the Republic's favor, cast a horoscope (a strategy commonly employed in the late Middle Ages and early Renaissance) which he interpreted as assuring Venice a successful outcome.[2] Marin Sanudo, who himself had included birth horoscopes

---

* I am grateful to the Newberry Library for a fellowship to complete part of the research, and to Loren Williams for generously sharing his knowledge of astrology in years past. Discussions with Edward Muir, Paul Kaplan, and Benjamin Kohl significantly improved the paper.

[1] See, for example, Frederic Lane, *Venice* (Baltimore: Johns Hopkins Univ. Press, 1973), 242–45 and Felix Gilbert, *The Pope, His Banker and Venice* (Cambridge: Harvard Univ. Press, 1980), 1–9. Unless otherwise noted, events of June and July are taken from Marino Sanuto, *I Diarii*, ed. Renato Fulin et al., 58 vols. (Venice: Visentini, 1879–1902), 8: cols. 335, 343–44, 351, 353, 368, 403, 419–20, 424, 435, 441, 446, 457, 480–81, 483–85, 487–88, 497–99, 507–8, 516, 519–21; for Sogliano see vols. 2–8 s.v. Ramberto (or Lamberto) Novello Malatesta, esp. 8: cols. 125, 139.

[2] Sanuto, 8: cols. 56–62; the practice was widespread: see Anon., "Sonetto fatto subito come i nostri prese Padoa," in *Antichi testi di letteratura pavana*, ed. Emilio Lovarini (Bologna, 1894), 55; Jean Lemaire de Belges, "Le Traicté: Nommé la legende des Venetiens, ou leur chronique abbregée," printed in October 1509 and now in *Oeuvres*, ed. J. Stecher (Louvain, 1885), 3: 363–64; Willy Hartner, "The Mercury Horoscope of Marcantonio Michiel of Venice," *Vistas in Astronomy* 1 (1955): 84–138; Innocenzo Cervelli, *Machiavelli e la crisi dello stato veneziano* (Naples: Guida, 1974), 149–63; Paola Zambelli, ed., *"Astrologi hallucinati": Stars and the End of the World in Luther's Time* (Berlin: Walter de Gruyter, 1986).

of Venice in several works, duly reported the count's predictions.

A key element in the horoscope was Jupiter's transit of its rulership sign Sagittarius. This position of the benefic (benevolent planet) linked to dominance, expansion, and the active life would complete one of the most favorable astrological formations, the grand fire trine, with the city's natal sun in Aries and ascendant in Leo.[3] However, Sogliano warned, the 1509 transit was blocked by a square (90°) angle to Saturn, the malefic (malign planet), whose association with loneliness, melancholy, and slowness persisted despite recent efforts by Neoplatonists to rehabilitate it.[4] Negative effects were exacerbated by the planet's position in Virgo (correlated with injurious communication, illness, and long-held grudges) and retrograde (reverse) motion, "il che proprio significha molte promesse fictitie, piene de veneno et de hypochresia et occulto odio et pessima dispositione" ("which means many false promises, full of poison and hypocrisy and hidden hatred and very bad attitudes"), particularly in the case of the pope. Moreover, the movement of Jupiter would also remain retrograde until late July, prompting the advice: "Fino che Jove non se diriga, le cose de quella illustrissima Signoria staranno suspense alquanto; et laudaria, che fino adicta a directione, possendo far di mancho, non lassino far facto d'arme" ("Until Jupiter resumes direct movement, the affairs of the most illustrious Signoria will remain suspended; and I would recommend that, until such a forward movement, if you are able to do without it, you not permit military activity"). Sogliano concluded with a prediction that,

---

[3] For the traditional founding time of noon March 25, 421, which first appeared in histories of the city in the fourteenth century (and seems to have been chosen for its astrological propitiousness), see Giovanni Monticolo, "Per l'edizione delle *Vite dei dogi* di Marin Sanudo," *Archivio Muratoriano* 1 (1906): 153–70; Vittorio Lazzarino, "Il preteso documento della fondazione di Venezia e la cronaca del maestro Iacopo Dondi," in *Atti dell'Istituto Veneto di Scienze, Lettere ed Arti*, Classe filosofia e scienze morali 99 (1939–40): 1263–81; Edward Muir, *Civic Ritual in Renaissance Venice* (Princeton: Princeton Univ. Press, 1981), 70–71. For Leo as ascendant of Venice: Niccolò Trevisan, *Cronaca di Venezia*, Biblioteca Nazionale Marciana, Venezia (hereafter BMV), It. VII, 519 = 8438, fol. 34v; Zorzi Dolfin, *Cronaca di Venezia*, BMV, It. VII, 794 = 8503, fol. 19v; Marin Sanudo, *De fundatione urbis Venetiarum*, BMV, Lat. XIV, 266 = 4502, fol. 301; id., *Vite dei dogi*, BMV, It. VII, 800 = 7151, fols. 3v–4r. For the sign in general, Johannes [Mueller] Regiomontanus, *Ephemerides* (Venice: Ratdolt, 1481), no pagination (hereafter abbreviated as n. pag.) but fols. 5v, 6r; Ali Ibn Abi al-Rijal, Al-Shaibani, *Preclarissimus in judiciis astrorum* (Venice: Jo. Baptista Sessa, 1503), fol. 3r; Nicola Ivanoff, "Il problema iconologico degli affreschi," in Carlo Guido Mor et al., *Il Palazzo della Ragione di Padova* (Venice: Neri Pozza, 1964), 82.

[4] Raymond Klibansky, Erwin Panofsky, and Fritz Saxl, *Saturn and Melancholy: Studies in the History of Natural Philosophy, Religion and Art* (New York: Basic Books, 1964), 158–59; printed versions of older treatises perpetuated the negative view: see Ali Ibn Abi al-Rijal, fols. 3v, 61v.

after the retrograde, Venice would triumph as a result of the greater dangers facing her enemies.

Most cinquecento astrologers would have read the formation even more negatively, as causing the (perhaps temporary) loss of rulership through entrapment, anxiety, and an inability to translate thought into action.[5] Sogliano bolstered the more positive interpretation by recalling his earlier successful prediction of Venice's resistance to a military challenge during an imposing conjunction in Cancer, also inimical to Aries. But the crushing Venetian defeat at Agnadello in May proved his forecast disastrously mistaken, and could well have increased anxiety about correct readings among the many members of the Venetian ruling class seeking portents from planetary movements, whose numbers included Pietro Bembo and Francesco Priuli. The war continued to go badly for the Republic, forcing the successive relinquishment of mainland cities. Between June 4 and June 6, at the time of a lunar eclipse, the Venetian army withdrew even from Padua, the jewel of the mainland state, crossing the Brenta to the Mestre side.[6] By early July, however, civic leaders, particularly *provveditore* of the army Andrea Gritti, decided to move the troops out again and attempt to reconquer the mainland. They received support from Venetian landlords whose attempts to harvest the ripening grain of the Paduan plain (increasingly important after the loss of Venetian possessions in grain-rich Puglia and Romagna) had been rebuffed by peasants.

Such a move, of course, would antagonize Venice's enemies and expose the army afresh, a situation to which Renaissance civic leaders commonly responded by consulting the heavens for guidance. The configuration of the planets indicated a massive stalemate between the forces of good and ill. Saturn, having resumed direct (forward) motion in April, was gaining on the position it had occupied before the retrograde, crippling the still-stalled Jupiter, a situation favorable to Libra, associated with Padua through the feast of its patron St. Justina on October 7.[7] However, Jupiter too was about to right itself; swifter in its

---

[5] See Ivanoff, 84; citations of Ali Ibn Abi al-Rijal in n. 4 and fol. 4r; for 1509 planetary positions see Johannes [Mueller] Regiomontanus, *Ephemerides sive Almanach perpetuum*, colophon: Petri Liechtenstein coloniensis . . . 1498 Idibus Octobris Venetiis; William D. Stahlman and Owen Gingerich, *Solar and Planetary Positions for Years −2500 to +2000 by 10-Day Intervals* (Madison: Univ. of Wisconsin Press, 1963), 491; Bryant Tuckerman, *Planetary, Lunar and Solar Positions A.D. 2 to A.D. 1649 at Five-Day and Ten-Day Intervals* (Philadelphia: American Philosophical Society, 1964), 772.

[6] For the eclipse, see Regiomontanus, *Kalendarium*, colophon: Johannes Helbronnensis [but Erhardus Ratdolt] . . . Anno S. 1485 Idus Octobri Venetiis, n. pag. but predictions of eclipses, 1509.

[7] For connections among Libra, St. Justina and Padua, see, e.g., the Libran glyph

movement, it would soon outstrip its stern enemy. Sun (rulership), Mercury (communication and movement), Venus (public life), and Mars (war) united forces in Cancer, a conjunction which most astrologers would have perceived as blocking both Arietan Venice and Libran Padua in all of those fields.[8]

Specifically, the square between postequinoctial Aries (associated with the waxing of the sun's power) and postsolstitial Cancer (the constellation that appears on the horizon as the days begin to shorten) could easily have prompted fears among Venetians that the period of mainland expansion had ended, to be followed by one of loss.[9] The equal hindering of autumnal Libra could have been interpreted as hampering Padua's pursuit of justice, intellectual endeavors, and the preservation of an independent past. The configuration acquired additional significance from the cardinality of Aries, Libra, and Cancer, which, with Capricorn, mark the solstices and equinoxes, thereby initiating the great seasonal shifts. As Carlo Ginzburg noted in his work on the *benandanti*, it was believed that at those four transitional points the entire new season could be oriented to either the benefit or the detriment of the subject.[10]

Astrological images began to be incorporated into works of art in the Middle Ages with the depiction of heavenly bodies as human beings in technical astrological treatises, an iconography stressing the immediacy of astral influences. Humanizing iconography soon spread to public religious art,[11] its influence peaking as a mood of competition, deprivation, and anxiety, induced by overpopulation, inspired the search for

---

on the astrological wheel in Giulio Campagnola's Paduan cityscape *Sage, Death and Devil* (also known as *Astrologer 1509*), in Edgar Wind, *Giorgione's "Tempesta" with Comments on Giorgione's Poetic Allegories* (Oxford: Clarendon Press, 1969), fig. 27; and the fresco of St. Justina located beneath the degrees of Libra and activities of October in Padua's Palazzo della Ragione, in Mor et al., *Palazzo*, plate 6 and here, fig. 5.

[8] See Regiomontanus, *Ephemerides* (1481), n. pag. but fol. 8r; Agostino Nifo, *De diebus criticis seu decretorijs aureus liber* (n.p.: Argentorati per Henricum Sybold, n.d. but Folger Shakespeare Library BF/1718/N5/D3/1528/Cage), dedicated to Vincenzo Querini, n. pag. but fols. 29r–30r, 56r; Rudolphus Goclenius, *Astrologiae generalia, Libri II* (Marburg: Paulus Egenolphus, 1614), 1: 21, 23, 37–38, 41; 2: 49, 59–60, 62, 87–88, 132, 136, 139.

[9] Cf. Hartner, 86.

[10] *I benandanti: Stregoneria e culti agrari tra Cinquecento e Seicento*, 3rd ed. (Turin: Einaudi, 1979), 36–38. The link with cardinal signs in Nifo, n. pag. but fols. 42 ff. and Goclenius, 1: 40–41. This characterization explains the association of cardinal signs with anxiety.

[11] Fritz Saxl, "Macrocosm and Microcosm in Medieval Pictures," in *Lectures*, 2 vols. (London: Warburg Institute, 1957), 1: 58–72; "The Revival of Late Antique Astrology," 1: 73–84; "The Belief in Stars in the Twelfth Century," 1: 85–95; "Illuminated Science Manuscripts in England," 1: 109.

other unorthodox spiritual remedies.[12] In the fourteenth century, zodiacal images were introduced into civic contexts. Their focus shifted to the influence of planetary rulers upon astrological signs at the same time that challenges to established power caused earthly rulers to become more concerned with maintaining political domination,[13] a development that would exert significant influence over political thought through the early sixteenth century.

The seat of the communal government in Padua, a center of astrological scholarship located in a region with a strong popular interest in cosmology, was frescoed with astrological images immediately prior to the severely strained commune's accession to the Carrara.[14] A century later, as Venice was beginning to conquer the mainland, Venus (often associated by the Venetians with their city) was depicted as a *castellana* and Mars as a doughty warrior set to defend her in the astrological capital of the Ducal Palace column.[15] When the vast Paduan cycle, which had been destroyed by fire, was repainted after the Venetian conquest, its planets and constellations mingled with heaven's Christian inhabitants and their political affiliations. A large fresco of St. Mark enthroned was placed in the midst of the Leonine activities of August, dislocated from the normal feast day (April 25) by a powerful association with Leo, sign of dominion and Venice; a St. Justina of much smaller physical dimensions is located beneath the activities of Libra.[16]

A double threat of political upheaval and high population materialized again in the late fifteenth and early sixteenth centuries,[17] with considerably more ruinous consequences for Italy's place in the power

---

[12] For the latter see David Herlihy, "Alienation in Medieval Culture and Society," in *Alienation. Concept, Term, and Meaning*, ed. Frank Johnson (New York: Seminar Press, 1971), esp. 136–39. This section was prompted by Saxl's observation that interest in astrology increased prior to World War I: "Revival," 73.

[13] Cf. Eugenio Battisti, *L'antirinascimento* (Milan: Feltrinelli, 1962), 61, 103–4.

[14] Camillo Semenzato, "L'architettura del Palazzo," in Mor et al., *Palazzo*, 30–36; Lucio Grossato, "La decorazione pittorica del Salone," ibid., 48, n. 2; Antonio Barzon, *I cieli e la loro influenza negli affreschi del salone in Padova* (Padua: Tipografia del Seminario, 1924), 187–94; Battisti, 72–73, 101–3, 143–44, 156–57, 392 n. 38, plate 4 item C; Francesca Guerra D'Antoni, "A New Perspective on the Veronese Riddle," *Romance Philology* 36 (1982): 185–200. The Michiel Mercury (see below) was sculpted by Paduan Antonio Minelli. For the Friuli see Ginzburg, and Cividale, Duomo, Museo Cristiano, stone carving of about the eighth century which I interpret as a sun symbol flanked on either side by a bull and calf and by a lion and cub (i.e., Taurus and Leo).

[15] For the mainland state and army see M. E. Mallett and J. R. Hale, *The Military Organization of a Renaissance State* (Cambridge: Cambridge Univ. Press, 1984), 7–33.

[16] Grossato, 51 ff; cf. Ivanoff, 83.

[17] David Herlihy, "Popolazione e strutture sociali dal XV al XVI secolo," in *Tiziano e Venezia* (Venice: Neri Pozza, 1980), 71–74, which informs this paragraph.

balance of western Europe. Fear of the threat seems to have generated anxiety over the inadequacy of life in the material world, contributing to the appeal of Neoplatonism and philosophies of self-denial. The contrasts between the early quattrocento flourishing of birth trays and their decline in the early cinquecento,[18] and between the promotion of marriage by Francesco Barbaro and its rejection by his grandson Ermolao seem symptomatic, as does the favorable reevaluation of Saturn.[19] A world swarming with too many people, states and, soon, religious groups engaged in a destructive competition for the most advantageous position may have seemed dangerously unstable, and a prudent abstention from activities that would aggravate such problems, a reasonable alternative.

As the need to maintain control over swiftly changing social and political conditions increased, both Neoplatonic and Hermetic astrology grew in importance. The scholarly seriousness with which the technical and metaphysical aspects of planetary influences were probed is exemplified by the research of Marsilio Ficino. In the late fifteenth and early sixteenth centuries, astrological knowledge became readily available through the printing of Pietro d'Abano's *Astrolabium planum*, Johannes Regiomontanus's *Kalendario* and the *Almanach nova* of Johannes Stoeffler and Jacob Pflaum. Each enjoyed numerous editions in Germany and in Venice, established as a leading center of scientific publishing by German printers.[20] Copious margin notes in Renaissance hand indicate the extent to which surviving copies were consulted. A relatively large proportion of the population having become familiar with the precepts of astrology, pamphleteers soon began issuing predictions which served as tools of political and religious propaganda.

Signs of the zodiac, which had earlier appeared on the clock tower in Padua were, by the turn of the sixteenth century, prominently displayed on the new one in Piazza San Marco, and on the pulpit of the Parma baptistery. Horoscopes provided the basis for art commissioned by Agostino Chigi while he was engaged in difficult loan negotiations with the Venetians during the Wars of Cambrai, by Marcantonio Michiel before he began his inventory of Venetian paintings, and by Kylian Weybeck in a church tower constructed in a Danubian village in 1514.

---

[18] See Mary Fitzgerald, "*Deschi da Parto*: Birth Trays of the Florentine *Quattrocento*" (Ph.D. diss. Syracuse University, 1986).

[19] Cf. Klibansky et al., 151–59; Amelia Carr and Richard Kremer, "Child of Saturn: The Renaissance Church Tower of Niederaltaich," *Sixteenth Century Journal* 17 (1986): 401–34.

[20] Carlo Maccagna, "Scienza e cultura scientifica nell'ambiente veneto tra Quattrocento e Cinquecento," in *Giorgione e l'Umanesimo veneziano*, ed. Rodolfo Pallucchini, 2 vols. (Florence: Olschki, 1981), 1: 37–50.

Esoteric glyphs appeared on the hat of a youth sitting for his portrait, and, in a Campagnola print, on the astrological wheel marked 1509 held by a dejected sage seated before the Paduan Salone.[21]

Giorgione's *Tempest* [fig. 1], which recent scholarship has associated with the Wars of Cambrai and specifically with Venice's 1509 defense of Padua,[22] appears to be another of the many attempts to ascertain through the positions of the planets whether the Republic would retain its mainland state. In astrological terms, the painting seems to work on several levels. Two towers of the somewhat fanciful Paduan cityscape [fig. 2], marked respectively with lion and cart, appear to represent long-term relations between Venice and Padua. The aggressive frontal posture of the Lion Tower, whose totemic image resembles both the Venetian symbol and its astrological counterpart [fig. 3],[23] seems to correlate with formal Venetian dominance. The Cart Tower, as Paul Kaplan has noted, bears the mark of the Carrara; its greater bulk, partially hidden by the side view and shrubbery, may allude to sustained clandestine anti-Venetian activities. The co-existence of the symbols, rare because the victor swiftly obliterated the mark of the vanquished, seems to signal conflict. The space between the towers equals that on an astrological chart between the sign of Leo and the figure of the Cart [fig. 4], one of the degrees of Libra popularized by Abano's *Astrolabium planum* and present in the Salone frescoes above St.

---

[21] For Chigi see Gilbert, 37–62 and Saxl, *La fede astrologica di Agostino Chigi* (Rome: Reale Accademia d'Italia, 1934), 39; for prophecies, see Ottavia Niccoli, "Profezie in piazza. Note sul profetismo popolare nell'Italia del primo Cinquecento," *Quaderni Storici* 41 (1979): esp. 503–4; Zambelli, ed., "*Astrologi hallucinati*"; Cervelli, 149–63. The youth's hat in a drawing by Bartolomeo Veneto (Vienna, Albertina; Otto Benesch, *Meisterzeichnungen der Albertina: Europäische Schulen von der Gotik bis zum Klassizismus* [Salzburg: Galerie Welz, 1964], cat. no. 13) bears several symbols including a St. Andrew's cross like that in Giorgione's *Three Philosophers*, linked with the Heavenly Temple and the Pythagorean system (T. Zaunschirm, "Giorgiones *Drei Philosophen*," *Alte und moderne Kunst* 21 [December, 1976]: 8–9); the symbols seem to be limiting evil and increasing good by pointing wedges in at a snake and out from the crosses. Hartner, in an otherwise superbly informed article, assumes the horoscope statue to have been planned for the conception of Michiel's first child, but, as Mercury is the planet of scholarly endeavors, I believe it is more likely to have been related to his study of art works.

[22] Peter Meller quoted by Piero Zampetti, "La quiete dopo la Tempesta," in *Giorgione e l'Umanesimo*, 1: 286, n. 18; Deborah Howard, "Giorgione's *Tempesta* and Titian's *Assunta* in the Context of the Cambrai Wars," *Art History* 8 (1985): 271–89; Paul H. D. Kaplan, "The Storm of War: The Paduan Key to Giorgione's *Tempesta*," *Art History* 9 (1986): 405–27.

[23] Cf. Antonio Rizzi, "I leoni marciani lapidei a Venezia," *Ateneo Veneto* 19, no. 1–2 (1981): 8 and Joha[n]ne Angeli [but Pietro d'Abano], *Astrolabium planum* . . ., colophon: Impressus Venetiis per Luca[m] Antoniu[m] de Giunta florentinu[m]. Anno salutis millesimo quingentesimo secundo kal. decembris, fol. K1r.

Fig. 1. Giorgione, *Tempesta*, Venice, Accademia (photo Boehm)

Fig. 2. Giorgione, *Tempesta*, detail of towers (photo Boehm)

Prima facies leonis est sa-　　Scda ẽ iouis: z ẽ rixaʒ nesci　　Tertia facies est martis: et
turni z ẽ crudelitatis: male-　entiũ: z necessitatis miſoʒ　est amoris: societatis nõ ce-
ficio. z violẽtiaʒ sustinẽdi　victorie viliũ p nescios: oc-　dendi z dimittẽdi de suo p
laboꝛes: audacie z libidis.　casionũ trahẽdi enses z plioʒ　rixis vitandis.

Ascendit vir tenens caput leonis　　　　　　　　Nauis vna parte inclinata in
in manu dextera.　　　　　　　　　　　　　　aquam.

℟ Homo fortis erit.　　　　℟ Hom disfortunatus erit in aquis.

Fig. 3. Anonymous, *Sign of Leo*, fol. K1r, Johan[n]e Angelis [but Pietro d'Abano],
Astrolabum planum . . . , Venice, 1502 (by permission of the Folger Shakespeare Library)

Fig. 4. School of Niccolò Miretto [?], *Cart* (astrological degree), Padua, Palazzo della Ragione (photo Museo Civico, Padua)

Fig. 5. Giusto de' Menabuoi [?], *St. Justina*, Padua, Palazzo della Ragione (photo Museo Civico, Padua)

Justina's head [fig. 5].²⁴ Thus, the overall impression conveyed by the background of the *Tempest* is one of contested Venetian rule.

The foreground figures, on the other hand, seem to embody the situation of Venice and Padua in early July, 1509 after the Serenissima's troops had retreated. The naturally mandated dominion of Venice over Padua has been truncated, like the wall. A soldier observes the nourishment which a mother, seated on the opposite bank of a river across from him, provides for her child, much as Venetian landlords eyed their crops. The two figures seem also to represent the sundering of Cancer's principal personifications, the defender of the homeland and the nursing mother. Their positions at the approximate midpoints of a circle (three quarters of which appears in the painting) correspond to several icons of masculine authority: the placements, on the zodiacal wheel, of Aries (ruled by Mars) and Libra (ruled by Venus),²⁵ as well as those of sun and moon during a lunar eclipse (illustrated in the sage's wheel in Campagnola's print). The placements of husband's and wife's shields on twelve-sided marriage *deschi* are similar, possibly due to astrological influences. Moreover, they resemble those of the marital coats-of-arms of sovereigns of different domains, recalling the widespread use of marriage as a metaphor for political dominance.²⁶ A *desco* origin sug-

---

²⁴ Mor et al., *Palazzo*, plate 6; an astrological interpretation of another landscape painting was discussed by Anthony Colantuono, "The Halcyon Days and Giovanni Bellini's *Feast of the Gods*," at the Sixteenth-Century Studies Conference, October 1987, Tempe, Arizona.

²⁵ See Gregorius Reisch, *Margarita philosophica nova*, colophon: vir Joa[n]nes Gruningerus operis excussor ... Ex Argentorato veteri pridie kalendas Aprilis. Anno redemptio[n]is n[ost]re octavo supra mille quingentos, Liber 7 Tractatus 1 n. pag. but fol. 8r; Joha[n]ne Angeli, fol. 3ii-v.

²⁶ Paul Kaplan has affirmed independently that the cityscape is not a literal rendering of Padua; alterations include the single cupola of the basilica, the visibility of the Carrara emblem (which was in fact covered), and the westerly rather than easterly direction of the bridge; for metaphor, see Muir, 119–34; for *deschi*, see John Pope-Hennessy and Keith Christiansen, "Secular Painting in Fifteenth-Century Tuscany: Birth Trays, Cassone Panels and Portraits," *Metropolitan Museum of Art Bulletin* 38 (Summer 1980): 6, and Paul F. Watson and Victoria Kirkham, "Amore e Virtù: Two Salvers Depicting Boccaccio's *Comedia delle Ninfe Fiorentine* in the Metropolitan Museum," *Metropolitan Museum Journal* 10 (1975): 38 and fig. 6; see also various examples in Fitzgerald. Pope-Hennessy and Christiansen note the shape of the *deschi*, whose astrological implications have been remarked upon by Dr. Fitzgerald in an interview. For royal marital arms see Jan Gossaert, *The Holy Family with Coats of Arms of Charles V and Isabella of Portugal* (St. Louis: St. Louis Museum of Art). For the lunar eclipse, see also Dante *Paradiso* 29.1–9; Edward Muir suggested the link between infant and *desco* traditions. A study of the popularity of the *Madonna lactans* in the western mainland state in conjunction with the population studies of David Herlihy and the iconographical work of Margaret Miles seems promising.

gests that the child derives from the birth trays' conventional *putto*. In metaphorical terms, it carries implications for the future of political rule, in connection with which the child's location on the Padua side assumes importance, confirming other evidence that Venetian governance of the mainland had been broken. Such iconographical traditions seem to have taken precedence over geography, which, with the sun setting on the left and Padua above, would place Venice on the right, a position occupied by the man in a number of contemporary works with similar figures.[27]

But more specific astrological correspondences may be noted, indicating that the painting functions as a horoscope in its primary, natural elements, rather than as one executed on paper. The three-quarter circle around which the *Tempest*'s cityscape, figures, and riverbanks are disposed resembles the moon on the sheet held by the elderly man of Giorgione's *Three Philosophers*, both configurations echoing the zodiacal path. Shadows thrown up from the soldier's legs identify the sun's location in the lower left, where it nears the end of its Cancer transit. The white flesh and clothing of the mother indicate the site of moon in Aquarius, fixing the time as sunset on July 3, 1509, the hour in which the Venetian government decided that the army would move camp from Mestre to retake the mainland. The thunderbolt of Jupiter, about to resume direct motion, rises on the right, while stern Saturn, whose Greek counterpart Cronos was overthrown in a revolt of his children led by Jupiter, sets near the broken wall at the soldier's head. Mercury stands below his flexed knee. Mars and Venus occupy the unfathomable space near his feet, their placement deep in Cancer increasing astrological tension as it blocks both their rulerships of Aries and Libra, and their functions as archetypal spouses and analogues of authoritarian governance.

An astrologer attempting to predict the fortune of an imminent military advance from such a horoscope would focus attention on whether the number and force of the planets transiting out of Cancer would be sufficient to counteract the negative influence of those lingering there and the continued retrograde motion of Jupiter. The sign

---

[27] See, for example, attributed to Giorgione, *Idillo campestre* (Padua, Museo Civico); *Idillo* (Compton Wynyates, Marquis of Northampton), *Giorgione e i giorgioneschi*, ed. Pietro Zampetti, 2nd ed. (Venice: Ferrari, 1955), cat. nos. 13 and 26; Giovanni Cariani, *Gli amanti* (Rome, Museo di Palazzo Venezia), cat. no. 96; and Palma Vecchio, *The Peaceable Warrior* (Philadelphia, Philadelphia Museum of Art). For storm as division of kingdom, see Angus MacKay, "Ritual and Propaganda in Fifteenth-Century Castile," *Past and Present* 107 (1985): 8; for storm as loss of luck, see Matteo Maria Boiardo, *Orlando innamorato*, bk. 2, canto 8, stanzas 58–63.

following Cancer, Leo, would add a highly positive element to the Venetian equation: the city's rising sign and favorable to its sun in Aries, Leo is also more forceful than Libra. Mercury would transit the earliest, about July 7, followed by the powerful sun on approximately July 14. Venice would not have the advantage of Venus's benevolence until July 19, however, and that of Mars, crucial to the fortunes of war, until August 13. The stalemate of outer planets Jupiter and Saturn would last until the end of September. Thus, there would have been good reason for anxiety over the reading of such opaque and contradictory signs, and reluctance about moving too quickly, an attitude that the painting seems to express.

It is impossible to know how the war affected Giorgione, who was born on the mainland but worked in Venice.[28] Some of those viewing the painting, aware that the knightly saint of his 1504 Castelfranco altarpiece carried an imperial standard, may have wondered whether the lightning bolt in the recent canvas was about to bless the Lion Tower or to destroy it. But the war clearly generated tensions and conflicts among Venetians, whose solutions to the crisis ranged from relinquishing the mainland to enlisting Turkish help in retaking it. The painting's probable patron, Gabriele Vendramin, was closely linked to the war effort by his brothers and his uncle, Andrea Gritti.[29] When compared to the Paduan cycle, the small, private nature of Giorgione's work seems to echo the concentration of power over the Venetian Republic in the hands of a few patricians during the course of the war—as noted by Felix Gilbert—as well as the tendency to read in a horoscope the vocation to rule.[30] Numerous birth horoscopes of Venice

---

[28] Giorgione has been connected with astrology by G. F. Hartlaub, in *Giorgiones Geheimnis: Ein kunstgeschichtlicher Beitrag zur Mystik der Renaissance* (Munich: Allgemeine Verlagsanstalt, 1925); Wind, *Giorgione's "Tempesta"*; and to some extent by Zaunschirm. The *fregio* in the Casa Marta-Pellizzari, regarded by some as an early work (Adriano Mariuz, "Appunti per una lettura del fregio giorgionesco di Casa Marta Pellizzari," in *Liceo Ginnasio Giorgione Castelfranco Veneto* [1966], 50–51) shows many tools of astrology but many errors as well (e.g., the constellations Pisces, Cancer, and Scorpio follow one another). The sheet in the *Three Philosophers* bears a word under critical dispute which when read on a transparent reproduction seems to be "eclsse." It is unclear if the alteration of the painting to include soldier and cityscape is related to the present interpretation. Giorgione's associate, Giulio Campagnola, used astrological themes in *Sage* and *Saturn*, see Klibansky, 210–14.

[29] Kaplan, "Storm," 408–9 and for lightning 414; for imperial standard, cf. Ludovico Zorzi, "Note," in Angelo Beolco, *Ruzante Teatro*, ed. L. Zorzi (Turin: Einaudi, 1967), 1369, n. 45.

[30] Felix Gilbert, "Venice in the Crisis of the League of Cambrai," in *Renaissance Venice*, ed. J. R. Hale (London: Faber and Faber, 1973), esp. 290; Claudia Rousseau, "The Yoke Impresa of Leo X," *Mitteilungen des Kunsthistorisches Instituts in Florenz* 33

in patrician chronicles dating from the late fifteenth and early sixteenth centuries, the period during which the city experienced the greatest challenge to its existence and the greatest consolidation of authority, indicate that Venice's collective aristocratic identity functioned as personal identity did in other Italian cases.

Years afterward, Francesco Guicciardini wrote his account of a speech delivered by Doge Leonardo Loredan later in the summer of 1509, when Padua was again assaulted by imperial troops. In Guicciardini's report, Loredan urges the Senate to defend Padua and regain the place in history lost with that city. Thus, "cancelleremo la infamia ricevuta; e vedendo non essere perduta in noi l'antica generosità e virtù, si ascriverà più tosto quel disordine a *una certa fatale tempesta*, alla quale né il consiglio né la costanza degli uomini può resistere, che a colpa e vergogna nostra" (emphasis added; "we will erase the infamy received thereby; and, seeing that we have not lost our ancient generosity and strength, people will ascribe that unrest to *a storm brought by fate*, against which the good advice and steadfastness of men are helpless, rather than to any fault or shame of ours").[31] Although, as Paul Kaplan has noted,[32] the quotation must be taken with caution because of

---

(1989): 113–26, which lends new vitality to Jacob Burckhardt's theory that the Renaissance was a period in which individuals made special efforts to create personal identity, an interpretation to be understood in sixteenth-century terms, i.e., a personal identity whose function was the domination of a social or artistic system. The conflict between Burckhardt's theory and more recent views, therefore, may be one of sources; the records with which he dealt were more likely to have been made or commissioned by those in control of the social structure and thus more aware of personal identity.

[31] *Storia d'Italia*, bk. 8, chap. 10, although Guicciardini appears to have intervened in the text. His version resembles more a letter from the Signoria to the *provveditori* of Padua (Sanuto, 9: cols. 114–15) than the speech (Sanuto, 9: col. 126), which was actually given to the Maggior Consiglio; and he seems to incorporate another speech made by Lorendan to the Maggior Consiglio on July 8 during the retaking of Padua (Sanuto, 8: col. 497): the events described are those of early not of late July and the language used is similarly colloquial rather than Latinizing (in these several sentences there are four instances of post-clitic reflexive pronouns as opposed to two in the rest of the speech, and the lexicon includes tough words such as "colpa" and "vergogna"). The eminence of *virtù* over *fortuna* also indicates Guicciardini's intervention in the text. It is also possible that the *Tempest* was painted during the second siege of Padua, auguring a second victory by reminding the Venetians that they had emerged triumphant from even less certain circumstances. A woodcut depicting events of June 1509 was used to illustrate a prognostic of 1510: see Mark Zucker, "An Allegory of Renaissance Politics in a Contemporary Italian Engraving. The Prognostic of 1510," *Journal of the Warburg and Courtauld Institutes* 52 (1989): 236–40.

[32] "Storm," 413–14 and n. 88; for "storm" as metaphor for war, see also BMV, It. 1, 66=6730, fols. 46v, 91r.

the late date of its writing, and the origin of the image cannot be identified with certainty, it is clear that *tempesta* was a metaphor current in Venice that conveyed a widespread attitude about the city's situation during the Wars of Cambrai.

Newcomb College, Tulane University

WENDY STEDMAN SHEARD

Giorgione's Portrait Inventions c. 1500: Transfixing the Viewer
(With Observations on Some Florentine Antecedents)

IN THE DECADE FOLLOWING 1500, GIORGIONE WAS RESPONSIBLE FOR A number of new inventions in the field of portraiture that challenged the traditional functioning of portraits in Venice.[1] Both the *Portrait of a Man* in Munich [fig. 1][2] and the badly damaged but

---

[1] Our current knowledge about Giorgione's portrait inventions owes much to the work of Jaynie Anderson, in particular her dissertation, "The Imagery of Giorgione" (Bryn Mawr College, 1972), 143–82, and "The Giorgionesque Portrait: From Likeness to Allegory," in *Giorgione, Atti del Convegno Internazionale di Studio per il 5° Centenario della Nascita* (Castelfranco Veneto, 1979), 153–58. Greater precision in defining Giorgione's artistic personality was made possible when the attribution to him of *La Vecchia* (Venice, Accademia Galleries) was at last made certain by Anderson's publication of the 1601 inventory, "A further inventory of Gabriel Vendramin's collection," *Burlington Magazine* 121 (1979): 639–48, see esp. 643. — This paper was substantially completed in March 1989. Not all the subsequent literature dealing with its several topics has been surveyed, but references to obviously relevant and important publications have been added to the footnotes.

[2] Alte Pinakothek München, *Gemäldekataloge*, vol. 9: *Venezianische Gemälde des 15. und 16. Jahrhunderts,* pt. 1 (Munich, 1971), no. 524, 202–5, *Brustbild eines jungen Mannes,* panel, 69.4 x 53.6 cm. (attributed to an unspecified Venetian painter, first quarter of sixteenth century). The painting is inscribed on the back in a late sixteenth-century hand: "Giorgion De Castel Franco. F Maestro De Ticiano." The portrait was engraved in 1650 by Wenzel Hollar while in the Antwerp collection of Van Veerle. The print's first state was identified as a portrait of Bonamico Buffamalco, painter in Venice, and its second as the portrait of a German of the house of Fugger, an identification which could go back to Vasari's mention of a painted portrait by Giorgione in his own collection: "É nel nostro libro una testa colorito a olio, ritratta da un Todesco di casa Fucheri, che allora era de maggiori mercanti nel Fondaco de' Tedeschi; la quale è cosa mirabile" ("There is in our book [viz. Vasari's collection of drawings] a head colored in oils, a portrait of a German of the Fugger house, who in those days was one of the major merchants in the Fondaco de' Tedeschi, which is a thing to be wondered at"); see *Le vite de' più eccellenti pittori scultori ed architettori,* ed. Gaetano Milanesi (1568; Florence, 1906), 4:99. See further Klára Garas, "Bildnisse der Renaissance. II. Dürer und Giorgione," *Acta historiae artium* 18 (1972): 128. Garas makes the attractive proposal that the portrait of a German of the House of Fugger once in Vasari's collection is the *Portrait of a Man* now in the San Diego Museum of Art, known as the "Terris Portrait," Garas, 128–29, fig. 2. The decisive importance of

still legible *Portrait of Gerolamo Marcello* in Vienna [fig. 2][3] demonstrate how Giorgione transformed the portrait from an advertisement of class, status, wealth, power, or holiness into a far more ambitious, more complex image whose relationship to the viewer was correspondingly altered. The concept of an individual's self or identity implied by Giorgione's new portraits embraced an emotional component which was not limited to the suggestion of a single "humor" or character type, but attempted to render the sitter's ongoing mood or other interior experience as if crystallized by the painter in a single instant. From a static image that summed up a person's character, role, and/or achievements, the portrait became a "slice of life" that showed this single moment in time. Correspondingly, a direct, urgent appeal to the viewer was achieved by strategies such as the violent turn of the head in the Munich portrait [fig. 1], which implies that the viewer is interrupting the sitter and is thereby triggering his alerted or attentive response. What follows is a demand that the beholder enter into a newly intimate psychological relationship with the sitter—and in the case of self-portraits, with the artist—which is tantamount to a demand that the beholder respond to an artifact as though it were a person. With these pictorial concepts, the magic-like element, or element of magic, in a painter's ability to represent what he saw with increasing literalness or accuracy as the fifteenth century progressed, achieves a new dimension, paralleled by the spell-casting potential of the full-face or three-quarter positioned human visage rendered with psychological realism.

The Munich portrait is a "turning portrait": a subcategory of one of Giorgione's most provocative inventions, the action portrait. The debate about attribution does not affect the history of portrait types which concerns us here; the weight of the evidence indicates that Giorgione was the moving force behind a host of new pictorial inventions around 1500. This claim is independent of the complex question of which painters in Venice adopted his inventions and when they did so.

The picture was described by Carlo Ridolfi in 1648 as "un Tedesco di casa Fuchera con pelliccia di volpe in dosso, in fianco in atto di

---

portraiture in Giorgione's overall oeuvre emerges clearly from Vasari's account of his life (*Le vite*, 4:91–100). — The identification of the Munich portrait with the self-portrait by Palma Vecchio that Vasari mentioned (5:246 f.) has been rejected by several scholars and by Rolf Kultzen, author of the Munich catalogue, in his summary of the painting's attribution history (*Venezianishe Gemälde*, 203–4).

[3] Kunsthistorisches Museum, no. 1526. See Teresio Pignatti, *Giorgione*, trans. Clovis Whitfield (London: Phaidon, 1971), no. A.64, 142–43, "*Portrait of a Warrior (Gerolamo Marcello)*," canvas, 72 x 56.5 cm. Listed in Kunsthistorisches Museum, Wien, *Verzeichnis der Gemälde* (Vienna, 1973, paper), 78 as "Giorgione (?), *Ein Krieger*."

girarsi"[4] ("a German of the Fugger house wearing a fox fur on his back, seen from the side, in the act of turning"). The last four words, "in atto di girarsi," in the act of turning, point to the definition of Giorgione's invention as perceived over a century later, with the accent on interrupted movement or action.[5] The axis through the shoulders lies at a three-quarters angle to the picture plane from lower right to left rear, while the head swivels sharply to the man's right. His right arm is raised to display the voluminous sleeve of a quilted jacket emerging from his fur cloak, and a glove he holds up in his clenched fist completes his "glass of fashion" aspect. The sharply turned head sets up a dialogue between the viewer and the sitter, encouraging the fiction that the spectator has suddenly interrupted and startled him, causing him to stare at us out of the ideal realm of the picture. The device triggers the illusion of a breakdown between the actual and the fictional worlds while implying that the truth of the sitter's personality is disclosed more fully than would be possible if a more formal, abstract, and "composed" portrait type had been employed. The sharply turned head thereafter became a hallmark of the romantic portraiture convention as employed from Titian to Van Dyck, Salvator Rosa and later by Gericault and Delacroix.[6]

The *Portrait of Girolamo Marcello* [fig. 2] represents a variant of Giorgione's action portrait in which the sitter is defined by engagement in a dramatic action or interaction.[7] Marcantonio Michiel in 1525 described it in the collection of Girolamo Marcello as "M(esser) Ieronimo armato che mostra la schena, insino al cinto, et *volta la testa* [italics added], fo de mano de Zorzi da Castelfranco"[8] ("Messer Gerolamo in armor, who shows his back down to the waist and turns his head, was

---

[4] *Le Maraviglie dell'arte*, ed. Detlev Hadeln (Berlin, 1914), 1:106.

[5] Anderson, "Giorgionesque Portrait," 155, discusses the concept and provides several examples of its use by Giorgione's followers.

[6] Sheard, "The Romantic Portrait as a Venetian Renaissance Invention," talk delivered at the National Gallery of Art, Washington, D.C., 26 October 1986.

[7] *The Three Ages of Man* and *The Concert*, both in the Pitti Palace Museum, Florence, belong to this type, which obviously lends itself to double or triple portraits, with one subject actively engaged in drawing the viewer into the action, often by means of "the look out of the picture." See Pignatti, *Giorgione*, nos. 28 (pl. 111) and A. 11 (pl. 180). For *The Three Ages of Man*, see 'Le tre età' dell'uomo della Galleria Palatina, Florence, Centro Di, 1989 (with text by Mauro Lucco). Attribution of *The Concert* is divided between Giorgione and Titian. Cf. the *Concert* at Hampton Court, attributed by John Shearman to Giovanni Bellini's workshop (*The Early Italian Pictures in the Collection of Her Majesty the Queen* [Cambridge: Cambridge Univ. Press, 1983], no. 38, 44 f.).

[8] *Notizia d'Opere del Disegno*, ed. Theodor Frimmel (Vienna, 1888), 88. Anderson pointed out how Michiel's description identifies the turning portrait as Giorgione's invention ("Giorgionesque Portrait," 151).

Fig. 1. Venetian Painter, *Portrait of a Man*, Munich, Alte Pinakothek

Fig. 2. Giorgione, *Portrait of Girolamo Marcello*, Vienna, Kunsthistorisches Museum

Fig. 3. Titian, *Il Bravo*, Vienna, Kunsthistorisches Museum

by the hand of Giorgio da Castelfranco"), noting both Marcello's unusual position with his back partly turned to the spectator, and his emphatically turned head. Marcello is clothed in antique armor as a victorious Roman warrior, wearing a laurel wreath on his head. To his right, now rather illegible owing to the painting's deteriorated condition, is the profile of an older man with a prominent, beak-like nose who peers intently at Marcello, gripping his wrist as it lies on the parapet.[9] As Jaynie Anderson has pointed out, the motif of a noble profile contrasted with a grotesque head is Leonardesque in origin.[10] But it is doubtful that Leonardo conceived of the configuration in terms of portraiture.

In making such a dramatic interaction between two figures an

---

[9] An engraving made by David Teniers in 1658 for his Theatrum Pictorium reveals that the painting has been cut down on the right. Originally more of the old man's body was included, as well as the end of the parapet and a staff or stick that Marcello held in his right hand. It was this engraving (although its author was misidentified) that enabled William Suida to identify the portrait described by Michiel with the painting in Vienna ("Spigolature Giorgionesche," *Arte Veneta* 8 [1954]: 165).

[10] "Giorgionesque Portrait," 154. In "The Imagery of Giorgione," Anderson provided the best account to date of how Giorgione's inventions responded to the art and thought of Leonardo (passim; in the case of portrait inventions see esp. 144–46, 151–52, 159–60). Anderson showed how Giorgione's invention of the turning portrait fulfilled three of Leonardo's criteria for successful portraiture: (1) the incorporation of movement or animation; (2) the revelation of the subject's soul or inner being through such depiction of movement or action; and (3) a more direct and intimate relationship to the viewer than earlier conventions permitted. — Note that Giorgione could have interpreted the portrait composition recorded in the Oxford copy of Leonardo's design for a portrait of Isabella d'Este as a "turning portrait," because of the contrast between the head in profile and the bust placed nearly frontally, angled just slightly away from the picture plane, as if Isabella has just turned her head *away from* the viewer. Isabella's pointing finger suggests that Leonardo intended to animate the image and motivate the retardataire use of a profile (which Isabella had probably insisted on out of conservative concern for the propaganda functions of her portrait) by portraying her as if in the midst of a conversation. For an illustration see John Pope-Hennessy, *The Portrait in the Renaissance*, Bollingen Series 35, vol. 12 (Washington, D.C.: National Gallery, 1966), 164, fig. 180. This possibility is not so evident if the better-known drawing for the Isabella d'Este portrait in the Louvre is considered without the Oxford variant which shows more of her figure. See Arthur E. Popham, *The Drawings of Leonardo da Vinci* (New York: Harcourt Brace, 1945), pl. 172. About Leonardo's studies for a portrait of Isabella, see now David Alan Brown, "Leonardo and the Ladies with the Ermine and the Book," forthcoming in *Artibus et Historiae*. For Leonardo's comments on body movements as expressive of emotions see *Leonardo da Vinci's Treatise on Painting*, trans. A. Philip McMahon (Princeton: Princeton Univ. Press, 1956), sections 111, 251, 388, 401, 402, 404, 405, and Hans Klaiber, "Leonardo da Vincis Stellung in der Geschichte der Physiognomik und Mimik," *Repertorium für Kunstwissenschaft* 28 (1905): 321–39, esp. 326 ff. — The influence of Leonardo on Giorgione has been discussed in the art historical literature ever since it was introduced by Vasari (*Le vite*, 4:11 and 92). See the recent articles by Ballarin and Pedretti, nn. 14, 75 below).

essential part of a portrait, Giorgione fused portraiture with history painting, again disregarding the traditional separation between the two genres and demanding a more complex set of responses from the viewer. Here the viewer is transfixed by the evident intensity of the exchange between the two men, regardless of whether its content is recognized. The narrative alluded to—but not illustrated literally, since telescoping devices are employed—is most likely the story of the virtuous Trebonius repulsing the homosexual advances of Caius Lucius. Edgar Wind called attention to Ridolfi's identification of the text from Valerius Maximus that explains the event portrayed in Titian's compositionally similar "*Il Bravo*" (Vienna, Kunsthistorisches Museum).[11] That "*Il Bravo*" [fig. 3] is a variant of the Marcello portrait is rarely noticed. Thus, the narrative that underlines the former probably also applies to its source: *Girolamo Marcello* becomes an allegory of virtue as well as a portrait, and the possibility that "*Il Bravo*" is a portrait as well as a historical narrative and an allegory of virtue should also be considered. The ramifications of this proposal are interesting with respect to the

---

[11] *Giorgione's Tempesta with Comments on Giorgione's Poetic Allegories* (Oxford: Clarendon Press, 1969), 7–11. See 31 n. 44 on the confusion surrounding the passage from Valerius Maximus and how it arose. In his catalogue entry on "*Il Bravo*," Harold E. Wethey, *The Paintings of Titian*, vol. 3, *The Mythological and Historical Paintings* (London: Phaidon, 1975), 130, summarizes the story, in which the handsome hero (Trebonius) slays his homosexual attacker (Caius Lucius). The wreath that crowns both Trebonius in "*Il Bravo*" and Girolamo Marcello (figs. 2 and 3) alludes proleptically to the garland given in recognition of his valor by Marius, Trebonius's commanding general (who was also the uncle of the assailant, so that the story illustrates Justice as well as the virtues of courage and chastity). Wethey points out that although in the seventeenth century "*Il Bravo*" was regarded as a major example of Giorgione's art, it may still have been the painting Michiel referred to in 1528 as "two figures attacking each other, by Titian" (130). In her dissertation, Anderson connected the Marcello portrait to "*Il Bravo*" in proposing that Giorgione appropriated to portraiture what had hitherto been the prerogative of history painting, action between several figures, and suggested that "*Il Bravo*" is "half-portrait, half-history painting," based on an invention by Giorgione ("Imagery of Giorgione," 154–55. But in her *Giorgione Convegno* article she admitted not being able to identify the "particular historical incident" being depicted in the Marcello portrait ("Giorgionesque Portrait," 155). — A new interpretation of "*Il Bravo*" has been published by Sylvia Ferino in her catalogue entry (credited to Bruce Sutherland): *Titian. Prince of Painters*, exhibition catalogue, Washington, National Gallery (Venice: Marsilio, 1990), no. 13, 178–80. Ferino suggests that it represents Bacchus's arrest by order of Pentheus, a scene from Euripides' *Bacchae*. Should this theory be accepted, the visual connection between "*Il Bravo*," a painting of 1515–20, and Giorgione's Marcello portrait from the first decade would be explained by Titian's use of Giorgione's "action portrait" concept as a point of departure for inventing a scene of intense interchange between two antagonists in a classical scene. Despite Ferino's rejection of the story of Trebonius as the narrative that underlies the Marcello portrait, I believe it to be the best explanation so far offered for the tense confrontation between the two men.

so-far unexplored topic of homoerotic themes in Venetian portraiture.

Giorgione's invention of the knight and page portrait combined the double portrait, in which the major subject is given clear predominance over the secondary figure, with the narrative elements of an "action portrait," in which the principal subject interacts with a subordinate.[12] This particular variant of "the action portrait," moreover, introduced potentialities for homoerotic subjects in yet another way. The *Knight and Page* at Castle Howard[13] is susceptible to an idealizing, romantic interpretation that would connect it, for example, to the chivalric themes in Carpaccio's full-length *Portrait of a Young Man in Armor* (Lugano, Thyssen collection), which is dated 1510.[14] But sexual overtones become

---

[12] An important source for Giorgione's double portraits was the sculpted double portrait relief *all'antica*, a new type invented by Tullio Lombardo, of which two examples are known, in Venice and Vienna. Both Tullio's double portraits give roughly equal emphasis to the man and the woman, and both are "psychological action" portraits, which, like Giorgione's slightly later, combine narrative with portraiture. In each case the couple is shown responding dramatically to an (unexplained) event lying outside the boundaries of the art work. See Sarah Wilk, "Tullio Lombardo's 'Double-Portrait' Reliefs," *Marsyas* 16 (1972–73): 67–86 and idem, *The Sculpture of Tullio Lombardo. Studies in Sources and Meaning* (New York: Garland, 1978), 55–84; and Sheard, "Giorgione and Tullio Lombardo," *Giorgione, Atti del Convegno Internazionale* (Castelfranco Veneto, 1979), 201–11, where an example of Giorgione's "tutor and pupil" double-portrait type is discussed in relation to Tullio Lombardo's prior inventions (205–6). Tullio's Venice double-portrait is illustrated as fig. 169 (and in articles cited in n. 26 below). Both Tullio and Giorgione seem to have known Flemish examples of double portraits which were also "action portraits": for example, Jan van Eyck's *Portrait of a Noble and His Agent Making Up Accounts*, which was in the Lampognano family collection in Milan (Marcantonio Michiel, *Notizia*, as in n. 8, 54); Wilk, *Sculpture of Tullio Lombardo*, 59–67, discusses Tullio's northern sources.

[13] Pignatti, *Giorgione*, no. C. 4, 147 (pl. 228), panel, 21 x 18 cm.

[14] Allen Rosenbaum, *Old Master Paintings from the Collection of Baron Thyssen-Bornemisza*, exhibition catalogue (Washington, D.C.: International Exhibitions Foundation, 1979), no. 6, 88–90 (pl. 6, in color), *Young Knight in a Landscape (Francesco Maria della Rovere, Duke of Urbino)*, canvas, 218.5 x 151.5 cm. Rona Goffen, "Carpaccio's Portrait of a Young Knight: Identity and Meaning," *Arte Veneta* 37 (1983): 37–48, argues that the knight is not Della Rovere but Antonio da Montefeltro, illegitimate son of Duke Federigo and husband of Emilia Pia, a central character in Castiglione's *Cortegiano*.—The *Warrior with a Page-boy* known as "*Gattamelata*" (Uffizi 911) Pignatti, *Giorgione*, no. A. 13, 121 (pl. 126), canvas, 90 x 73 cm., has been given a fascinating interpretation as a theoretical painting dealing with Plinian questions about different categories and effects of light, given currency in Venice by Leonardo during his documented visit in 1500 (but possibly during an even earlier visit), by Alessandro Ballarin, "Una nuova prospettiva su Giorgione: la Ritrattistica degli anni 1500–03," in *Giorgione, Atti del Convegno*, 232–34. Ballarin's hypothesis provides a new understanding of what may have motivated the Uffizi picture, which I believe is not by Giorgione but by a follower of Giorgione, based on a composition the master invented. Most of Giorgione's portraits are interpreted by Ballarin, dating them to circa 1500–1503, as theoretical demonstrations of Leonardo's ideas about light (227–52).

more overt in versions of the type created by Giorgione's followers, for example Sebastiano del Piombo. His *Portrait of a Man in Armor* in the Wadsworth Atheneum, Hartford, was unrecognized as a knight and page portrait until recently because Sebastiano had overpainted the head of the black page, originally located on the left.[15] Now it is possible to discern that the page's facial expression of romantic pathos indicated an emotional involvement between the two men. Its subsequent overpainting leads one to ask whether the erotic overtones of the original composition led the sitter to change his mind and request the more conservative portrait type, striking thought it remains as a powerfully romantic image. Caravaggio's *Alof de Wignacourt with a Page* (Louvre) is an audacious elaboration of the knight and page type.[16]

Giorgione's *Self-portrait as David* in Braunschweig [fig. 4] is regarded as a true record of Giorgione's self-portrait concept even by critics who do not accept the painting itself as the original.[17] The engraving made

---

[15] Sheard, "Sebastiano's *Portrait of a Man in Armor* and the Birth of Romantic Portraiture in Venice," talk delivered at the Wadsworth Atheneum, Hartford, Conn., 15 May 1986. The head of the black page can be detected clearly through the veil of green paint now that excess layers of varnish and dirt have been removed from the painting. The cleaning was performed in 1980 by the Paintings Conservation Laboratory at the Metropolitan Museum. — An abundance of literary sources testifies to erotic relationships between masters and servants in the sixteenth century; James Saslow, *Ganymede in the Renaissance* (New Haven: Yale Univ. Press, 1986), esp. 155–60. Although Saslow illustrates a particularly provocative example of the "man and his page" portrait type as his fig. 4.8 (158: *Alessandro Alberti with a Page*, National-al Gallery, no. 1159), he does not discuss its portrait type (or the related one of "knight and page"), probably because he believes (oddly enough) that "homosexuality was prevalent but not expressed artistically in sixteenth-century Venice" (7).

[16] *The Age of Caravaggio*, exhibition catalog (New York: Metropolitan Museum, 1985) no. 94, 328–31, canvas, 194 x 134 cm. (catalogue entry by Mina Gregori). Wignacourt, portrayed full length in the dress armor of the Grand Master of the Knights of Malta holding a baton of command, stares off to his left while his page, splendidly attired in maroon satin and vermilion stockings and holding Wignacourt's impressive parade helmet and cape, casts a forthrightly erotic glance at the viewer (and by implication at the painter). Perhaps this aspect of Caravaggio's employment of the knight and page format is unprecedented. Although Gregori comments on the rarity of including a page in early seventeenth-century portraits, the precedents in Venetian and Lombard sixteenth-century painting, and Wignacourt's habit of surrounding himself with a multitude of young pages, she is silent on the page's disturbing erotic gaze.

[17] Ulrich-Museum Braunschweig, *Selbstbildnisse und Künstlerporträts von Lucas van Leyden bis Anton Raphael Mengs*, exhibition catalogue (Braunschweig, 1980) no. 1, 38–42 (with ill. in color), canvas, 52 x 43 cm.; bibliography, 42. The catalogue entry by Sabine Jacob accurately assesses the enormous importance of this picture. The exact date of Giorgione's *Self-portrait as David* is unknown, but we need not presume that its use of the David and Goliath metaphor depends on Michelangelo's *David* of 1501–1504. On the question of Michelangelo's and Giorgione's influence on each other, see Craig Hugh Smyth, "Michelangelo and Giorgione," in *Giorgione, Atti del*

of the painting by Wenceslas Hollar in 1650 [fig. 5] shows the work intact before its lower section was cut off.[18] The Hollar engraving indicates the surprising size and prominence of the head of Goliath, allowing the identification of the portrait with one mentioned in a 1528 inventory of the collection of Giovanni Grimani in Venice: "un ritratto di Zorzon di sua mano fatto per David e Golia" ("a portrait of Giorgione by his own hand, in the guise of David and Goliath").[19]

By portraying himself in the armor of David, Giorgione deemphasized the requirement of literal likeness that had prevailed in the mainly conservative tradition of Venetian portraiture up until that time. His self-image demonstrates his rejection of the typical concept of the artist as a respectable citizen, dignified, sagacious, and responsible—worthy of the respect of the oligarchs who were dispensing the patronage. As Giovanni Bellini's drawing of his brother Gentile suggests, this "respectable artist" image had been cultivated by Venetian artists who had been given important state and civic commissions.[20] Giorgione's *Self-portrait as David* [fig. 4] can thus be seen as a manifesto declaring a new definition of the artist and his relationship to society.

Convegno, 213–20, citing earlier opinions. Beverly Louise Brown, "Giorgione, Michelangelo and the 'Maniera Moderna,' " in *Renaissance Studies in Honor of Craig Hugh Smyth*, ed. Andrew Morrogh et al. (Florence: Giunti Barbèra, 1985) 2:97–108, disagrees with Smyth. — Ballarin breaks new ground in discussing the dark background of the Braunschweig *Self-portrait* as an aspect of Giorgione's reception of the art and thought of Leonardo: "Una nuova prospettiva su Giorgione," 232, 243–44 (nn. 25–27). — The present article deals only with independent self-portraits, not with ones that occur in narrative or religious contexts.

[18] G. Parthey, *Wenzel Hollar, Beschreibendes Verzeichnis seiner Kupferstiche* (Berlin, 1853), no. 1408.

[19] Pignatti, *Giorgione*, 145. The fact that Giorgione's *Self-portrait as David* was in Giovanni Grimani's collection may suggest the specific agency by which Giorgione came to be influenced by the painting procedures, formats (for example, the half- or bust-length religious narrative close-up), and some individual disquieting motifs in the work of Hieronymus Bosch (George M. Richter, *Giorgio da Castelfranco* [Chicago: Univ. of Chicago Press, 1937], 50 and 65). Lorne Campbell has recently drawn attention to a plausible explanation for the presence of four panels and two triptychs by Bosch in the Palazzo Ducale, Venice: i.e., that they went to the Venetian *Signoria* as part of the donation of ancient and modern art works made to his native city by Cardinal Domenico Grimani in 1523. "Notes on Netherlandish pictures in the Veneto in the Fifteenth and Sixteenth Centuries," *Burlington Magazine* 123 (1981): 473. Grimani's nephew Marino, also a cardinal, owned two additional Bosch panels in 1528 (Campbell, n. 46, citing the basic article by Paschini). Without postulating that Giorgione saw paintings by Bosch owned by the Grimani, Bosch's visit to Venice soon after 1500 suggests another avenue of interchange between the two painters. See Leonard J. Slatkes, "Hieronymus Bosch and Italy," *Art Bulletin* 57 (1975): 335–45.

[20] Peter Dreyer, *Kupferstichkabinett Berlin, Italienische Zeichnungen* (Stuttgart and Zurich, 1978), no. 13 (KdZ 5170), pl. 13. I will discuss the "respectable artist" image in Florence at a later point.

Giorgione's self-portrait combines the "look out of the picture," which as far as we know was first employed for an extant, independent self-portrait by Jan van Eyck, with an overt expression of emotion, something that was exceedingly rare in earlier self-portraits. That the emotion was meant to be interpreted as melancholy is suggested by the scowl. Yet a scowl was also a mark of watchfulness and determination—as used for example by Donatello in his *St. George*, made for the Armorers' Guild niche at Or San Michele in Florence[21]—and thus a sign of courage and strength.

The scowl as an emblem of courage, strength, and determination was exaggerated to the point of caricature by Verrocchio in his bronze equestrian portrait of *Bartolomeo Colleoni*, an obvious source for Giorgione.[22] One of the *Warriors* on the Tomb of Doge Andrea Vendramin by Tullio Lombardo (Venice, SS. Giovanni e Paolo), carved by 1494, wears a scowl which is less emblematic, more believable than *Colleoni*'s.[23] Perhaps as an implied improvement on the one-dimensionality and artificiality of Verrocchio's famous scowl, that of Tullio Lombardo's *Warrior* is complex and nuanced, combining anxious watchfulness with determination to be steadfast, the promise of force as necessary with the reality of sorrow.[24] The possibility that the *Warrior*'s face contains

---

[21] H. W. Janson, *The Sculpture of Donatello*, 2 vols. (Princeton: Princeton Univ. Press, 1957), 1: pls. 26–32. 2: 23–29. More recently, Mosche Barasch, "Character and Physiognomy: Bocchi on Donatello's *St. George*. A Renaissance Text on Expression in Art," *Journal of the History of Ideas* 36 (1975): 413–30 and Bonnie A. Bennett and David G. Wilkins, *Donatello* (Mt. Kisco, New York: Moyer Bell, 1984): 199–200, with references in notes.

[22] *The Equestrian Monument to Bartolomeo Colleoni* was set up on the Campo SS. Giovanni e Paolo in Venice by 19 November 1495 and ceremonially unveiled on 21 March 1496. Verrocchio had completed the model before his death in the summer of 1488, and the work was cast and gilded by Alessandro Leopardi (d. 1522/23), a Venetian goldsmith, jeweler, die engraver, bronze caster, and architect. See Gunther Passavant, *Verrocchio*, trans. Katherine Watson (London: Phaidon, 1969), cat. no. 17, 185–87, and figs. 62 ff., esp. 67, a detail of the head. For the convention of the leonine scowl in ancient and Renaissance ruler portraiture see Peter Meller, "Physiognomical Theory in Renaissance Heroic Portraits," in *The Renaissance and Mannerism. Studies in Western Art. Acts of the Twentieth International Congress of the History of Art* (Princeton: Princeton Univ. Press, 1963), 2:67–69.

[23] Sheard, "The Tomb of Doge Andrea Vendramin in Venice by Tullio Lombardo" (Ph.D. diss., Yale University, 1971), 205–9. For illustration, see John Pope-Hennessy, *Italian Renaissance Sculpture* (New York: Phaidon, 1958), pl. 140. The photograph in the 1985 paperback edition of Pope-Hennessy's book (New York: Vintage) is less clear. It is highly likely that, during the interval between Verrocchio's death and the Vendramin *Warrior*, Tullio Lombardo had a chance to study Verrocchio's model for the *Colleoni*.

[24] In this case the melancholy or sorrow must be understood in the figure's context as a tomb mourner or *pleureur*. Tullio Lombardo modernized this originally

elements of self-portraiture[25] suggests yet another motivation for its scowl; its closeness to the male head portrayed in Tullio's *Double Portrait* relief in Venice (Ca' d'Oro) is one reason Alison Luchs has concluded that the relief is a self-portrait of Tullio with his wife.[26]

The association between the artistic temperament and melancholy, which became commonplace in the sixteenth century, was still rather new when Giorgione employed it in his self-portrait, probably painted shortly after 1500.[27] Because of the association, the virtue of courage to

---

medieval tomb feature by transforming it into a remarkably correct reconstruction of a Roman antique cuirassed statue with a facial expression of anxiety, tension, and sadness rendered with striking psychological naturalism.

[25] Sheard, "The Tomb of Doge Andrea Vendramin," 209. Anne Markham Schulz suggests that the *"Mars"* carved by Antonio Rizzo for the Arco Foscari in the Ducal Palace, Venice, contains elements of self-portraiture. *Antonio Rizzo Sculptor and Architect* (Princeton: Princeton Univ. Press, 1983), 30, figs. 36 and 37. She dates the *"Mars"* to the late 1460s (28), but this seems more precise than the visual evidence warrants. A dating of circa 1469–1475 is more reasonable. From the standpoint of the appearance of psychological naturalism in Venetian sculpture, the *"Mars"* is a pioneering work. One wonders whether Rizzo's experience as a military engineer during Venice's war with the Turks (at the seige of Scutari in 1474) could have played some part in his achievement of the expression of anxiety in the *"Mars."*

[26] "Tullio Lombardo's Ca' d'Oro Relief: A Self-Portrait with the Artist's Wife?," *Art Bulletin* 71 (June 1989): 230–36; also see Sarah Wilk, n. 12 above, and Sheard, "Giorgione and Tullio Lombardo" (n. 12). For the resemblance between the Vendramin *Warrior*'s face and the man in the Ca' d'Oro relief, see Sheard, "Tomb of Doge Andrea Vendramin," 209. — A scowling expression, with furrowed brow, employed in a portrait of a man who was not a soldier or military commander, is extremely rare in the fifteenth century. I believe that Mantegna's examples (see below and n. 29) established the tradition of the scowling self-portrait in fifteenth-century north Italy, so that by the time Tullio carved the Venice *Double Portrait* in the early to mid 1490s, a few years before Giorgione's Braunschweig *Self-portrait as David*, the scowl was beginning to be understood as an attribute of the artist, with the meanings discussed below (see nn. 27 and 37). It is important to note that Mantegna's influence on Tullio's artistic thinking was decisive, beginning when Tullio was a boy in Padua during the four years his father was in residence there (1464–1467/68).

[27] The painting documents the presence in Venice of the idea that the melancholic temperament was a concomitant of exceptional artistic ability, an ancient notion revived by Marsilio Ficino in his *De vita triplici*, first published in 1489: for a critical text and translation with scholarly commentary, see Carol V. Kaske and John R. Clark, *Marsilio Ficino: Three Books on Life*, Medieval & Renaissance Texts & Studies, 57 (Binghamton, NY, 1989). The best discussion of Ficino's attitudes to melancholy, including *De vita*, is Raymond Klibansky, Erwin Panofsky, and Fritz Saxl, *Saturn and Melancholy: Studies in the History of Natural Philosophy, Religion and Art* (New York: Basic Books, 1964), 42, 251–74. Stanley W. Jackson, M.D., *Melancholia and Depression. From Hippocratic Times to Modern Times* (New Haven and London, Yale Univ. Press, 1986) places Ficino's thought in a long chronological perspective of the history of medicine. Jackson, relying on Klibansky et al., points out that Ficino, possessed of a melancholy temperament himself and born under the sign of Saturn, veered between bemoaning this Saturnine nature as a burdensome curse and appreciating it as a "source of probing intelligence and creativity" (100). — The idea that genius and

which the scowl alludes can be interpreted as a wished-for bulwark against the onslaughts of the artist's own double-edged temperament. An artist's struggle must be directed both within and without, Giorgione's adoption of the metaphor of David's persona suggests. He combats persecution born of envy, the fate of the victorious David at the hands of Saul.[28] Anger at unjust calumny born of envy was a recurrent leitmotif in the life of Andrea Mantegna; and Mantegna's self-portrait bust of about 1480 in his funerary chapel in S. Andrea, Mantua [fig. 7] is an earlier instance of a scowling self-portrait.[29]

---

melancholy go together can be traced to pseudo-Aristotle (*Problemata* 30.1): "The question raised in the Aristotelian *Problemata* was 'Why is it that all those who have become eminent in philosophy or poetry or the arts are clearly of an atrabilious temperament, and some of them to such an extent as to be affected by diseases caused by black bile?'" (Jackson, 31–32). Klibansky, Panofsky, and Saxl's brilliant and penetrating discussion of Problem 30.1, in which the authors show how Platonism and Aristotelianism interpenetrate and balance one another in putting together the conception of frenzy accompanying the highest creative gifts with Aristotle's humoral theory and theory of the "mean" (Klibansky et al., *Saturn and Melancholy*, 3–43, esp. 37–42), has never been surpassed and Jackson's treatment of the subject draws on it extensively. — In Venice during the 1480s and 1490s, received ideas about Aristotle's thought were undergoing a radical transformation, led by Ermolao Barbaro and Girolamo Donato, humanists who were equally interested in Neoplatonic ideas, especially as articulated by contemporaries in Florence. See Vittore Branca, "Ermolao Barbaro and late Quattrocento Venetian Humanism," in J. R. Hale, ed., *Renaissance Venice* (London: Faber and Faber, 1973), 218–43, and Margaret King, *Venetian Humanism in an Age of Patrician Dominance* (Princeton: Princeton Univ. Press, 1986), 168, 182–91, 322–23, 366–68.

[28] Jaynie Anderson was the first to suggest that Giorgione's use of the persona of David alluded to phases of the biblical story that take place *after* his victory over Goliath ("Giorgionesque Portrait" 154).

[29] Ronald Lightbown, *Mantegna* (Berkeley: Univ. of California Press, 1986) cat. no. 62, 455–56, and 130–32, furnishes a sensitive and detailed discussion of Mantegna's bronze self-portrait, yet, curiously, he fails to mention the striking and unusual feature of its scowl, and omits from his references an article by David Summers which elucidates contemporary meanings of the scowl: "David's Scowl," in Sheard and Paoletti, eds., *Collaboration in Italian Renaissance Art*, 113–24. The frowning gigantic head Mantegna painted on the left exterior face of the apse arch in the Ovetari Chapel (Eremitani Church, Padua) as a signature and pendant to the self-portrait head of Nicolò Pizzolo on the right-hand side, between 1450 and the death of Pizzolo in the summer or early autumn of 1453 (executed most likely in 1450 or 1451), may be the earliest scowling self-portrait to have survived into our century—both were destroyed in the bombing of 1944. See the illustration in Sergio Bettini and Lionello Puppi, *La Chiesa degli Eremitani di Padova* (Vicenza: N. Pozza, 1970), fig. 137. Lightbown seems to believe that the head on the right (cf. Bettini and Puppi, fig. 119, captioned as "N. Pizolo, Testa gigantesca"—also illustrated on the right in Lightbown's own fig. 8), is Mantegna's self-portrait. That head is more stylized and tightly painted than its pendant, and lacks not only its vigor and painterly freedom, but its frown, furrowed forehead, and more naturalistic rendering of the eyes. It is hard to see how this confusion could have arisen, since it is quite

Fig. 4. Giorgione, *Self-portrait as David*, Braunschweig.

Fig. 5. Wenzel Hollar, Giorgione's *Self-portrait as David*, engraving

Fig. 6. Giorgione, *Self-portrait*, Budapest, Szépművészeti Múzeum

Fig. 7. Andrea Mantegna, *Self-portrait bust*, Mantua, Sant'Andrea

Fig. 8. Caravaggio, *David with the Head of Goliath*, Rome, Galleria Borghese

But the artist's most demanding struggle must be directed within, against melancholy itself, melancholy that generates incapacitating lassitude even as its reveries may be nurturing profound insights. The artist's imperative to grapple with his melancholy announces a modern theme that seems remote from the era of Duccio and Giotto, although not altogether alien by the late quattrocento.[30]

So many allusions and themes are condensed within this new kind of self-image, then, that the kinds of analogies with the density and compression of poetic meaning that gave rise to the term *poesia* appear to apply to Giorgione's self-portrait and his other portraiture *concetti* as well as to his pastoral scenes and unusual combinations of religious and secular narrative with allegory. Unlike Mantegna's bronze bust which was set within a stone and porphyry tondo on the wall in his funerary chapel [fig. 7], Giorgione's *Self-portrait* lacked a funerary context that would provide the occasion for self-immortalization. Thus, it avoided most of the conventions of heroic or idealizing self-portraiture or portraiture of poets that had so far been established using models from classical antiquity. Yet the sharp turn of the head in both Mantegna's and Giorgione's self portraits, a device whose effects in setting up a new psychological intimacy between sitter and viewer have already been discussed, was in fact a revival of an antique portraiture convention, invented originally by Hellenistic sculptors to convey just such an allusion of an interrupted moment.[31]

However, Mantegna's bust employs the device literally [fig. 7] to convey the effect that he is turning abruptly to scrutinize the visitor who enters the funerary chapel. The effect of the sharp turn of the head in Giorgione's *Self-portrait* [fig. 4] does not depend upon a specific location of the painting in space. Intensified animation results from the vigor of the head's movement as judged in relation to the three-quarter position of the body, which forces a more extreme twist of the head to the figure's right than in Mantegna's bust. Giorgione's decision to

---

clear, from the way both heads face (inwards), which side of the arch each occupied, and Lightbown accepts earlier scholars' arguments that Mantegna's self-portrait would naturally occupy a position corresponding to the left side of the chapel where the stories of St. James, that were delegated to him, were to be painted (*Mantegna*, 396).

[30] On Dürer's *Melencolia* I, see now Philip Sohm, "Dürer's *Melancolia* I: The Limits of Knowledge," *Studies in the History of Art* 9 (1980): 13–32, with references to past literature in notes.

[31] In Gisela M. A. Richter, *The Portraits of the Greeks*, ed. R. R. R. Smith (Ithaca: Cornell Univ. Press, 1984), cf. the following: *Alexander the Great* (Louvre), fig. 191, 227; "*Aesop*" (Villa Albani), fig. 43, 79; *Chrysippos* (British Museum), figs. 71 and 72, 106–7; *Karneades* (cast-Ravenna), fig. 113, 153; *Pseudo-Seneca* (Naples), fig. 151, 191; *Xenophon* (Alexandria), fig. 179, 216.

heighten this contrast can be inferred by comparing his Braunschweig *Self-portrait* to a small oil sketch on paper in Budapest [fig. 6] that shows the artist in contemporary dress with an open collar and white shirt; an area of deep shadow separates the brightly lit shirt from the jutting chin.[32] According to Klára Garas's authoritative evaluation, this painting's quality is exceptionally high, despite its poor condition.[33] That it was an independent self-portrait, or a study for one, and not a copy of the Braunschweig picture, is suggested by its relationship to the engraved portrait of Giorgione in Giorgio Vasari's collection of artists' portraits, in which he also wears contemporary dress.[34] The oil sketch, which can be dated about 1503, gives the impression of being a more literal record of Giorgione's features than the Braunschweig *Self-portrait*, and in it the painter's angry, sullen look is even more exaggerated. An idealized version of Giorgione's melancholy self-image is, I believe, present as the head of St. Sebastian in Titian's *St. Mark Enthroned*.[35]

---

[32] Andor Pigler, ed., *Museum der Bildenden Künste Szépművészeti Múzeum, Budapest, Katalog der Galerie Alter Meister*, 2 vols. (Tübingen: E. Wasmuth, 1968) 1: no. 86, 266–68; ill. in 2, pl. 76, oil on paper on panel, 31.5 x 28.5 cm. (cut down from a larger format), attributed to a follower of Giorgione. The earliest inventory reference, while the painting belonged to Bartolommeo della Nave, called it "his picture made by himself" (Pigler, 266).

[33] "Giorgione et Giorgionisme au XVIIe Siècle," *Bulletin du Musée Hongrois des Beaux Arts* 25 (1964): 77–78. A similar assessment of the small painting's quality and high degree of interest is that of Ludwig Baldass, in "Eine Porträtskizze vom jungen Tizian," *Zeitschrift für Kunstwissenschaft* 9 (1955): 193, an article about a comparable portrait sketch attributed to Titian in the Kunsthistorisches Museum, Vienna. Baldass stressed the Budapest painting's rapid and sketchy handling, which implies a directness and immediacy possible only if it had been made directly in front of the model. — Jaynie Anderson believes the handling in the Budapest sketch is too crude to permit its attribution as an autograph Giorgione (verbal communication, February 1988) but to me this crudeness or directness is intentional and may be thought of as part of the willed aggressivity that the image shares with the Braunschweig *Self-portrait*. Another determining factor in the Budapest *Self-portrait*'s style is its status as a rough sketch on paper, only later laid down on panel.

[34] See Wolfram Prinz, *Vasaris Sammlung von Künstlerbildnissen* (Florence, 1966), 109. The presence of the Budapest painting in its larger format (before being cut down) in two paintings of Archduke Leopold Wilhelm's Picture Gallery by David Teniers likewise suggests its existence as an independent self-portrait. See Pignatti, *Giorgione*, fig. 219. I cannot agree with Pignatti's opinion that a person other than the model for Giorgione's Braunschweig *Self-portrait* is represented (Pignatti, *Giorgione*, 146). Moreover, this is not, as he claims, Garas's opinion (cf. article cited in n. 33). — Vasari did not take his cue from his engraved portrait of Giorgione, frowning and pathos-filled, when composing his literary portrait, in which Giorgione appears as a suave, charming, handsome, ingratiating, elegant, and sociable "courtier," who mingled with wealthy patrician patrons, played the lute and sang at their dinner parties, and carried on an active love life which ultimately resulted in his death when he contracted plague from a companion in 1510 (*Le vite*, 4:92).

[35] *St. Mark Enthroned* (Venice, S. Maria della Salute) was painted as a memorial

The importance of this largely overlooked work is not confined to its status as one of the earliest oil sketches for a painting that has survived. It demonstrates that Giorgione's projection of a scowling, fierce self-image, and its theoretical implications for a conception of the power of art and the artist, were independent of the biblical figure of David. The pseudo-Aristotelian *Physiognomonica*, in which a "cloudy brow" is interpreted as a symbol of audacity or anger, has been claimed by David Summers as a literary source in the background of the scowl Michelangelo carved on the face of his *David* of 1501–1504.[36] Cesare Ripa built on the Aristotelian foundation when he defined *Audacia* as "the vice of those who little consider the difficulty of some great act, and presuming too much of their own powers, believe that they will easily attain their end."[37] Anger and audacity, as well as melancholy,

---

to the cessation of the plague in 1510, according to Joseph Crowe and Giovanni Battista Cavalcaselle, *Life and Times of Titian*, 2 vols. (London, 1877), 1:144–48. If so, the commission provided a suitable occasion for a funerary portrait and memorial to Giorgione in the form of a romanticized likeness of his mentor, colleague, and (perhaps) rival. For catalogue entry and color illustration after its recent cleaning and restoration, see *Titian. Prince of Painters*, as in n. 11, 151–53. David Rosand, *Titian* (New York: Abrams, 1978), 68, argues that *St. Mark Enthroned*, identified as Titian's first independent monumental commission, was painted earlier than 1510, about 1508–1509. To him, the figures of Roch and Sebastian testify to Titian's study of Giorgione's art in their romantic physiognomies, a valid observation even if the painting postdated Giorgione's death. The reader is urged to compare the face of St. Sebastian with Giorgione's Braunschweig *Self-portrait*. St. Sebastian may, on the other hand, be an homage to Giorgione executed while the older painter was still alive. If my interpretation is correct, Titian softened the angry, melancholic expression Giorgione chose to hand down to posterity and rendered his face and body as nobly beautiful, creating in visual terms an alternative tradition that Vasari later followed in his verbal portrait.

[36] "David's Scowl," as in n. 29, 113–16.

[37] Summers sets forth the uses of the term *audacia* in classical texts to reveal its connotations of highly skilled artifice and the artist's claim to the perfection of his art and the overcoming of all difficulties, predecessors and rivals, "David's Scowl," 116–17. Michelangelo, in projecting his self-conception onto his marble *David*, wittily compared his own seemingly insurmountable task of carving a gigantic statue of David from a too shallow, damaged marble block (itself an *Audacia*, following Pliny's usage), to the daunting prospect of a shepherd boy having to attack a giant with only a sling and a stone. There is also the implication that David/Michelangelo *becomes* a giant *because of* the *Audacia* that spurs him on to risk all with the hope of triumphing ("Davicte cholla fromba e io collarcho. Michelagniolo" is what the sculptor jotted on a sheet of studies for the bronze and marble *Davids*, now in the Louvre). The *David* is thus a metaphorical self-portrait. The basis for such a reading of the statue was laid down by Charles Seymour, Jr., *Michelangelo's David* (Pittsburgh: Univ. of Pittsburgh, 1967); and it has been enlarged and deepened by Kathleen Weil-Garris Brandt, "Michelangelo's Self-Portraits," a talk delivered at the Boston Museum of Fine Arts, 20 November 1985. Tullio Lombardo's Vendramin *Warrior* seems to have been among Michelangelo's sources for the scowl of his *David*.

are proclaimed as necessary emotional baggage for the artist. Giorgione's Budapest self-portrait sketch thus suggests that now, paradoxically, what is a vice for ordinary men becomes for the artist a necessary *virtue*—prideful *Audacia*—if the difficult problems art poses are to be overcome.[38] The role of *Audacia* in an artist's self-created image thus parallels that of melancholy—a vice for ordinary people (*acedia*, lassitude or lethargy), but a virtue for the artist. Seeds of the future release of the artist from the norms and boundaries of commonplace morality may be glimpsed here.

Caravaggio's *David with the Head of Goliath* in the Borghese Gallery[39] [fig. 8] prompts a somewhat different reading of Giorgione's *Self-portrait as David*, although I would argue that the interpretations are not mutually exclusive but co-exist as legitimate associations with the biblical parallel. Caravaggio's picture draws attention to the influence on him of several of Giorgione's pictorial ideas.[40] In Caravaggio's painting the head of Goliath is a self-portrait, while David portrays a shop assistant—in the words of Iacomo Manilli, the custodian of the Villa in 1650, "in quella testa volle ritrarre se stesso, e nel David ritrasse il suo Caravaggino" ("in that head [viz. Goliath's] he wished to portray himself,

---

Michelangelo would have encountered it during his brief stay in Venice in October of 1494 (Sheard, "Tomb of Doge Andrea Vendramin," 209). Cf. Craig Hugh Smyth, "Venice and the Emergence of the High Renaissance in Florence: Observations and Questions," in *Florence and Venice: Comparisons and Relations: Acts of Two Conferences at Villa I Tatti in 1976/1977*, 2 vols. (Florence: La Nuova Italia, 1979–1980), 1:211–13. Smyth elaborates on an earlier suggestion made by the writer that Tullio Lombardo's *Adam* from the Vendramin Tomb (New York, Metropolitan Museum) likewise inspired several features of Michelangelo's *Bacchus*. Smyth and Charles Seymour, Jr. had arrived at these conclusions independently, during the mid-1960s.

[38] Summers drew this same inference from Michelangelo's *David*, "David's Scowl," 117. Twentieth-century psychiatric thinking about clinical depression, our term for what was formerly thought of as pathological melancholy (see n. 27) has come increasingly to stress the emotions of anger and rage as components of depression (Michael Sheard, M.D., Professor of Psychiatry, Yale, verbal communication). Michelangelo's and Giorgione's self-portraits, in their combining of the two states, anticipate these modern conclusions, where artists' personalities are concerned.

[39] *Age of Caravaggio*, no. 97, 338–41 (detail in color, 340), canvas, 125 x 101 cm. (cat. entry by Mina Gregori).

[40] Caravaggio's uses of Giorgione's pictorial inventions are mentioned by Gregori in her essay on "Caravaggio Today," for example: "Implicitly Caravaggio indicated Giorgione as the recognized authority and theoretical reference point—the inspiration for his method of representing nature and for painting directly from life without preparatory drawings" (*Age of Caravaggio*, 31). The early homoerotic paintings Gregori refers to as "compositions of half-length figures, which reevoke the poetic aura of Giorgionesque painting, and seem to possess an erotic or homosexual significance" (32). See Donald Posner, "Caravaggio's Homo-erotic Early Works," *Art Quarterly* 34 (1971): 301–24.

and, as David, he portrayed his 'little Caravaggio' ").[41] The head of Goliath in Giorgione's *Self-portrait*, by contrast [fig. 5], may represent someone who had "lost his head" over the artist, just as in Giorgione's *Judith* in Leningrad, where the head of Holofernes is most likely a portrait of the lover of the lady for whose cabinet he commissioned the panel.[42]

To give a full account of Giorgione's many and varied sources of inspiration in the invention of so many new portrait types and strategies for engaging the viewer in novel relationships of intimacy, and eliciting new categories and combinations of response, is obviously not possible here.[43] To shed further light on the originality of Giorgione's self-portraits may, however, be possible by comparing them to two famous Florentine sculpted self-portraits and to one of the most decisively influential northern self-portraits, Jan van Eyck's. In consequence of a fresh consideration of the "look out of the picture" that Van Eyck's self-portrait introduced, I will argue that Andrea del Castagno's *Portrait of a Man* in the National Gallery, Washington [fig. 11] is also a self-portrait. The point at which the "look out of the picture" became disassociated with self-portraiture in Italian painting can, I further propose, be precisely defined as the portraits of Antonello da Messina.

The traditions of self-portraiture in fifteenth-century Italy that Giorgione was working against had their origins in Florence around mid-century, in the art of sculpture. Ghiberti's example was decisive for this development. He placed the later of his two bronze self-portraits on the frame of the Gates of Paradise [fig. 9], his second set of doors for the Florentine Baptistry, completed in 1452. Richard Krautheimer dated this second self-portrait to *circa* 1448, when Ghiberti was about seventy and had recently completed his autobiography.[44] The self Ghiberti

---

[41] His shop assistant, who modeled himself on the painter. *Age of Caravaggio*, 338.

[42] Basic information about the picture, with the report of the technical examination that revealed a keyhole (demonstrating that the panel once served as a cabinet door), is in Tamara Fomiciova, "The History of Giorgione's 'Judith' and its Restoration," *Burlington Magazine* 115 (1973): 417–20. I cannot agree with Teresio Pignatti's proposal that the head of Holofernes in the *Judith* is a self-portrait of Giorgione ("La 'Giuditta' diversa di Giorgione," *Giorgione, Atti del Convegno* [as in n.1] 269–71).

[43] For example, it is necessary to omit the crucial topic of the role of religious painting in generating devices like the "look out of the picture" and the sharply turned head as an expression of pathos, that were originally employed as strategies for engendering religious experiences. There is much suggestive material on this topic in Sixten Ringbom, *Icon to Narrative. The Rise of the Dramatic Close-up in Fifteenth-Century Devotional Painting*, 2d. ed. (Doornspuk, The Netherlands, Davaco, 1984).

[44] *Lorenzo Ghiberti*, 2d. ed., 2 vols. (Princeton: Princeton Univ. Press, 1970), 1:9–11. For Ghiberti's earlier self-portrait, placed (as a kind of signature) on the North Door,

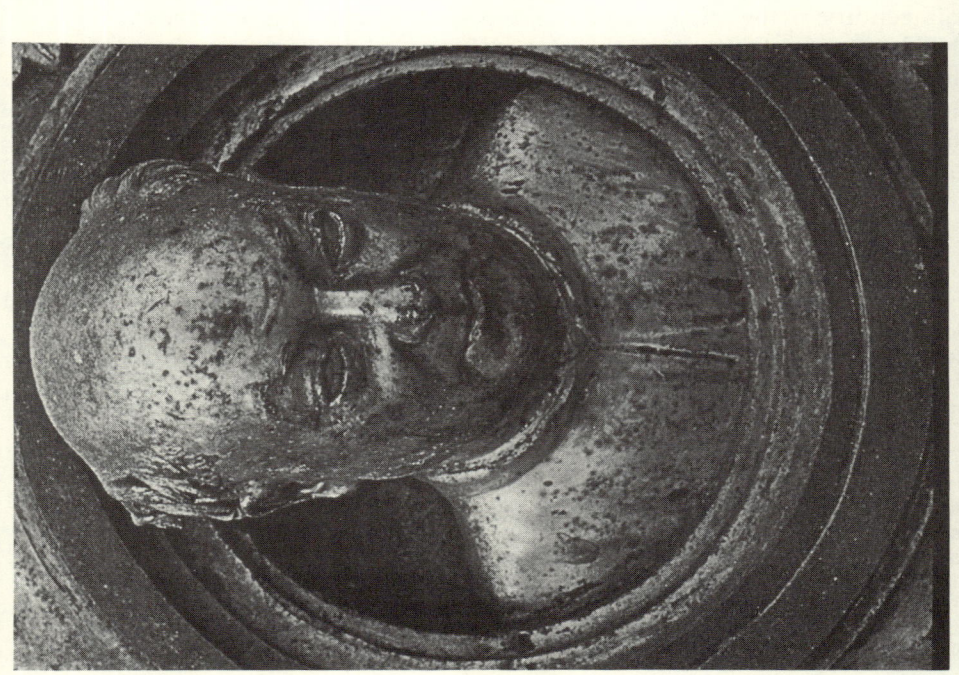

Fig. 9. Lorenzo Ghiberti, *Self-portrait*, Florence, Baptistry,

Fig. 10. Leon Battista Alberti, *Self-portrait*, National Gallery

Fig. 11. Andrea del Castagno, *Portrait of a Man*, National Gallery of Art, Andrew W. Mellon Collection, 17

portrays is made up of character traits, like intelligence and sagacity, that were expected to accompany the outstanding professional achievement that, it was hoped, would lead an artist to some degree of social and material security. Ghiberti's innate artistic talent was nurtured by his stepfather Bartolo di Michele, who trained him as a goldsmith. By 1450, the sculptor's superb technique in the casting and chasing of bronze reliefs had made him famous. Despite his contemporaries' belief that his birth was illegitimate, Ghiberti's artistic triumphs enabled him to acquire the status of a respected citizen and a degree of material wealth, including a small château, that surpassed what most artists of his time or the previous century managed to accumulate.

Ghiberti's own conception of himself, his achievements, and his status can be deduced from his *Commentarii*.[45] There we find the image of a "creative intellectual" whose insightful intelligence is ranked highest on the implicit scale of values, an artist no longer looked down on as a mere practitioner of mechanical arts, even though his particular *virtù* demands "a delicate and profound control of the hand." This image of an artist corresponds to the one that Filippo Villani had publicized in his *De origine civitatis Florentiae et eiusdem famosis civibus*. The idea that an artist's self-definition could include emotion or a representation of ongoing conscious experience is foreign to the concept of the artist as respected, wise citizen. No particular emotion registers on Ghiberti's countenance in his self-portrait [fig. 9], even though as a sculptor Ghiberti was a pioneer in the depiction of believable expressions of emotion on the faces of his *Prophets*.[46]

Alberti's *Self-portrait* plaque [fig. 10] shows that the bust of a clean-shaven man about thirty years old with "noble, forceful head" and flame-shaped curls that recall antique bronzes.[47] To the right is Alberti's abbreviated signature in revived Roman lettering, and a winged eye, Alberti's *impresa* with the motto "*Quid tum?*," appears between the chin and the knot at his throat.[48] Addressing the image to his fellow citi-

---

2: pl. 136a. Ghiberti's sculpted self-portraits are independent of the biblical personages they accompany on the frames of his Baptistry doors.

[45] *Lorenzo Ghibertis Denkwürdigkeiten (I Commentarii)*, ed. Julius von Schlosser, 2 vols. in 1 (Berlin: J. Bard, 1912); cf. Krautheimer, *Ghiberti*, vol. 1, chap. 20.

[46] English translation of excerpts from Villani quoted in John Larner, "The Artist and the Intellectuals in 14th-Century Italy," *History*, n. s., 54 (1969): 26. According to Larner, it is not possible to date the composition of Villani's *On the famous citizens of Florence* any more precisely than to the period 1376–1404.

[47] G. F. Hill, *Portrait Medals of Italian Artists of the Renaissance* (London: Medici Society, 1912), 30; John Pope-Hennessy, *Renaissance Bronzes from the Samuel H. Kress Collection* (London: Phaidon, 1965), no. 1, 7.

[48] Joan Gadol's reference to the hieroglyph of the winged eye as "Alberti's

zens in Florence, as Ghiberti did with his self-portraits,[49] would have been impossible for Alberti since his family had been exiled from Florence before his birth. Instead, Alberti speaks to a restricted circle of cultivated patrons and humanists to which his position as a secretary in the papal chancery had given him access. These men would have understood the visual allusions to classical art that the hairstyle, the bust in profile, and the knotted toga were meant to convey, and the reference to the mysteries of Egyptian hieroglyphs evoked by Alberti's personal *impresa* of the winged eye. Yet the profile presentation separates him from the viewer and locates the artist in an ideal realm apart. It is not an intimate portrait, even if addressed to intimates.

Is victory in the competition between the moderns and ancients being announced here also? Written in 1436, probably about the time this plaque was made, the dedication of *Della pittura*, the Italian translation of *De pictura*, tells how, on his first visit to his family's native city, Alberti had been overwhelmed by the beauty and technical brilliance of Florence's contemporary art and architecture. He especially praises Brunelleschi, the dedicatee, and singles out Donatello, Ghiberti, Luca della Robbia, and Masaccio as other artists able to "discover unheard-of and never-before-seen arts and sciences without teachers or without any model."[50] Since they have surpassed the ancients in *ingegno*, "our fame," he says, reflecting his sense of membership in this group, should outstrip that of the ancient artists. Whereas the *all'antica* mode of Alberti's *Self-portrait* has often been taken as a sign of his evident admiration for his classical predecessors in architecture and literature, a feeling of superiority and triumph over these revered antecedents ought also to be acknowledged. After all, the invention of single-point perspective which Alberti set forth in *De pictura* had been unknown to them.

Ghiberti, on the other hand, as we know from the *Commentarii*, al-

---

symbol of [the] quasi-divine act of 'rational seeing', a mode of imaginative vision which came to encompass all his aesthetic ideas in its gaze," alluding to the eye as symbol of the Divine in the fourth-century *Hieroglyphica*, sums up its likely meaning: *Leon Battista Alberti. Universal Man of the Early Renaissance* (Chicago: Univ. of Chicago Press, 1969), 69, with an illustration of the portrait medal of Alberti by Matteo de' Pasti (fig. 21) that permits comparison between the literal likeness/profile mode employed by De' Pasti and the heroic, *all'antica* mode Alberti himself chose for his self-portrait. Cf. Renée D. Watkins, "L. B. Alberti's Emblem, the Winged Eye, and His Name, Leo," *Mitteilungen des Kunsthistorischen Instituts in Florenz* 9 (1960): 256–58, and (still essential) Edgar Wind, *Pagan Mysteries in the Renaissance* (New York: Norton, 1968), 231 ff.

[49] Fig. 9 and Krautheimer, *Ghiberti*, 2: pl. 136a.
[50] Alberti, *On Painting*, trans. John R. Spencer, rev. ed. (New Haven: Yale Univ. Press, 1966), 40.

though justifiably proud of his creation of a new kind of pictorial relief, seems not to have conceived of his art as something fundamentally new, but rather as a continuation of what had been begun by illustrious trecento predecessors, executed in a personal style that was uniquely his own. The radical cultural advance that Alberti associates with his own generation, Ghiberti locates at the beginning of the trecento, with the renewal of art brought about by Giotto.

In Alberti's *Self-portrait* [fig. 10], perhaps the superiority being claimed is not restricted to the realm of art. Its forms and style suggest an allusion to Stoic moral superiority reminiscent of Alberti's remark that "Fortune yokes only those who submit to her,"[51] a remark which appears to be a veiled, but proud, reference to the overcoming of the disaster Alberti and his brother suffered when unscrupulous family members deprived them of their inheritance after the deaths of their father and uncle. The Stoic virtues of forbearance and tenacity enabled Alberti to overcome this blow of fortune and eventually to triumph, albeit in a sphere different from the wealth and social prominence the Alberti family had formerly enjoyed. Here the *all'antica* profile convention is not accompanied by the literalism of representation that often appears in profile portraits of quattrocento rulers;[52] its new expression in a classical style yields a complexity and richness for the artist's presentation of an expanded self, a self which reaches out to claim intellectual and moral superiority in rivalry with both ancient art and philosophy, and which emphasizes *ingegno* more than technical prowess, as may be deduced from the prominence of a cryptic *impresa* so close to the head in profile.

Once we turn to painted portraits, and attempt to trace the interrelationships between an artist's self-presentation and what he expects or demands from the viewer, the point of departure for Italian Renaissance developments must be sought in Flanders. Jan van Eyck's bust length *Man in a Red Turban* in London is the earliest known portrait whose sitter looks directly out at the spectator.[53] The combination of this out-

---

[51] Alberti, *I primi tre libri della famiglia*, ed. F. C. Pellegrini and R. Spongano (Florence: Sansoni, 1946), 9; quoted in trans. by Joan Gadol, *Leon Battista Alberti*, 4.

[52] See John Pope-Hennessy, *The Portrait in the Renaissance*, chap. 4 "The Court Portrait," esp. 155–72 and figs. 170, 173–76, 178–79, 184–89. A recent treatment of this same material is: Joanna Woods-Marsden, "'Ritratto al Naturale': Questions of Realism and Idealism in Early Renaissance Portraits," *Art Journal* 46, no. 3 (1987): 209–16. Woods-Marsden stresses the component of idealization in the equation "recognizability/encomium."

[53] Elisabeth Dhanens, *Hubert and Jan van Eyck* (New York: Tabard Press [1982?]), provides an up-to-date overview of the portrait (188–92, with two illustrations in color). Martin Davies, *Early Netherlandish School*, 3d ed. (London: National Gallery,

ward gaze with the three-quarter view of the head required a sideways glance, which intensifies the sharpness of the eyes' focus. The picture is signed on the frame's lower edge in Latin, "Jan van Eyck made me. 1433. 21 October," and, on the upper edge, "Als ich can," Jan's motto. The motto must be intended ironically here, considering the brilliant but ostensibly effortless virtuosity of the literal rendering of every detail of face and costume, which yet does not detract from the dynamically balanced architecture of the whole.

Despite the fact that the external evidence in favor of classifying this painting as a self-portrait is limited to a seventeenth-century inventory reference, the audacity of its innovation in incorporating the confrontational look leaves little room for doubt on this score.[54] Because Van Eyck enjoyed the same degree of artistic freedom for his wife's portrait as for his own, he could choose this new mode of presentation for her portrait of 1439 as well, and for the 1437 portrait of his friend, the goldsmith Jan de Leeuw.[55]

Jan's *Self-portrait* combines certain features of both Ghiberti's and Alberti's sculpted self-portraits, neither of which existed in 1433. The character traits projected by Jan's face—intelligence, capacity for shrewd judgment and evaluation, sagacity, and worldliness—are reminiscent of the self-image Ghiberti wanted to communicate. In fact, Ghiberti's and Jan's social positions were in some ways similar despite the many salient differences between Florence and the Burgundian court. Jan's extra-artistic responsibilities as adviser to and emissary for Philip the

---

1968), no. 222, 53–54, is the most recent museum catalogue reference.

[54] Professor Larry Silver of Northwestern University assures me that this is now the general consensus. Already Panofsky had noted, "It is more natural to assume that the important innovation, the 'look out of the picture,' first suggested itself to a painter observing his own face in a mirror than to a painter facing another person," *Early Netherlandish Painting*, 2 vols. (New York: Harper and Row, 1971), 1:198. The earliest instance of the "look out of the picture" in Italian portraiture known to Panofsky was the ideal group portrait of *Famous Florentine Artists* (Louvre), usually dated to the 1440s and associated with Paolo Uccello, which portrays Giotto, Uccello, Donatello, Manetti, and Brunelleschi. See now Christianne L. Joost-Gaugier, "Uccello's 'Uccello,' " *Gazette des Beaux Arts* 84 (1974): 233–38. In that work, both Giotto and Donatello stare out at the spectator, implying that soon after its invention, the "look out of the picture" was associated with portraits of artists, whether painted by themselves or by other artists. This device could have been considered a "natural attribute" of artists, since they must scrutinize the world intensely in order to practice their art; moreover, the common sense association that Panofsky made between the "look out of the picture" and an artist looking at himself in a mirror is probably part of a long tradition.

[55] Larry Silver, "Face as Figure: Portraits as Exempla in Northern Europe," typescript, 1; cf. Kurt Bauch, "Bildnisse des Jan van Eyck," *Studien zur Kunstgeschichte* (Berlin: de Gruyter, 1967), 79–122.

Good, duke of Burgundy, demanded the traits just mentioned—so did his many executive tasks as head of the major workshop in Bruges during the later 1420s and early 1430s.[56] Like Ghiberti's Jan's achievement of material wealth, despite being dependent on the good will of a noble patron rather than stemming from civic commissions, was exceptional in its time.

In a way that recalls Alberti's *Self-portrait* more than Ghiberti's, however, Jan uses aspects of iconography and style to expand the artistic self as well as to glorify it; one such use is the turban, painted in brilliantly modulated reds, whose piled-up shapes and mysterious folds and crevices function as a visual metaphor for the scale of the artist's personality and power of invention, a scale that dwarfs the sense of self-satisfaction that an artist could derive from possessing nothing but solid bourgeois virtues.[57] As with Alberti's plaque, perhaps we can interpret Jan's meticulously accurate style as a boast, like the double-edged *all'antica* language in which Alberti simultaneously praises and disparages the glorious "ancients." Style itself, then, can be part of the language of portraits.[58] The "modesty" of Jan's motto, "Als ich can," moreover, becomes an ironic commentary on the humility expected of a medieval craftsman in the light of the artist's dawning acknowledgement of his godlike powers.

From a longer historical perspective, the history of portraiture received a seismic jolt when the *Man in a Red Turban* was created, as much from its implication of a new intimacy between painting and onlooker, its demand that the onlooker participate in a dialogue, as from its aggrandizement of the artist's self-image. "We feel observed and scrutinized by a wakeful intelligence,"[59] as Panofsky observed, yet, what is even more remarkable, our own self-consciousness is pricked as we return the artist's gaze, and an interaction is set up in which the impact of a fictive presence takes on an eerie reality—painting thus becomes a branch of magic.[60] Conversely, the painting overtly

---

[56] Dhanens, *Van Eyck*, 34–59.

[57] Panofsky's observation that the turban "gives an impression of studied informality" (*Early Netherlandish Painting*, 198) is in my opinion incorrect and misleading, since it obscures the issue of how the turban may allude to the artist's desired aggrandizement of his role just at this key point in time (1433).

[58] Format and style as essential ingredients of the visual language of portraits is a theme explored by Larry Silver (see n. 55). Important for background is the work of Kurt Bauch (also as in n. 55). These issues were addressed from a different angle by Mark W. Roskill in his paper, "Character in Jan van Eyck's Portraits and the Language of Signs," delivered at the 1987 conference.

[59] Panofsky, *Early Netherlandish Painting*, 198.

[60] Cf. Bert Hansen, "The Complementarity of Science and Magic before the Scientific Revolution," *American Scientist* 74 (March–April 1986): 128–36.

"recognizes", so to speak, an element external to itself as intrinsic to its existence. It sets in motion a process far more complex than the simplistic cognitive "recognition" discussed in some theoretical analyses of the creation of visual art works which do not start out by asking how the picture as object *operates*. A painting's three-dimensional physicality elicits complex operations of perception that distinguish its *modus operandi* from that of a written or printed text, rendering ineffective methods which are based on the structure and function of verbal language when employed as the sole means of analysis.

It Italy, the implications of the "look out of the picture" for increased psychological realism in the portrayal of non-artists were first systematically exploited during the 1470s by Antonello da Messina, in such works as the *Portrait of a Man* in London and the one in the Galleria Borghese, Rome.[61] In Antonello's work, the device is no longer associable with self-portrayal. Although some writers have regarded the London painting as a self-portrait because of it, several of Antonello's subjects stare at the onlooker, and the painter combined the resulting intimacy between sitter and viewer with various emotional states. The half-smile and quizzical look of the man in the Borghese Gallery portrait are noteworthy in this connection. The *Portrait of a Man* at Cefalù[62] exemplifies the smiling portrait that Antonello created, apparently the first artist in Italy to do so. Antonello's inventions are crucial to an understanding of the history of the portrait in Venice, since he is known to have worked there during 1475 and probably early 1476.

The combination of the "look out of the picture" with the achievement of monumentality in a portrait image is owed to Andrea del Castagno. It is seen in the *Portrait of a Man* in Washington [fig. 11], the only known portrait by him, datable about 1450 by analogy with Castagno's *uomini famosi* frescoes in the Villa Carducci.[63] In it the dense, massive, sculptural quality sought by painters working in the tradition established by Masaccio early in the quattrocento in Florence is combined with a look of confrontation or challenge directed out of the picture at the spectator, resulting in a portrait of exceptional psychological force. Although Alberti is recorded as having made a lost self-portrait using the three-quarter view[64] and Castagno himself either

---

[61] *Antonello da Messina*, exhibition catalogue, Messina, Museo Regionale, 22 October 1981–31 January 1982 (Rome: De Luca, 1981), no. 19, 120–21 (ill. 121) and no. 20, 122–23 (ill. 123); see illustrations of all of Antonello's portraits, passim.
[62] Ibid., 107.
[63] Fern Rusk Shapley, *Catalogue of the Italian Paintings*, 2 vols. (Washington, D.C.: National Gallery, 1979), 1, no. 17, 127–29, wood, 54 x 40.5 cm.; Marita Horster, *Andrea del Castagno* (Ithaca: Cornell Univ. Press, 1980), 32, 50, 180–81.
[64] Prinz, *Vasaris Sammlung* (as in n. 34), 24; Cristofano dell'Altissimo's copy of

made or planned another portrait which included the "look out of the picture,"⁶⁵ the Washington panel may well be the earliest surviving Italian portrait of a single individual to make use of it.⁶⁶ Its possible status as a manifesto of avant-garde portraiture suggests itself, when we consider that its additional innovative elements include the extension of the figure from bust- to half-length, the omission of a head covering, and the inclusion of a hand performing an action—grasping the rim of the heavy mantle, a gesture which underlines the man's air of power and authority. I conclude that the man portrayed here is Castagno, and the painting is therefore a self-portrait. If that is so, the implications for self-assertion in the form of challenge and scrutiny of the viewer, similar to the impact of Mantegna's *Self-portrait* bust of thirty years later [fig. 7] are striking, and Castagno's portrait could be considered an additional stimulus to Mantegna's thoughts about self-portraiture.

The visual impact of the modelling of the sitter's body in Castagno's *Portrait of a Man* [fig. 11] is so dramatic that the figure seems to swell outward beyond the true two-dimensional limits of the picture plane and thereby to impinge on—even to assault—the space of the viewer. In this combination of aggressive plasticity with compelling personal

---

Alberti's self-portrait in the collection of Cosimo I is illustrated as fig. 10, 25.

⁶⁵ Castagno's only known drawing for a portrait, the *Head of a Man* in the Uffizi, 250E, 19.5 x 17.7 cm. (Horster, *Castagno*, fig. 88), shows its subject staring out at the viewer with a slight frown and a penetrating gaze.

⁶⁶ The portrait of Uccello included in the ideal group portrait of *Famous Florentine Artists* cited in n. 54 must be based on an early model, perhaps a self-portrait by Uccello which employed the "look out of the picture." However, an even earlier picture may have associated the device with artists: this is the (lost) model for the panel showing a *Self-portrait with Portraits of Taddeo Gaddi and Gaddo Gaddi*, originally executed by Agnolo Gaddi and preserved in a copy attributed to Domenico di Michelino (1417–1491). *Gli Uffizi: Catalogo Generale* (Florence: Centro Di, 1979), no. A309, 861, tempera on panel, 47 x 89 cm. In this picture, both the artist's father (Taddeo) and grandfather (Gaddo di Zanobi, a famous mosaicist) are shown looking out of the picture, while the artist himself, interestingly, is shown in a profile view, allowing the inference that the "look out of the picture" when employed before 1400 alluded to a look from beyond the grave, reminiscent of the frontally deployed heads on Roman provincial funerary monuments. Oddly enough, this fascinating conception of an artistic dynastic portrait, appearing apparently as early as the 1370s or 1380s in Florence, is not discussed by Bruce Cole in *Agnolo Gaddi* (Oxford: Clarendon Press, 1977), despite its anticipation of future developments, for example Titian's use of a similar format. Wolfram Prinz called attention to Harald Keller's conjecture that the Gaddi dynastic portrait was a composite of three portraits that had originated elsewhere (*Vasaris Sammlung*, 62). This method of constructing a dynastic group portrait of painters could have been employed by Uccello or whoever created the original on which the Louvre *Famous Florentine Artists* is based, even though there the assembly is "dynastic" only in an ideal or theoretical sense. For a more legible illustration of the Gaddi portrait, see Pascal Bonafoux, *Portraits of the Artist: the Self-portrait in Painting* (New York: Skina/Rizzoli, 1985), 44.

assertiveness expressed in the direct gaze at the spectator, Castagno established a tradition to which Perugino had recourse in his portrait of *Francesco delle Opere* [fig. 12] dated on the back July 1494.[67] Perugino is documented in Venice during the summer of 1494 in connection with paintings for the Scuola di San Giovanni Evangelista and an even more prestigious commission for work in the Ducal Palace. Francesco delle Opere was a Florentine, the brother of a gem-engraver and a gem engraver himself, who died in Venice in 1496.[68] Both the portrait's inclusion of so much of the body, as well as both hands, and its gesture that contributes to the characterization, depart from Venetian custom. Yet the setting of the massive figure against a landscape of an amplitude and serenity that could rival those of Giovanni Bellini would have impressed Venetian painters.[69]

That the Florentine tradition of the monumental portrait was adopted by Giorgione at least once, in a work that provided a point of departure for Titian's highly individual development of the type, is demonstrated by his *Portrait of a Young Man of the Giustiniani Family* in Berlin [fig. 13], a work that is universally accepted as autograph, although undocumented.[70] Perhaps dating from about 1500, the format of this

---

[67] *Gli Uffizi: Catalogo Generale*, no. P1159 (inv. no. 1700), 406, panel, 52 x 44 cm. See Pietro Scarpellini, *Perugino* (Milan: Electra, 1984) 64 (document summary) and no. 60, 88 (catalogue entry on the painting).

[68] Gaetano Milanesi discovered (1878–1881) the identity of the sitter, whose family was known for the manufacture of luxury fabrics "ad opera." The motto on the scroll held in the sitter's right hand, "TIMETE DEUM," might seem more appropriate for a commemorative, posthumous portrait. Considering that Francesco delle Opere died in Venice and that Perugino is documented as being there on 9 August 1494 soon after the portrait's date, there is no reason to believe that this portrait was executed in Florence. — Ballarin, as in n. 14, 237–38, summarized the known data about Perugino's stay in Venice; simultaneously Smyth, as in n. 37, 233, evaluated the influence on Perugino of his experience in Venice.

[69] The Flemish quality of the landscape was noted by Luisa Becherucci in Mario Salmi, ed., *The Complete Work of Raphael* (New York: Reynal, 1969), 14. Perhaps Perugino's portrait was one means by which Giorgione could study the Flemish landscape mannerisms which are so prominent in several of his works. — The half-length portrait with both hands included remained rather rare in the 1490s. Leonardo's *Ginevra de' Benci* (National Gallery, Washington, no. 2326; see n. 73 below) of the early- to mid-1470s was a noted early example (it now lacks the lower portion with hands). David Brown draws attention to the use of this format by Andrea Solario, a Milanese painter working in Venice during the first half of the 1490s, in his exceptionally forceful *Man with a Carnation* (London: National Gallery, no. 923), which Brown dates to the same period as *Francesco delle Opere*, implying that Solario and Perugino reached independently the sculptural and monumental conception of portraiture that both works share: *Andrea Solario* (Milan: Electra, 1988), 41–48.

[70] Staatliche Museen Preussischer Kulturbesitz, Berlin, *Catalogue of Paintings, 13th–18th Century* (Berlin-Dahlem, 1978), no. 12, 177, *Portrait of a Young Man*, canvas, 58 x 46 cm., attributed to Giorgione. Recently David Rosand has attributed the painting

Fig. 12. Pietro Perugino, *Francesco delle Opere*, Florence, Uffizi

Fig. 13. Giorgione, *Portrait of a Young Man of the Giustiniani Family*, Berlin, Staatliche Museen Preussischer Kulturbesitz

work departs radically from the type established in Venice by Antonello and developed by Giovanni Bellini, and by reflecting the mediation of Perugino's *Francesco delle Opere*, it reveals Giorgione's receptivity to the most up-to-date trends in painting outside of his native Venice. In this experimental work Giorgione combined the monumentality, sense of plastic solidity, and half-length format of Perugino's Venetian portrait with a Flemish portrait motif, the parapet, a space-creating device that separates the figure from the picture's front plane. A monochromatic background that concentrates all attention on the figure is used instead of a landscape. As in *Francesco delle Opere* (compare fig. 12), a hand anchors the composition at lower left. Giorgione's employment of this deliberately too-small hand, based on a motif popularized by Hans Memlinc,[71] seems calculated to enlarge the apparent volume of the rose-hued padded jacket. How remarkable this pink jacket with its elegant ties must have seemed, we can judge by contrasting it with the black clothes worn by young patricians in most earlier Venetian portraits.[72] Black was considered the appropriate attire for young nobles after admission to the Maggior Consiglio, as if it proved their sobriety and sense of civic responsibility. Quite a different spirit permeates this image of a youthful member of the Giustiniani family, anticipating elders' complaints about the newly headstrong and rebellious mood of youth around the time of the War of the League of Cambrai.

Other differences between Giorgione's and Perugino's portraits (figs. 12 and 13) are equally indicative. Compared to the more static figure of the gem-engraver, Giustiniani's body displays a hint of movement: his right shoulder recedes into the picture space. The beginnings of a *contrapposto* can be glimpsed in the balance of the retreating shoulder with the advancing head, and this nascent movement is continued by the turn of the head to the figure's proper right, while the glance,

---

to Titian (*Titian*, as in n. 35). The painting was in the collection of the Giustiniani family in Padua until 1884. For a plausible interpretation of the inscription "VV" on the front of the parapet, see Nancy Thomson de Grummond, "VV and Related Inscriptions in Giorgione, Titian and Dürer," *Art Bulletin* 57 (1975): 346–56.

[71] See, e.g., the *Portrait of a Young Man* in the Accademia Galleries, Venice: *Gallerie dell 'Accademia di Venezia* (Milan: Electra, 1985), no. 177, 138, with color illustration, 25. On Flemish pictures available in Venice, see Lorne Campbell, "Notes on Netherlandish Pictures in the Veneto in the Fifteenth and Sixteenth Centuries," *Burlington Magazine* 123 (1981): 467–73. Anderson offers the best discussion of this portrait's relationship to Memling, and she comments on its importance in supplanting the older bust-length schema ("Imagery of Giorgione," 147–49). — The new appreciation of Andrea Solario's Venetian portraits (in Brown, *Andrea Solario*, chap. 1, 25–67 and cat. nos. 2, 7) points to that painter's work as a potential additional stimulus to Giorgione in his experimental portraits.

[72] Anderson, ibid.

focussed directly outwards, accentuates the "look out of the picture" in a fashion reminiscent of Jan van Eyck's self-portrait. Even Giorgione's stepped parapet, a novel feature, contributes to the incipient animation. These unobtrusive steps in the direction of animating the figure would prove highly significant for the future development of Giorgione's portraiture ideas, and they suggest his awareness of and positive reaction to Leonardo's theories about animation as the key to life-like representations. In fact, the importance for Giorgione's portraits of Leonardo's inventions in this field, works like the portrait of *Ginevra de' Benci* in Washington[73] and the *Portrait of a Musician* in the Ambrosiana,[74] was of the highest order, comparable to the influence on him of what Vasari called Leonardo's "alcune cose molto fumeggiate e cacciate terribilmente di scuro" ("certain things that were smokily indistinct and dramatically hidden by darkness").[75]

---

[73] Shapley, *Catalogue*, as in n. 63, vol. 1, no. 2326, 251–55, wood, 38.8 x 36.7 cm. (obverse); illustrated in vol. 2, pls. 171, 171A. The portrait has been cut down by about eight inches; originally both hands were included (as suggested by Leonardo's Windsor sketch for the hands and Verrocchio's bust of Ginevra de' Benci in the Bargello—see catalogue entry). Shapley discusses the possibility that this portrait had been confiscated from the Sforza palace in Milan and sent to France by Louis XII, or given to the king by Leonardo himself after the king's triumphal entry into Milan in 1499, suggested by an inventory entry recording a portrait labelled "Genevra" in Queen Anne of Brittany's collection (255). However, Ginevra was a popular name in the fifteenth century. — Unaccountably, Shapley omitted from her references the most thorough discussion of *Ginevra de' Benci* to date, written by the director of the National Gallery at the time of the acquisition of the work (February 1967), John Walker: "*Ginevra de' Benci* by Leonardo da Vinci," *Report and Studies in the History of Art* (Washington, D.C.: 1968), 1–23, where the painting is called "the earliest of all psychological portraits" (7), and the possibility that the portrait was commissioned from Leonardo by Bernardo Bembo, the (apparently Platonic) lover of Ginevra during his tenure as Venetian ambassador in Florence (1475–1476, 1478–1480), and subsequently taken to Venice, is considered (8). Jennifer Fletcher has discovered evidence virtually proving that Bembo was the portrait's commissioner (see Fletcher, "Bernardo Bembo and Leonardo's Portrait of Ginevra de' Benci," *Burlington Magazine* 131 [1989]: 811–16). The consequences of Fletcher's discovery for comprehension of Giorgione's reception of Leonardo's portraiture ideas have yet to be investigated.

[74] Ludwig Goldscheider, *Leonardo da Vinci*, 7th ed. (Greenwich, Conn.: Phaidon, 1959), no. 26, 155, wood, 43 x 31 cm., color illustration, fig. 26. Goldscheider supported the portrait's identification as Franchino Gaffurio which had been made by Luca Beltrami. Gaffurio's concern with music as an aspect of cosmic harmony and his definition of harmony as a union of opposites ("harmonia est discordia concors," the words printed on a scroll issuing from his mouth in the woodcut frontispiece to the 1518 edition of his *De harmonia musicorum instrumentorum* [Milan: G. Pontanum]) offered a notable example of the artist as first and foremost an intellectual creator. Leonardo shows the musician as lost in thought, isolated in an active, but private, realm of psychic processes to which the viewer has no access.

[75] The exact sense of "fumeggiate" is difficult to render in English. Leonardo's "sfumato" is usually understood as a blurring of the edges of forms to render the

Comparing the facial expression of *Giustiniani* with that of *Francesco delle Opere* (figs. 13 and 12) underscores the shift in the theoretical basis for portraiture brought about by Leonardo: the young man's eyes are full of a dreamy reverie utterly foreign to the steady, neutral, and mask-like face of the gem-engraver, however communicative of a distinctive individuality the latter may be. Giorgione, like Leonardo before him, opens up to us "the motions of the mind":[76] the delineation of *character* according to prescribed types, humors, or social roles is no longer the intention.[77] Perugino's construct of Francesco delle Opere is removed and remote from the viewer, allowing him or her a comfortable distance. By contrast, Giustiniani regards us with irresistible intimacy, proffering an invitation to share the mood and the moment, to become an object of *his* experience in a reciprocal relation that blurs the boundaries of the art work. In Giorgione's variation on the "look out of the picture," the Romantic portrait is unveiled.

Stony Creek, Connecticut

---

effect of objects seen through a hazy atmosphere or one with reduced visibility, as during twilight. See n. 10 above and Carlo Pedretti, "Ancora sul rapporto Giorgione-Leonardo e l'origine del ritratto di spalla," *Giorgione. Atti del Convegno* (as in n. 1), 181–85. — Vasari's remark can be found in *Le Vite*, 4:92.

[76] Leonardo, *Treatise on Painting*, ed. cited in n. 10, 1: 58, paragraph 92.

[77] On the other hand, in this case Giorgione does not seem to have followed Leonardo's ideas concerning the completely idealized portrait, in which the element of likeness is totally suppressed. But an attentive study of Giorgione's portraits from this point of view might yield interesting results. Cf. David Alan Brown, "Leonardo and the Idealized Portrait in Milan," *Arte lombarda* 67 (1983–84): 102–16.

JAMES V. MIROLLO

"Where'er you walk": My Lady's Beautiful Foot and Generative Footsteps: The Literary Context of Parmigianino's Madonna del Bel Piede

IN 1535, ACCORDING TO VASARI, PARMIGIANINO RECEIVED A COMMISsion to paint a Madonna and Child for the Baiardi Chapel of the Church of Santa Maria de' Servi in Parma. The resulting work shows a Madonna holding a sleeping child. To the side, continues Vasari, Parmigianino depicted some angels, one of whom grasps a crystal urn in which there glows a cross contemplated by our Lady. He adds that the painter was not pleased with the work and so left it unfinished. Nevertheless, it was much praised as being typical of the artist's "maniera piena di grazia e di bellezza" ("manner full of grace and beauty").[1]

This painting was, of course, the celebrated *Madonna of the Long Neck*, or what I am retitling for this essay the *Madonna of the Beautiful Foot*, now widely regarded as a crucial document of the Mannerist style in Renaissance art. Although Vasari tells us a good deal about it in his brief account, there are some oddities that puzzle. For example, it is by no means clear that there is a crucifix glowing in the urn, or that the Madonna is contemplating it, or that the child is asleep rather than dead—a proleptic image of the Crucifixion fused with the Nativity. If the latter is the intention, then the isolated figure in the background looking away from an unfolded scroll would complete the temporal fusion by suggesting the prophecies that preceded the birth of Christ. The row of unfinished classical columns would then possibly refer to the world of pagan antiquity in which the Messiah appeared.

Nor does Vasari remark upon the work's shocking deviations from the compositional and figural norms of High Renaissance painting, as one might expect—assuming that he was aware of the modern theory of Mannerism that emphasizes such deviations. Of course it is certain that Vasari was *not* privy to our ideas about Mannerism, but it is also

---

[1] Giorgio Vasari, *Le Vite*, ed. Licia and Carlo L. Ragghianti (Milan: Rizzoli, 1976), 3: 299 ff.

possible that he overlooked the deviations because he did not know the work itself very well, or, more likely, that he knew about and took for granted some literary context or meaning, a verbal conceit that required a matching visual wit evident in the eccentric subversions of norms startlingly flaunted by Parmigianino and described by one modern art historian, Cecil Gould, as follows:

> Everything is ambiguous. The scene is neither indoors nor in the open air. The angels on the left are only three-quarters of the height of the Madonna (whose body is elongated to a point where it begins to bear little relation to a human form). Yet they are standing and she, at first, appears seated. But, characteristically, she is in fact only half-seated: her very attitude is as ambiguous and uncomfortable as if she were supported merely on a shooting stick, while the Child (no longer an infant but a sizable boy) seems ready to fall off the inadequate lap provided. Then again, the Madonna's cloak flies out at the back as though defying the laws of gravity. But if we look carefully we see an accumulation of loops under the Madonna's left hand suggesting that the chair (or whatever it is) she sits on, has an arm which may furnish some support further back. Finally, the most perverse liberties are taken with space. Five angels are crowded together on the left, and close behind them a curtain falls. The accumulation of the five bodies in so small an area would in fact result in pulling the curtain well out of the perpendicular. Yet there is no sign of this: under the looped portion it falls straight. As to the right side of the picture, the vastness of the unfinished columns is indicated by the small size of the man in front of them. He appears a long way back, and a long way below us, yet the relation of the court where he stands to the foreground is disquietingly undefined.... Most perverse of all, the edge of the cushion at the Virgin's feet is only an inch or two from the edge of the picture. But as it is her heel which rests on it her toes must project actually beyond the picture plane—in other words they must be on our side of the canvas—an effrontery which breaks the basic convention of a framed picture.
>
> Whatever may have been the nature of the religious experience which inspired such a work, there can be no doubt that these disquieting elements finally convey to the spectator an impression very different from what its superficial elegance has suggested at first sight.[2]

---

[2] *An Introduction to Italian Renaissance Painting* (London: Phaidon, 1957), 212.

Fig. 1. Parmigianino, *Madonna del Bel Piede*, Florence, Galleria Pitti (Alinari/Art Resource 9029).

In response to Cecil Gould's comments on the "effrontery" of the Madonna's protruding foot and the nature of the religious experience that inspired the work as a whole, I offer the following hypothesis of a literary context or verbal conceit that may clarify the meaning and purpose of Parmigianino's alleged ambiguities and eccentricities.

In a recent article entitled "Gesture in Painting: Problems in Semiology," André Chastel reminds us that in a work like Giovanni Bonifacio's 1616 *L'arte di cenni* (*The Art of Gesture*), "the intention is not to study the phenomenon of 'expressive gesture' ... but to pursue the repertory of body language that bears messages and that is thus apt to be assimilated into a sort of coherent 'para-language' or, better still, a rhetoric of non-verbal communication."[3] One might say, then, that of the four significant gestures made by Parmigianino's Madonna—the downward glance of her eyes, the right hand pressing against her breast, the body apparently sitting but also seeming to rise, and the protruding of her right foot—only the first two are quite conventionally expressive of her inner thought and emotion, but the last two belong to another, less conventional language aimed more directly at the viewer or the viewer's world. I say "more directly" because it can be objected that the gesture of the Madonna's right hand, by pressing inward in obvious opposition to the right foot extending outward, communicates something to the viewer as well as it expresses her inner experience. And at least one of the things it communicates is that the two gestures are antithetically related. This dual function of a gesture finds an obvious analogy in the rhetorical tradition, where physical and verbal gestures could establish the ethos and at the same time emphasize the message of the speaker. Bonifacio himself, in his subtitle, says that his treatise "si tratta della muta eloquenza, che non è altro che un facondo silenzio" ("deals with mute eloquence, which is no other than a garrulous silence"). This is of course the language of *ut pictura poesis*, and in particular of an intermedia rhetoric of gesture. In the second book of his *Institutio oratoria*, Quintilian had provided the theoretical basis for such an intermedia rhetoric based on deviation from a norm by comparing varied poses of the human figure in painting and sculpture to the deviations from ordinary linguistic usage in rhetorical figures of speech and thought.[4] While this comparison would echo in other and later *paragoni* of the sister arts of poetry and painting, and undoubtedly influenced actual composition in both arts, modern interpreters tend to

---

[3] André Chastel, "Gesture in Painting: Problems in Semiology," *Renaissance and Reformation* 10 (1986): 9.

[4] Quintilian, *Institutio oratoria*, trans. H. E. Butler (Cambridge: Harvard Univ. Press, 1966), vol. 1, bk. 2, 293–94.

shy away from such discredited exercises in *ut pictura poesis* in favor of semiotic and anti-Lessing formalist interpretations of literary and art works. But while we eschew traditional and facile intermedia equivalencies, we should not ignore the historical literary and visual contexts of either art, especially when purely formal analyses do not satisfy. In the case of Parmigianino and his ambiguities we might feel especially encouraged by Gombrich's remark that "It is in the nature of things that images need much more of a context to be unambiguous than do statements."[5] As for literary contexts, as I will demonstrate, the phenomenon of Petrarchism offers valuable insights into both the formal and thematic ambiguities of the *Madonna of the Long Neck* or *Beautiful Foot*.

Commenting upon Parmigianino's subjection of his figures to forced abstract shapes and curves, S. J. Freedberg has instanced the Madonna's feet and toes but does not speculate as to why the Madonna's right foot protrudes, not only breaking the painting's frame but also creating the troubling illusion that she is taking a step when she is, or seems to be, seated.[6] Adding to these ambiguities is the undoubted beauty of the foot, which indeed they highlight and emphasize. If, as Elizabeth Cropper has shown, the shape of the Madonna's head and neck echo the vase to her right and the column to her left (in accordance with analogies drawn by Vitruvius and Firenzuola), we might find in literary tradition a similar explanation or justification of that beautiful foot, seemingly stepping into our world while retaining its link to the inner world of the painting, which thereby assumes the ontological status of a spiritual realm.[7]

In a brief article published in 1969, James Villas surveyed what he characterized as the Petrarchan *topos* "bel piede," tracing the conceit that the beloved's footsteps are generative—possessing an "animating power . . . over herbal nature"—to passages in Lucretius, Persius, and Claudian.[8] These are the sources for the half-dozen occurrences of the *topos* in Petrarch's *Canzoniere*, which in turn guaranteed a European-wide diffusion. Since he was primarily concerned with supplementing Joseph G. Fucilla's surveys of Petrarchism in Spain, Villas listed instan-

---

[5] Ernst H. Gombrich, "The Evidence of Images," *Interpretation: Theory and Practice*, ed. Charles S. Singleton (Baltimore: Johns Hopkins Univ. Press, 1969), 97.

[6] Sydney J. Freedberg, *Parmigianino. His Work in Painting* (Cambridge: Harvard Univ. Press, 1950), 80: "The feet have become elongated, sinuous shapes; the toes are demarcations of the foot into minor curving rhythms."

[7] Elizabeth Cropper, "On Beautiful Women, Parmigianino, *Petrarchismo*, and the Vernacular Style," *Art Bulletin* 58 (1976): 374–94.

[8] James Villas, "The Petrarchan Topos 'Bel Piede': Generative Footsteps," *Romance Notes* 11 (1969): 167–73.

ces of the *topos* in Garcilaso, Figueroa, de Sota, and Lope de Vega, then concluded with single examples from Tasso, Du Bellay, and Ronsard, and the observation that undoubtedly it could be found in many other works.

As far as I am aware, neither Villas himself or anyone else has speculated further on the *topos* itself or followed up Villas's understatement of its diffusion and influence, although the subject is so rich, as I have discovered, that it demands a much more extensive treatment than I can offer in this essay, given my necessary focus on Petrarch and Parmigianino.

A glance at the classical sources—the three adduced by Villas and others I have found—is revealing. In the first book of *De rerum natura*, Lucretius includes in his "Invocation to Venus" the assertion that Earth will greet her arrival by sending up its flowers to honor her.[9] In Persius's second satire, however, the *topos* occurs in a passage ridiculing foolish prayer, as when an old nurse prays for her baby boy that, among his other future blessings, roses may appear wherever he treads.[10] Claudian's *Laus Serenae* similarly transfers the conceit from a divinity, in this case applying it to the addressee of his panegyric, whose footsteps cause roses and lilies to blossom.[11]

The additional sources mentioned make it clear that the *topos* arose as an adaptation, for purposes of praise of extraordinary mortals, of a divine attribute or power especially associated with fertility and regeneration. In *Iliad* 14.346–49, for example, the earth flowers spontaneously into thick and soft grass under the amorously embracing Zeus and Hera.[12] And Hesiod says to Venus that grass grew under her step.[13] In the Homeric "Hymn to Demeter," Rhea tells Demeter to restore fertility to the earth by making the seeds sprout, and soon the earth teems with leaves and flowers.[14] In the *Greek Anthology*, also, there are examples like the epigram of Rufinus Domesticus, who praises Melite's feet by identifying them with the feet of Thetis.[15] Virgil also echoes the

---

[9] Lucretius, *De rerum natura*, 2d. ed., trans. W. H. D. Rouse; rev. ed. Martin F. Smith (Cambridge: Harvard Univ. Press, 1982), 2–3.

[10] Persius, *Satirae* 2.37–38, *Juvenal and Persius*, trans. G. G. Ramsey (Cambridge: Harvard Univ. Press, 1979), 338–39.

[11] Claudian, "Laus Serenae," lines 89–91, *Claudian*, trans. Maurice Platnauer (Cambridge: Harvard Univ. Press, 1972), 244–47.

[12] Homer, *Iliad*, trans. A. T. Murray (Cambridge: Harvard Univ. Press, 1976), 2: 93.

[13] Hesiod, *Theogony*, 194–95, in *Hesiod, The Homeric Hymns and Homerica*, trans. Hugh G. Evelyn-White (Cambridge: Harvard Univ. Press, 1977), 93.

[14] "Hymn to Demeter," lines 469–472, ibid, 322–23.

[15] Trans. W. R. Paton (Cambridge: Harvard Univ. Press, 1969), 1:153.

trope in his fourth eclogue, where he asserts that against her wonted habits, Earth, untilled, will bring forth flowers as gifts to the child whose birth he is celebrating.[16] And in the later *Pervigilium Veneris*, generative power is restored to the footstep of a goddess.[17] Thus there is no doubt that Petrarch was adapting a familiar classical motif, mythic and panegyric, and gender-neutral to boot, when in his *Triumph of Fame* he says of Cicero that the grass flowered where he walked, or when in the *Canzoniere* he attributes to Laura that same power made manifest by her fertile footsteps.[18]

Since Petrarch himself and his subsequent critics have stressed Laura's veiled face and gloved hand, it is surprising to discover that there are some twenty references in the *Canzoniere* to Laura's "bel piede" and generative footsteps. Several of these references to Laura's beautiful foot invoke its imprint upon the ground, traces of which the poet searches out or recalls. Thus, in poem 108, he speaks of leaning down "a ricercar de l'orme / che 'l bel pié fece in quel cortese giro" (lines 10–11: "to seek out again the print her beautiful foot made in that courteous walking").[19] In poem 125, he addresses the shore of the river Sorgue, reminding it that so beautiful a foot never touched earth as Laura's did on that day when she "signed" ("segnata") it by her step.[20] But no sign remains, no vestige of her presence that might console, so the poet is forced to rely upon memory of that event and thus accept the reality of its loss.

The opening of poem 162 combines the motifs of envy and praise:

> Lieti fiori et felici, et ben nate erbe
> che Madonna pensando premer sòle,
> piaggia ch'ascolti sue dolci parole
> et del bel piede alcun vestigio serbe.[21]

Joyous and happy flowers, and well-born grass on which my lady is wont to walk deep in thought, shore that listens to her sweet words and preserves some vestige of her beautiful foot.

---

[16] Virgil, *The Eclogues*, ed., trans. Guy Lee (Harmondsworth: Penguin, 1984), 56–57.

[17] *Pervigilium Veneris* 4.2–3, *Catullus, Tibullus and Pervigilium Veneris*, trans. J. W. Mackail (Cambridge: Harvard Univ. Press, 1976), 350–51.

[18] Francesco Petrarca, *Triumphus Famae* 3.18, *Rime, Trionfi e Poesie Latine*, ed. Ferdinando Neri (Milan-Naples: Ricciardi, 1951), 543.

[19] The numbering and text citations are from Robert Durling, ed. and trans., *Petrarch's Lyric Poems* (Cambridge: Harvard Univ. Press, 1976); the translations are my own. Poem 108 is the sonnet "Aventuroso più d'altro terreno," 216–17.

[20] Poem 125 is the canzone "Se 'l pensier che mi strugge," line 55, ibid., 242–43.

[21] Ibid., 308–9.

But a few poems later, the sonnet numbered 165 makes the first flat assertion in the *Canzoniere* that Laura's footsteps are generative:

> Come 'l candido pié per l'erba fresca
> i dolci passi onestamente move,
> vertu che 'ntorno i fiori apra et rinove
> de le tenere piante sue par ch'esca.[22]

As her white foot virtuously makes it sweet steps through the fresh grass, a power seems to issue from her tender soles that opens and renews the flowers all about her.

And in poem 192, the assertion is reinforced by the claim that, recognizing her power, the natural world craves her presence:

> L'erbetta verde e i fior di color mille
> sparsi sotto quell'elce antiqua et negra
> pregan pur che 'l bel pié li prema o tocchi.[23]

The green grass and the flowers of a thousand colors scattered beneath that black oak beg that her beautiful foot press or touch them.

Thus a subtle shift has occurred in the poet's presentation of Laura's absence. Seeking her purely human traces, transient signs of her former presence, he can experience only frustration and loss. By associating her with, indeed assimilating her to, Nature and the natural cycle, however, he can see her in the fertile and regenerative bloom of grass, flower and tree on those shores and in those woods which she frequented; this evidence of her power, while not compensating entirely for her human absence, is consoling as a wonder to contemplate.

But if she is more than human, Laura is also something more than a generative force; like pagan fertility goddesses she is both immanent in, and transcendent of nature, "sopra Natura," a "lume che 'l Cielo in terra mostra" (poem 192: "a light that shows Heaven on earth").[24] And since it is the Christian heaven that is refulgent in her, she must also be something more than an agent of natural regeneration. Another shift is required if Laura's first human, then divine footsteps are to be recognized finally as holy or saintly. In the last invocation of Laura's "bel piede" before her death is announced by the poet, he refers again to grass signed ("segnata") by her beautiful foot, but now reiterates that

---

[22] Ibid., 310–11.
[23] Poem 192 is the sonnet "Stiamo Amor, a veder la gloria nostra," lines 9–11, ibid., 338–39.
[24] Ibid., line 4, 338–39.

she testifies here on earth to celestial spirits, recalling though not paralleling Dante's Beatrice, who, herself a sign, made and left behind no signs of her presence in the natural world.

The transition from beautiful to saintly feet occurs in poem 268, a *canzone* that is among the opening lyrics of the second half of the collection, concerned with Laura dead. Addressing the natural world, now deprived of her, the poet says that it is now fallen, its glory lost, because it was not worthy to be touched by her "santi piedi" (line 26: "holy feet").[25] This motif is repeated in poems 306 and 325. The former, a sonnet, is especially interesting because its opening lines assert that Laura's footsteps were "gloriosi" and show the way to heaven. Thus in the closing tercet he can state that although he seeks her in vain in those places where he once saw her, he does see her "santi vestigi tutti rivolti a la superna strada" ("holy footprints all turned toward the Heavenly path").[26] While Laura maintains her humanness in the poet's dreams and visions of her after her death, the purely human being and the wondrous natural agent of fertility have obviously been transcended and fulfilled in the heavenly guide to salvation, their final cause. The modulation from human footprint made by beautiful feet to holy footsteps making their blessed way to heaven is then confirmed by the final prayer to the Virgin, who is the final cause of Laura and all beautiful and virtuous women, and the love they inspire.

Needless to say, Petrarch's creative adaptation of a classical *topos* to his own literary and spiritual purposes will not be echoed by his later followers, who tend to treat it as indeed a *topos* to be dutifully imitated and exploited rather than an opportunity for creative exploration of philosophical, moral, or poetic issues. Still, the subsequent fate of the *topos*, reaching a kind of culmination in the neoclassical elegance of Pope's "Where'er you tread the blushing flowers shall rise," is fascinating and informative, as I hope the few examples I cite here that were not mentioned by Villas will demonstrate.[27]

The earliest Italian echoing of the Petrarchan *topos* I know of occurs in Poliziano's *Stanze per la giostra*, and thereafter it is heard everywhere.

---

[25] Poem 268 is the *canzone*, "Che debb'io far? che mi consigli, Amore?" line 26, ibid., 438–39.

[26] Ibid., 484–85.

[27] Alexander Pope, *Pastorals*, "Summer," in *Poetical Works*, ed. Herbert Davis (London: Oxford Univ. Press, 1967), lines 73–76, pp. 22–23:
    Where'er you walk, cool gales shall fan the glade,
    Trees, where you sit, shall crowd into a shade:
    Where'er you tread, the blushing flow'rs shall rise,
    And all things flourish where you turn your eyes.

Here is the coda to the fair Simonetta's epiphany to the previously resistant Iulio in the first book of Poliziano's *Stanzas for the Joust*:

> Poi con occhi piú lieti e piú ridenti
> tal che 'l ciel tutto asserenò d'intorno,
> mosse sovra l'erbetta e passi lenti
> con atto d'amorosa grazia adorno.
> Feciono e boschi allor dolci lamenti
> e gli augelletti a pianger cominciorno;
> ma l'erba verde sotto i dolci passi
> bianca, gialla, vermiglia e azurra fassi.[28]

Then with happier and more laughing eyes, so that the sky became serene all about her, she moved with slow footsteps over the grass, an act adorned with amorous grace. Then the woods made sweet laments and the birds began to weep; but the green grass beneath her sweet steps bloomed white, yellow, vermillion, and blue.

At the other end of the Italian tradition there is Tasso's *Gerusalemme liberata*, where Rinaldo is assigned generative footsteps (canto 18, octave 23), and the infernal fury Alecto the negative power of withering the meadows where'er she treads.[29] And Petrarch's great nineteenth-century annotators, Carducci and Ferrari, cite not only the usual classical sources but also the influence of our *topos* on popular Tuscan *canti*, appropriately enough, since popular love song is the graveyard of Petrarchism. And so we find in these canti repetition with little variation of the basic motif, "Dove passate voi l'erba ci nasce" ("Where you tread, the grass blooms").[30]

One typical adaptation of the *topos* by more sophisticated poets occurs as an embellishment of *blazons* of female anatomy, as when Sidney in the *Arcadia* includes among perfections no tongue can tell a foot "Whose step on earth all beauty sets."[31] Another example involves a Mannerist kind of witty exploitation of the Petrarchan text, as when in Lope de Vega's *Dorotea*, Fernando's poem extols the beloved's slippered feet by invoking the other Petrarchan *topos* of gloved hand, and so the tiny slippers are said to be the white gloves of her feet,

---

[28] *The "Stanze" of Angelo Poliziano*, trans. David Quint (Amherst: Univ. of Massachusetts Press, 1979), octave 55, pp. 28–29.

[29] *Opere*, ed. Bruno Maier, 5 vols. (Milan: Rizzoli, 1963–1965), vol. 3, p. 602 (Rinaldo) and canto 9, 1.5–6, p. 289 (Aletto).

[30] Francesco Petrarca, *Le Rime*, ed. Giosue Carducci and Severino Ferrari (Florence: Sansoni, 1960), 252n.

[31] *Arcadia*, ed. Maurice Evans (Harmondsworth: Penguin, 1977), 290.

which imprison them. Moreover, when she moves about in slippers, her footstep is so light the flowers are not crushed, but they are offended because she leaves no print for them, which they crave.³²

Spenser provides examples of both *topos* and anti-*topos*. In *Mutabilitie Canto* 7, stanza 10, the poet says of Dame Nature, appropriately enough, that "all the earth far underneath her feete / Was dight with flowers, that voluntary grew / Out of the ground, and sent forth odours sweet."³³ In his *Amoretti*, sonnet 20, Spenser surely is playing off the *topos* in the first quatrain:

> In vaine I seeke and sew to her for grace,
> And doe myne humbled hart before her poure:
> The whiles her foot she in my necke doth place,
> And tread my life downe in the lowly floure.³⁴

In a more fully Baroque vein, Milton's Eve will find the flowers she tends spring at her coming in *Paradise Lost* 8.44–47: when she

> Rose, and went forth among her fruits and flow's,
> To visit how they prospered, bud and bloom,
> Her nursery; they at her coming sprung
> And touched by her fair tendance gladlier grew.³⁵

In his *Adone*, Giambattista Marino endows the male protagonist with the familiar *bel piede* and generative footsteps, but as is his wont, he tries desperately to exploit the metaphoric potential of the trope, if only by multiplication:

> Là dove il vago passo o fermi o mova
> ogni erba ride, ogni arboscel s'indora;
> ringermoglia la terra e si rinova
> e quanto può le care piante onora;
> spunta di rose amorosette a prova
> schiera lasciva e le bell'orme infiora
> e 'l piè fregiato di celeste lume
> corre a baciargli e ne trae fiamme il fiume.³⁶

There where his lovely step pauses or moves, every blade of

---

³² *La Dorotea*, ed. Edwin S. Morby (Madrid: Castalia, 1968); *La Dorotea*, trans., ed. Alan Trueblood and Edwin Honig (Cambridge: Harvard Univ. Press, 1985), 35–37.
³³ *Faerie Queene*, ed. A. C. Hamilton (London: Longman, 1980), 725.
³⁴ *The Anchor Anthology of Sixteenth-Century Verse*, ed. Richard S. Sylvester (Garden City: Anchor, 1974), 353.
³⁵ *Paradise Lost*, ed. Scott Elledge (New York: W. W. Norton, 1975), 168.
³⁶ *L'Adone*, ed. Giovanni Pozzi (Milan: Mondadori, 1976), canto 15, oct. 26, p. 905.

grass rejoices, every shrub gilds itself; the earth blossoms and renews itself again and honors those dear feet as much as it can; a wanton band of amorous little roses blooms in turn and enflowers the beautiful footprints, while a stream runs to kiss, and become inflamed by, a foot embellished with a celestial glow.

A more imaginative and rather spectacular version of the *topos* occurs in Góngora's *Polifemo*, and in particular stanza 47, when the monster addresses his beloved Galatea, urging her to leave the sea and come ashore in these words:

> Pisa la arena, que en la arena adoro
> quantas el bianco pie conchas platea,
> cuyo bello contacto puede hacerlas,
> sin concebir rocío, partir perlas.[37]

Tread upon the sand, for on the sand I adore all the shells your white foot silvers, whose beautiful touch can make them, without the conception of dew, give birth to pearl.

Since Góngora's wit has taken the *topos* about as far as it can be exploited this side of utter obscurity, it was perhaps inevitable that its rehabilitation would come in the form of Pope's comparatively lucid though equally literary version quoted above, and that its life would be prolonged to our own day in the relatively unsophisticated language of popular song.

Returning now to Parmigianino's painting and the Madonna's *bel piede*, we can speculate with some confidence that there is a Petrarchan context that explains its meaning satisfactorily. Between one extreme of interpretation, which sees the foot as another of the painting's disturbing violations or playful manipulations of compositional norms, and another extreme, which sees it as combining with other features to present a Christian as well as alchemical paradox, "conception" *in vitro*, a Petrarchan explanation is both sensible and fruitful. It also provides an answer to the question why the Madonna is made to be not only humanly, stunningly beautiful, but sexy, an ambiguity that Vasari did not mention and Gould ignores in his otherwise detailed reading of the picture but has baffled this and other viewers. Note for example the Madonna's modish and bejewelled coiffure, her elegant hands, her clinging garments, not to mention the gratuitously shapely leg of the foremost angel to her right, which contributes to the curiously erotic tone of the painting as a whole.

---

[37] Luis de Góngora y Argote, *Obras Completas* (Madrid: Aguilar, 1956), lines 373–76, p. 629.

The key to this paradox is perhaps also to be found in Petrarch and especially in the Laura-Mary relationship. The fact that in Italian the word *madonna* is used for both the Virgin and the beloved of lyric poetry is a convenient indicator of the commerce of attributes that could easily occur between them. From a negative point of view, the assimilation of *madonna* and *Madonna* could cause temporary but dangerous confusion through neglect of Mary's superior status as final cause or transcendent ideal. But from another, more positive view, the emphasis on Mary's beautiful humanity, including her sexuality, makes her more accesible and enhances our in-so-many-other-ways frail and debased nature. Like the Christ child, who is a composite image of birth and death, Mary is also a composite image, of the beautiful young woman who arouses desire and the divine Virgin and Mother who is the ultimate goal and satisfaction of that desire.

In Parmigianino's painting, the ambiguities can be understood not only in terms of these Petrarchan amatory motifs but also of those mythic resonances that Petrarch incorporated from classical sources, quite consciously, in his initial modulation of the figure of Laura from that of beautiful young woman to that of nature deity. These mythical and amatory meanings, as well as the transit of attributes between human madonna and divine *Madonna*, manifest themselves in the *bel piede* thrust forward at us from the enclosed world of the painting, which, by a typical piece of Mannerist ontological juggling, becomes the spiritual realm which Mary inhabits *now* but which also represents in surreal fashion something that happened *then*. The *bel piede* of Mary thus links then and now, our world and hers, the humanly and divinely beautiful, by piercing the frame. Parmigianino may also be echoing Petrarch's bold attempt to assimilate the discourses of antiquity and Christianity, blending or at least uniting the two eras and their cultures. Thus we see in the painting that, once again, in a cycle of mythical return, a sacred female deity steps into and reanimates, rehabilitates, and redeems the natural world.

Columbia University

THOMAS S. FREEMAN

From Catiline to Richard III: The Influence of Classical Historians on Polydore Vergil's Anglica historia

At first glance it would seem that little remains to be said about either Polydore Vergil or his *magnum opus*, the *Anglica historia*. Ever since the last decade of the nineteenth century, when Wilhelm Busch in a meticulously thorough survey of the materials for early Tudor history pointed out the *Anglica historia*'s value as a source and proclaimed its superiority to other sixteenth-century English historical works, Vergil's role in the development of English historical writing has been recognized and acknowledged.[1] And while some of the praise has been recently qualified, there seems to be little disagreement with the assessment of Vergil's modern biographer, Denys Hay, that "it might be fair to call the *Anglica historia* one of the most important histories of England which have ever been published."[2]

One reason for this prominence is that the *Anglica historia* was the first English history written in accordance with the new standards of historical scholarship developed by the Italian humanists. As such, it attained international recognition as the standard work on the history of England even by those who were antagonistic to it on religious or nationalistic grounds.[3] Vergil's assessments of the major figures of late

---

[1] Wilhelm Busch, *England Under the Tudors*, trans. Alice M. Todd (London, 1895), 1:396.
[2] Denys Hay, *Polydore Vergil: Renaissance Historian and Man of Letters* (Oxford, 1952), ix.
[3] When Cardinal Campeggio sent his brother Marcantonio on a mission to try to reconcile Henry VIII with the papacy, he urged Marcantonio to study Vergil's *Anglica historia* to gain an understanding of past difficulties between kings and popes. (See William E. Wilkie, *The Cardinal Protectors of England: Rome and the Tudors Before the Reformation* [Cambridge, 1974], 229.) The Protestant polemicist, John Bale, also relied heavily on the *Anglica historia*, despite his criticisms of Vergil for "polluting our English Chronicles most shamefully with his Romish lies and other Italish beggarys" (quoted in Hay, *Polydore Vergil*, 158). Yet Bale repeated—on Vergil's authority—the erroneous report that Wycliffe went into voluntary exile in Bohemia.

medieval and early Tudor England—the boyish, decent, but weak-willed Richard II, the saintly Henry VI, the sinister, cruel Richard III, the avaricious Henry VII, and the arrogant, ostentatious, vainglorious Cardinal Wolsey—became a part of the English historical tradition and remained largely unquestioned until this century.[4] Finally, Vergil set forth in the *Anglica historia* a providential interpretation of fifteenth-century English history in which the kings of England were deposed or enthroned as a result of direct divine intervention, as a reward for virtue or a punishment for previous misdeeds. This interpretation, first formulated by Vergil, was borrowed and elaborated on by Hall and then by Grafton and Holinshed, and was finally used by Shakespeare as the central theme of his history plays. One is hard put to think of another historian who has made such a pervasive and enduring impression not only on English historiography but on English culture as well.

Some significant aspects of Vergil's historical writing have nevertheless gone virtually unnoticed. Since almost everyone writing about Vergil has been interested in him largely as a forerunner of bigger and better things such as the more "scientific" histories of the seventeenth century and the history plays of Shakespeare, there has been little discussion of the influence of earlier historians on Vergil. Students of English historiography have tended to regard the *Anglica historia* as being without antecedents, as having sprung, like Athena, fully grown from its creator's brow. Yet, as with all Renaissance historians, Vergil regarded the classical historians as the pre-eminent models to follow. Although Vergil knew Greek and was familiar with an impressive number of ancient writers, historiography in his lifetime was dominated by Latin models.[5] At that time, the most popular Roman historical seem to have been Livy, Valerius Maximus, Caesar, Curtius, Florus,

---

(See Margaret Aston, "John Wycliffe's Reformation Reputation," *Past and Present* 30 [1965]: 25 n. 5.) That Bale could have drawn on the *Anglica historia* for a subject of such importance—even though Vergil was openly hostile to Wycliffe—is a clear indication of the reliance placed upon this work.

[4] See Hay, *Polydore Vergil*, 164–65. For Vergil's role in helping to create the long prevalent image of Richard II as "an errant minor," see Margaret Aston, "Richard II and the Wars of the Roses," in *The Reign of Richard II: Essays in Honour of May McKisack*, ed. F. R. H. Du Boulay and Caroline M. Barron (London, 1971), 308.

[5] Hay, *Polydore Vergil*, 54–58 and 85–86. Similarly, although Thomas More was fluent in Greek and in *Utopia* made a point of having Hythloday read the great Greek historical writers, he never mentioned or quoted them in his other writings but turned to the Latin historical writers as his models. (See Thomas More, *The History of King Richard III*, ed. Richard S. Sylvester, in *The Complete Works of St. Thomas More* [New Haven, 1963] 2:lxxxv–lxxxvi. Hereafter the Yale edition of More will be referred to as CW.)

Sallust, Tacitus, and Suetonius.[6] Of these writers, Valerius, Caesar, Curtius, and Florus were of little use (apart from Caesar's description of Britain and his campaigns there) to someone writing a history of England. Livy, on the other hand, would have been a natural model for Vergil to follow, both because of the widespread admiration for his style and because he was the only one of these historians to undertake the task that Vergil attempted, that is, to narrate the entire history of a people from their origins to the present. Yet the influence of Livy on the *Anglica historia* was nil. The remaining writers, however—Sallust, Tacitus, and Suetonius—had a considerable influence on Vergil.

All the surviving works of both Sallust and Suetonius had been printed in widely read editions during the second half of the fifteenth century. Sallust had been immensely popular throughout the medieval period and this popularity had, if anything, increased in Vergil's day. Suetonius had been widely imitated since Einhard's biography of Charlemagne. Platina's influential papal biographies (modeled on Suetonius's imperial biographies) made the latter a model for fifteenth- and sixteenth-century historians and biographers.[7] Tacitus, on the other hand, had been neglected throughout the Middle Ages and was only rediscovered in the fourteenth century. His works would not attain real popularity in England until the seventeenth century, and Vergil was somewhat ahead of his time in using him as a model. The first printed text of Tacitus's works appeared in 1470 and contained books 11–16 of the *Annals*, all that remains of the *Histories* together with the *Germania* and the *Dialogue on Orators*. An edition that included books 1–6 of the *Annals* was not printed until 1515, just after Vergil had completed the manuscript of the *Anglica historia*, although Vergil would have been able to consult it before he undertook the revision of his work in which he most extensively developed his providential view of English history.[8]

These three historians had one important feature in common: they were all considered to be authorities on civil war, factionalism, tyranny,

---

[6] Peter Burke, "A Survey of the Popularity of Ancient Historians, 1450–1700," *History and Theory* 5 (1966): 136.

[7] See Beryl Smalley, "Sallust in the Middle Ages," in *Classical Influences on European Culture AD 500–1500*, ed. R. R. Bolgar (Cambridge, 1971), 165–75; Burke, "Popularity of Ancient Historians," 136–37; Eric Cochrane, *Historians and Historiography in the Italian Renaissance* (Chicago, 1981), 256; and J. E. Sandys, *A History of Classical Scholarship*, (Cambridge, 1908), 2:73, 93, 97 and 103. For an indication of Sallust's pervasive impact on Renaissance historiography see Cochrane, *Historians and Historiography*, 4, 26, 140, 143, 166, 232, 235, 279–80 and 441.

[8] Sandys, *Classical Scholarship*, 2:32–33, 36, 103 and 108; CW2:xxxix–xci; Kenneth C. Schellhase, *Tacitus in Renaissance Political Thought* (Chicago, 1976), 12 and 103, and Ronald Martin, *Tacitus* (Berkeley, 1981), 237–38.

rebellion, and their attendant evils. It was a cardinal tenet of humanist historiography (and much of medieval historiography, for that matter) that one could profitably apply lessons drawn from past events to similar problems and situations in the present. Thus, for example, Erasmus saw striking parallels between the world described by Suetonius and his own, and in the preface to his edition of the *Lives of the Caesars* Erasmus urged contemporary princes to study the work carefully in order to avoid the tyranny which characterized, and the calamities, that befell imperial Rome.[9] Similarly, the sixteenth-century Dutch scholar Justus Lipsius, editor of and commentator on Tacitus's works, maintained that Tacitus had a special relevance to the present age, an age of calamities, an opinion which Montaigne echoed when he claimed that Tacitus was particularly valuable "in sick and troubled state, like our present situation."[10]

Fifteenth-century England was also considered to be a sick and troubled state, and the parallels between England's misfortunes and the turmoil and strife of late republican and early imperial Rome did not escape contemporaries.[11] It is hardly surprising, then, that the first two histories of the period written according to humanist ideals and standards—More's *History of Richard III* and Vergil's *Anglica historia*—were deeply influenced by Sallust, Suetonius, and Tacitus.[12]

On the most obvious level, Vergil cited or quoted directly from Sallust's *Jugurthine War*, from Suetonius's *Lives of the Caesars*, from Tacitus's *Annals*, and from his *Agricola*.[13] More significantly, Vergil

---

[9] *Opus epistolarum*, ed. P. S. Allen (Oxford, 1910), no. 586.

[10] See Arnaldo Momigliano, "The First Political Commentary on Tacitus," in his *Essays in Ancient and Modern Historiography* (Middletown, CT, 1977), 206 and Burke, "Popularity of Ancient Historians," 152.

[11] Note for example the second Crowland continuator's comparison between Richard III's suppression of Buckingham's rebellion and the proscriptions of the Second Triumvirate. (*The Crowland Chronicle Continuations: 1459–1486*, ed. Nicholas Pronay and John Cox [London, 1986], 170. Hereafter this book will be referred to as Crowland.)

[12] For More's classical models see CW2:xxxvi–xcviii.

[13] A list and brief discussion of the extensive borrowings Vergil made from the *Annals* and the *Agricola* for the first two books of the *Anglica historia* is given in Mary Frances Tenney, "Tacitus in the Middle Ages and the Early Renaissance and in England to about the year 1650" (Ph.D. diss., Cornell University, 1931), 90–99. Direct references to the *Lives of the Caesars* and the *Jugurthine War* are in Polydore Vergil, *Anglica historia* (Basel, 1555), 10 and 17. Hereafter this book will—following the usage of Hay, *Polydore Vergil*—be referred to as C. This was the last of the four distinct versions of the *Anglica historia* that Vergil produced. The first was the manuscript, written in 1514. Around 1521–1524 Vergil extensively revised the still unpublished manuscript, and this version was published in Basel in 1534. (Hereafter this edition will be referred to as A.) Another substantially rewritten edition of the *Anglica*

followed Suetonius (or, more probably, followed Platina who followed Suetonius) in arranging his history biographically,[14] in his detailed descriptions of the physical appearances and characters of the kings of England which ended each post-Conquest book of the *Anglica historia*, and possibly also in his use of colorful anecdotes. To give but one example, his description of Richard III's reaction to Henry Tudor's invasion (at first self-confident and contemptuous, then filled with panic and rage) is very similar to Suetonius's description of Nero's reaction to the news of Vindex's revolt.[15]

The influence of Tacitus on the *Anglica historia* was more a matter of shared assumptions and attitudes about history and human character than of direct imitation, but Sallust's influence is pervasive, particularly for the reign of Richard III. For one thing, Vergil, who normally wrote restrained, lucid, relatively unrhetorical prose, suddenly began in his account of Richard to construct more impassioned and elaborate sentences while he also dropped the detached point of view he had previously maintained, and began to include the highly emotional, melodramatic, indeed almost overwrought descriptions of suffering humanity that are a feature of the *Conspiracy of Catiline*.[16] At the same time, many

---

historia was published in Basel in 1546. (Hereafter this edition will be referred to as B.) An anonymous English translation of the first twenty-five books of this edition—covering events up to 1485—was prepared in the mid-sixteenth century and the first eight and last three books of this translation were published by Sir Henry Ellis, Camden Society 36 (London, 1846) and 29 (London, 1844). (Hereafter these will be referred to as C. S. I and C. S. II respectively.) The only significant difference between B and C was an additional book chronicling the reign of Henry VIII down to the year 1537. A translation of this book together with an edition and translation of the manuscript of the *Anglica historia* for the years 1485–1513 (collated with the different editions of the *Anglica historia*) was published by Denys Hay, Camden Series 74 (London, 1950). (This will be referred to as C. S. III.) No published translation exists for the remaining fourteen books of the *Anglica historia* which cover English history from the reign of William the Conqueror to the death of Henry V. For the reader's convenience, references—where applicable—will be given for A and C together with the English translation in C. S. I or C. S. II. (Since C. S. I and C. S. II are very faithful translations of B it seemed redundant to supply references to that as well.) The spelling and punctuation of all quotations from C. S. I and C. S. II will be modernized. All translations not specifically credited are my own.

[14] See Hay, *Polydore Vergil*, 96.

[15] Compare A, 554; C, 561; or C. S. II, 218–19 with Suetonius *Lives of the Caesars* 6.40.4–41.2. According to C. D. Ross, Vergil's account is inaccurate and "runs entirely counter to the careful if slightly feverish and anxious manner of Richard's defensive preparations" (*Richard III* [Berkeley, 1981], 213).

[16] Compare, e.g., Sallust's lurid description of the panic which swept Rome during Catiline's conspiracy (31.3) with Vergil's account of the horror Londoners felt at Shaw's sermon (A, 538; C, 545; or C. S. II, 184) or their reaction to the news of the death of Edward IV's sons (A, 540; C, 547 or C. S. II, 189).

features of Sallust's literary style appear throughout Vergil's narrative of Richard's reign, notably an increased use of alliteration, the grouping together of like-sounding words, a more abrupt and jagged rhythm to the sentences, a terser style, and the increased use of graphic and vivid language—all of which contrasts markedly with Vergil's earlier style.

The best examples of these features appear in the speeches which Vergil composed and put into the mouth of Richard III. Sallust was famous for the rhetorical speeches in his works, and although Vergil tended to avoid writing these (and several of the ones he did write are based on speeches found in his sources), Richard III delivers not one, but two orations in the *Anglica historia* for which there are no known sources: his address to the nobility in which he urges that the duke of York be removed from sanctuary (one of the longest and most elaborate speeches in the *Anglica historia*), and his speech denouncing Hastings (a short but very eloquent and effective oration.)[17]

The second of these speeches is very Sallustian not only in its style but in its flamboyant rhetoric:

> Vos hoc hodierno die principes arcessendos ea duntaxat de causa curavi, ut vobis ostenderem, in quanto mortis periculo verser: ego enim abhinc paucos dies, neque noctu, neque interdiu quiescere, neque bibere, aut cibum capere queo, quare sensim me sanguis, me vires, me spiritus deficit, supraque modum omnia iam membra, ut videtis (brachium enim ostendebat) exiliora fiunt: quod utique malum in me proficiscitur ab illa malefica muliere Elizabeth regina, quae suis veneficiis me infecit, quibus laesus paulatim dissolvor.
>
> My lords, I have troubled to assemble you all today for no other reason than that I might show you in how much danger of death

---

[17] A, 534–35 (534 is misnumbered as 536 in this edition) and 536; C, 541–42 and 543; or C. S. II, 176–78 and 180–81. (There are minor differences in both these speeches between the different editions—e.g., in the speech against Hastings where the word "graciliora" was changed to "exiliora" and "mihi proficiscitur" became "in me profisiscitur." All the quotations from these two speeches are from C.) On the relative lack of rhetorical speeches in the *Anglica historia* see Hay, *Polydore Vergil*, 105–6. It should also be pointed out that the first of these two speeches, in all probability, had some factual basis since Dominic Mancini—the author of an eyewitness account of Richard III's accession to the throne which was almost certainly unknown to Vergil—states that Richard did make such an oration and Mancini's description of the substance of the speech agrees with the topics of the speech given in the *Anglica historia*. See Dominic Mancini, *The Usurpation of Richard III*, trans. C. A. J. Armstrong (Oxford, 1969), 89. Nevertheless, the wording of this speech is unquestionably Vergil's invention, and, as for the other speech, no account before Vergil has Richard making a speech just before Hastings's arrest.

> I am placed; for the past few days I am able to rest neither by night nor by day, nor drink, nor take food, wherefore my strength, my energy and my spirit gradually ebbs and beyond that, moreover, all [my] limbs, as you see (he displayed his arm) are emaciated because the evil is coming into me all over from that witch Queen Elizabeth, who corrupted me with her poisons, by which I, having been injured, am gradually being destroyed.

Another feature of this speech, which is typical of Sallust but not of most classical—or Renaissance—historical writers, is its terseness. In fact, Vergil's narrative of the episode of which this speech is an integral part—the downfall of Lord Hastings—moves along with considerable speed and vigor to end, a mere eleven lines after Richard's denunciation concludes, with this drumroll of a sentence: "Gulielmo [Hastings] vero vix dato confitendi peccata spatio, caput cervicibus abscinditur"[18] (William [Lord Hastings] was scarcely given sufficient time to confess his sins before his head was struck from his neck).

Richard III's speech demanding York's release from sanctuary (which is too long to reproduce in full here) also bears the hallmark of Sallust's style. In addition to the features discussed above, this speech employs the Sallustian device of having the speaker ask a series of rhetorical questions which are climaxed by an emphatic answer.[19] Also very Sallustian is the derisive force and sharply ironic tone of the speech, as this excerpt from it illustrates:

> Sed ecquid dicemus de malo consilio ab illis qui me semper pessim oderunt, dato Elizabeth reginae, quae nulla iusta de causa, tam imprudenter metum simulans, ausa est filios regis tanquam facinorosos, miseros, perditos, in asylum unicum in terris perfugium egestatis, aeris alieni, nequitiae, rapere, perinde ac si no iremus eos perditum, et iam omnia spectarent ad violentiam.[20]

But what shall we say of the evil counsel, given to Queen Elizabeth, [from those who have always most hated me], who without any just cause, simulating terror so recklessly, has dared to carry the king's sons, like criminals, paupers [and] wretches, into sanctuary, the sole refuge on earth for poverty, debt, and worthlessness, just as if we were about to exterminate them and that now everything might lead to violence.

---

[18] A, 536; C, 543. For another English translation, see C. S. II, 181.
[19] For examples see Sallust *Conspiracy of Catiline* 20.2–17 and 51.1–43.
[20] A, 534–35; C, 541. For another English translation see C. S. II, 177.

A double irony is being employed here which is very similar to that Sallust uses in Micipsa's speech to Jugurtha and the Numidian nobility, an irony which stems from both the speaker's deliberate and flagrant hypocrisy and from the absolute inaccuracy of the speaker's assurances and predictions.[21]

Vergil's Richard III is himself a conflation of Sallust's Jugurtha and Catiline. The similarities between Jugurtha and the historical Richard III were sufficiently striking: both men were usurpers who deposed their kinsmen, both had possessed exemplary reputations before their treasons and both were men of substantial courage and martial prowess. Vergil's Richard was also like Jugurtha in his suave, glib hypocrisy, his ready recourse to bribery, his ruthless slaughter of his friends, his troubled conscience, his paranoia, and his restless energy.[22]

But there is an even closer resemblance between Vergil's Richard and Sallust's Catiline. First of all there is a similarity in their mannerisms, for according to Sallust, Catiline was restless, frenzied, ravaged by remorse; he had a pale complexion, hideous eyes, and a walk which alternated from rapid to slow, whereas Vergil claimed that Richard III, "while he was thinking of any matter, he did continually bite his nether lip, as though that cruel nature of his did so rage against itself in that little carcass. Also he was wont to be ever with his right hand pulling out of the sheath to the midst, and putting in again, the dagger which he did always wear."[23] Sallust asserted that Catiline had great strength of mind and body and remarkable powers of endurance but that he was a man of burning passion, with a vicious and depraved nature, capable of any pretense and dissimulation and goaded by a monstrous ambition.[24] Vergil cast Richard in this same mold by stating that "he had a sharp wit, provident and subtle, apt both to counterfeit and dissemble, his courage also high and fierce...."[25] And at Bosworth, when Vergil's Richard refused to flee from the battle, determined to settle the issue once and for all, Vergil recreated not only the mood but the very thoughts of Sallust's doomed archvillain.[26] Finally, Vergil's description of Richard's death—"Tum vero temporis puncto, reliquis in fugam se dantibus, Ricardus inter confertissimos hostes praelians interficitur"

---

[21] Micipsa's speech is given in Sallust *Jugurthine War* 10.1–8.
[22] See Sallust *Jugurthine War* 11.8–9, 12.3–5, 15.1–16.4, 23.1, 28.1, 32.1–35.10, 72.1–2, 74.1 and 76.1 and compare with A, 535, 537, 547, 550 and 555; C, 542, 544, 557 and 562; or C. S. II, 178–79, 182–83, 204, 211 and 222.
[23] Sallust *Conspiracy of Catiline* 15.4–5 and C. S. II, 227. (Also see A, 558; C, 565.)
[24] Sallust *Conspiracy of Catiline* 5.1–5.
[25] C. S. II, 227. (Also see A, 558; C, 565.)
[26] Compare A, 557; C, 564; or C. S. II, 225–26 and Sallust *Conspiracy of Catiline* 58.6–21.

("then truly in a moment the rest [of his army] fled, and Richard was slain fighting in the thickest of the enemy [ranks]")—strikingly echoes Sallust's description of the death of Catiline: "Catilina postquam fusas copias seque cum paucis relictum videt, memor generis atque pristinae suae dignitatis in confertissumos hostis incurrit ibique pugnans confoditur" ("After Catiline saw that his troops were dispersed and that he was left with [just] a few men, remembering his lineage and former status he charged into the thickest of the enemy [ranks] and fighting there he was run through").[27]

The extent of Sallust's influence on Vergil and, incidentally, the extent to which Vergil drew upon Roman history to understand fifteenth-century England, is demonstrated by Vergil's discussion of the origins of the Wars of the Roses. Sallust had stated that the conclusion of the Punic wars removed the fear of external enemies which had hitherto united the Romans, and in the ensuing period of peace and prosperity, buried grievances surfaced, and two factions, the nobility and the people, tore the state apart.[28] Vergil, in turn, stated that the conclusion of the Hundred Years War removed the fear of external enemies which had hitherto united the English and in the ensuing

---

[27] A, 556-57; C, 563 (also see C. S. II, 225-26) and Sallust *Conspiracy of Catiline* 60.7. What is particularly interesting is that there were two well-established traditions concerning Richard's death on which Vergil could have drawn. The first is what could be called the chivalric tradition, and it praised Richard's courage and prowess in battle. It is notably represented by the author of the second continuation of the *Crowland Chronicle* (182) and by John Rous in his *Historia regum angliae* who wrote—just after a sentence in which he compared Richard III to the Antichrist—that Richard "conducted himself like a noble warrior and . . . defended himself most illustriously" (*Joannis Rossi Antiquarii Warwicensis Historia regum Angliae*, ed. Thomas Hearne [Oxford, 1716], 218). The second interpretation, which could be termed the official interpretation, is represented by the *Vita Henrici VII* of Bernard André, Henry VII's historiographer royal. Although André does not describe the battle of Bosworth itself, he paints an unfavorable picture of Richard's demise, ascribing the king's conduct during the battle to bloodlust and ferocity rather than courage. This is made clear in an oration which André has Richard address to his men before the battle, in which the king "inflamed with rage" screams that the enemy soliders should be crucified and slaughtered to a man and that Henry Tudor should be butchered "without any respect either for his blood or noble rank" or, if possible, captured alive so that Richard, with his own hands, could "slaughter, butcher [and] kill him" (*Memorials of King Henry the Seventh*, ed. James Gairdner, Rolls Series, vol. 10 [London, 1858], 31-32). There were very good reasons for Vergil to have adopted either of these interpretations. The chivalric interpretation was widely held—it is striking that Rous and Crowland continuator present it although they are otherwise hostile to Richard—while André's version of events had the merit of being completely acceptable to the Tudors. It is thus highly significant that Vergil rejected such firmly entrenched views and instead modeled his version of this notable event on Sallust.

[28] Sallust *Jugurthine War* 41.1-5.

period of peace, buried grievances surfaced, and two factions, the Yorkists and Lancastrians, contended for power and brought the kingdom to ruin.[29]

In using Suetonius, Tacitus, and Sallust as models, Vergil drew a number of lessons from these writers about history, historical writing, and politics. Vergil has been praised as "the first chronicler of English history to be seriously concerned with cause and effect," and it has been claimed that he "differed from his predecessors in his increased emphasis on human character."[30] It is possible to exaggerate Vergil's originality; the second continuator of the *Crowland Chronicle*, in particular, displayed a similar interest in character and motive.[31] But no one had been as consistent and rigorous in searching for the motives behind important actions—even the Crowland continuator was capable of describing the duke of Buckingham's revolt against Richard III without supplying any indication of why Buckingham turned on his ally.[32]

Vergil's concern with cause and motive was a legacy from the Roman historians and it derived from a particular view of government and politics, the chief concerns of the Roman upper classes and the historians they produced or patronized. The Romans regarded public life as being nothing more than an extension of the moral life of the individuals who made up the government and believed that as long as its leaders behaved morally, society would flourish and thrive, whereas if they became corrupt, society would also become corrupt and ultimately perish.[33] The persistence of this attitude among Roman historians can be seen in Tacitus's astonishment that men like Petronius, Licinius Mucianus, and Titus Vinius were dissolute in their private lives but able and energetic in public affairs, and in Sallust's confident declaration that Rome's conquest of the Mediterranean was due solely to the pre-eminent *virtus* of her citizens.[34] Because of this attitude, "it was a peculiarity of Roman thought generally to represent political

---

[29] A, 496; C, 502; or C. S. II, 94.

[30] E. M. W. Tillyard, *Shakespeare's History Plays* (New York, 1946), 35 and F. J. Levy, *Tudor Historical Thought* (San Marino, 1967), 68.

[31] Thus, for example, he claimed that Warwick's pro-French foreign policy stemmed from the earl's personal hatred of Charles the Bold, and took great care to explain that Hastings's insistence that Edward V come to London with only a small escort was due to Hastings's fear that the Woodvilles—the king's maternal kinsmen and his enemies—would use a large escort to seize power. *Crowland*, 114 and 154.

[32] See *Crowland*, 162.

[33] For a good discussion of this see Donald Earl, *The Moral and Political Tradition of Rome* (Ithaca, 1967), 11–43.

[34] See Tacitus *The Annals* 16.18 and *The Histories* 1.10 and 48 as well as Sallust *The Conspiracy of Catiline* 53.4.

crises as moral ones,"[35] and consequently to view human character as the great causative force in history and to become fascinated with the motives which underlie human behavior.[36]

In Sallust, Suetonius, and Tacitus the emphasis on character became an acute (perhaps over-acute) awareness of the power of self-interest and, following Thucydides, an eager readiness to give the worst motive for a course of action—no matter how far-fetched or incredible—the most credence.[37] Thus Tacitus could argue that Augustus chose Tiberius as his successor, knowing the latter's unworthiness, so that his reign would look all the better by comparison, and that Augustus's recommendation that the empire not be further expanded was also made out of a jealous concern for his reputation.[38] Similarly, Tiberius only feigned reluctance to succeed to the principate so that he could observe how people reacted to the news, and Tacitus darkly suggests that Antonius Primus incited mutinies in his armies in order to wrest sole command from his colleagues.[39] The legacy of these historians was a fascination with hidden causes and base motives which seems to have affected both the readers and writers of history in the Renaissance. Thus, for example, Dominic Mancini apologized to his readers that he did not stay in England long enough to learn "the secret designs of

---

[35] Donald, Earl *The Political Thought of Sallust* (Cambridge, 1961), 44.

[36] Note, for example, Suetonius's detailed discussion of Caesar's motives in crossing the Rubicon or his discussion of all the possible reasons for his refusal to employ adequate security precautions or his analyzing the motives behind Tiberius's retirement to Rhodes. Suetonius *Lives of the Caesars* 1.30.2–5, 1.86.1–2 and 3.10.1. It is interesting to note that Livy was the most deficient of the major Roman historical writers in his examination of the causes of events. Perhaps this is one of the reasons why he exerted so little influence on Polydore Vergil.

[37] For Thucydides see Meyer Reinhold, "Human Nature as Cause in Ancient Historiography," in *The Craft of the Ancient Historian: Essays in Honor of Chester G. Starr*, ed. John W. Ealie and Josiah Ober (Lanham, 1985), 23. For Sallust's adherence to this view, 27–28; Ronald Syme, *Sallust* (Berkeley, 1964), 56; and Smalley, "Sallust in the Middle Ages," 172. For Sallust's influence on Tacitus in this, see Syme, *Sallust*, 296, and also see Rheinhold, "Human Nature," 29–30. For examples of Suetonius's willingness to write down highly improbable stories that reflect his subjects in the worst possible light see *Lives of the Caesars* 3.42.1–2 and 7.22.1.

[38] Tacitus *The Annals* 1.10–1.11. It is, of course, difficult to know how seriously Tacitus intended these charges to be taken and the extent to which he made them up or was repeating common rumors. Nevertheless, although it seems far fetched to modern readers, the story that Augustus selected Tiberius as his successor solely in order to enhance his own reputation was sufficiently well known, and gained enough credence, that Suetonius specifically rebutted it and felt obliged to quote from Augustus's letters to Tiberius to prove that it was false. Suetonius *Lives of the Caesars* 3.21.2–7.

[39] Tacitus *The Annals* 1.7 and *The Histories* 3.11.

men" involved in Richard III's seizure of the crown.[40]

This obsession with motives was a fascination that Vergil shared, and given the scarcity of information that he (or anyone else) had about the inner lives of the main figures in fifteenth-century England, he had considerable freedom to speculate on the base and self-interested motives that lay behind the important events of the period. Thus, previous accounts had given two basic reasons for the breach that developed between Richard Neville, earl of Warwick, and Edward IV: opposition by the Nevilles to Edward's marriage to Elizabeth Woodville[41] and Warwick's opposition to the marriage alliance of Edward's sister to the duke of Burgundy.[42] Vergil, however, downplayed the first reason and specifically rejected the second as "a mere fable of the common people" on the ground that it was incredible that "a matter of so small importance [as the nation's foreign policy] could or ought to have alienated the earl from his liege lord."[43] Like the good Sallustian he was, Vergil knew that personal motives alone were important, and sought among these for the causes of the quarrel. Thus he conjectured that the root of the trouble lay in the king's jealousy of the earl (whose support had placed him on the throne) and the ingratitude people generally show to their benefactors. Additionally, Vergil (demonstrating the classical propensity to give the most credence to the most scandalous rumor) thought there was probably some truth in the report that Edward IV angered Warwick by assaulting a woman in the earl's household.[44]

Vergil also rejected the second Crowland continuator's statement that the earl of Warwick voluntarily released Edward IV from captivity because he needed the king's support to suppress Sir Humphrey Neville's rebellion. Vergil found this incredible and instead described

---

[40] Mancini, *The Usurpation of Richard III*, 57.

[41] The first Crowland continuator holds this view (*Ingulph's Chronicle of the Abbey of Croyland with the Continuations by Peter of Blois and Anonymous Writers*, trans. Henry T. Riley [London, 1854], 445), as does Robert Fabyan, *The New Chronicles of England and France*, ed. Sir Henry Ellis (London, 1811), 654 and the *Great Chronicle of London*, ed. A. H. Thomas and I. D. Thornley (London, 1938), 202.

[42] This is the opinion of the Burgundian chronicler Jean de Waurin (*Recueil des chroniques et anchiennes istoires de la Grant Bretaigne, a present nomme Angleterre*, ed. Sir William Hardy and Edward L. C. P. Hardy, Crowland Rolls Series, 39:5 vol. [London, 1891], 543–44) and of the second Crowland continuator (Crowland 114).

[43] C. S. II, 118. (Also see A, 507; C, 514.)

[44] A, 507; C, 514; or C. S. II, 117. Mancini, another Italian humanist observer of fifteenth-century England—as Rosemary Horrox points out—similarly perceived the Hastings/Woodville feud "in exclusively personal terms, and explains the animosity between Hastings and Dorset as rivalry over mistresses." *Richard III: A Study in Service* (Cambridge, 1989), 123.

how Edward bribed his guards and escaped, with such impressive circumstantial detail that the unwary reader could hardly suspect that Vergil had no source for this version of events.[45] Vergil even questioned such an apparently self-evident motivation as the passion for hunting which led the Norman kings to establish the New Forest; in his eyes this was simply a cunning pretext for clearing people hostile to their regime from the vulnerable southern shore.[46]

Vergil had complete freedom in ascertaining the causes of yet another quarrel, that between Richard III and his chief supporter, the duke of Buckingham, since his sources gave no explanation for the estrangement or simply threw up their hands and admitted that they were baffled.[47] Vergil, in Sallustian fashion, ascribed only self-interested motives to Buckingham, although he dismissed as common rumor the report that Buckingham was plotting to seize the throne himself (probably because Vergil wanted to downplay royal claimants other than Henry Tudor, and the Stafford claim to the crown was a particularly sensitive issue). Vergil instead claimed that Buckingham turned against Richard because the king had refused to grant the duke certain lands to which the latter had a claim and that (a nice Sallustian touch here) in refusing he had taunted the duke until Buckingham was "moved much with ire and indignation."[48] Here again, great events do not have great causes but are undertaken from petty motives of self-interest and injured pride.

Another important legacy of the Roman historians was their view of human character not only as being dominated by self-interest in many cases, but also as being beyond change or development in all cases. As Ronald Syme has observed, "the way of thought of the ancients was prone to conceive a man's inner nature as something definable and immutable. A change in observed behaviour was therefore not a change in essence, but only a manifestation of what was there all the time."[49] This conception of human character stemmed from and reinforced the

---

[45] A, 510; C, 517; or C. S. II, 124. Also see Crowland, 116. For Vergil's use of the second Crowland continuation see n. 72 below.

[46] A, 157; C, 160.

[47] See, for example the author of the *Great Chronicle*'s admission that he doesn't know why Richard III and Buckingham fell out (*Great Chronicle*, 234).

[48] C. S. II, 192–95. Also see A, 541–43; C, 548–50. As a matter of fact, the lands claimed by the duke (part of the old Bohun earldom of Hereford) had been provisionally granted to Buckingham in July 1483. For this and for discussions of Buckingham's reasons for rebellion see Ross, *Richard III*, 113–15, and Carol Rowcliffe, *The Staffords, Earls of Stafford and Dukes of Buckingham* (Cambridge, 1978), 30–32.

[49] Ronald Syme, *Tacitus* (Oxford, 1958), 421. This opinion has been endorsed and supported in Martin, *Tacitus*, 105–6, and Reinhold, "Human Nature," 29.

pessimism and suspicion with which classical historians viewed human motivations, since the character change these historians usually had to discuss was a degeneration, not an improvement, in the character of someone holding high office.[50] Such a degeneration is almost invariably described not as an erosion of a person's character under strain or pressure but rather a revelation of a person's true character which had hitherto been successfully hidden. Once again, human character is seen as being shot through with hidden vices which should be detected by the astute historian. This is why the great villains of Roman history were constantly portrayed as consummate hypocrites, and why Vergil, More, and Mancini all stressed dissimulation as the central element in the character of Richard III.[51] It is not simply a matter of propaganda or even of direct imitation of the ancients; it is the only resolution of the problem raised by trying to apply the concept of unchanging character to the career of a man of hitherto blameless reputation who was believed to have suddenly committed monstrous crimes.

The hold this idea of human character had on classical historians is readily apparent in the writings of Sallust who, as Donald Earl has pointed out, "seems to have been incapable of conceiving a slowly developing situation or character."[52] Thus his Catiline was always a villain who from his youth took pleasure in civil war, murder, and robbery and who spent the greater part of his life planning to overthrow the Republic.[53] Similarly, Suetonius's portraits of the Roman emperors are dominated by a view of human character as unchanging. Signs of Tiberius's cruel and dour character were discernible even in his childhood, although he disguised it partly to gain popular favor and partly from respect for and fear of his virtuous brother, Germanicus.[54] Tiberius was himself aware of his flawed character and thus refused various honors offered to him at the beginning of his reign, for fear that they would only increase his humiliation when his evil nature was ultimately discovered. Finally escaping from public scrutiny by retiring

---

[50] Tacitus commented that Vespasian was the only Roman emperor whose character changed for the better in office and strongly implied that this improvement astonished everyone (*The Histories* 1.50).

[51] See A, 558; C, 565; or C. S. II, 227 and CW2:xciv for Sylvester's point that "Dissimulation, therefore, lies behind every act of both [Tacitus's] Tiberius and Richard [III]." Mancini also characterizes Richard as "ad dissimulandum aptior" ("more suited to dissimulation") than his brother Clarence (Mancini, *Ursurpation of Richard III*, 62).

[52] Earl, *Political Thought of Sallust*, 87.

[53] Sallust *The Conspiracy of Catiline* 5.2. Also see Syme, *Sallust*, 75–77 for Sallust's antedating Catiline's revolutionary plans and activities.

[54] Suetonius *Lives of the Caesars* 3.57.1 and 4.6.2.

to Capri, he gave free reign to all the base lusts and vicious passions he had tried so long and so unsuccessfully to hide.[55] Similarly, even when young, Caligula could not conceal his inherent cruelty and dissipation, while Suetonius comments that Nero's boyhood lusts and cruelties were not merely adolescent behavior but revealed the true Nero.[56] Nevertheless, Suetonius was open-minded enough to declare that Domitian (whose reign, unlike those of Tiberius, Caligula, and Nero, he had actually lived through) was not inherently evil but that lack of funds made him greedy and fear of assassination made him vicious.[57]

Tacitus was, if anything, more rigid in his assessments of human character and constructed even more elaborate explanations of hypocrisy and dissimulation. In his view, Tiberius, despite his best efforts, could not completely conceal his cruel nature and when in temporary retirement at Rhodes his secret thoughts were solely on dissimulation and his covert lusts. His seclusion at Capri was really caused by his wish to conceal his vicious and depraved desires.[58] Tacitus sums up his opinion of Tiberius by observing that he led a blameless life under Augustus and that he had hidden his real character while Germanicus and Drusus lived. But as time passed and the restraining influences of Livia and Sejanus were removed, Tiberius's unchecked crimes and perversions brought his true personality to light.[59] The young Caligula was also regarded by Tacitus as a hypocrite who successfully concealed his evil nature, just as Nero in his adolescence concealed latent vices which only came to the fore upon the death of his mother.[60] The adult Nero was enabled by both nature and experience to become a master of hypocrisy and treachery, and the youthful Domitian ingeniously hid his true character and posed as a harmless youth devoted to the study of literature and poetry.[61] Nothing could be more revealing of Tacitus's view of human character as something fixed and immutable than his statement that Otho's unexpected ability and good conduct as an emperor—Otho had been known for his hedonism and sloth before his accession—unnerved everyone because they distrusted pretended virtues and vices that would inevitably return.[62]

The Roman historians' presentation of individual character as un-

---

[55] Ibid., 3.42.1 and 3.67.2-4.
[56] Ibid., 4.11.1 and 6.26.1.
[57] Ibid., 12.3.2.
[58] Tacitus *The Annals* 1.4 and 4.57.
[59] Ibid., 6.51.
[60] Ibid., 6.20, 13.1 and 14.13.
[61] Ibid., 14.56 and Tacitus *The Histories* 4.86.
[62] Tacitus *The Histories* 1.71.

changing powerfully influenced their Renaissance successors. Following classical models, humanist biographers "continued to assume, in spite of abundant evidence to the contrary, that the character of an individual person was indelibly established at the moment of birth, or even, as in the case of Giovio's Bernabò Visconti, at the moment of conception."[63] That Vergil also felt this influence can be seen in his treatment of Richard III. According to the *Anglica historia*, on receipt of the news that Edward IV had died, Richard, who coveted the crown, cleverly dissembled his true feelings to allay suspicion. When he met Buckingham at Northampton, his plans for usurping the throne were so firmly established, and he was able to impart them to the duke so persuasively, that the latter became his willing henchman.[64] Vergil dismisses Richard's positive accomplishments as king as being nothing more than an attempt, made out of fear of rebellion, to make people accept his rule. "But hard it is to alter the natural disposition of one's mind, and suddenly to extirp[ate] the thing therein settled by daily conversation," and Richard's "counterfeit" benevolence was unsustained and unsuccessful.[65] In the margin of his manuscript Vergil added the Tacitean comment that "Richard was not able to change his savage nature, and did not long persevere in goodness but immediately returned to evil and did everything thenceforward, as is evident in the case of his wife's death, under a cloak of hypocrisy."[66]

Vergil also viewed the career of Richard of York through Sallustian eyes and claimed that from the time of Cade's rebellion, York plotted to seize the throne for himself.[67] To contemporaries and foreign observers there were many causes of the Wars of the Roses but to Vergil there was but one sole cause for the civil wars: Richard of York's "outrageous lust of principality."[68] Where modern historians have seen in Richard of York a man first seeking redress for grievances and only driven to claim the crown after years of losing struggles with his enemies, Vergil

---

[63] Cochrane, *Historians and Historiography*, 415.
[64] A, 533; C, 540; or C. S. II, 173–74.
[65] C. S. II, 191–92. (Also see A, 541; C, 548.)
[66] Quoted in Kelly, *Divine Providence*, 101.
[67] A, 493; C, 499; or C. S. II, 86–87. Interestingly, Vergil makes a point here of maintaining that Richard of York attracted restless youths to his cause. There is no support for this strange assertion in either fact or Vergil's sources but Sallust had claimed that Catiline was especially successful in winning the support of the young (*Conspiracy of Catiline* 14.4–7).
[68] C. S. II, 94. Here is another example of the influence Sallust had on the *Anglica historia*. Vergil wrote that "hunc enim libido invaserat potiundi regni" (A, 496; C, 502) where Sallust had written of Catiline that "lubido maxuma invaserat rei publicae capiundae . . ." (Sallust *Conspiracy of Catiline* 5.6).

saw a man with an evil ambition which he steadily and consistently pursued until the end of his life.[69] Although there is no suggestion of it in any of his sources, Vergil did not hesitate to accuse York of trying to usurp Henry VI's powers and then kill or depose him during the duke's second protectorate.[70] Vergil was also clearly in the thrall of the classical historians when he claimed that Warwick dissembled his anger at Edward IV and plotted to restore Henry VI to the throne as early as 1467.[71]

Yet Vergil was flexible enough—or inconsistent enough—to disregard preconceived ideas on certain occasions when they came into conflict with what he knew to be facts, and there are a few cases in which Vergil did describe an individual's character slowly developing under the pressure of circumstances. Following the second Crowland continuator, Vergil hints that after the execution of the duke of Clarence, Edward IV might have turned into a tyrant from lack of opposition to his rule, had death not intervened.[72] Baffled by the fact that the same sources (including William of Malmesbury, a chronicler Vergil held in high regard) could present William the Conqueror as at once pious, magnanimous, cruel, and brutal, Vergil tentatively advanced the theory that the Conqueror's natural character was coarsened by the hardships of this youth and further hardened by the precariousness of his hold on England and the constant opposition to his rule.[73]

In the printed editions of the *Anglica historia* Vergil also described how Henry V, on coming to the throne, renounced his former lascivious lifestyle and evil companions, banished the latter from the kingdom,

---

[69] For strong statements that Richard of York did not initially seek the crown see, e.g., K. B. McFarlane, "The Wars of the Roses," *Proceedings of the British Academy* 50 (1964): 94 and R. L. Storey, *The End of the House of Lancaster* (New York, 1967), 69–73 and 162. Although T. B. Pugh has stated that "there can be little doubt that he [Richard of York] had long regarded himself as the rightful king of England" ("The Southampton Plot of 1415," in R. A. Griffiths and J. W. Sherbone [eds], *Kings and Nobles in the Later Middle Ages* [Gloucester, 1986], 86), it has been pointed out that as late as the first battle of St. Albans, Richard could have killed Henry VI with impunity and seized the Crown if he had wished to do so (P. A. Johnson, *Duke Richard of York 1411–1460* [Oxford, 1989], 157–58).

[70] A, 498; C, 504; or C. S. II, 97.

[71] A, 507–508; C, 514; or C. S. II, 118.

[72] Compare A, 530; C, 537; or C. S. II, 168 with *Crowland*, 146. For a summary of arguments on the possibility that Polydore Vergil consulted the second continuation of the Crowland Chronicle see *Crowland*, 34 n. 1. If the second Crowland continuator is not the source for this comment, then Vergil must have received it from one of his oral sources and it must have represented a common view of Edward IV. In either case, it would be a well-attested judgement that Vergil would have to take seriously.

[73] A, 157–58; C, 160.

and instead appointed wise, honest, and sober men to advise him.[74] Yet, despite the fact that Henry V's reformation was well attested to by several of Vergil's sources,[75] the classical concept of unchanging human behavior exerted a strong enough influence on Vergil for him to write nothing about Henry's youth in the manuscript of the *Anglica historia* except the comment that he had shown good hope from his earliest days.[76] Hence Henry's apparent *volte-face* on becoming king was a change of advisors and behavior, not of character and personality.

The most interesting description of a character change in the *Anglica historia* occurs in the manuscript when Vergil stated that Henry VII, in the latter part of his reign, became avaricious, and presented this as a slowly developing process. "It is not indeed clear whether at the start it was greed; but afterwards greed did become apparent ... he *gradually* laid aside all moderation and sank into a state of avarice"[77] (my emphasis). Here as with Suetonius's similar description of Domitian's gradual degeneration into despotism, an unusual perception may have been achieved because the historian was actually acquainted with people who intimately knew the person he was describing. Vergil also arrived in England in 1502 and although he would have been aware of the unpopularity of Henry's exactions from the time he arrived there, he depended on Reginald Bray and other early counsellors of Henry VII for information about the earlier period of the king's reign. These men had, as G. R. Elton has pointed out, a vested interest in presenting the period in which they wielded power in the best possible light and throwing the blame for Henry's unpopular measures upon later counsellors such as Empson and Dudley.[78] But if exceptions to the classical concept of unchanging character occur in the *Anglica historia*, they are exceptions which demonstrate how powerful a hold this concept had on

---

[74] A, 433–34; C, 439.

[75] Of these sources both the *Brut* and Psuedo-Elmham depict Henry V as leading a riotous youth and undergoing a sudden transformation on his accession to the throne, while if Vergil did consult Tito Livio's biography of the king, he would have read Livio's comment that Henry had committed indiscretions in his youth as all young soldiers did. (See *The Brut or the Chronicles of England*, ed. Friedrich W. D. Brie, vol. 2, Early English Text Society, no. 136 [London, 1908], 494; *Thomae de Elmham Vita et gesta Henrici quinti, Anglorum regis*, ed. Thomas Hearne [Oxford, 1727], 12–13, and Tito Livio, *Vita Henrici quinti, regis Angliae*, ed. Thomas Hearne [Oxford, 1716], 5.)

[76] See Kelly, *Divine Providence*, 91 n. 19.

[77] C. S. III, 127.

[78] See G. R. Elton, "Henry VII: Rapacity and Remorse," *Historical Journal* 1 (1958): 34–35. It is worth noting that in the printed editions of the *Anglica historia*, Vergil stated that Reginald Bray and John Morton were in "vulgi opinio" evil counsellors of Henry VII, a charge that Vergil emphatically denied (C. S. III, 128*-29*).

Vergil; for although he was capable of envisioning and describing a gradual change of character, he only did so when trusted sources, written or oral, had already presented him with just such a characterization. Left to his own devices he continued to view human character as fixed and immutable.

But now that we have seen how deeply Vergil's historical writing was influenced by his Roman predecessors, what is the interest and importance of this information? For one thing, although most people repeat the truism that Renaissance scholarship was influenced by classical models, this is a useful reminder of just how pervasive and profound this influence often was. For students of English history, this influence is a factor that must be taken into consideration when assessing the accounts of humanist historians, such as Vergil or More, or the later historians they influenced. If this is not done several misconceptions result. In the first place, several of the vivid and apparently realistic details that Vergil presents—such as Richard III's restless mannerisms or his desperate, fatalistic mood at Bosworth—are taken as facts whereas they are more probably the result of Vergil's conflating the heroes and villains of ancient Rome and medieval England.[79] Caution should also be exercised before accepting the motives behind events which are often supplied by humanist historians. As we have seen, humanist historians, following their classical exemplars, confidently attributed motives to their subjects based on nothing more than their preconceived ideas about individual character. Mancini, for example claimed that after Clarence's execution Richard III "was overheard to say that he would one day avenge his brother's death" at the hands of the Woodvilles—thus establishing an easily understood personal motive for Richard's seizure of the crown and his destruction of the Woodvilles.[80] Although Mancini is the only authority for this, certain scholars have accepted Richard's supposed outrage at Clarence's death as a virtual article of faith.[81] Yet how likely is it that Richard would have made such a dangerous remark? And if he had made it, how did it escape the attention of all other contemporary writers, particularly the second Crowland continuator, with his strong interest in human motivation and inside knowledge of Edward IV's court? And how did Man-

---

[79] See the similar but more general comments of Hanham (*Richard III*, 194), although even Hanham states that "there is no difficulty in believing that Vergil's concluding description of Richard [III] came, in its essentials, from people who had known him" (ibid., 130–31).

[80] Mancini, *Usurpation of Richard III*, 63.

[81] See, for example, Paul Murray Kendall, *Richard III* (New York, 1955), 147–49 and 305.

cini, who probably had difficulty understanding English and who does not seem to have had any informants close to Richard himself, come to hear about this remark?[82]

In the second place, a misleading and inaccurate picture of Tudor historiography has emerged from the readiness of scholars to conclude that obviously hostile and biased characterizations of Richard III are the result, directly or indirectly, of government propaganda. It is instructive to note that three humanist historians of Richard III's reign—Vergil, More, and even the relatively impartial Mancini—all come to the same conclusions about the plans of Richard III to seize the crown. More claimed that wise men thought Richard "long time in King Edward's life, forethought to be king," while Mancini's modern editor claims that Mancini's "assumption that the duke of Gloucester was all along aiming for the crown" is the only example of prejudice in his work.[83] One of the most important reasons—and one that has been completely overlooked—for Richard III's horrific reputation was the fact that the most influential accounts of his career and reign were written by men who were not only deeply influenced by the Roman historians but were also imbued with their ideas about character and motivation. On the other hand, it is equally wrong to assert—as C. D. Ross, in what is now the standard biography of Richard III, has done—that Vergil's praise of Richard's intelligence and courage is a mark of grace and intellectual honesty.[84] Rather, it is, as we have seen, part of an attempt to model Richard III on Sallust's Catiline.

Vergil's characterization of the important figures of fifteenth-century England was sometimes at variance with or even diametrically opposed to the ways they were described in his sources. When this occurred it was often because Vergil saw events from the standpoint of his classical models. Yet because of the tremendous influence of the *Anglica historia*, Vergil's interpretations often completely superseded the earlier ones and formed a new historical tradition. Thus, for example, Vergil's sources and fifteenth-century chroniclers in general were quite sympathetic to Richard of York and usually presented his career in a favorable light. In particular, they did not regard his claiming the throne as the culmination of a lifetime of ambitious scheming. As we have seen, Vergil, dominated by the classical conception of unchanging human

---

[82] For Mancini's ignorance of English and lack of information about Richard III see Mancini, *Usurpation of Richard III*, 16.

[83] CW2:8 (also see Thomas More, *Historia Richardi tertii*, ed. Daniel Kinney, in CW15:327, and Mancini, *Usurpation of Richard III*, 17.

[84] Ross, *Richard III*, xxv.

character, did suspect Richard's motives; and his authority, together with the coherence and consistency of his portrait of Richard of York, insured that his version of the duke's career was accepted without question by all the subsequent Tudor chroniclers.[85]

Vergil's adherence to classical models significantly influenced both the content of English history and the way it was written. One of the chief lessons Tudor historians drew from the *Anglica historia* was one Vergil had drawn from his classical models—the importance of indicating the motives and causes that lay behind events. As we have seen, Vergil's English predecessors generally had been content to record the deeds of men without worrying about what had caused their actions. By the middle of the sixteenth century, however, Vergil's example had triumphed to such an extent that the *Mirror for Magistrates*—a work that accurately reflected public tastes and was far from being the product of an intellectual avant-garde—could declare that "causes are the chiefest things that should be noted of the [hi]story writers" and could criticize earlier English chroniclers, such as Robert Fabyan, for failing to realize this.[86]

Beyond this, the *Anglica historia* served as an inspiration to other English writers to produce historical works which closely adhered to classical models. The most obvious example is More's *History of King Richard III*,[87] but Vergil's work also contributed to the "politic" histories that arose in the late sixteenth and early seventeenth centuries.[88]

---

[85] Edward Hall, *The Union of Two Noble and Illustre Families of Lancastre and York*, ed. Sir Henry Ellis (London, 1809), 233; Richard Grafton, *A Chronicle at Large*, ed. Sir Henry Ellis (London, 1809), 1:654; and Raphael Holinshed, *Holinshed's Chronicles of England, Scotland and Ireland*, ed. Sir Henry Ellis (London, 1808), 3:242.

[86] *The Mirror for Magistrates*, ed. Lily B. Campbell (Cambridge, 1938), 198.

[87] Note in this connection Alison Hanham's intersting hypothesis that More not only used the manuscript of the *Anglica historia* "as basis of his *History*" but that he was parodying Vergil's history in his work (*Richard III*, 159–61 and 164). Admittedly, Daniel Kinney has tentatively suggested that Vergil may have drawn on More's work rather than the other way around (CW15:626–27 note to 448/7–8). But since the manuscript of the *Anglica historia* was written in Italy, during Vergil's trip there in 1513–1514 (see Cecil Clough, "Federigo Veterani, Polydore Vergil's 'Anglica historia,' and Baldassare Castiglione's 'Epistola . . . ad Henricum Angliae Regem,' " *English Historical Review* 82 [1967]: 776–77), while Sylvester has dated the composition of More's history to 1514–1518 (CW2:lxiii–lxv)—and Kinney himself has pointed out indications that it was composed after 1515 (CW15:613 note to 344/6–346/23)—this seems unlikely.

[88] Vergil's contribution to Bacon's *Henry VII*, in particular, is still too readily overlooked, creating a misleading impression of the originality of Bacon's historical writing. Thus, when Edwin I. Berry argues that Bacon's description of Henry VII's increasing avarice marked a clear departure from the canons of humanist historical

Probably the most important classically inspired innovation Vergil brought to English historical writing, however, was his organization of his history by reigns instead of by years, by the six ages of man or any of the other medieval chronological arrangements. This regnal structure is not only an obvious difference between the works of chroniclers such as Robert Fabyan who preceded Vergil and subsequent chroniclers such as Edward Hall and Raphael Holinshed, but it laid the groundwork for later histories of individual reigns such as More's *History of King Richard III*, John Hayward's *The First Part of the Life and Raigne of King Henrie the IIII*, Francis Bacon's *History of the Reign of Henry VII*, and Edward Herbert's *The Life and Raigne of King Henry the Eighth*.

The conceptions of history and character that Vergil drew from his classical predecessors also contributed significantly to the formation of Vergil's providential interpretation of history. Vergil's classically inspired efforts to analyze the causes behind events and the importance he and his models attached to character and personality as causative factors in history merged with the classical conception of history as a series of moral crises, and naturally led to the passing of moral judgments on historical figures. They also fostered the conviction that there was an absolute correlation between the morality of a state's leaders and the prosperity and peace of that state. With these assumptions, it became easy to believe that the disasters which struck fifteenth-century England were the result of monstrous immorality among its rulers. The Sallustian emphasis on self-interest and hidden motives would naturally lead a historian to look for—and place credence in—secret crimes that had to be avenged before peace could be restored.

These classical conceptions of character also fostered Vergil's providential thinking in another way. G. R. Elton once commented that Vergil's "mind worked in stereotypes" and many of Vergil's characterizations are indeed one-dimensional portraits of people almost purely good or purely evil.[89] This tendency to stereotyping is a natural out-

---

writing ("History and Rhetoric in Bacon's *Henry VII*," in *Seventeenth-Century Prose: Modern Essays in Criticism*, ed. Stanley E. Fish [New York, 1971], 295–96), it is obvious that Berry was unaware of Polydore Vergil's earlier description of this process. Similarly, John F. Tinkler, after quoting Bacon's statement that some people thought that Henry VII's avarice was part of a deliberate policy to weaken his subjects' desire and capacity to rebel, points to Aristotle as the inspiration for Bacon's observation ("The Rhetorical Method of Francis Bacon's *History of the Reign of King Henry the VII*," *History and Theory* 26 [1987]: 41). What Tinkler does not mention is that this view had already been expressed by Hall (499), who was, in turn, merely transliterating the *Anglica historia* (C. S. III, 132*).

[89] Review of S. B. Chrimes, *Henry VII* (*Historical Journal* 16 [1973]: 627).

growth of the classical view of human nature as immutable, which, by eliminating an individual's internal conflicts and tensions as well as the hesitations, inhibitions, and ambiguities that mark anyone's career and aspirations, often led to the portrayal of human character as dominated by a single overriding virtue or vice, and of an individual's career as a single-minded effort to gratify the desires which arose from this virtue or vice. Once the central appetite or desire of an historical figure was established, the Roman historical writers generally tended to describe that figure only in terms of that desire. Tacitus's Messalina is little more than an embodiment of lust and his Vitellius an incarnation of gluttony. Furthermore, once people are pictured as embodying absolute vices it becomes natural to portray their rivals or opponents as embodying absolute virtues. Thus Tacitus idealized the younger Germanicus in order to denigrate his uncle, Tiberius; one reason why Vergil presented Richard of York in such an unfavorable light was his desire to portray Richard's opponent, Henry VI, in a favorable one.

This process of contrasting good and evil personalities, once started, easily built on itself. This happened in the *Anglica historica* where, since Henry VI was virtuous and Richard of York wickedly ambitious, Edmund Beaufort (in flat contradiction of Vergil's sources) was portrayed as a man of integrity trying to save his king from York's evil schemes. Similarly, because Humphrey of Gloucester was portrayed as a noble and upright statesman, his determined opponent the duke of Suffolk is described as an utterly corrupt and evil politician. This process continues until practically every important fifteenth-century figure in the *Anglica historia* is aligned with one of the two opposing moral camps. (But not political camps—Vergil did not describe one "party" as being righteous and the other evil; rather there were good and bad Yorkists and good and bad Lancastrians.) Having viewed fifteenth-century England as a battleground between virtuous and villainous leaders, it was only natural for Vergil to see the vicissitudes of the period as God's retribution or reward for such spectacular iniquity and pre-eminent virtue.

The importance of classical conceptions of history and human character in the development of Vergil's providential system should, however, be seen in perspective and not be exaggerated. These conceptions were not the reasons he adopted a providential viewpoint; to understand fully why Vergil did adopt one it is necessary to examine carefully the functions the *Anglica historia* was meant to serve—a task well beyond the limits of this paper. Nevertheless, the manifold influence of Sallust, Suetonius, and Tacitus upon Vergil greatly facilitated his acceptance of a providential viewpoint and helped him to form a systematic providential interpretation of English history, an interpretation which would form the theme for the plays of England's greatest dramatist and which would not be the least of the many debts England owed Italy during the Renaissance.[90]

Rutgers University—New Brunswick

---

[90] I would like to thank the Richard III Society for their grant of a Schalleck Memorial Fellowship, which assisted in the research for this paper. I would also like to thank Rutgers faculty members John Lenaghen, Jack Cargill, Traian Stoianovich, Karl F. Morrison, Martha Carlin, and especially Maurice D. Lee, for the valuable criticisms they made of earlier versions of this paper.

KENNETH LLOYD-JONES

From Sewers to Triumphal Arches: Dolet's Ideal of Civic Oratory

AMONG THE TEXTS GENERATED BY THE QUARREL OVER CICEROnian style, Etienne Dolet's *De imitatione Ciceroniana*[1] stands out for the dynamism of its attack on the Erasmian approach to the emulation of classical authors. Although not published until Dolet had established himself in the humanist printing circles in Lyons, the *Erasmianus* was in all likelihood begun as early as 1528 while he was a student at Padua under such distinguished Ciceronians as Villanovanus, himself a disciple of the recently deceased Longolius—hence the work's subtitle: "adversus Desiderium Erasmum Roterodamum, pro Christophoro Longolio." 1528 was of course the year that had seen the publication of Erasmus's brilliant and devastating attack on the Ciceronians, the *Ciceronianus*,[2] and it is this text, deriding as it did those very Latinists whom the young Dolet was striving to follow, that forms the necessary background to the present discussion.

It is too easy to dismiss the protagonists in the quarrel over the imitation of Ciceronian style as hidebound formalists, bickering over the *minutiae* of linguistic fidelity and structural rigor, while losing sight of whether what was being said was in fact worth saying. That such a view became widespread is, to a large degree, a tribute to the wit and polemical exuberance of Erasmus's condemnation of those whose veneration of Cicero's thought and language led them to little more than mindless aping. Erasmus's attack had centered on two basic issues—one esthetic or stylistic in nature, the other ideological. The first argument is straightforward enough: modern times and modern sensi-

---

[1] (Lyons: Gryphius, 1535); facsimile and commentary in E. V. Telle, *L'Erasmianus sive Ciceronianus d'Etienne Dolet* (Geneva: Droz, 1974).

[2] (Basel: Froben, 1528); text and translation in A. Gambaro, *Dialogus, cui titulus Ciceronianus, sive De optimo genere dicendi* (Brescia: La Scuola Editrice, 1965). See also B. I. Knott's annotated translation in the *Collected Works of Erasmus*, vol. 28, *Literary and Educational Writings*, ed. A. H. T. Levi (Toronto: Univ. of Toronto Press, 1986), 323–603.

bilities call for modern modes of expression, and it is both anachronistic and stylistically improper to use Ciceronian Latin to argue and explore today's issues. Good style calls for us not to freeze Latin into an excessively reverential kind of *rigor mortis*, but to grant it all the spontaneity and capacity for growth of a truly living language. Erasmus's second argument goes much farther: to express the mysteries and truths of Christianity while insisting on limiting oneself to the language of pagan Latinity is, inevitably, to fall into paganizing oneself.[3] Writing in 1528, barely ten years after Luther's break with Rome, Erasmus contemplates a Christendom increasingly divided: thought is inseparable from the means of its expression, and the promotion of Ciceronian Latin—the language of a writer and a culture from whom God in his wisdom has chosen to withhold the benefits of revealed Truth—can only exacerbate the intellectual disarray now threatening Christian unity.

Dolet's answering *Erasmianus* seeks to refute Erasmus's arguments by positing the superiority of Cicero as both a conceptual and a stylistic model, and by insisting on the distinction between rhetorical strategies (which properly constitute a basis for the dialectic of argument and discussion) and issues of belief and conscience. The *Erasmianus* argues that rhetoric deals with the formal arrangement of ideas as a means of persuasion, whereas faith is ultimately a matter for the privacy of a man's heart; as such it is not subject to the judgment of others less intimately acquainted with the inner justification of our beliefs.[4]

Inasmuch as Dolet's polemical text answers argument with argument, it engages Erasmus theoretically, on the terrain of ideology. Destiny had, however, provided Dolet with the opportunity, some five years after the publication of Erasmus's volume, to respond on the level of practice. While an aspiring law student at the University of Toulouse,

---

[3] Erasmus's jocular presentation of the "scrupulous Ciceronian's" dilemma was not meant to mask the grave doctrinal issues at stake: "Quid faciet? quo se uertet hic ille superstitiose ciceronianus? An pro patre Christi dicet 'Iuppiter Optimus Maximus,' pro filio dicet 'Apollinem' aut 'Aesculapium'; pro uirginum regina dicet 'Dianam'; pro ecclesia 'sacram concionem,' aut 'ciuitatem' aut 'rempublicam'; pro ethnico 'perduellem'; pro haeresi 'factionem'; pro schismate 'seditionem'; pro fide christiana 'christianam persuasionem'...? Quid hic faciet ciceronianiae phraseos candidatus? Utrum'ne tacebit, an ad hunc modum immutabit recepta Christianis uocabula?" (*Ciceronianus*, ed. Gambaro, lines 1931-56: "What will our Ciceronian do here with his scruples? Where will he turn? Will he say 'Jupiter Optimus Maximus' for the Father of Christ, 'Apollo' or 'Aesculapius' for the Son? Will he say 'Diana' for the Queen of Virgins; 'sacred assembly' or 'state' or 'republic' for the Church; 'betrayer' for pagan; 'faction' for heresy; 'sedition' for schism; 'the Christian persuasion' for the Christian faith...? What will he who aspires to Ciceronian phraseology do here? Will he keep silent, or will he transform in this manner the vocabulary accepted by Christians?")

[4] See Telle, *Erasmianus*, introduction, 15-63.

Dolet gave, in the fall and winter of 1533, two public speeches in Latin, which he published in Lyons the following year under the title *Orationes duae in Tholosam*.[5] These speeches are clearly intended to refute Erasmus's criticisms by providing a dazzling demonstration of what can be achieved through the skillful deployment of Ciceronian oratory. As such they reveal how one of the most important humanists of the French Renaissance viewed the issues raised by Erasmus and sought to integrate classical rhetorical techniques and values into the major cultural and political concerns of the 1530s.

Dolet's first speech was delivered on October 9, in his capacity as official orator of the guild of French students at the University of Toulouse ("French" meaning from north of the Loire, as opposed to the Gascons or Aquitains). He spoke to protest the frequent (and ultimately futile) attempts of the city fathers to close down the various national associations of students, chiefly on account of their boisterousness and occasionally murderous rivalry. There is also good reason to believe that many student guilds were hotbeds of the "new learning" that was clearly so threatening to a bastion of Catholic orthodoxy like Toulouse, and Dolets's identification with such groups surely tagged him as someone henceforth to be eyed with suspicion.[6]

Dolet's main argument lay in his assertion of the self-evident and universally celebrated superiority of the French over the Gascons, these latter being the source of every misdeed committed throughout the known world. Not surprisingly, an answering speech was delivered by a Gascon orator, Pierre Pinache, a few weeks later. While this speech is now lost to us, it was clearly of an insultingly personal nature and stung Dolet into responding by means of his *Oratio secunda*, delivered not in his capacity as official orator this time, but rather as a personal *apologia*.

More particularly for our purposes, it was Pinache's jibe, reported in the *Oratio secunda*, that Dolet was no more than a "fervent imitator of Cicero" (2.35) that went to the heart of Dolet's immediate purposes as an orator, and, as such, to the heart of his larger quarrel with what he judged to be the Erasmian understanding of rhetoric. Pinache's sneering remark was of course potentially very dangerous. In Toulouse, home of the Dominican order and the Inquisition, even the hint of paganism was not to be taken lightly. Barely a year before his speeches, Dolet had witnessed the burning of one of the law professors, Jean de Caturce,

---

[5] *Orationes duae in Tholosam. Eiusdem epistolarum libri II. Eiusdem carminum libri II. Ad eundem epistolarum amicorum liber* (Lyons: Gryphius, 1534). M. van der Poel and I hope to publish an annotated edition and translation of the *Orationes* soon.

[6] See Telle, *Erasmianus, Appendice VIII*, 435-37, and passim.

accused of "blasphemy and Lutheranism," an event that was to prompt Rabelais's young giant Pantagruel to study elsewhere, "when he saw that [in Toulouse] they caused their professors to be roasted alive, like smoked herrings."[7] Indeed, not even at the Sorbonne was the new humanism more in jeopardy than in Toulouse. In light of such a situation, the striking thing is that far from seeking to deflect the dangerous nature of Pinache's remark, Dolet was in fact to delight in his having been characterized as a "religiosus Ciceronis imitator."

In a purely formal sense, Dolet's fidelity to the norms of Ciceronian rhetorical practice in the two *Orationes* is total. In keeping with the principles outlined in the major treatises of Cicero and Quintilian, Dolet's speeches are models of rhetorical organization. Both the first speech, conforming to the *genus deliberativum* (meant to persuade the public of the city fathers' improper actions in suppressing the student associations), and the second, exemplifying the *genus demonstrativum* (in which Dolet defends his own name and seeks to cast blame on Pinache), follow clearly the classically prescribed divisions from *exordium* through *conclusio*. Each speech contains numerous examples of the approved "figures of speech" and "figures of thought," and Dolet's Latin itself is replete with echoes and imitations of Cicero's rhetorical strategies and oratorical idiosyncracies. These stylistic devices range from typical imprecations to *clausulae* (although he never uses "esse videatur"!) and draw heavily on the forensic speeches: there is scarcely a characterization of Antonius, Catilina, Vatinius, or Verres that is too good to apply to Pinache. Dolet's vocabulary eschews neologisms, accumulation and parallelisms abound, and the three registers of *oratio gravis*, *oratio media*, and *oratio tenuis* are carefully alternated to provide variety and esthetic satisfaction.[8] However, to raise such matters as these is to speak only of externals, whereas it is the conceptual implications of Dolet's Ciceronianism that matter, if we are to appreciate his understanding of the role that classical rhetoric must play in the turbulent days ahead.

"By the immortal god," exults Dolet, "what could be more magnificent for me, more beautiful, more blessed" than to be called a fervent imitator of Cicero? In a barely veiled allusion to the Erasmian notion of imitation and the role it plays in original composition, he agrees that if he were incapable of finding sufficient inspiration for his eloquence

---

[7] "mais il n'y demoura guères quand il vit qu'ilz faisoyent brusler leur régens tous vifz, comme harans soretz ..." (*Pantagruel*, chap. 5).

[8] For a more detailed discussion of these technical matters, see K. Lloyd-Jones, "Dolet et la rhétorique: les *Orationes in Tholosam*," *Etienne Dolet (1509–1546), Cahiers V. L. Saulnier* no. 3, (Paris: Univ. de Paris-Sorbonne, 1986), 79–92, and idem, "Renaissance Rhetoric: Dolet's *Orationes in Tholosam (1533–1534)*," *Neo-Latin Bulletin* 4, 2 (1988): 14–18.

among the writings of Cicero, he would indeed deserve Pinache's sarcasm:

> [I say this because] if I were to wander indiscriminately through all the categories of writers and orators of our time in search of an example, and not find a single one among them whom I could imitate, or if (like you and the Dutch rhetor) I considered Cicero's inexhaustible abundance and richness to be so scanty and parsimonious that I should despair of being able to supply everything that was needed to those desirous of speaking Latin, then you could rightly destroy me with your laughter. You could indeed compare me to those who practice the sort of eloquence where things are made up of a pile of words drawn from all over, and flung together in a huge heap of stories, examples and adages, like a piece of gaudily colored material sewn together with bits of cloth taken from wherever they could be found. You could indeed accuse me of having practiced an eloquence devoid of refinement, charm, or significance, whose form lacks organization and consistency, as if—in its futility—it were bloated with an excess of words, and overflowing with the number of topics treated.[9]

When, echoing Cicero's portrayals of the debauched Marcus Antonius, Dolet accuses Pinache of comparable intemperance—

> Once he had done these obscene and repulsive things, nothing could destroy the madness of this obscene and repulsive creature. He has foully vomited over me a harangue embellished with no ornament of rhetoric, but rather one composed in the course of so many nightly drinking bouts that now, as if suffering from a hangover, and with his belly and his brain huffing and puffing with indigestion, and on the point of befouling himself, he spews it over us too.[10]

---

[9] "quid me per deum immortalem lautius? quid pulchrius? quid denique beatius? ... Quod si per omnia scriptorum genera inconsulte nostri temporis oratorum exemplo vagarer, nec aliquem unum mihi imitandum proponerem, aut si tuo Batavique rhetoris iudicio inexhaustam Ciceronis copiam atque ubertatem, ita tenuem contractamque arbitrarer, ut latine loqui cupienti non omnia abunda suppeditare posse diffiderem, risu me iure proscinderes, ab iis non dissimilem, qui eo orationis genere utuntur, quae ex verborum undique accersitorum corrogatorumque congerie, et immenso historiarum, exemplorum, adagionumque cumulo, velut cento undequaque consutus, constet: quaeque nullam neque elegantiam, neque venustatem, neque gravitatem prae se ferat, formamque inconditam habeat, et minime aequabilem: sicque verbis distenta sit et exuberans, rerum pondere inanis" (2.35-36).

[10] "Illa sic obscoene et turpiter facta, obscoeni turpisque hominis furorem non extinxere, concionem non ullo rhetoricae ornatu expolitam, sed tam multis compota-

—we are not simply dealing with a conventional manner of censuring one's adversary, but rather with the judgement of a Ciceronian contemplating the Erasmian model. What we have here is an exactly *opposite* conception from what Terence Cave has so precisely defined as the governing concern of Erasmus's Folly:

> from the beginning of her demonstrative exercise, [she] will repeatedly reject rhetorical planning in favour of extempore speech; immediacy, in her view, is a sign of nature and consequently a guarantee of authenticity.[11]

Erasmian authenticity stems from the personal, spontaneous quality of the text, where the author's *self* is the generator of authority, whereas Dolet's sense of authenticity stems from a more objective notion of what constitutes, in all senses of the word, the *auctoritas* of the text. Authorial *auctoritas* cannot be better guaranteed than by fidelity to the greatest of the authorities, Cicero. To speak directly, from the heart, instinctively and naturally, is what matters for Erasmus:

> the issue of extempore speech is decisive in determining the opposition between a written (Ciceronian) and a spoken (Erasmian) model of discourse.... The project of Ciceronian imitation is enclosed within the space of the written; its commitment to the past, to isolation and to absence, excludes it from life, presence, the accident of the moment.[12]

But for Dolet, and those like him, there is a different ideal, in which we bring the best of our advocacy and of our most competent skills to the defense of morally and ethically defensible values. Because the essence of rhetoric lies in the art of persuasion, the first merit of Ciceronianism lies in its ability to help us defend the good, and the classical model of the orator as a "vir bonus peritus dicendi" seems ever more urgently needed in the France of the early 1530s.

In one of the more impassioned moments of the *Oratio secunda*, Dolet taxes Pinache with a complete failure to understand what he had been

---

tionibus nocturnis elucubratam, quam crapulam, et stomachi cerebrique cruditatem exhalantem, in me foede evomuit, eademque nos se contaminaturum dissipat" (2.67). Cf. for example *Philippicae* 2.63 and 5.20. Among many other imitations, cf. Cicero's cry of outrage, "O rem non modo visu foedam, set etiam auditu!" (*Ph.* 2.63), echoed in Dolet's "O rem cum auditu crudelem, tum visu nefariam" (2.47); Pinache's Latin is found wanting ("non Latine candidoque animo dicentem" [2.25]), as was that of Antonius (*Ph.* 13.43).

[11] T. Cave, *The Cornucopian Text: Problems of Writing in the French Renaissance* (Oxford: Clarendon Press, 1979), 127.
[12] Ibid., 139.

trying to do in his first speech. Of course he had had harsh words for the Toulouse Parliament which, in its attempt to ban the student unions, was destroying the nature of friendship and fraternity itself. But, he proclaims, "the fact remains that it is not what might be said, but in what spirit it is said, that must be carefully considered."[13] Is Pinache's mentality so deranged, he asks, that he does not know that orators must use a style adapted to the circumstances, the time, and the place?

> Can you doubt that, from time to time, it is granted to an orator, and indeed a matter for his discretion, to fashion things to his own liking, sometimes (in line with his duty) not to speak the truth, to pretend, to dissemble, to have us take sewers for triumphal arches, to debase the sublime, to exalt the ignoble, sometimes to argue according to the letter of the law and sometimes to step back from it, to shade everything, to turn it upside down, to change everything around?[14]

Such a passage as this might surely seem to argue for considerably less than the ideal of the "good man skilled in the art of speaking": there is without a doubt something alarming in the proposition that it is permissible for an orator, whose chief function it is to persuade us, "*not* to speak the truth, to pretend, to dissemble." Indeed, the danger posed by the specious orator ready to hire out his technical abilities in the name of ignoble causes is constantly stressed by the classical theoreticians, and lies at the very basis of their insistence that rhetorical competence be anchored in the notion of appropriateness—that the style be appropriate to the occasion. As Cicero declares in the *De oratore*:

> It is up to the orator to use identical embellishments of style in ways that are on one occasion more powerful, and on another more subdued; and whereas to be able, in all things, to do what is appropriate is a matter of both skill and talent, to know what

---

[13] "Etenim non quid dicatur, sed quo dicatur animo accurate videndum est" (2.63).

[14] "Tune, Pinachi, absurdo ita ingenio ... ut multa interdum vel fingere, vel officiose nonnunquam mentiri, ut simulare, dissimulare, arcem [sic] ex cloaca facere, sublimia deprimere, abiecta attollere, summo iure aliquando agere, de iure quandoque decedere, omnia denique variare, pervertere, transferreque, concessum oratori, atque solutum dubites?" (2.64). Cicero uses the proverbial expression "arcum [sic] facere ex cloaca" (*Pro Plancio* 95); the version used by Dolet (*arx* [citadel] for *arcum* [triumphal arch]) is now generally considered as stemming from an early misreading of the manuscript tradition.

is appropriate, and when it is so, is a matter of practical wisdom.[15]

Scire quid quandoque deceat prudentiae.... Classical rhetoric clearly implies a kind of contractual understanding between orator and listener as to what the rules of engagement are. The orator's function and duties cannot be separated from the listener's, who also has the responsibility of distinguishing between what is said and the manner in which it is said; as Dolet goes on to argue, the "contract" requires that the listener too be able to distinguish between the orator speaking in false accusation and the orator speaking to protect the innocent.[16] Unlike the spontaneous and highly personalized eloquence of an Erasmus, which we cannot evaluate without fully knowing the personal values of the orator, the objective and universally appreciable skills that underpin Ciceronian eloquence serve to protect the interests of truth and justice, as long as both players and spectators know and respect the conventions.

The *Orationes in Tholosam* show Dolet's moral ideal to be inseparable from his Ciceronian, rhetorical ideal; his defense of the orator is fully congruent with his defense of the values he must argue for, if the new learning is to prevail over the old, tolerance over intolerance, humanism over superstition. Dolet's imitation of Cicero, from start to finish in the *Orationes*, serves to convey the vision of a world rendered less insecure when it is apprehended through the structures and values of classical rhetoric. This vision is composed of three principal elements: first, a particular concept of the social order, based on Cicero's notion of the relationships between eloquence, friendship, and the notion of *humanitas*; second, consideration of the damage done to the social order when rhetorical principles are betrayed by those who would follow the Erasmian model of discourse; and third, a certain idea of his own art, in which the values of classical rhetoric are rethought and reaffirmed in a world in which the wisdom of the ancients seems in increasingly short supply.

Adhering closely to the opening pages of the *De inventione*, Dolet in turn argues that the orator inspired by wisdom, putting his talents at

---

[15] "Ornamentis eisdem uti fere licebit alias contentius, alias summissius; omnique in re posse quod deceat facere artis et naturae est, scire quid quandoque deceat prudentiae" (*De oratore* 3.212).

[16] "Hoc inter constantem et inconstantem, hoc inter prudentem et ignarum hoc inter aequum iudicem, et calumniatorem interest, quod hic omnia detorquet, recte dicta calumniatur, innocentissimo cuique invidiam periculumque intendit. Constans autem et prudentia praeditus, innocentem de reis eximit, aequum se rebus praebet, imprudenter lapsis non superbe ignoscit, diligenter omnia accurateque discutit, ut suum quisque ius atque aequum bonum obtineat, non dolosa verborum interpretatione in discrimen vocetur" (2.64–65).

the service of his country and of his fellow citizens, can in fact be the embodiment of the civic ideal. Just as the opening pages of the *Orationes* resound with cries of appreciation toward those who have welcomed him into their confraternity, so their closing pages echo with reiterated calls for his listeners to grant him their love and friendship. The final words of the *Oratio secunda* explicitly connect the notion of the *amicitia* that binds the orator to his fellow citizens with his own responsibility to defend his community:

> It is not right, when you have been so prompt in revealing the respect you bear me, that I should be slow to declare my gratitude. And so, gentlemen, I shall conclude my oration. For your part, as indeed you do, grant me your love forever. For my part, as indeed I do, I shall ever defend and protect your dignity from the violence and the insults of your enemies.[17]

Such is indeed the *credo* of one who seeks to be both *utilissimus* and *amicissimus* in his dealings with the state, fully in keeping with Cicero's definition of the ideal citizen-orator:

> But the man who arms himself with eloquence, not to oppose the well-being of his country, but so that he might fight to defend it—such a man will, in my opinion, be seen to be the citizen who is the most helpful and the most devoted to both his own interests and those of the state.[18]

In attempting to strike down the student associations, the authorities of Toulouse are destroying an essential part of the social fabric: it was the need for fraternity and friendship that first brought primitive peoples together into families, clans, and nations, and the intelligence that led them thus to group together could have had nothing of what Cicero refers to as a "silent wisdom, lacking in eloquence":

> As far as I am concerned, it seems impossible that the wisdom that succeeded in suddenly turning mankind away from the force of habit, and in bringing us to a different way of living, could have been silent and lacking in eloquence.... For from eloquence many advantages accrue to the state, on condition that wisdom

---

[17] "Non aequum est, cum vos ad promerendum officium tam fueritis expediti, me ad referendam gratiam esse tardum. Iam finem dicendi faciam, Viri Amplissimi, vos quod facitis, perpetuo me amate, ego, quod facio, dignitatem vestram in perpetuum ab inimicorum vi atque iniuriis defendam, et tuebor" (2.74).

[18] "qui vero sese armat eloquentia, ut non oppugnare commoda patriae, sed pro his propugnare possit, is mihi vir et suis et publicis rationibus utilissimus atque amicissimus civis fore videtur" (*De inv.* 1.1).

be at hand as the mistress of all things. Through eloquence, glory, honor, and great esteem come to those who have acquired wisdom. Through eloquence they can also provide the surest and safest protection for their friends.... Therefore it seems to me that the man who excels among mankind itself in that ability by which men surpass the beasts has indeed acquired something of excellence.[19]

Wisdom needs the skillful orator for it to be propagated as the necessary bond in a well-ordered *civitas*, and the ability to speak wisely, to give voice to wisdom, is in turn the very basis of our *humanitas* and our *virtus*.

It is this high notion of the orator's civic function that underlies the other two dimensions of Dolet's humanist vision as it is expounded in the *Orationes*, and as enacted in his remaining dozen or so years of creative activity. "The fact remains that it is not what might be said, but in what spirit it is said, that must be carefully considered." Erasmus's call for spontaneity and "sincerity" as the true basis of eloquence jeopardizes the social bond: who can truly know an individual's deepest convictions but that individual himself? What truly matters is indubitably the spirit in which things are said—but when we cannot be certain of knowing that spirit, we must not persecute and torture and kill, we must not imperil the social fabric in the mistaken assumption that any man can be privy to the conscience of another. It is precisely such a conviction that leads Dolet to his vibrant condemnation of the burning of Jean de Caturce; the cruelty of the authorities is denounced not only on fundamental humanitarian grounds, but also because what happened represented a betrayal of the very social compact that eloquence seeks to secure:

> Since he was in the process of climbing out of the whirlpool and the abyss of his error, and eager to reach the haven of the good, why did they not all agree to enable him to bring his vessel back to port? These were his last words, his appeal of the archbishop's sentence and of the City Parliament's verdict of capital punishment; who could deny, according to any law whatsoever, that such an appeal should have been held to be valid, and should

---

[19] "Ac mihi quidem videtur hoc nec tacita nec inops dicendi sapientia perficere potuisse ut hominis a consuetudine subito converteret et ad diversas rationes vitae traduceret.... Nam hinc ad rem publicam plurima commoda veniunt, si moderatrix omnium rerum praesto est sapientia; hinc ad ipsos qui eam adepti sunt laus, honos, dignitas confluit; hinc amicis quoque eorum certissimum et tutissimum praesidium comparatur.... Quare praeclarum mihi quiddam videtur adeptus is qua re homines bestiis praestent ea in re hominibus ipsis antecellat" (*De inv.* 1.3–5).

have been granted? But, in the end, it availed him nothing to have sought to return, after having erred, to the right path. No change of mind, which is commonly the haven of the penitent, could keep his life safe from the savagery of the unjust.[20]

The orator's function, as Roman law consistently assumed, is to persuade, not to reveal the truth, and even the most specious orator can only affect our grasp of the *appearance* of things: all the more reason, then, to be extremely careful when we make of appearances—of what we believe to be the beliefs of others—matters of life and death. Appearance is a very different matter from truth; even when we are persuaded to take sewers for triumphal arches, the truth stands unimpaired, and the sewer remains a sewer. If the end is social good, and upon the absolute condition that the advocate is indeed "a good man, skilled in the art of speaking," then society, in the civic vision that permeates the conclusion of the *Oratio secunda*, can afford to allow the end to justify the means. We are not so far here from that other, exactly contemporary, civic vision that Rabelais incorporates into his abbey of Thélème, where it will become possible to build a society based on the single law that free citizens need observe, "Do what thou wilt"—"Fay ce que vouldras,"

> because free men and women, born to good families, well educated and discussing matters in honest good-fellowship, possess by nature an instinct, something that spurs them on, that always encourages them to behave virtuously, and dissuades them from vice, and this instinct is what they would call "honor."[21]

For Dolet as for Rabelais, a proper understanding of eloquence and rhetorical arrangement, enabling us to deal with each other while "conversans en compaignies honnestes," remains a condition of the ideal *civitas*.

The *sine qua non* of Dolet's vision is, of course, the requirement that the orator be indeed a good man. Erasmus would have us follow the

---

[20] "Quare ex erroris vortice voragineque emergenti, et se ad portum frugemque bonam recipere cupienti, non omnium consensu data est navem inhibendi facultas? Fuit haec ultima illius vox, et a pontificis sententia, et a senatus iudicio capitali provocatio: quam quis probabilem acceptamque haberi debuisse iure ullo inficietur? Profuit tamen nihil post erratum in viam redire voluisse: nec, quae portus poenitenti esse solet, mutatio consilii, vitam illi incolumen ab iniquorum immanitate servare potuit" (2.56). For Dolet, the need for separation of church and state, for distinction between private conscience and public power, is clearly paramount.

[21] "parce que gens libères, bien néz, bien instruictz, conversans en compaignies honnestes, ont par nature un instinct et aguillon, qui tousjours les poulse à faictz vertueux et retire de vice, lequel ilz nommoient honneur" (*Gargantua*, chap. 57).

inclinations of our own nature—so obviously unstable, so necessarily self-directed as to be highly suspect as the basis for our ability to speak wisely, to give voice to wisdom. Dolet would have us follow Cicero, the most articulate and persuasive voice that classical wisdom brought forth, yet also one whose sense of the good is such that even Erasmus readily grants that he would have been a saint, were he to have lived after the revelation:

> He was the best craftsman in the art of speaking, and as good a man as could be found among the pagans. I think that if he had studied Christian philosophy, he would deserve to have been counted among those who, nowadays, on account of their having lived in a blameless and pious manner, are venerated as saints.[22]

The immediate aftermath of Dolet's two speeches was a short period of imprisonment, followed by his banishment from Toulouse, but this temporary victory of the "barbarians" over the spokesman for the new republic of letters was not to be allowed to stand. He left Toulouse with the avowed intention of returning to Italy, more precisely to Padua, where the triumph of Ciceronianism and all its values must have seemed a far surer thing.[23] Dolet was to travel only as far as Lyons, however, capital of the French printing industry. He immediately became an employee of one of the most prestigious of the humanist printers established there, Sebastianus Gryphius, and within less than two years had availed himself of Gryphius's presses to publish the volume containing his speeches, poems, and letters, the *Erasmianus*, and the first of his two massive tomes of *Commentaries on the Latin Language*.[24] For Dolet, leaving Toulouse for Lyons was to mean moving from the study and eventual practice of jurisprudence to devoting his life to the advocacy of the new values. The spoken word must necessarily yield henceforth to the written, and this was in turn to alter, dramat-

---

[22] "Dicendi artifex optimus, atque etiam ut inter ethnicos vir bonus, quem arbitror si christianam philosophiam didicisset, in eorum numero censendum fuisse, qui nunc ob vitam innocenter pieque transactam pro divis honorantur" (*Ciceronianus*, ed. Gambaro, lines 4374–78).

[23] Writing to his protector, Jean de Langeac, from his prison cell in a letter dated 1 March 1534, Dolet states, "addam hoc solum, in animo esse mihi, Patavium ad ineuntem autumnum proficisci, illic ut studiorum meorum legitimorum rudimenta ponam, & cursum in literis susceptum conficiam" (*Epistolarum liber II* [see n. 4, above], 137): "I will merely add that it is in my mind to proceed to Padua next fall, in order to begin afresh on my legal studies there, and to complete my course of studies in the realm of scholarship." There can be little doubt as to where the bulk of his time would have been spent!

[24] See above, notes 4 and 1 respectively; vol. 1 of Dolet's *Commentarii linguae Latinae* appeared in 1536 (vol. 2 appeared two years later).

ically and unexpectedly, Dolet's understanding of what his heroic conception of the orator could lead to in the France of his day. It ultimately brought him to choose, and indeed to become one of the strongest proponents of the vernacular over Latin as the most persuasive means of propagating ancient wisdom: the new age called for the Latin orator to become one of the foremost printers and publishers in the French language.[25]

In France perhaps more poignantly than elsewhere, given the times, the growing threat to both the new learning and to the *res publica* from the 1530s onward called urgently for the future to be built on the best of the past—and no matter how reactionary the Ciceronians might now seem to us, that is in the end what the more thoughtful among them hoped to achieve. To deliver, and especially to publish, the *Orationes* constituted Dolet's first steps along a path that was to lead to the gallows and end among the flames in 1546. But for the moment we are still in 1533. In his two speeches, Dolet gives voice, both structurally and conceptually, to an authentically humanist civic vision, in which the promise of the future is guaranteed by all that is sure and good in the past. Given the harshness of the times, the very act of publishing his *Orationes* is an act of faith—faith in the capacity of the *res publica* to move toward a better world, in which, as Cicero has it (*Brutus* 45), society has only to privilege the orator and empower him to speak persuasively, for the handmaiden, and indeed the ward, of peace, order, and civic harmony to be revealed as none other than Eloquence herself.

Trinity College

---

[25] Within three years of Dolet's execution, Joachim Du Bellay was to hail him as a "man of good judgment in our national language" ([un] homme de bon jugement en notre vulgaire) (*La Deffence et illustration de la langue françoyse* [Paris, 1549], ed. H. Chamard [Paris: Didier, 1948], 86). The reasons for Dolet's eventual championing of the vernacular are complex. Over and above the issue of national values implicit in Du Bellay's appreciation, there is little doubt that psychological complications following the delivery of the speeches in Toulouse, his imprisonment and his subsequent exile played a major role in his evolution; cf. C. Longeon, "Etienne Dolet: Années d'enfance et de jeunesse," *Réforme et Humanisme* (Montpellier, 1977), 37–61, and idem, "Cohérences d'Etienne Dolet," *Acta Conventus Neo-Latini Sanctandreani*, ed. I. D. McFarlane, Medieval & Renaissance Texts & Studies, vol. 38 (Binghamton, NY, 1986), 363–69.

PATRICIA FRANCIS CHOLAKIAN

Signs of the "Feminine": The Unshaping of Narrative in Marguerite de Navarre's Heptaméron, Novellas 2, 4, and 10

THE SEARCH FOR "FEMININE WRITING"[1] SHOULD BEGIN WITH AN attempt to discover how early women's texts interact with the narrative conventions of men's fictions about gender relations. In other words, early women's narratives should be read as autobiographies which encode the experiences of historical women, and as palimpsests which write over the pre-existing male narratives.[2]

One of the first women to write fiction in French was Marguerite d'Angoulême (1492–1549), sister to King François Ier and Queen of Navarre.[3] Exceptionally well educated and conversant with several languages, she was the leading lady of the French Renaissance. Her best known work, the Heptaméron, is a self-announced imitation of Boccaccio's Decameron.[4] It consists of seventy-two tales, told by ten narrators, and framed by conversations and a Prologue. Her decision to work in the novella genre is in some ways surprising—for the early novella was given to gross sexual exaggeration and scabrous detail,[5] whereas she

---

[1] For a definition of "feminine" writing, see Hélène Cixous, "The Laugh of the Medusa," Signs (1976) 1, 4: 875–93. She argues that "feminine" writing does not yet exist because women are not free to write about their bodies. I agree that women's writing originates in the attempt to "write the body" but I also believe that traces of it can be found in early women's works.

[2] I use the word "palimpsest" in the sense defined by Gérard Genette in Palimpsestes: La littérature au second degré (Paris: Seuil, 1982).

[3] Marie de France (twelfth century) may or may not have been a woman. Christine de Pisan's writings were largely didactic and allegorical. Two other women who wrote fiction in the early French Renaissance were Hélisenne de Crenne and Jeanne Flore, although there is no definitive proof that the latter was a woman either.

[4] Marguerite de Navarre, L'Heptaméron, edited by Michel François (Paris: Garnier, 1945). All references in parenthesis are to this edition. English translations of this and other French texts are my own. The most recently published translation in English is The "Heptameron," trans. by P. A. Chilton (Harmondsworth: Penguin, 1984).

[5] For a definition of the French novella, see Patricia Francis Cholakian and Rouben Charles Cholakian, The Early French Novella (Albany: SUNY Press, 1972), 17–73. For a more general discussion of the genre in the Renaissance, see Robert J.

was a high-born lady of impeccable reputation whose other works treat mainly of moral and spiritual concerns. Although purporting to instruct by example, the genre's main goal was to entertain, usually by eliciting laughter—and its butt was frequently a woman. Descended from the medieval *fabliau* and heavily imbued with the virulent anti-feminism of such works as Jean de Meung's *Roman de la Rose* and *Les Quinze Joies de mariage*, it routinely depicted Eve's descendants as deceptive, lascivious, and unfaithful.

Furthermore, Gallic short fiction was aimed at a male audience. Philippe de Vigneulles situated his *Cent Nouvelles Nouvelles* (1505–1515?) in a military garrison, and Bonaventure Des Périers hinted that his *Nouvelles Récréations et Joyeux Devis* (published posthumously in 1558) were unsuitable for female readers. Nicolas de Troyes's *Le Grand Parangon des Nouvelles Nouvelles* (1537) offers a striking example of the genre's phallic preoccupations: his novella 27 tells of a ring which increases the size of the male organ by half a foot every time its wearer makes the sign of the cross.

How then was it possible for the Queen of Navarre to write within a genre so clearly masculine in its construction of gender relations? Was it not inevitable that the tension between her refined femininity and the novella's coarse ribaldry would result in a warping of the narrative fabric? What is more, would not the double standard imposed on sexuality during the Renaissance mark her retelling of both comic and tragic stories about women in love?[6]

On the surface the *Heptaméron* appears to resemble its predecessors in its depiction of sexual peccadilloes; but as the Prologue makes clear, this "French Decameron" set out to be *different*. First, all of the tales were to be true. To be sure French novellas of the fifteenth and sixteenth centuries frequently made such assertions, but in most cases their claims of veracity were nothing more than a rhetorical convention, a traditional way of introducing an old tale that had been around for centuries.[7] In the *Heptaméron*, however, many stories *are* verifiably true, and novella four, a story of attempted rape, is believed to be based on what happened to the writer in her own bed. Secondly, its narrators were not to be "gens de lettres" (professional writers), and their tales were not to be spoiled by "art" or "rhetoric" (9). In the *Heptaméron*,

---

Clements and Joseph Gibaldi, *Anatomy of the Novella: The European Tale Collection from Boccaccio and Chaucer to Cervantes* (New York: New York Univ. Press, 1977).

[6] See Ian Maclean, *The Renaissance Notion of Woman* (Cambridge: Cambridge Univ. Press; 1980), especially chap. 2.

[7] See Krystyna Kaspryzk, *Nicolas de Troyes et le genre narratif en France au XVIe siècle* (Paris: Klincksieck, 1963), 38.

therefore, narrative is predicated on the rejection of art/fiction as it had been produced in earlier times.

Traditional scholars have tended, however, to concentrate on verifying the historicity of the tales and to disregard the Prologue's assertion that the stories would be told *in a new way*. As a result, some have even looked upon the work's gaps, prolixities, and ambiguities as proofs of the female author's amateurism. Reviewing a new edition of Marguerite's stories, the nineteenth-century critic Sainte-Beuve dismissed it as "without art, composition, or the sense of an ending."[8] To Jourda Marguerite de Navarre is "as little a writer as possible ... form does not count for her."[9]

More recent critics have come to see that her departures from narrative conventions constitute her originality,[10] but her disconcerting lapses are usually explained in terms of the Renaissance conflict between old and new values. "The usual meaning of words disintegrates ... through paradoxes and contradictions, thus reflecting at the stylistic level the uncertainty which the writer witnesses around her," writes Tetel.[11] Her text is split "between inductive and deductive knowledge —or rather between collective assessment of truth and individual apprehension of a transcendent reality," writes Lyons.[12] Winn discerns in these stories "Marguerite's skillful narrative moves" which lead to the "reader's inability to grasp the 'true' meaning or meanings," but she also attributes this phenomenon to "the disconcerting feeling that modern man experiences, when facing the inscrutable Other and the irreducible ambiguity of the Word."[13] Kupisz explains the apparently irreconcilable contradictions of the text as a "coming to terms with the misery and weakness of man which brings to bear a painful explanation of his existential contradictions."[14]

---

[8] *Causeries du lundi*, 3rd ed. (Paris: Garnier, n.d.), 7, 449. Cited in Ann R. Jones and Nancy J. Vickers, "Canon, Rule and the Restoration Renaissance," *Yale French Studies* 75 (1988): 9–25.

[9] Pierre Jourda, *Marguerite d'Angoulême* 2 vols. (Paris: Champion, 1930), 2:978.

[10] See, for instance, Michel Olsen, *Les Transformations du Triangle Erotique* (Universitetsforlaget I Copenhagen: Akademisk Forlag, 1976), 152–82.

[11] *Marguerite de Navarre's "Heptaméron": Themes, Language, and Structure* (Durham: Duke Univ. Press, 1973), 184.

[12] John D. Lyons, "The *Heptaméron* and the Foundation of Critical Narrative," *Yale French Studies* 70 (1986): 63.

[13] Colette H. Winn, "An Instance of Narrative Seduction: The *Heptaméron* of Marguerite de Navarre," *Symposium* 39, 3 (1984): 217–26. See especially 222 and 224.

[14] Kazimerz Kupisz, "A Propos de l' 'Honneste' dans l'*Heptaméron*," *Kwartalnik Neofilologiczny* 31 (1984): 125–48. The citation is from 147–48: "c'est la constatation désabusée de la misère et de la faiblesse de l'homme qui apporte une explication douloureuse de ses contradictions existentielles."

By and large, scholars have not analyzed the unshaping of the narrative line in terms of the effort to tell the truth. Likewise relatively little has been made of the fact that to the author telling the truth meant, in a large number of cases, writing as a woman about rape. A study of what Nelly Furman calls "the politics of language" remains to be done in the *Heptaméron*.[15] Deborah N. Losse's work represents a partial exception to this, but although she examines the "scenes of sexual assault" she does not consider the author's gender as a category of analysis, nor does she take into account her personal stake in depicting male sexual aggression.[16] Curiously, no one has studied how Marguerite de Navarre's gender may have unshaped the narrative line of her stories.[17]

Stories about ladies who are surprised in their beds are common enough to the novella genre. But whereas a typical heroine in the *Decameron* or the *Cent Nouvelles Nouvelles* would have welcomed such an adventure, Marguerite de Navarre claims to have fought off her attacker so vigorously that he dared not show his face the next day. Her own ordeal thus contradicted both the fictional representation of such situations and the implication that they represented reality. Her reputation as a noble and virtuous lady made it impossible for her to denounce her attacker, however, and even when she wrote about the incident many years later, she had to conceal the fact that she was its heroine and endorse the ideology which made it necessary for her to do so.

One of the principal semantic difficulties facing the Renaissance woman was the unstable meaning of the word "honor" which shifted its definition as it applied to men vs. women and to the public vs. the private.[18] A man's honor signified physical courage, a woman's signi-

---

[15] Nelly Furman, "The Politics of Language: Beyond the Gender Principle?" in *Making a Difference: Feminist Literary Criticism*, ed. by Gayle Greene and Coppélia Kahn (London and New York: Methuen, 1985).

[16] Deborah N. Losse, "Distortion as a Means of Reassessment: Marguerite de Navarre's *Heptaméron* and the "Querelle des Femmes," *Journal of Rocky Mountain Medieval and Renaissance Association* 3 (1982): 75–84. See especially 76 and 84.

[17] Olsen does study the way Marguerite tranforms narrative formulae and argues that she comes close to abandoning a genre which is imperfectly suited to her purposes (181). However, he explains this in terms of the conflict between divine and terrestrial love rather than that between masculine and feminine signifying systems.

[18] For an examination of the shift in meaning between public and private honor see Jean-Claude Carron, "Les Noms de l'honneur féminin à la Renaissance : Le nom tu et le non dit," *Poétique* 67 (September 1986): 269–80; also Kupisz (n. 14 above) and Nicole Cazauran, *L'Heptaméron' de Marguerite de Navarre* (Paris: Société d'Edition d'Enseignement Supérieur, 1976).

fied chastity. This double meaning of "honor" also blurred the meaning of a related concept—rape. In French, "elle est ravie" can mean either "she is ravished" or "she is delighted"; and in English, the word "rapture," which contains "rape" as its root, also connotes sexual pleasure. Thus the English word "rape" (sexual violation) and the French word "rapt," or abduction, both carry the presumption of women's rapturous collaboration in the undoing of the male line. The "honorable" woman was the one who was not subject to "ravissement" or sexual desire.

So long as fiction was written by men, these shifts in the meaning of "honor" and "ravissement/rapture" caused no problem. The conventional plot of male desire, *boy wants girl* (or to put it in terms of transformational grammar: subject > verb > object), could equate the honor of the subject with his desire for victory.[19] The successful conquest of the military objective was really no different from the successful conquest of a woman. In order for a woman to create fiction, however, the object would have to become the subject; and such a reversal would immediately call into question the meaning of both honor and desire, creating ambiguities and paradoxes in the narrative.

In this essay I want to examine three novellas (four, two, and ten) in which the heroine struggles to defend her honor against a rapist. The first of these tells how as a young woman Marguerite herself had narrowly escaped being raped in her own bed by one of the luminaries of her brother's court, the Seigneur de Bonnivet.[20] Far from collaborating like the typical novella heroine in the cuckolding of a husband whom she did not love, Marguerite had fought tooth and nail to defend her honor. It is altogether possible that this shattering adventure inspired her to contest the cynical assumptions of the novella tradition and to make a collection of "true" stories, a high percentage of which depicted similar episodes.[21] This seems therefore a fitting place to begin the search for "feminine" writing in the *Heptaméron*.

---

[19] See A. J. Greimas, *Sémantique structurale* (Paris: Larousse, 1966), 173: "The content of the actions changes all the time, the actors vary, but the enunciation-spectacle remains always the same, for its permanence is guaranteed by the fixed distribution of the roles."

[20] See Brantôme, *Les Dames galantes* (Paris: Garnier, 1960), 422–23. He says that his grandmother, who was Marguerite's lady-in-waiting, told him the facts behind this novella.

[21] If we include what is now called "acquaintance rape," the following novellas all contain instances of rape: 2, 4, 5, 7, 8, 10, 12, 14, 22, 23, 26, 27, 31, 42, 46, 48, 62, 72. One of the problems in studying rape in fiction has been scholars' inability or unwillingness to identify it. See Kathryn Gravdal, "Camouflaging Rape: The Rhetoric of Sexual Violence in the Medieval Pastourelle," *Romanic Review* 76 (1985): 360–73.

To Tell the Truth: Novella Four

In this story, an admirer first tries to interest a princess in an "honest friendship."[22] This offer she forcefully declines, making him promise never to repeat it. Nevertheless, as is often the case, the gentleman is unwilling or unable to believe that she really means the "no" with which she meets his advances. At the heart of the rape attempt, therefore, is a breakdown in communication which turns around the question of the woman's sexual desire.

He next invites her and her brother to a hunting party at his château. There he lodges her in a room which is connected with the one beneath it by a trap door concealed under a rug. This room he occupies himself, and one night after she has retired, he sneaks into her room through the trap door and attacks her in her bed. The princess succeeds in fighting him off, but when she vows to bring him to justice, she is discouraged from doing so by her lady-in-waiting who warns that if she denounces him she will jeopardize her own reputation. The older woman's advice interrupts the story. The dénouement (what happened) is trivialized by the sheer length of her utterance. And, in fact, the soundness of her counsel sets aside the "crime and punishment" plot envisioned by the princess, making the tale end inconclusively. The public unmasking of the rapist never takes place. The next day when she and her brother depart, their mutilated host pleads illness, thus confirming the lady's suspicion that he was the culprit. But the real point seems to be the practical lesson in how to deal with such an adventure, for the narrator concludes by saying,

> Voylà, mes dames, qui devroit donner grande craincte à ceulx qui presument ce qu'il ne leur appartient et doibt bien augmenter le cueur aux dames, voyans la vertu de ceste jeune princesse et le bon sens de sa dame d'honneur. Si à quelqu'une de vous advenoit pareil cas, le remede y est ja donné. (34)

Ladies, that should put fear into the hearts of those who presume to take what doesn't belong to them and increase ladies' courage, considering the virtue of this young princess and her

---

[22] It is very difficult to determine exactly what is meant by a "perfect" or "honest" friendship in the *Heptaméron*, for the conflict over what it signifies is at the heart of these stories. The term would seem to indicate what is loosely called a "courtly romance" but it may also indicate a "platonic" friendship. In the 1540s there was renewed interest in the definition of love found in Plato's *Symposium* as expounded by Marsile Ficino. This found its expression in Antoine Héroët's *Parfaicte Amye* (1544). Héroët was a personal friend and protégé of Marguerite's.

lady-in-waiting's good sense. If a similar case should happen to you, the remedy has already been given.

In form as well as content, this story of attempted rape, as written by a woman, shifts away from linearity at the moment when the heroine's desire to punish the rapist interferes with her honor. The princess is silenced by the wise lady's "motherly" advice. Her maternal discourse disrupts the narrative at the precise point where the reader expects closure. What is more, implicit in her advice is the threat of female desire:

> Vous estes belle et jeune, vivant en toute compaignye bien joieusement; il n'y a nul en ceste court, qu'il ne voye la bonne chere que vous faictes au gentil homme dont vous avez soupson: qui fera juger chascun que s'il a faict ceste entreprinse, ce n'a esté sans quelque faulte de vostre costé. (32)

> You are beautiful and young, given to enjoying all sorts of company; there is no one in this court who does not see how warmly you treat the gentleman you suspect, which will make everyone conclude that if he attempted such a deed, it was not without some fault on your part.

She urges the princess never to speak of what has happened, lest she find herself "remembering things which are so pleasant to the flesh" (33). Many, she says, have fallen the second time, and even the most chaste have been unable to keep from feeling a few "sparks" in such circumstances. Desire is thus projected as a possible consequence of rape, a danger from which the virtuous woman is never safe. This has the effect of making the victim's innocence dependent upon a lack of desire, and reinforcing silence as the only sure way to deny her guilt. In terms of the story's structure, the disproportionate amount of space devoted to the "remedy" constitutes a makeshift answer to an insoluble problem, the substitution of female desire for male desire, or how to make a woman's story out of a man's.

In the discussion which follows the novella, another narrator, Hircan, criticizes the story from a man's point of view. Far from being impressed by the princess's valiant defense of her honor or the way in which she dealt with the aftermath of her adventure, Hircan concentrates in his remarks on the role of the hero, and censures the gentleman for his lack of perseverence.

> Il me semble, ce dist Hircan, que le grand gentil homme, dont vous avez parlé, estoit si despourveu de cueur, qu'il n'estoit digne d'être ramentu; car, ayant une telle occasion, ne debvoit, ne pour vielle ne pour jeune, laisser son entreprinse. (34)

It seems to me, said Hircan, that the great gentleman of whom you spoke was so lacking in courage that he was not worth being remembered; for having such an opportunity, he should not for young or old have abandoned his enterprise.

If Hircan had gotten that far, he would have considered himself *dishonored*, he says, had he not carried out his intention, even if that meant killing the old woman in order to frighten the young one into submission! To him, sexual intercourse is an "enterprise," a military conquest whose success or failure determines a man's honor. Hircan's remarks (written for him to utter by a woman) point out the way a man would alter the dénouement of the Fourth Novella to make it conform to his plot. His ending would obliterate the woman's right to say no. This passage demonstrates how a man *fictionalizes* a woman's *true* story to produce *his* "happy ending."

The Cult of the Victim: Novella Two

The fourth novella may be based on a true happening, but the wise woman's advice which unshapes it also condemns it as a story which cannot be told. The fiction of the princess's Flemish identity must disguise the truth. The second novella may be read as another attempt to rework the autobiographical event narrated in the fourth. This time the narrator is Oisille, who functions within the frame as the "mother" of the company.[23] Her heroine has also firmly refused the propositions of a servant who has tried to seduce her. Seized by a "fantasy," this "varlet" (like the princess's gentleman-lover) finds a way to enter her bed. He makes a hole in the wall which is concealed by the bed curtains, and when the heroine has fallen asleep, he crawls into her bed and tries to take her by force, while she resists his attack with all her might.

Unlike the heroine of the fourth novella, however, the muleteer's wife is unsuccessful in her efforts to fight off her aggressor and he stabs her with his sword. He then rapes her as she lies dying, and escapes. This is rape from the woman's perspective—an assault with a deadly weapon from which there is no escape. Had Marguerite de Navarre not been successful in fighting off her attacker, her fate might have been the same. Indeed, in the conversation following the fourth novella, Hircan asserts that he would have murdered the Princess's attendant and threatened her too. In novella two, however, this omnipresent threat is

---

[23] Scholars have identified her variously as the author's mother, Louise de Savoie, or as Marguerite herself, as she was in her later years.

deflected to a man whose lowly occupation makes him "more bestial than the beasts with which he had spent so much time" (19).

Up to this point, the narrative which tells the truth about rape from the woman's point of view has proceeded in a straightforward manner. The wife's moral superiority should now logically be rewarded by a satisfactory dénouement which punishes the culprit. Instead, the villain flees and is never apprehended. As in novella four, he escapes scot free, and attention is refocused on the heroine through a detailed account of her pious end. Realizing that she is dying, the muleteer's wife turns to God, naming him "her strength, her virtue, her patience and her chastity," comparing her blood to Christ's and continuing to give signs of faith with her eyes and hands after the power of speech has left her. Offering her soul to God is a way of *not offering her body* to the rapist, and the vocabulary describing the *joy* which she experiences is, like that of so many mystical visions, the vocabulary of orgasm. We recall that the lady-in-waiting of the fourth novella suggests the same substitution/sublimation, when she insists on attributing her mistress's successful resistance to God and tells her that she should "humiliate herself" and pray that God will give her "grace ... to continue in the honest ways" which he has placed in her heart (32-33).

The focus then shifts again, this time to the unsuspecting husband, who returns to find his wife's body awaiting burial in front of his house. When he learns the cause of her death, he discovers that he has "a double reason to grieve." Her tomb becomes a local shrine venerated by the townswomen. Eventually even the "foolish and light" among them "seeing the honor paid to this body" are inspired to change their ways (21). The heroine's body has not been raped in vain. On the contrary, her attempt to defend it has earned it a status it could not have enjoyed if she had lived. Of double value dead, the muleteer's wife miraculously inspires other women to choose the path of chastity.

Here too narrative closure is replaced by a maternal discourse which counsels collaboration with the prevailing mores. This is the same phenomenon which takes place in the fourth novella when the lady-in-waiting's monologue prevents the princess from unmasking the gentleman who attacked her. The maternal narrator offers an example of how honorable women should act when threatened with rape at the point of a sword; and in order to encourage them to remain steadfast in the face of this danger, she holds out hope of fame and glory. Oisille's heroic revision of the rape scenario transforms the nightmare of *real rape* into a "good dream," a moral victory culminating in a posthumous reward. The wife's mutilated body, deprived of speech and venerated in its grave, becomes the signifier not of what has been done to it, but of benefits which it can neither know nor enjoy. In the land of the living, however, her deed, like Lucretia's, benefits men—her husband, who has a "double reason" to grieve, and the husbands of the "foolish and light" women who are transformed by her example into faithful wives. In fact, the heroine's apotheosis is not really *her* story at all. It is a camouflaging device which draws attention away from the horrible events which Oisille has just described. The "true" story is about a woman who is raped and stabbed to death, while her murderer remains at large, presumably capable of doing the same thing to others. It should instill terror into all women's hearts, for they are equally vulnerable to such an attack, which takes place in the woman's own bed. They are distracted from their terror, however, by the narrator's exhortations to fight for their chastity and the promise of an unearthly reward. The story does not permit women to exorcize their fear by seeing justice done. Instead it makes them morally responsible for a situation which is totally beyond their control.

Oisille distracts her female listeners from the horrible truth about rape in another way; she emphasizes the gap which separates them from the muleteer's wife, who is far beneath them in station. Piqued by Oisille's implied indictment of female virtue in high society, they envision themselves rivaling the muleteer's wife in heroism. By situating the defense of chastity in the masculine register of physical courage, Oisille successfully arouses their desire not only to emulate the raped woman but to compete with her. They express no outrage at her fate or at her assailant's escape. Women's choice is limited to compliance or heroic resistance unto death.

When we analyze this story we see that once again at the precise moment when the reader/listener expects a satisfactory resolution of the plot's conflict, it veers off course. Oisille's "piteous tale" attempts to depict the real truth about rape, a project necessitating symbolic entry into the "feminine." In order to define the raped woman as virtuous, however, it is necessary to use a masculine heroic vocabulary that equates death with victory. That is why, as Olsen has remarked, we find a lack of "narrative logic" in this tale.[24]

From Fact to Fiction: Novella Ten

In the tenth novella, Marguerite de Navarre rewrites her encounter with Bonnivet in the form of a romance. This version explores the problems inherent in the medieval ideal of "courtly"[25] love from the perspective

---

[24] Olsen, 167.

[25] The word "courtly" is actually a nineteenth-century adjective for *fine amor*, the highly ritualized servitude of a knight for a lady found in troubadour lyrics and medieval romances.

of the female object. Its narrator Parlamente begins by saying that the story has been told to her by "un ami" (a male friend) in praise of the man he loved most in the world (54). As the novella unfolds, however, she progressively situates "his story"—the narrative which previously circulated among men—in female territory, transposing it into a woman's story about a woman.

It is the tale of Amadour, a valiant but penniless knight who falls in love with the virtuous Floride and plots to win her love. From the beginning, the hero, who is described as the "best talker" in Spain, is depicted as a maker of devious plots. He marries Floride's companion Avanturade in order to be near Floride, and soon his charms have won for him the confidence and affection of Floride's mother, the countess d'Arande. He then persuades Floride to enter into a "perfect friendship," which he swears will remain honorable.[26] Both lovers carefully dissimulate their feelings, as decreed by the rules of "courtly" love, and Floride's mother, who suspects the true nature of Amadour's attachment, looks the other way.

This agreeable *modus vivendi* comes to an end, however, when the countess arranges, without consulting her, for Floride's marriage to a man she hates, and Floride accepts her mother's decision without question. This female collaboration in the exchange of women results in the estrangement of mother and daughter. The silence which both have observed with regard to Amadour widens and Floride withdraws into isolation, secretly consoling herself with thoughts of Amadour's "perfect friendship."

This is, of course, hopelessly naive on her part. Amadour's wife dies, and he decides that the time has come to be "paid . . . what he thinks he deserves." He therefore feigns illness and Floride, who believes he is dying, goes to visit him in his bedroom. At first he acts the part of a man "whose strength has deserted him," but when Floride attempts to console him, he is "rendered so much stronger" that "pretending to be half dead . . . he tried to seek that which ladies' honor forbids" (72).

When we compare the attempted rape of the tenth novella with that in the fourth, we see that there are decided similarities. In both, a man who has promised to respect a woman's honor betrays his promise and tries to take advantage of her in a bedroom. In the tenth novella, however, the positions of the man and the woman are reversed. Here it is the heroine who visits the hero. Furthermore, unlike the rapist, she comes openly and honorably, trusting in their "perfect friendship." Floride's visit to Amadour's chamber attempts to replay the rape scene of the fourth novella according to the woman's rules. Amadour is not,

---

[26] See note 22.

however, the ideal object of Floride's sublimated desire. Horrified when she realizes what he is doing, she confronts him with the disparity between action and word:

> Amadour, quelle follye est montée en vostre entendement? et qu'est-ce qu'avez-vous pensé et voulu faire...? Et où est l'honneur, dist Floride, que tant de foys vous m'avez presché? (73)
>
> Amadour, what madness has seized you? what do you think you are doing and what do you want...? And where is the honor, said Floride, which you have so often preached to me?"

Amadour's lengthy reply reveals the semantic differences which are at the root of their misunderstanding. He argues that it is impossible to love her honor more than he does. As long as she was not married, he concealed his passion so well that she was not even aware of it. But now that she is married and "her honor can be covered," why shouldn't he enjoy the fruits of a love which he has won by long service? He even argues casuistically that such a passion is not sinful. It is at this point in the novella that the split over female honor, which is the true signified behind the rape attempt, makes it impossible for the plot to move forward in a coherent manner. Amadour's unwillingness to accept Floride's definition of honor leads to a breakdown not only in communication but in the relationship itself. Floride thus finds herself completely isolated within a social structure which simultaneously arouses and thwarts all forms of female desire.

Having sent Amadour away, Floride continues to "love him with all her heart," but "obeying honor," she never gives him any sign of it. Although Amadour's project (*boy wants girl*) remains unchanged, the heroine's plot can no longer exist within the signifying system to which she is confined.[27] The story thus illustrates the cogency of Freud's celebrated question, "What do women want?" From this point on, Floride's actions and reactions become more and more difficult to understand, as do those of the other woman in the story—her mother. Amadour goes to see the countess in the hope of enlisting her aid and finds her "very sick from sorrow at her daughter's absence" (76). He tells her about his friendship with Floride, thus breaking the rule of

---

[27] I am alluding to Nancy K. Miller's idea of a "heroine's text." See *The Heroine's Text: Reading in the French and English Novel, 1722–1782* (New York: Columbia Univ. Press, 1980). Miller's theory that female desire takes the form of desire for power also underlies my analysis of the role of female desire in these stories. "Emphasis Added: Plots and Plausibilities in Women's Fiction," *PMLA* 96 (1981): 36–48.

secrecy, whereupon the countess agrees to arrange a rendezvous for him. When Floride realizes that she cannot count on her mother for protection, she decides on a desperate step.

> [Floride] pensa que souvent Amadour l'avoit louée de sa beaulté ... parquoy, aymant mieux faire tort à son visaige, en le diminuant, que de souffrir par elle le cueur d'un si honneste homme brusler d'un si meschant feu, print une pierre qui estoit en la chappelle, et s'en donna par le visaige si grand coup, que la bouche, le nez et les oeilz en estoient tout difformez. (77)

> Floride thought that Amadour had often praised her for her beauty ... so that preferring to do harm to her face in order to lessen it, rather than to allow such an honest man's heart to burn with such a wicked fire, she took a stone which was in the chapel and struck such a great blow to her face that her mouth, nose, and eyes were quite deformed.

The failure of the heroine's plot (love with honor) leads Floride to mark her own body as undesirable. This episode constitutes yet another attempt on Floride's part to remake the hero as she would like him to be. In order to do so, however, she must destroy the very attribute traditionally associated with the heroine of romantic fiction—her beauty. Her mother finds her bleeding, bandages her up, and sends her in nonetheless to Amadour, who soon makes it clear that he intends to pursue his "wicked desire" despite all her pleas.

> Et quant Floride veid que prieres, raison ne larmes ne luy servoient ... se ayda du secours qu'elle craingnoit autant que perdre sa vie, et, d'une voix triste et piteuse, appella sa mere le plus hault qu'il luy fut possible. (79)

> And when Floride saw that neither prayers, reason, nor tears would serve ... she sought the aid which she feared as much as losing her life, and in a sad piteous voice called her mother as loudly as possible.

The countess rushes in, but the wily wordsmith pretends that all he wanted to do was kiss Floride's hand and Floride stubbornly refuses to tell her mother the truth. Unable to understand why Floride is acting as she does, the countess turns against her and punishes her by refusing to speak to her for seven years, only relaxing her harsh treatment when she learns that Amadour is involved with a new mistress.

Although I have had to summarize hastily a very complicated story, I hope that I have made clear that the reader has little doubt about what Amadour is up to, while the actions and motivations of both Floride and the countess are increasingly difficult to understand. They both know that Amadour is not what he appears to be, yet neither admits this to the other. Furthermore, instead of uniting against a common enemy, each of the two women dissimulates what she knows about him and allies herself with him against the other. For instance, the "virtuous" countess, who already knows that Amadour loves Floride, encourages a rendezvous which will certainly compromise her daughter's reputation. And although she pines for Floride when they are separated, she refuses to speak to her for seven years. Floride's actions are equally inconsistent. We are told that her moral principles have been instilled in her by her mother, yet she would rather die than call on her for help when her honor is in jeopardy.

It is of course possible for the modern reader to explain this behavior by various hypotheses based on the psychoanalytical model; but the text itself speaks only of both women's preoccupation with Amadour's "virtue," a curious displacement of what is really their own concern. The narrator offers no good reason why a mother would prefer a relationship with a younger man to one with her own daughter. Nor does she explain why a daughter would mutilate herself or risk rape in order to protect her lover's good name.

In the second and fourth novellas, the narrative veered off at the point where female desire should have been. In the fourth, the princess's resolve to denounce the rapist is thwarted by the older woman's advice. In the second, the rapist's punishment is replaced by religious fervor. In both cases, this is accomplished by a type of maternal discourse which collaborates with patriarchal politics. In the tenth novella, which is the romanticized version of the rape adventure, the short-circuiting of the linear plot takes the form of inexplicable hostility between mother and daughter.

I would like to suggest that the incoherent behavior of the female protagonists in the tenth novella signifies their inability to achieve status as subjects within the narrative. The fictional plot which we all know and expect to read in narrative fiction is the fixed plot of male desire (the one outlined by Hircan). When a woman tells the story of male desire, however, she cannot do so without being painfully conscious of its dark underside, the destruction of female autonomy, which in this novella takes the form of Amadour's assault on what Floride values most—her honor. To put it another way, fictional plots are moved forward by desire (what the *actant* wants); but since there is no room in the sexual economy of patriarchy for female desire, there is no way for the heroine to pursue her plot. Confined by their "virtue" to silence, the women in the story have no means of formulating a coherent counterplot. The reader, whose narrative expectations have been formed on the male model, is in turn disconcerted by behavior which seems to have no rational explanation.[28]

The man's story about a man is deconstructed by the woman's story about a woman. The transposition of object and subject reveals the constraints of the female condition which make it impossible to determine the nature of female desire. Since what the women want is to love and not to love at the same time, they cannot act as subjects who are the owners of their desire. They can only react to Amadour's initiatives in unpredictable and incoherent ways. The only form of closure possible for the heroine's story is retreat to a space where she can no longer be threatened by the plot of male desire:

> sans en parler ne à mere ne à belle-mere, s'en alla randre religieuse au monastere de Jesus.... Ainsy tourna toutes ses affections à aymer Dieu si parfaictement, que après avoir vescu longuement religieuse, luy rendit son ame en telle joye, que l'espouse a d'aller veoir son espoux. (83)

> without speaking to mother or mother-in-law, she became a nun in the monastery of Jesus.... Thus she turned all her affections to loving God so perfectly, that after having lived a long time as a nun, she gave him her soul as joyously as a wife goes to see her husband.

The ideal hero is out of this world. Only God can satisfy Floride's desire for both love and honor. This dénouement parallels closely, of course, the final pages of *La Princesse de Clèves*, a later piece of women's writing which also projects the denial of desire as the only happy ending for the heroine's plot.[29] The curious and seemingly gratuitous reference to mother and mother-in-law reminds us even here, however, that there is another conflict in this story—the conflict among women who live under patriarchy, which manifests itself in lies, secrets, and silence.[30]

This version of the rape narrative attempts to retell the woman's adventure as a "courtly" romance. What was a man's story about a

---

[28] See Peter J. Rabinowitz, *Before Reading: Narrative Conventions and the Politics of Interpretation* (Ithaca and London: Cornell Univ. Press, 1987) for a discussion of how reading is influenced by preconceived notions based on narrative conventions.

[29] See Miller's "Emphasis Added" cited above. For an analysis of the unspoken conflict between mother and daughter in *La Princesse de Clèves*, see Marianne Hirsch, "A Mother's Discourse: Incorporation and Repetition in *La Princesse de Clèves*," *Yale French Studies* 62 (1981): 67–87.

[30] The expression "lies, secrets, and silence" is an allusion to Adrienne Rich's *On Lies, Secrets, and Silence* (New York: W. W. Norton, 1979).

knight and his lady is transformed by the woman's point of view, creating a dizzying example of the narratological phenomenon known as the "mise en abyme." The ensuing breakdown in narrative coherence sends a distress signal to the reader in the form of bizarre and disconcerting female behavior. The tenth novella subverts the male plot in the only way it can—not by reversing male and female roles as subject and object, but by revealing that it is impossible to do so.

When Marguerite de Navarre proposes to write a different decameron, she says she will create a non-fictitious, non-rhetorical, non-artistic text. Such a text (novella four) turns out to be untellable as truth because it represents a threat to female honor. Her desire to speak enters into direct conflict with the way Renaissance society confers on women their good name. Her true story can only be told as a fiction. She must disguise herself as a Flemish princess, and even then her story will be unshaped by patriarchal ideology disguised as motherly advice. In novella two, she works through the nightmare of rape to a happy ending, but only at the cost of freeing her villain and sublimating her desire to punish the rapist. She then attempts to retell her story as a "courtly" romance, but the gender-linked meaning of "honor" once again interferes, this time with the functioning of her female protagonists. Her determination to tell the truth has created a text which demonstrates what happens to narrative syntax when male and female roles are reversed. Although men can pretend to be women, there is simply no way for a woman to appropriate male desire and pretend to be a man. Because so many of the concepts involved in fiction (honor, desire, rape) mean different things as they apply to men or women, the context in which a woman writes fiction is necessarily different from a man's. Although the specific historical context and personal circumstances of the writer will vary, close attention to such linguistic contradictions and dislocations pinpoint one of the ways in which women's writing is *different*.

What I have tried to suggest is that the ambiguities, lapses, and awkwardness found in the *Heptaméron* are the signs which mark it as a woman's text. Marguerite de Navarre's effort to tell the truth about rape changes the shape of narrative. It encodes the female body in "feminine" writing.[31]

Hamilton College

---

[31] This essay is an earlier and abridged version of the first section of my book *Rape and Writing in the Heptaméron* (Carbondale: Southern Illinois Univ. Press, 1991).

SHEILA FFOLLIOTT

A Queen's Garden of Power: Catherine de' Medici and the Locus of Female Rule

POLITICAL UNREST—CAUSED BY RELIGIOUS DISSENT CULMINATING in civil war, combined with King Henri II's accidental death in 1559 followed less than two years later by the early death of his son and heir (François II)—left the French monarchy in a vulnerable position. The succession of ten-year-old Charles IX required a regency. Henri's widow, Catherine de' Medici, was the most likely candidate, but the prevailing cultural assumption that women were inferior beings and therefore subject to men made it difficult for the Queen Mother—as it would for any potential woman ruler—to establish her authority.[1] However, not only did she serve as regent from 1562–1565, but she also continued to influence policy at the French court until her death in 1589. In fact, she is often credited for having preserved the institution of the French monarchy during this period of extreme tension. Typically for the Renaissance, the French court employed the metaphor of art, literature, and pageantry to represent the mystique of rule. The purposefully designed permanent setting, filled with iconographically charged works of art, provided the stage for symbolic or political action; the festival and triumphal entry, whether commissioned by the sovereigns themselves or by subjects wishing to express their expectations of the monarchs, employed similar imagery, often involving mythological prototypes. Analysis of the imagery devised for court art can reveal attitudes about rulers and rule—both their own and those of others toward them. As I have argued elsewhere,[2] the analysis of works of art made for a woman regent is revealing of contemporary attitudes towards women in positions of authority.

---

[1] See Ian Maclean, *The Renaissance Notion of Woman* (Cambridge: Cambridge Univ. Press, 1980).

[2] "Catherine de' Medici as Artemisia: Figuring the Powerful Widow," in *Rewriting the Renaissance: The Discourses of Sexual Difference in Early Modern Europe*, ed. M. Ferguson, M. Quilligan, and N. Vickers (Chicago: Univ. of Chicago Press, 1986).

In this essay I shall argue that in addition to the prototype's costume, pose, and gesture, an analysis of the setting in which the idealized queenly prototype appears is important in understanding the nature of an acceptable representation of the paradox of a ruling queen. Artists could not simply adopt the traditional imagery of the male monarch; they needed to invent an imagery to accommodate the anomaly of the female ruler. The setting in which the ruling queen appears is an important component in inventing an imagery that could sanction an anomaly without advocating abandonment of what was considered to be the norm.

It is not surprising to find a courtier-on-the-make, in this case the apothecary Nicolas Houel, seeking to gain favor from Queen Catherine by providing her with an appropriate image for a ruling female to employ in large-scale works of art. His contribution fills a void, for the Salic Law prohibited female succession to the French throne and prevented the establishment of a real tradition of women rulers. Houel's vision of the ideal queen appears in a body of written and visual materials detailing the life of an ancient queen, Artemisia, which Houel assembled for presentation to Catherine de' Medici beginning in 1562: fifty-nine drawings intended for enlargement into tapestry, mostly by the French court painter Antoine Caron (c. 1521–1599), accompanying sonnets, and a lengthy and well annotated manuscript biography of Artemisia (*L'Histoire de la Royne Arthémise*), the sonnets and manuscript from the pen of Houel himself.[3] Houel made clear his intent to provide the queen with an appropriate *exemplum* for female rule in an ancient prototype: Artemisia was a widow who, like Catherine, governed her kingdom after her husband's death.

Studies of court imagery often consist of an investigation of the resonances of the match between ruler and prototype: Charles V and Neptune, Francis I and Mars, Elizabeth I and Astraea.[4] In attempting to gain a greater understanding of the purpose, extent, and function of court imagery, I shall explore the significance of one of the settings in which the artist Caron places Artemisia, the prototype chosen for Catherine. Through the examination of one tapestry design in particular, I argue that the discovery of a model ancient queen was but one step in creating an imagery of authority for the unlikely concept of a female

---

[3] *L'Histoire de la Royne Arthémise*, Bibliothèque Nationale MS. fr. 306. The drawings and accompanying sonnets are divided between the collections of the BN, Éstampes, Résérves, AD 105 and the Musée du Louvre, Cabinet des Dessins.

[4] See, for example, my *Civic Sculpture in the Renaissance: Montorsoli's Fountains at Messina* (Ann Arbor: UMI Research Press, 1984) for discussion of Charles V as Neptune and Francis I as Mars; see also Frances Yates, *Astraea: The Imperial Theme in the Sixteenth Century* (Harmondsworth: Penguin, 1975).

ruler in sixteenth-century France. In order to be effective, a prototype, even when a convincing match, needed to be seen in action. An attempt to define not only an imagery but also a wider culture of queenship must account for the setting in which the prototype appears. The artist depicts the queen, acknowledged by Houel as an idealized Catherine, performing a range of activities appropriate to the queen regent: overseeing the education of the young king, administering the government, and waging war. Many of the queen's official activities take place in garden settings. Her son learns about art and music in an elaborate garden. Philosophers discourse amid carefully planned parterres. The regent and her son visit a sculpture garden and a menagerie. Artemisia holds a banquet for the young king, consults with architects and astrologers on the design of her deceased husband's tomb, and receives petitions, all in gardens. Why does the garden figure as the setting for so many of the ideal queen's activities? How do these garden settings contribute to an imagery of queenship? Considering the range of activities that Caron places in garden settings, the banquet and philosopher scenes coincide directly with the Renaissance view of how the garden functioned in antiquity. The visits to sculpture garden and menagerie clearly require garden settings. Investigation of the other activities taking place in garden settings, therefore, is more likely to be productive in assessing the particular relevance of the garden to Catherine de' Medici and to the concept of female rule.

The garden played a highly significant role in the culture of the ruling class in early modern Europe. Renaissance princes planned their gardens in conscious imitation of those of the ancients.[5] It comes as no surprise, therefore, to find that Nicolas Houel considered the villa and garden central to the life of an ancient queen, nor that Catherine de' Medici and her contemporaries invested a great deal in building gardens and country houses. Seeing the garden so frequently represented in an idealized version of Queen Catherine helps to clarify her possible motivation for the actual expenditures on gardens and demonstrates the ways in which she may have planned to use the spaces. It is important to question here not only why garden imagery appears in the Artemisia drawings, but also how an analysis of the use of garden-related themes in that series informs us about the garden's significance for the queen. Is the fact that Caron so frequently turns to the garden significant in creating an imagery of female, as opposed to male, rule?

Houel, trained in the herbal tradition as an apothecary, would immediately associate Artemisia with the garden before considering her

---

[5] See James S. Ackermann, *The Cortile del Belvedere*, Studi e documenti per la storia del Palazzo Apostolico Vaticano, 3 (Vatican City, 1954).

historical accomplishments. This queen belonged in a garden because "Artemisia," as recorded by Pliny and others, is the name of a plant related to what would today be called the daisy family—a fact that may explain Houel's fascination with the ancient queen in the first place. *Artemisia* (wormwood) is an essential ingredient of vermouth and absinthe. Charles Estienne, a sixteenth-century encyclopedist and one of Houel's acknowledged sources, says the plant *Artemisia*, in fact, took its name from the ancient queen.[6] He also notes the medicinal properties of the plant in alleviating female problems like painful menses and in promoting fecundity and easy passage of the fetus.[7] Fertility had eluded Queen Catherine during her first ten years of marriage. She sought treatment from apothecaries and probably began her association with Artemisia in this manner.

Interest in herbal medicines combined with the introduction of new plant species brought by voyages of discovery prompted the formation of botanical gardens in the 1540s.[8] Houel was himself involved in the creation of the first botanical garden in Paris.[9] Writing slightly later in the sixteenth century, Girolamo Porro, a Venetian publisher, said that the ideal botanical garden should contain, among other things, a statue of Artemisia.[10] For Houel, therefore, the association of queen with plant made her location in the garden logical.

Houel's professional interest in the garden cannot, however, explain Caron's way of staging Artemisia in that space. Because Houel described his *Histoire* as a conscious idealization of Queen Catherine's life, can we assume that Caron's drawings are an ideal projection of the ways in which she used the spaces around her? Do they record the queen's own practices or her aspirations? (Catherine de' Medici's inter-

---

[6] *De Latinis et Graecis nominibus arborum, fructicum, herbarum . . . ex Aristotele* (Lutetiae, 1547), 13.

[7] *De re hortensi libellus, vulgaria herbarum, florum* (Lugduni, 1536), 47.

[8] Dennis Rhodes, "The Botanical Garden of Padua: The First Hundred Years," *Journal of Garden History* 4 (1984): 327. The Italian universities at Pisa, Padua, and Florence founded the first botanical gardens in the decade 1540–50. Padua appointed Daniele Barbaro in 1545 to superintend the construction of the garden, known as the "horto dei semplici."

[9] Perhaps Houel hoped that the queen would become his patron in promoting the botanical garden for Paris. His source for information on plants, Charles Estienne in a brief "Discourse on nicotine," states that "some people called it the Queen Mother's herb, because M. Nicot sent it first to the Queen Mother" ([1536], 123).

[10] Rhodes, 329. Girolamo Porro was a Venetian publisher specializing in books on architecture and ancient monuments; his 1591 publication contained a description of the ideal botanical garden. It "needs a fountain, and 4 statues: Aesculapius, Hippocrates, Mithridates, and Galen; above four corners of the loggia will be placed statues of Circe, Artemisia, Medea, and Helen; on the sides, Apollo, Mercury, Janus, and Pan. Above the cupola, Minerva."

est in building or improving gardens is well known.)[11] Or, on the other hand, do the tapestry drawings suggest what she ought to do, from Houel's or Caron's point of view? Providing a simple answer for these questions is not a straightforward matter since we are confronted with male artists working for a male entrepreneur providing imagery for a potential female patron. The argument that the drawings suggest how the queen should act is strengthened by Caron's use of perspective. The use of perspective reflects the practice of contemporary stage design seen in the work of the Italian architect Sebastiano Serlio, then active in France. Caron infuses theatricality into his staging of Artemisia's life and the garden is one of his principal sets.[12]

Queen Catherine regularly used the garden as a place to talk day-to-day politics. In 1562 for example, the year in which Houel presented her with his *Histoire*, the queen's secretaries of state reported to her regularly in the gardens of the Louvre.[13] Her reasons for choosing this location may have been purely practical: the garden provided a quiet place to talk and possibly minimized the chances of being overheard. But it is apparent from remarks made by contemporaries that Catherine's use of garden spaces for political purposes was understood as distinguishing her arena from those chosen by others. As regent, or later as someone acting from behind the scenes, her role was marginal. The palace was the real—or male—locus of power; the garden was its annex.

While no drawing in the series illustrates Artemisia "talking politics," Houel describes and Caron illustrates the new regent receiving petitioners at her country house [fig. 1].[14] This is the one composition in which Caron shows the queen herself actively involved in governmental administration and not just watching her son. The queen appears at the left standing under a portico supported by Ionic columns, the order Vitruvius considered appropriate to the female, as opposed to the male Doric Order.[15] The French court architect Philibert de L'Orme confirmed the continued validity of the tradition in the sixteenth century by stating that the palace under construction in Paris for the queen mother would employ the Ionic Order because it is feminine, having been constructed according to the proportions of ladies and goddess-

---

[11] See Anthony Blunt, *Philibert de L'Orme* (London: Zwemmer, 1966).

[12] See Anthony Blunt, *Art and Architecture in Italy: 1500–1700* (Harmondsworth: Penguin, 1973), 72.

[13] N. M. Sutherland, *The French Secretaries of State in the Age of Catherine de' Medici* (London: Methuen, 1962), 125.

[14] Houel, *Histoire*, fol. 39v.

[15] Vitruvius, *The Ten Books on Architecture*, M. H. Morgan, trans. (New York: Dover Publications, 1914), 198.

Fig. 1. Antoine Caron, *Les Placets / The Petitions*, c. 1560s, pen and ink and wash,

es.[16] In Caron's drawing, Artemisia's son stands in front while she transacts business with a petitioner via an intermediary. The petitioner's right hand, extended toward the queen, appears at an important place in the composition, accented by the intersection of perspective lines that underscore the significance of her involvement in this interaction. The presence, in back, of a man carrying a spade and hat, similar in appearance to gardeners in Caron's other drawings, suggests that the queen closely supervised the planning of her gardens. Houel here drew upon a tradition linking great monarchs from the past who felt close to the land. As he explained it,

> All the great people from past times have had such an affinity to agriculture. Even our first kings like David.... The great Cyrus was much given over to country work,... he made a large parterre formed of trees planted in a line. This [accomplishment] gave him no less pleasure than the victories that he won.[17]

Houel's reference to Cyrus reminds us that he acknowledged Xenophon's *Cyropaedia* (*The Education of Cyrus*) as the model for his *Histoire d'Arthémise* (fol. 3r). The Persian king had built a famous garden known as the *pairidaeza*, an Old Persian word meaning "walled garden" that has entered English with all of its ideal associations as "paradise." Ancient sources inform us that Cyrus's garden "united the official and residential palaces. The geometric plan of the garden was defined by a decorative, carved stone watercourse; trees and shrubs were planted symmetrically in plots."[18]

Illustration of the queen's official duties takes up only half the

---

[16] Philibert de L'Orme, *L'Architecture* (Rouen, 1648; Gregg reprint, 1964; earlier editions exist), fol. 155v. His book was dedicated to Catherine de' Medici.

[17] Houel, *Histoire*, fol. 87v.

[18] Elizabeth Moynahan, *Paradise Is a Garden* (New York: George Braziller, 1980), 1: "The English word 'paradise' is simply a transliteration of the Old Persian word *pairidaeza* referring to a walled garden. It comes to us through Xenophon, the Greek essayist and historian, who heard it in 401 B.C. in Persia where he fought with Greek mercenaries. In Xenophon's socratic discourse, the *Oeconomicus*, Socrates explains that the Persian king not only excelled in the art of war but in cultivation, and regarded it as a noble and necessary pursuit.... Socrates follows this statement with an illustration by repeating a story told by the Spartan Lysander, commander of the Peloponnesian Fleet and victor in the war. He visited the Persian Cyrus the Younger at his palace in Sardis. Lysander was shown the pleasure garden.... Some years after his Persian expedition when he settled on his estate in Scillus, he laid out a garden. He included a *pairidaeza* similar to Cyrus' by planting a grove of symmetrically arranged fruit trees surrounding a temple dedicated to Artemis. These writings had great influence on the Romans.... The oldest garden for which it is possible to make a schematic reconstruction is that built by Cyrus the Great at Pasargadae, ca. 546 B.C."

composition. On the right hand side is a garden typical of the French Renaissance style. It is enclosed in an arcaded wall of the type found at Blois and other Loire châteaux. The garden is subdivided into parterres, according to contemporary taste, and decorated with a large and prominent fountain, the specific imagery of which I discuss in another paper. As Caron's other works demonstrate, he is not an artist who loads his work with insignificant details. His compositions generally appear crowded, but each figure, building, or sculptural decoration contributes to the overall imagery.[19] It is safe to assume, therefore, that the emphasis on the garden here is significant.

As Castiglione remarks in the third book of *The Courtier*, the principal problem of describing an ideal behavior lies in the discovery of an appropriate prototype.[20] Constructing a visual imagery of authority for a female is made difficult by the fact that so few prototypes occur in the corpus of narrative art. The one important woman for whom an extensive visual tradition exists is the Virgin Mary, the most famous queen of Heaven. Representations of women in the visual arts often refer to Marian prototypes, consciously or unconsciously.[21] Marina Warner has noted, for example, the similarity of the gesture made (in a manuscript) by Blanche of Castille, thirteenth-century queen-regent for King Louis IX of France, to that of the Virgin in contemporary cathedral portals.[22] The structure of Caron's composition resembles, in a general way, illustrations of the life of Mary. First, the Annunciation, in which characteristically a female figure stands under the protection of a portico with a kneeling figure in front and a garden visible behind. Second, the Adoration of the Magi, in which kneeling figures approach the Virgin, who presents her son to them. Caron has succeeded in inventing a composition in which the queen appears to be the focus of attention. His invention, however, does not threaten conventional notions of rulership because it fits into the visual tradition of Marian imagery in which a woman is also the focus of attention.

Two literary works, cited as sources by Houel, provide us with further queenly associations with the garden other than Marian. Boccaccio begins the *Decameron* with a female character proposing that each day a queen (and later a king) be chosen to decide upon the activities to

---

[19] "Casting a Rival into the Shade: Catherine de' Medici and Diane de Poitiers," forthcoming in *The Art Journal*.

[20] *The Book of the Courtier* (Harmondsworth: Penguin, 1975), 110.

[21] Deborah Marrow, *The Art Patronage of Marie de' Medici* (Ann Arbor: UMI Research Press, 1982), 61–63.

[22] Marina Warner, *Alone of All Her Sex: The Myth and Cult of the Virgin Mary* (New York: Vintage, 1976), 114.

be followed within the confines of the villa and garden where the Florentine aristocrats sought refuge from the plague.[23] In Fra Francesco Colonna's romance, the *Hypnerotomachia Polifili*, which appeared in a newly-illustrated French edition in 1546, Queen Eleutherillida holds court in a series of different enclosed gardens.[24] Even though Queen Artemisia, presumably, and Queen Catherine, definitely, exercised authority over their entire kingdoms, the perception, as fostered in the imagery of the drawings and in these literary queens, is that they act within confined spaces. In the Renaissance, the garden—an idealized version of nature—was always enclosed. Not only in Persian, but in almost every language, the word used for the concept garden derives from the word for fence/enclosure.[25] Caron figures an authoritative queen, but mitigates the potential challenge of that authority by setting her in the midst of an enclosed garden. At this point, the question of audience arises. Is Caron, under the supervision of Houel, attempting to create an imagery that will appeal to the queen regent so that she will ask him to enter her employ? Does the queen regent understand the nature of the discourse of power in sixteenth-century Europe so well that she would appreciate the subtleties of Caron's power message that does not substantially challenge the patriarchal assumptions of contemporary political culture?

Caron's positioning of the figures in a garden setting is reminiscent of Marian scenes, like the Annunciation and the Adoration of the Magi, and of the rule of literary queens from Medieval and Renaissance fiction. Caron fits Artemisia into this female tradition while giving her the prominent position and active pose appropriate to a ruler. Instead of presenting the actively administrating queen in the predominantly male space of the palace hall (like Pope Sixtus IV in Melozzo da Forli's portrait of c. 1474–1477 [Vatican, Pinacoteca]) or the public square (like Titian's *Allocution of Alfonso D'Avalos, Marquese del Vasto* [Madrid, Prado] of c. 1540–1546), Caron employs a visual language that relates to a queenly tradition, permitting Artemisia to appear in an authoritative position without seeming to usurp a kingly role. I would argue that Houel's writings and Caron's drawings first made the potential of the garden as an arena for staged politics apparent to Catherine de' Medici.

---

[23] In Pampinea's proposal, women seem to have equal footing with men. Natalie Zemon Davis, in "Women on Top," in *Society and Culture in Early Modern France* (Stanford: Stanford Univ. Press, 1975), 141, has noted that "queens" were elected for things like harvest festivals and May Day, both of which also have connections with nature, flowers, and gardens.

[24] Fra Francesco Colonna, *Hypnerotomachia Polifili* (Paris, 1546).

[25] Anne van Erp-Houtepen, "The Etymological Origin of the Garden," *Journal of Garden History* 6 (1986): 227–31.

Caron's sensitive handling of narrative composition in these drawings shows his concern for the problems inherent in showing a woman in a position of authority—given patriarchal political culture. Queen Catherine took Caron's imagery and translated it into direct action.

The triumphal entry, in which visiting sovereigns or dignitaries were welcomed into specially decorated cities, provided frequent opportunity in the Renaissance for the public display of the monarchs. This vehicle for political image-presentation took place in cities whose city fathers planned—and paid for—the events. Catherine chose to take control of the public staging of rule by changing the locus for display from city street to royal garden. She transformed Caron's ideal visions into live action and herself assumed the role of artist as choreographer of the political festivals that have come to characterize the public face of French politics in the late sixteenth century. The queen regent exploited the garden—the space where a woman could be in control—as the locus for her court to act out the ideal politics of conciliation that she espoused.[26] She achieved this beginning with fêtes in the gardens at Chenonceau in 1563, continuing at Fontainebleau the next year, welcoming the Spanish royal family at Bayonne as part of the Royal Tour of France in 1564–1565, and culminating with the lavish reception for the Polish ambassadors who came to offer her second son—the future Henri III—the crown of Poland in 1573.

Houel devoted a great deal of space in the *Histoire* to a discussion of the importance of country life. He, through Caron, permitted Artemisia/Catherine to exercise her regent's power within the confines of the garden, but he has other plans in mind for her later life that also involve the country house. Writing in 1562 when the queen was just beginning her public life as regent for her son Charles IX, Houel suggests, through his description of how her prototype Artemisia lived, that it would be appropriate for Catherine to retire from public life to her country house when the king comes of age, marries, and is able to rule on his own.[27] Artemisia can be an ideal queen only as long as she does not interfere with the normal course of events—the male ruler. Catherine clearly did not take this advice, for she remained close to the center of royal authority for the rest of her life and played an important role in the reigns of all her sons.

While Houel's description of Artemisia's retirement indicates what he, and probably others, expected of the queen mother, she surprised them by seeing in the very imagery they proposed for her the potential

---

[26] Roy Strong, *Art and Power: Renaissance Festivals 1450–1600* (Berkeley: Univ. of California Press, 1984), 98–125.

[27] Houel, *Histoire*, fol. 94.

of the garden as the locus for promoting her own political agenda through lavish politically charged festivals *she* staged, but in which *others* were the visible actors.

George Mason University

DORA E. POLACHEK

Imagination, Idleness and Self-Discovery: Montaigne's Early Voyage Inward

THIS PAPER FOLLOWS IN THE QUIET REVOLUTION THAT IS TAKING place in Montaigne studies by offering further evidence to challenge the long held contention that, as far as Montaigne's early essays are concerned, "Tout ce qu'on peut dire de la plupart de ces chapitres, c'est qu'il n'y a rien à en dire."[1] More specifically, it takes to task a perspective which relegates the "A" level essays[2] to the realm of "premiers tâtonnements de Montaigne,"[3]—tentative gropings wanting in personal substance and psychological depth—and which proposes that one has to look towards the later essays in order to find strong evidence of introspection in Montaigne's work. In order to demonstrate the complexity and richness of the early texts, I take as my point of departure "De l'oisiveté," one of the earliest essays, which a growing number of critics are beginning to believe was written even prior to 1572 and may have been envisioned by Montaigne

---

[1] Pierre Villey, *Les Sources et l'évolution des 'Essais' de Montaigne* (Paris: Hachette, 1933), 2:40 ("All that one can say about most of these chapters is that there is nothing to be said about them"). For studies demonstrating the complexity of the deceptively short early essays, see Barbara Bowen, *The Age of Bluff: Paradox and Ambiguity in Rabelais and Montaigne* (Urbana: Univ. of Illinois, 1972), 138; see also her "Speech and Writing in the 1580 text of 'Du parler prompt ou tardif'" in *Montaigne (1580–1980): Actes du colloque international*, ed. Marcel Tetel (Paris: Nizet, 1983), 54–74; see also Raymond C. La Charité, "Montaigne's Early Personal Essays," *Romanic Review* 62 (1971): 5–15; and his "The Coherence of Montaigne's First Book," *Esprit Créateur* 20 (Spring 1980): 36–45; also Marianne S. Meijer, "'Des postes' et 'Des pouces': Plaisanteries ou points de repère?" in *Columbia Montaigne Conference Papers*, ed. Donald M. Frame and Mary B. McKinley (Lexington: French Forum, 1981), 105–18.

[2] For one of the clearest descriptions of the composition of the *Essais*, its "A," "B" and "C" strata, and the text's publication history, see R. A. Sayce, *The Essays of Montaigne: A Critical Exploration* (London: Weidenfeld and Nicolson, 1972), 8–24.

[3] Pierre Villey, 1:397.

as the introductory chapter.⁴ Through textual analyses of Montaigne's early encounters with the powers of his own imagination, I stress the highly nuanced psychological aspects of the 1580 level of the *Essais*, and demonstrate how even at this early stage the startling discoveries afforded by the egocentric vantage point relate to Montaigne's literary undertaking.

As "De l'oisiveté" clearly shows, startling discoveries about himself were the last thing Montaigne expected when he decided to retire from life in society. The firmness of his resolution (*"deliberé"* is the adjective he uses) to pass the remainder of his life "à part" (1.8.33)⁵ depended

---

[4] The notion of the prefatory characteristics of "De l'oisiveté" is claimed by Donald Frame, *Montaigne's Essais: A Study* (Englewood Cliffs, NJ: Prentice Hall, 1969), 75. The idea is lent further support by Carol Clark, *The Web of Metaphor* (Lexington: French Forum, 1978), 124; Raymond C. La Charité, "Montaigne's Early Personal Essays," *Romanic Review* 62 (1971): 8.

[5] All textual reference will be to Pierre Villey, *Les 'Essais' de Michel de Montaigne: Edition conforme au texte de l'exemplaire de Bordeaux* (Paris: Presses Universitaires, 1965). In the body of this article parenthetical information after a quotation will refer to book, chapter, and page number. English translations will be my own unless otherwise noted. In those instances they will be those of Donald Frame, *The Complete Essays of Montaigne* (Stanford: Stanford Univ. Press, 1958). Since I cite from "De l'oisiveté" so often, what follows is the portion of the Donald Frame translation reflecting the "A" level of the essay, "Of Idleness" 20-21:

> Just as we see that fallow land, if rich and fertile, teems with a hundred thousand kinds of wild and useless weeds, and that to set it to work we must subject it and sow it with certain seeds for our service; and as we see that women, all alone, produce mere shapeless masses and lumps of flesh, but that to create a good and natural offspring they must be made fertile with a different kind of seed; so it is with minds. Unless you keep them busy with some definite subject that will bridle and control them, they throw themselves in disorder hither and yon in the vague field of imagination.
> And there is no mad or idle fancy that they do not bring forth in this agitation:
> > Like a sick man's dreams,
> > They form vain visions.   Horace
>
> The soul that has no fixed goal loses itself; for as they say, to be everywhere is to be nowhere....
> Lately when I retired to my home, determined so far as possible to bother about nothing except spending the little life I have left in rest and seclusion, it seemed to me I could do my mind no greater favor than to let it entertain itself in full idleness and stay and settle in itself, which I hoped it might do more easily now, having become weightier and riper with time. But I find—
> > Ever idle hours breed wandering thoughts   Lucan
> —that, on the contrary, like a runaway horse, it gives itself a hundred times more trouble than it took for others, and gives birth to so many chimeras and fantastic monsters, one after another, without order or purpose, that in

largely on what he felt sure he could expect from himself and what he felt sure he could expect from retirement. If we examine Montaigne's early descriptions of his personality, we see that he conceives of himself as, above all, predictable. By claiming that he has an "esprit ... devenu avec le temps plus poisant et plus mur" (1.8.33: "[a] mind ... having become weightier and riper with time"), he also underlines the mental maturation that has come along naturally with age. Terms such as "poisant," denoting solidity and down-to-earthness, abound in similar descriptions he offers in other early essays. In "De l'institution des enfans," for example, Montaigne says that he sees himself as "poisant ... et endormy" (1.26.146: "heavy ... and sluggish"). Later, he recalls that as a child he was "si poisant, mol et endormi, qu'on ne me pouvoit arracher de l'oisiveté non pas pour me faire jouer" (1.26.174: "so heavy, weak and sluggish, that one couldn't pull me out of idleness, not even in order to take me to play"). And in "De la solitude" he describes himself as having "l' apprehension molle et lâche" (1.39.242: "a weak and lax disposition").

The congruence between his personality and what he envisions the solitary life to be results in the initially strong belief that he is bound to succeed. He compares his mind to a rich and fertile field which he has intended to let lie fallow ("le laisser en pleine oysiveté" [1.8.33]) in order to attain his goal of restful tranquility through a retreat into himself. Retirement will enable him to "passer en repos" what remains of his life. And according to Montaigne, not much time remains. In his "Au Lecteur," for example, he sees his death as imminent. In "De l'oisiveté" he refers to "ce peu qui me reste de vie" (1.8.33). Montaigne's use of reflexive verbs in the essay points not only to a retreat into one's self ("s'arrester et rasseoir en soy") but also to a desire to live in a solipsistic universe very much akin to death. In a sense, Montaigne's initial retreat from society is designed to create a *mise-en-scène* resembling death while he is still alive. The opening image of fertile, fallow land teeming with weeds (1.8.32) can be interpreted as one of a graveyard, thus reinforcing the motif of death.

It would be hard to imagine the writer of "De l'oisiveté" claiming, as he does in later essays, that "nous sommes nés pour agir" (1.20.89) or insisting, "Je veux qu'on agisse" ("We are born to act; ... I want man to act"). At this point he sees his life as over. With nothing left to discover, what he desires is akin to a dialogue with a good, familiar

---

order to contemplate their ineptitude and strangeness at my pleasure, I have begun to put them in writing, hoping in time to make my mind ashamed of itself.

friend, a dialogue devoid of shocks or surprises.[6] On a deeper level, it is a lulling state of existence that will make the transition toward death a smooth and peaceful one.

Given his expectations, Montaigne is surprised to find that he is totally unprepared to deal with what ensues in indolent solitude. Instead of calm, he encounters the full impact of the faculty of imagination, the picture-producing part of his mind.[7] Through the unexpected nature of its productions, he is thrust into "le vague champs des imaginations" (1.8.32) and is forced to realize that he has an inherently counterfeit portrait of himself. What he has believed he already knows still remains to be learned: "La plus grande chose du monde, c'est de sçavoir estre à soy" (1.39.242: "The greatest thing in the world is to know how to belong to oneself" [1.39.178, Frame translation]). Instead of a grave, mature mind, he finds one behaving like a runaway horse (1.8.32). Instead of offering rest and retirement, he finds his mind "se donne cent fois plus d'affaire à soy mesmes, qu'il n'en prent pour autruy" (1.8.33). The energy of his mind per se does not pose a problem; what does, however, are the startling and potentially frightening things it bodies forth—"chimères et monstres fantasques." To belong to oneself (1.39.242), Montaigne's prime goal, can thus be seen as a virtual impossibility since Montaigne neither recognizes what his imagination is pouring out, nor does he see a way of predicting what will issue forth next.

Montaigne's use of hyperbole underlines the dominating and overpowering quality of the imagination. At the beginning of "De l'oisiveté" he stresses the overwhelming number of imagination-inspired thoughts by comparing them to "cent mille sortes d'herbes sauvages et inutiles" (1.8.32). At the end of the essay he uses the same rhetorical device: "[mon esprit] faisant le cheval eschapé ... se donne cent fois plus d'affaire à soy mesmes, qu'il n'en prenoit pour autruy" (1.8.33). In both instances he places emphasis on the untamed qualities of the productions of his mind in solitude. As we have seen, he compares his mind

---

[6] On this point it is interesting to note the recent critical emphasis on Montaigne's creation of the *Essais* as a means of replacing the presence of La Boétie. See in particular Richard Regosin, *The Matter of My Book: Montaigne's Essais as the Book of the Self* (Berkeley: Univ. of California Press, 1977), especially chapter 1, "Friendship and Literature," 7–29. Also Raymond C. La Charité, "The Coherence of Montaigne's First Book," *L'Esprit créateur* 20 (1980): 36–45.

[7] For a fuller treatment of Montaigne's views of imagination in relation to moral, epistemological, and psychological issues, see Dora E. Polachek, "Montaigne and the Concept of Imagination: A Synchronic Reading" (Ph.D. diss., Univ. of North Carolina, 1984).

to an unbridled, runaway horse acting instinctively, spontaneously, and impulsively. Montaigne stresses most heavily, however, the lawlessness of what issues forth, since what he encounters negates his initial belief in the unicity of his mind and the consistency, orderliness, and predictability that the word implies. What he finds is unruly, thrusting itself (the verb *se jeter*, and not *se présenter* is used) hither and yon, giving birth to chimeras and fantastic monsters "les uns sur les autres, sans ordre, et sans propos" (1.8.33).

As one critic has put it, this marks Montaigne's "initiation to the contemplative life."[8] Instability, fragmentation, unpredictability, disorder—wasn't this Montaigne's appraisal of life in society? Here in solitude, with himself as companion, the initial assessment of the situation is strikingly similar. As John O'Neill points out, Montaigne discovers that "retirement, so far from leaving him in peace, left him prey to all the wanderings of his imagination so that he was less at home with himself than he had been in public life."[9] Whereas in society man is a plaything of fortune, in his private life he can, potentially at least, fare worse by being dominated by an errant imagination.

Instead of the peaceful mind he longed for, Montaigne discovers the inner chaos of his unexplored and uncharted psyche. That Montaigne finds no comfort in it is clear. Because of his imagination he is in a continual state of "agitation" (1.8.32) and the never-ending variety of "folie" and "rêverie" are classified by Montaigne as things of which to be wary, indicative of something closer to pathology than mental health. His citation from Horace underlines the unhealthy quality of these visions, and his comparison of his mind's productions to deformed, aborted fetuses reinforces this point.

Up to now one could easily claim that Montaigne is treading familiar ground. We see how he is continuing in the tradition of the Middle Ages, and its distrust of the imagination.[10] Even the image of the inactive mind as a fertile field, abounding in disorderly and variegated burgeonings, is a stock one.[11] For example, in a passage remarkable for

---

[8] Glyn Norton, *Montaigne and the Introspective Mind* (The Hague: Mouton, 1975), 26.

[9] John O'Neill, *Essaying Montaigne: A Study of the Renaissance Institution of Writing and Reading* (London: Routledge & Kegan Paul, 1982), 104.

[10] For the historical legacy see Murray Wright Bundy, *The Theory of Imagination in Classical and Medieval Thought*, University of Illinois Studies in Language and Literature, 12 (Urbana: Univ. of Illinois Press, 1927).

[11] See Carol Clark, *The Web of Metaphor*, 58–61, where she traces the development of the agricultural image, showing the similarities in passages from Montaigne, La Primaudaye, and Meurier.

its similarity to the opening of "De l'oisiveté," Gabriel Meurier in 1583 writes:

> l'oiseux ... doibt estre condemné pour mauvais, car comme la terre à default de culture et d'estre bechée ou cultivée ... nourrit force orties, griesches et ortiantes, espines picantes et autres herbes inutiles et nuisibles. Ainsi advient de l'oisiveté vray chevet et oreiller du diable.[12]

> the idle one ... must be condemned as wicked, for like an untended land which nourishes nettles, thorns and other useless and harmful weeds, so too it is with idleness, veritable resting place of the devil [translation mine].

Meurier's passage is important because it typifies the prevailing attitude as well, an attitude that Montaigne does not share. Montaigne's use of the stock image is merely a "gesture in the direction of convention."[13] His subsequent reevaluation of the image can thus be construed as a fairly radical undertaking. Whereas Meurier and others make the link between idleness and the diabolic portent of the lawless imagination, Montaigne's attitude differs markedly. Even though he stresses the dangers of the imagination, nowhere does he call for its condemnation on moral grounds. While what is springing forth in this period of inactivity certainly cannot be called good and natural, "une generation bonne et naturelle" (1.8.32), Montaigne gives not sign of his considering it evil. It is, after all, a part of him and nowhere does he utilize what some have termed the "fiercely punitive imagery favored by so many of his contemporaries—no cutting or burning, no uprooting of weeds...."[14] If he were to have his "pruning knife always at the ready to eliminate any signs of unregenerate nature,"[15] Montaigne would be maiming himself. And even at this early stage, Montaigne demonstrates an intuitive sense that the productions of these internal, irrational forces which cause him to see and experience things not visible merit closer examination.

Thus, these "chimeres et monstres fantasques" are treated almost paternally by Montaigne. Issuing forth from him they are his offspring (something which the birth image in "De l'oisiveté" underlines). His attitude toward them brings to mind his remarks about a father's

---

[12] Gabriel Meurier, *La Perle de similitudes*, cited in Clark, *The Web of Metaphor*, 60.
[13] Clark, *The Web of Metaphor*, 60.
[14] Ibid., 125.
[15] Ibid., 60.

attitude toward his son in the opening paragraph of "De l'institution des enfans" (1.26.145–6): "Je ne vis jamais pere, pour teigneux ou bossé que fut son fils, qui laissast de l'avoüer. Non pourtant ... qu'il ne s'aperçoive de sa défaillance; mais tant y a qu'il est sien" ("I have never seen a father who failed to claim his son, however mangy or hunchbacked he was. Not that he does not perceive his defect ... but the fact remains that the boy is his" [1.26.106, Frame translation]). His attachment to them will cause him to treat them gently.

The decision to examine them is made possible by Montaigne's subsuming belief that order is attainable. To say, as Montaigne does, that if we do not bridle and restrain the wild and untamed, they will "throw themselves in disorder hither and yon" (1.8.32) implies that one can be fairly well assured that bridles and restraints can make order out of disorder. This is echoed in a statement such as "L'ame qui n'a point de but estably elle se perd" (1.8.32). The solution is simple: fix a goal. In this way, the imagination can be conquered. But for Montaigne triumph over the imagination does not involve the bludgeoning or eradication described by his contemporaries. Disturbing and unbalancing as this discovery of the shadowy chaotic realm may be, Montaigne recognizes that it "demands expression and release in a substantial form."[16]

What strategies, then, does Montaigne develop? The process of recording these chimeras and fantastic monsters, *"les mettre en rolle"* (1.8.33) establishes control over them by casting an impediment to their rhythm. What characterizes the imagination is the breakneck speed with which it is able to produce and thus overwhelm. It leaves no time for discourse (they spring forth in full bloom, "sans propos"). By recording the productions of his imagination, Montaigne will first of all slow it down. On a very fundamental level, then, he will modify the numbers involved. As we saw earlier, Montaigne's use of hyperbole strongly suggests his discomfort with the fecundity of the imagination, which is able to pour forth continually a hundred thousand kinds of useless weeds. Secondly, keeping this record will serve as a palliative to the "agitation" his mind, and therefore he, as well, are experiencing. It will enable him to "contemplate at ease" (1.8.33) the peculiar nature of his imaginary monsters, and will thus make possible the *repos*, the *arrêt*, and the *rassisement en soi* which he fully and unquestioningly expected initially.

Even though his initial premises about the voyage inward were erroneous, Montaigne's method of dealing with the imagination makes

---

[16] Norton, *Montaigne and the Introspective Mind*, 29.

possible the reestablishment of dialogue—*propos*—which he deems so essential. This is echoed later in that famous passage from "De la solitude":

> Il se faut reserver une arriereboutique toute nostre, toute franche, en laquelle nous establissons notre vraye liberté, et principale retraicte et solitude. En cette-cy faut-il prendre nostre ordinaire entretien de nous à nous mesmes.... Nous avons une ame contournable en soy mesme; elle se peut faire compagnie; elle a dequoy assaillir et dequoy defendre, dequoy recevoir et dequoy donner: ne craignons pas en cette solitude de nous croupir d'oisiveté ennuyeuse.... En nos actions accoustumées, de mille il n'en est pas une qui nous regarde (1.39.241).

> We must reserve a back shop all our own, entirely free, in which to establish our real liberty and our principal retreat and solitude. Here our ordinary conversation must be between us and ourselves.... We have a soul that can be turned upon itself; it can keep itself company; it has the means to attack and the means to defend, the means to receive and the means to give: Let us not fear that in this solitude we shall stagnate in tedious idleness. Among our customary actions there is not one in a thousand that concerns ourselves [1.39.177; Frame translation of "A" level text].

The dialogue will result from a turning inward ("une ame contournable en soy mesmes") that must inevitably lead to an exploration of the self as opposed to others, who are always entangled and imprisoned by socially governed actions ("nos actions accoustumées"), tending to mask rather than to reveal. Given this opposition between inner self/outer world which Montaigne underlines throughout this essay, we can extrapolate and extend Montaigne's logic in the last sentence quoted in the passage (a passage similar in construction to those we examined in "De l'oisiveté"). Thus Montaigne is saying that "En nos actions privées, de mille chacune nous regarde." The activity he refers to also encompasses thoughts, for it will be the life of the mind that will sustain him in his retreat. The dialogue is made possible by a splitting of the self into experiencer and analyzer. Paradoxically, if Montaigne were to remain at the level of experiencer, the end result would be fragmentation, for, as we have seen, he would be tossed about without end by the power of his imagination. The anchoring effect that he seeks in *repos* can come about only by distancing from the self. This is essentially what the following image borrowed from Seneca implies for Montaigne: "... vous et un compagnon estes assez suffisant theatre l'un à l'autre ou vous à vous mesmes" (1.39.247: "you and one companion are an adequate theater for each other, or you for yourself" [1.39.182, Frame translation]).

In theory, nothing could be simpler. But as Montaigne discovers throughout his essays, putting into practice any philosopher's insights is fraught with difficulty. Seneca's image of becoming a theater onto one's self is a stock commonplace, but due to Montaigne's discovery of the force of the faculty of the imagination, a complex transformation takes place. The actor/spectator dichotomy can be construed as one involving the difference between activity and passivity. For Montaigne, however, the actor is the one acted upon, and the true power for action lies only with the scriptor/spectator. The kind of theater—and therefore the kind of dialogue which will ensue—is perhaps best articulated in *Le Théâtre et son double*, a twentieth-century work which resonates with what Montaigne is discovering.[17] As Artaud puts it, "Il est dur quand tout nous pousse à dormir . . . de nous éveiller et de regarder comme en rêve, avec des yeux qui ne savent plus à quoi ils servent, et dont le regard est retourné vers le dedans" ("It is hard when everything is pushing us to sleep . . . to wake ourselves up and look as if in a dream, with eyes that no longer know their purpose and whose gaze is turned inward").[18]

Montaigne realizes that he will have to look with new eyes upon the vast, unexplored dream and nightmare-like terrain with which his imagination is constantly confronting him. *Repos*, which Montaigne originally anticipated as having the calm of an almost lifeless state, will acquire a new meaning for him, given his physical and mental stages of development. In terms of his physical point in time he senses that his life is almost over—a notion which, as we have seen, he brings with him when he decides to live "à part" (1.8.33). In terms of his mental point in time, he comes to the realization that there is an entire world—that is, himself—about which he knows virtually nothing, and that ultimately this knowledge which he lacks is the only kind of knowledge that is worthwhile. The chasm between his physical and mental maturation is something which he will have to bridge in order to attain a meaningful harmony of body and mind. To pass in full idleness the little time which remains—what Montaigne initially envisioned as the desired state—is not only impossible, but also inappropri-

---

[17] To my knowledge, no other analyses exist exploring the affinities between these ideas of Montaigne and Antonin Artaud's, in such essays as "Le Théâtre et la culture" and "Le Théâtre et la cruauté," for example.

[18] Antonin Artaud, "Le Théâtre et la culture," in *Le Théâtre et son double* (Paris: Gallimard, 1964), 16. All translations from Artaud are mine.

ate and potentially harmful. As his encounter with the faculty of imagination has shown him, one cannot replicate a state of death while still alive. "Nous sommes nés pour agir" (1.20.89) applies to the contemplative life as well, if not more so. The kind of *mise-en-scène* needed is clearly not one that will lead to an "engourdissement inefficace, où paraissent sombrer toutes nos facultés" ("ineffectual torpor, in which all our faculties seem to sink").[19] It cannot comprise a comfortable dialogue between two friends preordained by destiny to meet, whose spirits are so attuned that one can complete the other's thoughts effortlessly. This, after all, typified the relationship between Montaigne and La Bóetie. From the outset, then, Montaigne is forced to realize the impossibility of resurrecting his friend. The kind of dialogue necessary will require effort.

If Montaigne is to be an adequate enough theater unto himself, it will have to be with the realization that this is a "théâtre qui nous réveille: nerfs et coeur" ("a theater which awakens us: nerves and heart"),[20] for it will consist of a dialogue between two diametrically different forces, each pulling in the opposite direction: one aiming for unbounded flight, the other clearly earth-directed. And yet, as Montaigne realizes, the two are inextricably connected. Together they constitute the totality of his being—the qualities of one are heightened by the presence of the other (1.39.241: "elle a de quoi assaillir et de quoy defendre, de quoi recevoir et de quoy donner"). Their interaction generates a dynamic equilibrium consisting of energy which is constantly being generated and put to use.

In his role of scriptor, Montaigne will give body to his chimeras by transforming them into words. In this way they will cease being "inutiles" (1.8.32). The internal dialogue will change idleness into a state of activity which renders the useless useful ("pour nostre service"). As Artaud will say later on, "Il s'agit donc de faire du thèâtre, au propre sens du mot, une fonction ... quelque chose d'aussi localisé et d'aussi précis que ... le développement, chaotique en apparence, des images du rêve dans le cerveau, et ceci par un enchaînement efficace, une vraie mise en servage de l'attention" ("It becomes a question, then, of making theater into a function in the true sense of the word ... something as localized and as specific as ... the development, in appearance chaotic, of dream images in the brain, and this via an efficacious involvement, a true enslavement of the attention").[21]

---

[19] Artaud, "Le Théâtre et la cruauté," 129.
[20] Ibid.
[21] Ibid., 139.

Paradoxically, the effect will be one of liberation. Instead of being enslaved by the imagination, the constant vigilance needed to record them, "les mettre en rolle," will prevent the mind from dissipating its energy—"l'ame qui n'a point de but estably, elle se perd" (1.8.32). The development will have the appearance of being chaotic, but to talk of appearances is to bring into play the evaluation by others whom Montaigne rejects as inappropriate interpreters of his actions. As he states in "De la solitude": "Or c'est assez vescu pour autruy, vivons pour nous ... ramenons à nous ... et à nostre aise non pensées et nos intentions" (1.39.368: "We have lived enough for others.... Let us bring back our thoughts and plans to ourselves and our well-being" [1.39.178, Frame translation]). What others see as chaotic—and have trained us to see as chaotic—may not be so at all, just as what they discern as a courageous act may be just the opposite. By looking inward, Montaigne will be freed from the prejudicial and distorting vision of others. His inner-directed energy will cause him to be a world unto himself.[22] It will be a world where the action will emanate from the imagination—those chimeras and fantastic monsters, those wild and useless weeds—and its interplay with his other faculties, whose full potential for usefulness will unfold the more they deal and grapple with the productions of the imagination. In Baudelaire's words, imagination is that "Mystérieuse faculté ... [qui] touche à toutes les autres; elle les excite, elle les envoie au combat" ("Mysterious faculty ... [which] touches all the others: it excites them, sends them into combat" [translation mine]).[23]

The most important faculty that will be called into play will be judgment, and it is through judgment's intervention that things *fantasques* and *inutiles* will be enlisted into Montaigne's service. The dialogue that will ensue between imagination and judgment will have a strong psychological dimension. As La Charité has remarked, judgment's role in introspection will be less one of ruler than that of fathomer of psychological disturbances.[24] As we have seen, the recording process will slow down the imagination. Judgment will continue this process of *ralentissement* further by its ability to "seize and fix in time mental ... phenomena."[25] In this way it will fulfill one of its major

---

[22] This will be articulated fully after Montaigne has had considerable practice in this kind of activity. In the "B" strata of "Du repentir" he will say, "J'ay mes loix et ma court pour juger de moy, et m'y adresse plus qu'ailleurs" (3.1.807).
[23] "Salon de 1859," in *Oeuvres complètes* (Paris: Pléiade, 1966), 1037.
[24] Raymond C. La Charité, *The Concept of Judgment in Montaigne* (The Hague: Nijhoff, 1968), 57.
[25] Ibid., 36.

functions—"to snatch, pick out ... pieces of information and analyze and display them for what they are."[26]

The involvement of judgment, then, will render the strange familiar, for it will take a step further the process begun by recording. Whereas recording arrests the imagination's products for observation, judgment will enable their evaluation. The importance of evaluation is paramount; without it one runs the risk of literally getting carried away by the imagination, for will and the concomitant ability to take action become paralyzed. Perhaps Montaigne's most powerful description of imagination devoid of evaluation is the following: "Nous tressuons, nous tremblons, nous pallisons, et rougissons aux secousses de nos imaginations ... quelques fois jusques à en expirer" (1.21.98: "We drip with sweat, we tremble, we turn pale and turn red at the blows of our imagination ... sometimes to the point of expiring" [1.21.69, Frame translation]). Even if death does not occur (and given Montaigne's description of his personality this outcome is highly unlikely), the outgrowth of this state of fear and trembling is perhaps the most pernicious: it can result in a looking outward for an explanation of these productions, and a belief in forces beyond our control. What operates so often on the level of man in society can easily take place in solitude: "le principal credit des miracles, des visions, des enchantemens, et de tels effects extraordinaires, vienne de la puissance de l'imagination, agissant principalement contre les ames du vulgaire, plus molles. On leur a si fort saisi la creance, qu'ils pensent voir ce qu'ils ne voient pas" (1.21.91: "It is probable that the principal credit of miracles, visions, enchantments, and such extraordinary occurrences comes from the power of imagination, acting principally upon the minds of the common people, which are softer. Their belief has been so strongly seized that they think they see what they do not see" [1.21.70, Frame translation]). Not only does one suffer from mental agitation, but physical disturbances (for example, seeing what is not there) begin to mirror the psychological disorder. Finally, the belief in the supernatural renders this state of disharmony potentially permanent, since man views himself as powerless to change the situation.[27]

In the final analysis, the one frontier Montaigne finds worthy of

---

[26] Ibid., 38.

[27] For a detailed discussion of Montaigne's scornful attitude concerning his society's belief in the interrelationship between human phenomena and supernatural forces, see Dora E. Polachek, "Montaigne and Imagination: The Dynamics of Power and Control," in *Le Parcours des Essais: Montaigne 1588–1988*, ed. Marcel Tetel and G. Mallary Masters (Paris: Aux Amateurs de Livres, 1989), 135–145.

exploration is the world within. As described so aptly in "De l'oisiveté" it is limitless, uncharted, teeming with vitality. By focusing on the productions of his imagination, Montaigne will succeed in transforming the outside world and incorporating it within his private universe. Seen from this perspective, Montaigne's early essays cease to be disjointed recountings of anecdotes, historical accounts, and matters devoid of interest. When Montaigne resuscitates stories about preachers, lawyers, ambassadors, kings, soldiers, he has one question in mind: what do these people and incidents have to tell me about myself? Thus, even the most hackneyed tale becomes renewed, for it is emptied of its traditional lessons. It enters into the all important domain of *inscience*, ready to be scrutinized and reevaluated by the active interplay of all the faculties.

In conclusion, it is because of his encounter with the powers of his own imagination that Montaigne, as early as 1572, becomes aware of the world within himself and creates a work rich in the complexity of its psychological insights. As we have seen, it would not be an exaggeration to claim that it was because of his encounter with the faculty of imagination that Montaigne decided upon his literary undertaking. The choice, in a sense, was to write or to go mad. Once Montaigne discovers the tempering qualities of the recording process, however, imagination's potentially overpowering lawlessness becomes transformed into a life-affirming fecundity. The *Essais* comes into being as a result of the dynamic interplay between the imagination and the limitless body of knowledge and unfathomed material that it activates. Montaigne realizes, too, that the rhythm of imagination is the rhythm of living—fast, sudden, full of the unexpected. Instead of fearing imagination, as others of his day do, he discovers a method of making full use of it. By linking *repos* and *propos*—discourse—he establishes the inner harmony characteristic of his primary goal in writing and more importantly, in life: to live more at leisure and at one's ease, "vivre plus à loisir et à son aise" (1.39.238).

Cornell University

LAWRENCE F. RHU

Young Tasso's Reckoning with the Orlando furioso

TASSO'S EFFORTS TO COME TO GRIPS WITH THE PROMINENCE OF Ariosto and the triumph of the *Orlando furioso* in the literary tradition that he sought to inherit are complex and multifarious, and they begin to appear early and often both in the young poet's theories of heroic poetry and in his own narrative practice. In the preface that Tasso addressed to the readers of his *Rinaldo* in 1562, he enlists Aristotle to sanction authorial anonymity and the example of Homer in narrative verse; and Ariosto's frequent self-reference in the proems to individual cantos of the *Furioso* is the precedent to be eschewed in this regard according to Tasso's neoclassical norms.[1] Shortly thereafter, when the young poet again raises this issue in the *Discorsi dell'arte poetica* of 1564 or thereabout and warns against the intrusion of authorial commentary upon an advancing story, the abundant editorializing in Ariosto's romance is the obvious, though unnamed, object of his critical caveat.[2]

But the evidently irresistible appeal of chivalric material like that in the *Furioso* significantly influences Tasso's argument for the appropriate subject of a heroic poem: in the early *Discorsi*, he maintains that the proper period in time for such a composition should be neither too ancient nor too modern, but in the middle distance, like the age of Charlemagne and Arthur. Even when Tasso later recasts this opinion in the *Discorsi del poema eroico* of 1594, his assertion that love is a suitable subject for epic allows him ready access to central concerns of the very tradition that he appears to question and reject on other grounds.[3]

Other early reflections of Tasso's on the *Furioso* and poems of its kind frequently reveal a comparable sort of double dealing that mixes

---

[1] Tasso, *Rinaldo*, a cura di Luigi Bonfigli (Bari: Laterza, 1936), 5–6.
[2] Tasso, *Discorsi dell'arte poetica e del poema eroico*, a cura di Luigi Poma (Bari: Laterza, 1965), 20–21.
[3] Ibid., 9–10, 104–8.

rejection and reclamation in odd combinations. In his discussion of fidelity to historical facts, young Tasso shows a tolerant acceptance of Ariosto's irreverent rewriting of Homeric legend. Although he cannot accept the story of Troy that none other than St. John the Evangelist proclaims in the thirty-fifth canto of Ariosto's poem, he does admit that he can see how the assertions that the Greeks really lost and that Penelope was a whore serve Ariosto's particular purpose when taken in context.[4] In the early *Discorsi* other citations from the *Furioso* are regularly condemned in the name of decorum; for example, Tasso quotes three scabrous passages to indict their stylistic impropriety. Likewise, when he considers the issue of wholeness of plot, he concedes that the *Furioso* satisfies this requirement when read together with the *Orlando innamorato*; but he then turns promptly to the matter of size and labels the very merger, which he initially condoned on other grounds, as a *monstrum in excessu*, given his new criterion.[5] Such shifts between approval and censure are characteristic of the general attitude the young poet adopts toward his formidable precursor.

Furthermore, consideration of the right size of an epic also leads Tasso to broach the issue of episodes as increments to the overall body of the plot. Episodes can proliferate endlessly in romance, and this capacity of that form plainly unsettled Tasso, as his nervous treatment of just such a possibility reveals in his subsequent discussion of unity in the early *Discorsi*.[6] But this preliminary concern with episodes, as well as Tasso's later expression of uneasiness about them, readily give rise to thematic questions in addition to problems of structure. For knight-errantry in the *Gerusalemme liberata*, besides supplying multiple opportunities for digressive exploits, also occasions nearly all of the poem's episodes and certainly accounts for its most contested content. Thus, these elements appear almost tainted at the source with a double poison—their structural multiplicity *and* their dangerous themes. Tasso employs a kindred metaphor in a letter to Orazio Capponi in July, 1576, in which he outlines the argument of his poem.[7] As he proceeds sequentially through the cantos, the fourth elicits this summation:

> Consigli de' demoni. Venuta d'Armida. Da questo canto, *come da fonte*, derivano tutti gli episodi. (emphasis added)
>
> Assemblies of the devils. Arrival of Armida. All the episodes derive from this canto, as from a fount.

---

[4] Ibid., 18–19.
[5] Ibid., 41, 20 ff.
[6] Ibid., 24.
[7] *Le lettere di Torquato Tasso*, a cura di Cesare Guasti (Florence, 1852), 205.

Leaving out the other major contributor of episodes in his poem, the adventures of Erminia (as Tasso understandably does in this context), this particular wellspring of romance unmistakably arises from a dubious or clearly evil source: the assembly of devils who decide to use Armida to thwart the progress of the Crusade. Thus, the recognition of Tasso's anxieties over form, which certainly make themselves felt in his early poetics, ramifies into the region of content when we take into account his avowed sense of the substance of his poem's romantic adventures. However, this double burden challenges his virtuosity in a notably productive way, and no matter how conscious our investigation makes us of Tasso's problems, we cannot overlook how masterfully he solves them on this occasion. For Tasso shrewdly affiliates the dark forces of his poem with the pagan mythology that he derives from classical literature, and he manages thereby to exploit this questionable version of divine life aesthetically while he devalues it morally.[8]

Tasso's Hell is full of ancient monsters such as Harpies and Centaurs (4.5), which he derives from the first creatures we encounter in Virgil's underworld (*Aen.* 4.286-9). He names his Satan Plutone (4.6), and he has him protest his wounded pride (4.12) in the tradition of outraged honor among pagans like Ajax and Achilles. Other classical monsters, such as Cerberus and Hydra, also appear in this grim locale where Cocytus serves as a landmark (4.8). Armida's beauty inspires comparison with Helen of Troy as well as with Roman goddesses like Juno, Venus, and Diana by mention of places traditionally connected with them: Argos, Cyprus, and Delos (4.29). And when Armida appeals to God, she calls him Jove (4.42), while her voice reminds the poet of that of a Siren and her wiles exceed those of both Circe and Medea (4.86). Finally, Tasso caps this crescendo of classical associations with an emphatic conclusion unmistakable in its implications, particularly in light of all that has gone before to define the drift of this canto. Once we have seen that some Christian warriors have been led astray by the sort of tricks that Armida plays, it becomes no wonder that the pick of pagan heroes fell prey to love:

> Qual meraviglia or fia s'il fero Achille
> d'Amor fu preda, ed Ercole e Teseo,
> s'ancor chi per Giesù la spada cinge
> l'empio ne' lacci suoi talora stringe?   (4.96)

Now what kind of marvel will it be if fierce Achilles was the

---

[8] Judith Kates's essay, "The Revaluation of the Classical Heroic in Tasso and Milton," *Comparative Literature* 26 (1974): 299-317, has in part guided my reading of canto 4 of the *Liberata*.

prey of Love, and Hercules and Theseus, if even him who buckles on the sword for Christ the impious fellow catches in his toils?[9]

Key complications of character as well as those of faith also deepen and clarify themselves through the encounter between Armida and Goffredo over using Christian knights to help her out in her apparent distress. The captain of the Crusade is quite clear about religious differences between Islam and Christianity, and he warns the knights who depart to assist Armida in similar terms (4.65.5–6 and 5.78.1–3). However, compassion is awakened in him and makes him have second thoughts, giving his ambivalence a worthy source, unlike the lust which inflames the knights. Practical utility also influences him because Damascus, Armida's home, could offer much strategic support to his cause (4.65.7–8, and 66). Still, he finally does say no. But he has revealed in the process of making that decision a nature of genuine depth and complexity. In Tasso's creation of a high-minded and generally irreproachable hero, it is certainly worth wondering if the alternative to clay feet is no feet at all. Therefore, we should note that Goffredo has second thoughts here, and his feelings vie for the upper hand in determining his decision. However, by and large he does fit the Virgilian mold rather tightly and thus inherits some of the abstractness and rigidity that typify Aeneas's *pietas* and the duty-bound single-mindedness of his sense of purpose despite temporary lapses.

Goffredo and Armida also dramatize a study in contrasting faiths, for where he assents to the priority of God's claim upon him (4.69.7–8), she indicts the heavens for her harsh fate (4.71.7–8). She then announces suicide as the apt solution to her dilemma, following the direction that a pagan philosophy such as Stoicism might advise; and she cuts a noble figure in the process (4.73.7–8 and 74.1–2). In presenting this crucial conflict Tasso again draws tellingly upon Virgil; for the knights' unspoken, interior indictment of Goffredo's apparent hardness of heart toward his evidently distraught petitioner echoes Dido's accusations of Aeneas when the latter claims he is obliged by divine command to leave her and Carthage (*Aen.* 4.365–7; 4.77.5–7). Further, these same lines from the Roman poet are re-echoed in Armida's subsequent vilification of Rinaldo (16.57.1–4), after he says that he must abandon her in her garden and return to battle in Jerusalem. Tasso thus brilliantly complicates the drama of sin and redemption by this verbal association of the erring Christians and the pagan enchantress, and Goffredo's

---

[9] Throughout this essay I use Ralph Nash's translation, *Jerusalem Delivered* (Detroit: Wayne State Univ. Press, 1987).

forgiveness of the errant knights can be seen in this connection to prefigure Armida's conversion and so prepare us for one of the most disputed turns in the plot as it draws to a close.

Ample evidence of the considerable weight that Tasso means his discussion of unity of plot to carry emerges at its outset in the early *Discorsi*, because he introduces this topic as a subject of widespread and intense controversy. On one side stand proponents of Aristotle's authority as a preceptor in this regard as well as the convincing examples of antecedent classics whose structure depends on this principle; and Tasso, of course, belongs to this party. On the other side, contemporary habits of composition and the present taste of the courts both indicate a strong preference for multiple plots such as Ariosto contrived in his masterwork. And the overwhelming popularity of the *Orlando furioso*, by comparison with the complete neglect of Trissino's efforts in the alternate mode, and their consequently dismal failure, signals the triumph of romance. Although Tasso demonstrates a measured skepticism about Ariosto's theoretical defenders, whose motives he plainly questions, his esteem for his precursor as a supremely skillful poet sounds a clear note in his otherwise disapproving assessment. However, Ariosto's example should be avoided in the matter of multiple plots.[10]

A great deal is at stake here for Tasso, and critical readers of both his poetics and his poem have sensed his defensiveness and ill-concealed vulnerability as he aims to justify this crucial claim for his doctrine of composition. Robert Durling and Sergio Zatti exemplify the most cogent proponents of this response to young Tasso's theoretical and practical struggles with the issue of unity;[11] and a most relevant passage in the *Discorsi dell'arte poetica*, which effectively serves their turn in this discussion, warrants citation as we take up the same theme:

> suppose the plot is the poet's main purpose, as Aristotle affirmed and no one has yet denied. If the plot is single, his purpose will be single; if there are many and diverse plots, there will be many and diverse purposes. However, since diverse purposes distract the mind and hinder labor, he who sets himself a single goal will work more effectively than the imitator of a multitude of actions. I add that multiple plots cause confusion, which could go on and on forever if art did not set and prescribe limits. The poet who treats one plot attains his goal when that one plot is finished; he

---

[10] Tasso, *Discorsi*, 22–23.
[11] See Robert M. Durling, *The Figure of the Poet in the Renaissance Epic* (Cambridge: Harvard Univ. Press, 1965), 200–210; and Sergio Zatti, "Erranza, infermità e conquista: le figure del conflitto nella *Liberata*," *Lettere italiane* 33 (1981): 191–97.

who weaves together more may weave together four or six or ten: he is no more obliged to one number than to another. Thus, he can have no sure sense at what point he best stop.[12]

Tasso's personal sense of the consequences that ensue from misjudgment in this vital manner makes itself strongly felt because he implicates himself in the act of composition as he envisions it for the poet whose poem contains multiple plots. His own feelings of peril in the face of the uncontrollable ramifications of a plot unconstrained by the principle of unity become apparent as he imagines the distraction, confusion, and insecurity that multiple plots must inevitably entail for the artist who takes this sort of liberty with his compositions.

Tasso's later career and its famous episodes of undeniably psychopathological behavior encourage us to read such a passage from an exclusively psychoanalytic perspective, which would emphasize its latent content rather than its manifest claims and would aim to tell us as much about the author as about his text. This approach can help readers with biographical concerns to secure a seductively consistent interpretation of Tasso's character because they can here perceive signs of the coming storm that their own chronologically privileged position enables them to read accurately, without any of the risks that attend the forecaster's role. However, without disclaiming the insights that such a method can provide, honesty requires a forthright acknowledgement of the limitations of some of its standard procedures.

Without question, anxieties breathe uneasily beneath the surface of Tasso's text as he attempts to capture in theory the ultimate principles that underlie the making of an epic while he must simultaneously face and account for the undeniable triumph of a previous poem that routinely breaks all the rules. When we read in Tasso's defense of plot unity the absolute assertion that "there is surely no poetic genre today in use, nor was there such in ancient times, nor will such arise again in a long cycle of the centuries, which Aristotle did not fathom,"[13] we can

---

[12] "presupponendo che la favola sia il fine del poeta (come afferma Aristotele, e nissuno a sin qui negato), s'una sarà la favola, uno sarà il fine, se più e diverse saranno le favole, più e diversi saranno i fini; ma quanto meglio opera chi riguarda ad un sol fine che chi diversi fini si propone, nascendo dalla diversità de' fini distrazione ne l'animo e impedimento nell'operare, tanto meglio operarà l'imitator d'una sola favola che l'imitatore di molte azioni. Agiungo che dalla moltitudine delle favole nasce l'indeterminazione, e può questo progresso andare in infinito, senza che le sia dall'arte prefisso o circonscritto termine alcuno. Il poeta ch'una favola tratta, finita quella, è giunto al suo fine; chi più ne tesse, o quattro o sei o dieci ne potrà tessere; né più a questo numero che a quello è obligato. Non potrà aver dunque determinata certezza qual sia quel segno ove convegna fermarsi." *Discorsi*, 24.

[13] "che spezie di poesia non è oggi in uso, né fu in uso negli antichi tempi, né

certainly sense the extreme need for ultimate solutions and final authorities that governs his appeal to the ancient philosopher.

The same high tension and over-compensatory advocacy of his own choice of sanctions make themselves felt in Tasso's poetic practice when he broaches subjects reminiscent of the controversial realm of romance. During the opening muster of the Crusaders, Tasso introduces the band of adventurers who, at this utterly Homeric moment, bring the feudal customs of knight-errantry and the exploits of medieval chivalric romance into the world of his epic. Tasso emphatically upgrades their status in regard to the rival traditions whose heroes they completely supersede.

> Squadra d'ordine estrema ecco vien poi
> ma d'onor prima e di valor e d'arte.
> Son qui gli aventurieri, invitti eroi,
> terror de l'Asia e folgori di Marte.
> Taccia Argo i Mini, e taccia Artú que' suoi
> erranti, che di sogni empion le carte;
> ch'ogni antica memoria appo costoro
> perde: or qual duce fia degno di loro? (1.52)

Lo then comes a band the last in order but first in honor and in courage and skill. Here are the Adventurers, invincible heroes, the terrors of Asia and thunderbolts of Mars. Let Argus be silent about the Minyans, and Arthur be silent about his errant knights, that fill the pages with dreams. For every memory from antiquity loses by comparison with these. Now what leader will be worthy of them?

Taken literally, Tasso's assertion here leaves no doubt about the superiority of this squad of paladins who import the excitement of freelancers into the (temporarily) disciplined ranks of the Christian army. Taken "personally," however, with an ear attuned to the author's own story, it can readily make Tasso seem to protest too much the comparative excellence of these wandering knights who seem to have strayed into an enterprise of an altogether other order than their usually solitary feats of generous heroism.

Given young Tasso's special and self-evidently vexed concern over the poetics of romance, we can see how the stanza in his poem quoted above may be carrying more than the merely thematic burden that its contents openly declare. This passage may, in addition, convey what a

---

per un lungo volger di secoli di novo sorgerà, nella cui cognizione non si debba credere che penetrasse Aristotele...." Ibid., 28.

psychoanalytic reader would deem Tasso's "unresolved conflict" over the legitimate presence of chivalric heroes on epic occasions. When we note that both the main thrust and the final conclusion of Tasso's theoretical argument over unity of plot assert the generic identity of epic and romance,[14] we can also speculate with some confidence about the blend of literary and personal motives that define Tasso's dilemma as a poet consciously trying to reconcile a complex inheritance in theory as well as in practice. Obviously, if epic and romance are one and the same kind of poem, Tasso can have unqualified access to the sort of material that excited his imagination enough to inspire some of his loveliest poetry and some of his most committed theorizing. However, if his art and his aesthetics regularly betray the insecurity of their own foundations, which rest on the basis of an uneasy marriage between two quite different narrative and religious traditions, innumerable and fiercely maintained qualifications of both theory and practice become necessary in order to sanction Tasso's decisions as an author. In fact, these qualifications, in their turn, become evidence of the very insecurity that necessitates them.

Although circular, the above argument at least makes the same assertion throughout the whole of its compass! Psychoanalytic motive-hunting, however, can quickly invert my earlier contentions about Tasso's skillful management of his options and force a bald paradox upon us. Rather than bearing witness to artistic choice and control, the very emphasis with which Tasso associates classical mythology with Satan and the forces of evil in his poem's fourth canto may seem "over-determined" or "compulsive" and thus disclose an unacknowledged attraction to the powers of darkness that he is straining to overcome or to camouflage. Likewise, Goffredo's mixed emotions in his response to Armida's petition may seem negligible enough in the end to justify labeling the conflict between good and evil in Tasso's epic as virtually "Manichaean" on that occasion as well as more generally throughout the whole work.[15] The ideological purism of a simplistic code of right and wrong may, in its turn, seem an unconvincing cover for profound "ambivalence" in the poet's feelings about key aspects of his own creation. Since conflict and the unconscious are givens of the psychoanalytic approach, fundamental axioms of its version of our nature, such an outlook will tend to discover these factors wherever it trains its gaze. Even in an atmosphere of public controversy and repression, like that of the times which Tasso lived through, these phenomena

---

[14] Ibid., 26–29, 34–37.
[15] See Sergio Zatti, "L'uniforme cristiano e il multiforme pagano nella *Gerusalemme liberata*," *Belfagor* 31 (1976): 405.

will often be perceived as exclusively private conditions of particular psyches offering discrete confirmation of a generally ahistorical and individual anthropology. That a perspective of this sort cannot help but degrade young Tasso's accomplishment should go without saying.

Further, sustained comparison of Tasso with Ariosto, although obligatory when we mean to study the former's critical and creative designs, can only underscore the emotional turmoil that characteristically attracts our attention in reading the later poet's works. Ariosto was Tasso's most eminent precursor, and the young poet's *Discorsi* show him struggling to come to grips with that legacy just as numerous other aspirants had to reckon with it. However, Ariosto is also duly famous for keeping his cool; throughout the *Furioso* he is usually as tranquil as the Buddha, and outbursts of genuine passion or scenes of sustained pathos are extremely few and far between in that text. For instance, in the proem to canto 14 (stanzas 7–9), his lament over the outrageous acts of violence committed by the French troops during the sack of Ravenna in 1512, which tempers and finally undermines his celebration of Duke Alfonso d'Este's triumph there, sounds one of the rare notes of entirely credible indignation in the whole *Furioso*. Likewise, in the proem of canto 34 (stanzas 1–3), after Astolfo has successfully sequestered the harpies in their infernal abode, Ariosto breaks forth with a stinging denunciation of Ludovico il Moro, who first opened the doors of Italy in 1494 to invasions by rapacious foreigners who have ravaged the country, driven to continual violence by their insatiable greed. But this too is an exceptional occasion; and even at the highest pitch of outrage or pathos, Ariosto is likely to reverse the flow of feeling or compromise the emotion of the moment with ironic and down-to-earth matter-of-factness. Isabella is the namesake of Ariosto's devoted friend, Isabella d'Este, the sister of his patron; and she epitomizes the feminine virtues of fidelity and chastity. Like her loyalty and her loss in love, her readiness to die and thereby save her honor from the stain of forced intimacy with the brutal Rodomonte makes a powerfully moving spectacle. However, once she is willingly beheaded in an act of ultimate self-sacrifice for her lofty ideals, Ariosto does not resist the most prosaic and deflationary sort of observation (24.36.1): after the decapitation, her severed head bounces three times when it hits the ground, and this occasion of high seriousness similarly loses a lot of altitude at that moment, landing with a bit of a thud.

Therefore, Tasso's readings of Ariosto often impose serious constructions upon passages where such feelings are utterly alien to the spirit of their composition, and the earlier text reaches us through a compromising filter of foreign concerns. Thus, while Tasso may appear as a poet forever engaged in passionate conflicts of questionable outcome, Ariosto comes to seem an irreverent iconoclast and a biting satirist. Both, however, distinguish themselves from the confines of these stereotypes, especially as our awareness of the conditions that create these misreadings increases; and Ariosto becomes a worldly ironist shrewdly gaging the instrument of his art to register and expose excess and defect of all sorts, while Tasso achieves frequent reconciliation and balance of the rival elements that he seeks to blend in his poem.

Ariosto wrote no formal poetics. He and his age had no need of the self-conscious neoclassicism of Tasso and his contemporaries, so the pressure to legitimize himself theoretically hardly constrained Ariosto with the labor of self-justification that Tasso felt obliged to accomplish. Of course, there is no denying that Ariosto reflected deeply upon the craft that he practiced. The success of his efforts adequately testifies to that fact, but the only apparent form such reflections take are occasional asides, parenthetical poetics imbedded in the flux of this author's ongoing narration. The issue of unity of plot, for example, little interests him theoretically; and the practice plainly would bore him. At one such juncture, where a theoretical concern does momentarily engage Ariosto, and which can also typify the numerous arbitrary turns in the plot of his poem, he develops a brief rationale for the constant shifts in his attention as a story-teller. When Bradamante, once again in quest of her beloved Ruggiero, falls prey to Atlante's enchantment and joins the captive company of Neoplatonic strivers in the hall of mirrors that keeps them continually deceived yet determined to attain their illusory goals, Ariosto peremptorily abandons her there in the magician's castle and directs his interest elsewhere.

> Ma lascià n Bradamante, e non v'incresca
> udir che cosí resti in quello incanto;
> che quando sarà il tempo ch'ella n'esca,
> la farò uscire, e Ruggiero altretanto.
> Come raccende il gusto il mutar esca,
> cosí mi par che la mia storia, quanto
> or qua or là piú varïata sia,
> meno a chi l'udirà noiosa fia.
>
> Di molte fila esser bisogno parme
> a condur la gran tela ch'io lavoro.
> E però non vi spiaccia d'ascoltarme,
> come fuor de le stanze il popol Moro
> davanti al re Agramante ha preso l'arme,
> che, molto minacciando ai Gigli d'oro,
> lo fa assembrare ad una mostra nuova,
> per saper quanta gente si ritruova.   (23.80–81)

> But let us leave Bradamant: be not dismayed to hear that she remains imprisoned in the spell—when time is ripe for her to be released from it, I shall bring her away, and Ruggiero too. As varying the dishes quickens the appetite, so is it with my story: the more varied it is the less likely it is to bore my listeners. / To complete the great tapestry on which I am working I feel the need for a great variety of strands.
>
> Suffer me, then, to tell you about the Saracens assembling from their encampments to pass in review before King Agrament: a dire threat he poses to the Golden Lilies as he summons his troops to this latest review in order to assess their numbers.[16]

Tasso, who claims in the early *Discorsi* that narrative artistry depends more on the manner an author adopts to stitch together the fabric of a plot than on the novelty of the material he uses, would have responded with ready sympathy to Ariosto's figurative language in this theoretical gloss on the tale he is telling. However, the procedure that it aims to defend, a sudden and capricious change of subject for the mere sake of amusement, would have surely aroused the young poet's strong disapproval—though one can easily imagine an Ariosto who could not have cared less about such an objection! In fact, it would not overstrain the credibility of critical intuition to invent an Ariosto *redivivus*, hypothetically endowed with a vision of the second half of his own century, who might see, in young Tasso's *Discorsi* and the pursuit of the ultimately perfect poem that they propose,[17] another phantom like his own Angelica. That such a self-created spectre of perfection might haunt its own author to the point of madness and beyond would seem to the earlier poet a familiar story indeed.

Such Ariostan insouciance, as well as the calm acknowledgment and acceptance of human fallibility that regularly accompany it, ill accord with the passionate high-mindedness so typical of Tasso; and they markedly distinguish Ariosto's temperament from that of the later laureate. Decisive differences like these betoken the tension, if not the futility, that any effort at the reconciliation of such opposite types of poets and poetry must face; and they thus signify the grim odds inherent in the challenge that Tasso himself undertook. Contemporary theories, like Harold Bloom's, which speculate on the psychology of intertextuality in clearly Freudian terms, can find ready confirmation in the pervasive anxieties that seem both "free-floating" throughout the

---

[16] Throughout this essay I use Guido Waldman's translation: *Orlando Furioso* (New York: Oxford Univ. Press, 1983).

[17] *Discorsi*, 20.

whole of Tasso's epic and intensely local at specific moments. But the "influence" of romance upon a neoclassical epic narrator undeniably entails problems and even "anxieties" that transcend personal psychology by virtue of their objectively discernible reality: the two literary forms, epic and romance, differ notably in elements of both theme and structure, even though the sum of these differences may still not define them as two distinct genres; and these key discrepancies require acknowledgment. Although in his theorizing Tasso labors to establish the shared identity of epic and romance, he also means to announce and exploit their dissimilarities in his poem, as he testifies in the previously quoted octave that introduces the *aventurieri* (1.52).

Ariosto's attitude toward preceding texts and literary precursors betrays little of the competitive edge that Tasso displays on such an occasion, although the issue of priority is certainly alive for him. Ariosto makes a forthright and immediate claim for his own originality during the induction at the very start of his poem (1.2.1–2), and he does so in a high register of the epic voice. But he soon lapses into much more characteristic tones and topics; and, once we encounter Ferraù unsuccessfully searching for his helmet, which he has accidentally dropped into a river, the deflationary project of undermining the pretenses of chivalry is already well under way. This prosaic misadventure determines the activities of the first knight whom we actually encounter in the text (1.14); and, shortly thereafter, we witness this same Spanish champion striking a thoroughly practical bargain with his adversary Rinaldo in the name of their shared appetite for a woman. This business-like partnership that subordinates their rivalry in love and war and faith to immediate sexual self-interest occasions Ariosto's mock-laudatory outburst,

> Oh gran bontà de'cavellieri antiqui! (1.22.1)
>
> Great was the goodness of the knights of old!

In this instance, like many another, Ariostan irony undercuts the chivalric idealism that Tasso's Christianity means to supersede by virtue of an even higher code of conduct.

The strain of high-mindedness creates tensions in Tasso's text where it promotes laughter and release in the *Orlando furioso*. For example, each poet rewrites for his own purposes the myth of Perseus and Andromeda; Ariosto derives his version from book 4 of Ovid's *Metamorphoses* while Tasso's source is the fourth chapter of Heliodorus's *Ethiopica*. The assimilation of this pagan myth poses a serious challenge to Tasso's religious scruples; so, he transforms it into the Christian legend of St. George and the dragon (12.23), and he uses it as the motivating force behind the ultimate conversion of Clorinda, thereby winning for the faith the most appealing warrior among the Saracens and eliminating some discomfiting ambiguities about the forces of good and evil in his poem. The only such scruples that Ariosto's adaptation of Ovid seems to have challenged were those of his readers, who may have been tempted to consecrate the classical text by the routine means of Christian allegoresis—a commonplace legacy of the medieval approach to the *Metamorphoses*—and thus visit their own acceptable preconceptions upon pagan sensuality.[18] Ariosto, therefore, stresses the erotic comedy in the encounter of Ruggiero with Angelica on the isle of Ebuda, which depends on the Ovidian model, far beyond any similar inclinations in his source. As the cinquecento ran its course down to Tasso's times and the audience he had to address, the young poet almost instinctively felt the scandalized outrage that such lascivious highjinks might arouse in his more censorious readers. In his early poetics, when he considers the matter of decorum, the memory of Ariosto's irreverence requires a reckoning, and he cites a sequence of suggestive or simply lewd moments in the *Furioso* as exemplary transgressions of the epic norm for style that he means to clarify in the third of his initial *Discorsi*.[19] Ruggiero's irrepressible urge to assault the rescued maiden figures prominently in these selections that all serve both as a warning against such extremes of vulgarity and as a chance for Tasso to dissociate himself decisively from what inevitably struck him as a profoundly disturbing quality in Ariosto's attitude toward his material.

But continuity and closure—knowing both how to focus and sustain a given storyline and when to bring it to a conclusion—are the two artistic problems with multiple plots that particularly vex Tasso, and the *Furioso* especially exemplifies this pair of difficulties. On one hand, Ariosto willfully violates aesthetic values inherent in certain classical models that he evokes via imitation, and such intentional transgressions clearly make known his egalitarian bias against any literary hierarchy that ranks ancient paragons almost out of the reach of contemporary rivals. But on the other hand, he invokes unforgettable moments of pagans heroism to dignify his own efforts by echoing their achievements. This paradox, which shows Ariosto first as a dauntless leveller of literary authorities and then as a shrewd summoner of their ultimate sanction, must certainly betoken something of the extreme frustration young Tasso experienced in his efforts to sort out in theory the contradictory valences that obtain in Ariosto's masterwork and the traditions

---

[18] See Daniel Javitch's "Rescuing Ovid from the Allegorizers," *Comparative Literature* 30 (1978): 97–107, for an interesting discussion of Ariosto's strategy to avoid this pious and conventional appropriation of this text.

[19] *Discorsi*, 41.

it draws upon. And his own most brilliant crystalization of his thinking in this regard—discordant concord[20]—by no means signals any final reconciliation or profound agreement between the two poets. Rather, it demonstrates the conceptual flexibility that young Tasso had to strive to achieve and the distance he had to go to attain it in contrast to the more intuitive artistry of Ariosto, who was spared the burden, if not the curse, of any such concomitant theoretical mission.

Ariosto's intention to reduce romance and epic material to a common level becomes notably clear during his presentation of the siege of Paris in cantos 14-15 when the beleaguered Christians are nearly overcome by the Saracens. Numerous aspects of this narrative are obvious reminders of the final four books of the *Aeneid* and their account of the war between the Trojans and the Latins. The assault on Paris evokes the Trojan camp under attack by the Rutulians; Rinaldo's arrival with reinforcements from England and Scotland parallels Aeneas's return with Arcadian and Etruscan auxiliaries; Dardinello's single combat with Rinaldo recalls Pallas's fatal encounter with Turnus, whose exploits are otherwise suggested by the solitary marauding of Rodomonte within the city walls and his last-minute withdrawal from the threatening approach of his foes; and the nocturnal debacle of Cloridano and Medoro reflects elements of the poignant misadventures of Nisus and Euryalus, although their more immediate source is Statius's imitation in the *Thebaid* of this Virgilian passage. The cumulative effect of all these echoes must surely impress the reader with the epic nature of this occasion, but Ariosto structures his account of these events in a manner that regularly weakens their overall impact and dissipates the power that could accrue from a sustained sequence of such obvious signs. He frequently turns his attention away from Paris to the exploits of Astolfo and other wandering paladins in the Middle East, to heroes and adventures reminiscent of romance. He interrupts the continuity of this epic-in-progress and intersperses it with knight-errantry in remote locales—even or, perhaps, pointedly, at moments of great excitement and for long enough to dispell any suspense that a briefer break might allow him to build.[21]

In contrast, Tasso holds the geographic center of his narrative with remarkable tenacity. Certainly, there is a journey to distant shores; but, when we examine, for example, cantos 4-12 (which as an unbroken sequence amounts to almost half the poem), we can note that, after the

---

[20] Ibid., 36.

[21] Daniel Javitch's essay, "The *Orlando Furioso* and Ovid's Revision of the *Aeneid*," *Modern Language Notes* 99 (1984): 1023–36, contains much illuminating analysis of the qualities of plot structure that I touch upon in this paragraph.

infernal council at the opening of the first of these cantos, there is no significant departure from the theatre of war around Jerusalem, with the exception of Erminia's night sortie and her pursuit by Tancredi. Erminia's flight and her interlude with the shepherds, Tancredi's search for her and his duel with Rambaldo—altogether these occupy forty-seven octaves in a sequence of nine cantos otherwise situated entirely in the immediate vicinity of the city under seige. And it is worth mentioning that Tasso was censured for that one disturbance in his steady focus, if we wish to emphasize the remarkably different climate of opinion that distinguishes his audience from Ariosto's.[22]

The closure that Ariosto does at last exercise upon his rambling text comes in terms of epic finality that resonate with memorable decisiveness, but they still cannot avoid a somewhat hollow ring. By this time Ariosto has so frequently emptied occasions of high seriousness of their conventionally meaningful contents that a straight-faced allusion to a moment of unforgettable grandeur strains credulity in keeping its countenance even though no evident indications of irony in the immediate context raise any such doubts. Ariosto directly appeals to Virgilian gravity by concluding his final canto with an obvious climactic reference to the end of the *Aeneid*. The death of Rodomonte at the hands of Ruggiero transpires in terms that plainly echo Aeneas's triumph in single combat over Turnus, his arch-enemy among the Rutulians. Nothing in this last octave can deny it the genuinely epic stature that it clearly aspires to, in the same way that nothing in this poem's very opening stanza undercuts the epic pitch that it promptly attains—especially if we join with Tasso in considering love a suitable subject for heroic verse.[23] However, so much of an entirely other order has taken place between these two distant poles of this lengthy narrative that the seasoned reader might readily cast a suspicious glance in both directions.

Before questioning the muliplicity of Ariosto's plot, young Tasso first wondered about its wholeness, asserting that it lacked a beginning no matter whether the reader identified its main action as the dynastic or as the military theme. Of course, this limitation came with the subject matter Ariosto chose as his own because the origins both of the war between Charlemagne and Agramante and of the love between Brada-

---

[22] See Riccardo Bruscagli's essay, "Il campo cristiano nella *Liberata*," in *La corte e lo spazio: Ferrara estense*, a cura di Giuseppe Papagno e Amedeo Quondam (Rome: Bulzoni, 1982), for much useful discussion of Tasso's strategies to establish and maintain a geographical center for his narrative.

[23] *Discorsi*, 104–8.

mante and Ruggiero are presented in the *Orlando innamorato*.[24] But, wholeness aside, each of these actions reaches a conclusion in the *Furioso*; for we witness the marriage of the heroic Estense ancestors, and then the bridegroom delivers the *coup de grâce* to the last formidable challenger among the pagan heroes. Thus, in regard to structural finality, Ariosto's text apparently plays by the rules whose potential violation so unsettled young Tasso in the poem of many actions. But the sprawl of the *Furioso*'s manifold episodes and Ariosto's arbitrary and incessant interruptions of one after another of them make such evident closure seem far too little too late. Further, the irrepressible irony and wit that characterize Ariosto's attitude throughout the entire fabric of his poem must have struck Tasso as no negligible cause of its enviable popular success. But his own temperament seems neither a match nor even an acceptable contestant for Ariosto on those grounds, and the Counter-Reformation as an era can hardly claim levity as its dominant humor! Thus, young Tasso's unavoidable reckoning with his major precursor seems in many ways a curious encounter indeed where such radically divergent personalities and periods struggle for a synthesis almost doomed at the outset by the fundamentally disparate natures of all the elements involved.[25]

University of South Carolina

---

[24] Ibid., 19–20.

[25] Patricia Parker's chapter on Ariosto in *Inescapable Romance* (Princeton: Princeton Univ. Press, 1979) warrants notice for its suggestive commentary on the *Furioso* and especially for her remarks on the problem of closure (31–39).

BARBARA ODABASHIAN

Thomas Wyatt and the Rhetoric of Change

JUST AS THE CONTENT OF WYATT'S LOVE LYRICS INVOLVES THE DEVELopment of the speaker's view of love and women, the form of Wyatt's love lyrics embodies the logical process by which this development is effected. The use of logic in writing love lyrics, especially on the subjects of the unfairness and fickleness of women (and also on the subordinate theme of the changefulness of Fortune), makes the reader highly conscious not only of the tension between the subjects of reason and love but also of the tension between content and form—the tension that is essential to the art of poetry. In choosing to provide form for an especially chaotic content, love, Renaissance poets are involved in making their readers conscious of the poetic process. In choosing the rhetorical technique of argument instead of imagery to control and order an irrational subject matter, Wyatt makes his readers especially conscious of the fact that the art of poetry is his real subject matter. Wyatt's rhetorical techniques embody the themes of his love lyrics. Indeed, as is true of all good poets, it is impossible to separate his form from his matter.

Wyatt's rhetorical structure embodies both his primary theme of change, in particular the changefulness of women, and his secondary theme of reciprocity in relationships with women. In reading Wyatt's best poems, one not only traces the development of his speaker's thoughts by following his argument but also experiences what he is talking about. If the speaker's subject is woman's changefulness, Wyatt's rhetorical structure, using such techniques as change of tense and manipulation of refrain, enables the reader to experience the changes the speaker has undergone. If the speaker's subject is his demand for a reciprocal relationship, Wyatt's rhetorical structure, supported by such devices as parallel structure, repetition, and such metrical devices as "alliterative" verse, enables the reader to experience the balance and equality of roles he is seeking.

In the following selection of Wyatt's original poems[1] we can see the speaker developing his own attitude about women and revealing to his reader the steps by which he has arrived at his conclusions. Each poem reveals a logical progression of the speaker's thinking from the acceptance of the traditional mistress-servant relationship to its rejection and the corresponding development of the demand for an equal or reciprocal relationship with a woman.

The topic of E71, "In eternum I was ons determed,"[2] is the development of the speaker's view of women and love, and, ultimately, the matter of change. The speaker not only reveals the woman's changefulness and as a result his own change in attitude but also directly confronts the larger issue of the possibility of permanence versus the reality

---

[1] The first problem that has to be confronted in a discussion of Wyatt's love poetry is the question of the canon. The general critical position is that the Egerton MS. 2711 (British Museum) can be accepted *in toto*, and thus is the keystone of the canon. Richard Harrier (*The Canon of Sir Thomas Wyatt's Poetry* [Cambridge: Harvard Univ. Press, 1975], 1–92) goes so far as to say that a true picture of Wyatt can only be drawn from an analysis of the Egerton poems. (H. A. Mason voices his strong opposition to this view in his article "Editing Wyatt," *The Sewanee Review* 84 [Fall 1976]: 675–83, where he criticizes Harrier for accepting the Egerton MS *"en bloc."* Mason is generally critical of the historical approach and feels there should be much less emphasis on the manuscripts and much more emphasis on a selection of only "the best poems" of Wyatt.) The Egerton MS is the only one containing poems in Wyatt's own hand; they appear in both fair and working copies. As far as the other extant manuscripts associated with Wyatt (primarily the Arundel Harington, Devonshire, Blage, and Park-Hill MSS) are concerned, the Devonshire MS. 17492 (British Museum) is considered second in importance. Harrier also argues convincingly that no one has been able to put the manuscripts successfully in chronological order. Therefore, there is no way to know which came first—the Devonshire or the Egerton. Tottel's *Miscellany* is an entirely different matter. The *Miscellany* was published in 1557 (fifteen years after Wyatt's death) and contains 271 poems, of which 96 are Wyatt's. And fifteen of these poems are unique to the *Miscellany*. The problem with the *Miscellany* is its editor's attempts to make Wyatt's poetry read more smoothly. — Since my subject is the aesthetics of Wyatt's love poetry, my selection of poems for analysis was made cautiously. Therefore, my discussion is based, ultimately, on an analysis of poems taken primarily from the Egerton MS and secondarily from the poems that Harrier, carefully and logically, provides good reason for validating in the Devonshire MS.

[2] I base my analysis on Kenneth Muir's first edition of Wyatt's poems (*Collected Poems of Sir Thomas Wyatt* [London, 1949; repr., The Muses' Library, Cambridge: Harvard Univ. Press, 1963]). Subsequent citations from Wyatt are from this edition; with the exception of modernizing i/j and u/v, I maintain the old spelling. Each poem will be designated by its manuscript number in the text: E (Egerton MS), D (Devonshire MS). However, I also refer closely to the later edition by Muir and Patricia Thomson (*Collected Poems of Sir Thomas Wyatt* [Liverpool: Liverpool Univ. Press, 1969]) for its collations of the text, but more importantly for its commentary on the sources of Wyatt's translations, and, finally, to the modernized edition by Joost Daalder (*Sir Thomas Wyatt: Collected Poems* [Oxford: Oxford Univ. Press, 1975]) for the comparison of its version of the text and for its annotations.

of change. The form of the poem, at first glance, seems deceptively simple; however, just as there is more than one level of meaning in this poem, there is more than one device to support those levels. On one level the structural device of narration supports the logical process, step by step, by which the speaker developed his view of women and love; and on another level diction—in particular the poet's choice of verbs and adverbs to reflect either movement or stability—enhances the contrast between change and permanence. In addition, Wyatt manipulates the tense of his verbs not only to support his narration and to show how his past experiences resulted in his present beliefs but also to emphasize the concept of time and to point out its relation to change, as opposed to the timelessness of eternity.

Finally, Wyatt highlights change by using the techniques of the refrain and repetition. Again, at first glance, his use of the refrain seems almost simplistic, even tedious, in this poem; however, unlike his more obvious manipulation of the refrain in the following poem in the Egerton MS, "Syns ye delite to knowe," this time the significance of the refrain changes, from stanza to stanza, literally without changing a word. The ultimate irony of the poem lies in Wyatt's subtle manipulation of the refrain: for six stanzas the words of the refrain never change, "in eternum"; however, the significance of the refrain changes with the meaning of every stanza until the paradoxical conclusion takes the reader as far away from the original intention of the refrain, as put forth in the first stanza, as he can possibly get.[3]

In both the first and last stanzas Wyatt imitates a device used in the rondeau; the opening phrase of each of these stanzas is the same as the refrain: "In eternum." In the first stanza he uses this device to emphasize, from the outset, what the speaker was "determed" to have and, therefore, what "the story" of the poem is going to relate; in addition Wyatt imitates the traditional opening for a story, "once upon a time," to emphasize that the speaker is actually going to tell a story:

> In eternum I was ons determed
> For to have lovid and my minde affermed,

---

[3] C. S. Lewis (*English Literature in the Sixteenth Century Excluding Drama*, vol. 3 of the *Oxford History of English Literature*, ed. F. P. Wilson and Bonamy Dobrée [London: Oxford Univ. Press, 1954], 228–29) says that Wyatt's best poems "carry in themselves the reason for their length or for the order in which the stanzas come" and that this poem is a "success" because its "refrain is given a slightly different meaning at each repetition." On the other hand, Thomson (*Sir Thomas Wyatt and His Background* [Stanford: Stanford Univ. Press, 1964], 135–36) believes that Wyatt does not prepare the reader for the speaker's change in attitude.

> That with my herte it shuld be confermed
> In eternum.

The speaker, however, indicates the ultimate negative outcome of his search for eternal love by his choice of verb tense; he states that he "was ons determed" "to have lovid" "in eternum." His use of the past tense followed by the present perfect infinitive, which indicates action that occurred before that of the main verb, suggests that what he "ons" desired to have accomplished did not in fact come true. In addition, his use of the auxiliary "should" indicates that, at the time, the speaker believed that what he desired indeed ought to be "confermed" ("ratified").[4] The participial adjective "determed" ("finally and firmly resolved") and the verb "affermed" ("maintained or asserted strongly") support this conviction. The diction of the first stanza reflects the speaker's belief in the importance of establishing the permanency of love whereas the connotation of his verbs in the immediately following stanzas reflects the driven nature of his reckless pursuit for permanency in an object—woman—that is, by nature, mutable.

The first word of the second stanza indicates that the speaker did not waste any time in putting his thought into action:

> Forthwith I founde the thing that I myght like,
> And sought with love to warme her hert alike,
> For, as me thought, I shulde not se the like
> In eternum.

Wyatt follows the adverb "forthwith" with the verbs "founde" and "sought" to indicate that the speaker promptly, if precipitately, as the remaining words in the stanza indicate, took hot pursuit of a woman. The refrain here changes its meaning from a story-book forever and ever into a more worldly notion of never being able to find another one to replace her.

In the third stanza the speaker continues to describe how he drove himself in the vain pursuit of this lady:

> To trase this daunse I put my self in prese;
> Vayne hope ded lede and bad I should not cese
> To serve, to suffer, and still to hold my pease
> In eternum.

He put himself "in prese" and was led by "vayne hope," who (in the semblance of a personification of a vice in a morality play, or in an allegorical poem) urged that he "should not cese." And what was it that

---

[4] All definitions cited in the text derive from the *Oxford English Dictionary*.

he was actually driving himself to do? What he hoped to be productive energy spent in progressive motion in the pursuit of eternal love actually turns out to be wasted energy spent in the repetitive motion of the dance of short-lived love. Ironically, he was pushing himself "to trase this daunse," "to tread" the steps of the dance of courtly love, or perhaps "the olde daunce" (of fleshly love) of the Wife of Bath. The refrain "In eternum" is now used to measure his suffering.

"Still," at the beginning of stanza 4, the speaker describes himself as continuing to follow the code of courtly love and continuing to be deceived by the false belief that he was "swiftly" moving ahead:

> With this furst rule I fordred me apase,
> That, as me thought, my trowghthe had taken place
> With full assurans to stond in her grace
>   In eternum.

Indeed, finally, in this stanza, the speaker, employing a variant of the literary device of dramatic irony, relates how he had reached the point where he believed, "as [he] thought," that his troth had been plighted[5] and that, therefore, he had arrived at his goal and no longer had to chase after her. Wyatt replaces the verb "fordred" and the adverb "apase" in the first line with the verbs "had taken place" and "to stond" in the second and third lines to indicate the end of the speaker's pursuit and the end of the "daunse" and the beginning of eternal love by contrasting words signifying movement (and therefore a state of transiency) with words signifying stability (and therefore a state of permanency). Note that Wyatt uses the rhyme words for emphasis of his theme; his first "a" rhyme in this stanza, "apase," reemphasizes the forward movement of the previous stanza and the haste of his pursuit whereas his second "a" rhyme, "had taken place," emphasizes his change over to the stability appropriate to eternal love. Wyatt's choice of verb in the middle of the third line simply reaffirms his newly found stability: "With full assurans to stond in her grace."

However, in the very first line of the following and penultimate stanza, Wyatt uses the negative adverb "not" to point out that, in contradiction to the thought expressed in the last lines of the preceding stanza, and unlike the existence of eternity itself, the speaker's hopeful state did not last long:

> It was not long or I by proofe had found
> That feble bilding is on feble grounde;

---

[5] Daalder translates "trowghthe" as "truth" (61).

> For in her herte this worde ded never sounde,
> In eternum.

This is the climax of the drama he is unfolding: the turning point of the action the speaker has decided upon in the first stanza and then precipitated in the second. In comparison to what the speaker so quickly "founde" in the second stanza, "the thing that I myght like," "it was not long" before he "had found" the truth, "That feble bilding is on feble grounde." In the climax of his poem Wyatt replaces possibility with harsh reality. Furthermore, he reinforces the speaker's realization by suddenly, and momentarily, changing tense in the second line of this stanza, from the past (which Wyatt has used until now and will continue to use in this stanza, with the exception of this line) to the present in order to contrast the ephemeral nature of the speaker's former delusion or "vayne hope" with the constant nature of the homely truth. Finally, this is an extremely good choice of proverb not only because it metaphorically describes the speaker's action but also because it literally evokes the poem's underlying concern with the contrasting states of change and permanency in that a building's essential quality is its fixed or stationary state.

The speaker, however, obviously had the need to confirm the truth of this proverb through his own experience, by the evidence of his own eyes. Wyatt's use of logic surfaces as his speaker points out that he "by proofe had found" that his original assumptions were false and indeed "That feble bilding is on feble grounde." Looking back from this vantage point, the reader can see new meaning in the speaker's statement in the third line of the second stanza, "For, as me thought, I shulde not se the like"; perhaps Wyatt is even implying, at this climactic point, that the speaker should have known all along, as the proverb indicates, that it was neither logical nor realistic to have faith in this woman, "For in her herte this worde ded never sounde, / In eternum."

Wyatt echoes the refrain of this stanza in the beginning of the first line of the final stanza to emphasize that the woman's changefulness is the cause of the speaker's change of attitude and that, because "in her herte this worde ded never sounde," he "then" banished the thought of permanency from his "herte":

> In eternum then from my herte I kest
> That I had furst determined for the best;
> Nowe in the place another thought doeth rest,
> In eternum.

This is the dénouement of the drama: the outcome of the action the speaker had decided upon in the opening stanza. The final stanza, on the one hand, imitates the structure and diction of the first stanza and, on the other hand, contradicts its content. In the final stanza the speaker acknowledges that what he "had furst determined for the best," he subsequently rejected; by emphasizing the word "furst," Wyatt is pointing out not only the erroneous decision of the first stanza but also the erroneous belief of the fourth stanza: "With this furst rule I fordred me apase."[6]

Then, in the penultimate line of the last stanza, Wyatt emphasizes the difference between the speaker's past attitude and his present attitude by replacing the adverb "ons," used in the first stanza, with the adverb "nowe," and by changing from the past tense (which he used from the beginning of the poem to this point, with the exception of the proverbial line) to the present tense. Note that the verb "kest" emphasizes the paradoxical action of removing the immovable, "In eternum," whereas the noun "place" and the verb "doeth rest" emphasize the paradoxical action of establishing the thought of change. What the speaker wanted to confirm, in the first stanza, was the establishment of eternal love; "nowe" this is replaced, in the last stanza, by "another thought": the establishment of the paradoxical concept of eternal change.[7]

In casting out "In eternum" from his heart, as a consequence of experiencing the reality of his lady's changefulness, the speaker took the logical step. His ultimate conclusion is just as logical: the only thing that he can depend on, that never changes, is change itself. He must reject his senseless pursuit of eternal love in favor of the practical wisdom of the changefulness of women and love, and he must accept the worldly belief in the permanence of change alone. And so, the speaker describes how he arrived at his new attitude towards women and love; his constant repetition of the short refrain "In eternum," which consists of two feet as opposed to the five feet contained in each of the preceding three lines of every stanza, creates the dramatically ironic effect of a bell tolling the hours of a love that was supposed to be eternal but turned out to be ephemeral.

It is a short but bitter leap of faith to Wyatt's poem "To rayle or geste ye kno I use yt not." In D139, in the guise of a calm rational man, the speaker undertakes a scathing attack on his faithless beloved. His guise is appropriate for the writer of irony, and the speaker in this poem is obviously trying to display the restraint that is the hallmark of the writer of irony; however, as his argument unfolds, the speaker is

---

[6] Thomson sees this poem as being "dominated by Chaucer's antithesis between convention and experience, or, in Wyatt's own words, 'rule' and 'proofe' " (135).

[7] To the contrary, Lewis concludes that the speaker's new thought is "the thought of eternity" or, in other words, that "he is doing his palinode" (229).

unable to maintain this pose and in alternate pairs of lines we will see first the mask of indifference that the speaker is trying to hide behind and then his true face, which reveals his feelings of anger and bitterness. Although the structure of the poem is ironic, its content is not; indeed, because this poem is a frontal attack on the feminine vice of changefulness, the speaker wants to appear to be a reasonable, disinterested man so that his fiercely single-minded attack will not be disregarded as the monomaniacal ravings of a madman.

In the octave the speaker tells the lady that he hates her changefulness, but, although he hates it, he does not want her to change her changeful ways. He sets the ironic tone by stating in the first two lines that, although there is cause enough for anger, he is not the uncontrollably emotional kind, as she knows: "To rayle or geste ye kno I use yt not, / Though that such cause some tyme in folkes I finde." Furthermore, in lines 5 and 6, he goes on to state that her reform is nothing to him since he has no personal gain from it: "And if ye ware to me as ye are not, / I wolde be lothe to se you so unkinde." However, in contradiction to this pose, he says in lines 3 and 4: "And tho to chaung ye list to sett your minde, / Love yt who liste, in faithe I like yt not." The contradiction becomes more emphatic in lines 7 and 8 in which he moves from dislike to hate: "But sins your faithe must nedes be so, be kinde: / Tho I hate yt, I praye you leve yt not." Lines 5 and 6 parallel 1 and 2, and 7 and 8 parallel 3 and 4, in both content and rhyme scheme; and therefore the octave consists of four alternating pairs of lines which contradict each other.

In addition, within this ironic structure there are also verbal contradictions. In line 4, referring to her faithlessness, expressed in line 3, "And tho to chaung ye list to sett your minde," he says, "Love yt who liste, in faithe I like yt not"; then in line 7, he concludes, "But sins your faithe muste nedes be so, be kinde." It is significant that Wyatt's speaker chooses to play with the word "faithe"; contrasting his faithfulness with her faithlessness, he states that "in faithe" he does not approve of her changefulness but then concludes that, if her "faithe" must indeed be changefulness, then she should continue to be faithful to her faithless ways, especially with "other lovers." In lines 6 and 7 Wyatt's speaker plays with the word "kind":

> I wolde be lothe to se you so unkinde;
> But sins your faithe muste nedes be so, be kinde.

Seemingly, in line 7 he is contradicting what he is saying in line 6 in that "kinde" is the positive form of "unkinde"; however, in actuality, the speaker is confirming what he has just said because, in telling her to "be kinde," he is telling her to be true to her nature, which is to be "unkinde" or uncaring.[8]

As the sestet opens, Wyatt continues the alternating pattern of his rhetorical structure; lines 9 and 10 echo 1 and 2 and 5 and 6. The speaker claims he would not think of making any big demands but only makes a small request: "Thinges of grete waight I never thought to crave: / This is but small—of right denye yt not." The emphasis is on how reasonable his demand is; he is not inclined to excess. Then lines 11 and 12 parallel 3 and 4 and 7 and 8: "Your fayning wayis as yet forget them not, / But like rewarde let other lovers have." His request has ironic overtones: in most of Wyatt's love poems the speaker is demanding that the lady change her changeful ways, but in this poem he is asking her to be true to her nature and not to change her changeful ways; in particular the phrase "as yet forget them not" recalls the refrain of D130, "Fforget not yet," but, whereas that refrain refers to his honest and faithful ways, this phrase refers to her deceitful and changeful ways. The speaker goes on to clarify his request in the final couplet: "That is to saye, for servis true and faste, / To long delaies and changing at the laste." The speaker in this poem is disgusted not only with the lady's conduct but also with his own naïveté in expecting her to play by the "rules" of courtly love; he is trapped between two worlds: the dream world of courtly love and the real world of his love relationships. In the end his bitterness is completely unmasked; he wants her "other lovers" to receive the same reward as he: faithlessness in return for faithfulness.

By now it is evident that Wyatt's attitude towards women is neither that of the troubadors nor that of Petrarch. In the poems discussed there is one underlying theme: change, in particular the changefulness of women. However, his subject matter consists of more than the mere reiteration of this given; Wyatt takes this given and creates poems which describe the evolving consciousness of the speaker so that the content of the lyrics really consists of the dramatic development of the speaker's view of women rather than just the static presentation of the view as a *fait accompli*. Logical argument becomes a crucial part of Wyatt's subject matter since the steps by which the speaker arrives at his conclusions are more important than the conclusions themselves,

---

[8] William H. Wiatt ("Sir Thomas Wyatt's Wordplay," *Annuale Mediaevale* 1 [1960]: 96–101) points out the importance of wordplay in Wyatt's poetry and also stresses that, from a historical perspective, "Wyatt's wordplay is a neglected but important facet of that wit for which he was esteemed by his contemporaries." He cites the play on the word "kind" in this poem as an example of *"significatio"* or in other words "the pun"; his source for the definitions of the three different types of wordplay he discusses is the *Rhetorica ad Herennium*.

which are always one and the same: women are changeful. And so, ultimately, the logical structure and the various rhetorical devices that support it are the real subject matter of Wyatt's love poetry.

And nowhere is his argument more dramatic or more dazzling than in the justly famous E37, "They fle from me."[9] In this poem Wyatt stresses a secondary theme found in his love lyrics: his desire for a reciprocal relationship with a woman—reciprocal in affection and reciprocal in responsibility. (Wyatt's emphasis is, strictly speaking, not on mutuality, but on reciprocity.) However, the impossibility of having such a relationship is predetermined by his basic premise that women are, by nature, changeful.

The rhetorical structure of the poem reveals the speaker's desire for reciprocity in love; he expresses this desire simply by relating, and therefore comparing, both sides of the story: what he does versus what the woman does (and what women, in general, do), what he wants versus what the woman wants (and what women, in general, want), what he gets versus what the woman gets (and what women, in general, get), what the speaker deserves versus what the woman deserves (and what women, in general, deserve). In the final couplet of the poem the speaker explicitly expresses his desire for reciprocity in love:

> But syns that I so kyndely ame served,
> I would fain knowe what she hath deserved.

The underlying theme of change, in particular the changefulness of women, is also embodied in the rhetorical structure of the poem; Wyatt employs the organizing principle of reversal in his argument in order to realize the concept of change: reversal of time (past versus present), reversal of the roles of the speaker and his beloved, reversal of the speaker's fortune in love. The poem consists of three stanzas: stanza 1 proceeds by reversing the time period four times (present/past/present/past/present) and, correspondingly, reversing the roles of the speaker and the women he has loved and his fortune in love; stanza 2 describes past time and, correspondingly, the speaker's good fortune in love in one specific case, but, in contradiction, it describes the speaker

---

[9] Among the many discussions of this poem, I find these five articles to be the most pertinent, and therefore acknowledge in advance any debt I may incur in the following discussion: Albert S. Gérard, "Wyatt's 'They Fle from Me,'" *Essays in Criticism* 11 (1961): 359–66; Leonard E. Nathan, "Tradition and Newfangleness in Wyatt's 'They Fle from Me,'" *ELH* 32 (1965): 1–16; Arnold Stein, "Wyatt's 'They Flee from Me,'" *The Sewanee Review* 67 (1959): 28–44; Robert G. Twombly, "Beauty and the (Subverted) Beast: Wyatt's 'They Fle from Me,'" *Texas Studies in Literature and Language* 10 (1969): 489–503; Leigh Winser, "The Question of Love Tradition in Wyatt's 'They Flee from Me,'" *Essays in Literature* 2 (1975): 3–9.

and his beloved as having the reversed roles belonging to the present time period; stanza 3 begins in past time but then reverses to the present and, correspondingly, describes the speaker and his beloved as having reversed roles and bad fortune in love. It is not until the line preceding the final couplet that the speaker actually expresses the changefulness of his beloved: "And she also to use new fangilnes." The rhetorical structure serves one other important purpose, and that is to reveal the reasonable nature of the speaker and, therefore, of his final remark. The poem has the structure of a logical argument; the speaker proceeds by employing deductive reasoning and inquiry from the general to the particular, from speaking of his relationships with women, in general, in the first stanza, to speaking of his relationship with one woman, in particular, in the second and third stanzas.

The first thing that Wyatt does in "They fle from me" is to reverse the traditional roles of men and women by playing with the Petrarchan metaphor of the hunt. The first words of the speaker in this poem are "They fle from me. . . ." Then, later in this stanza, continuing to describe his present situation, he speaks of them "That nowe are wyld and do not remembre." So the speaker, in the present time, adopts the role of the unsuccessful hunter. On the other hand, also in the first stanza, Wyatt reverses the role of the speaker so that he describes himself as a successful hunter in the past. In the second half of the first line he says that he did not have to pursue these animals, who symbolize women, because they ". . . sometyme did me seke / With naked fote stalking in my chambre." And, as opposed to being "wyld," they were "gentill tame and meke." He would just sit there and they would come to him and willingly place themselves "in daunger." This is one of several words that have a double meaning in the poem: Wyatt uses the device of the pun to support the rhetorical structure of the poem by imitating both the "two-sided" nature of the "story" and its pattern of reversal. "Daunger" signifies both a state of risk and a state of domination. In suggesting that the woman submitted to the speaker's domination, Wyatt is reversing the traditional medieval notion that it is the role of the lover to put himself in the lady's domination. The word "stalk" also has a double meaning: "to walk softly, cautiously, or stealthily," the connotation which corresponds with women's subservient position in the speaker's past, or "to pursue game by the method of stealthy approach," which hints at their hidden instinct to become hunters themselves. This instinct is fully, and openly, realized in the speaker's present time, as he duly notes in the final line and a half of this stanza: ". . . and nowe they raunge / Besely seking with a continuell chaunge." The speaker recognizes that it is no longer enough for them "to take bred at my hand" or to confine themselves to his "chambre"; the two meanings of "raunge" in this poem are "to move hither and thither over a comparatively large area," referring both to persons and animals ("*esp.* of hunting dogs searching for game"), and "to change from one attachment to another; to be inconstant."

Wyatt also uses metrical devices to support his rhetorical structure, the rhyme royal stanza, a seven-line stanza written in iambic pentameter and rhymed *ababbcc*, and, simultaneously, the alliterative line. The effect of a caesura dividing each line into two hemistichs supports the rhetorical structure once again by imitating both the "two-sided" nature of the "story" and its pattern of reversal, as is demonstrated by line 1, "They fle from me that sometyme did me seke," and line 6, "To take bred at my hand; and nowe they raunge." To emphasize the reciprocity he advocates, Wyatt makes every literary device doubly effective in this poem, even going so far as to use the combined effect of two metrical systems, the accentual and the accentual-syllabic.[10]

In stanza two Wyatt reverses the meaning of the Petrarchan metaphor of the hunt by making the speaker the hunted animal and the lady the hunter. Furthermore, as the speaker describes the situation, she was neither the unsuccessful hunter he is in the present nor the passive hunter he was in the past:

> In thyn arraye after a pleasaunt gyse,
>   When her lose gowne from her shoulders did fall,
>   And she me caught in her armes long and small.

She lured him and then she caught him. To emphasize her success, as opposed to the male speaker in "Who so list to hount," who refers to his lady as "an hynde" and "the Diere," Wyatt has the speaker in this poem recall the exact words that the lady used to address him, "*dere hert, howe like you this?*" "Dere hert" can be interpreted both as a term of affection and as a reference to the male deer. In addition, the speaker in "Who so list to hount" never caught his "hynde," who carried the warning "*Noli me tangere,*" whereas the lady in this poem was not afraid to catch and hold the apparently all-too-willing speaker "in her armes long and small." Obviously, unlike "the Diere" and his present women, but like the women in his past (with this one exception, "but ons in speciall"), he is not "wyld" but "gentill tame and meke." He has exchanged roles with this particular lady; she is now the hunter and he is the docile beast.

---

[10] See D. W. Harding, "The Rhythmical Intention in Wyatt's Poetry," *Scrutiny* 14 (1946): 90–102; for related views on Wyatt's metrics also see Lewis, "The Fifteenth-Century Heroic Line," *Essays and Studies* 24 (1938): 28–41, and Alan Swallow, "The Pentameter Lines in Skelton and Wyatt," *Modern Philology* 48 (1950): 1–11.

In the first line of the third and final stanza, the speaker recalls, "It was no dreme: I lay brode waking," but in the second line he reveals that the happy past is gone, "But all is torned thorough my gentilnes." He specifically uses the words "but all is torned" to signify yet another reversal in his situation and the words "my gentilnes" to describe the cause of his present unhappiness. "Gentilnes" has two different connotations, the medieval meaning of "gentilesse," courtesy or chivalry, which is considered to be a desirable quality for a man, and the meaning of "gentill" in the first stanza, tame or docile, an undesirable characteristic for a man. There is an implied criticism of courtly love in the pun on "gentilnes" in that, by taking up the appropriately subservient role of a courtly lover, the speaker has put himself in the unhappy position of being forsaken by the lady.

As the speaker recalls at the beginning of this stanza, he consciously adopted a passive role in his relationship with this lady: "I lay brode waking." And now he realizes that his passivity has caused him to be forsaken in "a straunge fasshion":

> And I have leve to goo of her goodenes,
> And she also to use new fangilnes.

Unlike the "wyld" women in stanza 1 who "fle" him, he has been given permission to go when he obviously wants to stay; and, on the other hand, the lady is all too ready for new action. Throughout the poem Wyatt uses verbs signifying motion to describe the acts of the women. In the first stanza, the women "seke" and "fle" and "stalk" and "raunge" and are ultimately described as "Besely ["actively, briskly"] seking with a continuell chaunge"; their only static moment was when "they put theimself in daunger." In the second stanza the speaker describes how the lady's "lose gowne from her shoulders did fall" and then, dramatically, "and she me caught." The contrast between his passive state and her active state is succinctly expressed by Wyatt's choice of verbs in the final couplet:

> But syns that I so kyndely ame served,
> I would fain knowe what she hath deserved.

The choice of the passive voice to describe the speaker and the active voice to describe the lady is suited to their reversed roles of subservience and domination. He is "served" by her, signifying he is "treated in a specified (usually unpleasant or unfair) manner" by her, whereas she has "deserved" he knows not what, signifying she has "acquired or earned a rightful claim, by virtue of actions or qualities, to (something)." He is at her mercy, but she is obviously not at his. The word "kyndely" has two meanings here: "with sympathy, benevolence, or good nature" or "properly, fittingly." "Benevolently" carries an ironic implication for this line: she treats him kindly or benevolently in that she trapped him and now she is letting him go. "Fittingly," however, carries a literal implication for this line: he is rewarded in kind, or fittingly, for behaving as if he were a tamed animal, a subservient beast.

In the final couplet the speaker is comparing his just deserts with hers. He is stating that, since he is so appropriately requited for his subservient behavior (having behaved as if he were a docile beast and therefore being treated as if he were one), he would like to know what she has earned or merited for her "service," for her forward behavior (as related in detail in the second stanza). He is simply asking to be treated equally or reciprocally, since she seems to have escaped unscathed. By reversing the roles of men and women and by making women as aggressive as men in general, and more aggressive than the speaker in this poem, Wyatt prepares the way for the woman to take equal responsibility for the success or failure of a relationship. At the same time, however, by describing women as "wyld" animals and himself as "dere hert," innocent victim, the speaker undermines his own cause. Furthermore, how is it possible for reciprocity to exist alongside "new fangilnes"? Apparently, the very nature of woman prohibits the possibility of a reciprocal relationship, but this knowledge does not stop the speaker from wondering.

The excitement of reading Wyatt's best poems comes from the tension he creates by controlling chaotic subject matter with logical form. The reader is able to realize intellectually the emotional turmoil that the speaker has undergone. The rhetorical structure of Wyatt's love poems enables the reader not only to follow the logical process by which the speaker's view is developed, and be convinced of the truth of the speaker's conclusions, but also actually to experience that truth.

John Jay College
City University of New York

NITA KREVANS

Print and the Tudor Poets

STUDENTS OF THE ENGLISH RENAISSANCE HAVE LONG BEEN INTERested in how the arrival of print affected Tudor authors. The exceptional documentation provided by the registers of the Stationers' Company offers investigators a rich and detailed view of what was printed, but the role played by print in the literary system remains controversial. In part this is because some of the most famous authors of the period seem to display such contrasting attitudes towards print—for example, Sidney avoids it and Shakespeare's poetry is printed only under protest, while Jonson and Drayton produce editions of their own complete works. Studies of the question have tended to focus on differences between the various poets to explain these contrasts, and one of the most influential theories has been Saunders's theory of the stigma of print.[1] Saunders argues that the courtier-poets such as Sidney, Wyatt, and Surrey scorned print and published only in manuscript for a closed circle of friends; moreover, aspiring poets who hoped to win preferment through their writing were forced to pay lip-service to the distaste for print expressed by the aristocracy. In support of this theory Saunders cites prefaces which apologize for printing, or which claim that friends requested publication of the work,

---

[1] J. W. Saunders, "The Stigma of Print: A Note on the Social Bases of Tudor Poetry," *Essays in Criticism* 1 (1951): 139–64. The argument was taken up again in his *The Profession of English Letters*, Studies in Social History, ed. Harold Perkins (London: Routledge and Kegan Paul, 1964). See also Richard Helgerson, "The Elizabethan Laureate: Self-Presentation and the Literary System," *ELH* 46 (1979): 193–220 and his 1983 monograph, *Self-Crowned Laureates* (Berkeley: Univ. of California Press). Most recently, Arthur Marotti has addressed this topic; see his "The Transmission of Lyric Poetry and the Institutionalizing of Literature in the English Renaissance," in *Contending Kingdoms*, ed. Peter Rudnytsky and Marie-Rose Logan (Detroit: Wayne State Univ. Press, forthcoming). I am grateful to the author for showing me a draft of his essay.

or that the work was pirated. In addition, he points to the prevalence of anonymous publication during this period.

Much of this makes good sense. It appears that some of the courtier-poets shunned any type of publication which would compromise their status as gentlemen amateurs.[2] I say "appears," because a closer look at the evidence brings out one of the problems with Saunders's interpretation: the absence of printed work does not necessarily denote avoidance of print by an author. In spite of the eagerness of printers for material, the complexities of the two-tiered publication system created situations in which authors anxious to print lost access to their own work while it was circulating in manuscript. That is, failure to print certain types of work might have resulted not from authorial reluctance (even feigned reluctance) but from conventions which required that the work be presented to the patron or addressee.

Consider the case of Thomas Churchyard. At the beginning of *Churchyards challenge* (1593), he places a list of his books, entitled "The bookes that I can call to memorie alreadie Printed: are these that followe."[3] He then lists in roughly chronological order (by reign) thirty-two works, giving the subject or short title of each, and, in most cases, the patron. Following this is an even more interesting list: "These workes following are gotten from me of some such noble freends as I am loath to offend."

> *Aeneas* tale to *Dydo*, largely and truely translated out of *Virgill*, which I once shewed the Qu.[een's] Ma.[jesty] and had it againe.
>
> A book of the oath of a Iudge and the honor of Law, delivered to a Stacioner, who sent it to the L. cheefe Baron that last dyed.
>
> A book of a sumptuous shew in Shrovetide, by sir Walter Rawley, sir Robart Carey, M. Chidly, and M. Arthur Gorge, in which book was the whole service of my L. of Lester mencioned, that he and his traine did in Flaunders, and the gentlemen Pencioners proved to be a great peece of honor to the Court: all which book was in as good verse as ever I made: an honorable knight dwelling in the black Friers, can witnes the same, because I read it unto him.
>
> A great peece of work translated out of the great learned

---

[2] See Saunders, *The Profession of English Letters*, 31 ff.; Helgerson, *Self-Crowned Laureates*, 26–34.

[3] STC 5220, sig. *3v.

French Poet Seignior Dubartas, which worke treated of a Lady and an Eagle, most divinely written on by Dubartas and given by me to a great Lord of this land, who saith it is lost.

An infinite number of other Songes and Sonets, given where they cannot be recovered, nor purchase any favour when they are craved.[4]

There are several interesting points here. The first, and most obvious, is that Churchyard feels it necessary in writing this bibliographical notice to distinguish between printed works and those which had not been printed, even if they were performed publicly or circulated in manuscript. Seventy years earlier Skelton had set a similar poetic bibliography into his *Garland of Laurell* (1170 ff.);[5] both lists serve as a kind of advertisement for the poet, a claim to literary authority. But Skelton places the list inside the poem in the mouth of a fictional character, joining the other allegorical arguments in defense of his poetry which he has marshalled there. He makes no distinction between printed and manuscript works, and so many of the titles mentioned are otherwise unknown that they may be as fictional as the narrator.[6]

Churchyard, by contrast, has already grasped the modern spirit of bibliography. He places his list outside the text of the work, in a position analogous to other items in the editor's province: lists of *errata*, tables of contents, commendations of the book by other authors. He orders the items neatly and provides enough information to identify each one precisely. He writes not, as Skelton does, from a purely poetic point of view, but half as poet, half as editor; and from this point of view, the distinction between what is printed and what is not becomes crucial, because the editor's work perishes easily when the book has no permanent form.

We should note that Churchyard is not closely associated with booksellers or printers. His literary models are Surrey (whom he once served as a page), Sidney, and Wyatt.[7] In spite of his associations with

---

[4] STC 5220, sig. **.

[5] E.g., lines 1173–74, "Item the boke how men shulde fle synne / Item royall demenaunce worshyp to wynne" (Skelton, *A ryght delectable tratyse upon a goodly garlande or chapelet of laurell*, 1523 = STC 22610).

[6] Cf. John Scattergood, ed., *John Skelton, the Complete English Poems* (New Haven: Yale Univ. Press, 1983), 7; see also his comments *ad loc*.

[7] Churchyard's translations reflect his desire to follow in the footsteps of these courtier-poets: Surrey had attempted Virgil and Sidney du Bartas. (Surrey's partial version of the *Aeneid* exists in both manuscript and printed form; on Sidney's lost translation see W. A. Ringler, Jr., *The Poems of Sir Philip Sidney* [Oxford: Oxford Univ. Press, 1962], 339.)

the court, however, Churchyard clearly believes that print confers a stamp of approval. In each case where something is not printed, he feels compelled to offer some excuse: the work is lost; the stationer lent it out; Churchyard is too polite to request its return from a certain lord, etc. The role of the noblemen granted private glimpses of these works is not simply that of patron, but that of witness to the work's existence and quality: "I once shewed the Qu. Ma."; "An honorable knight dwelling in the black Friers can witnes the same, because I read it unto him." Without print, there is no proof that the book exists, or that Churchyard wrote it.[8]

One lesson to be learned from this list, then, is that the existence of works in manuscript only is no guarantee that the author did not want to have them printed. It is clear that Churchyard would have printed these items if he had been able to do so, and in fact, the stationer must have recovered the manuscript sent to the dead baron, because a book entitled *The honor of the lawe* appears in 1596.[9] Churchyard's main problem seems to be an inability to recover manuscripts from eminent patrons without offending them, and this suggests that there is still during this period a conflict between presentation to a patron and print publication. If this is so, then the patron and the printer are competing for jurisdiction over the text, and the patron's opinions on print may have as much weight as the author's in determining how a piece is published.

Another lesson lies in the fate of Churchyard's "infinite number" of songs and sonnets, "given where they cannot be recovered." Even in the age of print, lyric poetry is especially liable to remain unpublished and eventually to disappear.[10] If Churchyard, an indefatigable collector of his own writing, is unable to preserve many of his lyrics, we must imagine that the printed poetry of other, less zealous authors represents a very small portion of their lyric *oeuvre*.

---

[8] There were accusations that his most famous poem, *Jane Shore*, was by someone else; in the preface to the *Challenge*, Churchyard makes a veiled allusion to this problem as part of a wish that his printed books will confer a kind of immortality on him: "Many sorrowfull discourses in my dayes I have written, and numbers of bookes I have printed: and because they shall not be buried with me, I challenge them all as my children to abide behinde me in the worlde ... hoping they shall not be called bastards, nor none alive will be so hardy as to call them his" (STC 5220, sig. A2, dedication to Sir John Wolley).

[9] STC 5238.

[10] As noted by Marotti (above, note 1), with an extensive discussion of the conflict between "occasional" composition and performance of lyrics and their emergence as a serious literary form in the printed collection.

This brings us to the second problem with Saunders's theory. Do the apologetic prefaces, the claims of piracy, and the prevalence of anonymity signal a distaste for print, specifically—or a distaste for publication? For example, consider the cases cited by Saunders in which the insistence of friends is given as an excuse for printing.[11] Does this really prove that each of these authors felt "obliged to excuse his appearance in print"?[12] Or is this a much older phenomenon, a *topos* of prefaces from the classical period through the twentieth century? We find such sentiments already in the dedicatory letter to Clarus prefacing Pliny's *Epistles*: "You have often urged me to collect and publish any of my letters which I had written especially carefully...."[13] Complaints about pirate publication are not unknown in antiquity, either: both Galen and Quintilian claim that they have reluctantly published editions of private lectures to disciples in order to replace pirate versions which were full of errors.[14]

The classical examples suggest not only that it is important to distinguish fear of print from fear of publication, but also that we should look more closely at the reluctance to publish, whether feigned or genuine. In the case of Pliny, Galen, and Quintilian, the material which is published is ostensibly private, written for specific readers or listeners. Even though collections of letters had been part of Greek and Roman literature for several centuries before Pliny, there is an inherent contradiction in collecting and publishing pieces whose existence depends on a premise of secret communication. Pliny as editor undermines Pliny as letter writer.

These reflections raise the possibility that the varying attitudes toward print/publication which we find in the Elizabethan period may be associated more with differences between genres than differences between authors.[15] It is, in fact, quite instructive to catalogue by genre

---

[11] Saunders, "The Stigma of Print," 145–46.

[12] Saunders, 144.

[13] "Frequenter hortatus es ut epistulas, si quas paulo curatius scripsissem, colligerem publicaremque" (Pliny *Ep.* 1.1). See also Pliny *Ep.* 6.15: an elegiac poet, beginning his recitation with the excuse "Prisce, iubes" ("Priscus, you command me ... [to publish/write poetry]") is interrupted by the startled patron, who exclaims: "Ego vero non iubeo!" ("But I don't command!").

[14] Galen, ed. Kuehn, vol. 17: 80, 576, 822; vol. 19: 9, 10, 13, 17, 41, 50. Quintilian *Inst.* proem ad Marcellum 7.

[15] The assumption that a poet should not acquiesce in the publication of certain kinds of poetry forms part of the distinction Helgerson proposes between amateur poets (such as Sidney), professional writers for the theater, and what Helgerson calls "laureates." See, for example, his discussion of Jonson's attitude towards publishing his epigrams (*Self-Crowned Laureates*, 31, 168).

the printed and unprinted output within the corpus of individual writers. Such an examination reveals that most courtier-poets see their lyrics printed (if at all) only as commendatory verses or in miscellanies. They are, however, represented in print during their lifetime by other types of writing. Sir Thomas Wyatt, Sir John Cheke, and Nicholas Udall all publish printed translations.[16] Sir Walter Raleigh's prose treatises on history and exploration began appearing in print as early as 1591.[17] Nicholas Grimald prints several Latin works in Cologne and writes an English translation of Cicero's *De officiis*, which appears in 1556.[18] Thomas Sackville, although renowned as a sonneteer among his contemporaries, is known to modern readers only as the author of parts of *Gorboduc* (1565) and *A myrroure for magistrates* (1559), both printed before his death in 1608.[19]

A parallel pattern can be seen in the genre distribution of anonymous versus attributed works for certain authors. Sir John Davies's *Nosce Teipsum*, a religious poem, bears his name on all three editions (1599, 1602, 1608), but the more secular *Orchestra* (1596) and *Hymnes of Astraea* (1599) appear anonymously, and his *Epigrams* (1599?), bound in the same volume as Marlowe's translations of Ovid, give only his initials.[20] A similar situation holds for Giles Fletcher, Richard Lynche, and Nicholas Breton: prose works, translations, religious poetry carry the author's name while sonnet sequences and lyric collections are anonymous or at most signed with initials.[21]

The attractions of anonymity are explained by Francis Davison, who undertakes the publication of some sonnets by himself, his brother, and a friend, but rebukes the printer for revealing the authors' names:

> My friendes name I concealed, mine owne, and my brothers, I willed the Printer to suppresse, as well as I had concealed the other, which he having put in, without my privity, we must both

---

[16] Cheke's translation of Chrysostom appeared in 1544 (STC 14637); Wyatt's version of Plutarch, the *Quyete of mynde*, probably in 1528 (STC 20058.5); Udall's selections from Terence, *Floures for Latine spekynge*, in 1534 (STC 23899).

[17] *A report of the truth of the fight about the iles of Açores* (Anon., 1591), STC 20651.

[18] *Thre bokes of duties* (STC 5281).

[19] STC 18684, 1247.

[20] STC 6355, 6356, 6357, 6360, 6351, and 6350 respectively.

[21] Giles Fletcher, *Of the Russe common wealth* (1591), STC 11056 vs. *Licia* (Anon., 1593?), STC 11055; Richard Lynche, *An historical treatise* (1601), STC 17092 and Cartari's *The fountaine of ancient fiction* (1599), STC 4691 by "Richard Linche, Gent." vs. *Diella* ("R. L.," 1596), STC 17091; Nicholas Breton, e.g., *Pilgrimage to paradise* (STC 3683, printed with signed dedication, 1592) vs., e.g., *A floorish upon fancie Compiled by N. B. Gent.* (1577), STC 3654.

now undergoe a sharper censure perhaps than our nameles works should have done, & I especially. For if their Poems be liked, the praise is due to their invention, if disliked, the blame both by them, and all men will be derived uppon me, for publishing that which they meant to suppresse.[22]

Davison's general argument in favor of anonymity derives special force in his case from the type of poetry in the collection. Lyric, and especially love lyric, participates in the rhetoric of privacy which we mentioned earlier in connection with collections of letters. Indeed, the conventions of both classical elegy and Renaissance sonnet sequences demand that the name of the mistress be replaced by a poetic pseudonym, and the poet often gives himself a matching alias within the text, as Sidney does in *Astrophil and Stella*. The suppression of the author's name brings forward the fictional persona of the masked lover and helps obscure the conflict between the poet's editorial role and his amatory one.[23]

The association of anonymity and reluctance to publish with these "private" genres is reinforced by another model inherited from classical antiquity: the ideal career of the poet. In this model, the poet exercises his fledgling talents on lighter personal poetry in his youth and then moves on to weightier forms—a program based on the life of Virgil, who, in the extreme versions of this interpretation, produced the pastoral *Eclogues* and the didactic *Georgics* only as training for the *Aeneid*.[24] Many Elizabethan poets who wished to make a name for themselves

---

[22] *A poetical rapsody, containing diverse sonnets* . . . (1602), STC 6373, "To the reader," sig. A2v.

[23] A similar convention applies to Renaissance pastoral, which is fond of mingling political and religious allegory (requiring the use of pastoral disguises for prominent contemporaries) with the love themes found in sonnet sequences. Spenser's *Shepheardes Calender* (published anonymously) is a good example. On the conflict between secrecy and publication inherent in the sonnet sequences, see most recently Patricia Fumerton, " 'Secret' Arts: Elizabethan Miniatures and Sonnets," *Representations* 15 (1986): 57–97.

[24] Helgerson discusses the influence of the Virgilian model on the Elizabethan poets at length in *The Self-Crowned Laureates*, and the poets themselves frequently mention Virgil's career as a paradigm. One famous example is "E. K." in the "Epistle to Harvey" preceding *The Shepheardes Calender*, who claims that Spenser writes pastoral

> following the example of the best and most aunciten Poetes, which devised this kind of wryting . . . at the first to trye theyr habilities: and as young birdes, that be newly crept out of the nest, by little first to prove theyr tender wyngs, before they make a greater flyght. So flew Theocritus. . . . So flew Virgile, as not yet well feeling his winges. (*The Poetical Works of Edmund Spenser*, ed. J. C. Smith and E. de Selincourt [Oxford: Oxford Univ. Press, 1912], 418.)

pondered the Virgilian career and the strictures against publishing the "toys and amorous devises" of youth[25] and emerged with an ingenious compromise: the first book appears in print anonymously, but new books or subsequent editions of the first appear under the author's name. Richard Barnfield's *The affectionate shepheard* (1594) is anonymous,[26] but in a signed preface to *Cynthia* (1595) he takes retroactive credit for the book:

> Gentlemen; the last Terme there came forth a little toy of mine, intituled, the affectionate *Shepheard*: in the which, his Country *Content* found such friendly favor, that it hath incouraged me to publish my second fruites.[27]

Similarly, the printer tells the reader of Barnabe Barnes's *Parthenophil and Parthenophe* (1593) that

> the Author though at the first unknowne, yet enforced to accorde to certaine of his friends importunacy herein, to publish them by their meanes, and for their sakes: [is] unwilling (as it seemeth) to acknowledge them, for their levity, till he have redeemed them with some more excellent worke hereafter.[28]

The book is not genuinely anonymous, however, since one of the dedicatory sonnets at the end of the sequence is signed.[29] Barnes does then acknowledge his second book of verse, *A divine centurie of spirituall sonnets* (1595).[30] Compare George Peele, whose earliest work, a pastoral drama, is printed anonymously in 1584, but whose *Polyhymnia*, in 1590, bears his name on the title page.[31]

The works of Samuel Rowlands provide a fuller example of this pattern. His earliest work, a book of religious verse, is printed in 1598

---

[25] William Percy, *Sonnets to the fairest Coelia* (1594), STC 19618, sig. A2. For examples of the Elizabethan association between youth and light verse see Saunders, "The Stigma of Print," 144; Helgerson, "The Elizabethan Laureate," 201–2.

[26] STC 1480; the dedicatory poem is signed in character by "Daphnis."

[27] STC 1483 sig. A3.

[28] STC 1469 sig. A2.

[29] STC 1469 sig. *2v (sic, ante V2).

[30] STC 1467.

[31] *The araygnement of Paris*, STC 19530; *Polyhymnia*, STC 19546. James VI attempts a modest namelessness in accord with the title of his *Essayes of a prentise in the divine art of poesie* (1584; STC 14373), though the commendatory verses, including a Latin acrostic of his name (sig. A1), leave no doubt as to the author's identity. His second book of verse, however, is entitled *His Maiestie's poeticall exercises* (1591; STC 14379).

under his initials, "S. R."[32] Over the next seven years, his satires, epigrams, and prose pieces are all similarly published, with initials only: *The letting of humors blood in the head-vaine* (1600); *Tis merrie when gossips meete* (1602); *Looke to it, for Ile stabbe ye* (1604); *Hell's broke loose* (1605).[33] Another book of religious verse, printed around this time, is "by Samuel Rowlands."[34] Then, in the prefatory poem to *A theater of delightfull recreation* (1605), which contains commendatory verses addressing the author by name, Rowlands takes retroactive credit for his less pious works—but only as he renounces them, and satire as a whole:

> No minute more to *Satyrs* I will lend
> Nor drop of inke on *Epigram* Ile spend:
> Let Humorists do as themselves thinke good,
> My pen hath done with *Letting Humors blood*:
> Ile show no more to each fantastique asse
> His pourtraiture in *Humors Looking-glasse* ...
> *Deaths Challenge*, with *Ile Stab*, has pass'd the Presse,
> and so I leave him to his powerfulnesse:
> With *Hell broke loose* I have no more to doo....[35]

The renunciation of satire is not of long duration. But again, as the poet returns to satiric verse in his "knave" series, we find the same pattern. *The knave of harts* (printed 1612) appears anonymously; *The knave of clubbes*, the first in the series (1609) and *More knaves yet? The knaves of spades and diamonds* (1613) bear only initials; however, a subsequent edition of the latter (?1613), "with new additions," is signed in full.[36]

Rowland's repeated impulse to test the critical waters under his initials before acknowledging his work is again genre-related. Satirists, like political and religious writers, might well view anonymity as a form of protection rather than simply a literary convention. And yet to say that the Elizabethan satirists withhold their names purely out of concern for their safety, as the Jesuit poet Robert Southwell did, fails to explain the impulse which led Rowlands to return to anonymity when beginning his "knave" series. Consider the case of another satirist, John Marston. His first book, *The metamorphosis of Pigmalions image* (printed

---

[32] [*The betraying of Christ*], STC 21365.
[33] STC 21392.7, 21409, 21398, 21385.
[34] *A terrible battell betweene the two consumers of the whole world, time and death* (?1606), STC 21407.
[35] STC 21408 sig. A2 ff. = Samuel Rowlands, *Uncollected Poems*, ed. F. O. Waage, Jr. (Gainesville: Scholars' Facsimiles and Reprints, 1970), 51.
[36] STC 21390, 21387, 21392, 21392.3.

1598), bears only the initials "W. K."[37] In *The scourge of villainie* (1598), which appeared shortly afterward, the full pseudonym, "W. Kinsayder," appears.[38] Thus Marston duplicates the pattern of publishing anonymously or under initials only and then revealing the full name—but using a pen name instead of his own, thereby combining two different conventions governing disclosure of authorship.

The problem of pirate printing is closely connected to this phenomenon of anonymous publication. On the one hand, over-modest authors may find their works claimed by others who rush in to fill the void,[39] and pirate printing is a well-known annoyance during this period.[40] On the other hand, most claims of piracy are very suspicious when examined closely, and begin to fall into patterns similar to those we have seen in the case of anonymous publication. Nicholas Breton and Samuel Daniel complain bitterly about the unauthorized printing of their poems—especially because their work has been mixed in with poems by others.[41] Yet Breton continues to give the larcenous printer Richard Jones the rights to many other books, and Daniel is a close friend of Nashe, the editor of the offending edition of *Astrophil and Stella*. Gascoigne, like Breton, reprints a corrected edition of his book with the "pirate," Richard Smith,[42] and a year later is the prime mover in the pirate publication of a friend's manuscript.[43] The printer of Thomas Blenerhasset's *The seconde parte of the mirrour for magistrates*

---

[37] STC 17482.

[38] STC 17485. On this name, which may be a pun on Marston, see A. Kernan, *The Cankered Muse* (New Haven: Yale Univ. Press, 1959), 96; Helgerson, *Self-Crowned Laureates*, 135. The epilogue, "To him that hath perused me," is signed "Theriomastix" (sig. I 3v).

[39] E.g., Robert Tofte, whose title pages rarely carry more than his initials, complains in his translation of Varchi's *The Blazon of Jealousy* (1615, STC 24593, by R. T., Gentleman) that an earlier translation of Ariosto (1608, STC 744) has been printed "unknowne to mee ... in another man's name" (p. 6 = sig. C3v, note v).

[40] The miscellanies are the most notorious offenders; the editors of *Englands Helicon* (1600, STC 3191) even defend the reprinting of other publishers' copy in their preface (sig. A4); pirated works are also more likely to be miscellanies in fact if not in name, since the printers would add poems by other authors to the stolen manuscript. Examples are the 1594 edition of Henry Constable's *Diana* (STC 5638); *Brittons bowre of delights* (1591, STC 3633); the 1591 edition of *Astrophil and Stella*, with sonnets by Daniel appended. On this question see, e.g., H. S. Bennett, *English Books and Readers* (Cambridge: Cambridge Univ. Press, 1952–70), 2:19–26.

[41] Breton, preface to *The pilgrimage to paradise* (1592, STC 3683, sig. ¶3); Daniel, dedicatory epistle to *Delia* (1592, STC 6243.2, sig. A2); see above, note 40.

[42] *A hundreth sundrie flowres* (1573), STC 11635; reissued in 1575 as *The posies of G. Gascoigne corrected and augmented*, STC 11636.

[43] See Bennett, 2:22.

(1578) obligingly includes a letter from Blenerhasset, "The Authour's Epistle vnto his friende," in which Blenerhasset, having supposedly entrusted the manuscript to this friend before going abroad, writes: "Keepe these trifles from the view of all men, and as you promysed, let them not raunge out of your private Study."[44] Barnaby Googe also leaves his poetry in the hands of a friend and returns to find it about to be printed; since "it coulde not withoute great hynderaunce of the poore Printer be nowe revoked" he allows the printing and hastily appends a signed dedication.[45] A similar mishap befalls William Percy in the 1594 *Sonnets to the fairest Coelia*:

> Courteous Reader, whereas I was fullie determined to have concealed my sonnets as thinges privie to my selfe, yet of courtesie having lent them to some, they were secretlie committed to the Presse and almost finished before it came to my knowledge, Wherefore making as they say, *Vertue of necessitie*, I did deeme it most convenient to praepose mine Epistle, onely to beseech you to account of them as of toyes and amorous devises.[46]

It is not only modern scholars who find these claims of piracy suspicious. When Harvey complains that the letters between Spenser and himself were printed against his will by "undiscreete friends,"[47] Nashe accuses Harvey of sending them to the press himself and of writing the "welwillers epistle" praising himself for the *Four Letters*: "the compositor that set it swore to mee it came under his owne [Harvey's] hand to be printed."[48]

When speaking of piracy, then, it is important to distinguish three different types: (1) genuine piracy involving an author who is unwilling to print his work; (2) genuine piracy involving an author who is *not* reluctant to print. This type of piracy reflects the struggle between authors and printers for control over the format and content of the published work; (3) Claims of piracy involving authors who wish to avoid responsibility for publishing their work.

This last category (which in my opinion covers the great majority of piracy cases) seems to have certain analogies to anonymous publication;

---

[44] STC 3131 sig. *4v.
[45] STC 12048, *Eglogs epytaphes and sonettes*, 1563, sig. A6 ff.
[46] STC 19618 sig. A2. On this passage see Bennett, 2:257.
[47] Gabriel Harvey, *Works*, ed. A. B. Grosart (London: printed for private circulation by the Huth Library, 1884–1885), 1:180.12.
[48] Thomas Nashe, *Works*, ed. R. B. McKerrow (London: A. H. Bullen, 1904–1910), 1:296; 3:127.

that is, the "pirated" work is usually the first book published. Like anonymity, piracy provides a screen for an author as he first ventures into print. The unauthorized publication allows him to repudiate the work, or revise it and take retroactive credit for it once it has been well received. The "pirated" works of Blenerhasset, Lodge, Percy, Daniel and Gascoigne are all the first printed publications of these authors.[49] In fact, Blenerhasset's printer openly suggests that a favorable reception will encourage the author to publish further efforts: "It may be (good Reader) that the friendely acceptyng hereof, wyll encourage the Authour to set thynges of greater price in Print."[50] Similarly, Percy, after insisting that the *Coelia* has been sent to press without his consent, nevertheless promises in his hastily prefixed epistle that "ere long I will impart unto the worlde another Poeme which shall be both more fruitfull and ponderous."[51] We may compare the verse preface to the *Shepheardes Calender*, where we find a similar claim:

> But if that any aske thy name,
> Say thou wert base begot with blame:
> For thy thereof thou takest shame.
> And when thou art past ieopardee,
> Come tell me, what was sayd of mee
> And I will send more after thee.[52]

This third type of piracy seems to involve poetry rather than prose, just as anonymity is more common for books of verse than for other types of writing. Among the Tudor writers I examined, only Harvey claims to have been unwilling to publish a prose work: significantly, it is the *Letters*, and most of the verse "pirate" publications are sonnet sequences or lyric miscellanies. This suggests that these claims of piracy may be motivated less by the author's attitude towards print than by the genre of the book he is publishing. Sonnets, like letters, propose the fiction of a private addressee.

In conclusion, I would argue that what has been seen as evidence of

---

[49] Although Daniel had published a translation of Giovio's *Imprese* in 1585 (STC 11900).

[50] STC 3131 sig. *2 ff.

[51] See above, note 46.

[52] Spenser, *Shepheardes Calender*, "To his booke," lines 13–18. Note also the remarks of "E. K." in the "Epistle to Harvey" (p. 418, Smith and de Selincourt): "Which [works] albeit I know he nothing so much hateth, as to promulgate, yet this much have I adventured upon his frendship, him selfe being for long time furre estraunged, hoping that this will the rather occasion him, to put forth divers other excellent works of his, which slepe in silence."

a court-based stigma attaching to *print* may sometimes be evidence of a genre-based stigma attaching to the *publication* of certain kinds of poetry and prose. Authors find anonymity and accusations of piracy a convenient detour around the incongruities involved in collecting and publishing the lighter, more private genres. Some courtiers, like Sidney, do seem to have a general reluctance to publish their work, and the example of Churchyard's lost manuscripts reminds us that there was on occasion a practical, if not ideological, conflict between manuscript presentation and print. But others, like Surrey, may escape print because they are lyric poets rather than because they are courtiers. The coyness of their baser-born imitators stems not from a socially-based bias against print *per se*, but from an understanding of the conflicts between public and private in certain genres—conflicts which are exacerbated by the advent of print, but which have their roots in antiquity, where the hierarchies of genre first make their mark on the Western literary tradition.[53]

University of Minnesota

---

[53] I would like to thank Alvin Kernan, who inspired the earliest version of this paper, and Gordon Teskey, who generously assisted with this revision.

DONALD FRIEDMAN

Bottom, Burbage, and the Birth of Tragedy

THE SECOND CONGRESS OF THE INTERNATIONAL SHAKESPEARE Association, meeting in Stratford-upon-Avon in 1981, chose as its topic "Shakespeare: Man of the Theatre," thus setting its seal on a change in the way we read Shakespearean plays.[1] It was an approach that had been urged for some time, to be sure; but the Stratford conference signaled not only that it had survived the disintegrationists and decades of close textual criticism, but also that full parity with Caroline Spurgeon's thematic images, G. Wilson Knight's expanded metaphors, Northrop Frye's archetypal forms, and other holistic interpretive formulas had been achieved by the notion that the plays should be read always in the imagined context of performance and in the awareness of the theatrical conditions surrounding their genesis.

For the understanding of Shakespeare, among the most important of these conditions are the nature and design of the Elizabethan adult companies of players and the unusual circumstance of the playwright's having been not only an actor but also a long-time sharer (i.e., a permanent owner-partner) in the company for which he wrote. One piece of evidence frequently used to illustrate the significance of these unique circumstances is the detectable differences in the parts he wrote for clowns after Will Kempe's departure from the Lord Chamberlain's Men around 1599, and with the accession of Robert Armin. We may point to the correspondence between the character of the parts we know Kempe to have played, such as Peter in *Romeo and Juliet* and Dogberry in *Much Ado*, and his own much-admired talents for buffoonery, verbal play, and physical clowning. We may then note the very different qualities of such jesters as Feste and Fool in *Lear*, who sing ballads and antique songs, bandy witticisms with young gentlemen and corrupt words for their employers, and speak in mixed tones of bitterness and melancholy.

---

[1] The proceedings, edited by Kenneth Muir et al., were published under this title by the Univ. of Delaware Press in 1981.

In thinking about the effect on Shakespeare's daily stint of his close, full, and long-standing knowledge of the senior members of his acting company, we assume, quite reasonably, that the playwright worked to capitalize on their traits of voice and movement, their range of gesture and inflection, their height, their temperament, perhaps their memories, and even their powers of understanding. In short, we take it for granted that he was trying to show them to their best advantage. But, ironically, one sort of actor presents a problem for this paradigm, a mote to trouble the mind's vision of the idyllic playwright-actor relationship—it is the clown. From roughly 1594 to 1599 that would have been, for the Lord Chamberlain's Men, Will Kempe, who followed Dick Tarlton in the favor of the public and the queen, famous for his dancing and his doggerel recitations, and who loved to play upon the laughter of his audiences—as we can judge from his own reports of the throngs who surrounded him daily on his nine days' morris to Norwich. The problem lies in the tension that is likely to have arisen between an author involved in the staging of his own scripts and a prominent colleague whose popularity is based on his skills of improvisation.

What follows rests on two assumptions, one perhaps more reasonable than the other. The first is that Shakespeare shared some of Hamlet's distaste for the clowns who speak "more than is set down for them"; in this instance the fastidious prince and the playwright jealous of his prerogative seem to be at one, although Shakespeare, the practical man of the theatre, surely knew the value of Kempe's way with an audience.[2]

The second assumption is that the role of Bottom in *A Midsummer Night's Dream* was written for the company's leading clown, and therefore that it is very likely that is was performed by Kempe. Of course, there is no proof that this was the case, not even the atypical speech-headings that demonstrate his participation in *Romeo* and *Much Ado*. But he had played Peter shortly before, he would act Dogberry within a few years, and the role calls for his style and known talents. So suited to Kempe's comic skills is the role of Bottom, in fact, that I want to suggest

---

[2] The most comprehensive survey of Kempe's career and his place in Shakespeare's history is David Wiles, *Shakespeare's Clown. Actor and Text in the Elizabethan Playhouse* (Cambridge: Cambridge Univ. Press, 1987). Wiles argues there (ix–x) that Prince Hamlet does not speak for Shakespeare since his "neo-classical aesthetic," while appropriate to a university-educated aristocrat, does not fit the needs or the temperament of a "commercially minded actor-manager." But Andrew Gurr, in *Playgoing in Shakespeare's London* (Cambridge: Cambridge Univ. press, 1987), sees Kempe's departure as a crucial moment in the company's history, one that led to weighty changes in its overall style and repertory; "Shakespeare's fellows," he says, "may well have shared Hamlet's view of clowns" (152).

that Shakespeare has fashioned a role for the clown that is virtually indistinguishable from what Kempe would have done in any case if he had been allowed to plump up his part at will in his usual way with his usual devices. Indeed, the character of Bottom is in some ways an anatomy of Kempe the clown (or at least of the kind of clown Hamlet deplores), a projection of his best-known traits as a performer, and thus a kind of mirror in which the clown can find only his own image and cannot establish an identity apart from his role, which was a privilege the clown had always claimed, and which, no doubt, was the head and source of the distemper Shakespeare gives voice to in Hamlet's lines to the Player King.

What better way to restrain the clown from setting on some quantity of barren spectators to laugh, though in the meantime some necessary question of the play be then to be considered, than to create a role in which the clown must always appear to be himself, in which every improvised line or gesture appears to be part of the character he is playing, in which, in short, the clown in both displayed perfectly and, in a sense, imprisoned?

W. A. Armstrong has suggested that in his creation of Dogberry, Shakespeare revealed something like a desire to prevent Kempe "from dominating the stage as Tarlton had done." He points out that "the bumbling discursiveness of the characterization seems designed to accommodate such digressions, by-play and improvisations as Kempe may have brought to the role."[3] Now Bottom shows signs of kinship to the egregious constable in his passion for order, his decorous pomposity, and his limitless, genial self-love. But he also goes beyond such traits, as he demonstrates the moment the mechanicals enter and he begins to grasp at the reins of authority which should be held by Quince, the putative author of their lamentable comedy.

Even as Shakespeare expands and re-invents the clown's role, he draws it more firmly about the actor who inhabits the role, in a kind of systole and diastole of permission and restraint. For example, we know from a number of contemporary sources that clowns were wont to make ludicrous and grotesque faces at suitably incongruous moments. Imagine the opportunities for such mugging provided by the scene in Titania's bower. The actor who played Bottom must surely have felt that the ass's head was a restriction on his ability to mug it up; but at the same time it was a transcendently ludicrous and grotesque "face" itself. Slightly more subtle is the restraint placed upon the clown by licensing Bottom's bergomask immediately after the performance of *Pyramus and*

---

[3] "Actors and Theatres," in *Shakespeare Survey* 17 (Cambridge: Cambridge Univ. Press, 1964), 194–95.

Thisby. Both the part and the decorum of the occasion thus require Kempe to do what he is famous for doing, and what the audience has been waiting for him to do—to perform the jig that follows the end of the play. But there is still the epilogue to be spoken by Puck; and the transition to a jig is made more difficult by the concluding sequence of dance and speech.

One of the traditional clowns' skills was mimicry, and they were often given speeches in which they could feign or imitate a number of types, or other characters in the play. Shakespeare has transformed a conventional occasion for the display of special histrionic skills into the analysis of the character of an actor: Bottom offering to play Thisby (or any other part going, for that matter) is a fairly transparent trope of the clown as mimic. But when he offers to "roar you as gently as any sucking dove," or to play the lion in the form of a nightingale, we have gone beyond simple mimicry toward recognizing the appetite of the protean actor. The clown is of all the company the one best able to cross the boundaries between discrete personae; and if the playwright cannot manage to patrol all the borders against the incursions of a Kempe, what better device than to cast him as an actor who wants to play every part?

The other hard thing is to find a way to control improvisation, especially in the form of back-chat with the audience. Repartee feeds upon itself, and the play must needs come to a stop while Kempe plays off the lines thrown at him by the spectators.[4] Unless, of course, the impromptu exchange is built into the script and Kempe's jibes and responses are inscribed in Bottom's own lines, as in his gentle corrections to the Duke's misapprehensions about the wall.[5] This is improvisation both indulged and severely curtailed; Bottom is whenever Kempe is not, so to speak.

Thus the clown is granted all the opportunities he could wish for, to dance, to mimic, to address the audience, to quibble over the meanings of words, and to draw the eyes of all in the most absurd of costumes, while lying in the arms of the Fairy Queen. The audience saw Will Kempe reveling in his repertoire of tricks and gambits. Will Kempe saw himself in a part which anticipated his best moves, setting down for him the kind of lines he would have uttered if he had been able to depart from them. What Shakespeare saw was a way to dominate the clown who would otherwise dominate him, by subverting him with his own technique.

---

[4] Cf. Gurr, *Playgoing*, 126, for a description of Tarlton's excursions in this manner of playing.
[5] *A Midsummer Night's Dream* 5.1.350 ff.

This, I am almost persuaded, is what Shakespeare did when he wrote the part of Bottom for Kempe; "almost" because I am reluctant to believe that he could have been guilty of so cold and ingenious a revenge. But he undoubtedly had the opportunity to learn Kempe's ways and to perceive his vulnerability to such control, precisely because the clown's actions were generically predictable and because his preeminence depended so much on keeping his known personality clearly distinguishable from the role in which he was cast.

This was less obviously so in the case of the tragedian, because he was bound intrinsically to the plot. Even he was subject to the claims of notoriety, and could become identified with what T. W. Baldwin called a "line" of acting, a particular sort of role or style of performance;[6] this was true of the best-known actors of the time. Nevertheless, the differences among them are even more important for an understanding of the development of Shakespearean drama. It was not entirely fortuitous that he wrote the great tragic roles after the year 1599.

What we know about Shakespeare's career permits us a few plausible surmises about his interests and activities around the time Kempe left the company. Meres tells us that he had written some of the sonnets by then; and very shortly he was to write *Hamlet*, and thus begin the series of tragedies that emerged within six or seven years, culminating in *King Lear, Antony and Cleopatra*, and *Coriolanus*. It would be foolhardy to attempt to summarize, let alone enumerate, the reasons for Shakespeare turning at this time from the comedies and histories on which his not inconsiderable reputation was already established. They may range from those personal sorrows which C. J. Sisson dismissed as mythical more than fifty years ago, to the national and local effects of the death of Elizabeth and the accession of James I,[7] to developments in blank verse,[8] to changes in the composition of the Lord Chamberlain's Men. Shakespeare's company, although the most stable over its

---

[6] The *locus classicus* for this account of actors and roles is *The Organization and Personnel of the Shakespearean Company*, (Princeton: Princeton Univ. Press, 1927), passim. Baldwin's schematic assignment of "lines" to members of the company, and his assumptions about the stability of role-typing, have often been attacked, notably by David Bevington in *Mankind to Marlowe* (Cambridge: Harvard Univ. Press, 1962), 108–10. But Andrew Gurr is less skeptical about Baldwin's theories; in *The Shakespearean Stage, 1574–1642* (Cambridge: Cambridge Univ. Press, 1970), 76, he notes that the demands of the repertory system might well have required some such allocation of "lines."

[7] Cf. Leonard Tennenhouse, *Power on Display* (New York and London: Methuen, 1986), 99–101 and chapter 3, passim.

[8] Cf. Bernard Beckerman, *Shakespeare at the Globe. 1599–1609* (New York: Macmillan, 1962), 127.

long life of the public groups, nevertheless went through several transformations before the construction of the first Globe and the purchase of the Blackfriars' theatre; but its original membership and its majority in those years consisted of comic actors, suited to its predominant repertory of plays. The primacy in tragic drama was conceded perforce to the Admiral's Men, to their leading player Edward Alleyn, and to the plays of Marlowe. Alleyn began to act when he was still in his teens, in the 1580s; and by the time he left the stage in 1597 he had achieved so consummate a success that he could build the Fortune theatre three years later and resume some of his most famous roles for a few years more. The most popular of these, undoubtedly, was Tamburlaine; and the various adulatory mentions of Alleyn make it clear why. His admirers cite most vividly his stature, the strength of his voice, the energy of his stage manner, and generally the powerful impression of heroic vigor he brought to his monolithic Marlovian roles. The plays and the style of performing them continued to be associated with the Fortune and with the Red Bull theatre, a tradition which persisted until the closing of the theatres in 1642, although not without incurring some mockery of its old-fashioned strutting and bellowing.[9]

It is not clear whether it is a quirk of history or a quirk embedded deep in the national character, but there always seem to be at any one time two leading actors in the English theatre, representing differing styles of characterization or "personation." Alleyn's junior competitor was Richard Burbage, who worked beside him briefly in the early 1590s when Lord Strange's Men and the Lord Admiral's occupied the Rose. From 1594, when the Lord Chamberlain's troupe was reformed, Burbage was the leader among the actor-sharers, the player for whom Shakespeare wrote all his great tragic parts, and the actor whose fame rivaled Alleyn's, though for rather different excellences. Both men, inevitably, were praised as Roscius *redivivus*, and both were called Proteus for their ability to change shapes. But it is noticeable in the several allusions, notes, elegies, and the like that have survived, that where Alleyn's image is one of extraordinary force and dominance, Burbage is most often praised for his facility in disappearing into a character, for the conviction and lifelikeness of his portraits, in short for his "natural" style of playing.

Detailed reports or descriptions of Alleyn's performing style are very sparse; but they are sufficient to suggest the strong personal impression he made in roles such as Tamburlaine, Faustus, and Barabas. Ben Jonson, in his epigram, "To Edward Allen," forges a distinction to ex-

---

[9] Cf. Gurr, *Playgoing*, 149–51.

plain how Alleyn "present worth in all doth so contract" when he says that "as others speak, only thou dost act."[10] Everard Guilpin, in *Skialetheia*, remembers Alleyn's "gait" while performing the (lost) eponymous role of Cutlack;[11] and Fuller singles out for praise the actor's ability to make a "majestick" role become him.[12]

By contrast, the memorials of Burbage are consistent in their emphasis on his ability to sink into a role so completely "as had he truly been the man he seem'd."[13] It seems fairly clear that what Burbage brought to the very late Elizabethan theatre was an art of supple, lucid, and realistic speech and gesture, a style that did not call attention to itself but to the personation of character that it served. It is impossible to decide whether Burbage's talents presented to Shakespeare the opportunity to create characters of a complexity hitherto unknown on English stages, or whether the playwright's shaping of those roles nourished the talents and created the style that earned Burbage his reputation. It is nevertheless fair to say that these things happened together, and that there is a strong possibility that they influenced one another.

---

[10] No. LXXXIX.

[11] Epigram 43.

[12] Thomas Fuller, *History of the Worthies of England*, 2 vols. (London: Printed for F. C. and J. Rivington, 1811), 2:14.

[13] The lines are from Thomas May's *The Heir* (1622), 1.1, in which Roscio asks Polimetes whether he has seen "a player personate Ieronimo" (one of Burbage's renowned roles); he replies that he has indeed "seen the knave paint grief / In such a lively color, that for false / And acted passion he has drawn the tears / From the spectators' eyes. Ladies in the boxes / Kept time with sighs, and tears to his sad accents." The mention of painting and acting together is a complimentary allusion to Burbage, who was known as an artist in both media; a well-known elegy on him, whose authorship is disputed, begins by lamenting the loss of one who could best "both limn / And act my grief," and goes on to recall his powers of naturalistic mimesis:

> Oft have I seen him leap into the Grave
> Suiting the person, which he seemed to have
> Of a sad lover, with so true an eye
> That there I would have sworn he meant to dye,
> Oft have I seen him play this part in jest,
> So lively, that Spectators, and the rest
> Of his sad crew, whilst he but seemed to bleed,
> Amazed, thought even then he died in deed.

See E. Nungezer, *A Dictionary of Actors* (New Haven: Yale Univ. Press, 1929), 74. I have modernized the text. The character *Of an Excellent Actor* (1615; attributed to John Webster), which Chambers believed was modeled on Burbage, specifies that "he doth not strive to make nature monstrouse, she is often seene in the same Scaene with him," and observes that "what we see him personate, we thinke truely done before us." Cf. *The Elizabethan Stage* (Oxford: Clarendon Press, 1923), 4:257-58. Chambers prints the anonymous elegy quoted above on pp. 308-9.

That Shakespeare was conscious of differences in dramatic and performing styles, perhaps between the two competing companies, we can infer from several kind of evidence. Among the most compelling is act 2, scene 2 of *Hamlet*, in which the Prince prescribes for members of an adult company rules and principles of playing which take as a pejorative contrast those players who "have so strutted and bellow'd" that they "imitate humanity ... abominably." Whether Hamlet may be adverting to Alleyn as Tamburlaine is less important to decide than it is to notice that it is Burbage who delivers these lines, presumably in the natural and unobtrusive manner for which he is already known, and thus "trippingly" as he recommends, suiting his own verbal action to the word as he utters the word and acts the part, holding himself (as Hamlet) as a mirror up to his own nature as an actor. The same sort of confrontation had occurred to Shakespeare years before, when Burbage created the role of Richard III, the first of the major tragic characters he played to dwell at length and at heart on the interweaving of playing roles and manipulating reality. However theatrical Richard tells us he is, from his first soliloquy forward, he is clearly not meant to display his role-playing skills in the manner of the "deep tragedian" described by Buckingham in act 3, scene 5, who trembles and starts at the "wagging of a straw," and who calls upon his stock of gestures, "ghastly looks," and "enforced smiles" to imitate emotion and conceal stratagems. If this describes the professional actor, what is the contrasting image we are to fashion of the professional actor Richard Burbage? What does the new deep tragedian personate, now that the excesses that both Bottom and Mistress Quickly remind us of, in the 'Ercles' and Cambyses' vein, have been reformed altogether?

In many cases, he personates a madman; or, rather, a heroic figure so divided within or so ill-suited to the role he must act that he begins to exhibit the behavioral characteristics of madness. That is, what distinguishes Shakespeare's tragic roles, as contrasted with what Lawrence Danson has called in Marlowe's heroes the "sheer tenacity of their will always to be themselves,"[14] is instability of characterological identity, the sudden shifts and slippages, the uncertainties and indecisions that Hamlet and Lear and Othello and Antony both experience and exhibit. The first thing we are told of Antony is that his captain's heart has become "the bellows and the fan / To cool a gypsy's lust"; the first thing we are told to see when he appears is that the "triple pillar of the world" is "transform'd / Into a strumpet's fool." The actor must

---

[14] "Continuity and Character in Shakespeare and Marlowe," *Studies in English Literature* 26 (1986): 217. See also Danson's *Tragic Alphabet* (New Haven: Yale Univ. Press, 1974), 176–77, on the language of madness in Shakespearean tragic heroes.

convince us of the transformation, and must thus show us both the pillar and the fool. Othello must descend from marmoreal nobility to frothing fury, Lear from vigorous command to feeble, passive dependence—and back again—passing through hysterical rage and naked derangement along the way. Laurence Olivier recently warned the actor attempting Hamlet for the first time that he must be "aware that it's a sporadic collection of self-dramatizations";[15] the keynote is "sporadic," and it is struck most clearly in the soliloquies.[16] If it is there that we are to find direct access to the character's thinking, then in *Hamlet* pre-eminently we are presented with the lightning changes of mood and diction, the reversals of logic and rhythm, the passionate near-inconsequentiality of addresses to the audience which are in truth debates within the self. More, they are debates about the self, carried on by a player attempting to create the illusory consistency of a dramatic character out of materials which in themselves are inconsistent because of their faithfulness to the appearances of lived reality.

To project a central personality through such materials requires of the player technical skills of a particular kind. He must, for example, be able physically to shift from one level of diction or tonal register to another swiftly and unfalteringly, and to adjust stance and bodily gesture equally quickly. He must give voices to the polyphony of such speeches as Hamlet's act 2, scene 2 soliloquy, which moves in little more than fifty lines from self-lacerating despair to rhetorical rage, to ironic self-regard, to coolly calculating plot-making, and all the while commenting on the relation between passion and action, exhibiting at the same time a rhythmic range that extends from "Remorseless, treacherous, lecherous, kindless villain!" to "the play's the thing / Wherein I'll catch the conscience of the King." Lear's arias on the heath or in the great storm are no more precariously constructed on points of change and modulation than his tirades in act 2, scene 4, where, although not "alone" like Hamlet, he addresses an audience not limited to his daughters, and where his struggles to comprehend the events he is undergoing are played out in internal debates, logical reversals, and finally in the disintegration of the control he could still muster in "I will not trouble thee, my child: farewell" into the frustrated fury of "I will do such things— / What they are yet I know not, but they shall be / The terrors of the earth!" Othello's return to "himself" is commonly identi-

---

[15] *On Acting* (New York: Simon and Schuster, 1986), 77.
[16] Francis Barker in *The Tremulous Private Body* (New York: Methuen, 1984), 36, names the soliloquy as the "rhetorical form proper" to what he views as Hamlet's "anachronistic subjectivity." The soliloquy may also be thought of as a version of the Kempish clown's direct address to the audience.

fied with the return of his stately and visionary speech in act 5, scene 2, in which he reconciles finally his images of Venetian warrior and disruptive alien by killing himself as he had once the "turban'd Turk" who had "traduc'd the state"; that return is measured for us by its distance from "Pish! Noses, ears, and lips. Is't possible? Confess? Handkerchief? O devil!"

To play these speeches an actor would need at a minimum the ability to pronounce lines of widely varying rapidity and density, to utter them, so to speak, "trippingly on the tongue"; and he would want to create the illusion of characters succeeding one another with occasionally bewildering speed. What we know of Burbage's diction and of his knack for submerging himself in a role (albeit that knowledge is fairly slender) suggests that he was particularly well equipped for these tasks. Moreover, those skills made it possible for Shakespeare to conceive his tragic heroes as exemplars of role-playing, in both its triumphs and its perils, and perhaps to explore madness as the expressive form of the hero's troubled implication in the society of the stage.

For the division of self from identity (or, one might say, character from role), was probably the most weighty determinant of madness in Shakespeare's time, perhaps because it advanced the most threatening challenge to established ideas of social structure and the place of individuals in it. Proteus was the god most often invoked to describe both actors and madmen; I doubt that it is without significance that Shakespeare's full-scale study of a melancholic as hero should also be steeped in meditation about the art of playing and the ontology of illusions. Michael MacDonald's book on Richard Napier, the Buckinghamshire physician who specialized in the treatment of mental disorders and who began his practice just about the time that Shakespeare began his career in the theatre, shows that the forms of behavior most directly associated with madness were those that offered to disrupt the orderings that held human relationships in some stable structure.[17] Violence against members of one's family, or acts that repudiated familial roles, were regarded as both dangerous and criminal, and so were almost certain proofs of madness. Other ways of disregarding or showing disobedience to convention or to conventional symbols of status were equally menacing to agreements about identity, and therefore equally mad by definition. Tearing one's clothes, for example, or wearing rags, or going naked were understood as rejections of the signs of social hierarchy, castings off of the bonds of society, and thus in some sense as "acts of self-de-

---

[17] Cf. *Mystical Bedlam. Madness, Anxiety, and Healing in Seventeenth-Century England* (Cambridge: Cambridge Univ. Press, 1981).

structive violence, a kind of social suicide."[18] Lear's unbuttoning in the storm is but one version of the separation of self from role, as is Othello's farewell to his occupation, Hamlet's declaration to Laertes that Hamlet "from himself be ta'en away," and Macbeth's realization that what he must not look to have is "honor, love, obedience, troops of friends." And as if to show how familial Shakespeare's tragic characters seem to be with Richard Napier's patients, we may find in his clinical notes that those symptoms of madness most frequently observed were "frantic energy, fits of wildly inappropriate laughter, or rage, restless wandering or aimless running, and titanic physical strength." "Laughter," says MacDonald, "was the special token of antic madness";[19] "O God, your only jig-maker," says Hamlet.

What Napier remarked most of all in his patients were the quicksilver changes in their moods. Alexander Leggatt speaks of Burbage as "capable of quick passions and sardonic wit."[20] The connection I wish to make is fairly simple: a few years after Richard Burbage joined the newly-formed Lord Chamberlain's company and won for himself the position of primary tragic player, Shakespeare was beginning to experiment with modes of character representation that were intensely involved with his continuing speculation on the nature of playing and of theatrical illusion. He had touched upon the self-conscious role-playing character in Richard III, Richard II, and elsewhere; but in creating Hamlet and the major tragic roles that succeeded it, his thinking about the art of playing developed into more comprehensive explorations of the ways of identity, explorations which imitated some of the symptomology of madness while trying to create an illusion of stable identity in characters notable for inner conflicts, rapid changes, and the awareness of their own shifting and unsuitable relationship to their roles. To create such an illusion required an actor whose speech could be molded to quick and successive imitations, one who could make variousness convincing, one who did not rely on singleness and strength to make the impression he needed. From what we know by contemporary reports of Burbage's playing, these are the abilities he provided, and at a level of excellence unapproached by any others.

Joel Fineman has suggested recently that in moving within the sonnet from the fixed and externalized visual iconography of the Petrarchan tradition to the ambiguous, fleeting, and intrinsically ironic mode of speech, Shakespeare invented the literary subject, and set the

---

[18] *Mystical Bedlam*, 131.
[19] *Mystical Bedlam*, 139.
[20] *Revels History of Drama in English. 1576–1613* (London: Methuen, 1975), 3:98.

terms for the modern understanding of subjectivity.[21] It seems to me unlikely that such a discovery, so radical a break with the history of consciousness up to 1599, would have occurred only in the little room of the sonnet stanza. The invention of the modern subject was taking place at the same time, I submit, in the creation of the Shakespearean tragic hero, divided within and from himself, his madness of indecision mirrored in the nimble and transparent medium of the player of parts. In a British Academy lecture delivered more than fifty years ago, Richard David admitted modestly that while he did not "say that Shakespeare switched from comedy to tragedy solely because Burbage had developed into a superb tragic lead," he did feel that "the existence of Burbage is likely, nevertheless, to have provided the initial stimulus."[22] I think he may have been right.

University of California—Berkeley

---

[21] *Shakespeare's Perjured Eye* (Berkeley: Univ. of California Press, 1986).

[22] "Shakespeare and the Players," in *Studies in Shakespeare. British Academy Lectures*, ed. P. Alexander (Oxford: Oxford Univ. Press, 1964), 33–55.

DOUGLAS E. GREEN

Shakespeare's Violation: "One face, one voice, one habit, and two persons"

However much we may argue about Shakespearean texts, we never doubt that they mean something—and they do, although not quite in the way the old introductory Shakespeare course descriptions once implied. Because "Shakespeare is," according to Alan Sinfield, "one of the places where ideology is made,"[1] we have lately had a proliferation of multiply explicated Shakespeares, deconstructing and deconstructed Shakespeares, Marxist Shakespeares, psychoanalytic Shakespeares, new historicist Shakespeares, and feminist Shakespeares.[2] In her book *The Social Production of Art*, the Marxist-feminist theorist Janet Wolff discusses the implications of this sort of "interpretation as re-creation": "What is far more important than the fact that, as a literary critical exercise, we may attempt to recover an author's meaning, is the fact that this meaning is effectively dead. What an author intended, or even meant to his or her contemporary public and first readers, is only of interest insofar as that original meaning has historically informed the present reading of the text."[3] For many Shakespeareans that is a particularly bitter pill.[4] But as much recent feminist and new historical criticism has shown, the various constructions of gender in Shakespeare's plays do not transcend their historical determinants.[5] In connection with *Twelfth Night*, the

---

[1] Alan Sinfield, "Introduction: Reproductions, Interventions," in *Political Shakespeare*, ed. Jonathan Dollimore and Alan Sinfield (Ithaca: Cornell Univ. Press, 1985), 132.

[2] See the excellent bibliographies—and commentaries—in Edward Pechter's "The New Historicism and Its Discontents: Politicizing Renaissance Drama," *PMLA* 102 (1987): 292–303, and in Phyllis Rackin's "Androgyny, Mimesis, and the Marriage of the Boy Heroine on the English Renaissance Stage," *PMLA* 102 (1987): 29–41.

[3] Janet Wolff, *The Social Production of Art* (New York: New York Univ. Press, 1984), 95, 102.

[4] See Pechter, passim.

[5] See, for instance, Lisa Jardine's *Still Harping on Daughters: Women and Drama in*

kind of romantic comedy still admired for the pluck of its heroine, I shall suggest at least one of the dangers of persisting in the myth of a transcendent Shakespeare.

The construction of gender in *Twelfth Night* raises special issues for the modern reader or audience, which the mere insertion of women into roles originally written with boy-actors in mind does not eradicate, but further complicates. Stephen Greenblatt has recently argued that "licit sexuality in *Twelfth Night*—the only craving that the play can represent as capable of finding satisfaction—depends upon a [natural] movement that deviates from the desired object straight in one's path toward a marginal object, a body one scarcely knows." Thus, fortunately for Olivia and Viola, Sebastian and Orsino (or rather Antonio?), this deviating "nature is," according to Greenblatt, "an *unbalancing* act."[6] But even if we endorse wholeheartedly Greenblatt's intertextual conjunction of Renaissance medical discourse and *Twelfth Night*'s construction of gender and identity, we modern readers still face our own problematic transcription of the text's construction of gender: how do our diverse re-constitutions of the women's roles, usually without regard to the textual residue of the original mode of production, affect the representation of women on the stage, not to mention their place in the world? The question reminds us that, for feminist critics as well as others, interpretation has present, as well as past, historical and political

---

the Age of Shakespeare (New Jersey: Barnes and Noble, 1983); Leah Marcus's "Shakespeare's Comic Heroines, Elizabeth I, and the Political Uses of Androgyny," in *Women in the Middle Ages and the Renaissance*, ed. Mary Beth Rose (Syracuse: Syracuse Univ. Press, 1986), 135–53; and such essays by Adrian Louis Montrose as "*A Midsummer Night's Dream* and the Shaping Fantasies of Elizabethan Culture: Gender, Power, Form," in *Rewriting the Renaissance: The Discourses of Sexual Difference in Early Modern Europe*, ed. Margaret Ferguson, Maureen Quilligan, and Nancy J. Vickers (Chicago: Chicago Univ. Press, 1986), 65–87, 329–34, and " 'The Place of a Brother' in *As You Like It*: Social Process and Comic Form," *Shakespeare Quarterly* 32 (1981): 28–54. Jean Howard's excellent article "Crossdressing, the Theater, and Gender Struggle in Early Modern England," *Shakespeare Quarterly* 39 (1988): 418–40, an early version of which was delivered at the 1987 CEMERS conference, rigorously discusses from a feminist-historicist perspective several issues addressed here.

[6] Stephen Greenblatt, *Shakespearean Negotiations: The Circulation of Social Energy in Renaissance England* (Berkeley: Univ. of California Press, 1988), 68. Not long after I had presented the original version of this paper at the CEMERS conference (October 1987), Greenblatt's controversial essay on "Fiction and Friction" appeared in the foregoing collection of essays (66–93, 175–84) and has since become the center of a debate among feminist and new historical critics of *Twelfth Night*, not least for the authority it grants Renaissance medical discourse on gender and for the effect its general acceptance might have on political and, in particular, feminist criticism. (See, for instance, Jean Howard, 422–23.) Therefore, since I am addressing concerns relevant to the current debate, it seems appropriate to note some points of agreement and disagreement between Greenblatt's views and mine.

import. In her provocative psychoanalytic account of gender and genre in Shakespeare, Linda Bamber has claimed that, even in the comedies, "insofar as the Self is within drama and human, it counts itself a member of the dominant social group," whereas "the feminine is Other to society's rules and regulations, to its hierarchies of power, and to the impersonality of its systems and sanctions."[7] But if, as Luce Irigaray asserts, "any theory of the subject has always been appropriated by the 'masculine,'"[8] then Shakespeare's *Twelfth Night,* insofar as it aims to represent versions of woman as desiring subject, not only suggests anxiety about feminine identity and desire, but ultimately denies any Other consciousness at all—that is, any consciousness not constituted in masculine terms. Thus, unlike her literary cousin Rosalind, Viola never returns from boyhood to even the illusion of womanhood; instead she remains Cesario—a colony of that "little Caesar," the *boy-actor inscribed in the text,* sign of the masculine as prototype of subjectivity.

Twelfth Night essentially exiles all but traditionally deceptive and erratic images of women from the stage; the puckish Maria, weaver of Toby's beloved "device," is the rule, not the exception. Her deceptive letter to Malvolio replicates various postures and disguises of Olivia and Viola, but with a difference: it exposes the dangers of feminine wiles and desire, as do Maria's appeal to Sir Toby and her own attraction to him. On the one hand, as her handwriting indicates, Maria is her mistress's diminutive double; as such, she suggests problems with Olivia's rule over the house and indirectly implicates her mistress in the deception of Malvolio. Though her household seems to respect and even fear Olivia, the chaos of the subplot undermines the illusion of her governance. And since Maria uses her mistress's "being addicted to a melancholy" as part of the ruse,[9] Olivia's own excesses are at least tangentially linked to Malvolio's cruelly comic imprisonment.

On the other hand, like Viola, Maria masquerades, albeit in the written word only. As in the obvious anagrammatic play among the names Viola, Olivia, and Malvolio, there is in Maria's writing a material illustration of the slipperiness of words that Viola and Feste note and employ in witty quibbles:

Viola. Thy reason, man?

---

[7] Linda Bamber, *Comic Women, Tragic Men* (Stanford: Stanford Univ. Press, 1982), 27-28.

[8] Luce Irigaray, *Speculum of the Other Woman,* trans. Gillian C. Gill (Ithaca: Cornell Univ. Press, 1985), 133.

[9] William Shakespeare, *Twelfth Night,* ed. J. M. Lothian and T. W. Craik, Arden Edition (London: Methuen, 1975), 2.5.202-3 (p. 73). All further references to this work appear in the text.

Clown. Troth, sir, I can yield you none without words, and words are grown so false, I am loath to prove reason with them.
(3.1.22–25)

Furthermore, like Viola but with greater impetus, Maria maneuvers her way into marriage through her clever deception. True, she *uses* a "device" (2.5.182), whereas Viola merely *assumes* a disguise. Still, the audience's sense of Viola's cleverness derives at least in part from her convincing masquerade; subliminally, Viola's clever deception belies her virginal innocence, which has to be reintroduced through the duel *manque* with Sir Andrew. Finally, the anti-romantic marriage between Maria and Toby exposes many of the artificial conventions of *Twelfth Night*'s romantic main plot—both its chaotic courtships and its protean marital resolutions. Though I do not wish to overstate the importance of Maria, I do want to unmask the disguised implications of the subplot for issues of gender in the main.

Needless to say, the subplot's innuendoes hardly tell us everything we need to know about characters in the main plot; in particular, they seem to cast but a shadow of a doubt on Olivia, that remarkable characterization of a woman in love. Olivia recognizes and, unlike Orsino, takes responsibility for the swiftness and instability of her own passion and acknowledges that under its influence "ourselves we do not owe" (1.5.296). From her first encounter with Cesario, Olivia recognizes the pitfalls of the path down which she is headed: "I do not know what, and fear to find / Mine eye too great a flatterer for my mind" (312–13). In each successive encounter, she articulates her own precarious position as a female suitor and yet persists in her desires: "Under your hard construction must I sit, / To force that on you in a shameful cunning / Which you knew none of yours. What might you think?" (3.1.117–19). Like Viola, she submits to her fate as an unrequited lover (1.5.314–15); but, unlike the disguised female orphan and rather like Maria, she exercises her powers—feminine (she unveils her face [1.5.237]) and aristocratic (she arranges the betrothal [4.3] and later calls the priest as witness [5.1])—to get what she wants. Olivia is adept both at disguise and deferral—just why has she adopted that excessive posture of mourning that she so readily discards when the right love comes along?[10]—and at assertive forthright action—her most effective commands to Toby and his cohorts occur when having mistaken the be-

---

[10] For an answer to the question, see Coppélia Kahn's "The Providential Tempest and the Shakespearean Family," in *Representing Shakespeare: New Psychoanalytic Essays*, ed. Murray M. Schwartz and Coppélia Kahn (Baltimore: Johns Hopkins Univ. Press, 1980), 226.

sieged Sebastian for Cesario, she defends her beloved: "Rudesby, be gone!" (4.1.50).

But repressed anxiety about such headstrong women surfaces in the text. Finally, Olivia's attraction to the gentlemanly but impoverished Cesario also indicates a desire to retain the kind of authority in marriage that union with Orsino, a social superior, precludes; as Sir Toby remarks, "She'll none o' the' Count; she'll not match above her degree, neither in estate, years, nor wit; I have heard her swear't" (1.3.106–8). Olivia's superior social standing seems to guarantee, if not an equal place in the marriage she wants (Sebastian does, after all, beat her kinsman [5.1.207]), at least a better place than most married women could hope for.[11] As we shall see, though this nearer equality between husband and wife is offered as an ideal,[12] the final scene casts some doubt on its extra-theatrical efficacy and, from the masculine perspective of one such as Orsino, even on its desirability.

The debate between Viola and Orsino addresses the issue of difference between feminine and masculine desire. As a lover, Orsino claims at times an imaginative capaciousness and mutability as great as the "sea" (1.1.9–15; 2.4.101–2), an image whose feminine associations many critics have noted.[13] If Olivia has to adopt the uncharacteristic role of female suitor, Orsino often speaks of being in love as a feminine disposition: "Our fancies are more giddy and unfirm, / More longing, wavering sooner lost and worn / Than women's are" (2.4.33–35). By universalizing aspects of the love experience traditionally associated with one or the other gender, Shakespeare seems to eradicate the difference between men and women in love. What Viola, in a moment of solitary candor, says of the smitten Olivia applies equally to the masculine fancy of Orsino: "How easy it is for the proper false / In women's waxen hearts to set their forms!" (2.2.28–29). In this instance, both man and woman are erratic, unstable, unpredictable—in other words, conventionally feminine.

But Viola's remark is only half the story; it belies her later claim, in the person of Cesario, that women "are as true of heart as we [men]" (2.4.105). Though the play suggests that men in love are as erratic as women—we should note that Orsino, like many another Renaissance misogynist, considers fickleness essential to women whether or not they are in love—Shakespeare is also claiming in turn that women can be as

---

[11] Marilyn L. Williamson, *The Patriarchy of Shakespeare's Comedies* (Detroit: Wayne State Univ. Press, 1986), 38–41.
[12] Marianne L. Novy discusses this view in *Love's Argument: Gender Relations in Shakespeare* (Chapel Hill: Univ. of North Carolina Press, 1984), 32–44.
[13] E.g., Kahn, 225.

faithful as men: "She [Cesario's fictive sister] sat like Patience on a monument, / Smiling at grief. Was not this love indeed?" (2.4.115-16). By conjuring up the Patient Griselda—that feminine prototype of steadfastness—Viola-Cesario and Shakespeare undercut the masculinist sentiments of Orsino.[14] In this way, virtue in love is extended to women; love's transforming power is made universal. The fact that the contradictory statements about women's faith and fickleness in comparison to men's come from the girl-boy Viola-Cesario helps to create the illusion that, at least in matters of the heart, men and women are more or less on an equal footing. Through the boy-actor masquerading as a woman imitating a man, Shakespeare attempts to erase sexual difference: "I am all the daughters of my father's house, / And all the brothers too" (2.4.121-22).

But because this illusion of universality requires the skills of a boy-actor, the mode of production itself accords the masculine a peculiar privilege. Here we see a very basic sense in which "any theory of the subject has always been appropriated by the 'masculine'"; in this Elizabethan script, subjective experience is constituted in masculine terms by men.[15] Thus, afflicted with his own version of Malvolio's self-love, Orsino too claims the "trick of singularity" in love (2.5.151), by defining himself as lover in the very manner that men in patriarchal society have defined themselves, the self, and subjectivity itself—as not feminine.[16] Indeed, in the key exchange with Cesario, cited earlier, Orsino predicates the depth of his desire and his very being on his

---

[14] For the reference to Patient Griselda and further implications of this image, see Catherine Belsey's "Disrupting Sexual Difference: Meaning and Gender in the Comedies," in *Alternative Shakespeares*, ed. John Drakakis (New York: Methuen, 1985), 186-87.

[15] Notable among the treatments of masculine appropriation are such diverse ones as those by Peter Erickson in *Patriarchal Structures in Shakespeare's Drama* (Berkeley: Univ. of California Press, 1985), 1-13; by Lisa Jardine, 9-36; by Phyllis Rackin, 31-32; and by Linda Woodbridge in *Women and the English Renaissance: Literature and the Nature of Womankind, 1540-1620* (Urbana and Chicago: Univ. of Illinois Press, 1984), 152-56.

[16] Greenblatt notes that "if a crucial step in male individuation is separation from the female, this separation is enacted inversely in the rites of cross-dressing; characters like Rosalind and Viola pass through the state of being men in order to become women. Shakespearean women are in this sense the representation of Shakespearean men, the projected mirror images of masculine self-differentiation" (92). But when is Viola seen as a woman *again*? Whereas she remains Cesario, the boy-actor has undergone the passage through femininity to masculinity—and in this case, he never closes the circle by re-appearing in female guise. At the end of *Twelfth Night* the boy-actor remains true to himself; indeed, even in developing the heroine, the text manifests an unconscious association between individuation and maleness.

difference from the woman, the mere object of desire.[17] In contrast to Olivia's, Orsino's passion makes him more himself: "Make no compare / Between that love a woman can bear me / And that I owe Olivia" (2.4.100-102).

Of course, it is not quite so simple; as we have seen, Orsino likes to have it both ways. Even his appropriation of the oceanic capacity of the feminine exposes the extent to which this "man is the measure of all things," including femininity. There is no lack of self-possession here, but a fruitless attempt to possess or appropriate all through the imaginative capacity (often for role-playing or at least posturing) that love occasions. Unfortunately for Orsino, who seems to believe his protestations at least as much as he presumably believes that Olivia is the only socially suitable match in town (5.1.110 ff.), his love's fancy does not extend much beyond the Petrarchan conceits and conventional courtly attitudes of the masculine lover.[18] Moreover, since Orsino's various declarations, unlike Olivia's or for that matter Viola's, are made *in absentia* and in isolation or in company supposedly of his own sex, they underscore masculine self-absorption and self-affirmation in love.[19]

Certainly, given Orsino's rather sudden change of heart at the end, Viola's comment on women's being "as true of heart as we [men]" (2.4.105) suggests the instability of all desiring subjects, masculine as well as feminine. But it is through the image of woman that Shakespeare figures this lack of control, as we see in Orsino's long-awaited confrontation with Olivia in the final scene. Only when he has been repeatedly and undeniably thwarted, does he come in person and then prove the depth of his unrequited love by the will to murder—not the unfaithful woman herself but the object of ostensibly feminine desire: "But this your minion, whom I know you love, / And whom, by heaven, I swear I tender dearly, / Him will I tear out of that cruel eye / Where he sits crowned in his master's spite" (5.1.123-26). Orsino's violent verbal attack on Olivia and his threat against Cesario reveal almost as much as the play's omission of Cesario's transformation back into Viola. Most obviously, they cast all responsibility for his troubles on women, actual or disguised. They expose, furthermore, what Coppélia Kahn calls "his fear of losing himself in passion." That fear—particularly masculine, as I see it—is underscored by the threat against Cesario, the annihilation of Orsino's own ambiguous object of desire; Orsino unmasks once again his need to "defend against Eros as a threat

---

[17] Relevant to this point is Toril Moi's discussion of Kristevan "positionality" in *Sexual/Textual Politics: Feminist Literary Theory* (New York: Methuen, 1985), 166-67.
[18] Williamson, 35.
[19] Kahn, 226-27.

to the integrity and stability of the self."[20] Whereas Olivia hauls forth a priest to declare and ratify the love relation she wants (a marital one both we and undoubtedly Queen Elizabeth might question),[21] Orsino's anti-social behavior, which culminates in the threat of violence against the boy-girl he loves, exposes masculine paranoia about the loss of self in love and about the indefinition of his own desire. Indeed, the indeterminacy of his own desire is suggested by Cesario (the boy playing a girl playing a boy), the target standing in for Olivia—who by the way is also played by a boy. Though the play certainly exposes many of the inconsistencies and contradictions of masculine love like Orsino's, the Shakespearean solution, the play's resolution, is nonetheless problematic, especially from a modern perspective.

The problems derive in large part from the comedy's mode of production; the boy-actor who plays Viola-Cesario remains a boy even after Orsino has declared his "share in this most happy wrack" (5.1.258). I cannot quite agree with Coppélia Kahn about "what Viola herself never forgets: that no matter how the duke and countess see her, she is not androgynous but irreducibly a woman."[22] In fact, Viola's witty disclaimer—"a little thing would make me tell them how much I lack of a man" (3.4.307-9)—is a two-edged sword, not only undercutting the female character's masculine bravado but also underscoring the boy-actor's irreducible, or at least incipient, manhood.[23] Though Orsino seems to deny it in his last lines, he finds his "mistress and his fancy's queen" in the boy Cesario, and not in Viola (5.1.377)—at least in terms of the visual tableau, a fact somewhat obscured in Phyllis Rackin's excellent article.[24] The theatrical presence of the boy-actor as a boy manifests what, in *The Daughter's Seduction*, Jane Gallop calls "homosexuality" or the "sexuality of sames"—precisely the effect that Lisa Jardine claims the boy-players generally evoked, according to Renaissance commentators, both homophobic and otherwise.[25] The dramatic resolution of the sexual play and the sexual tensions belies any accep-

---

[20] Ibid.

[21] On the issue of Elizabeth and marriage, see Marcus, passim, as well as Greenblatt, 68-69.

[22] Kahn, 228.

[23] In contrast, Rackin notes the boy-player's economic dependency, an extra-dramatic extension of the feminine role, which underscores the indeterminacy of the boy-heroine both on and off the stage (33).

[24] Rackin, 38.

[25] On "homosexuality" in this sense, see Jane Gallop's "Impertinent Questions," in *Psychoanalysis and Feminism: The Daughter's Seduction* (Ithaca: Cornell Univ. Press, 1982), 80-91, especially 84. On the matter of the erotic effect of the boy-players, see Lisa Jardine's provocative argument (9-36).

tance of an Other by Orsino; it still relies on what Peter Erickson sees in *As You Like It* as the "security of male bodies mirroring and confirming a common physical identity."[26] Oddly enough, by having Orsino accept his lover untransformed (in some ways a radical move compared to *As You Like It*'s conservative ritualism and mystification of marriage),[27] Shakespeare replicates the very narcissism and self-absorption of masculine love that the play supposedly unmasks. In this sense, the self-expulsion of the ill-willed, vengeful, self-loving Malvolio is the text's greatest deception.

Furthermore, Erickson's claim that the comedies' narcissistic mirroring "depends precisely on relief from the specifically genital demand associated with the opposite sex" is especially applicable to *Twelfth Night*, where the appearance of Viola's male twin Sebastian underscores the all-male mode of production.[28] According to Kahn, "In *Twelfth Night* ... the twin and other doubles function at first as projections of emotional obstacles to identity and then, in Viola and Sebastian, as the fulfillment of a wish for a way around the obstacles."[29] But the all-male Elizabethan production and its textual inscription in Orsino's remarks—that in Cesario "all is semblative a woman's part" (1.5.34) and that only "other habits" make the woman (5.1.386)—complicate the fulfillment of Viola's, the play's, and the critic-reader's wish that "imagination ... prove true" (3.4.384). As Phyllis Rackin explains, "without the illusion (Viola's disguise as a boy), the right characters would not have fallen in love; without the reality, they could not have married. In the figure of Sebastian, gender and sex correspond, both within the play world and between the play and the audience."[30] Sebastian apparently resolves the play's problems because in him theatrical and actual sexual identity are one and the same; for the same reason, I maintain, the object of Orsino's transferred affections never transforms himself from Cesario back to that theatrical illusion—the girl Viola. Even though the transformation only requires the boy-actor's resumption of his "woman's weeds" (5.1.271), there is in a meta-dramatic sense more truth in the undisguised Viola's remaining Cesario, in her showing herself—like Sebastian, but in another way—both "maid and man" (5.1.261).

---

[26] Peter Erickson, 5.

[27] Regarding the ending of *As You Like It* and that play's quite different construction of gender, see my article on "The 'Unexpressive She': Is There Really a Rosalind?," *Journal of Dramatic Theory and Criticism* 2, no. 2 (1988): 41–52.

[28] Peter Erickson, 5. Erickson's insightful comments have meta-dramatic significance that he suggests but often does not discuss in detail.

[29] Kahn, 225.

[30] Rackin, 38.

The uneasy Renaissance conflation of two "contradictory accounts of the origin of gender" that Greenblatt outlines in his discussion of the play may underlie some of the "slippage" in identities. In one version, the domination of male or female seed determines identity; "a double nature becomes single." In the other theory, "the unitary genital structure," conceived as essentially male, "divides into two distinct forms, internal [female] and external [male]"; "a single nature becomes double."[31] But how do we explain the relative values the play assigns to and by gender? Along with Malvolio's accusations of "Notorious wrong" by Olivia (5.1.327-28), who is at the end the one theatrically disguised boy remaining on stage, the image of Orsino with Cesario corroborates the traditional privilege the text accords to masculinity, as well as its imputation of duplicity to femininity. The bias of the text in this case is not nature's "bias" (5.1.258), but the culture's—akin to men's age-old wish for a single-sex utopia, a world without women.[32] The minor Sebastian-Antonio plot exposes this sub-text. Antonio's homoerotic infatuation with Sebastian, his "willing love" (3.3.11), is an unmasked version of Orsino's attraction to Cesario and, again, given the mode of production, even of the relationship between Sebastian and Olivia. In fact, it brings to the fore the all-male mode of production. When Antonio mistakes Viola-Cesario for the adored Sebastian, the error involves an indictment not only of beauty without virtue, but also of the disjunction between exterior and interior—in other words, of Viola's masquerade as "unkind" or unnatural: "Thou hast, Sebastian, done good feature shame. / In nature there's no blemish but the mind; / None can be call'd deform'd but the unkind" (3.4.375-77, 377n). Is it an accident that Antonio directs his accusations at a female character, who has already acknowledged her disguise "a wickedness" and herself a "monster"?[33]

---

[31] Greenblatt, 84.

[32] See Greenblatt's explanation of the "metaphor from the game of bowls" and nature's bias; heterosexuality is conceived as a normal, "happy swerving" (68). Greenblatt's argument is fascinating, and the pattern he describes does indeed resemble the plot of a Shakespearean comedy (86). But unlike Greenblatt I would argue that, however problematic the Renaissance accounts of gender, the valuation of the genders is less so; at the very least the second theory of gender—with its play upon the male organ, the latter's inward or outward, hidden or open, disposition—is less ambiguous about the primacy of male nature and hence of masculinity. Indeed, if one combines this view of sexuality with Viola's and Antonio's talk about truth, the correspondence between interior and exterior, one finds that women are never quite themselves. *Twelfth Night*, as well as the context that gave rise to it, tends to promote the truth that shows itself—in Sebastian and in Viola-Cesario, emblem of the theater of boys and men that represents the world of women and men. For a provocative historicist reading that differs from Greenblatt's, see Howard, 430-33.

[33] Rackin, 37.

The moment recalls Viola's own words to the Captain in act 1, words that conjure up the traditional masculine suspicion of feminine beauty: "There is a fair behaviour in thee, Captain; / And though that nature with a beauteous wall / Doth oft close in pollution, yet of thee / I will believe thou hast a mind that suits / With this thy fair and outward character" (1.3.47–51). Indeed, the proof that Viola is a virtuous woman, that she is worthy to be loved, and that she is everything she claims and seems to be requires not only her reunion with the brother she imitates to the life (3.4.389–93), but also her conforming to the masculine standards of truth reiterated by Antonio—an absolute correspondence between interior and exterior, spirit and body, even word and thing. Is it then an accident that Antonio, whose very presence exposes the inability of the theatrical illusion to achieve such a correspondence, "is left out in the cold," displaced by a second boy-actor masquerading as a woman, the Lady Olivia, without any authority calling to "entreat *him* to a peace" (5.1.379; emphasis mine)?[34] The ultimate corroboration of social order and expectations through the mediation of laws conceived as natural or providential makes this text's intersection with our own culture a problematic one. Though the "pleasure" of the play is less concerned with "truth of identity" than the "titillation" aroused by the "dangers that follow from the disruption of sexual difference,"[35] this comedy also closes down the possibilities implicit in Viola-Cesario's admission of sexual indeterminacy—"I am not what I am" (3.1.143)—and in Antonio's undisguised and unresolved homoerotic attraction.

Why then has Shakespeare refused to return to the initial illusion in

---

[34] Greenblatt notes that, though Renaissance church and state sanctioned only the heterosexual consummation of desire, "it did not follow that desire was inherently heterosexual. The delicious confusions of *Twelfth Night* depend on the mobility of desire. And if poor Antonio is left out in the cold, Orsino does in a sense get his Cesario" (93). But though Greenblatt mentions also the way in which the all-male cast of Shakespeare's theater embodies a double-sided Renaissance view of gender, he eschews the implications, for us, of the inscription in the text of this mode of production and this construction of gender. What values are inherent in these "delicious confusions," this "set of exchanges and transformations"? To formulate the matter at its most extreme, do the play's exile of the explicitly homosexual and the enforced masquerade of woman within marriage (or, in another sense, the absence of women altogether) recommend themselves, as immediately and unequivocally as Greenblatt implies, to the modern reader? What does it mean to accept Greenblatt's brilliant "corollary" theory about the play—"that men love women precisely *as representations*, a love the original performances of these plays literalized in the person of the boy actor" (93)? Pleasurable, "delicious confusions" perhaps—but not neutral ones, not ones without present ideological efficacy, given the place of Shakespeare in our culture.

[35] Belsey, 185.

which boy plays girl, the illusion that corroborates the traditional social union of male and female in marriage? I propose that, although other Shakespearean comedies may also manifest uneasiness toward their feisty heroines, *Twelfth Night* exiles its heroine—perhaps more thoroughly than it exiles Malvolio himself. Herein lies the danger of a supposedly transcendant Shakespeare, and herein lies as well the problem for the modern reader (or viewer or performer), who wishes to avoid complicity in this text's "bias." Ultimately there is not even the pretense of a sovereign female consciousness. Viola remains in masculine guise because that is the sign of her truth; Orsino can trust her only insofar as she is "masculine." Indeed, in the end, we realize that the play's model for true love is not heterosexual, but rather "homosexual" in Gallop's sense—the love of Antonio for Sebastian and, by a comforting displacement, of Orsino for Cesario *nee* Viola. In contrast to the androgynous epilogue of *As You Like It*, the last of Shakespeare's high comedies elevates the heroine by eradicating her, by letting her be absorbed into the masculine; for as Viola herself says, and as the play's dramatic illusion underscores, women "die, even as they to perfection grow" (2.4.40).

Augsburg College

REBECCA BUSHNELL

Tyranny and Effeminacy in Early Modern England

RENAISSANCE STATECRAFT LITERATURE IS DEEPLY SCARRED BY THE image of the depraved tyrant, meant to serve as a mirror to a virtuous king. Erasmus's picture of the tyrant is positively apocalyptic; speaking of the duty of the prince's tutor to illustrate vividly the horrors of tyranny, the author commands:

> Now let him bring out the opposite side by showing a frightful, loathsome beast, formed of a dragon, wolf, lion, viper, bear and like creatures; with six hundred eyes all over it, teeth everywhere, fearful from all angles, and with hooked claws; with never satiated hunger, fattened on human vitals, and reeking with human blood.[1]

In statecraft rhetoric, the king is the man of reason, while the tyrant is one driven by passion, and desire for sex and money, to waste and pillage his country. La Primaudaye's strictures in his *French Academie* typify such an opposition:

> As a good king conformeth himselfe to the laws of God and nature, so a tyrant treadeth them underfoote ... the one spareth the honor of chaste women, the other triumpheth in their shame ... the one burdeneth his [people] as little as may be, and then upon publike necessitie, the other suppeth up their blood, gnaweth their bones and sucketh the marrow of his subjects to satisfie his desires.[2]

What, then, can be called "feminine" in this image of the tyrant, who

---

[1] *The Education of A Christian Prince*, trans. Lester K. Born (New York: W. W. Norton, 1968), 163.
[2] *The French Academie ... by Peter de La Primaudaye, ... newly translated into English by T. B.* (London: 1589), 637.

runs rampant through his country, stealing, murdering, and doing violence to women? Recall that at the same time as they dwell on women's frailty and vulnerability, the numerous attacks against women in the sixteenth and seventeenth centuries also express a fear of women's power over men, invested in women's very irrationality and capacity for voracious desire. Natalie Davis succinctly summarizes the usual charges against women in the period: "The female sex was thought the disorderly one par excellence in early modern Europe. 'Une beste imparfaicte,' went one adage, 'sans foy, sans loy, sans craincte, sans constance [an imperfect beast, without faith, without law, without fear, inconstant]'."[3] With the exception of fearlessness, this description exactly matches the typical portrait of the tyrant, who is a monster and a shifter of shapes, who rules without rule, law, trust, or reason. The tyrannical indulgence of pleasure was itself thought to be "effeminate"—even if that indulgence involved violence against women.

While the connection between tyranny and femininity is mostly implicit in statecraft literature, in Renaissance drama tyrants are explicitly identified with women. This identification gave the male playwright a way of showing how frightening a tyrant is, as something irrational, uncontrollable, and fundamentally incomprehensible. At the same time, the contradictory cultural value of the feminine, whereby women are strong in their irrationality and yet weak and thus easily mastered by men, also permitted the playwright to suggest that tyrants *are* eventually controllable. Tracts on tyranny allow us to define the dimensions of the Renaissance descriptions of tyranny and femininity which can be aligned. However, in some early modern English plays, and particularly in *Macbeth*, the stage tyrant is directly "feminized" by being subjected to a powerful woman who is at the same time his double; that is, the tyrant is "feminized" by being mastered by a woman and by resembling a woman: irrational, passionate, disorderly, hypocritical. (I prefer to make a distinction between the figure of the female ruler in the Renaissance and the figure of the feminized tyrant, although they are related in a mind such as John Knox's: That is, I am concerned with how the rise to power and failure of the male stage tyrant is traditionally linked to his "unmanning." Obviously, the link between tyranny and femininity in Elizabethan drama is complicated by the presence of Elizabeth herself.)

Statecraft treatises take it for granted that the virtues of the prince will be "masculine" virtues. Tyndale, in *The Obedience of a Christian Man*, proposes that a conventional tyrant would be better than an

---

[3] Natalie Zemon Davis, *Society and Culture in Early Modern France* (Stanford: Stanford Univ. Press, 1975), 124.

"effeminate" king, implying, in effect, that effeminacy is a worse sort of tyranny:

> For a tyrant, though he do wrong unto the good, yet he punessheth the evil and maketh all men obeye.... A kinge that is soft as silke and effeminate / that is to saye turned to the nature of a woman / what with his owne lustes / which are as the longinges of a woman with child / so ... shal be moch moare grevous unto the realme then a right tyrant.[4]

Elizabeth herself was careful to circumvent the problems raised by her sex, emphasizing, as Montrose says, the

> masculine strength of her body politic, so that she might pronounce to her people: "I have always so behaved myself that, under God, I have placed my chiefest strength and safeguard in the loyal hearts and good will of my subjects.... I know I have the body of a weak and feeble woman, but I have the heart and stomach of a king, and of a king of England, too."[5]

Thus, while she admits that her body is that of a woman, she stresses that her "affections" or emotions are masculine, thus implicitly at once both strong and under control.

The most notorious and explicit tract associating femininity with tyranny is John Knox's *First Blaste of the Trumpet Against the Monstrous Regiment of Women*. Knox liberally cites Chrysostom in making his argument that women's rule is inherently tyrannical, not only because they cannot be anything except usurpers, but also because their minds and bodies are given to vice, desire, and irrationality. While he may start from the premise that women are inherently "weak and feeble" and thus not suited to rule, Knox quickly reveals his deeper fears: "Nature, I say, doth paint them furthe to be weake, fraile, impacient, feble and foolishe, and experience hath declared them to be unconstant, variable, cruell, and lacking the spirit of counsel and regiment."[6] It is clear that for Knox, although women's vices in "nature" are those associated with their weakness or childishness, once they are in power, those vices are transformed into precisely the typical vices of "mascu-

---

[4] William Tyndale, *The Obedience of a Christian Man* (London: 1528), fol. xxxiv r.

[5] Cited by Louis A. Montrose, "*A Midsummer Night's Dream* and the Shaping Fantasies of Elizabethan Culture: Gender, Power, Form," in *Rewriting the Renaissance: The Discourses of Sexual Difference in Early Modern Europe*, ed. Margaret W. Ferguson, Maureen Quilligan, and Nancy J. Vickers (Chicago: Univ. of Chicago Press, 1986), 80.

[6] John Knox, *The First Blaste of the Trumpet Against the Monstrous Regiment of Women* (1558), 10.

line" tyrants: cruelty, irrationality, and changeability. The transformation results from women's "frailty" being equated with irrationality, which engenders vice. Citing Chrysostom, Knox writes that, as in the case of the tyrant whose soul is overruled by desire,

> woman can never be the best governour, by reason that she, being spoiled of the spirit of regiment, can never attein to that degree to be called or judged a good governour; because in the nature of all woman, lurketh such vices, as in good governours are not tolerable. Which the same writer expresseth in these words: Womankind (saith he), is rashe and foolhardy, and their covetousness is like the golf of hell, that is, insaciable.[7]

At the same time as they dwell on their frailty, the numerous attacks against women in the sixteenth and seventeenth centuries also emphasize women's improper power, called "shrewishness," which originates in lust and irrationality.[8] Woman is represented as framed in nature as what the "male" tyrant becomes: the principle of the lower and ferocious power of desire usurping the sovereignty of reason.[9] In their review of the controversy about women in England from 1540 to 1640, Katherine Henderson and Barbara McManus cite as the two most popular stereotypes of woman that of the whore, "enticing, sexually, insatiable, and deceitful in the service of her lust," and that of the shrew, "willful, scolding and domineering."[10] The two images are often found conjoined, since women's sexuality is linked to the power they are seen to exert over men (partly because a free tongue is associ-

---

[7] Knox, 25. John Aylmer, in *An Harborowe for Faithfull and Trewe Subjectes, agaynst the late blowne blaste concerning the government of women* (Strasbourg: 1559), is forced ultimately to make the kind of arguments that are offered by later formulators of absolute sovereignty. Aylmer at first will not concede that it is "unnatural" for women to rule, using history against Knox's argument for nature; the only inferiority of women he conceded in nature is physical weakness. Yet he is ultimately brought to argue that the character of the person is irrelevant to rule: so, as he says, "Wherefore, though there be some faults to be found in this Theodora and other: yet proveth it not that thei may not reigne, for it is a fallax *ab accidente* to say she was naught: ergo, she might not rule: for that hangeth not uppon the rule, that she was naught, but upon the persone" (sig. f2r).

[8] See Linda Woodbridge, *Women and the English Renaissance: Literature and the Nature of Womankind, 1540–1620* (Urbana: Univ. of Illinois Press, 1984), 214.

[9] Davis comments: "The lower ruled the higher within women, then, and if she was given her way, she would want to rule over those above her outside"(125).

[10] Katherine Usher Henderson and Barbara F. McManus, *Half Humankind: Contexts and Texts of the Controversy about Women in England, 1540–1640* (Urbana: Univ. of Illinois Press, 1985), 47.

ated with sexual incontinence).[11] The woman who controls a man through her sexuality is seen as committing an outrage equivalent to the tyrant's rape of wives and daughters: in each case uncontrolled sexuality is the image and expression of an improper power. So Henry Hutton, in his *Follie's Anatomie*, presents a satire on a woman in whom sexuality, monstrosity, and sovereignty are seen as inseparable: in this "woman creature most insatiate / See the incarnate monster of her sex, / Play the virago, unashamed, perplext, / See Omphale her effeminated king, / Basely captive make him do anything."[12] One of the most popular images of female sovereignty in the medieval and early modern period was that of Phyllis riding Aristotle, where Aristotle is shown so overcome by the seductiveness of Phyllis that she can persuade him to let her ride him as she would a beast. As Davis comments on this image: "Here youth overthrows age, and sexual passion, dry sterile philosophy; nature surmounts reason, and the female, the male."[13]

As Hutton's image of Hercules and Omphale and the story of Aristotle and Phyllis indicate, "shrewish" behavior in women was seen to be complemented by "effeminacy" in men,[14] where effeminacy could mean many things. In some cases, as in Tyndale, effeminacy means weakness, submissiveness, or lack of courage. In other cases, it is a love of pleasure which is seen to make a man "effeminate": The author of the *Vindiciae contra tyrannos* speaks of a tyrant's introducing pleasure to his people by setting up a "multiplicity of taverns, gaming houses, masks, stage plays, brothel houses, and all other licentious superfluities that might effeminate and bastardise noble spirits."[15] La Perrière, in the *Mirrour of Policie*, often observes that pleasure makes a man womanish;[16] he cites the example of the tyrant Sardanapulus,

who did wind thred, spinne yearne, used his looking glass, and

---

[11] See Lisa Jardine, *Still Harping on Daughters: Women and Drama in the Age of Shakespeare* (Sussex, England : Harvester Press, 1983), 123–24.

[12] Henry Hutton, *Follie's Anatomie, or Satyres and Satyricall Epigrams* (London: 1619), sig. b6v.

[13] Davis, 135–36; see also Arlene W. Saxenhouse, *Women in the History of Political Thought: Ancient Greece to Machiavelli* (New York: Praeger, 1985), 153.

[14] See Woodbridge, who notes that "comment on male effeminacy in Renaissance literature was complemented, if immensely overshadowed, by comment on aggressiveness in women" (171). Woodbridge also describes how "two prominent literary traditions dealing with love and marriage, the courtly love tradition and the women wearing the breeches, portray men as weaklings helplessly languishing under the tyrannous rule of formidably powerful women" (218).

[15] *A Defense of Liberty Against Tyrants: A Translation of the Vindiciae contra tyrannos*, by Junius Brutus, intro. and ed. by Harold J. Laski (New York: Burt Franklin, 1924; repr. 1972), 185.

[16] Guillaume La Perrière, *The Mirrour of Policie* (London: 1598), sig. c2r–v.

was skilfull in nothing else but in eating, drinking, wantonesse, and sleeping, and never performed any manly act in all his life, but when he burnt himself, by which act he delivered his subjects from a monstrous Hermaphrodite, who was neither true man nor true woman, being in sexe a man and in heart a woman.[17]

A more general equation between vice and effeminacy can also be found in many tracts of the age. The "Hic Mulier, Haec Vir" conflict in 1620, waged in pamphlets between the mannish woman and the womanish man, ended with the final word of Hic Mulier in *Mulde Sack or the Apologie of Hic Mulier*, listing categories of men who have fallen into vice as the "monstrous broode of the feminine masculine";[18] here all kinds of vices, from those of the lawyer to those of Papists and Puritans, are lumped together as rendering a man "effeminate." Finally, Erasmus, in his *Education of a Christian Prince*, suggests that "it is the mark of the tyrant—and womanish, too—to follow the unbridled will of your mind."[19] Thus, "effeminacy" in man matches the figure of the "disorderly" woman, who is ruled by the lower power of desire rather than the masculine principle of reason. The humanist makes the connection with tyranny and effeminacy far more explicit in his piece on kings and fools, where he complains,

> The guardians of a prince aim never to let him become a man. The nobility, battening on public corruption, endeavor to make him as effeminate as possible by pleasure lest he should know what a prince ought to know. Villages are burnt, fields are devastated, temples pillaged, innocent citizens slaughtered, all things temporal and spiritual are confounded, while the king plays dice, or amuses himself with fools, or with hunting or drinking.[20]

The prince's "effeminate" indulgence in pleasure is thus seen as inevitably accompanied by the kind of cruelty and destruction commonly attributed to tyrants.

The association between femininity and tyranny in Renaissance culture can thus be perceived in two related images: the figure of the lustful and shrewish woman as the mirror image of a tyrannical ruler, and the figure of the prince subjected to his desire as he rules others

---

[17] La Perrière, sig. h2r.
[18] *Mulde Sack or the Apologie of Hic Mulier* (London: 1620), sig. c2v.
[19] Erasmus, 190.
[20] Cited and translated by Robert P. Adams, *The Better Part of Valour: More, Erasmus, Colet and Vives, on Humanism, War and Peace, 1496–1535* (Seattle: Univ. of Washington Press, 1962), 91.

tyrannically.²¹ The use of femininity as a representation of tyranny works on several levels of Renaissance analogical political thinking. First, insofar as the body, pictured as a hierarchy of head and body, is a symbol of the state, the "naturally" irrational woman becomes a symbol in herself of the tyrannical rule of desire. Second, insofar as the family was considered a symbol for the state and its essential building block, the "mannish" authority of the shrew and the submission of the husband to her served as a model of tyranny, which is the opposite of legitimate sovereignty.²² The image of "the woman on top" is not just a figure of a rebellion from beneath, from the lower orders of society; it is symbolic of the problem at the heart of sovereignty, located in the uncertainty of reason's mastery of desire, when the "weakness" of the lower part is itself strength, breaking the bonds of rule and law.

While statecraft literature thus implies the effeminacy of the tyrant in terms of the culture's definitions of tyranny, it is only in the drama that we see the "womanish" tyrant fully figured, when the tyrant's passion is staged through his subjection to a woman. In the English theater, even when we see the tyrant unlawfully seize a woman—usually a sister, a cousin, or another's wife—it generally results in his marrying her and being enslaved by his passion for her. This comes up quite early on in sixteenth-century tragedy in a play such as Thomas Preston's *Cambyses*; this tyrant's original vice is drunkenness, which then leads him into an extraordinary list of violent crimes, including killing a baby before his parents and flaying a man alive on stage. This list climaxes in his incestuous infatuation with and marriage to the nameless "Lady" who is his first cousin.

In *Cambyses*, the occasion of Cambyses' attraction to the Lady is his being struck by Cupid's arrow, for Venus's amusement. Cambyses interprets the metaphor (as we have, in fact, seen it literalized):

My meaning is that beauty yours my heart with love doth wound;

---

²¹ There are even some cases of mothers who usurp the proper authority from their princely sons, while introducing them to soft pleasures: the author of the *Vindiciae contra tyrannos* attacks women "who so educated their sons (as the queens of the house of the Medicis in these latter times) during their minority, that attaining to more maturity, their only care was to glut themselves in pleasures and delights, so that the whole management of their affairs remained in the hands of their mothers, or of their minions, servants and officers" (184).

²² Cf. Davis, 127–28: "In the little world of the family, with its conspicuous tension between intimacy and power, the larger matters of political and social order could find ready symbolization.... Kings and political theorists saw the increasing legal subjection of wives to their husbands (and of children to their parents) as a guarantee of the obedience of both men and women to the slowly centralizing state."

> To give me love mind to content, my heart hath you out found;
> And you are she must be my wife, else shall I end my days.
> Consent to this and be my queen, to wear the crown with praise.
> (9.63–66)[23]

Cambyses' statement presents a contradictory image of who is controlling whom here. On one level, he has been presented as Venus's plaything, the object of her amusement. Rhetorically, the actions of Cupid and Venus are translated into the beauty of the Lady; thus it is suggested that she dominates him, and if he cannot have her, he shall end his days. Yet the tyrant in turn insists that she must be his wife. He commands her to consent. When she refuses, saying that he "may not" in this case have his request, for it is against "nature's course," Cambyses fumes: "May I not? Nay then, I will, by all the gods I vow; / And I will marry thee as wife. This is mine answer now" (9.77–78). Thus his being overcome by love and beauty here is transformed into an expression of his will, implicitly combining the two meanings of sexual desire and simple volition. He is mastered by the Lady, but then his desire for her, in turn, becomes a means of dramatizing his power in the face of anyone who might resist his wishes.

Cambyses' infatuation with and marriage to his Lady, then, marks the apex of his tyrannical career, representing the epitome of his power and the fundamental instability of his power, since it is invested in his love for his Lady. It is true that this tyrant is not so infatuated that he cannot condemn the Lady to death at once when she complains about Cambyses' murder of his own brother Smerdis. He reacts to her saying that he should have shown love and not cruelty to his brother with a hatred as intense as his former love. Immediately after the murder of his Lady Cambyses himself dies, "accidentally" killed by his sword—a coincidence which suggests the Lady's death is closely linked with his own. Cambyses' taking of the Lady is thus both the stunning climax of his lawlessness, which expresses his power, *and* the apparent source of his defeat, insofar as it figures the weakness in his link to a feminine other.

A much later play, Philip Massinger's *The Roman Actor*, takes the crude outlines of the Cambyses tyrant and explores it with more subtlety. This play tells the story of the Roman emperor Domitian, notorious for his lust as well as his cruelty, who falls passionately in love with another man's wife, the lady Domitia. This relationship goes beyond the threat of Cambyses' incest to emphasize the tyrant Domitian's infatua-

---

[23] Text is that of *Drama of the English Renaissance*, Vol. 1: *The Tudor Period*, ed. Russell A. Fraser and Norman Rabkin (New York: Macmillan, 1976).

tion with what is in essence his female double, the Domitia to his Domitian, for, unlike Cambyses' good Lady, Domitia parallels Domitian in cruelty and lust in the course of the play. Further, she taunts Domitian constantly with her knowledge of her power over him, boasting: "yet I to thy teeth / When circled with thy guards, thy rods, thy axes, / And all the ensigns of thy boasted power / Will say, Domitian, nay add to it Caesar, / Is a weak, feeble man, a bondman to / His violent passions, and in that my slave" (5.1.44–49).[24] Domitian, in turn, compares himself to the hero Hercules who served and labored under the Lydian Omphale, when he notoriously did women's work in woman's garb (5.1.55–56). Thinking to free himself finally of Domitia, Domitian signs her death warrant, which amounts to the signing of his own, insofar as the death warrant is the catalyst to a revenge plot on the part of all those whom Domitian has wronged. Having attempted to destroy Domitia, Domitian believes he has regained his sovereignty and autonomy, but in effect he destroys himself because he *is* Domitia (who is herself hauled off to judgment at the end).

The Shakespearean version of the uxorious tyrant characteristically complicates this basic pattern of the tyrant who finds himself, as Hercules to Omphale, slave to a woman and identified with a female self. I am referring, of course, to Macbeth and his Lady. Along with Richard III, Macbeth can be pointed to as one of Shakespeare's most unequivocal tyrants. When Malcolm gives Macbeth the full complement of labels traditionally associated with tyranny, he accuses him of being luxurious; however, we see no direct evidence in the play of Macbeth's supposed "luxuriousness" or lustfulness. The relationship with his wife can be read as luxuriousness insofar as he is uxorious: that is, according to the pattern exemplified in the earlier sixteenth-century plays, as well as in misogynist tracts, subjection to one's wife signals one's being mastered by lust for her.

At the same time that the tyrant's uxoriousness is introduced, however, it is complicated by the confusion as well as opposition between masculinity and femininity.[25] When Lady Macbeth asks the spirits to unsex her and fill her from top to toe full of direst cruelty, her plea is usually interpreted as a rejection of her femininity in favor of a

---

[24] Text is that of *Drama of the English Renaissance*, Vol. 2: *The Stuart Period*, ed. Russell A. Fraser and Norman Rabkin (New York: Macmillan, 1976).

[25] Robert Kimbrough, "Macbeth: The Prisoner of Gender," *Shakespeare Studies* 16 (1983): 175–90, offers a good example of the liberal version of the tragedy's depiction of the "personal and social destructiveness of polarized masculinity and femininity" (177); for him Shakespeare's "works move toward liberating humanity from the prisons created by inclusive and exclusive gender labeling" (175). I would suggest rather that Shakespeare uses gender as a critique of political conventions.

masculine code of blood and ambition. Yet, while Lady Macbeth asks the spirits to unsex her, she also asks them to convert her female sexuality into a form of cruelty—milk to gall—to change what is seen in her as "feminine" weakness into feminine power, thus fulfilling John Knox's fear that while women in nature are weak, in experience they are "variable and cruel."[26] More than simply "manly," her actions are shrewish, when she commands her husband to "hie thee hither, / That I may pour my spirits in thine ear, / And chastise with the valor of my tongue / All that impedes thee from the golden round" (1.5.25-28).[27] Her behavior is not entirely "unfeminine" but rather a fulfillment of men's fears of what happens when the nature of women is freed.[28]

The Lady's scene with Macbeth that follows this invocation emphasizes Macbeth's effeminacy which accompanies her shrewishness, even as she fashions a model of manliness for him to follow.[29] Any movement that Macbeth makes away from murdering Duncan his Lady marks as unmanliness, although it is implicitly unmanly or effeminate that he should submit to her plans for the murder. When he first begins to resist going ahead with the murder, she challenges him in a contradictory way with an accusation of effeminacy (being so green and pale)[30] and of an implicit failure in his love for her—a love which defines his uxoriousness: if he fails, she says, "From this time / Such I account thy love" (1.7.38-39). Macbeth clearly perceives the content of this speech as a threat to his manliness. Indeed, it is threatening that she

---

[26] Janet Adelman, " 'Born of Woman': Fantasies of Maternal Power in *Macbeth*," in *Cannibals, Witches and Divorce: Estranging the Renaissance: Selected Papers from the English Institute, 1985* (N.S. no. 11), ed. Marjorie Garber (Baltimore: Johns Hopkins Univ. Press, 1987), argues that in the image of inviting the spirits to suck gall from her breast, Lady Macbeth "localizes the image of maternal danger" (98).

[27] The texts of Shakespeare used here are from *William Shakespeare: The Complete Works*, ed. Alfred Harbage (Baltimore: Penguin, 1969).

[28] Harry Berger, Jr., in "Text Against Performance: The Example of *Macbeth*," in *The Power of Forms in the English Renaissance*, ed. Stephen Greenblatt (Norman: Pilgrim Books, 1982), argues that in the case of the Witches and Lady Macbeth, "contending so vigorously against milky weakness and naked frailty, their language expresses a 'lust for maleness' which, as Joel Fineman ingeniously observes, is itself female. They can no more defeminize themselves than can Lady Macbeth" (73). Dennis Biggins, "Sexuality, Witchcraft and Violence in *Macbeth*," *Shakespeare Studies* 8 (1975): 255-77, also suggests that "witchcraft is associated with sexual domination and unnatural sexual infatuation" (263).

[29] Cf. Peter Stallybrass, "Macbeth and Witchcraft," in *Focus on Macbeth*, ed. John Russell Brown (London: Routledge and Kegan Paul, 1982) on the Witches' association with "female rule and the overthrowing of patriarchal authority, which in turn leads to the 'womanish' (both cowardly and instigated by women) killing of Duncan, the 'holy' father who establishes both family and state" (201).

[30] See Adelman, 101.

says it at all: "Prithee, peace!" he begs, "I dare do all that may become a man; / Who dares do more is none"(1.7.45–47). His defense of his masculinity is as much a reaction to her shrewishness as a gesture against the murder. Lady Macbeth, in turn, diverts attention away from gender by interpreting his response in terms of the opposition of man and beast, rather than man and woman; thus, he can feel less that he is overcome by her and his own weakness than that he is embracing a more inclusive concept of manliness. In the end, Macbeth appears sufficiently convinced that he has not really given into her. He does not praise her as a man, but rather as a woman who is capable of creating men: "Bring forth men-children only; / For thy undaunted mettle should compose / Nothing but males" (1.7.73–75).

The audience has thus seen Macbeth giving in to his wife and her "sexual blackmail,"[31] but by saying that he will be the manly one in doing what she proposes, his Lady has prevented him from seeing that he has assumed an effeminate role. While Macbeth's decision to proceed with Duncan's murder clearly echoes Cambyses' infatuation with his Lady and double as a sign of unmanliness,[32] it is also different, because in following his wife Macbeth is supposedly upholding masculine values. Insofar as Cambyses' love for his Lady is expressed in threats and cruelty, this conjunction of masculinity and effeminacy may be implied; in *Macbeth*, however, the relationship is explicitly expressed in terms of gender difference.

Further, in Cambyses' case, the tyrant's infatuation with a woman represents, or at least parallels, the climax of his bloody and vicious career; in *Macbeth*, however, Macbeth's submission accompanies his rise to the throne. *After* the murder of Duncan, Macbeth drifts apart from Lady Macbeth.[33] In his terror after committing the deed, he barely seems to hear her, when she chides him to "consider it not so deeply" (2.2.29). When she commands him to take the daggers back to the place where Duncan lies, too, Macbeth refuses to do it. The moment following the murder scene thus signals his drawing away from her influence,

---

[31] D. F. Rauber, "Macbeth, Macbeth, Macbeth," *Criticism* 11 (1969): 59–67, at 61.

[32] Michael Hawkins, in "History, Politics and Macbeth," in *Focus on Macbeth*, notes that uxoriousness is an essential part of Macbeth's image as a tyrant (164–65). Also see Coppélia Kahn, *Man's Estate: Masculine Identity in Shakespeare* (Berkeley: Univ. of California Press, 1981), for a psychoanalytic interpretation of Macbeth's "dependency on women": "The kind of manly action to which she successfully incites her husband by taunting him with his failure to be as resolute as she is originates, then, in a profound passivity, a suffusion by a liquid feminine element that drowns whatever compunctions oppose it" (178).

[33] Kahn, however, suggests that during this time "Macbeth moves to passive identification with the mysterious, evil feminine powers" (185).

insofar as he both disregards and disobeys her; the next time we see them together in private, Lady Macbeth complains that Macbeth keeps alone (3.2.8). While before the banquet scene he still addresses her with endearments, he does not tell her his secrets (3.2.45–46). In the banquet scene, when Macbeth is crazed by his vision of Banquo's ghost, Lady Macbeth taunts him again with the accusations of unmanliness: "Are you a man?" she asks (3.4.58). Is Macbeth "quite unmanned in folly"? (3.4.73). She sees his actions as feminine "flaws and starts" which "would well become / A woman's story at a winter's fire / Authorized by her grandam" (3.4.62–66). While Macbeth attempts to confront the specter "like a man," this time he cannot give in to her vision of himself and of events as he did before the murder. Even though he might appear here to be at his most "unmanly" when gripped by fear and illusion, at the same time he is detaching himself from her influence completely, and as such, is no longer uxorious.

After the banquet scene in Act 3, we never see husband and wife together again, and Macbeth takes the news of her death completely without emotion or reaction. When he hears the cry of women, he says, "I have almost forgot the taste of fears" (5.5.9). While fear above all dominated his first actions as a tyrant, here even fear seems to have left him as he is surrounded by Malcolm's troops. The only identifiable emotion he has left is a warrior's anger, a sanctioned "manly" emotion.[34] Macbeth's development as a tyrant in this play, in contrast to that of a Domitian or Cambyses, thus ends with his being emptied of passion and feeling, the hallmarks of the feminine—and of the traditional tyrant.[35]

Linda Bamber suggests that in Shakespeare "the tragic process," or tragic experience of the male self, is paralleled by a process of separation from the feminine, the consequent abuse of women, and then a moving beyond anger and loss to a new vision of the self—but, as she notes, that pattern does not occur in *Macbeth*.[36] Bamber sees that there is no real dialectic between feminine and masculine in the play, because Lady Macbeth values "the world of men above everything else."[37] But the feminine is not, as she claims, "irrelevant to the dialectic of the trag-

---

[34] On the "newly homeric valorization of anger" in the Renaissance, see Gordon Braden, *Renaissance Tragedy and the Senecan Tradition: Anger's Privilege* (New Haven: Yale Univ. Press, 1985), 75.

[35] See Kahn, 191, on Macbeth's use of the verb "cow" in his response to Macduff's announcement that he is not of woman born.

[36] Linda Bamber, *Comic Women, Tragic Men: A Study of Gender and Genre in Shakespeare* (Stanford: Stanford Univ. Press, 1982), 105.

[37] Bamber, 91.

edy"[38]: it is located in Macbeth's uxoriousness, which he sheds in the course of the play.[39] Macbeth's portrait as tyrant is accented by his gradual separation from his wife, and in the end we are shown his lack of desire as the proof of his tyranny.

In this suggestion that Macbeth pays both too much and not enough attention to his wife, the play thus exposes the contradictions of gender typing in the construction of the tyrant. While the Cambyses type of tyrant transforms uxoriousness into cruelty and domination over others, Macbeth challenges our expectations about the use of gender categories in political imagery, insofar as uxoriousness and tyranny are ultimately separate, when Macbeth is a tyrant both as he is mastered by effeminate desire and in his *rejection* of the emotions which are traditionally feminine. The doubleness of the feminine in which passion is strength and weakness surfaces in Lady Macbeth, whose excessive "femininity" is converted into shrewishness, but also in her husband, who is at his most "manly"—and most depleted—in his full tyranny. Even if Macduff is not of woman born and Malcolm is a virgin, by the end of the play Macbeth's condition establishes that separation from women is not an absolute virtue: Malcolm and Macduff must share that state with the tyrant, Macbeth.

In an earlier play, *Richard III*, Shakespeare also deviates from the traditional description of the tyrant, in a much more radical way. In *Macbeth* Shakespeare uses and twists the old model; in *Richard III* he shows Richard himself consciously manipulating the traditional associations between tyranny and uxoriousness. Shakespeare's Richard III's credentials as "that excellent grand tyrant of the earth" are well-established.[40] If the epithets of tyrant hurled at him by the other characters were not enough, scholars have demonstrated that he is, in Bacon's words, a "Tyrant both in title and regiment," that is, as a usurper as well as in his wicked rule.[41] Yet, unlike Macbeth, Shakespeare's Richard does avoid attribution of that most common of the tyrannical vices, which is lust. Instead, Richard accuses Edward of lust to paint him as a tyrant. At the same time, he fashions an image of himself as a maid

---

[38] Bamber, 107.

[39] Adelman sees the play ultimately enacting a fantasy of the exclusion of the power of the female: "Initially construed as all-powerful, the women virtually disappear at the end," where "the natural order of the end depends on the exclusion of the female" (109).

[40] As Moody Prior says, in *The Drama of Power: Studies in Shakespeare's History Plays* (Evanston: Northwestern Univ. Press, 1973), 131, "only in *Macbeth* do the words 'tyrant' and 'tyranny' appear more frequently."

[41] Cited by W. A. Armstrong, "The Elizabethan Conception of the Tyrant," *Review of English Studies* 22 (1946): 161–81 at 166.

who must be desired, to strengthen his claim to the throne.

Far from being obsessed by his own lust, the hideous Richard describes himself as lacking sexual desire (because he finds that women do not respond to him); instead, his "soul's desire" is sovereignty (*3 Henry VI* 3.2.128), not women. The corollary of this argument is Richard's evident misogyny: to him, women are not worth desiring, since they do not care for him.[42] When seeking sovereignty, in fact, Richard carefully manipulates the traditional association between lust and tyranny to undermine the claims of Edward IV, who was supposedly overfond of women. Practically, in his representing Edward as lustful, Richard wants to "infer the bastardy of Edward's children" (*Richard III* 3.5.75). But strategy goes further than this to suggest Edward's own character as a tyrant:

> Moreover, urge his hateful luxury
> And bestial appetite in change of lust,
> Which stretched unto their servants, daughters, wives,
> Even where his raging eye or savage heart,
> Without control, lusted to make a prey.   (3.5.80–84)[43]

Richard's appearance in Act 3, scene 7, supported by two holy fathers, dramatizes the contrast:

> Ah ha, my lord! this prince is not an Edward.
> He is not lulling on a lewd love-bed,
> But on his knees at meditation;
> Not dallying with a brace of courtesans,
> But meditating with two deep divines;
> Not sleeping, to engross his idle body,
> But praying, to enrich his watchful soul.
> Happy were England, would this virtuous prince
> Take on his grace the sovereignty thereof.   (3.7.71–79)

Richard's manipulation of statecraft's description of tyrannical desire thus converts his own exclusion from the pleasures of sexual desire into a virtue, legitimizing his claim to sovereignty on "natural" terms, against Edward's "unnatural" desire.

---

[42] See Madonne M. Miner, " 'Neither mother, wife, nor England's queen': The Roles of Women in *Richard III*," in *The Woman's Part: Feminist Criticism of Shakespeare*, ed. Carolyn Ruth Swift Lenz, Gayle Greene, and Carol Thomas Neely (Urbana: Univ. of Illinois Press, 1980), on Richard's misogyny: "Implicitly, the quality of the present which Richard finds so onerous is its femininity" (36).

[43] Richard also paints a picture of Edward as uxorious: in response to Clarence's complaining that such a "toy" such a prophecy should send him to the Tower, Richard carps, "Why, this it is, when men are rul'd by women" (1.1.62).

In the central scene, which Buckingham has engineered to make the Lord Mayor and citizens not simply accept, but want Richard for their king, Richard himself is in fact figured as eminently and femininely desirable in both erotic and political terms. Buckingham sets this up as a scene of seduction, with Richard as the one who is to be seduced to be king, when he is brought out holding a Bible and supported by two holy men. Buckingham instructs Richard: "And be not easily won to our requests. / Play the maid's part: still answer nay, and take it" (3.7.50–51). They scheme thus to create an image of a passive, effeminate and desirable Richard, one filled with "tenderness of heart / And a gentle, kind effeminate remorse" (210–11). The very desirability of this "sweet Prince" is supposedly wrapped up in his lack of desire; he submits, even at the end, unwillingly: "For God doth know, and you may partly see, / How far I am from the desire of this" (3.7.235–36). As Heilman puts it, at least from a man's point of view, this is "language that might be used by a woman coyly yielding to seduction."[44] The amorous rhetoric of the scene is familiar from the erotic politics of Elizabeth's court, but here the "virgin Queen" is the chaste Protector, Richard. Shakespeare presents a case in which femininity construed as weakness and desirability is used by an avowedly misogynistic tyrant as a strength, to fashion a persuasive and powerful political image. At the same time that Richard, the aspiring tyrant, rejects lust and hates women, he draws on the Petrarchan image of the reluctant mistress, making himself look like a woman who must be seduced into power.

Both *Macbeth* and *Richard III*, in different ways, take us back to the doubleness of femininity, being both beyond and subject to male control in the imagery of tyranny. In Macbeth's case, Macbeth becomes a tyrant when he is mastered by a woman, thus by irrationality and perversity; yet Shakespeare also suggests that he is as fully a tyrant in his distance from the weaknesses which are culturally feminine. Exploiting the double image of woman and tyrant, Richard manipulates the usual ideas about lust to distance himself from tyranny; at the same time, he constructs an image of himself as a woman who must be wooed to create an image of his power. From the perspective of the male self, tyrant and woman are powerful insofar as they escape rationality and abandon "civilized" values; the strategy of philosophy and plays is to control this threat by representing it and defeating it. Characteristically, in plays tyrant and woman are turned against each other, each defeat-

---

[44] Robert B. Heilman, "Satiety and Conscience: Aspects of *Richard III*," in *Essays in Shakespearean Criticism*, ed. James L. Calderwood and Harold E. Toliver (Englewood Cliffs: Prentice-Hall, 1970), 142. Heilman also notes how Richard finds "largest gratification in the style of his own surrender" (141).

ing the other: the tyrant rapes, but the woman subdues him. Both are thus bound together inextricably in the power and vulnerability of desire.[45]

University of Pennsylvania

---

[45] This essay appears as part of my book, *Tragedies of Tyrants: Political Thought and Theater in the English Renaissance* (Ithaca: Cornell Univ. Press, 1990).

DYMPNA CALLAGHAN

Wicked Women in Macbeth: A Study of Power, Ideology, and the Production of Motherhood

SINCE THE ADVENT OF FEMINISM IN THE ACADEMY, ISSUES OF POWER and empowerment, subversion and recuperation have been crucial components of critical discourse. I wish to examine the complexities of power, patriarchal oppression, and the structures of resistance as they constellate around Renaissance discourse on witchcraft in Shakespeare's *Macbeth*.

It is helpful to address witchcraft not only as the victimization of women by the forces of patriarchal hegemony, though it is primarily that, but also as a manifestation of both the symbolic power attributed to women and the cultural dynamics of resistance. While resistances necessarily occur within the terms of the dominant cultural and political framework and while the subversive forces represented by witchcraft may well be produced by patriarchalism's endeavors at repressive self-legitimation (by the very mechanism intended to foreclose it),[1] we cannot ignore the destabilizing impact of strategies which are designed to circumvent the order of patriarchal logic, specifically the fact that, in the witch, resistance is figured as feminine. Thus, power is double-edged; oppression both produces and responds to resistance, so that it becomes difficult to discern the boundary that demarcates one from the other. This is particularly so in the case of witchcraft, a privileged nexus of desire, power, and an "other place" of cultural consciousness, the crucial component of the Renaissance fantasy of "woman," which serves both to endorse and undermine the fantasy patriarchy has of itself.[2] Mechanisms of power place women in postures of victimization

---

[1] My working definition of patriarchalism as the patriarchal justification of political authority follows that of Gordon Schochet in *Patriarchalism and Political Thought: The Authoritarian Family and Political Speculation and Attitudes Especially in Seventeenth Century England* (New York: Basic Books, 1975). See also James Daly, *Sir Robert Filmer and English Political Thought* (Toronto: Univ. of Toronto Press, 1979).

[2] My thinking here is indebted to Peter Stallybrass and Allon White's *The Politics and Poetics of Transgression* (Ithaca: Cornell Univ. Press, 1986) who comment on "the

or resistance, both literally and symbolically, roles which have recuperative and subversive implications for patriarchal structures.[3]

That women were the primary victims of witch persecutions has been amply demonstrated by scholars.[4] The fact that the witch represents a unique juxtaposition of femininity and power in a period which debarred women from access to legal, economic and political power, however, has not been addressed. Traditional critical analyses of *Macbeth* in particular have focussed on witchcraft as supernatural fiction, and more recently critics have argued that witchcraft in the play represents the male fantasy of feminine power.[5] C. L. Barber and Madelon Gohlke have noted that overpowering feminine forces threaten vulnerable masculinity, and in a fascinating and important essay, Janet Adelman has examined the play in terms of an insistent and recuperative fantasy of escape from maternal power, an apparently "universal condition."[6] All these readings, however, deprive the play's representa-

---

nexus of power and desire which regularly reappears in the ideological construction of the low-other" (4) and to Jacqueline Rose's essay "Hamlet—the 'Mona Lisa' of Literature," in *Sexuality in the Field of Vision* (London: Verso, 1986), 123–40, which elucidates the concept of the fantasy of woman.

[3] Catherine Clément, in a brilliant analysis of Freud's comparison between the hysteric and the witch, argues: "Deviants, who are not hysterics, but clowns, charlatans, all sorts of odd people ... occupy challenging positions foreseen by the social bodies, challenging functions within the scope of all cultures. That doesn't change the structures, however. On the contrary, it makes them comfortable." Hélène Cixous and Catherine Clément, *The Newly Born Woman*, trans. Betsy Wing (Minneapolis: Univ. of Minnesota Press, 1986), 155.

[4] It is important to note that the idea of woman as witch is not universal. See Christina Larner, *Enemies of God: The Witch-Hunt in Scotland* (Baltimore: Johns Hopkins Univ. Press, 1981), 9. James I offered his own explanation for this phenomenon: "The reason is easie ... as that sexe is frailer than men is, so is it easier to be intrapped in these grosse snares of the Devill, as was well proved to be true, by the Serpents deceiving of Eve at the beginning, which makes him the homlier with that sex ever since." Quoted by Marilyn J. Boxer and Jean H. Quataert, ed., *Connecting Spheres: Women in the Western World to the Present* (New York: Oxford Univ. Press, 1987), 33. Notably in England a higher proportion of those accused of witchcraft were women than in Scotland or on the Continent (33).

[5] Janet Adelman's brilliant psychoanalytic essay " 'Born of Woman': Fantasies of Maternal Power in *Macbeth*," in *Cannibals, Witches, and Divorce: Estranging the Renaissance*, ed. Marjorie Garber (Baltimore: Johns Hopkins Univ. Press, 1987), 90–121, argues that Macbeth plays out the fantasy of escape from the powers of the mother and that he is punished for his fantasy of eluding feminine reproductive power, while at the same time the play endorses another version of the fantasy in Macduff. Robert Kimbrough posits that the characters in the play are severely confined by the respective categories of manhood and womanhood, and that Shakespeare demonstrates the value of striving toward a fuller and more androgynous range of being; see "Macbeth: The Prisoner of Gender," *Shakespeare Studies* 16 (1983): 175–90.

[6] See C. L. Barber, "The Family in Shakespeare's Development," in *Representing*

tions of powerful femininity of any substantive or subversive force and obscure its staging of the complex dynamics of power, particularly the unauthorized power witches were regarded as possessing which could kill, maim, and generally undermine the fabric of society. Witches represented the demonic antithesis of godly rule, produced by a hierarchy prone to invert itself and by a system of antithetical thinking wherein systematic substitutions of the top of any given hierarchy for its opposite were imminent. Yet, the logical antithesis of James's patriarchal, patrilineal government is not actually demonism at all, it is matriarchy; government by women in a social system where descent is traced through the line of the mother.[7]

In *Macbeth*, two crucial cultural conflicts are played out: one between patriarchy and the rule of the mothers, represented by the witches, and the other between skepticism about witchcraft practices and witch belief. I also suggest that *Macbeth* participates in the production of yet a third category, namely, the dominant ideology of motherhood in nascent modernity. This directly counters gender-oriented readings of the play which posit the patriarchal recuperation of an already constituted category of femininity.[8] Thus, while James's *Daemonologie* is crucial in setting the ideological perimeters of *Macbeth*, it does not simply replicate its ideological project, namely, "the legitimation of, the hegemony of patriarchy."[9] Further, the advent of skepticism and the advent of femininity are closely related aspects of emergent modernity since both reflect contested understandings about the location of political power—either in demonic femininity or in divinely ordained sovereignty—as well as its instability. *Macbeth* is an arena of ideological contest more than one of ideological legitimation and is instrumental in the cultural production of femininity rather its repudiation.

That the witches in *Macbeth* are understood as possessing genuine power is crucial to any understanding of the play as more than elabo-

---

Shakespeare: New Psychoanalytic Essays, ed. Murray M. Schwartz and Coppélia Kahn (Baltimore: Johns Hopkins Univ. Press, 1980), 196; Madelon Gohlke, "'I wooed thee with my sword': Shakespeare's Tragic Paradigms," in *Representing Shakespeare*, 177; Adelman, 90–121. Harry Berger Jr. also explores the theme of sexuality in terms of the dialogue between text and performance criticism; see "Text Against Performance in Shakespeare: The Example of Macbeth," *Genre* 15 (1982): 49–79.

[7] "If kingship is legitimated by analogy to God's rule over the earth, and the father's rule over the family and the head's rule over the body, witchcraft establishes opposite analogies, whereby the Devil attempts to rule over the earth, and the woman over the family, and the body over the head." Peter Stallybrass, "*Macbeth* and Witchcraft," in *Focus on "Macbeth*," ed. John Russell Brown (Boston: Routledge and Kegan Paul, 1982), 192.

[8] This is the flaw in Adelman's analysis.

[9] Stallybrass, "*Macbeth* and Witchcraft," 189–209.

rate didacticism. That mother-power was seen as a real threat can be understood from William Perkins's *Discourse on the Damned Art of Witchcraft* (1608) where the demonic pact makes a witch more powerful than even a monarch.[10] Witches, though often old, celibate, and devoid of kin, were imaged as the mother in an idea which has strong associations with the ancient fertility goddess under whose auspices all procreative power was placed.[11] In witchcraft, dynastic motherhood is seen as threatening to the reign of the father, and the battle is neither universal nor archetypal; rather, it is intrinsic to the metaphysics of Divine Right,[12] the dominant conception of government in the Jacobean state wherein Godly rule was thought to be actively opposed by those who practiced witchcraft.[13] The threat of matriarchy in *Macbeth* is actually *produced* and magnified by the antithetical thinking which characterizes patriarchalism itself. Stevie Davies, despite somewhat idealizing the function of the feminine in Elizabeth's reign, makes an important point about the new king's endeavor to reinforce patriarchy: "though in James I and VI's reign ... white Isis-magic ... was reinterpreted by that woman-hating, hag-ridden Scot as black and demonic, and under his influence witch-hunting flared, the feminine power was still in the air."[14] Female rule, rather than being merely an element of demonism, becomes its very embodiment. In order to negate the symbolic threat of matriarchy, a number of deft ideological maneuvers were required to subsume the threat of female power amid a wider preoccupation with the legions of hell. Thus, the "fantasmatic omnipotence" ascribed to (demonic) maternality necessitates its sublation.[15]

In *Macbeth* the kingdom of darkness is unequivocally female, un-

---

[10] Selma R. Williams, *Riding The Nightmare: Women and Witchcraft* (New York: Atheneum, 1978), 111.

[11] See Williams, 20; Larner, 3. Another important feminist treatment of this subject is Barbara Ehrenreich and Dierdre English's *Witches, Midwives and Nurses: A History of Women Healers* (New York: The Feminist Press: SUNY/College at Old Westbury, 1973), which places the witch-hunts in the context of the establishment of a male dominated medical profession. A recent brief account of Renaissance witchcraft, deeply indebted to Larner's work, is in Boxer and Quataert, 32–38.

[12] Stuart Clark, "King James's Daemonologie: Witchcraft and Kingship" in *The Damned Art*, ed. Sidney Anglo (London: Routledge and Kegan Paul, 1977), 156–57.

[13] See Stuart Clark, "Inversion, Misrule and the Meaning of Witchcraft," *Past and Present* 87: 98–127, and "King James's Daemonologie." James I's *Daemonologie* (Robert Waldsgrave: Edinburgh, 1597; repr. New York: Da Capo Press, 1969) showed the rule of Satan to be the logical and direct antithesis of godly rule, which meant not merely the rule of God, but more specifically the reign of James himself.

[14] Stevie Davies, *The Feminine Reclaimed* (Lexington: Univ. Press of Kentucky, 1986), 28.

[15] See Sara Kofman, *The Enigma of Woman: Woman In Freud's Writings*, trans. Catherine Porter (New York: Cornell Univ. Press, 1985), 72.

equivocally matriarchal, and the fantasy of incipient rebellion of demonic forces is crucial to the maintenance of the godly rule it is supposed to overthrow. Significantly, at the start of the play the tragic heroine is firmly aligned with the witches who lead her husband to perdition.[16] In fact, by seventeenth-century standards, not to mention those of the statute of 1604, prior to her hysterical somnambulism, Lady Macbeth is a witch.[17] Macbeth, on the other hand, is initially presented as the good son, one who defies those who try to usurp the royal authority of his king. He is at this stage a defender of the state, capable of the violence necessary to the maintenance of patriarchal authority. As Bellona's bridegroom Macbeth is unconquered by the reputedly softening, weakening qualities of Venus in the traditional opposition of love and war.[18] Yet it is neither valor nor love that entraps Macbeth, but power, which is clearly located among the insatiable forces of feminine misrule.

The manly Macbeth submits himself to female governance, to the mothers of the underworld. The play is full of opposing images of patriarchal blood and matriarchal milk, which symbolize antithetical ideologies of human generativity.[19] Blood in the play, notably Duncan's "golden Blood" (2.3.110) symbolizes patriarchy and can be equated with the life blood of a nation ("Bleed, bleed, poor country!" [4.3.32]), as we can see when Macbeth tells Donaldbain that his father, King Duncan, has been murdered:

> The spring, the head, the fountain of your blood
> Is stopp'd; the very source of it is stopp'd.
>
> (2.3.96–97)

Such blood is assured of vengeance as even the mute ghost of Banquo manages to convey to Macbeth: "It will Have blood, they say: blood

---

[16] See Catherine Belsey, *The Subject of Tragedy: Identity and Difference in Renaissance Drama* (New York: Methuen, 1985), 185.

[17] Anthony Harris, *Night's Black Agents* (Manchester: Manchester Univ. Press, 1980), 52. Coppélia Kahn also notes: "Shakespeare establishes the connection between Lady Macbeth and the witches by having her invoke the spirit of evil and ask her to fill her with their spirits." *Man's Estate: Masculine Identity in Shakespeare* (Berkeley: Univ. of California Press, 1981), 177.

[18] See Davies, 14–17.

[19] Coppélia Kahn points out in a discussion of *King Lear* that "patriarchal structures loom obviously on the surface of many texts, structures of authority, control, force, logic, linearity, misogyny, male superiority. But beneath them, as in palimpsest, we can find . . . 'the maternal subtext,' the imprint of mothering on the male psyche, the psychological presence of the mother whether or not mothers are literally represented as characters." "The Absent Mother in *King Lear*," in *Rewriting the Renaissance*, ed. Ferguson et al. (Chicago: Univ. of Chicago Press, 1986), 35.

will have blood" (3.4.121). Legitimate blood cries out even from the grave.[20]

Patriarchal blood is used symbolically to confirm paternity, "which is always a matter of belief, of deduction."[21] Such blood strives to evade "the inescapable female connection between creation and procreation, the destiny that is inexorably determined by anatomy."[22] It becomes ideologically necessary to deprive Macbeth of heirs in order to circumvent the problem of the production of progeny if patriarchalism were taken to its logical conclusions. Blood, not the milk of human kindness, allegedly in Macbeth's nature, nor that gall from Lady Macbeth's breasts, is the fluid of enduring generations in the patriarchal appropriation of the reproductive capacity.

Macbeth sheds royal blood but he cannot transfuse himself with it. Having killed the nurturing father/king, he also forgoes sleep, "Chief nourisher in life's feast" (2.2.38). He justifies his continued killings as an effort to gain lost nourishment; but nourishment does not emanate from Hecate's dug from whence comes only milk/gall, the antithesis of legitimate paternity's blood:

> Ere we will eat our meal in fear, and sleep
> In the affliction of these terrible dreams,
> That shake us nightly.   (3.2.17–19)

Macbeth displaces the legitimate reproductive function onto the phallic image of the snake, which also has ancient associations with fertility. "We have scorch'd the snake, not kill'd it" (3.2.13),[23] says Macbeth of the murder of Banquo: "There the grown serpent lies; the worm, that's fled,/ Hath nature that in time will venom breed" (3.4.28–29). Macbeth sees all legitimate progeny as evil because it threatens his usurped crown. As the "wayward son of Hecate" (who is of course ancient fertility goddess as well as protectress of witches), he makes his wife a matriarch, "Bring forth men children only."

---

[20] Kenneth Muir, ed., *Macbeth* (New York: Methuen, 1984), 97. All subsequent references to the play are taken from this volume.

[21] Kofman, 71. Interestingly, Kahn also notes that "Duncan the father-king has great symbolic resonance as an idealized figure of just paternity, but he stands aloof from aggression and competition. The two aspects of oedipal authority, might and right, are split off from another, leaving Duncan helpless under Macbeth's dagger." " 'Magic of Bounty': Timon of Athens, Jacobean Patronage and Maternal Power," *Shakespeare Quarterly* 38 (1987): 38.

[22] Sandra Gilbert, introduction to Cixous and Clément, xiii.

[23] Interestingly, critics have noted that the image might have been suggested by the serpentine trunk of the Banquo family tree in Shakespeare's source, the very emblem of patrilineality; see Muir, 81.

Notably, the images of children in the latter part of Macbeth vacillate between patriarchalism's legitimate babes and the evil specter of fatherless offspring like the "birth-strangled babe, / Ditch-delivered by a drab" (4.1.30–31). The bloody babe which should reify the connection with the maternal body instead represents the patriarchal mystification of "blood," since the babe is Macduff the man charmed by brutal severance with the maternal. It is similarly crucial to this project that Malcolm is "unknown" to woman. Jacobean patriarchalism requires absolute symbolic appropriation of feminine reproductive powers. Instead of revealing the fact that men without women can only be barren and fruitless, it posits the reverse. The forces of patriarchy endure, it seems, while maternal forces wreak death and destruction. The play thus represents an important facet of the dominant ideology of patriarchalism, which fears and punishes those it deprives of power. In James's emphasis on the king as father, this entails the symbolic usurpation of female generativity:

> The king towards his people is rightly compared to a father of children, and to a head of a body composed of diverse members, for as fathers the good princes and magistrates of the people of God acknowledged themselves to their subjects.[24]

James stresses the bloodline of patrilineality over the more obvious somatic connection between children and their mothers. Crucially, James also emphasizes his role as father *and nurturer* of his people:

> As the Father over one family, so the King, as Father over many families, extends his care to preserve, feed, clothe, instruct and defend the whole commonwealth ... so that all the duties of a King are summed up in a universal fatherly care of his people.[25]

This notion of the father as mother is thus used to justify and obfuscate patriarchal domination.[26]

Yet in *Macbeth*, this is contested—paternal forces are also seen to bring war and death. Siward's son "has paid a soldier's debt; / He only liv'd but till he was a man" (5.9.5–6) even though dying in the name of the fathers is regarded as noble, at least by his father: "Had I as many

---

[24] James I and VI, *The Trew Law of Free Monarchies* (1598), repr. in *Divine Right and Democracy: An Anthology of Political Writings in Stuart England*, ed. David Wootton (Harmondsworth: Penguin, 1986), 99.

[25] Quoted by Schochet, 148. Coppélia Kahn has paralleled James's patronage with maternal bounty in " 'Magic of Bounty,' " 34–57.

[26] For an account of the familial basis of patriarchal authority and its importance in critical studies of tragedy see Dympna Callaghan, *Woman and Gender in Renaissance Tragedy* (Atlantic Highlands: Humanities Press, 1989).

sons as I have hairs, / I would not wish them to a fairer death" (5.9.14-15). The pun on "hairs" and "heirs" contradicts any straightforward legitimation of patriarchy.[27]

Importantly, too, the structure of the antithesis between godly male rule and anarchic femininity is disrupted in *Macbeth*. The gender of the forces which represent the matriarchal order is undecipherable:

> What are these
> So wither'd and so mild in their attire,
> That look not like th'inhabitants of the earth,
> And yet are on't? Live you? or are you aught
> That man may question? You seem to understand me,
> By each at once her choppy finger laying
> Upon her skinny lips; You should be women
> And yet your beards forbid me to interpret
> That you are so.   (1.3.39-47)[28]

As bearers of power, indicated by the deformation of the phallus signalled by the choppy fingers, the witches are disturbingly androgynous. These are the feminine monstrosities John Knox clearly feared in the "monstrous regiment of women,"[29] and in ancient, tribal matriarchy: "Amazones were monstrouse women, that could not abide the regiment of men, and therefore killed their husbandes."[30] This fear has its parallel in the rash of men in this period who sought protection from their wives in the courts, a fact made remarkable by the lack of historical evidence that women even attempted to murder their husbands and by the fact that the strenuous subjugation of women would have made it difficult for them to do so.[31] Notably, while matriarchy merits careful distinction from any single instance of female sovereignty within patriarchal structure, such as that of Elizabeth,[32] her reign nonetheless

---

[27] See Kahn, *Man's Estate*, 190, for an alternative interpretation of the death of young Siward.

[28] Marjorie Garber has argued convincingly that "power in Macbeth is a function of neither male nor female but of the suspicion of the undecidable. The phallus as floating signifier is more powerful than when definitely assigned to either gender." *Shakespeare's Ghost Writers: Literature as Uncanny Causality* (New York: Methuen, 1987), 110.

[29] Although Knox was arguably more troubled by Catholic government than female rule, *The Woorth of Women* (1599) argued that "All the great Monarchies were instituted by the Councell of women." Quoted by Simon Shepherd in *Amazons and Warrior Women: Varieties of Feminism in Seventeenth-Century Drama* (New York: St. Martin's Press, 1981), 35.

[30] Quoted by Shepherd, 14.

[31] Belsey, 135.

[32] See Alison Heisch, "Queen Elizabeth I and the Persistence of Patriarchy,"

threatened patriarchy, a threat recuperated by the ideological construction of the good mother in the iconography of the pelican who feeds her young with blood pecked from her own breast,[33] which is transformed and extended in the Jacobean era. Femininity is thus unfixed by its problematic alignment with power. The powerful woman is monstrous in a culture that proposes the categories of woman and power as discrete and mutually exclusive entities.

The mother figure in patriarchy is invariably ambivalent: "the ... representation of supreme security and ultimate risk, life and death, gentleness and sensuality, virgin and whore. It is only through the effect of splitting that each of her attributes is cut off from its opposite."[34] Indeed the witches represent a form of femininity unrecognizable in terms of its subsequent historical development. This transformation of the feminine is figured in the character of Lady Macbeth.

Lady Macbeth becomes troubled with feminine remorse, guilt, and madness familiar in modern conceptions of femininity. Significantly, Lady Macbeth is finally unable to relinquish her maternality. She remains one who has "given suck" and knows "How tender 'tis to love the babe that milks me" (1.7.55); she is prey to the ravings of guilt and feminine remorse. Maternality as it is figured in human women rather than in supernatural witches is benign, symptomatic of the innate moral sensibility of the mother which is so characteristic of her appearance in nascent modernity's newly created private sphere.[35] In contrast, the witches' language is as devoid of moral sensibility as it is full of severed body parts: the pilot's thumb, Jew's liver, "Nose of Turk and Tartar's lips," and "Finger of a birth-strangled babe." Yet such dismemberment mimics the violent rituals of patriarchal valor: "he unseam'd him from the nave to th' chops, / And fix'd his head upon our battlements" (1.2.22–23). In terms of the dominant antithesis between godly rule and ungodly anarchy, patriarchy is de-privileged by the fact that the forces of matriarchy and patriarchy are almost paradoxically equat-

---

Feminist Review 4 (1980) and Robert Brustein "The Monstrous Regiment of Women: Sources for the Satiric View of the Court Lady in English Drama," in *Renaissance and Modern Essays*, ed. G. R. Hibbard (London: Routledge and Kegan Paul, 1966), 35–50.

[33] Peter Stallybrass, "Patriarchal Territories: The Body Enclosed," in *Rewriting the Renaissance*, ed. Ferguson et al, 131.

[34] Kofman, 73. Kahn comments on the parallel elements on maternal bounty and betrayal in royal patronage; see " 'Magic of Bounty,' " 35. On the parallels between martial prowess and motherhood, see Nancy Huston, "The Matrix of War: Mothers and Heroes," in *The Female Body In Western Culture: Contemporary Perspectives*, ed. Susan Rubin Suleiman (Cambridge: Harvard Univ. Press, 1986), 119–36.

[35] See Mary Beth Rose, *The Expense of Spirit: Love and Sexuality in English Renaissance Drama* (Ithaca: Cornell Univ. Press, 1988), on the creation and idealization of private life attendant upon the Protestant doctrine of marriage (ix–xi).

ed as equally balanced (rather then hierarchized) opposites in the terms of the antithesis.

Lady Macbeth's prior maternality is used in conjunction with Lady Macduff to polarize femininity into the consecrated mother and the witch.[36] Such ideological maneuvering counters the overwhelming power of female generativity. In the slaughter of Macduff's sentimentalized, perfect family of "pretty chickens and their dam" (4.3.218), *Macbeth* participates in a cultural shift, a new representation of maternality in patriarchal ideology. In Lady Macduff, the weak dependent woman appears rather less than a match for the wit of her precocious son. She is both sentimentalized and victimized.

> Wither should I fly?
> I have done no harm. But I remember now
> I am in this earthly world, where, to do harm
> Is often laudable; to do good sometime
> Accounted dangerous folly: why then, alas!
> To say I have done no harm?   (4.2.72–78)

With the invention of the ideology of motherhood, there is also the invention of childhood, in Macduff's valiant little son:

> L. Macd.   Sirrah, your father's dead:
>   And what will you do now? How will you live?
> Son. As birds do mother.
> L. Macd. What, with worms and flies?
> Son. With what I get I mean; and so do they.
>   L. Macd. Poor bird! thoud'st never fear the net, nor lime,
>   The pit-fall, nor the gin.   (4.2.30–35)

The comfort of domesticity has been juxtaposed throughout with the murderous battles over family power; thus, the apparition Macbeth sees at supper is "A woman's story at a winter's fire, / Authoris'd by her grandam" (3.4.64–65). Feminine power is tamed as an old woman's narrative, not the hellish tale woven by the weird sisters. Act 4, scene 1 is a turning point, marking as it does the decline of matriarchy. The scene begins with a wonderful depiction of demonic domesticity. The

---

[36] Julia Kristeva comments: "the *consecrated* (religious or secular) representation of femininity is absorbed by motherhood. If, however, one looks more closely, this motherhood is the *fantasy* that is nurtured by the adult, man or woman, of a lost territory; what is more it involves less an idealized archaic mother than the idealization of the *relationship* that binds us to her, . . . an idealization of primary narcissism." "Stabat Mater," in *Tales of Love*, trans. Leon S. Roudiez (New York: Columbia Univ. Press, 1987), 234.

witches at the cauldron[37] are inverted emblems of the matriarch's control of nurturance. They are presented as the forces of destruction, in a complete reversal of ancient associations with fertility and creativity.[38] From this point on there is a patriarchal recuperation of the errant feminine forces of the play.

Such domestication of the forces of maternality is perfectly congruent with the advent of rational skepticism. The eerie witches and their power are demystified by Macduff, the representative of the burgeoning forces of patriarchal rationalism. As he undoes the riddle of their prophecy, the witches become mere stage business. No man or woman born becomes no man the product of vaginal birth; Birnam wood rising forth to Dunsinane becomes every soldier marching with a branch in his hand. Thus, patriarchalism does not remain static as it produces a new model of femininity. That is, attempts to legitimate patriarchy also change the nature of patriarchy itself. Patriarchy no longer has as its emblem the blood of primitive warfare and the masculine forces of violence and butchery. Instead, patriarchy achieves its supreme rationalization in the quasi-metaphysical patriarchal bloodline, on which Filmer's *Patriarcha* was based: "paternal power cannot be lost; it may either be transferred or usurped; but never lost, or ceaseth. God who is the giver of power, may transfer it from the Father to some other."[39] Metonymic blood is reified in new ways. Notably, this is also the period in which Harvey discovers the circulation of the blood, and where the body becomes the site of scientific enquiry. Patriarchalism and witch persecutions were thus synonymous with the decline of magic rather than an indication of its brief but devastating revival.

In fact, Peter Stallybrass points out that James's interest in diabolism was not residual medievalism to be expected of the famed and eccentric "comic offspring" of Mary Queen of Scots and Lord Darnley, but rather an attempt to keep abreast of the dominant intellectual ideas of his day, such as those of Jean Bodin lately arrived from the continent.[40] Bodin was actually a skeptic who advocated a sophisticated empiricism known

---

[37] Muir quotes Robert Bridges' comment that "hell and home" are leagued against Macbeth, xvi.

[38] See Kahn, *Man's Estate*, 173, on the witches' alliance with destruction. They have lost all association with fertility and creativity.

[39] Schochet, 148.

[40] Stallybrass points out that James's interest in diabolism was not residual medievalism to be expected of the famed and eccentric "comic offspring" but rather an attempt to keep abreast of the dominant intellectual ideas of his day, such as those of Jean Bodin lately arrived from the continent: "*Macbeth* and Witchcraft," 191. Williams is mistaken, I think, when she describes James as "a mental mess," 95.

as the "common-sense theory of Theophrastus,"⁴¹ on which he based his theories of diabolism. Crucially, seventeenth-century skepticism did not mean disbelief in the central tenets of the Judeo-Christian religion, as it does today, but rather "a philosophical view that raises doubts about the adequacy or reliability of the evidence that could be offered to justify any proposition."⁴² Interestingly, Filmer, whom one might expect to be an advocate of witch belief, was actually dubious of it. Nonetheless, he arrived at this conclusion by utilizing a methodology not altogether dissimilar from that employed in Bodin's brand of skepticism. Taking the Bible as the source of his empirical evidence, he maintained that since devil worship was not to be found in Scripture, witchcraft did not exist.

Also, witchcraft practices, as Ernest Jones notes, were newly defined as heretical and the fact that they acquired this status was in no way the result of the evolution of popular fantasy. Carlo Ginzburg has shown in a recently translated study of the good walkers agrarian folk occultists of Italy that practices once existing in perfect symbiosis with the dominant religious ideology suddenly became shaped as its antithesis.⁴³ The role of witch was often forced upon society's victims at the merest suspicion of nonconformity or deviation among those at the very bottom of the social hierarchy.⁴⁴ Similarly, in 1604 certain witchcraft practices which had carried relatively lighter sentences during Elizabeth's reign suddenly became punishable with death.⁴⁵ As Christina Larner notes, "witch-hunting was an activity fostered by the ruling class; it was not a spontaneous movement on the part of the peasantry to which the ruling and administrative classes were obliged to respond."⁴⁶ Thus, although a witch was not usually a randomly selected

---

⁴¹ Richard H. Popkin, *The History of Scepticism from Erasmus to Spinoza* (Berkeley· Univ. of California Press, 1979), 83.

⁴² Popkin, xvii.

⁴³ Ernest Jones, *On the Nightmare* (New York, 1931; new ed. New York: Grove Press, 1951), 214; see also Carlo Ginzburg, *The Night Battles: Witchcraft and Agrarian Cults in Sixteenth and Seventeenth Centuries*, trans. John and Anne Tedeschi (Baltimore: Johns Hopkins Univ. Press, 1983).

⁴⁴ Keith Thomas, *Religion and the Decline of Magic: Studies in Popular Beliefs in Sixteenth- and Seventeenth-Century England* (London: Weidenfeld and Nicholson, 1971; repr. Harmondsworth: Penguin, 1980), 621–29.

⁴⁵ Although Elizabeth ruled within a patriarchy, and although there was never any real threat to inheritance through the father's line, any individual instance of female rule produced important culturally residual connotations of matriarchy. Elizabeth herself was characterized by Robert Cecil as "more than a man and in troth sometimes less than a woman."

⁴⁶ Larner, 1.

victim of the judiciary,[47] since she was usually atrabilious and voluble in her discontent, the nature of her crimes and the mechanisms whereby she was brought to so-called justice are to a large extent evidence of the fact that witchcraft *as a category of deviance* is produced from above at the instigation of those institutions of political and cultural prominence.[48] This is corroborated by the fact that while some elements of witchcraft practice are pan-cultural, witch-hunting is a quite culturally, geographically, and historically specific phenomenon "directed and organized by government elites for political purposes."[49]

The witch persecutions constituted the beginning of scientific rationalism, rather than its antithesis: "They were scientifically constructed and defined, although with the help of popular ideas ... developed in its elements by the systematic theology of the medieval Church, legally established in the laws of Church and State, and finally built up into a whole by means of ecclesiastical and lay criminal trials, first of all by the Inquisition of the Heretics."[50]

The sexual / mother of witchcraft persecutions also formulated a displaced but intricate body of sexual knowledge, perhaps only paralleled by the confessions that constitute the basis of modern psychoanalytic practice. Witch persecutions instigated a scientific investigation into a crucial component of mother power, namely, the demonic ferocity of female sexual desire. As Robert Burton, writing in 1621, put it: "Of Women's unnatural, insatiable lust what country, what village doth not complain."[51] Celibate old women in particular were thought to quench their insatiable appetites by means of sexual congress with the devil in a manner which threatens patriarchal potency—hence the disasters witches were believed to wreak on human and agricultural fertility.[52] As source of fertility the witch / mother has the power to deprive men of it.

It is interesting to note that women were persecuted *as mothers*: as bad old mothers for witchcraft, and as bad young mothers for infanticide. This is part of the effect of the emergence of "woman" as a catego-

---

[47] Larner, 1.

[48] Here I disagree with Barbara Rosen's assertion that English witchcraft was, in contrast to European witch beliefs, essentially a folk belief. As her evidence, Rosen cites the importance of Reginald Scot's skeptical treatise, ignoring the fact that James I ordered all copies of it burnt and ignoring all legislation on witchcraft practices as well as minimalizing the effect of the widely available *Malleus maleficarum*; see Barbara Rosen, ed. *Witchcraft* (London: Edward Arnold, 1969), 19–20.

[49] Boxer and Quataert, 33.

[50] Jones, 214.

[51] Quoted by Thomas, 679.

[52] See Harris, 6.

ry in early modern discourse. After 1560, this latter phenomenon became an "infanticide craze," "which may have resulted in more executions than the famous witch-craze."[53] Interestingly, children and sometimes even babies were used to indict witches, and the sadistic sexual curiosity[54] of witch "interrogations" involved elaborate searches of women's bodies for the witch's mark, a teat from which devils' familiars (a peculiarly English aspect of diabolism) were believed to suck the witch's blood.[55] This was often located in the genital area. Keith Thomas points out that in the English witch trials in particular the teat was, as early as 1579, stated to be "a common token to know all witches by."[56] Such a nipple was a sign of a maternal function, source of nourishment but also a source of sexual pleasure which had escaped patriarchal appropriation. In James's reign emphasis on devil's marks in witch trials increased.[57]

Witchcraft persecution thus utilizes a profoundly scientific, empirical method in many respects, one for which the female body is the principal object of knowledge. Lady Macbeth too is subject to the scientific scrutiny of the Doctor: "This disease is beyond my practice; yet I have known those which have walk'd in their sleep, who have died holily in their beds" (5.1.55–57). Lady Macbeth's instigation of the murder of Duncan is, in one sense, rationalized by her subsequent neurotic compulsions, "What will these hands ne'er be clean?" (5.1.41). The doctor's prognosis refers her to spiritual rather than physical remedy: "More needs she the divine than the physician" (5.1.171). Lady Macbeth remains a "fiend-like Queen" who was nonetheless subject to very feminine remorse. More importantly, Lady Macbeth becomes one of the most notable suicides in dramatic history, killing herself not because she has been violated, dishonored, grief-stricken, or the victim of unrequited love, but because she has descended to the depths of a peculiarly modern despair:

> 'tis thought, by self and violent hands
> Took off her life   (5.9.36–37)

---

[53] J. A. Sharpe, "The History of Crime in Late Medieval and Early Modern England: A Review of the Field," *Social History* 7 (1982): 200. Also quoted by Stallybrass, "Patriarchal Territories."

[54] Jones, 226; see K. M. Briggs, *Pale Hecate's Team: An Examination of the Beliefs on Witchcraft and Magic among Shakespeare's Contemporaries and His Immediate Successors* (New York: Humanities Press, 1962), 39.

[55] Thomas, 530.

[56] Thomas, 530.

[57] Alan Macfarlane, *Witchcraft in Tudor and Stuart England* (New York: Harper and Row, 1970), 19; see also Antonia Fraser, *The Weaker Vessel* (New York: Vintage Books, 1985), 110–15.

By about 1615 James joined the ranks of those skeptical about the existence of witchcraft, ranks which included Sir Reginald Scott and Sir Robert Filmer, both of whom were avid exponents of divine right.[58] James now declared that witches who had formerly merited the sternest punishment were merely afflicted with what we now call hysteria, what he called "the mother."[59] Like Lady Macbeth, the witch in Jacobean culture had become the hysteric, a scientific phenomenon rather than a disturbing threat to phallic power. The modernity of this transformation is apparent in that it is identical to Freud's diagnosis of the witch.[60] The witch had metamorphosed into a new creature, the ailing nurturer at a time when *childhood* is "discovered" and *motherhood* invented.[61] The breast, often exposed in seventeenth-century portraits of noblewomen, took on a new significance now symbolizing charity, nourishment, and selfless ardor.[62]

By 1609, the *Masque of Queens* represented female warriors as the antithesis of female demonism shown in the anti-masque.[63] Notably, Queen Anne played the rather lascivious Bel-Anna (with echoes of her antithesis, Spenser's chaste Bel-pheobe). Crucially, however, as Jonathan Goldberg has pointed out, Bell Anna's arrival is accomplished by Perseus, the embodiment of heroism, whose virtue is "described specifically as the power of giving birth."[64] Here, in the appropriation of female generativity, warrior masculinity is problematized, feminized, and destabilized. Simultaneously, Motherhood receives the ultimate patriarchal sanction. This complex historical shift in the gender categories, which is motivated by the scientific empiricist impulse to define femininity by its most obvious biological marker, the ability to give birth, is both recorded by and participated in by Shakespeare's *Macbeth*.

Syracuse University

---

[58] Preface to *The Daemonologie*.

[59] Williams, 115.

[60] Clément and Cixous, 12.

[61] Boxer and Quataert, 37. For feminist critiques of the dominant ideology of motherhood see *Mothering: Essays in Feminist Theory*, ed. Joyce Trebilcot (Savage, Maryland: Rowman and Littlefield, 1983) and *Women and Stepfamilies*, ed. Nan Bauer Maglin and Nancy Schniedewind (Philadelphia: Temple Univ. Press, 1989).

[62] Marina Warner, *Monuments and Maidens: The Allegorical Figure of the Female Form* (New York: Atheneum, 1985), 285.

[63] Quoted by Harris, 70.

[64] Jonathan Goldberg, "Fatherly Authority: The Politics of Stuart Family Images," in *Rewriting the Renaissance*, ed. Ferguson et al., 9.

AMY LECHTER-SIEGEL

Isabella's Silence: The Consolidation of Power in Measure for Measure

IN ACT 1 OF *MEASURE FOR MEASURE*, THE NOVICE ISABELLA FIRST APpears on stage in obedience before a religious authority of whom she requests a life of severe asceticism. In Isabella's first major speech, she makes closely reasoned pleas for the Christian principle of mercy. By contrast, in act 5 Isabella appears in supplication before a secular authority and first makes emotional and then poorly reasoned pleas for the secular principles of justice and equity. In the final scene, the novice, who had requested a cloistered life of chastity and severe simplicity, anticipates a public life of marriage and courtly opulence. A character who is first described to the audience as an eloquent and persuasive speaker is, in the final moment of the play, silent.

What transpires between acts 1 and 5 to bring about this reversal? Can we view Isabella as a developing dramatic character whose desires change from the beginning to the end of the play? Many critics imply that we can and argue that this alteration is a happy development brought about under the Duke/Friar's tutelage and testing. Some critics argue that Isabella receives a "moral education": she realizes that she was too severe at the start in refusing so resolutely to show mercy for her brother by sacrificing her chastity.[1] Other critics argue that Isabella receives a sexual education: Anne Barton, for example, argues that "beneath the habit of the nun is a passionate girl afflicted with an irrational fear of sex which she has never admitted to herself."[2] Similarly, many see the Duke's marriage proposition as a felicitous ending:

---

[1] Jonathan Dollimore, "Transgression and Surveillance in *Measure for Measure*," in Jonathan Dollimore and Alan Sinfield, eds., *Political Shakespeare* (Ithaca: Cornell Univ. Press, 1985), 87. Dollimore, in his footnotes, points to the many critics who see Isabella as too severe in refusing Angelo's bargain.

[2] Anne Barton, "*Measure for Measure*," in *The Riverside Shakespeare* (Boston: Houghton-Mifflin, 1974), 546. Barton further argues that finally "Isabella arrives at a newer and juster knowledge of herself."

Bullough notes, "Isabella yields and thereby proves herself too valuable to the world to immure herself in a convent."[3]

The problem with all these views, it seems to me, is that they are value judgments imposed from outside based on the critic's assessment of moral, or sexually healthy, or socially beneficial behavior and that they do not consider the ending in terms of Isabella's own behavior and expressed desires. If we consider these, there seems to be nothing in the play which leads us to conclude that she gains a new moral or psychic awareness or that her desires change from the beginning to the end. She never considered the concept of mercy to require that she commit a mortal sin, nor does her final plea for mercy at the end encompass that idea. And there is no hint, in word or deed, that Isabella develops any burgeoning awareness of her own sexuality. Finally, in the end, she does not willfully "yield" to the proposition of marriage; rather, in the face of command masquerading as a proposal, Isabella is silent.

Thus, if we cannot see Isabella as a developing dramatic character for whom the ending is a satisfactory resolution, we must look for the function of her character and the significance of the resolution elsewhere. I suggest that we see Isabella less as a character than as a representative of certain ideas. I am in agreement with Marcia Riefer, who has traced the process by which Isabella becomes increasingly directed by the patriarchal control of the Duke until her voice is "literally" lost.[4] Riefer persuasively argues that the anomalous ending represents "the incompatibility of sexual subjugation with successful comic dramaturgy."[5] I would like both to build on and to shift significantly the focus of that position by arguing that the Duke/Friar represents not generalized patriarchal control, but rather historically specific Jamesian-style control as James I outlines his concept of absolutist authority in the *Basilikon Doron*. In this context, Isabella can be understood to represent two specific challenges to Vincentio's absolutist position. First, in her adherence to religious authority, Isabella resists the secular control of the state; and second, in her adherence to virginity, she resists the social control of the Duke as both a private and public patriarch.[6]

---

[3] Geoffrey Bullough, *Narrative and Dramatic Sources of Shakespeare* (New York: Columbia Univ. Press, 1973), 2:416.

[4] Marcia Riefer, "Instruments of Some Mightier Member," *Shakespeare Quarterly* 35 (1984): 157–69. Riefer's argument, to which I am indebted, maintains that the Duke assumes the comic role of dramaturgical control previously assumed by females in Shakespeare's comedies and that deprived of this comedic leadership, Isabella comes under the control of the Duke. Riefer's emphasis is on genre.

[5] Ibid., 158.

[6] For a fuller and more recent discussion of how the choice of chastity represents an "alternative sexuality" to the dominant patriarchal forms represented in the play,

Further, as a highly articulate spokesperson of these ideas, her rhetoric is especially threatening to the state. If we understand Isabella in this way, we can understand her "development" as a process of containment whereby the challenges she represents are eliminated in the play's resolution.

Such a reading is based on already extensive scholarship which argues for the interrelationship of *Measure for Measure*, the *Basilikon Doron*, and James I and which maintains an identification of the Duke/Friar with King James.[7] First, I wish to add to this scholarship by arguing that the *Basilikon Doron* can be read as James's program for consolidating religious, secular political, and social power and that *Measure* can be read as a parallel text in which the same program is reproduced. Second, I wish to show how the process of containment is reflected in the Duke's ability to transform and to control Isabella's speech.

James opens the *Basilikon Doron* with a sonnet which defines his divine right style of rule. It begins:

> God giues not Kings the stile of *Gods* in vaine,
> For on his Throne his Scepter doe they swey: (3)[8]

This idea is echoed again when he urges his son "to know and love that God ... for that he made you as a little GOD that sit on his Throne, and rule ouer other men" (12).

James's program for the consolidation of religious, secular political, and social power in a divine right monarch is benignly couched as advice to his son on the proper behavior of a king in his three roles of good Christian, of good ruler, and of model virtuous social being—roles

---

see Susan Carlson, "'Fond Fathers' and Sweet Sisters: Alternative Sexualities in *Measure for Measure*," *Essays in Literature* 16 (1989): 13–31.

[7] For a discussion of how the play reflects James's theatrical style, see Jonathan Goldberg, *James I and the Politics of Literature* (Baltimore: Johns Hopkins Univ. Press, 1983), 230–39. For a discussion of how the actual language as well as the principles of kingship of the *Basilikon Doron* are reflected in *Measure*, see David Lloyd Stevenson, *The Achievement of Shakespeare's "Measure for Measure"* (Ithaca: Cornell Univ. Press, 1966), 134–66 and Elizabeth Pope, "The Renaissance Background in *Measure for Measure*," *Shakespeare Survey* 2 (1949): 66–82. For a discussion of how the play challenges the paternalistic and patriarchal notions set forth in the *Basilikon Doron*, see "Talking Back to the King: *Measure for Measure* and the *Basilicon Doron*," *College Literature* 12 (1985): 122–34.

[8] See *The Political Works of James* with an introduction by Charles McIlwain (New York: Russell and Russell, 1965), 3–52. All quotations from the *Basilikon Doron* will be from this edition, and the page number will follow the quotation in parentheses.

which correlate to the three areas of monarchal power. I would argue that it is by the consolidation of power through the use of these three roles that James attempts to establish his absolutist position, and it is further by the elimination of all challenges to this consolidation that James seeks to sustain this position. The treatise also reflects James's perception of the obstacles to this consolidation and his extreme anxiety over these.

Because the Renaissance notion of sovereignty demanded that all people must obey the sovereign without question *unless* his demands directly contradicted God's orders,[9] it is natural that it was the power of the church (whether Anglican, Protestant, or Catholic) which would pose the greatest threat to a monarch who saw a special divinity in his rule. In the *Basilikon Doron,* James seems to perceive the challenge to his divine right position coming from two sources: the first threat comes from those who would accuse him of insufficient religiousness; and the second comes from religious leaders who would assert the priority of *their* authority over the monarch's.

His greatest anxiety is over the Anabaptists who show "contempt for the civil Magistrate," and who advocate that "Christian Princes ... be resisted." These kind of men, James writes, "I wishe my Sonne to punish, in-case they refuse to obey the Law, and will not cease to sturre up rebellion" (7). The divisiveness created by the Anabaptists furthermore increases the power of the Catholics (Papists) to challenge the authority of the state (7, 8). James exhorts his son to suppress the power of church leaders in a language which dramatically conveys both the extent of his anxiety and his absolutist stance: "as well as yee represse the vain Puritaine, so not to suffer proude Papall Bishops ... so *chaine them with such bondes* as may preserve that estate from creeping to corruption" (24) [emphasis mine].

James begins the second book of the *Basilikon Doron* with an image which marvelously suggests the consolidation of religious and secular control in the person of the king: "But as ye are clothed with two callings so must ye be alike careful for the discharge of them both: that yee are a good Christian so yee may be a good King" (18). "Clothed with two callings" describes the Friar/Duke of *Measure* who is literally so clothed, and thus by his person contains both appeals to independent religious authority (made by Isabella) and claims of independent secular authority (made by Angelo). The Duke/Friar has not only to contain these competing elements, but also to reintegrate them into society through marriage, and he arranges these marriages through the third

---

[9] Elizabeth Pope, "The Renaissance Background," 71.

role James describes in the *Basilikon Doron*—his social role as both private and public patriarch of the realm.

In the *Basilikon Doron* James notes that a good king acts, in relationship to his subjects, "as their naturall father, and kindley Master" (22). In this role, James would undertake the arrangement of marriages as an absolutist strategy of social control in order to consolidate his political position.[10] In *Measure*, Duke Vincentio is, of course, the quintessential arranger of marriages. Also, James's remarks on marriage and the choice of a wife in the *Basilikon Doron* reflect how the double-edged quality of the new Protestant conception of marriage allowed the private and public patriarch to assume more direct power over women than he previously had. The Protestant marriage gave for the first time in history priority to married chastity over Catholic asceticism and virginity.[11] While many have seen this as a happy development for women, others have realized that, to the degree that the power of the priest was diminished, to an equal degree, the power of the family patriarch was increased.[12] In the Duke's proposal to Isabella after his dramatic unhooding by Lucio, Shakespeare provides a compelling *visual* representation of this very transformation from the priority of virginity to the priority of married chastity and of the quite literal transference of power from the priest (or friar) to the husband.

As a natural father, James could claim to be a Father to the realm more convincingly than could Elizabeth claim an analogous personal leadership role before him. The Duke in *Measure for Measure* uses marriage in the end to contain all subversive elements in the society, to suppress any challenges to his divine right position, and, in good comedic fashion, to reintegrate everyone back into his society—creating a union directed by a monarch who has gained control through the consolidation of his secular political, religious, and social roles.

Finally, I would like to suggest that in the *Basilikon Doron*, James perceives the threat to his control expressed through "slander." Those who would accuse him of irreligiousness or question his religious authority he accuses of "famous libels," "iniurious speeches," and dishonorable "inuectiue" against all Christian princes (7) and maintains that the "malicious lying tongues of some haue traduced me" (13). His

---

[10] Leonard Tennenhouse, "Representing Power: Measure for Measure in Its Time," in Stephen Greenblatt, ed. *The Power of Forms in the English Renaissance* (Norman: Pilgrim Books, 1982), 152–53. Tennenhouse compares Elizabeth's attitudes toward arranging marriages with James's.

[11] Juliet Dusinberre, *Shakespeare and the Nature of Women* (London: Macmillan, 1975), 3–5, 22–24, 32–33, 41–48 , 55.

[12] Walter Cohen, *Drama of a Nation: Public Theatre in Renaissance England and Spain* (Ithaca: Cornell Univ. Press, 1985), 188.

anxiety is so great that he advises his son, again in absolutist language, that the "remedie" for "vnreuerent speakers" is to "stop their mouthes from all such idle and vnreuerent speeches" (27). Although it is Lucio who most persistently represents the threat of slander, and it is Lucio's mouth which most obviously will not be stopped, Isabella too threatens and eventually does slander Angelo. Because her rhetoric challenges the power of the state, the Friar first directs, then effectively stops, her speech.

To reiterate, I have argued that Isabella challenges the Duke/Friar's absolutist position in two ways. First, by invoking religious authority over secular (in her arguments to the Duke's representative, Angelo), she challenges the secular political control of the state; second, by choosing virginity, she resists the social control of the monarch as patriarch of the realm. Now, I would like to argue that the play enacts the containment of those challenges and that the process of containment can be traced by following Isabella's changing discourse: first, Isabella generates reasoned arguments which challenge the state; next, under the Duke/Friar, her language is directed by the state; and finally, her speech is contained by the state.

In the early scenes of the play, Claudio says of his sister, "she hath prosperous art / When she will play with reason and discourse / And well she can persuade" (1.2.184). The first time we see Isabella she stands before a nun of whom she requires not a lesser, but a stricter restraint within the already strictly ascetic order of St. Clare. Further, we learn in this scene that once Isabella enters the order she must take a vow of silence forbidding her to speak to and be looked upon by men at the same time. Interestingly, while Isabella will *freely admit* to the imposition of silence in obeisance to religious authority, she will, in the meantime, use her arts of language brilliantly in the next scenes to challenge and inadvertently threaten secular authority.

In her first encounter with Angelo, Isabella challenges his secular authority by using logical appeals which show proficiency in close reasoning and the ability to make clear distinctions. She presses her case by making eight reasoned pleas. Each time she makes an argument based on Christian principles, Angelo counters with an argument based on secular legal authority. Thus, a dialectic movement is set up between these two sources of power. Finally, Isabella audaciously challenges Angelo's position by daring to project herself (woman and novice) into the role of the head of state: "I would to heaven I had your potency, And you were Isabel" (2.2.71). This bold assertion is based on her sense of power as a follower—and perhaps to a certain extent as a representative—of religious authority. In her final pleas, Isabella challenges the very legitimacy of secular authority itself, deploring the tyrannous exercise of power by "proud men dressed in a little brief authority" (2.2.118). Having reminded him that his authority is not absolute (an argument that implicitly interrogates the Jamesian absolutist position), she tells him to look inside himself. This argument inadvertently leads to Angelo's realization that her words have compelled him to love her and to his (quite liberal) loss of control. There is thus a correlation suggested here between loss of sexual control and loss of political control. Both the content and manner of Isabella's speech threatens the control of the representative of the state, and the rest of the play is concerned with containing that threat. Importantly, between Isabella's and Angelo's first and second meetings the Duke/Friar makes a brief appearance which seems to have little dramatic purpose. However, his appearance can function as a visual synthesis of the religious/secular dialectic, and thus it rehearses the ultimate consolidation of religious and secular power in the person of the monarch at the end of the play.

In her second meeting with Angelo, Isabella is forced from the offensive position of challenging secular authority to the rhetorically weaker defensive position of resisting that authority's attempts to possess her sexually. Again, the dialectic is resumed with Angelo invoking the authority of the state in order to propose that Isabella exchange her virginity for her brother's life, while she invokes the religious principle that death is better than eternal damnation. Her integrity of speech is maintained when Angelo suggests she respond in a more "womanly" way; she answers, "I have no tongue but one ..." (2.4.139). When Angelo presses further, she threatens slander: "Sign me a present pardon ... / Or ... I'll tell the world aloud / What man thou art" (2.4.152–85). But Angelo's retort that no one will believe her suggests that the punishment for the slanderer is rhetorical powerlessness: "you will stifle in your own report and smell of calumny" (2.4.158–59). This scene signals the beginning of the process by which Isabella's strength of speech is undermined.

When in the next scene the brother whom she trusts implies that she should submit, her rhetoric breaks down to a vituperative and aggressive hurling of epithets. This change suggests a breakdown of what one critic has called that "strong self" constituted by her rhetoric.[13] We might assume that Isabella, fleeing from Claudio, is rushing back to the convent when the Duke/Friar suddenly appears before her and bids a word. She responds, "What is your will?" (3.1.152). Humiliated by the forces of secular authority, she is anxious to cleave to religious authority, and when the Friar suggests a plan, she consents: "Show me how

---

[13] Dusinberre, 224.

good father" (3.3.238). At this point in the play we see not a development of Isabella's personality but a shift in her position from one of powerful and articulate resistance to secular authority to (though unbeknownst to her) submission to it. From now on the Duke/Friar maintains control over Isabella by making her believe Claudio is dead and then by scripting a scenario which requires her to announce publicly that she is a violated virgin—a remarkable request considering both her integrity of speech ("I have no tongue but one") and her vocation of chastity. As Riefer points out, despite Isabella's reluctance "to speak so indirectly" (4.6.1), she gives over rhetorical control when she vows to the Duke/Friar, "I am directed by you" (4.3.137).[14]

In act 5, Isabella's rhetoric demonstrates a changed relationship to the state. Whereas the use of close reasoning in support of mercy describes her first encounter with Angelo, here she is making a pathetic appeal for justice—the secular principle she renounced in act 1. Regaining her capacity for reasoned argument, however, she presses her charges against Angelo with careful distinctions and analogies once again: "'tis not impossible / But one, the wicked'st caitiff on the ground, / May seem as shy, as grave, as just, as absolute, as Angelo ..."(5.1.52–55). Ironically, her strong discourse constitutes slander, and the Duke—consistent with the Jamesian absolutist position—must contain the slander by imprisoning Isabella. This is a very interesting moment, for here we see the Duke constructig a threat to secular authority (in the role consigned to Isabella), and then through his consolidated secular/religious authority containing that threat. It will be marriage, not imprisonment, that is the final mode of containment; but, I would argue, the imprisonment of Isabella makes the final solution of marriage seem benevolent by contrast.

This same process of constructing the threat in order to contain it occurs again when Vincentio re-presents himself on stage as the Friar who slanders the Duke. Here he constructs a challenge by religious authority, not only to secular authority (as was the case with Isabella's challenge), but to divine right monarchy. Again a dialectic is played out between the "Friar" and Escalus (5.1.305) in which the Friar claims religious authority is not subject to monarchy ("The Duke / Dare no more stretch this finger of mine than he / Dare rack his own. His subject I am not" [5.1.313–15]). The Friar's challenge, which so compellingly echoes the threats James perceives from churchmen in the *Basilikon Doron*, is once again contained by Escalus, who accuses the Friar of "slander to the state" and orders his imprisonment.

---

[14] Riefer, 164.

At this point, Lucio unhoods the Friar to expose the Duke. At last, the consolidation of religious and secular power in the person of the Jamesian divine right monarch is visually represented in this brilliant coup de théâtre. Angelo confirms his divinity: "I perceive your Grace, like power divine" (5.1.369). But what of Isabella to whom he entreats, "Come hither, Isabel, / Your friar is now your prince"? When secular power (embodied in Angelo) was re-presented as religious power (embodied in the Friar) Isabella bent to its will. But after she cleaved unto religious authority, that authority re-presented itself once again as divine right absolutist authority. This visual transformation, suggestive of a magician's sleight, brilliantly conveys *how* Isabella comes under the sway of the state. *That* she comes under its sway is demonstrated in her final plea for Angelo.

In this plea, Isabella argues for mercy, but instead of grounding this argument on Christian principles as she had earlier, she now grounds it on the secular principle of equity: "His act did not o'ertake his bad intent / And must be buried but as an intent / That perish'd by the way" (5.1.450–54). While secular law makes a distinction between intent and action, theological law *does not*; an argument by Christ would see Angelo's transgression as a serious violation of God's law. Furthermore, Isabella's argument is illogical, for Angelo did not only intend to engage in illicit sex, but, in sleeping with his fiancée, he actually did the very same thing Claudio did. Isabella's inability to make that distinction, when her forte all along has been the ability to perceive distinctions, represents the final dissolution of that "strong self" constituted by her rhetoric.

In the final consolidation of power, the Duke uses the Jamesian social role of patriarch in order to reintegrate his citizens into society through marriage. But the Duke's use of marriage is an absolutist strategy which can be at variance with individual desire. Lucio makes this clear when he tells the Duke, who directs him to marry a whore, that he'd rather be whipped: "Marrying a punk, my lord, is pressing to death, whipping, and hanging" (5.1.522–23). The Duke replies, "Slandering a prince deserves it" (5.2.524). That the imposition of marriage is an absolutist strategy in this play, in contrast to most Shakespearean comedies, is suggested by the fact that of those who are married off in the end, fully half—Angelo, Lucio, and Isabella—do not desire it.

The problematic "deus ex machina" ending which troubles many critics becomes singularly appropriate if the play is understood as one about "ideas" more than about "characters" and about specifically Jamesian ideas—as these are articulated in *Basilikon Doron*—of consolidating secular political, religious, and social power by ruling (as the Duke/Friar does) in "the stile of *Gods*." The very contrivance of the ending, wherein the events do not seem to evolve naturally and dramatically from the desires of the individual characters, but rather are imposed from without (by a kind of god from a machine), suggests the very style of authoritarianism and absolutism which, I have maintained, the play is "about."

Isabella's silence at the end of *Measure for Measure* has provided a challenge for theatrical directors of the play. Jonathan Miller's National Theatre production had Isabella turn away in horror at the Duke's proposal of marriage;[15] by extreme contrast, another recent production had Isabella throw off her veil in a celebratory and liberating gesture. While Miller's interpretation is consistent with Isabella's "dramatic character," it contradicts the play's movement toward comic resolution. On the other hand, the second interpretation, while true to the play's movement towards resolution, is so totally contrary to Isabella's character that it altogether lacks dramatic veracity. Shakespeare gives us neither Miller's nor any other response from Isabella. He gives us silence. It is "silence," argues Pierre Macherey, that "the critic must make speak."[16] Isabella's silence speaks most convincingly, I believe, as an expression of the Jamesian Duke/Friar's successful containment of voices which challenge his absolutist claims to authority. However, containment does not imply any simple or comfortable acquiescence by those voices. Rather, speechlessness can also be interpreted as a *refusal* to assent positively to the control of an "other." It is for this reason, I believe, that Isabella's silence reverberates in our minds long after the play is done.

University of Maryland—College Park

---

[15] Arthur Kirsch, *Shakespeare and the Experience of Love* (Cambridge: Cambridge Univ. Press, 1981), 71.

[16] Pierre Macherey in Terry Eagleton, *Marxism and Literary Criticism* (Berkeley: Univ. of California Press, 1976), 35.

JYOTSNA SINGH

The Influence of Feminist Criticism / Theory on Shakespeare Studies, 1976–1986

I

IN THE INTRODUCTION TO THEIR COLLECTION OF ESSAYS, ENTITLED *The Woman's Part* (1980), the editors, Carolyn Swift, Gayle Green, and Carol Thomas Neely, announced their early agenda for feminist criticism of Shakespeare's works: "Feminists assume that women are equal to men but that their roles, more often than men's and in different ways, have been restricted, stereotyped, minimized." Therefore, "feminist critics are profoundly concerned with understanding the parts women have played, do play, and might play in literature as well as in culture." The purpose of such criticism, as they saw it, was to "compensate for a bias in a critical tradition that has tended to emphasize male characters, male themes, and male fantasies."[1] The agenda stated in this anthology had already been legitimized in a special session on feminist criticism at the 1976 MLA convention, and had been voiced at other MLA sessions and conferences from which some of the essays in this volume emerged.

Now, more than ten years later, feminist criticism marks a broad space in Shakespeare studies. Inclusive in its scope, often eclectic and provocative, feminist work on Shakespeare has incorporated a variety of approaches and methodologies: deconstruction, new historicism, and Marxism, among others. Its impact has been most striking in its critique and revision of a long tradition of liberal-humanist criticism that assumed as natural a scheme of gender relations in which women had stereotyped or subordinate roles. Shakespearean critics, until recently, often implicitly accepted the patriarchal value system and saw no significance in questioning the playwright's treatment of "timeless" institutions and practices such as the family and marriage—especially in the

---

[1] Carolyn Ruth Swift Lenz, Gayle Greene, Carol Thomas Neely, *The Woman's Part: Feminist Criticism of Shakespeare* (Urbana: Univ. of Illinois Press, 1980), 3, 4.

context of contemporary assumptions about women.

The feminist perspective on Shakespeare's works in the 1970s and 1980s, I will argue, has gradually challenged the ideology of the gender system that in criticism—as in social practice—has so long passed for the "truth." My purpose in this essay is to examine this collective feminist project by charting its history and looking to its future. I begin by briefly summarizing the two phases through which feminist criticism has transformed itself into an ideologically aware theoretical enterprise: the first feminist impact of the 1970s opened a new avenue of approach to the plays by bringing to the center those characters whose presence was considered marginal—for instance, by giving characters like Ophelia, Gertrude, and Desdemona an importance and existence beyond the tragic heroes' perceptions of them.[2] This criticism, closely aligned to liberal-cultural feminism, contested the misogyny often ascribed to the plays and that frequently surfaced in traditional readings of them. Its obvious purpose was to reappraise and reorder the values ascribed to men and women, specifically, by privileging qualities that were considered innately feminine.

The critical practice of the second phase, covering the 1980s, marks the development of feminist criticism into feminist *theory*—by which I mean that critics are not only incorporating the assumptions of other modes of critical inquiry to their readings, but are also beginning to theorize their own and others' critical positions. Contemporary feminist readings, *specifically* those emerging from the ideological grid of cultural materialism and new historicism—two related by increasingly diverging theoretical modes—acknowledge the value of the prior work, but radically question its assumptions and methods. Examining the earlier, "mimetic, essentialist model of feminist criticism," Kathleen McLuskie critiques it for "defining certain characteristics as feminine and admiring them as a better way to survive in the world." Marxist feminist critics such as McLuskie and Catherine Belsey critique the *essentialist* approach for trying to assert a "moral connection between the mimetic world of Shakespeare's plays and the real world of the audience" and for presenting the characters as representative men and women and the categories male and female as "essential, unchanging, definable in modern, commonsense terms."[3] The critical practice that they propose is more self-consciously multi-faceted: it assumes the social construction of human identity and gender as well as a complex, intertextual rela-

---

[2] Ibid., 4–5.
[3] Kathleen McLuskie, "The Patriarchal Bard: Feminist Criticism and Shakespeare," in *Political Shakespeare: New Essays in Cultural Materialism*, eds. Jonathan Dollimore and Alan Sinfield (Ithaca: Cornell Univ. Press, 1985), 89–90.

tionship between literary texts and their social and cultural contexts—a relationship in which literature is a "*part* of history, and the literary text as a much a context for other parts of cultural and material life as they are for it."[4] In stressing such an interactive relation between text and context, contemporary feminist critics show how the concept, the "nature of woman," becomes problematic as one tries to reconstruct it from various social and ideological positions, as well as from the various discursive modes and practices, of the Renaissance.[5]

II

When the anthology *The Woman's Part* was published in 1980, it marked the initial impact of the political feminist movement of the 1960s and 1970s on the literary criticism of Shakespeare. The essays in this volume clearly align themselves to the cause of feminism in the different functions they perform: "they liberate Shakespeare's women from the stereotypes to which they have too often been confined; they examine women's relations to each other; they analyze the nature and effect of patriarchal structures; and they explore the influence of genre in the portrayal of women."[6] Despite their diversity of methods, the contributors to *The Woman's Part* are unified by the task of restoring female identity to the plays. What they also share is a positive image of the playwright: taking a generally *ahistorical* approach, the different critics focus on dramatic strategies and themes which represent women in a favorable light and question male values. Shakespeare is, in effect, co-opted by feminist critics who construct him as a sympathetic author challenging the orthodoxies of his culture, and often taking "the woman's part."

Catherine Stimpson's powerful essay, "Shakespeare and the Soil of Rape," typifies the tone and methodology of the anthology with its emphasis on Shakespeare's sympathy for women—in this instance for women as rape victims in an era when rape meant loss of virtue. The playwright, according to Stimpson, "never falters, never hedges, as he shows how defenseless women are before sexual violence," and neither does he seem imaginatively obsessed by the act. While Stimpson's essay

---

[4] Jean Howard, "The New Historicism in Renaissance Studies," *English Literary Renaissance* 16 (1986): 25.

[5] Kathleen McLuskie pertinently suggests that "far from being an unproblematic concept, the 'nature of woman' was under severe pressure from both ideological discourses and the real concomitants of inflation and demographic change" (91).

[6] *The Woman's Part*, 4.

makes a case for Shakespeare's feminist leanings, it also acknowledges that it is the perversion of patriarchal authority that is under attack in Shakespeare's works, and not patriarchy itself—and that the playwright never ceases to remind his audiences of "the boundaries that marriage places on female sexuality."[7]

Thus the issue of rape is linked to prevailing conceptions of female sexuality in Renaissance England, but Stimpson only briefly touches upon the socio-historical conditions underlying Shakespeare's treatment of sexual violence. Instead, she concerns herself with rape as a source and emblem of a number of conflicts in his works: between "unnatural disorder and natural order";[8] between the honorable and dishonorable exercise of power, the "good" and "bad" selves in the rapist's mind; and above all, between a woman as helpless victim and the rapist male aggressor. The conflict between male and female is spelt out in terms of predetermined moral categories in which the identities of men and women figure forth as unmediated entities. Stimpson's reading, while illuminating, is thus limited by its binarism and by its exclusion of historically-specific considerations of female sexuality.

A few essays, however, look beyond this kind of simple dualism and seem more aware of the cultural ideals and premises which influence gender definitions. Among these, a particularly provocative study is "The Miranda Trap: Sexism and Racism in Shakespeare's *The Tempest*." Examining Miranda's role within the frame of sexual and racial politics in the play—which reflect the Christian-humanist race and gender divisions in the seventeenth century—Lorie Jerrell Leininger concludes with an epilogue in which a twentieth-century Miranda dismantles Prospero's assumptions of a predetermined hierarchical order: "My father is no God-figure.... My father is a man, and fallible, as I am.... There is no such thing as a 'natural slave'.... I will not be used as the excuse for his [Caliban's] enslavement."[9]

Through the voice of a contemporary Miranda, the critic makes a significant move to rewrite Prospero's fatherly scheme of social relations predicated on racism and sexism. Despite Leininger's obvious political intent in exposing relations considered natural—such as those between father and daughter or master and slave—as being a part of an arbitrary system of domination and oppression, she also finally essentializes the characters into a transhistorical community of "real" people, possessing unchanging attributes that make them either victims or oppressors.

While this study of *The Tempest*, and, it seems to me, a few other

---

[7] In *The Woman's Part*, 59, 62.
[8] Ibid., 57.
[9] In *The Woman's Part*, 291–92.

essays in *The Woman's Part*, attempt to look beyond a simple binary view of gender relations, the anthology as a whole is limited by the fact that its focus remains on *reversing* patriarchal values. Thus, boundaries marking sexual difference remain intact as the essays assume the existence of an "irreducible feminine identity."[10] However, despite our present critique of it, the feminist criticism of the 1970s made a significant breakthrough in revealing that criticism prior to or coinciding with early feminism was not *gender neutral* as is, perhaps, perceived by some. Feminist readings of the 1970s were quick to note how prior critics often conveniently judged the women characters through the misogynistic perspective of some male characters—and like them, condemned what they believed to be the "nature of women."

L. T. Fitz's famous article, "Egyptian Queens and Male Reviewers: Sexist Attitudes in *Antony and Cleopatra* Criticism" (1977), is one such critical landmark that first exposed sexist assumptions underlying traditional approaches to Shakespeare. Fitz makes her point effectively by demonstrating how Cleopatra has been cut off from serious consideration as a tragic protagonist by being compared to other heroines, most of whom inhabit the comedies. Related to this habit of prior critics to discuss women characters as a group is the tactic of describing Cleopatra as an archetypal "woman—a practicer of feminine wiles, mysterious, childlike, long on passion and short on intelligence."[11] Thus, using labels like "eternal woman" and "quintessential woman," generations of critics, Fitz argues, have never been considered the political dimensions of Cleopatra's role as a ruler—in part because they had no model for discussing her as a tragic hero of the same stature as the male figures. Fitz's exposure of the implicit sexist bias of earlier readings typifies the work of the critics of the 1970s who first identified the gender inflections of a seemingly unbiased and innocent criticism.

III

The feminism of the 1980s came into being via a new awareness of gender as a social and historical product. Jonathan Dollimore, in *Political Shakespeare* (1985), outlines the matrix of this new interest in cultural analysis, which drew the interest of feminists, among others, and labels it "cultural materialism" as it is known in Britain and "new histori-

---

[10] See Catherine Belsey's discussion of this term in "Disrupting Sexual Difference: Meaning and Gender in the Comedies," in *Alternative Shakespeares*, ed. John Drakakis (London: Methuen, 1985), 188–90.

[11] *Shakespeare Quarterly* 28 (1977): 298.

cism" in America. In examining the convergence of "history, sociology, and English in cultural studies" Dollimore successfully counters the conventional view that Shakespeare's "universal" genius enables his works to transcend history and politics. Instead, Dollimore places the literary texts within the historical and social process, demonstrating materialist criticism's urgent concern with "the way that beliefs, practices, and institutions legitimate the dominant social order or status quo—the existing relations of domination and subordination—" and, in the process, naturalize the existing social and political order.[12]

The impact of such an emphasis on the influence of ideological and social structures had already been felt on the feminist criticism of Shakespeare in the 1980—most significantly, in Lisa Jardine's seminal work from Britain, *Still Harping on Daughters* (1983). Explicitly setting out to correct the deficiencies of the ahistorical and realist bias of earlier criticism, Jardine gave a radically new direction to the feminist project. Earlier approaches, according to the critic, were limited by their acceptance of the characters as "real people," and, more importantly, by their assumption that Shakespeare's "female characters reflect accurately the whole range of specifically female qualities which are supposed to be fixed and immutable from Shakespeare's age to our own."[13]

To remedy the limitations of such a transhistorical perspective, Jardine proposes a critical practice that would read "the relationship between real social conditions and literary representation." Drawing on diverse historical documents ranging from antitheatrical tracts to contemporary accounts of Elizabeth I's intellectual skills, the critic explores the ways in which Elizabethan attitudes and expectations about femaleness and maleness shaped and were shaped by a network of cultural influences. In her provocative opening chapter, for instance, Jardine examines the tradition of the boy player—and the history of the polemic against cross-dressing—to make us wary of ascribing "real" female virtues and insights to women characters. "The boy player," according to the critic, "armed with his arsenal of female characteristics and mannerisms mimes out acceptable forms of [what may be considered] as real womanly feelings," but are in fact stereotype representations of women—for instance, of heroic womanhood prostrate with grief.[14]

The significance of Jardine's critical practice to feminism is noteworthy: in showing how notions of femininity and masculinity are pro-

---

[12] Jonathan Dollimore, "Introduction: Shakespeare, Cultural Materialism and New Historicism," in *Political Shakespeare*, 2–15.

[13] *Still Harping on Daughters: Women and Drama in the Age of Shakespeare* (Brighton: Harvester Press, 1983), 3.

[14] Ibid., 7, 33.

duced and managed through cultural discourses, the critic exposes the gender system as being a social and political construct rather than a "natural" entity—a construct often involving an arbitrary relation of domination and oppression between the sexes. One drawback to Jardine's study, however, is that even while promoting a pluralistic perspective, the critic seems to privilege history over literature and ignores the formal elements of the literary text.

Howsoever we might judge the merits of individual critical works, it must be clear by now that feminist critics of Shakespeare in the 1980s increasingly see themselves as engaged in an ideological critique of the social practices and discursive modes by which any culture perceives and represents its world. And in emphasizing how sexual difference is constructed within social and cultural traditions, feminist studies broadly conform to what feminist historian Joan Kelly has defined as the imperative need for any study of female experience: they have a "multi-faceted focus on sexual ideologies, on women's ... social, political, and cultural ... activities."[15] Such a practice characterizes a number of significant critical studies in recent years—for instance, those of Karen Newman, Coppélia Kahn, Kathleen McLuskie, Peter Stallybrass, and Catherine Belsey. Here, it is important to note that while the surge of interest in cultural analysis is being felt in Shakespeare studies as a whole—both in Britain and America—the new historicist treatment of gender differs from the feminist concerns of the British Marxist critics.[16]

Until recently, cultural/ideological criticism, both in terms of its assumptions about the relationship between history and literature and in its methodology, had been thought to encompass new historicism in America and cultural materialism in Britain.[17] The current debate in Shakespeare studies, however, makes it apparent that the major new historicist scholars in America—Stephen Greenblatt, Louis Montrose, and Jonathan Goldberg—unlike feminist critics, subordinate concerns of

---

[15] Joan Kelly, cited in Mary Beth Rose, *Women in the Middle Ages and the Renaissance* (Syracuse: Syracuse Univ. Press, 1986), xiii.

[16] See Walter Cohen's "Political Criticism of Shakespeare," in *Shakespeare Reproduced: The Text in History and Ideology*, ed. Jean E. Howard and Marion F. O'Connor (London and New York: Methuen, 1987), 18–46. In this essay the critic clearly charts the diverging trends in the feminist critical practice of the two countries. The work of British Marxist critics such as McLuskie and Belsey, according to Cohen, represents an alliance between Marxism and feminism that Gayle Greene had called for in 1981 (26). This critic's implication is that such work has not yet been initiated in America—in part because of the new historicist emphasis on power relations among males.

[17] Dollimore, 2–5, and Howard, in "The New Historicism," 12–20, view cultural materialism in Britain and new historicism in America as part of one movement.

feminism to general concerns of power—specifically, state power as manifested in institutions and in the person of the monarch—and reflect on various forms of representation as they questioned established ideologies. Therefore, seen from a feminist perspective, new historicism is primarily interested in power relations between men.[18] Walter Cohen succinctly defines this feminist critique when he states that "new historicists understand gender in relation to the body or to power more than in relation to women. The orientation toward the court only accentuates the tendency. Thus in the extreme case women cease to be historical actors or subjects. They can be victims or objects, but it is not, however complexly, their experience that matters."[19]

In some current work in America, attempts have been made to merge the concerns of new historicism and feminism. Coppélia Kahn recently made a strong case for a collaborative scholarship between the two critical modes: "[although the feminists write] about gender, sexuality, marriage, and the family, the historicists about power, ideology, and politics," Kahn argues, "theoretically, they share the same terrain, for questions of power cannot be separated from questions of gender."[20] Marilyn Williamson's *The Patriarchy of Shakespeare's Comedies* (1986) is one recent work that combines the two approaches. Marking a significant shift in emphasis from the new historicist concern with the power of the state institutions to the power relationships and sexual politics within the family, Williamson traces the changes in representations of patriarchal power in the comedic sub-genres and in the romances: the romantic comedies of the 1590s, according to the critic, dramatize a fantasy of a marriage with a powerful woman—a fantasy that had particular historical relevance in the Elizabethan period when young aristocrats had few professions and depended on the patronage of the queen. The problem comedies dealing with a patriarchal ruler and enforced marriages replace the idealization of a powerful woman with an anxiety about the unregulated sexuality of the young. Such fears were pertinent to Jacobean society when protests against enforced

---

[18] For a discussion of the tensions between new historicists and feminists on the issue of gender, see Peter Erickson's "Rewriting the Renaissance: Rewriting Ourselves," *Shakespeare Quarterly* 38 (1987): 327–37. This ongoing debate is also the subject of two important recent essays: see Lynda Boose, "The Family in Shakespeare Studies; or—Studies in the Family of Shakespeareans, or, The Politics of Politics," *Renaissance Quarterly* (1987): 707–42 and Carol Thomas Neely, "Constructing the Subject: Feminist Practice and the New Renaissance Discourses," *English Literary Renaissance* 18 (1988): 5–18.

[19] Cohen, 38.

[20] Coppélia Kahn, " 'Magic of bounty': *Timon of Athens*: Jacobean Patronage and Maternal Power," *Shakespeare Quarterly* 38 (1987): 1–17.

marriage raised issues of patriarchal control. And in the romances, Williamson argues, Shakespeare seems to valorize the power of the father/ruler by making it seem natural and necessary. Sexuality, once again, calls for control, but here the children are represented as naturally chaste.[21]

Overall, Williamson's historically-oriented reading of gender relations participates in the debate central to feminist Shakespearean criticism—a debate that questions the extent to which the patriarchal system contained and suppressed women in the Renaissance.[22] Thus, her methodology clearly marks a break from the essays in *The Woman's Part* and makes an important contribution to the current feminist-historicist trend in Shakespeare studies. Basing her analysis on Foucault's theories, the critic demonstrates how notions of sexuality and power are historically contingent—and how Shakespeare's varied representations of women are a result of changing social conditions and of differing forms of patriarchal ideology. While Williamson clearly focuses on the interaction between texts and their historical contexts, her marked tendency is to uphold her argument, sometimes even at the cost of overlooking the contradictions and gaps that may open up multiple perspectives on characters and their identities.[23] In conclusion, I would like to suggest that although Williamson's critical work has obvious literary and historical value, it does not give the feminist project any radically new direction. It would, however, have had greater political import if the critic had attempted to develop a paradigm for theorizing modern constructions of sexuality—focusing on the power "a society can exercise with regard to sexuality."[24] Her argument, undoubtedly, would have benefited from a sustained reflection on such issues.

The critical practice of the British Marxist critic Catherine Belsey differs from Williamson's work in its self-conscious theorization of its political agenda: Belsey's aim, explicitly demonstrated in *The Subject of Tragedy*, is to demystify the subject of liberal humanism—namely Man as the "unconstrained author of meaning and action. . . . Unified, knowing, autonomous." Tracing the origins of liberal humanism in the rise of the bourgeois class in the seventeenth century, Belsey persuasively

---

[21] Marilyn L. Williamson, *The Patriarchy of Shakespeare's Comedies* (Detroit: Wayne State Univ. Press, 1986), 20–22.

[22] For a fuller account of this issue see the introduction to *Rewriting the Renaissance: The Discourses of Sexual Difference in Early Modern Europe*, Margaret W. Ferguson, Maureen Quilligan, and Nancy J. Vickers (Chicago: Univ. of Chicago Press, 1986), xv–xxxi.

[23] See Phyllis Rackin, rev. of *The Patriarchy of Shakespeare's Comedies*, in *Shakespeare Quarterly* 38 (1987): 525–27.

[24] Williamson, 180.

claims that while "the autonomous subject of liberalism was in the making, women had no single or stable place from which to define themselves as independent beings." In this sense, they both "were and were not subjects."[25] If the essays in *The Woman's Part* privileged feminine identity by reversing the male/patriarchal power structure, Belsey's work clearly seems to argue for the destabilization of the whole notion of a fixed human identity.

In her original, provocative, deconstructive analysis in *The Subject of Tragedy* Belsey examines the "radically discontinuous" subject position of women in Renaissance discourses. But in that discontinuity she also finds occasions for a contest for the meaning of subjectivity and of gender, both in the different aspects of the social formation and in individual discursive practices such as drama. If women were absent in discourses defining power relations in the state, and lacked a clearly defined position in the discourses about family relations, the instability of their position also kept open the question of sexual difference—and the "meaning of what it is to be a woman." Similarly, in a number of tragedies of the period in which the definition of women in discourses controlled by men is inevitably patriarchal and reductive, characters like Cleopatra and Beatrice-Joanna, Belsey suggests, defy patriarchal inscriptions by allowing their audiences no single, unified position from which to judge them.[26] Thus, the critic notes, women's unstable positions on the margins of dominant discourses could be considered as sites of resistance, though never in our contemporary sense of the term.

In her essay "Disrupting Sexual Difference: Meaning and Gender in the Comedies," Belsey similarly turns to Shakespeare's comedies and draws our attention to the way they question "the inevitability of an antithesis between the terms masculine and feminine, men and women." Placing her reading within a social context, Belsey locates this disruption in the context of the opposition in the sixteenth and seventeenth centuries between two distinct meanings of the family: the dynastic family in which women assure its continuity; and the intimate, affective marriage where the wife is an equal partner. Even in this seeming opposition, however, "women were, once again, everything that men were not ... and their sphere of influence was the newly defined private retreat from the public world of work and politics," the home.[27]

Thus, in a period when both the family and femininity were being redefined, the artists' striking interest in female transvestism—in Ama-

---

[25] Catherine Belsey, *The Subject of Tragedy: Identity and difference in Renaissance drama* (London and New York: Methuen, 1985), 8, 150.

[26] Ibid., 148, 160–61.

[27] 167, 177.

zons, female warriors, and women disguised as pages—was not unusual. In Shakespeare's comedies, Belsey demonstrates, the comic heroines in male disguise disrupt the conventional organization of sexual difference. However, Rosalind and Viola, speaking from a position "not that of a full, unified gendered subject," do not achieve an androgynous identity which eliminates all distinctions, but instead, keep alive a sense of the multiplicity of human identity.[28]

Belsey's methodology in both works involves some marked tendencies: most significantly, she charts the construction of the subject—male or female—entirely through a range of cultural and literary discourses, which in a Foucauldian analysis of intellectual history, would be termed a "discursive field."[29] However, the drawback of applying such a methodology to an analysis of literary and social texts, as Belsey does, is that it tends to make the latter read like a history of ideas. In light of this consideration, it is not surprising that the debates that emerge in the work—about the place of women in relation to society, for instance—sometimes seem to be flattened into an intellectual argument. Even the plays themselves get subsumed within the framework of Belsey's political concerns as the critic pays limited attention to their dramaturgy, their formal design, and their conditions of performance in the theatre.

The strength of Belsey's critical practice, as I demonstrated earlier, lies in locating points of rupture in the seemingly monolithic patriarchal discourses of the sixteenth and seventeenth centuries, or more specifically, in undermining rigid notions of gender difference postulated by such discourses. It is not surprising then that the critic begins *The Subject of Tragedy* by affirming her reliance on deconstruction, both in her assumptions of the unstable nature of all discourses and in her use of it as a method of analysis:

> A specific discourse is always embattled, forever defending the limits of what is admissible, legitimate or intelligible, attempting to arrest the play of meaning as it slides toward plurality. Alternative discourses propose alternative knowledges, alternative meanings. For these reasons, signifying practice is also the location of resistances.[30]

Such a critical premise serves Belsey well in capturing those moments in Shakespeare's works when "the plurality of meaning is most insistent." As a result, this obviously "radical criticism"[31] avoids the bina-

---

[28] Ibid., 180–81.
[29] Cited by Cohen, 29.
[30] Belsey, *The Subject of Tragedy*, 6.
[31] Belsey, "Disrupting Sexual Difference," 178, 166–67.

rism and essentialism of earlier feminist readings, such as those in *The Woman's Part*, and marks a sharp break with New Criticism on which prior feminists were forced to rely.

The political implications of Belsey's methodology for feminism are significant: what she is offering us is a critical discourse whose primary aim is to unfix the existing categories of gender on which sexual stereotyping depends. At their most powerful moments, her readings produce gaps and ruptures in existing discourses in which "other modes of being for women are momentarily visible."[32] But are we to consider her perspective of a disruption in sexual differences as an Utopian ideal —an ideal that signals a world in which categories of gender are in a constant state of interplay?[33] The temptation is certainly there to advocate her practice, especially as it enables us to experience in literary and social texts "a plurality of places, of possible beings."[34] But we must realize that a playful disruption of sexual categories may also draw our attention away from seeing how the gender system—posited on hierarchy and domination—works and has worked. Thus, although Belsey affords us a new model for reading the Renaissance culture's constructions of gender, she seems to offer no means of transforming her Utopian vision into practical politics.

Concluding my survey and critique of feminist studies of Shakespeare by pointing to what is *not* accomplished by Belsey, my purpose is simply to suggest that there are new avenues left for exploration and that the feminist project does not, at any moment, suggest unity and stability. However, even as contemporary feminism grapples with its own limitations, few can deny its dramatic and provocative impact in reassessing the Shakespearean canon. Traditionally, as we are well aware, critics rendered the different works of the playwright into a revered body of "obviously meaningful works, embodying shared universal truths, recognizable by any thinking subject."[35] Contemporary feminist criticism of the 1980s, the most widely practiced form of

---

[32] Ibid., 178.

[33] The dangers of reading political meaning into a playful, deconstructive erasure of gender categories are apparent in Jonathan Goldberg's essay, "Shakespearean Inscriptions: The Voicing of Power," in *Shakespeare and the Question of Theory*, ed. Patricia Parker and Geoffrey Hartmann (London: Methuen, 1985), 116-37. Here Goldberg posits a postfeminist world that will enable "one to think oneself into the multiple forms of Shakespearean experience and beyond the divisions of gender" (137). Deconstructive wizardry such as Goldberg's can be deceiving as the critic wishfully erases all elements of patriarchialism by collapsing the distinction between the representations of the patriarchy on the stage and the culture off stage.

[34] Belsey, "Disrupting Sexual Difference," 189.

[35] James H. Kavanagh, "Shakespeare in Ideology," in *Alternative Shakespeares*, 144-64.

political criticism in Shakespeare studies, exposes these "coherent truths" as ideologies that stabilize and universalize a given social order, serving particular interests such as those of the patriarchy. Furthermore, if earlier critics viewed gender relations in Shakespeare's works as simple, immutable, and transhistorical, contemporary feminists read them as complex, changeable, and historically and socially bound. And finally, if Shakespeare was considered the touchstone of abiding human values, feminists have dismantled the assumptions of that value system.

That feminist critics have appropriated Shakespeare—the grand icon of the Anglo-American tradition—for political ends is apparent. But are the feminists, as they are accused by some, simply confusing literary criticism with politics? And shouldn't, as some would say, the two entities remain separate? My answer to this would be that if literary criticism is concerned with human experience, then how can it avoid being engaged with cultural/social beliefs about the nature of societies, interpretations of history, and problems of power, of sexuality, and of gender itself? Feminist criticism in Shakespeare studies, as in other fields, is only beginning to explore the possibilities of such an engagement. But given its record of the past ten years, the future holds promise.

Southern Methodist University

ALBERT H. TRICOMI

Shakespeare, Chapman, and the Julius Caesar Play in Renaissance Humanist Drama

THE VIEW OF SHAKESPEARE AS DISINTERESTED NATURAL POET HAS had an honored history. Mainline interpreters beginning with Johnson (who did not approve of what he saw) through J. Middleton Murry (who did) discovered a Shakespeare who eschews moral and political judgments (apart from those implied by general nature).[1] This is not to say that Shakespeare has usually been seen as indifferent to the tyranny of Macbeth or Richard III or that he takes no sides between Goneril and Cordelia, but that he declines to dismiss any character without some insight into or understanding of that character's conduct. The more exuberant, sentimental version of this theory, still current in the academy, which I do not accept—especially when I think of the prejudicial portrayals of religion or ethnicity in Shylock, Malvolio, Iago, and Joan Pucelle—is that Shakespeare possessed an unsurpassed breadth of sympathy for his characters, whatever their moral view or social station. In Dryden's famous formulation, Shakespeare possessed "of all modern, and perhaps ancient poets ... the largest and most comprehensive soul."[2]

In both versions, the view, fashioned by Jonson and Pope and developed by Schlegel, that Shakespeare was an "untutored natural

---

[1] Arthur M. Eastman, *A Short History of Shakespeare Criticism* (1968; New York: Norton, 1974), 26–30, 261–62. Traditional interpretations of the ideology of Shakespeare's political plays point to the dramatist's acceptance of the Great Chain of Being. This view functions to reinforce the perception that Shakespeare was "the Natural Order" reproduced, or in the case of G. Wilson Knight, the supernatural order. See Theodore Spencer, *Shakespeare and the Nature of Man* (New York: Macmillan, 1943; rev. ed. 1961); E. M. W. Tillyard, *The Elizabethan World Picture* (London: Chatto & Windus, 1943) and *Shakespeare's History Plays* (1942; New York: Collier, 1962), 146–47; and G. Wilson Knight, *The Wheel of Fire: Essays in Interpretation of Shakespeare's Sombre Tragedies*, 4th rev. ed. (London: Methuen, 1949).
[2] "A Critique of Dramatic Poetry," in *Essays of John Dryden*, ed. W. P. Ker (New York: Russell & Russell, 1961), 79.

poet" who possessed a supreme understanding of humanity has promoted Shakespeare's unique cultural position as the diviner of universal truths. Whatever Shakespeare's personal, political, or religious opinions may have been, whatever his relations to the Rival Poet or Dark Lady (if they ever existed)—they don't really matter because, the argument goes, Shakespeare transcended his environment. As Jonson said, he was "not of an age but for all time!"[3] The old New Criticism put it another way, claiming that Shakespeare's virtual "anonymity" as a person is not a fact to be recorded but a circumstance to be celebrated since the bard became each character he created.[4]

This apotheosis of Shakespeare is not universally upheld by scholars today, but the orientation is prevalent, not merely because tradition persists, but because this conception of the artist feeds our deepest wishes for the understanding acceptance of the world's wide range of humanity. But whatever the causes, this charismatic persona of Shakespeare continues to flourish as a suprarational phenomenon, despite our rationalist criticism.

Difficult as it may be to believe that there can be anything wrong with celebrating Shakespeare for his sympathy, understanding, and suspension of judgment, a proper answer may begin with the observation that the Shakespearean mystique, established now for over two hundred years,[5] has rigidified our sense of what the universal values are, if not foreclosed the more unsettling possibility that there are no universal values. Indeed, if this latter possibility were firmly to take hold, it could well prompt an academic *crise de conscience*: what, or whose, values have we instructors embraced all these years in praising Shakespeare's universality? Does the capacity to create character sympathetically and convincingly, and to write with unmatched fecundity of imagination and "verbal texture" constitute the essential values we seek in drama? Perhaps so.

Nevertheless, to interpret events from the point of view of character rather than from the economic, institutional, and ideological structures

---

[3] Ben Jonson, "On Shakespeare" (1.43), in *The Complete Poetry of Ben Jonson*, ed. William B. Hunter, Jr. (Garden City, NY: Doubleday, 1963). For the history of the idea that Shakespeare was a "natural poet," see Eastman, *Shakespeare Criticism*, 8-9, 20-23, 43-45.

[4] A striking example is W. H. Auden's Introduction to *The Sonnets* (New York: New American Library, 1964), xvii-xxi. Margaret Cavendish, duchess of Newcastle, first articulated the notion that Shakespeare became all his characters. See her *Letters* (1664), reproduced in *Four Centuries of Shakespeare Criticism*, ed. Frank Kermode (New York: Avon, 1965), 42-43.

[5] See Robert W. Babcock, *The Genesis of Shakespeare Bardolatry* (Chapel Hill: Univ. of North Carolina, 1931).

that shape behavior clearly reveals an ideological position all its own. We should ask whether there are other kinds of dramatic representation that we can or ought to cherish. Are ideological considerations pertaining to monarchism, jingoism, racism, class, and political orthodoxy (or heterodoxy) of incidental significance to us? Does it matter to us that several dramatists besides Shakespeare made the representation of social and political issues rather than character central to their art? Is there an identifiable aesthetic appropriate to the primary representation of *these* concerns, and would such an examination, if carried out in relationship to Shakespeare's plays, affect our assessment of Shakespeare?

I believe that reconsideration of these broad questions is needed to move us away from accustomed categories of perception and valuation. To apply the case, we must break a habit of author worship that centers English Renaissance drama on Shakespeare's relationship to that drama, thereby effectively devaluing the achievement of other playwrights. A ready-made antidote for this state of affairs, one would think, would be the New Historicism, whose project it is to treat literary discourse as a continuum among all other cultural discourses. Ironically, the problem is not one that even New-Historical revisionism is soon likely to redress. In fact, the present situation is full of irony, for even those dedicated to historically specific, materialist interpretations of Renaissance drama are centering their criticism on Shakespeare and finding in his plays hitherto unimagined heterodoxies, heterodoxies and transgressive impulses that of course address modern social concerns. Inadvertently, the movement has begun to foster a new kind of bardolatry, albeit in mirror image.[6] Thus, despite the purported aim to free criticism from effete orthodoxies, a good deal of revisionist criticism effectively works to demonstrate that Shakespeare is our contemporary after all, one whose rich textuality enables us to make him the focal point of our own cultural criticism.

Surely there must be a better way than to make thirty-seven plays

---

[6] I think of Stephen Greenblatt, *Renaissance Self-Fashioning: From More to Shakespeare* (Chicago: Univ. of Chicago Press, 1980); *Alternative Shakespeares*, ed. John Drakakis (New York: Methuen, 1987); *Political Shakespeare: New Essays in Cultural Materialism*, ed. Alan Sinfield and Jonathan Dollimore (Manchester: Manchester Univ. Press, 1985); several essays in *Shakespeare and the Question of Theory*, ed. Patricia Parker and Geoffrey Hartman (New York: Methuen, 1985); and *The New Historicism: Selections from English Literary Renaissance*, ed. Arthur F. Kinney and Dan S. Collins (Amherst: Univ. of Massachusetts Press, 1987). For a discerning critique of these critical developments, see David Norbrook, "*Macbeth* and the Politics of Historiography," in *Politics of Discourse: The Literature and History of Seventeenth-Century England*, ed. Kevin Sharpe and Steven N. Zwicker (Berkeley: Univ. of California Press, 1987), 78–81.

function like a Talmud for this secular age.⁷ Marlowe, Chapman, Heywood, Tourneur, Webster, and Jonson all composed during the very same Renaissance as did Shakespeare but variously dramatized critical views not easily found in Shakespeare's work of courts, class, and country. This all-too-evident observation leads me to seek a critical approach that will furnish Shakespeare's contemporaries with an academic stage in which they become actors alongside Shakespeare with something like an equal chance of gaining our attention, even our admiration.

I

I would like to begin by considering a kind of play in which the relative isolation of Shakespeare from his contemporaries is probably the *least* pronounced—the English histories and Roman plays. Comparative studies with Marlowe's and especially Jonson's plays have often been undertaken.⁸ Yet even here the need for integrating, comparative, dramatic studies is strong inasmuch as they hold out the promise of revealing a Shakespeare who was very much one of his time, a Shakespeare who registered his partisan outlook, his ideology.⁹

To treat comprehensively all the Roman plays of Shakespeare and his contemporaries would overextend this essay, but what is manageable is an exemplary study of Shakespeare's *Julius Caesar*, a work that has remained unexamined in the context of the Caesar plays of his contemporaries, except when they have served the purpose of Shakespeareans searching for potential sources for Shakespeare's own. The other English Julius Caesar plays of the period once numbered at least

---

⁷ Consider the views of Louis Marder, who both records this process and contributes to it in *His Exits and His Entrances: The Story of Shakespeare's Reputation* (London: John Murray, 1963), 362.

⁸ See, for example, S. Musgrove, *Shakespeare and Jonson* (Auckland: Auckland Univ. College, 1957); E. Honig, "*Sejanus* and *Coriolanus*: A Study in Alienation," *Modern Language Quarterly* 12 (1951): 407–21; Irving Ribner, "Marlowe and Shakespeare," *Shakespeare Quarterly* 15 (1964): 41–53; H. Rohrman, *Marlowe and Shakespeare: A Thematic Exposition of Their Plays* (Arnhem: Van Loghum Slaterus, 1952); F. P. Wilson, *Marlowe and the Early Shakespeare* (Oxford: Clarendon Press, 1953).

⁹ Among the few integrating dramatic studies are two fine ones comparing Chapman and Shakespeare by Richard Ide—*Possessed with Greatness: The Heroic Tragedies of Chapman and Shakespeare* (Chapel Hill: Univ. of North Carolina Press, 1980), and "Chapman's *Caesar and Pompey* and the Uses of History," *Modern Philology* 82 (1985): 255–68. The latter piece observes astutely that the status of Chapman's brand of tragedy is low because Shakespearean interpreters determine the rules of the game.

eight, but five of these—an anonymous *Caesar and Pompey* (1576–1582), a *Caesar's Fall (Two Shapes)* (1602) by Dekker, Drayton, Middleton, Munday, and Webster, a *Julius Caesar* (c. 1613–c.1630) by Thomas May, and the Admiral's plays *I and II Caesar and Pompey* (1594, 1595)—have been lost.

Beside's Shakespeare's tragedy, those English plays that survive include Sir William Alexander's closet drama, *The Tragedy of Julius Caesar* (1607), the anonymous *Tragedy of Caesar and Pompey, or Caesar's Revenge* (hereafter called *Caesar's Revenge*) (ca. 1595; printed 1606), and Chapman's *The Tragedy of Caesar and Pompey* (1604).[10] A related ninth English language play, Thomas Kyd's closet drama, *Cornelia* or *Pompey the Great, his faire Corneliaes Tragedie* (1594), is a translation of Robert Garnier's *Cornelie* (1574) and treats Caesar's career as a crucial, if secondary, subject. Additionally, two important continental Caesar plays appeared in the mid-sixteenth century—Marc Antoine Muret's *Julius Caesar* (1544) and Jacques Grévin's *César* (1561)—and are still extant.[11]

Each of these tragedies deserves consideration in its own right, but rather than try to treat each one at length, I propose to develop a view of the place of these tragedies in the tradition of the Julius Caesar play, with special focus on Chapman's *Caesar and Pompey* and Shakespeare's *Julius Caesar*. These two tragedies, along with the exemplary patterns provided by the other extant ones, enable us to see clearly two distinctive ideologies that Caesar's career and death were made to illustrate—support for Tacitean republicanism and for the providential nemesis that awaits traitorous homicides. From their contrasting perspectives, we will also see in the Caesar plays of Shakespeare and Chapman two powerful, fundamentally contrasting conceptions of tragedy.

II

In *Censorship and Interpretation*, Annabel Patterson established that intellectuals such as Jonson—but also, I would add, Chapman, Daniel, Greville, and Massinger—used their historical tragedies to provide edifying, analogical paradigms or "prognostic" analyses for the Elizabe-

---

[10] On the date of *Caesar* and *Pompey* see my "Dates of the Plays of George Chapman," *English Literary Renaissance* 12 (1982): 242–66. Composition and publication dates of the other English plays are from Alfred Harbage and Samuel Schoenbaum, rev. 3rd. ed. Sylvia Stolen Wagonheim, *Annals of English Drama 975–1700* (London: Routledge, 1989).

[11] Dates of Muret's *Julius Caesar* and Grévin's *César* are from Ellen S. Ginsberg, ed., *Jacques Grévin: César* (Geneva: Librairie Droz, 1971), 19–20.

than age.[12] To carry forward their Republican principles of government, these dramatists were likely to employ Tacitus or Suetonius as models. By contrast, Shakespeare repeatedly returned to the more psychological Plutarch. While the members of the first group have come to be identified with "Tacitean republicanism," Shakespeare, characteristically enough, has escaped any political identification with respect to his view of Roman history. Nevertheless, Shakespeare's *Julius Caesar* displays an unacknowledged relationship, even in tacit opposition, to the political ideologies dramatized by his more reform-minded contemporaries.

The history of Caesar's career offered playwrights two momentous critical events. The first was Caesar's march on Rome, which precipitated the fall of the Republic and ended in Caesar's elevation as dictator. The second, Brutus's assassination of Caesar, was an act that brought Rome to a second civil war and concluded in the calamitous defeat of Brutus's forces and the beginning of the reign of the emperors. Unless playwrights chose to treat their material as chronicle history, they had to decide which of these two major events to depict, or at least to organize their plays around. Of course, this choice was conditioned by dramatic considerations, but it was by no means value-free since the very selection suggested the playwright's political perspective. To organize one's play around Caesar's subjugation of Pompey and the Senate was to make the destruction of the Republic the crucial issue; to find the dramatic center in Caesar's murder and Brutus's suicide was, to the contrary, to make the assassination of a popular ruler and the moral retribution consequent to it the central issues.

Kyd in *Cornelia* and Chapman, who may have followed the lost *I and II Caesar and Pompey* in *Caesar and Pompey*, chose to portray the destruction of Pompey and the Republic. In so doing, both Kyd and Chapman made Caesar's name synonymous with vainglory and tyranny. Kyd, for example, allows the republican Cicero to articulate the tragedy Rome suffers at Caesar's hands:

> T'is thou (O Rome) that nurc'd his [Caesar's] insolence;
> T'is thou (O Rome) that gau'st him first the sword
> Which murder-like against thy selfe he drawes,

---

[12] Annabel M. Patterson, *Censorship and Interpretation: The Conditions of Writing and Reading in Early Modern England* (Madison: Univ. of Wisconsin Press, 1985), 49–58. See also her " 'Roman-cast Similitude': Ben Jonson and the English Use of Roman History," in *Rome in the Renaissance: The City and the Myth*, ed. Paul Ramsey, Medieval & Renaissance Texts & Studies, 18 (Binghamton, NY, 1982), 381–94. On the pervasiveness of the dissident Republican tradition see my *Anticourt Drama in England, 1603–1642* (Charlottesville: Univ. Press of Virginia, 1989), 72–92, 153–64.

> And violates both God and Natures lawes.
>
> (3.2.35–38)[13]

By contrast, Shakespeare, along with William Alexander and the French dramatists, restricted himself to the events surrounding Caesar's assassination, making the psychology and morality of killing Caesar crucial. As a kind of chronicle history, *Caesar's Revenge* portrays both Pompey's defeat as well as Caesar's murder and Brutus's suicide. Such an approach of itself signaled no special orientation; nevertheless this play too places its culminating emphasis on the retribution exacted upon the conspirators.

This latter moralized position holds that Caesar's assassination was morally unjustifiable and disastrous in leading Rome to internecine civil war. This orthodox, medieval view, as Ernest Schanzer describes it, filtered through medieval commentaries and Dante's *Inferno* and may be traced back to Plutarch himself (despite the latter's practice of presenting the pros and cons of issues).[14] The dispersal of this homiletic tradition in the Renaissance can be seen most starkly in the dramatic motifs of *Caesar's Revenge*. "Caesar's Ghost" is made a principal figure who repeatedly demands to be avenged (1971.1), and Brutus is shown to be overcome with fits of conscience and remorse:

> *Caesar* vpbraues my sad ingratitude,
> He saued my life in sad *Pharsalian* fields,
> That I in *Senate* house might worke his death.
> O this rememberance now doth wound my soule,
> More then my poniard did his bleeding heart.
>
> (2276–80)[15]

Caesar's Ghost also functions as a moralizing Senecan specter, as when it labels Brutus politically and morally as, "Accursed traytor damned *Homicide*" (2294).

This is not to say that playwrights in this tradition necessarily endorsed monarchic principles in any unqualified way or that they were Caesar enthusiasts. On that score there was room for ambiguity and debate. But the wrongfulness of murdering Caesar is not in doubt in *Caesar's Revenge* or in the other plays treating that crucial act in

---

[13] Frederick S. Boas, ed., *The Works of Thomas Kyd* (Oxford: Clarendon Press, 1901).

[14] For the view that Plutarch presented an ambivalent response to Caesar, see Ernest Schanzer, "The Problem of *Julius Caesar*," *Shakespeare Quarterly* 6 (1955): 298–99.

[15] Line citations from *The Tragedy of Caesar's Revenge* are to F. S. Boas' edition (London: Malone Soc. Rpts., 1911).

Roman history. Sir William Alexander, for example, carried his poem through Caesar's murder, but not Brutus's suicide or the civil war, and made the assassination of the prideful dictator a demonstration, in the tradition of the mirror for magistrates, of the insecurity of great estate. At the same time, however, he preserves the tradition from Seneca's *Hercules Furens*, which Muret first represented in his tragedy, that Caesar in death "rests deified" (3098).[16] Through the speeches of Cicero and Chorus, Alexander also underlines the "wounded state" (2804) in which the assassins have placed Rome, and through Calpurnia plants the idea that a providential nemesis will pursue the conspirators. At the same time, the Nuntius calls the conspirators "Unnatural men" because they "make Natures course to change" by "such a monstrous crime" (3069-70).

In a related treatment, the author of *Caesar's Revenge* depicts Caesar as repugnantly prideful and vain, a characteristic portrayal seen as well in Alexander and the French Senecan dramatists.[17] Still, Christian patterns of divine retribution suffuse the anonymous playwright's pagan materials so that the overarching judgement of Brutus and the depiction of Caesar's spiritual triumph is more explicit than in Alexander's tragedy. Thus the tragedy's concluding movement reveals a Brutus hounded by the furies of conscience, abjectly fearful of an infernal afterlife, while a gloating Ghost of Caesar, exultant and unafraid, anticipates walking among the "great *Heroes* of the Goulden age," relishing the pleasures of "sweete *Elysium*" (2559, 2569).

Summarily as I have described it, this is the moralized manner in which Renaissance playwrights variously depicted Caesar's assassination and its aftermath.

III

Shakespeare's enactment of these events would appear to be very

---

[16] Quotations are from L. E. Kastner and H. B. Charlton, eds., *The Poetical Works of Sir William Alexander* (Manchester: Manchester Univ. Press, 1921).

[17] Schanzer invokes Shakespeare's relation to the French Senecans both in "Problem of *Caesar*," 299, and "A Neglected Source of *Julius Caesar*," *N&Q* 199 (1954): 196-97. Emphasizing both Caesar's self-infatuation and Brutus's guilty conscience, Schanzer develops the view in "Problem of *Caesar*" that the French plays reveal an ambivalent, "divided response" that Shakespeare reflects. However, this perspective is not responsive to the manner in which Muret apotheosizes Caesar, setting him among the gods after his death, nor of the way that Grévin creates his tragic effect by tying Caesar's fate to the fate of Rome. For an astute analysis of these latter points see Jeffrey Foster, ed., *César de Jacques Grévin* (Paris: A. G. Nizet, 1974, 1974), 15-17.

different. It pares away this heavy moralizing and shifts the dramatic center toward an exploration of Brutus's psychology and the political consequences of the assassination. No Ghost of Caesar appears at Philippi in *Julius Caesar* to mock the conspirators, and when it does appear it utters no pronouncement that Brutus is an ingrate or a regicide. Yet Shakespeare retains the paradigm of *Caesar's Revenge* and other mainline treatments—in his handling of Caesar's ghost, his sympathetic but critical assessment of the conspirators' management of Rome's political affairs, and his insinuations that a poetic justice pursues Brutus and Cassius to the death.

This providential framework does not require a heavy-handed reading, nor does it need to challenge the received opinion that Shakespeare offers qualified views of his principals and renders the moral issues complexly. What does need to be challenged is that this manner of dramaturgy can plausibly be taken to demonstrate that Shakespeare is non-political or, in Vernon Hall's phrase, that *Julius Caesar* is "A Play Without Political Bias."[18]

The complexities of judgment in *Julius Caesar* have been reviewed systematically by Robert Miola, who offers a valuable consideration of the tragedy in the context of Reformation and Counter-Reformation polemics on the ethics of tyrannicide.[19] Miola demonstrates that although Shakespeare's Caesar must be judged a tyrant *ex defectu tituli* by virtue of his unconstitutional assumption of power, he can by no means clearly be shown to be a tyrant in practice, *de parte exercitii*. In Shakespeare's version, Caesar may display certain tyrannical inclinations, but he enjoys broad popular support, is on the verge of having a constitutional mantle conferred upon him (we are twice informed that the Senate wishes to crown him in the Capitol), and is magnanimous (not selfish as a conventional tyrant would be) in the legacy he leaves to Rome.

There is pattern to this complexity. The extremely qualified presentation of Caesar's character and his right to rule is strategic: without such complexity, even ambiguity, Brutus's conscience-laden anguish about

---

[18] Vernon Hall, "*Julius Caesar*: A Play Without Political Bias," in *Studies in the English Renaissance Drama*, ed. Josephine W. Bennett (New York: New York Univ. Press, 1959), 106–24.

[19] Robert S. Miola treats *Julius Caesar* in terms of contemporary treatises on tyrannicide in "*Julius Caesar* and the Tyrannicide Debate," *Renaissance Quarterly* 38 (1985): 271–89. The essay, to which I am indebted throughout the paragraph, makes an especially important contribution in treating *Julius Caesar* in terms of the cultural-political polemic that Caesar's career signified in the late Renaissance. My own approach emphasizes the need to treat Shakespeare's tragedy in terms of the dramatic representations of Caesar on Renaissance stages.

joining the conspiracy ceases to be compelling. Of necessity, the decision to murder Caesar must be well-intentioned, and it must be based on plausible anxieties. Yet as Shakespeare represents it, that fatal choice is contained within a providential overview which shows the conspirators to be self-deceived, sophistic, and fatally misguided.

There is no need to review in detail the articulation of this structure, except to observe that Shakespeare works to separate assessments of Caesar's efficacy as a ruler from those of his character. Thus Caesar is presented as a colossus who is yet hard of hearing, weak in swimming, superstitious, and repellingly vain. But he knows how to govern, and nothing in Cassius's denigrating assessments of his character effectively shakes that perception. Shakespeare's redirection of Plutarch effectively underlines the point: whereas Plutarch and Suetonius report Caesar's repeated disregard for the Republic and for constitutional precedent, Shakespeare ignores such proofs, emphasizing instead Caesar's personal weaknesses, vanity, superstition, and political posturing.[20] Moreover, he quietly makes Cassius—not Rome's citizens—the agent who throws the stones that call upon Brutus to "strike" (2.1.47).[21]

In strategic contrast to Caesar, Brutus is made more attractive as a person, even as the soundness of his judgment is held up to scrutiny. Dignified, gentle, and scrupulous, Brutus champions the humanist's ideal of Reason in public affairs and is endowed with an extraordinary capacity for friendship. Yet his decisions are flawed by unacknowledged ambition and self-righteousness, and he is revealed to be self-deceived and politically naive. Not only does Brutus's abstracting idealism prove to be incompatible with the effective exercise of political leadership,[22] but his personal virtue, including his narrow sense of fairness in insisting that the ambitious Antony be permitted to speak at Caesar's funeral, opens the way to factionalism and the conflagration of civil war. Similarly, Brutus is made a respected but gravely erring military leader, overruling a wiser Cassius on the time and place to do battle and then, in an interpretation not to be found in Plutarch, initiating the disaster at Philippi by giving the signal to attack too early.

---

[20] Suetonius, *The Twelve Caesars*, trans. Robert Graves (Harmondsworth: Penguin, 1957), 41–43. Quotations from Plutarch's *Life of Caesar and Brutus* are from Thomas North's original English translation, in *Shakespeare's Plutarch*, ed. T. J. B. Spencer (Harmondsworth: Penguin, 1964), 80–83. Page numbers follow quotations in my text.

[21] David C. Green, *Julius Caesar and Its Source* (Salzburg: Universität Salzburg, 1979), 13–14, makes the point. Quotations from *Julius Caesar* and other Shakespeare plays are from *The Riverside Shakespeare*, ed. G. Blakemore Evans (Boston: Houghton Mifflin, 1974).

[22] For the contrary view, see Ernest Schanzer, "The Tragedy of Shakespeare's Brutus," *ELH* 22 (1955): 1–15.

It is thus the overarching structure within this often-observed pattern of complexity that bears perusal, for it has solidity as well as moral point. Shakespeare's tragedy is shaped by a providentialist perspective that links it unmistakably to the homiletic of *Caesar's Revenge*, Alexander's *Julius Caesar*, and Plutarch's biography. To take the latter first, Plutarch, in his treatments of dignitaries who were assassinated, can be counted on to provide evidence that a divine presence presides over human affairs. His biography of Caesar directs attention to the wondrous "chance" that Cassius, after his defeat at Philippi, "slew himself with the same sword with the which he strake Caesar" (99). Making a similar point, Plutarch observes that "[Caesar's] ghost that appeared unto Brutus [before Philippi] showed plainly that the gods were offended with the murder of Caesar" (99). Alexander, in like homiletic vein, has the Nuntius proclaim, "the Gods by many a wondrous signe, / Did show (it seem'd) how against their will, / The destinies would *Caesars* dayes confine" (l. 3060–62).

Shakespeare's relationship to this ideology is striking. Despite the complex manner of dramaturgy, the depiction of a vainglorious Caesar and the climactic ordering of events clearly reveal an orthodox, theocidean orientation. Shakespeare, for example, follows Plutarch's report in giving dramatic life to Caesar's Ghost, who styles himself, "Thy evil spirit, Brutus" (4.3.282). He preserves Plutarch's freighted observation that Cassius died by the same instrument with which he had stabbed Caesar: "Caesar, thou art reveng'd, / Even with the sword that kill'd thee" (5.3.45–46). In effect, Shakespeare makes Cassius acknowledge the poetic justice of his defeat and death. He even goes beyond his Plutarch in underlining the significance of Caesar's spiritual presence at Philippi: "O Julius Caesar," Brutus laments, "thou art mighty yet! / Thy spirit walks abroad, and turns our swords / In our own proper entrails" (5.5.94–96). Through this handling of events the dead Caesar, unlike the Umbra of Bussy in Chapman's *The Revenge of Bussy D'Ambois*, remains a hovering, providential specter through the final act. All of these intimations Shakespeare gracefully gathers together in Brutus' dying invocation—"Caesar, now be still, / I kill'd not thee with half so good a will" (5.5.50–51; cf. 5.5.17–20). In this manner, Shakespeare's fabled, many-sided manner of depicting character asserts itself without ever constraining the tragedy's pervasive sense in which a divine, implicitly political, moral order works its subtle way in human affairs, "rough-hew them how we will" (*Hamlet* 5.2.11).

Although Shakespeare shows himself no unqualified supporter of absolutism either in *Julius Caesar* or his English histories, the dramatist's conservatism is implicit in his psychologizing approach to his materials, particularly in the probing dissection of Cassius's and Brutus's "noble" motives. This manner of dramaturgy, with the ideological predilection it contains, is highlighted in telling ways by comparison with the other Caesar plays. One example is Brutus's "serpent's egg" speech. Shakespeare's play alone, in contrast to the prose sources and the other dramatic treatments, including Muret's and Grévin's, puts in Brutus's mouth the admission, which in this play we are to take as fact, that Caesar has committed no tyrannies. Yet in an ironic turn of logic, Brutus concludes that Caesar must like "a serpent's egg" be killed "in the shell" before he hatches (2.1.32–34).[23]

Shakespeare's psychologizing representation of Cassius's motive is ideologically weighted in the same way. In fact, Shakespeare's psychological method of interrogation, by its very nature, discounts Cassius's political motives (and those of the more minor conspirators as well), substituting as the *real* cause deeper, irrational ones. This manner of portrayal moves several strides beyond continental representations. In Grévin's *Julius Caesar*, a play that builds sympathy and pity for Caesar, Cassius is portrayed as the blunt soldier, crude in expression and brutal in imagination, but stalwart in his opposition to Caesar and his tyrannies. Shakespeare, however, takes this individuating coloration to the point where he suggests that Cassius's feelings of personal slight at Caesar's elevation threaten to become his ruling passion. Through this interrogation of Cassius's self-aggrandizing motives, Shakespeare undercuts Cassius in at least five ways—as being venal, envious, and ambitious, and as having "a lean and hungry look" (1.2.194), and, Machiavellian-like, as enticing Brutus to lead the conspiracy. Clearly, this dramatization of Cassius's motives, and of Brutus's too, is not reconcilable with republican depictions of Caesar's death. And yet Shakespeare allows us to see a certain magnanimity in Cassius in the love he reveals for Brutus at their reconciliation.

If these contextual considerations possess any cogency, *The Tragedy of Julius Caesar* must be understood as occupying an ideological space that links it to Grévin's and Muret's Caesar plays and in its providentialist treatment of the events at Philippi to Alexander's *Caesar* and the anonymous *Caesar's Revenge*. But orthodox as the moral vision of Shakespeare's tragedy is, the manner of dramaturgy is distinctive because it eschews the declamatory manner of earlier treatments, allowing its moral outlook to insinuate itself throughout the tragedy. Moreover, through his patient presentation of the ambiguities and

---

[23] Drawing from Pierre Charron's treatise *Of Wisdome*, Miola, "Tyrannicide Debate," 276–77, concludes, I think strangely, in the context of Shakespeare's tragedy, that Brutus's resolve to kill Caesar before he becomes a true tyrant is "perfectly proper and expedient."

contradictions of character, Shakespeare develops a kind of tragedy in which we come to feel a disjunction between the unequivocal destiny his principals eventually meet and the many-sidedness of their being. By such means as these, Shakespeare's *Julius Caesar* begets a contemplative wonder about the nature of things, even as it perpetuates providentialist notions in its premonitory representations of the guilt, mischance, and ruin that dog Brutus and Cassius at every turn after their assassination of Caesar.

IV

The political ethics of Shakespeare's *Julius Caesar* offered a worthy target to reform-minded, humanistic interpreters of Roman history such as Jonson and especially Chapman, for whom Caesar was a tyrant and Cato, Pompey, and Brutus heroes of the Republic. Given Chapman's republican political perspective, his reliance upon Plutarch as *his* main source in *Caesar and Pompey* is as instructive as it is surprising.[24] This use not only links *Caesar and Pompey* to Shakespeare's *Julius Caesar* in unexpected ways, but it also underscores Chapman's originality in transmuting the ethical significance of Caesar's career, especially as contrasted with Plutarch's and Shakespeare's rendering of it.

Because Chapman assigns to "Fortuna"—rendered as a degenerate instrument of Nature—a prominent place in history, his understanding of history has appeared, in marked contrast to Shakespeare's (particularly in the second tetralogy with its emphasis on individual choice and character),[25] to be conventional, mechanical, even "medieval." In fact, however, Chapman's conception of Fortune, which is independent of Plutarch's, is central to a powerful idea of tragedy. Fortune in *Caesar and Pompey*, as in the D'Ambois tragedies, is Nature's blind goddess, an emblem of the alien, unrestrainable otherness of life, the force beyond the capacity of human beings to fathom or control. Malevolent Fortune is the indisputable given in a Job-like conception of experience that presents for contemplation the spectacle of virtuous individuals who

---

[24] On Chapman's use of Plutarch, see Peter Ure, "Chapman's Use of North's Plutarch in *Caesar and Pompey*," *Review of English Studies* 9 (1958): 281–84; T. M. Parrott, *The Plays of George Chapman: The Tragedies*, 2 vols. (London, 1910; repr. New York: Russell & Russell, 1964), 2:657; and Albert R. Braunmuller, "Chapman's Use of Plutarch's *De fortuna Romanorum* in *The Tragedy of Charles, Duke of Byron*," *Review of English Studies* 23 (1972): 178–79.

[25] But see Norman Rabkin who in *Shakespeare and the Common Understanding* (New York: Free Press, 1967), 119 ff., discerns Brutus's inability to make "history human rather than mechanical."

must face the failure of their ideals and institutions in a malignant world.

The absence of a reassuring teleology in *Caesar and Pompey* raises basic questions not about the character's psychology, but about humanity's relationship to the cosmos, the purpose of "being" in the world, and the nature of that world. In Chapman's tragedy no earthly providence is to be discerned in the fall of a sparrow. Cato's retainer Athenodorus articulates this view unequivocally—"The gods' wills secret are" since "heaven itself / Fails to reform" life's "digested villainy," its "eternal chaos" (5.2.70–81).[26] The best that Cato can envision is an afterlife in which "we shall know each other, and past death / Retain those forms of knowledge learn'd in life" (5.2.137–38). The questions, as compelling as they are uncharacteristic of Shakespeare's tragedy, then become, "How in a perfidious world ought virtuous human beings to conduct themselves?" and "How can they sustain the values of life when the issue of events lies beyond control?"

The fall of Rome is comprehended in this world view. As Chapman represents it (in contrast to Kyd's more circumscribed rendition), the Republic is of such significance to civilization that its *un-*fortunate fall at Caesar's hand presents an excruciating test of human ability to sustain a transcendent set of affirming values. Accordingly, Cato and Pompey, the champions of the Republic, become the focus of Chapman's tragedy while Caesar in his triumph is sneeringly identified as proud Fortune's child:

> Though some have said she [Fortune] was the page of Caesar,
> Both sailing, marching, fighting, and preparing
> His fights in very order of his battles;
> The parts she play'd for him inverting nature,
> As giving calmness to th' enraged sea,
> Imposing summer's weather on stern winter.   (1.2.167–172)

Since Chapman's conquering Caesar becomes the symbol of sub-lunar Nature, Cato and Pompey must learn how to prevail against the vulgar world. With the laws and sacred institutions of the commonwealth trampled by Caesar's troops, the Republican Cato champions a standard of conduct that is beyond "the law [which is], / Made for a sort of outlaws" and unswervingly chooses a Stoic suicide to preserve untouched the last repository of "just men's liberties" (5.2.3, 8–9).

How different are the ethics of Nature in this tragedy from those in *Julius Caesar*. Shakespeare's tragedy suggests that the Ghost of Caesar is

---

[26] Quotations from Chapman's tragedies are from Parrott's edition, vol. 2.

an expression of offended Nature, which seeks to reestablish the moral balance against a valiant and honorable but self-deceived Brutus. In fact, Shakespeare repeatedly represents the inversion of Nature in the ideals of the conspirators. Thus the supernatural portents of Caesar's death show the heavens angry. According to Casca, "It is the part of men to fear and tremble / When the mighty gods by tokens send / Such dreadful heralds to astonish us"; yet Cassius cunningly but erringly interprets this falling of things "from their ordinance, / Their natures, and preformed faculties" (1.3.54–56, 66–67) as applying to monstrous Caesar. For the audience and for Cassius himself, who fights at Philippi on a day presaging defeat after "Two mighty eagles fell" while "ravens, crows, and kites" look on (5.1.80–84), Cassius's divinations prove terribly ironic.

This same irony undercuts the entire project of the conspirators, whose misconstruction of reality and unnatural murder (cf. *Macbeth* 2.3.111–14) is emblematically represented and re-presented in Brutus's attempt to portray as a ritual act, with arms "Up to the elbows" bloodied, the murder of Caesar (3.1.107). The self-deception in this construction of events is exposed, of course, both by Caesar's ghost and by Antony, the hard-headed realist and opportunist who reminds Brutus of his "good words" and "bad strokes": "Witness the hole you made in Caesar's heart, / Crying, 'Long live! hail, Caesar!'" (5.1.30–32). Even the ideal of liberty, for which Chapman's Cato chooses death over life, is stripped of its inspiration power in Shakespeare's treatment and exposed as a political shibboleth: "Then walk we forth," urges Brutus, "And waving our red weapons o'er our heads, / Let's all cry, 'Peace, freedom and liberty!'" (3.1.108–10). The ironies of this defining moment are in fact not unlike those that expose with even greater trenchancy Caliban's cry, "Freedom, highday! highday, freedom! freedom, highday, freedom!" as that "deformed slave" champions the new order to be brought about by a drunken butler and a jester (*Tempest* 2.2.186–87).

To readers of Shakespearean tragedy, Cato's anguishless death has appeared untragic, even static. Parrot himself, an editor both of Shakespeare and Chapman, asserts backhandedly, "If ... ethical instruction were the true aim of tragedy, it would be hard to find in Elizabethan drama a truer and nobler tragic hero than Chapman's Cato."[27] But is it ethics merely, or a tragic sense of life that Chapman is dramatizing? The steadfastness of Cato's course expresses only the most accessible aspect of his tragic suicide. Cato must also suffer the fracturing of his

---

[27] Parrott, *Tragedies*, 660. For a fine analysis of Chapman's tragedy as positing a "tragic flaw" within the social order rather than the individual see K. M. Burton, "The Political Tragedies of Chapman and Ben Jonson," *Essays in Criticism* 2 (1952): 397–412.

original world view. The man who could speak of the gods, asking rhetorically, "Have not I / Their powers to guard me in a cause of theirs" (1.1.64–65), must in the end turn to a world beyond as the only place free from "tyrants' sceptres," a place where, he believes, "we shall know each other, and past death / Retain those forms of knowledge learned in life" (5.2.136–38). The very affirmation issues from the failure of Cato's temporal, humanistic faith. The world affords no place for virtuous individuals and there is no place for Roman liberty in Caesar's Rome. At one and the same time, Cato's suicide is a dauntless assertion of the autonomy of the virtuous self and a tragic demonstration of the puniness of the self in its attempt to direct the wayward world toward some virtuous end.

Nor is the scope of Chapman's tragic outlook comprehended by Cato alone. Pompey is more than Cato's irresolute Stoic follower. Despite the *sententiae* of Chapman's play (cf. Webster's in *The White Devil*), Pompey's life cannot be epitomized by the comforting notion that the defeated leader "learns that true greatness is inward goodness" (see 5.1.181–233). Pompey's assassination in front of his wife—the subject Garnier and Kyd chose for their tragedy of *Cornelia*—elicits an anguished indictment of the gods themselves who would permit such an unmerited, pitiless death. "[A]fter this / Who will adore or serve the deities?" (5.1.262–63), the dying Pompey asks. The spectacle of Pompey's outraged piety and of his erstwhile stoical wife swooning before the sight of her husband's bleeding body testifies to the insufficiency, the breakdown, of piety as it confronts an unmerited death and the shattering experience of the failure of a just cause.

Different as they are, Cato and Pompey share, along with Cicero and Cornelia in Kyd's tragedy, a contempt for Caesar's world-engrossing conquests and tyranny, however covered over. Caesar, for his part, unlike Shakespeare's thrasonical magistrate, is endowed with intelligence and magnanimity, fully cognizant that Pompey and Cato have exceeded him in the Roman virtue of their attainments.[28] As Chapman's ironic imagery makes clear, Caesar understands too well that his principal ideological opponents have more royally than he attained the crown of life, the inward empire of the spirit.[29] Finding only the life-

---

[28] Chapman's presentation of contrasting but complex and strategically balanced characters merits notice as Shakespeare does. Shakespeare darkens Caesar's character even as he underscores the unnaturalness of the murder; contrariwise, Chapman elevates his Caesar's character even as he underscores the hollowness of Caesar's material victory.

[29] On this crucial Chapman concept, see G. R. Hibbard, "Goodness and Greatness: An Essay on the Tragedies of Ben Jonson and George Chapman," *Renaissance and Modern Studies* 11 (1968): 5–54.

less body of Cato to greet him in victory, Caesar laments—"O Cato, / All my late conquest, and my life's whole acts, / Most crown'd, most beautified, are blasted all / With thy grave life's expiring in their scorn" (5.2.179-82). Knowing the world to be the unstable thing it is, Caesar must live with the emptiness of his material victory over it.

In this way Caesar, Pompey, and Cato enact not one, but three fundamentally different tragedies, each of which Chapman arrays in relation to two searching philosophical questions: "According to what laws does the world turn?" and "How, in the absence of a reassuring, providential destiny, are virtuous human beings to live in this world?"

V

From this comparison of Chapman and Shakespeare's dramatic treatment of Caesar's career, several further ironies emerge. The most jarring of these inverts our received conceptions of the kind of tragic art each practiced. Chapman, reputed as the age's finest composer of political tragedy outside Shakespeare,[30] ends by abjuring the political world. Through that abjuration Chapman affirms the transcendent importance of the inner life and being. In this way, the integrity of the self proves to be everything and the political world, as in a morality play, a mighty but empty vanity. In relation to the politics of the state, however, the ethics of *Caesar and Pompey* must still be reckoned heterodox, even radical, for Chapman eschews a standard of virtue that requires loyalty to Caesar or, indeed, to any merely temporal order.

With similar irony, we may observe that Shakespeare's sympathetic but exacting psychological exploration of Brutus's private motives is resolved within a framework that affirms a morality and cosmology congenial to the prevailing political order, for the violation of which Brutus and Cassius pay with their lives.

These political and ontological comparisons, I readily acknowledge, are not value-neutral; they express my point of view, which aims to move our dramatic criticism away from accustomed categories of evaluation and from modes of perception which, I have argued, effectively make Shakespearean value the standard. As a countermeasure, I have sought throughout this essay to place Shakespeare, not above, but among his contemporaries, and by positioning *The Tragedy of Julius Caesar* among Renaissance humanist plays of like subject I have sought

---

[30] I think particularly of Charles W. Kennedy, "Political Theory in the Plays of George Chapman," in *Essays in Dramatic Literature: In Honor of T. M. Parrott*, ed. Hardin Craig (Princeton: Princeton Univ. Press, 1935), 73-86.

to show that it does indeed take up an ideological space in contemporary dramatic treatments of kingship, obedience, republican political principles, and private virtue.

Having surveyed the modest field, I have lavished attention on Chapman's *Caesar and Pompey* because it discloses a noble conception of tragedy fundamentally different in technique and tragic outlook from Shakespeare's own. It reveals, furthermore, a conception of tragedy whose originality and power our culture has scarcely recognized and appreciates even less.

Caesar and Pompey is, I admit, only one play, but I have set forth its virtues in the belief that there are numerous other Elizabethan-Jacobean plays that ought to be examined alongside one or more of Shakespeare's own—not to make Shakespearean measure *the* measure, but to discover the distinctive space, ideological and dramatical, that other playwrights occupied so well.

State University of New York at Binghamton

ROBERT WILTENBURG

Donne's Dialogue of One: The Self and the Soul

MUCH HAS BEEN WRITTEN LATELY ABOUT THE FORTUNES OF the self in the Renaissance, its making and unmaking, its struggle to be known or heard. The analysis has depended upon several historical observations concerning the increased scope and urgency of individual choices: the fact of greater economic and social mobility; the climate of religious and political controversy; the discovery of the person (as well as the state) as a "work of art"; the Protestant doctrine of the priesthood of all believers, with its emphasis on the necessity of a personal faith. There are many choices to be made, and one becomes what one chooses. It is therefore not surprising to find John Donne, in a sermon of 1629, explaining man's essence as "a faculty of will, and election" (*Sermons*, 9.75).[1]

Coming at the end of a century notable, as has been argued, for self-fashioning and at the beginning of another notable, as has also been argued, for self-consuming,[2] Donne would seem to be a centrally, if somewhat precariously, placed test case for assessing the "inner life" of a Renaissance man. Anne Ferry has, for example, found in the Holy Sonnets the culmination of a process in which the adequacy of language to express the "inward self" becomes, for the first time, a recognizable and central concern.[3] But here I wish to address another question: not whether or how Donne's inner life is expressed, but how it is conceived and carried on in the first place.

---

[1] The sermons are quoted from *The Sermons of John Donne*, ed. George R. Potter and Evelyn M. Simpson, 10 vols. (Berkeley: Univ. of California Press, 1953–62).
[2] Stephen Greenblatt, *Renaissance Self-Fashioning: From More to Shakespeare* (Chicago: Univ. of Chicago Press, 1980); Stanley E. Fish, *Self-Consuming Artifacts: The Experience of Seventeenth-Century Literature* (Berkeley: Univ. of California Press, 1972).
[3] Anne Ferry, *The "Inward" Language: Sonnets of Wyatt, Sidney, Shakespeare, Donne* (Chicago: Univ. of Chicago Press, 1983), chap. 5.

It is often said that our inward sense of self is dialogical: formed, maintained, and experienced as differentiation, response, or opposition. But the dialogue of any particular inwardness becomes more or less idiosyncratic, depending not only upon its terms—who is responding to what?—but also on its subject, tone, direction, and degree of closure. In Donne's case there has been wide agreement on the characteristic tone of witty paradox; more complex agreement on the principal subject, love human and divine; and some disagreement on the direction, the degree of closure, and even on the fundamental terms. One possibility is to accept some version of the progressive, Augustinian pattern suggested by Donne himself and confirmed by Walton: Jack Donne vs. Dr. Donne, sinner vs. saint, unmarried vs. married, worldly ambition vs. religious devotion, and so on. Some recent critics have preferred to frame the dialogue as between Donne and his circumstances, whether personal, social, or institutional.[4] At the risk of being neither traditional nor fashionable, I wish to argue that, however strong Donne's own sense of before and after, the primary division is not between early Donne and late Donne; and whatever the stimulating, conditioning, or limiting influence of circumstance, it is not between inner Donne and outer Donne. Rather, Donne presents a fundamentally internal and non-progressive dialogue between two concepts of the inner life, the self and the soul—a dialogue that is exploratory, inconclusive, and thereby faithful to its subject, Donne in love.

Two preliminary cautions: first, I make no claim that my use of the terms "self" and "soul" reflects some perfectly consistent use of these words on Donne's part. As Ferry has shown, at this period the same inner phenomena may be variously attributed to heart, mind, spirit, or soul; and "self" may refer to the soul, the body, or the body and soul together.[5] (A shifting and ambiguous vocabulary is a great preserver of your "undissociated sensibility.") Donne sometimes makes or attends to such distinctions; sometimes ignores them; more often plays with them. Thus in one of the early paradoxes inverting the usual relation of body and soul:

> I say againe, that the *body* makes the *minde*, not that it created it a *minde*, but *formes* it a *good* or a *bad mind*; and this *minde* may be confounded with *soule* without any violence or injustice to *Reason* or *Philosophy*: then the *soule* it seemes is enabled by our *body*, not this by it. (Paradox 11)

---

[4] See, for example, Arthur F. Marotti, *John Donne, Coterie Poet* (Madison: Univ. of Wisconsin Press, 1986).

[5] Ferry, *"Inward" Language*, 39.

Or in a poem like "The Legacie":

> When I dyed last, and Deare, I dye
>   As often as from thee I goe,
>   Though it be an houre agoe,
> And Lovers houres be full eternity,
> I can remember yet, that I
>   Something did say, and something did bestow;
> Though I be dead, which sent mee, I should be
> Mine owne executor and Legacie.
>
> I heard mee say, Tell her anon,
>   That my selfe, that's you, not I,
>   Did kill me,'and when I felt mee dye,
> I bid mee send my heart, when I was gone;
> But I alas could there finde none,
>   When I had ripp'd me,'and search'd where heart should lye;
> It kill'd mee'againe that I who still was true,
> In life, in my last Will should cozen you.
>
> Yet I found something like a heart,
>   But colours it, and corners had,
>   It was not good, it was not bad,
> It was intire to none, and few had part.
> As good as could be made by art
>   It seem'd, and therefore for our losses sad,
> I thought to send that heart in stead of mine,
> But oh, no man could hold it, for twas thine.[6]

Here matters are not simply ambiguous, but deliberately confounded: life and death, I and you, I and me, executor and legacy, agent and patient, mine and thine. Whose is that artificial heart at the end? What does the speaker feel? What are we to feel? Commiseration with either lover? Wry amusement at the vagaries of love? Admiration for the poet's wit?[7] The experiences that interest Donne most—love in all its

---

[6] The paradox is quoted from *John Donne: Selected Prose*, ed. Helen Gardner and Timothy Healy (Oxford: Clarendon Press, 1967), 17. Texts from the *Songs and Sonnets* are from the edition of Helen Gardner (*The Elegies and The Songs and Sonnets* [Oxford: Clarendon Press, 1965]).

[7] For a stimulating account of "Donne as the master of ... poems that simply will not resolve" (5) who typically creates a "double voice" and a "double presence" (8), see Judith Scherer Herz, " 'An Excellent Exercise of Wit That Speaks so Well of Ill': Donne and the Poetics of Concealment," in *The Eagle and the Dove: Reassessing John Donne*, ed. Claude J. Summers and Ted-Larry Pebworth (Columbia: Univ. of Missouri Press, 1986), 3–14.

variety, self-consciousness, religious anxiety and yearning—demand for their accurate representation just this sort of confounding of terms and relations. The energies and motives involved are so volatile and ductile that a specious clarity must be firmly resisted: only paradox will serve.[8] The most that can be said is that Donne's usages are not *finally* inconsistent with each other; and I claim only that mine are not inconsistent with his.

Second, I assume—and will also argue—that neither term, neither "self" nor "soul" is reducible to the other. We can hardly hope to comprehend Donne's inner experience if we begin by regarding the soul as a fictional epiphenomenon, an idealized version of the self, or as a piece of false consciousness, a mystification imposed by institutional or other authority.[9] Nor will we do well to interpret (as Donne himself occasionally does) his obsessive self-concern and self-dramatization as mere symptoms of a disordered soul. Any attempt to fold one category into the other will, as Donne repeatedly shows, neither hold nor satisfy for long.

Why self and soul?[10] The *Oxford English Dictionary* records a burst of linguistic experimentation regarding "self" from the mid-sixteenth to the mid-seventeenth century.[11] Early and late, all sorts of object prefixes are tried, Donne himself employing, in the poems alone, "self-accusing, self-despising, self-fixed, self-flattery, self-life (2), self-love (2), self-murder (2), self-preserving, self-tickling, self-torment, and [alas] self-traitor." At the same time, self is increasingly being used as a freestanding substantive. Donne is involved here also: it is sometimes

---

[8] Rosalie L. Colie observes that Donne "found in paradox a decorum exactly right, since it 'exactly' matched inexactness, the shifting contours of his paradoxical subjects. . . . [and made possible the] imitation of a contradictory reality, of contradictory psychological states" (*Paradoxia Epidemica: The Renaissance Tradition of Paradox* [Princeton: Princeton Univ. Press, 1966], 129).

[9] Historically informed critics like Greenblatt and Marotti usefully remind us that personalities and poems take form not in the boundless aether, but in an atmosphere of multiple pressures and responses: social, ideological, rhetorical, esthetic. A too exclusive concentration on the submissions, evasions, and accommodations made to circumstance may, however, obscure the intense inner (not merely internalized) debate in which poets (and their readers) attempt to work out who they are and wish to be.

[10] The distinction has, of course, a long history—whether primarily descriptive and formal (*nous* and *psyche*) after Aristotle, or primarily ethical and theological (*ego* and *anima*) after Augustine.

[11] Quentin Skinner remarks that "the surest sign that a group or society has entered into the self-conscious possession of a new concept is that a corresponding vocabulary will be developed" ("Language and Social Change," in *The State of the Language*, ed. Leonard Michaels and Christopher Ricks [Berkeley: Univ. of California Press, 1980], 564).

difficult to decide whether "my self" (or "our selves") is best read as a reflexive pronoun (myself) or noun and pronominal adjective (my *self*). Donne arguably comes close to the full substantive in an early epistle to Rowland Woodward in praise of the religious uses of retirement:

> Seeke wee then our selves in our selves; for as
> Men force the Sunne with much more force to passe,
> By gathering his beames with a christall glasse;
>
> So wee, if wee into our selves will turne,
> Blowing our sparkes of vertue, may outburne
> The straw, which doth about our hearts sojourne.

He concludes:

> Wee are but farmers of our selves, yet may,
> If we can stocke our selves, and thrive, uplay
> Much, much deare treasure for the great rent day.
>
> Manure thy selfe then, to thy selfe be'approv'd,
> And with vaine outward things be no more mov'd,
> But to know, that I love thee'and would be lov'd.[12]

But this example is rare, and not perfectly conclusive.

Not until the mid-seventeenth century does it become possible to speak confidently of possessing "a self" in the modern sense of "that which in a person is really and intrinsically *he* ... a permanent subject of successive and varying states of consciousness" (O.E.D. C.1.3). Thus before 1550 no Englishman "had" a "self"; after 1650, they begin to be common. This is not to say that no one in Renaissance Europe had a self before 1550;[13] but the English are famously suspicious of and slow to adopt continental fads and fashions. Although lacking selves, they were not entirely unprovided with ideas about their innermost experiences. As John N. Morris has observed, before men had selves they had souls.[14] Indeed, they had had them for a long time, and the Protestant reformers had recently given fresh impetus to the examination and care of the soul. I suggest that for Donne and other equal heirs of the Renais-

---

[12] "Like one who'in her third widdowhood doth professe," cited from the edition of W. Milgate (*John Donne: The Satires, Epigrams and Verse Letters* [Oxford: Clarendon Press, 1967], 70) who suggests a date of 1597 (223).

[13] Thomas Greene, "The Flexibility of the Self in Renaissance Literature" (in *The Disciplines of Criticism*, ed. Peter Demetz, Thomas Greene, and Lowry Nelson, Jr. [New Haven: Yale Univ. Press, 1968], 241–64) identifies Petrarch as the first.

[14] John N. Morris, *Versions of the Self: Studies in English Autobiography from John Bunyan to John Stuart Mill* (New York: Basic Books, 1966), 6.

sance and the Reformation, to whom both ways of describing and organizing the inner life are available and urgent, there is a primary need to adjudicate, to satisfy, and, if possible, to reconcile, the competing claims—both compelling, both legitimate—of the self and the soul.

What are these claims? For a working sense of each we may look to their respective creation stories, that of the soul in Genesis, that of the self in Pico della Mirandola's revision of Genesis in his *Oration on the Dignity of Man*. Like all creation stories, these tell not only how things were in the beginning, but also how, at bottom, they continue to be.

In Genesis we see first the typical activities of the divine artist giving form to the world: creating, commanding and fulfilling, dividing, assigning, naming. And once the fundamental shaping and dividing is finished, he begins to fill, ornament, enrich, and enliven all the places he has made, exhibiting a meticulous care for each detail, and a concern for the continued flourishing of all living things, each of which is blessed and made fruitful, the whole culminating in the creation of man, formed in God's "own image," and placed in the garden.

This account stresses the deliberate order and harmony of the created world, the careful separation and balancing of elements, the adornment of the earth with each creature placed and continued "according to its kind." Everything has its place, and in that place is neither static nor dead, but complete, and fruitful. Man (and woman), in the "image of God," implicitly shares in the conclusion that all this is good—this is the world he would make, and the way he would make it, if he were God—and his later naming of the animals, the sign of his "dominion," indicates his sympathetic participation in it. Man's happiness, his soul's delight, is here depicted as primarily a state or place; his virtue the *filling* (and thus fulfilling), through obedience, of that place; and his reward, rest after labor.

Pico, who in his *Heptaplus* comments rhapsodically on the whole of the creation story, elaborates, in a famous passage of his *Oration*, on the climactic event, when God, having finished the creation of the world, "kept wishing that there were someone to ponder the plan of so great a work, to love its beauty, and to wonder at its vastness." Having made man a "creature of indeterminate nature" and having placed him "in the middle of the world," God addresses Adam:

> Neither a fixed abode nor a form that is thine alone nor any function peculiar to thyself have we given thee, Adam, to the end that according to thy longing and according to thy judgment thou mayest have and possess what abode, what form, and what functions thou thyself shalt desire.... We have made thee neither of heaven nor of earth, neither mortal nor immortal, so that with

freedom of choice and with honor, as though the maker and molder of thyself, thou mayest fashion thyself in whatever shape thou shalt prefer. Thou shalt have the power to degenerate into the lower forms of life, which are brutish. Thou shalt have the power, out of thy soul's judgment, to be reborn into the higher forms, which are divine.[15]

Pico always was a high flyer; Donne called him "a man of an incontinent wit, and subject to the concupiscence of inaccessible knowledges and transcendencies."[16] In an addendum to the *Heptaplus* he even undertakes to demonstrate that the whole plan of providential history is contained in the first word of Genesis, through an ingenious expounding and arranging of other words that may be anagrammatically discovered in it. Here, in this revisionist commentary on Genesis, his "extravagant assertion of human freedom," as Thomas Greene has called it,[17] man is placed not in Eden, but in some unspecified "middle," a placeless place, a point of vantage only, from which his observations, choices, and movements may be made. He is instructed not that the whole creation is "good," but rather, in typical Neoplatonic fashion, the higher the better, the lower the worse (notice the contempt for the brute). As there is no garden, so there is no tree, and no prohibition, no responsibility to govern, no necessary part to play, but only the optional delights of pondering, loving, wondering, and contemplating the whole—and fashioning himself. It is a heady story, all motion and no place, and it celebrates a new sense of the "image of God" less as the obedient soul responsive to God than as what we (and the later Renaissance) call the self: mobile, self-sufficient, free, falling and rising according to its choices alone, its nature and good summed in ceaseless activity.

Can these competing imperatives, the soul's desire for place and harmony, the self's demand for movement and liberty, both be accommodated? Can one, must one, give way to the other? Is the self merely the fallen soul? Or the soul in the making? Donne makes such questions central to his poetry by challenging not only the stylized poses of sonnet and sonnet sequence but also the Neoplatonic (or other) ladder

---

[15] *Oration on the Dignity of Man*, trans. Elizabeth Livermore Forbes, in *The Renaissance Philosophy of Man*, ed. Ernst Cassirer, Paul Oskar Kristeller, and John Herman Randall, Jr. (Chicago: Univ. of Chicago Press, 1948), 224–25.

[16] John Donne, *Essays in Divinity*, ed. Evelyn M. Simpson (Oxford: Clarendon Press, 1952), 13. M. M. Mahood reminds us of Walton's report that "Donne seemed to his contemporaries a second Pico della Mirandola in his youth and a second St. Augustine in his last years" (*Poetry and Humanism* [New York: Norton, 1970], 87).

[17] Greene, "Flexibility," 243.

of ascent (distance to intimacy, aspiration to fulfillment, sensible to intellectual) which such sequences assume, even when engaged in demonstrating and lamenting the poet's failure to climb successfully. Rather, the *Songs and Sonnets* assert that the experience of love is neither of successful nor frustrated ascent, but of vigorous claim and counterclaim, which no single form or sequence of forms can adequately represent. It is for this reason that Dame Helen Gardner's attempt to introduce a biographically based Augustinian sequence hinging on Donne's marriage to Ann More, a movement from earlier, technically and emotionally simpler expressions of male energy and cynicism to more complex, delicately nuanced expressions of mutual affection, while plausible (no decisive evidence is available) must be resisted.[18] For it is precisely the promiscuous juxtapositions of the traditional arrangement that make Donne's most important and characteristic points about the self and the soul in love.

Formally, the poems are the domain of the self, as Donne, with protean, kaleidoscopic brilliance dips and soars, assuming many moods, postures, and points of view "taming" and "fettering" his "pains" and "grief" through a great variety of "vexed" verses. One moment he will be all cynical mockery and witty misogyny, another all unbuttoned celebration of fleshly delights, a third devoted to the joys and sorrows of true lovers—or these and others mixed and counterchanged. Also of the self is the thematic emphasis on variety and inconstancy as not only inevitable but positively good. Most important is the continual rhetorical pressure exerted by the ego, the "I," the all but omnipresent, omnifacient first person singular. Sometimes, as in pieces of pure wit like "Goe, and catche a falling starre" or "Womans Constancy," it is merely playful:

> Now thou hast lov'd me one whole day,
> To morrow when thou leav'st, what wilt thou say?
> Wilt thou then Antedate some new made vow?
>   Or say that now
> We are not just those persons, which we were?
> Or, that oathes made in reverentiall feare
> Of Love, and his wrath, any may forsweare?
> Or, as true deaths, true maryages untie,
> So lovers contracts, images of those,
> Binde but till sleep, deaths image, them unloose?
>   Or, your owne end to Justifie,
> For having purpos'd change, and falsehood; you

---

[18] Gardner, "General Introduction," li–lxii.

> Can have no way but falsehood to be true?
> Vaine lunatique, against these scapes I could
>   Dispute, and conquer, if I would,
>   Which I abstaine to doe,
> For by to morrow, I may thinke so too.

Still more striking is the imperative mood, gigantic, engorged with the physical and emotional immediacy and sufficiency of its experience of love:

> She'is all States, and all Princes, I,
>   Nothing else is.
> Princes doe but play us; compar'd to this,
> All honor's mimique; All wealth alchimie.

Male energy and the ideal of mutual love are not so easily separated in fact, and in many of the best poems, including such celebrated instances of "mutuality" as "The Good-morrow," "The Sunne Rising," "The Anniversarie," or "The Canonization," it is the active and aggressive self we hear, the self discovering, through love, the power not only to shape itself ("And now good morrow to our waking soules"), but to shape the world to itself ("Princes doe but play us"), to shape its own world ("All other things, to their destruction draw, / Only our love hath no decay"), or to "extract" the "soule" of a world that still (and finally) resists its shaping, becoming a transcendent "patterne"—the self apotheosized in love—to "all" who follow:

> Wee can dye by it, if not live by love,
>   And if unfit for tombes or hearse
> Our legend bee, it will be fit for verse;
> And if no peece of Chronicle wee prove,
>   We'll build in sonnets pretty roomes;
>   As well a well wrought urne becomes
> The greatest ashes, as half-acre tombes,
>   And by these hymnes, all shall approve
>   Us *Canoniz'd* for Love.
>
> And thus invoke us; You whom reverend love
>   Made one anothers hermitage;
> You, to whom love was peace, that now is rage;
> Who did the whole worlds soule extract, and drove
>   Into the glasses of your eyes,
>   So made such mirrors, and such spies,
> That they did all to you epitomize,
> Countries, Townes, Courts: Beg from above

> A patterne of your love!

Such is the extravagant effect of love upon the self, and the extravagant power of the self in love, whether to dominate the world or to transcend it. Yet the soul, with its contrary needs for rest, assurance, consolation, an intimate mutual "forgetting" of the "He and Shee" ("The Undertaking"), is, as the ending of this poem shows, never long or completely neglected. For all the boisterous self-assertion of the opening ("For Godsake hold your tongue, and let me love"), the canonized lovers are those for whom love was, finally, peace.

Verbally, "soul" appears regularly in the *Songs and Sonnets*, though less frequently than "I" or the royal "we." Thematically, it may appear even in a libertine poem like "Loves Usury," in which the speaker, bargaining with the God of Love to be willing to be "inflam'd" when old if he can be free in youth to "travell, sojourne, snatch, plot, have, forget," ends on an equivocation at once cynical and unexpectedly touching:[19]

> This bargaine's good; If when I'am old, I bee
>   Inflam'd by thee,
> If thine owne honour, or my shame, or paine
> Thou covet, most at that age thou shalt gaine.
> Doe thy will then, then subject and degree,
> And fruit of love, Love, I submit to thee,
> Spare mee till then, I'll beare it, though she bee
>   One that loves mee.

In other poems, the soul takes center stage, as in "The Extasie" where, however one interprets the framing introductory and concluding sections, we have in the middle a picture of the soul in love:

> Our soules, (which to advance their state,
>   Were gone out,) hung 'twixt her, and mee.
>
> And whil'st our soules negotiate there,
>   Wee like sepulchrall statues lay;
> All day, the same our postures were,
>   And wee said nothing, all the day.   (15–20)

Here it is the soul that "moves," and the "Wee," the ever busy pronom-

---

[19] Marotti similarly comments on the "surprise" of the poem's conclusion, in which the revelation of the speaker's "sensitivity to the need for reciprocating affection . . . ironically undoes the comical bravado of the libertine stance" (*Coterie Poet*, 76).

inal self is, for an ecstatic moment, stilled in favor of a "soules language" in which both parties, in silent sympathy, "mean" and "speak" the same. They describe the effect of love upon the soul as it is and as it may be:

> When love, with one another so
>   Interinanimates two soules,
> That abler soule, which thence doth flow,
>   Defects of lonelinesse controules.
>
> Wee then, who are this new soule, know,
>   Of what we are compos'd, and made,
> For, th'Atomies of which we grow,
>   Are soules, whom no change can invade.   (41–48)

In this vision the soul finds the fulfillment of its longings in the creation of a "new," "abler" soul, as strong and pure as that of the unfallen Adam, and in the conviction that this experience provides the fundamental and unchanging core of identity, "th'Atomies of which we grow." Yet even here the soul cannot "speak" in a voice of its own, and, once the vision has been presented, the return to the body (and to the officious "we") immediately begins. The continuing critical debate over the poem's seriousness or "idealism" reflects both the instability of this vision, and our uncertainty as to which voice, the self or the soul, finally controls it.

Rarest of all are such poems as "A Valediction: Forbidding Mourning" in which the needs of both self and soul seem fully reconciled. Here is a pair of lovers so "refin'd" by their love, so perfectly "Interassured of the mind," their inner lives so thoroughly penetrated by love that they no longer "know what it is," no longer perceive it as something other than themselves. Self and soul being one, the contrary imperatives to motion and to rest can be accommodated in a single comprehensive image:[20]

> If they [our souls] be two, they are two so
>   As stiffe twin compasses are two,
> Thy soule the fixt foot, makes no show
>   To move, but doth, if the'other doe.
>
> And though it in the center sit,
>   Yet when the other far doth rome,

---

[20] For an analysis of the compass image's spiral reconciliation of rectilinear and circular motion (i.e., bodily and spiritual love), see John Freccero, "Donne's 'Valediction: Forbidding Mourning,' " *ELH* 30 (1963): 335–76; especially 337–56.

> It leanes, and hearkens after it,
> And growes erect, as it comes home. (25-32)

Both motion and rest, division and unity are reciprocally reconciled: the elements of the compass, seen to be two while at rest, become one in motion; divided while in motion, the epanaleptic subject and object ("It ... it") of the penultimate line resolve into a perfect equivocation as "it" comes home.

The divine poems show a similar pattern of claim and counterclaim, of dialectical imperatives in conflict, with the difference that the very fact of conflict is usually a source not of challenge or delight but of anxiety and melancholy. Here too, as Donne complains, "Oh, to vex me, contraryes meete in one" (H.S. 19).[21] He explicitly frames the dialectic as between self and soul and envisions a clear program: the overthrow of the self by whatever means necessary. His earnest desire is, as he says addressing God, to "resigne / My selfe to Thee" (H.S. 1); and similarly, looking inward:

> Then turne
> O pensive soule, to God, for he knowes best
> *Thy* true griefe, for he put it in *my* breast.
> (H.S. 8 [my emphasis])

The clearest (and most vehement) statement of this inner division comes in Holy Sonnet 14:

> Batter my heart, three person'd God; for, you
> As yet but knocke, breathe, shine, and seeke to mende;
> That I may rise, and stand, o'erthrow mee,'and bend
> Your force, to breake, blowe, burn and make me new.
> I, like an usurpt towne, to'another due,
> Labour to'admit you, but Oh, to no end,
> Reason your viceroy in mee, mee should defend,
> But is captiv'd, and proves weake or untrue,
> Yet dearely'I love you, and would be lov'd faine,
> But am betroth'd unto your enemie,
> Divorce mee,'untie, or breake that knot againe,
> Take mee to you, imprison mee, for I
> Except you'enthrall mee, never shall be free,
> Nor ever chast, except you ravish mee.

---

[21] Text cited from Dame Helen Gardner's edition of *The Divine Poems*, 2d ed. (Oxford: Clarendon Press, 1982); I retain, however, the traditional numbering for the Holy Sonnets.

The interplay of self and soul in this and in other of the divine poems is never simple, though Donne wishes it could be.[22] For all the huffing and puffing, the breaking, blowing, and burning, the Augustinian consummation so devoutly wished for is never quite achieved. The effect of "Batter my heart" depends precisely on its equivocal presentation of the "I" (and "me") who writes and speaks the poem: Is it the soul, crying *de profundis* in its desperate longing to be made "new," or is it the self, performing a star turn *as* the soul crying, etc.? Of course it is both at once, and the brilliant, inextricable mixture of motives and voices dramatizes man's inability, without divine help, to make conversion out of the interminable inner conversation. This is true even in Donne's "last" poem, "A Hymne to God the Father," in which the counterpointing of the two imperatives—the hectic, anxious self ("I") and soul ("Don[n]e") missing and, at last, finding itself fully possessed by God—ends on a note of maximal resolution:

> Wilt thou forgive that sinne where I begunne,
> Which is my sin, though it were done before?
> Wilt thou forgive those sinnes through which I runne,
> And doe them still: though still I doe deplore?
>   When thou hast done, thou hast not done,
>   For, I have more.
>
> I have a sinne of feare, that when I'have spunne
> My last thred, I shall perish on the shore;
> Sweare by thy selfe, that at my death thy Sunne
> Shall shine as it shines now, and heretofore;
>   And, having done that, Thou hast done,
>   I have no more.

Even here, and finally, when Donne himself is done, when the soul at last finds rest, it is the self that must close the scene; only through its voice can the soul be heard.

And this is as it must be. The soul is of necessity in the self's keeping: the motions of the self we live with every day; the satisfactions of the soul we glimpse only in extraordinary moments, if at all. Donne's

---

[22] Gardner speaks of a "conflict between his will and his temperament" (*Divine Poems*, "Introduction," xxxvi); Roger B. Rollin of a conflict between "ego" and "superego" (" 'Fantastic Ague': The Holy Sonnets and Religious Melancholy" [in Summers and Pebworth, *Eagle and Dove*, 131–46]); Richard Strier of a conflict between "Catholic" and "Calvininst" impulses ("John Donne Awry and Squint: The 'Holy Sonnets,' 1608–1610," *Modern Philology* 86 [1989], 357–84); Marotti observes that "The self in performance and the self in humble devotion seem ... throughout the *Holy Sonnets*, to be intractably, if creatively, at odds" (*Coterie Poet*, 257).

experience of human love has for him the status and the force of revelation, a revelation guaranteeing that the soul is not simply one more of the ego's many projections, but represents an insight into human nature and its fulfillment that the ego, in itself, could never attain. Moreover, this love provides an analogy, a foretaste, and a promise of the divine; as he says in Holy Sonnet 17, "Here the admyring her [his wife] my mind did whett / To seeke thee God." Donne's exploration of this experience necessarily assumes the form of a dialogue, not a progress. The self in pursuit of the beloved does not give way to the soul in pursuit of (or pursued by) God. Rather, Jack Donne and Doctor Donne, Pico and Augustine, self and soul, are present from the beginning and continue in pleasurable, anguished, fruitful, unresolvable conversation to the end. This is not perhaps the sort of ending we would like (though perhaps these days it *is*), yet it is Donne's peculiar quality and courage to insist throughout that we have both something like a self and something like a soul (as we have also both soul and body) and that the claims of both must be, if not quite satisfied, recognized. The reward of such a dialogue, that favorite Renaissance form, is, after all, not knowledge but wisdom, not a decisive result, not some particular accession of knowledge or change in behavior, but rather an understanding of the conditions under which certain kinds of knowledge—of others, of love, of oneself, of God—are held.[23] The purpose of Donne's continuing dialogue of love, carried on by the self and the soul, is to assert, even as it assesses, the centrality of love's revelation of the soul and its needs; to make that revelation active in his own life and in his reader's; and to make it finally prevail. Of course that "finally" is not yet, and even when it does come "in glory," what is envisioned is less the dissolution of the self, that essential "faculty of will, and election," than its "establishment," its final (re-)union with the soul.[24] As he explains in a sermon, in this world, at this moment:

> I am not all here, I am here now preaching upon this text, and I am at home in my Library considering whether *S. Gregory*, or *S. Hierome*, have said best of this text, before. I am here speaking to you, and yet I consider by the way, in the same instant, what it is likely you will say to one another, when I have done. You are

---

[23] K. J. Wilson, *Incomplete Fictions: The Formation of English Renaissance Dialogue* (Washington, DC: Catholic Univ. Press, 1985) observes that "Tudor dialogue evolved into a mode for the imitation of the interior world of thought and emotion" (179).

[24] Cf. Mahood, *Poetry and Humanism*, 161: "His final union is achieved, not through the denial, but through the affirmation of those things which would present insurmountable obstacles had not the Word been made flesh: his selfhood and his sins."

not all here neither; you are here now, hearing me, and yet you are thinking that you have heard a better Sermon somewhere else, of this text before.... I cannot say, you cannot say so perfectly, so entirely now, as at the Resurrection, *Ego,* I am here; I, body and soul; I, soul and faculties ... [but then] *Ego,* I, body and soul, soul and faculties, shall say to Christ Jesus, *Ego sum,* Lord, it is I ... and I the same man, shall receive the crown of glory which shall not fade. (*Sermons,* 3.110)

At which moment, the conflicting imperatives of the merely human dialogue of self and soul will be absorbed into a divine dialectic present from the beginning, a dialectic intimated in the word used in Genesis 1 to describe the "Action" of God's spirit, a word, as Donne remarks "of a double, and a very diverse signification":

for God had two purposes in the creation, *Vt sint, ut maneant,* That the creature should be, and be still; That it should exist at first, and subsist after; Be made, and made permanent.... The holy Ghost moves, he is the first author; the holy Ghost perpetuates, settles, establishes, he is our rest, and acquiescence, and center; Beginning, Way, End, all is in this word, *Recaph; The Spirit of God moved, and rested.* (*Sermons,* 9.99)

Washington University

DEBORAH RUBIN

"Let your death be my Iliad": Classical Allusion and Latin in George Herbert's Memoriae Matris Sacrum

ON JUNE 8, 1627, MAGDALEN HERBERT DANVERS WAS BURIED AT her home in Chelsea. Less than a month later, on July 7, a memorial volume was entered in the Stationers' Register that contained the text of a sermon delivered by John Donne—a close friend and great admirer of Lady Danvers—and *Memoriae Matris Sacrum*, fourteen poems in Latin and five in Greek by her seventh child, George Herbert. Although composed with extraordinary speed in response to an event of both public and personal importance, these poems cannot properly be described as occasional. In twenty-eight days, Herbert wrote nineteen poems that together form a moving autobiographical account of the process of grieving and a coherent lyrical sequence. The conditions of their precipitate creation and publication—so unlike those governing the production of Herbert's other poetic works—make them of special interest within the larger opus, and independently they deserve a more thorough reading than they have yet received in this century.[1] Their unique thematic content, exploration

---

[1] The standard edition of the Latin and English poems is still *The Works of George Herbert*, ed. F. E. Hutchinson (Oxford: Oxford Univ. Press, 1941), which provides a brief commentary, primarily glossing vocabulary and mythological references. McCloskey and Murphy's edition, *The Latin Poetry of George Herbert: A Bilingual Edition*, trans. Mark McCloskey and Paul R. Murphy (Athens, OH: Ohio Univ. Press, 1965), includes a free verse translation that is unreliable and conveys little of the quality of the Latin poetry. No book-length work on Herbert's Latin poems has yet appeared, and the number of articles is small. W. Hilton Kelliher's "The Latin Poetry of George Herbert" (in *The Latin Poetry of English Poets*, ed. J. W. Binns [London: Routledge, 1974], 26–57) provides a useful overview of *Musae Responsoriae, Passio Discerpta*, and *Lucus* as well as *Memoriae Matris Sacrum*, and Amy M. Charles, in *A Life of George Herbert* (Ithaca: Cornell Univ. Press, 1977), comments on the Latin sequences. Herbert H. Huxley's "The Latin Poems of George Herbert (1593–1633)," in *Acta Conventus Neo-Latini Amstelodamensis: Proceedings of the Second International Congress of Neo-Latin Studies*, Amsterdam 19–14 August 1973, ed. P. Tuynman, G. C. Kuiper, and E. Kessler (Munich: Wilhelm Fink Verlag, 1979), 560–65, briefly describes the contents and metrics of the Latin poems. Aside from translations of several

of classical prosody and reference, and strikingly intimate revelations about Herbert and his relationship to his mother are crucial to a complete understanding of the man and of his English poetry.

In contrast with the austerely anonymous and exemplary poems of *The Temple*—which avoid all proper nouns except those from the Scriptures and which refer to no contemporary figures—*Memoriae Matris Sacrum* is individual and public in its exposure of intimate psychic experiences. The publication of the sequence in conjunction with Donne's sermon ("A Sermon of Commemoration of the Lady Danvers, late Wife of Sir John Danvers. Preach'd at Chilsey, where she was lately buried. By John Donne Dean of St. Pauls, London. 1 July 1627")[2] names

---

poems, Edmund Blunden offers only casual comments in "George Herbert's Latin Poems," in *Essays and Studies by Members of the English Association* 19 (1934): 29–39; repr. London: Dawson, 1966.

The only articles devoted largely to *Memoriae Matris Sacrum* are E. Pearlman's "George Herbert's God," *English Literary Renaissance* 13 (1983): 88–112; Rhonda Blair's "George Herbert's Greek Poetry," *Philological Quarterly* 64 (1985): 573–84; and William Kerrigan's "Ritual Man: On the Outside of Herbert's Poetry," *Psychiatry* 48 (1985): 68–82. Pearlman touches upon many crucial and otherwise unexplored issues regarding Herbert's psychology, relationship to Lady Danvers, and conception of God, focusing primarily on *Memoriae Matris Sacrum*; Blair discusses the five Greek poems in *Memoriae Matris Sacrum*, tracing classical analogues and assessing Herbert's skill in Greek prosody. Kerrigan's article, psychoanalytic in emphasis, discusses *Memoriae Matris Sacrum* but focuses more broadly on Herbert's poetry. Other articles on individual Latin poems or sequences by Herbert include Edmund Miller's chapter on *Passio Discerpta*, Philip Dust's on "Triumphus Mortis" and *Passio Discerpta*, and Leicester Bradner's on Herbert's epithalamium for Princess Elizabeth and Frederick, the Elector Palatine. (Miller, *Drudgerie Divine: The Rhetoric of God and Man in George Herbert*, Salzburg Studies in English Literature, Elizabethan and Renaissance Studies 84 [Salzburg: Universität Salzburg, 1979]; Dust, "George Herbert's Pacifist 'Triumphus Mortis' and the Evolution of War," in *Acta Conventus Neo-Latini Turonensis: Troisième Congrès International D'Études Néo-Latines*, Tours, 6–10 Sept. 1976, ed. Jean-Claude Margolin, 2 vols. [Paris: Librairie Philosophique J. Vrin, 1980], 1011–18; Dust, "George Herbert's *Passio Discerpta* and Franciscus Lucas's Commentaries on the New Testament," in *Acta Conventus Neo-Latini Bononiensis: Proceedings of the Fourth International Congress of Neo-Latin Studies*, Bologna, 26 Aug. to 1 Sept. 1979, ed. R. J. Schoeck, Medieval & Renaissance Texts & Studies, 37 [Binghamton, NY, 1985], 451–58; Bradner, "New Poems by George Herbert: The Cambridge Latin Gratulatory Anthology of 1613," *Renaissance News* 15, 3 [1962]: 208–11.) — Two earlier articles briefly discuss the role Magdalen Herbert played in George's life: William Blackburn, "Lady Magdalen Herbert and her Son George," *South Atlantic Quarterly* 50, 3 (1951): 378–88 and Aubrey Noakes, "The Mother of George Herbert," *Contemporary Review* 183 (1953): 39–45.

[2] *The Sermons of John Donne*, ed. Evelyn M. Simpson and George R. Potter, 10 vols. (Berkeley and Los Angeles: Univ. of California Press, 1953–1962), 8:61–93. In this title and in my citations of *Memoriae Matris Sacrum* I have substituted v for u, i for j and j for i to conform with modern orthographical practice in Latin and English. I have also omitted the acute, grave, and circumflex accents Herbert employs in writing Latin.

the person commemorated and places the event squarely in secular history. With the identification of Lady Danvers, the speaker is identified also, not as any pious son but as George Herbert, born in 1593, currently residing in Chelsea, step-son and friend of John Danvers, younger friend and literary colleague of John Donne. As the sequence progresses, he will hint at developments within his small circle—criticisms of his extravagant grief made by acquaintances and prying observations into his strained physical health by a physician—and he will explore his relationship to the historical moment—a passive weeper on the shore as ships are launched and war waged.

The sequence is also more individual in its exposure of Herbert's relationship to his mother and the antisocial aspects of his grief. He praises Lady Danvers's character in terms that move beyond conventional elegiac tributes to female virtue; he describes her physical appearance and his own body, each in eccentric detail; he evokes his house and garden and invites his mother's shade to dwell in it with him, in the tradition of the passionate shepherd. *Memoriae Matris Sacrum* not only permits such specificity of reference; it shifts Herbert's object from the numinous to the human and carnal. In *The Temple*, human frailty and mortality are locked in combat with a grace-dispensing God; in *Memoriae Matris Sacrum*, forgiveness and salvation recede in the face of crushing grief, and the capacity of men and women to suffer takes on a secular dimension.

A companion in Herbert's grief is a world of pagan allusion that has been utterly excluded from his English poetry. While Milton and other English poets use classical materials in their English elegiac and sacred poetry, Herbert does not, and in *The Temple* he expresses ambivalence over even the use of rhetorical figures and fictions, which he finds unsuited to a sinner addressing himself to God. By choosing to write in Greek and Latin in *Memoriae Matris Sacrum*, Herbert has allowed himself access not only to other languages, with the prosodic options they allow, but also to a pagan literary tradition and to the classical mythology upon which it is constituted. In doing this, he deliberately removes himself from the language of the Church of England, of his major devotional poems, and of the largest part of his rational life. He turns instead to the ambivalent, eroticized matter of pagan myth, and to a tongue he identifies with the experience of the maternal.[3]

---

[3] His understanding of this sequence as a gift to his mother and an expression of her voice is the subject of another essay. While we do not know whether Magdalen Herbert knew Latin or to what degree she personally participated in her children's early care and learning of English, Herbert makes claims in poems 1 and 2 that suggest a symbolic identification between the poems' language and his mother.

Herbert's appropriations of pagan material initially appear startling. He describes Lady Danvers as "my Juno" and "Magna Mater," offers to hitch the horses of the Sun to her chariot, and equates his sufferings with those of Ulysses, exclaiming, "haec tua mors, Ilias esto mihi" ("Let this your death be my *Iliad*"). The idolatry, erotic content, and exaggerated despair of such representations seem to be violations of his English-speaking persona, psychologically, theologically, and aesthetically. In fact, the European Neo-Latin verse tradition is more tolerant of such materials than the Renaissance vernacular traditions are,[4] and Herbert exploited this alternate tradition to deal with a personal crisis. The classical allusions in *Memoriae Matris Sacrum* are consonant with his state of mind, and with the difficult position in which Herbert found himself in attempting to explore his relation to his mother in verse. The forbidden associations, expressed in a more private language, are evocative of forbidden emotions, which Herbert sought to explore and contain in verse. In moments of denial, rage, despair, and confusion he falls back upon the resources of pagan literature and philosophy.

Denial, rage, despair, and yearning to regain the lost beloved are of course well-documented stages of the mourning process as observed by twentieth-century social scientists, and there is evidence that Renaissance psychology did not differ fundamentally in this area.[5] Although social expectations for the behavior of mourner and consoler differed widely from our own in the sixteenth century and somewhat less widely in the early seventeenth century, as G. W. Pigman III's recent

---

[4] See the introduction to Fred J. Nichols, ed. and trans., *An Anthology of Neo-Latin Poetry* (New Haven: Yale Univ. Press, 1979), 1-2 and passim.

[5] Bowlby's *Loss: Sadness and Depression*, vol. 3 of *Attachment and Loss* (New York: Basic Books, 1980) is an important psychological study of contemporary expressions of loss and mourning. Pigman's psychoanalytic study of English Renaissance elegy (*Grief and English Renaissance Elegy* [Cambridge: Cambridge Univ. Press, 1985]) surveys the shift in conventions of mourning and consolation from the early sixteenth century to the mid-seventeenth century; George W. McClure's article on Italian humanist responses to the death of sons ("The Art of Mourning: Autobiographical Writings on the Loss of a Son in Italian Humanist Thought [1400-1461]," *Renaissance Quarterly* 39 [1986]: 440-75) traces a similar pattern in fifteenth-century Italy. Peter M. Sacks's study of English elegies from Spenser to Yeats (*The English Elegy: Studies in the Genre from Spenser to Yeats* [Baltimore: Johns Hopkins Univ. Press, 1985]) offers a literary/psychological perspective on the work of mourning, and Arnold Stein's *The House of Death: Messages from the English Renaissance* (Baltimore: Johns Hopkins Univ. Press, 1986) examines the treatment of death in Renaissance literature more broadly. For socio-historical findings on death in the Renaissance, see Lawrence Stone (*The Family, Sex, and Marriage in England 1500-1800* [London: Weidenfeld and Nicholson, 1977]) and Philippe Aries (*Western Attitudes toward Death: From the Middle Ages to the Present*, trans. Patricia M. Ranum [Baltimore: Johns Hopkins Univ. Press, 1974]).

work demonstrates, the underlying psychic processes appear to have been much the same.[6] Thus, what seems most extreme and indecorous in *Memoriae Matris Sacrum* viewed in relation to his English poems is understandable in terms of human reactions to stress and grief. Shaken by an intense personal crisis and apparently feeling isolated from those around him, Herbert undertook this sequence of poems as a therapeutic exercise, exploiting pagan materials for his own purposes.

Thus Herbert begins poem 2 with an invocation to "Corneliae sanctae, graves Semproniae," notable and grave mothers of past sons who will praise and bewail, and also mirror in their persons, the chaste dignity of Lady Danvers. Later in the same poem, Herbert likens her wisdom, skill with words, and business acumen to those of the Catos. A third passage claims "Pactoli arena tibi tumulus est unicus" (41). The famed golden sands of Pactolus would, Herbert suggests, provide a fitting gravesite and measure of her worth.[7] In the context of Herbert's elegant Latin, such modest concessions to the culture of the language are not obtrusive, especially in a poem almost totally devoid of Christian reference. One reason poem 2 is able to absorb such allusions readily is that its content is so secular. The majority of its sixty-five lines describe Magdalen Herbert's daily life, paying predictable tribute to private wifely virtues—modest attire, skill in household matters, generosity toward the poor, and good temper—but enumerating as well public attainments less often praised in a Renaissance noblewoman: witty speech, knowledge of business affairs, wisdom and elegance in writing. Up to line 49, the poem is almost pagan in tone, stressing ritual mourning and a just praise of the dead woman.

Unlike Jonson's "On My First Sonne," which Pigman places in the tradition of earlier sixteenth-century rigorism, poem 2 does not seek to "loose" the ties of family feeling or to place personal love for the departed in a larger, Christian perspective.[8] While Herbert credits his mother with vivid faith and refers to her music as "caelestis harmoniae breve praeludium" (44), a brief prelude to celestial harmony, the poem

---

[6] Pigman, passim.

[7] I have cited Hutchinson's edition throughout. All translations of *Memoriae Matris Sacrum* are my own. Jean Herrick kindly read my translations and helped me to tease out several passages.

[8] Rigorism, the most inflexible traditional Christian attitude towards grief, "condemns all grief for those who have died virtuously and are in heaven.... If one mourns, one either is guilty of the sin of despair or is admitting that the deceased is in hell" (Pigman, 27). By the early seventeenth century in England, such an absolute position as Jonson's was unusual. Christians permitted themselves and others a moderate expression of grief, although anxiety as to the appropriate amount did not abate greatly.

reveals little interest in her heavenly status, stressing, rather, his duty to sustain her glory and her name with earthly tributes: "Tu vero mater perpetim laudabere / Nato dolenti" (61–62: "You, indeed, Mother, will be praised perpetually / by a grieving son"). Where Jonson blames himself for the sin of "too much hope for thee, lov'd boy" and vows not to love too well again, Herbert concludes his poem with a rebuttal to an interlocutor who claims his feelings for his mother are inappropriate:

> At tu qui inepte haec dicta censes filio,
> Nato parentis auferens Encomium,
> Abito, trunce, cum tuis pudoribus.   (52–54)

But you who foolishly judge a son's words, depriving a child of his parent's praise, go away, idiot, with your shame.

Much more could be said about Herbert's concern in this poem with the gift of speech, and his compulsion to "restore a tongue" to his mother, whom he views as needing, even in heaven, a human voice and a passionate defense by her son (59). The position in which Herbert finds himself as he writes the entire sequence is difficult and painful. Biographical information suggests that his relation to his mother was an unusually close one,[9] and other poems in this sequence point toward an unresolved oedipal attachment. The facts that Herbert's father died when George was three years old, a crucial age in terms of the resolution of oedipal conflicts, and that Magdalen Herbert married Sir John Danvers, a man in his twenties, when George was not quite sixteen, support this possibility. The abandonment, anger, and yearning he feels for Lady Danvers are complicated by guilt at the expression of grief, and anxiety that others will criticize these emotions. He is unable to imagine severing his long and close ties with his parent. Out of his need

---

[9] Charles's biography of Herbert stresses Magdalen Herbert's careful supervision of all her children's education. Contrary to the general pattern of separation from the family during adolescence that Stone describes, the Herbert children were often close to their mother. After her own mother's death, Magdalen Herbert moved her entire household to Oxford to be near her son Edward, who was at school. George continued to live at home while he attended Westminster School as a day student, and lived principally in his mother's household until the time of her death. Only then did he enter the priesthood and marry. — Other recent accounts also stress Herbert's extraordinary involvement with his mother. Pearlman's article comments in similar terms on "the intensity of the maternal bond" between Herbert and Lady Danvers (98). Kerrigan argues conversely that Herbert lost a "nourishing mother" at an early age due to the birth of three younger children and to the responsibilities Lady Danvers assumed on the death of her first husband, and that "presexual mourning rather than oedipal violence" explains his adult psychology (73).

for her, he fabricates her continuing need for him, and constructs these verses as her monument.[10]

Poems 5, 6, and 7 comprise the psychic nadir of the sequence, confronting death at its most physical, exhibiting the most extreme form of avoidance, and exploring the poet's own physical illness. They are also the occasion for more startling evocations of the classical world. The corpse takes center stage in poem 5, where the odor of death seems to permeate all living things and the Christian afterlife recedes as a possible consolation:

> Horti, deliciae *Dominae*, marcescite tandem;
>   Ornastis capulum, nec superesse licet.
> Ecce decus vestrum spinis horrescit, acuta
>   Cultricem revocans anxietate manum:
> Terram & funus olent flores: Dominaeque cadaver
>   Contiguas stirpes afflat, eaeque rosas.
> In terram violae capite inclinantur opaco,
>   Quaeque domus Dominae sit, gravitate docent.
> Quare haud vos hortos, sed coemeteria dico,
>   Dum torus absentem quisque reponit heram.   10
> Euge, perite omnes; nec posthac exeat ulla
>   Quaesitum Dominam gemma vel herba suam.
> Cuncta ad radices redeant, tumulosque paternos;
>   (Nempe sepulcra Satis numen inempta dedit.)
> Occidite; aut sane tantisper vivite, donec
>   Vespere ros maestis funus honestet aquis.

Gardens, beloved by my mistress, droop at last; you have adorned the coffin, but cannot survive. See how your beauty bristles with sharp thorns, anxiously calling back the [female]

---

[10] In an essay in progress I consider these issues in more detail. The problem of how to understand Herbert's relationship with his mother has been a troubling one for several earlier critics. See, for example, Joseph H. Summers's comment: "The *Memoriae Matris Sacrum*, in conjunction with Walton's *Life* and Donne's funeral sermon, almost invariable arouses speculation today concerning the psychological relationship between Herbert and his mother. The literary critic without professional psychiatric training, however, can hardly hope for a greater success in medical diagnosis than the psychiatrist ignorant of literary conventions usually achieves in literary criticism" (*George Herbert: His Religion and Art* [Cambridge: Harvard Univ. Press, 1968], 205–6). See also E. Pearlman's caveat, 112. In the twenty years since the publication of Summers's book, the gap between professional training in psychoanalysis and literary theory has narrowed considerably, and while, as Pearlman argues, "the general psychological outlines of the late medieval world are only beginning to emerge" it is possible to base certain observations on the emotions displayed, the statements, and the images in a text such as *Memoriae Matris Sacrum*.

> gardener's hand. The flowers smell of earth and death; the mistress' corpse breathes on the nearby plants, and they breathe on the roses. Violas bend their dark heads to the earth, showing by their heaviness the home of their mistress. And so I call you not gardens but burial grounds, where every bed lays to rest the absent lady. Well done! now die, every one, and henceforth let no bud or plant seek out its mistress. Let all return to roots and fathering mounds; surely God has given enough free graves. Perish—or live just until dew adorns the corpse with its sad waters in the evening.

Flowers, which are customarily placed on the coffin to mask the corruption of death, are here themselves corrupted. The coffin doesn't smell of flowers; instead the flowers smell of death, and with their odor they infect the rest of the garden. The focus here is on decay, not eternal life, on the body not the spirit. A spiritual nausea seems to have seized the speaker: death's contagion threatens to engulf all life and beauty, and grief and depression prevail throughout nature. All the world has become a burial ground; every flower is a mourner. God, giver of life on earth and of everlasting life thereafter, has become the giver of "sepulcra inempta" ("free graves"), and all that Herbert longs for is the end of birth and growth (11–12).

Poem 5 represents a later stage of grieving than the first few poems: acknowledgment of the physical annihilation and loss of identity that death brings, and the depression that accompanies it. Herbert's initial denial of these facts accounts for the ingenuity of his posturings in the first few poems as he strives to compensate for and thus undo the death. The simplicity and emotional integrity of this elegy may take their impetus from Herbert's exhausted acceptance of some part of the truth—that death brings an end to life in the body, and that no amount of sacrifice, striving, or symbolic substitution will alter that reality.

Herbert's acknowledgment of death in its most physical aspect is accompanied by a more overt exploration through classical allusion of his erotic ties to his mother. Echoes of Catullus's sparrow poems in Herbert's first line contribute to the pathos of poem 5. The phrase "horti, deliciae Dominae" ("gardens, beloved by my mistress") closely follows "passer, deliciae meae puellae" ("sparrow, beloved of my mistress") in Catullus 2 and 3[11] and allows Herbert to evoke the pity, delicacy, and ambivalence of Catullus's poems. Lines 11–12 of Catullus 3, describing the sparrow setting forth on its journey to the underworld, "qui nunc it per iter tenebricosum / illuc, unde negant redire quem-

---

[11] Thanks to Brian Striar for drawing my attention to this echo.

quam" ("that now goes on that shadowy journey / from which they say that no one returns"), despite its mock-heroic dimension, deftly counterposes the theme of mortality to the erotic play that has preceded it. The sparrow gains dignity from its death-journey and from its fate that it was loved by Lesbia. Herbert, scanning Catullus for meters to explore in the sequence, may have read such lines as these with new eyes: "passer ... quem plus illa oculis suis amabat: / nam mellitus erat suamque norat / ipsam tam bene quam puella matrem" (5-7: "the sparrow that she had loved more than her own life / for it was sweet, and it had grown to know her / as well as a girl knows her own mother"). In its dual role as child pressed to Lesbia's breast, and erotic object, the sparrow serves as a subliminal image for Herbert in this poem.

Catullus's sparrow, setting out for the underworld never to return; the flowers of Lady Danvers's garden, withdrawn back to their roots and to the "tumulos ... paternos" ("fathering mounds"); and the corpse of Lady Danvers, sprinkled with evening dew and prepared, too, to enter the earth, connect the poems in their shared perception of the irrevocable aspects of death. The flowers of the garden, bristling with thorns, vainly call back the gardener's hand as formerly each plant and bud had searched out its mistress. Beneath this shared mythology of loss and epic search is the Orphic dream of retrieving the beloved and enjoying her company again on earth. This is most apparent in poem 7, where Herbert beseeches his mother's shade to assume the more loving form she had in life and come live with him. The theme appears in other poems as well. In poem 3, for example, Herbert debates whether Phoebus can send down his mother to earth on a golden ray of sun. For a Christian, these are illicit hopes to introduce into an elegiac sequence, here facilitated by Catullus's seemingly innocent sparrow.

In poem 5 we see only the merest traces of the erotic in the association of the garden's "domina" with Catullus's. In Latin, as in English, "mistress" has several meanings, but Herbert assigns the mistress here to the garden and not to himself: while Catullus writes "passer deliciae *meae* puellae," Herbert omits the possessive adjective ("horti, deliciae Dominae"), letting the plants stand in his stead. His reference to the absent lady as "hera" in line 10 is similarly ambiguous, for "hera" may mean mistress, Lady (as epithet to a goddess), sweetheart, or of course the goddess herself. In poem 7, however, a dramatic encounter between mother and son places Herbert's fantasies about their relationship in the foreground. In lines 1-21, the speaker confronts the shade of his dead mother in a hostile and unfamiliar form; in the second section, he attempts to "revoke" her in the Latin sense, to coax her back to her former appearance and to recall her from the liminal place where she now resides. He offers her a new home and garden, where they can share a life together:

> Pallida materni Genii atque exanguis imago,
> In nebulas similesque tui res gaudia nunquid
> Mutata? & pro matre mihi phantasma dolosum
> Uberaque aerea hiscentem fallentia natum?
> Vae nubi pluvia gravidae, non lacte, measque
> Ridenti lacrymas quibus unis concolor unda est.
> Quin fugias? mea non fuerat tam nubila Iuno,
> Tam segnis facies aurorae nescia vernae,
> Tam languens genitrix cineri supposta fugaci:
> Verum augusta parens, sanctum os caeloque locandum,
> Quale paludosos iamiam lictura recessus   11
> Praetulit Astraea, aut solio Themis alma vetusto
> Pensilis, atque acri dirimens Examine lites.
> Hunc vultum ostendas, & tecum, nobile spectrum,
> Quod superest vitae, insumam: Solisque iugales
> Ipse tuae solum adnectam, sine murmure, thensae.
> Nec querar ingratos, studiis dum tabidus insto,
> Effluxisse dies, suffocatamve Minervam,
> Aut spes productas, barbataque somnia vertam
> In vicium mundo sterili, cui cedo cometas   20
> Ipse suos tanquam digno pallentiaque astra.
>   Est mihi bis quinis laqueata domuncula tignis
> Rure; brevisque hortus, cuius cum vellere florum
> Luctatur spacium, qualem tamen eligit aequi
> Iudicii dominus, flores ut iunctius halent
> Stipati, rudibusque volis impervius hortus
> Sit quasi fasciculus crescens, & nidus odorum.
> Hic ego tuque erimus, variae suffitibus herbae
> Quotidie pasti: tantum verum indue vultum
> Affectusque mei similem; nec languida misce   30
> Ora meae memori menti: ne dispare cultu
> Pugnaces, teneros florum turbemus odores,
> Atque inter reliquos horti crescentia foetus
> Nostra etiam paribus marcescant gaudia fatis.

Pale bloodless shade of my mother's spirit, have my joys been changed to mists and things like you? Do you, cunning apparition, take my mother's place, breasts of air deceiving your gaping-mouthed child? Woe, cloud, heavy with rain not milk, mocking my tears, the color of water, why don't you go away? My Juno wasn't so gloomy, so slow a form, ignorant of vernal dawn, so languid a mother, substituted for fleeting ashes. Truly, she was a majestic parent; a sacred face worthy to be placed in the sky, like that Astraea bore when she was ready to forsake her marshy retreats, or that of kind Themis, raised aloft on her ancient throne, ending strife with keen judgment. Show that countenance, and with you, noble specter, I'll expend what remains of life. I myself will hitch the horses of the Sun to your chariot without a murmur. Nor will I bewail the thankless days that have passed by as I, wasting away, pursued my studies—Minerva strangled—or hopes postponed, and my maturer dreams I'll cast off into the barren world of mutability, to which, for it deserves them, I leave its comets and its pale stars.

I have a little paneled house in the country with twice five beams and a small garden where downy flowers contend for space. But a discerning owner would choose just such a place so that the compacted flowers might breathe in accord, and so that, impassible to uncouth feet, the garden might be like a blooming nosegay and a nest of odors. Here, you and I shall daily feast on the incense of many herbs. Only assume your true expression, similar in feeling to mine, and don't confuse this faint face with the one I remember, lest we, at odds because of different situations, confound the tender odors of the flowers, and lest, among the other fruits of the garden, our growing joys [the flowers] begin to droop because of fates like ours.

In poem 7, Herbert unites more troubling matter and more densely pagan allusions. In this elegy, addressed to "Pallida materni Genii atque exanguis imago," he reproaches an aloof, ungenerous shade, so unlike his mother when alive, and compares the latter to three deities—Juno, Astraea, and Themis—as well as calling her "augusta parens," an epithet whose associations reinforce the theme of divinity. Such identifications raise questions individually, and are problematic as a group. Themis—ancient goddess of justice, pity, and hospitality—seems a suitable classical emblem of Lady Danvers's qualities, and Astraea—last of the gods to abandon the earth after the Golden Age—provides an appropriate myth of death and translation to the heavens as a constellation. They are, however, both pagan and divine. While mourners customarily idealize the dead, to appropriate a goddess for a mother verges on idolatry, or requires an allegorical reading of the sequence that seems forced.

Juno, with her original identity as the female creative principle and her later definition in terms of spite and sexual jealousy, is still more difficult to assimilate.¹² Herbert's reference to "mea Iuno" is ambiguous. Does he view himself as a child of Juno, and if so, what attributes does he mean to confer upon Juno as parent? The possessive form, uncommon prefacing a parent's name, hints at other relationships or at a jealous focus on himself, as if their relationship were unique.¹³ Since Herbert elsewhere identifies Lady Danvers with Athena, with "Magna Mater," and with the Graces, the genealogical possibilities are numerous and provocative. An implied comparison between Herbert and Aeneas, which I will discuss later, introduces yet another divine parent, Venus, with her erotic associations.

The first half of poem 7 contains Herbert's anguished plea that his mother's shade assume a more familiar face and manner—that is to say, return to life—and engages in that kind of Orphic bargaining for the return of the dead that recent research into the grieving process has begun to describe. The speaker offers to hitch the horses of the Sun to her chariot, and to forsake all bitterness over unrealized worldly hopes ("suffocatamve Minervam" ["Minerva strangled"]). The bargain is inherently sacrilegious, as are many subconscious impulses. A fallen human being has nothing to bargain with before God, and to attempt to bargain with anyone else to undo God's will is a sign of confusion. The legal images in Jonson's epigram on his son make this point clearly: the child was lent to him and now is repaid; to wish to keep the boy—"too much hope of thee"—was a sin; even to lament his death is wrong. Herbert, conjuring up his mother's shade in terms that evoke epic

---

¹² Juno is associated with life, particularly sexual life, and assists women at marriage and childbirth, subsuming in her development the goddesses Lucina, Opigena, Iterduca, and Cinxia (*The Oxford Classical Dictionary*, ed. N. G. L. Hammond and H. H. Scullard, 2d ed., rev. [Oxford: Clarendon Press, 1972]). In her origins, she is the female aspect of the Latin Genius figure. According to Jane Chance, "The Genius of the head of the household was complemented by the Juno of the mother: the father begot the child, but the mother bore it, and this feminine spirit protected the wife's fertility and capacity for bearing children." She is also the "female cosmic" figure who, with Jupiter's seed, produces all things. "Magna Mater" is one of her names. (*The Genius Figure in Antiquity and the Middle Ages* [New York: Columbia Univ. Press, 1975], 9, 26–27.)

¹³ While Charles argues that Edward, the eldest child, was Magdalen Herbert's favorite (44), in *Memoriae Matris Sacrum* Herbert describes his role in praising and mourning for her as unique, and sometimes writes as if there were no other children. In poem 1, he writes, "*Tantum* istaec scribo gratus, ne tu mihi *tantum* / Mater (7–8) ("Grateful, I write these things *only*, lest you be Mother *only* to me"), implying that if he does not secure her reputation, her maternal virtues will only be known to him. In poem 2, he sends off an interlocutor critical of his extravagant grief, exclaiming, "Mihine matris urna clausa est *unico* . . ." (57) ("Is my mother's urn shut up to me *alone*?"). Here, Herbert emphasizes the fact that he alone is prohibited from mourning, a unique position of disadvantage. Pearlman comments both on Herbert's closeness to his mother and on his self-presentation as an only child (91).

descents to the underworld or European folkloric accounts of revenants (the unquiet dead returned from the grave),[14] has pitted his imagination and will against the power of God to give and to take away.

The shade of Lady Danvers—pale, cloudlike, deceiving, withholding, impossible to caress or to take nourishment from—has its origins in the descents of Odysseus and Aeneas to the underworld, and thereby draws the reader into a wider circle of possible referents. Odysseus, seeking Teiresias, encounters his mother, who has pined away out of longing for him. He tries to make amends but cannot:

> I bit my lip,
> rising perplexed, with longing to embrace her,
> and tried three times, putting my arms around her,
> but she went sifting through my hands, impalpable
> as shadows are, and wavering like a dream.
> Now this embittered all the pain I bore,
> and I cried in the darkness:
> "O my mother,
> will you not stay, be still, here in my arms,
> may we not, in this place of Death, as well,
> hold one another, touch with love, and taste
> salt tears' relief ...?" (191)[15]

Odysseus's responsibility for Antikleia's death becomes the justification for his mother's failure to respond to his caresses, to return to life. Aeneas, descending into Avernus to be reunited with his father, confronts as well the forsaken Dido. Here the parent and the betrayed have been split into two persons, Anchises, to whom Aeneas has been a pious son, and Dido, whom he has betrayed. The shade in poem 7 partakes of aspects of both apparitions but is more like that of Dido. Anchises' shade, like Antikleia's and Lady Danvers's, cannot be embraced (6.460), but it is welcoming in expression and gesture, extending loving arms, feasting on the sight of its son, and offering a consolation for past suffering in terms of future triumphs. Dido's shade—stubborn,

---

[14] Revenants, who occupy a transitional status between life on earth and the afterlife or grave, are distinguished in the European ballad tradition, for instance, by tokens such as wet clothing and hats of birch as well as by their pallor ("Sweet William's Ghost," Child 77; "The Unquiet Grave," Child 78; "The Wife of Usher's Well," Child 79). See Francis James Child, ed., *The English and Scottish Popular Ballads*, 5 vols. (1884–98; repr. New York: Dover, 1965). "mater ... uvida" in poem 4 and the pale, misty *imago* in poem 7 have their origins in this traditon as well as in the classical one.

[15] Page number refers to Robert Fitzgerald's translation of *The Odyssey* (Garden City, NY: Doubleday-Anchor, 1963).

stony, hateful, and devoid of its former love—greatly resembles Herbert's vision, impassive, mocking, and withholding. It is Dido, not Anchises, whom Virgil describes in terms of clouds and shadows, and it is Dido who elicits an ambivalent mixture of pity and guilt from Aeneas:

> "funeris heu tibi causa fui? per sidera iuro,
> per superos et si qua fides tellure sub ima est,
> inuitus, regina, tuo de litore cessi....
>   nec credere quiui
> hunc tantum tibi me discessu ferre dolorem.
> siste gradum teque aspectu ne subtrahe nostro.
> quem fugis? extremum fato quod te adloquor hoc est."
>   (6.458-60; 463-66)

> "Oh god! was it death I brought you, then? I swear by the stars,
> By the powers above, by whatever is sacred in the Underworld,
> It was not of my own will, Dido, I left your land....
>   I did not, could not imagine
> My going would ever bring such terrible agony on you.
> Don't move away! Oh, let me see you a little longer!
> To fly from me, when this is the last word fate allows us!"[16]

By comparing Lady Danvers to Athena, the Graces, Juno, Astraea, and Themis, Herbert diffuses the specificity of reference that any deity individually would have. But these allusions are not simply interchangeable evocations of the idealized, almost sainted, dead nor are these deities in combination merely an allegorical representation of human virtue. The poet's more dramatic confrontation with his mother's shade challenges such a general view, forcing the reader to confront Herbert's ambivalent attitude toward his mother, who in death has been split into many images. Chaste, accomplished, just, and pious, she is also an abandoning mother, and a love object who has rejoined her first husband in the afterlife, just as Dido has. In Aeneas's address to Dido, we can perceive both the desperate lover, afraid of being abandoned, and the guilty murderer. In Herbert's glancing tributes to Dido here and elsewhere, we read the poet's rage at abandonment, his sense that he has been injured by the departure of the dead, and his guilt at such a representation.

In the second half of poem 7, after a heart-stopping ellipsis, Herbert

---

[16] C. Day Lewis, trans., *The Aeneid of Virgil* (Garden City, NY: Doubleday-Anchor, 1953), 143. I quote the edition of R. A. B. Mynors, *P. Vergili Maronis Opera* (Oxford: Oxford Univ. Press, 1969), 241.

describes the idyll of his mother's return to live with him in a charming cottage and garden, a familiar pastoral scene. The psycho-sexual implications of this proposal are striking, as noted earlier. The sequence and this poem in particular, through an array of puns, literary allusions, and dramatic confrontations, suggest, if not an imagined erotic relationship between Herbert and his mother, at least a relationship of unusual intimacy and exclusivity. The final lines of poem 7, with their presentiment of star-crossed love blighting the flowers, offer one illustration:

> tantum verum indue vultum
> Affectusque mei similem; nec languida misce
> Ora meae memori menti: ne dispare cultu
> Pugnaces, teneros florum turbemus odores,
> Atque inter reliquos horti crescentia foetus
> Nostra etiam paribus marcescant gaudia fatis.
> (29–34)

Only assume your true expression, similar in feeling to mine, and don't confuse this faint face with the one I remember, lest we, at odds because of different situations, confound the tender odors of the flowers, and lest, among the other fruits of the garden, our growing joys [the flowers] begin to droop because of fates like ours.

Other illustrations may be found in poem 11, where Herbert compares himself to Ulysses by means of the simile of an uprooted oak, torn from its only support. The poem closes with a second comparison drawn from the natural world, this time to a clutching octopus, and with a second epic equation:

> Tu radix, tu petra mihi firmissima, Mater,
>   Ceu Polypus, chelis saxa prehendo tenax:
> Non tibi nunc soli filum abrupere sorores,
>   Dissutus videor funere & ipse tuo.
> Under vagans passim recte vocer alter Ulysses,
>   Alteraque haec tua mors, Ilias esto mihi.
> (9–14)

You are root, you are firmest rock for me, Mother. Like an octopus, with tentacles I clutch rocks, tenacious. The Sisters have not cut your thread, only; I seem unraveled also by your death. Whence, wandering here and there, I may rightly be called another Ulysses. Let this be your death be for me another *Iliad*.

The reader remembers Antikleia's parting words to Odysseus in the underworld—"Note all things strange / Seen here, to tell your lady in after days" (192)—for the point of his wanderings is to return, not to his mother, but to his wife.

The unexpected introduction of the *Iliad* as well as the *Odyssey* at the conclusion of the poem illustrates the instability of some of Herbert's classical allusions. The most sweeping claim of identification between his private life and classical literature, "haec tua mors / Ilias esto mihi," cannot be explained by reference to poem 11 or to *Memoriae Matris Sacrum* as a whole. Is the *Iliad* a model of tragedy on a heroic scale? Does Herbert see himself as resembling a figure in the epic, or does he see his mother as resembling one? The answer cannot be found in the sequence, and such an allusion remains hermetic, a private use of available classical material, perhaps more a reaction to the alternative Christian model than a full exploitation of the classical one.

The psychological state in which Herbert wrote *Memoriae Matris Sacrum* helps to explain the outpouring of difficult classical imagery in this work. Grieving for the loss of his mother, and probably also finding himself in a crisis particular to his relationship with her, Herbert appears to have suffered great pain and anxiety. In several poems, he responds to imagined interlocutors who criticize him for excessive grief and inappropriate praise of his mother, or who treat him as ill.[17] Under this unusual stress, he retreats temporarily from a Christian perspective and consolations and also from the language of Protestant worship.[18]

As Fred Nichols observes, Latin poetry in the Renaissance possessed an intimate, confessional quality often not present in the vernacular. "Perhaps they found it easier to be intimate in a language other than the one in which they had developed all the mental reticences and inhibitions formed as part of our earliest education," he speculates.[19] This seems to have been the case for Herbert, who is able to explore intimate aspects of his psychology and his relationship with his mother in the ritually controlled context of an ancient language, traditional

---

[17] Pigman's chapter "The Angry Consoler" offers evidence that a mourner in Herbert's time might indeed have been the recipient of such criticism (11–26). Rigoristic sanctions against obstinate grief appear in folklore as well as Christian works of consolation. See Child's discussion of revenants asking relief from the incessant weeping of their kin (2:234–36; subject index under "dead").

[18] This retreat is not total. Hutchinson cites several references to the Old and New Testaments, the most significant one occurring in poem 8. Here, an imagined speaker rebukes Herbert for raging at his fate: "Susurrat aure quispiam, / Haec fuerat olim potio domini tui. / Gusto proboque Dolium" (8–10) ("Someone whispers in my ear, / 'This potion once was your Lord's.' / I taste and approve the wine"). This poem alone of those in *Memoriae Matris Sacrum* would appear at home in *The Temple*.

[19] Nichols, *An Anthology of Neo-Latin Poetry*, 3.

verse forms, and a pagan mythology. Distancing himself from Christian culture also allows Herbert to experience stages of mourning that conflict with his ordinary beliefs. In poems 5, 6, and 7, he focuses obsessively on the physical remains of the dead woman, describing despair over the disintegration of the corpse, a strange identification with the female body of his mother, and an encounter with her shade. Later, he feels free to equate his sufferings with those of epic heroes. That Herbert viewed these poems as part of a temporary starategy for mourning and healing is suggested by the final poem, in which he denounces the muse for demanding from him these elegiac tributes, and by his haste to publish—a thing that he never did with his English poems—and thus to close the book forever:

> Eia, agedum scribo: vicisti, Musa; sed audi,
> Stulta: semel scribo, perpetuo ut sileam.
> (poem 19, lines 7–8)

Ok, I'm writing. You've won, Muse, but listen, foolish one: I'm writing once more, so that I may be silent forever.

What for thirty days he has permitted himself and what he now forbids is not merely the composition of a sequence in honor of his mother. It is a ritual of mourning and of regression, a seeming disintegration that actually allows many aspects of his emotional life to be reordered. This temporary dislocation involves not only emotions but language. In choosing to write in Latin, in opening up the possibilities of pagan allusion and association, in assigning the origins of this language to a woman, Herbert opens up another language and another context for interpreting experience. He writes, not from the shattered center of his past life or with a damaged remnant of his accustomed mode of speaking, but from a more primal emotional center and with another language that enables him to say other things. Latin, which has been characterized as the vehicle of a "[male] Renaissance puberty rite,"[20] has been appropriated by Herbert for a private, subversive exploration of experience and feeling that predates formal religion, patriarchal structures, and the acquisition of their language and symbols.

Nassau Community College

---

[20] Walter Ong, "Latin Language Study as a Renaissance Puberty Rite," *Studies in Philology* 56 (1959): 103–24.

LEE A. JACOBUS

Milton Hero:
The Rhetorical Gesture of Monody

IN *A PORTRAIT OF THE ARTIST AS A YOUNG MAN*, JAMES JOYCE DESCRIBES a progress from lyric, to epic, and dramatic in the evolution of literature. His ideal is the street ballad *Turpin Hero* which begins in the first person and ends in the third person. Ironically, *Portrait* begins in the third person and ends in the first person, defying Joyce's ideal, while in Milton's *Lycidas* the progress of the detachment of the speaker from his grief is dramatized by a shift in point of view which frames the event and separates the reader from the action, making the reader over into an audience. The emphasis on performance is affirmed by Milton's headnote (in the Trinity MS, 1645 and 1673 editions, but not in its original publication) describing his poem as a monody. This detail is an important clue to Milton's meaning in the poem. And in its allusion to revolutionary changes in modern music—chiefly centered in Italy—Milton makes a gesture of independence among his peers, accepting a position as a leader among poets. His heroic gesture is underscored in his resolving the poem, and detaching his own persona from it, in the ending *ottava rima*. Milton emulates the composer who evokes sympathetic response from his audience, but who distances himself by leaving the performance to a singer who is not himself but is part of a dramatic moment.

The Meaning of Monody

Most critics have limited Milton's designation of the poem as a monody. A. S. P. Woodhouse[1] connected it with Menander the Rhetorician, who

---

[1] A. S. P. Woodhouse, "Milton's Pastoral Monodies," in *Studies in Honor of Gilbert Norwood* (Toronto: Univ. of Toronto Press, 1952), 269-70. See also Woodhouse and Douglas Bush, eds., *A Variorum Commentary on The Poems of John Milton*, vol. 2, part 2 (New York: Columbia Univ. Press, 1972), 637: A note by John Crossett describes

mentions monody as a minor genre related to the epitaph and involving consolation, and with George Puttenham, who said in his discussion of obsequies, "Such funerall songs were called *Epicedia* if they were sung by many, and *Monodia* if they were vttered by one alone."² Woodhouse regarded *Epitaphium Damonis* and *Lycidas* as Milton's Christian pastoral monodies. He admits difficulties with this generic description, since the all-important digressions in *Lycidas* "depend not on the tradition of the pastoral monody, but on that of the eclogue, from which Milton lifts this feature for incorporation in his pastoral monody."³

The Variorum commentary suggests that Milton might have called his poem a threnody.⁴ Monody is rare in seventeenth-century usage and among its few citations there is dispute over its meaning. Johan Alstedius in his Ramist encyclopedia discusses it in terms of music and says there are two kinds of melody: simple and compounded; the simple is monody, the compounded is symphony.⁵ But Scaliger describes monody as occurring in any moment when a character steps forward in Greek tragedy and speaks alone.⁶ This is, in part, the way the term had been understood by the Florentine Camerata, which had been attempting to revive classical styles by studying the Greek tragedies. One of the lines of modern influence stemmed from the Camerata's experiments.

Musical monody is significant in part because it signalled the beginning of the move from the polyphony of early Renaissance music to the homophony of later music in which a single melodic line is supported by a (usually) triadic harmony. The style developed for two reasons. One was connected to the desires of composers to represent accurately in music the emotions excited by their text. Polyphonic styles made it impossible to imitate such emotions. Monody, with its single melodic line, made it possible for a text to be heard and understood, thereby allowing the words to express emotions with clarity. The first source of

---

monodia as a "song done by actors alone.... The form is discussed at length in the *Rhetoric* of Menander (*Rhetores Graeci*, ed. L. Spengel [Leipzig, 1856], 3, 418) where it is a branch of the *logos epitaphios* and allied with the speech of consolation, *logos paramythetikos* (Spengel, 413). The speeches of Andromache, Hecuba, and Helen in *Il.* 24 are called monodies (ibid. 434–37). Menander gives specific instructions for such a speech, including the injunction not to tire the audience by exceeding 150 verses."

² George Puttenham, *The Arte of English Poesy*, intro. Baxter Hathaway (Kent: Kent State Univ. Press, 1970), I: xxiv, 63.

³ A. S. P. Woodhouse, "Milton's Pastoral Monodies," 273.

⁴ *Variorum*, vol. 2, part 2, p. 549 n.

⁵ Johan Henry Alsted, *Templum Musicum: or the Musical Synopsis, of the Learned and Famous Johannes-Henricus-Alstedius* (London: 1664; orig. pub. 1620), 60.

⁶ Scott Elledge, *Milton's* Lycidas (New York: Harpers, 1966), 109.

monody is called "derived" because it was derived harmonically from the polyphonic techniques of the day. It is derived from harmonic musical practices rather than having its origin in literary or other theory.

For example, Monteverdi's monodies are derived because he developed them out of his own musical practices—which were largely polyphonic. He sought alternatives of expression for given texts. His was a search for an expressive style, one that permitted him to represent the emotions he perceived in his texts. In his sixth book of madrigals, his desire to subdue the distracting textural features of multiple melodic lines of polyphony resulted in his attempt to intensify a single line of melody to create a new kind of expressive madrigal.

The second source of monody was the Florentine Camerata's experiments in recitative led by Count Giovanni de' Bardi, who is credited with devising the masque[7] and Vincenzo Galilei, who is credited with having composed the first monodies in 1575.[8] Galilei, like Bardi, Ottavio Rinucini, Giulio Caccini, and others in the Camerata, sought the legendary effects achieved by Greek music. Their researches concluded that the only way these effects could have been achieved was by a blending of words and music, since music did not seem to achieve them alone. They further concluded that Greek tragedy must have been sung rather than simply spoken, and they developed a monodic *stilo recitativo* or *stilo rappresentativo*. Galilei began with two *lamenti*, one for Count Ugolino in Dante and one from the *Lamentations* of Jeremiah. *Lamenti* became one of the most durable genres of monody, including examples from Monteverdi in his powerful *Lamento di Arianna* and from Milton's collaborator Henry Lawes, whose *Ariadne* won special praise from Milton.

The question of imitation and representation in music concerned Galilei because he was dissatisfied with contemporary word-painting in the madrigals. Galilei, in his *Dialogo della musica antica e della moderna* (1581) complains

> that the music of their times produces none of the notable effects that ancient music produced, when quite the other way, they would have more cause for amazement if it were to produce any of them, seeing that their music is so remote from the ancient music and so unlike as actually to be its contrary and mortal enemy.... For its sole aim is to delight the ear, while that of

---

[7] See Gerald Abraham, *The Concise Oxford History of Music* (London: Oxford Univ. Press, 1979), 268.

[8] Nigel Fortune, "Italian Secular Songs from 1600 to 1635" (Ph.D. Diss., Gonville and Caius College, Cambridge, 1954), 77. See also Karl Gustav Fellerer, *The Monody*, trans. Robert Kolben (Cologne: Arno Volk, 1968), 5.

ancient music is to induce in another the same passion that one feels oneself.[9]

Milton's identifying the genre of his poem as a monody establishes him in the forefront of stylistic change, since only a small number of English composers had yet discovered the advantages of monody. Milton's father, for example, had written a "Teares and Lamentations," but it was in the polyphonic style. Milton's praise in 1646 for Lawes's *Ariadne* emphasized the way in which he fit the music to the text prepared by William Cartwright:

> Harry, whose tuneful and well measur'd Song
> First taught our English Music how to span
> Words with just note and accent, not to scan
> With *Midas'* Ears, committing short and long. . . .

Milton's praise for Lawes implies a special approach to English texts set to music, an approach that goes beyond the simple scansion of verse according to accented and unaccented syllables. "Committing short and long" is glossed by Todd as "offending against quantity and harmony" and by Carey and Fowler in the OED's figurative meaning of to "engage [parties] as opponents."[10] Milton complains of the discordant results of other composers, while praising the apparent system that the Italian monodists were using, which resulted in apportioning musical stress to the syllables that bore most of the weight of the text.

Italian monody was still a novelty in 1637 in England. Motets, madrigals, canzones, and other compositions in the late sixteenth century were invariably polyphonic. Monody had been established in Italy since the late sixteenth century as a promising new style. To have been aware of its significance in England in the 1630s was to have identified oneself as progressive and modern. That is why the contrast between the polyphonic conservatism of John Milton Sr. and the monodic progressivism of Henry Lawes in their approach to the genre of *lamenti* is instructive. Only someone who was keenly aware of what was happening in Italian music would have appreciated the achievement of monody. Elise Jorgens says: "Italian monody was essentially a musical revolution. . . . As a new musical style, it was definitely known in England, whether or not the English were aware of its goals and implications."[11]

---

[9] Translated in Oliver Strunk, *Sources in Music History* (New York: W. W. Norton, 1950), 317.

[10] See Henry John Todd, *The Poetical Works of John Milton*, 4 vols., 5th ed. (London: Rivington, 1852), 4:218 n. and Carey-Fowler, 292 n.

[11] Elise Bickford Jorgens, *The Well Tun'd Word* (Minneapolis: Univ. of Minnesota

The power of the early experiments of the Camerata was recorded by Bardi in a letter of 1634 to Doni, concerning the development of *stile rappresentativo* in the 1597 staging of *Dafne* by Jacopo Peri in competition with Giulio Caccini, who "brought the enterprise of the *stile rappresentativo* to light, and avoiding a certain roughness and excessive antiquity which had been felt in the compositions of Galilei, he sweetened this style, together with Giulio, and made it capable of moving the passions in a rare manner, as in the course of time was done by them both."[12] "The first poem to be sung on the stage in *stile rappresentativo* was the story of *Dafne*, by Signor Ottavio Rinuccini, set to music by Peri in few numbers and short scenes and recited and sung privately in a small room. I was left speechless with amazement."[13]

The efforts of the Camerata were directed toward imitation, as the term *stile representativo* implies, but it was not the imitation sometimes implied in word-painting. Representation, for the Camerata, centered on exciting the emotions of the text in the audience. The word "affetti" denotes the target of the musicians. An emphasis on the emotions of the audience naturally produced a strong interest in rhetoric, which explains in part why so many commentators talk about the relationship of music and rhetoric. As Peacham says, "Yea, in my opinion, no Rhetoricke more perswadeth, or hath greater power ouer the mind; nay, hath not Musicke her figures, the same which Rhetorique? What is a *Reuert* but her *Antistrophe?* her reports, but sweete *Anaphoras?* her counterchange of points, *Antimetabole's?* her passionate Aires but *Prosopopoea's?* with infinite other of the same nature."[14] John Hollander says one "notion that lies behind the seventeenth-century affective theory of music's power is an identification of music with rhetoric, rather than with philosophy, or rational discourse in general."[15]

Among the most obvious rhetorical gestures of the monodists was their use of specific modes and keys designed to produce a desired effect. An example is Monteverdi's *Sestina: lagrime d'amante al sepolcro dell'amata*, a moving monodic lament from the Sixth Book of Madrigals (1614). It was commissioned by the duke of Mantua, whose teenage mistress, Catarinuccia Martinelli, was to have performed the lead in *Arianna*, the opera whose music was lost in the sack of Mantua in 1630.

Press, 1982), 208.

[12] Strunk, 363.

[13] Strunk, 365.

[14] Henry Peacham, *The Compleat Gentleman* (London: Francis Constable, 1627), 103.

[15] John Hollander, *The Untuning of the Sky* (Princeton: Princeton Univ. Press, 1961), 176.

She died two months before its performance in May of 1608. Monteverdi's wife had also died just before he accepted the commission, and it is thought the exceptional power of the piece may derive from personal grief. It employs dissonance to allegorize anguish, and it employs repetition to intensify the emotion: each of the six stanzas is in a different key, but all are resolved on a strong D major chord. Since it is a sestina, it does not rhyme but repeats the endwords in each of its six stanzas and in its final three-line envoi. The narrative is the lament of Glaucus the shepherd for his nymph, and it includes dialogue and expostulation.

The monodic qualities of the *Lagrime* are masked by its being set for five voices in the form of the madrigal, a reflection of the taste of Mantua and the taste of Monteverdi's commissioner. After the stunning success of his *Lamento di Arianna* in its monodic operatic form, Monteverdi recast the piece in 1610 for five voices and included it also in the Sixth Book of Madrigals. Doni complains that he ruined the piece doing this, but Monteverdi was interested in pleasing his audience, which may be one reason why he straddled so fully the two opposing musical practices of his day. He later returned *Arianna* to monody by transforming it into a religious song, *Pianto della Madonna*, in *Selva morale e spirituale*, vol. 8 (1640), scored for a soprano and organ continuo. In this form, its true monodic qualities are best perceived, and its emotional range can be appreciated. In its secular monodic form, with a soprano voice and string continuo, and with the chorus's three-line response (drawn from the opera's libretto), the emotional power of the work is less apparent to a modern ear.

Monteverdi knew what he was doing. In a letter dated 1634, he said, "It is my intention to show, through the medium of our practice, what I was able to adopt from the spirit of the ancient philosophers to the advantage of the good art."[16] Even more importantly, Leo Schrade reminds us that "when he wrote the *Lament of Arianna*, there was no book available to explain the natural method of imitation nor any work, except Plato, that shed light on the proper functions of an imitator in art."[17] This point is crucial in seeing not only the originality of the work, but in understanding why it was so widely praised and so widely known. Monteverdi was inspired by the concept of imitation and informed by his reading of Plato. Like Galilei, he focused on representing the affections, examining the deep interior of the texts with which he worked. At its best, says Schrade, "the text must be such that

---

[16] Leo Schrade, *Monteverdi: Creator of Modern Music* (New York: W. W. Norton, 1950), 205.
[17] Schrade, 205.

all the emotional qualities of the poem could be reduced to one predominant affection."[18] The success of the *Lament of Arianna*, as Nigel Fortune puts it, "was phenomenal, and Bonini tells us that every musical household had its copy."[19] About monodies in general, Fortune tells us that they "were published not by the dozen but by the gross; they reached a far wider audience than operas ever did,"[20] and "within a few years the new style had been embraced by perhaps thousands of music-lovers, from the duke in his palace to the amateur in his humble music-room."[21]

Gretchen Finney has connected *Lycidas* with Monteverdi's *Orfeo*, produced in 1607. Reminding us that most of the early operas were connected to Orpheus, she says that "the story of *Lycidas* is the story of Orpheus."[22] Finney connects *Lycidas* with canzone, as does Prince, pointing to dramatic qualities, consonant with the character of the canzone, that seem to dominate the poem. She says "the signs point unerringly" toward "Italian musical drama."[23]

The connection made by Finney and Prince of *Lycidas* with the canzone must be measured against Joseph Wittreich's conclusion, after an analysis of the rhyme scheme, that Milton is influenced by the madrigal form.[24] This is significant because I see in Monteverdi a new approach to madrigal using monodic techniques designed to intensify the affects of the music. The question of how Milton might have come to be aware of the developments of Italian music, and how he might have conceived the connection of drama and poetic text is resolved in his connections, personal and professional, with Henry Lawes.

Henry Lawes was well known to the Milton family, and Milton's "Sweet Echo," for *A Maske* (1634), is a monody following a popular monodic pattern resulting in dialogues and echo songs, a volume of which was published by Lawes himself. In September of 1637, Milton was reading Italian history.[25] Lawes had been working with William Cartwright since 1635. As an undergraduate, Cartwright provided the

---

[18] Schrade, 241.
[19] Nigel Fortune, 8 n.
[20] Fortune, 1.
[21] Fortune, 147.
[22] Gretchen Finney, *Musical Backgrounds for English Literature: 1580–1650* (New Brunswick, NJ: Rutgers, 1961), 218.
[23] Finney, 207.
[24] Joseph Wittreich, *Visionary Poetics: Milton's Tradition and His Legacy* (San Marino: Huntington Library Press, 1979), 169.
[25] John Milton, *The Works of John Milton*, ed. Frank A. Patterson (New York: Columbia Univ. Press, 1936), 12:29.

words for *Ariadne* which Lawes wrote between 1637 and 1643.[26] If he wrote the song in 1637, the monodic influence on Milton would have been intense during the composition of *Lycidas*. Lawes's influence on Milton was strong at this time. Not only did Milton praise Lawes in print, but he also seems to have gotten his Italian passport through the influence of Lawes in 1638.[27]

Lawes's Italian musical connection begins with his teacher, Giovanni Coperario, who was studying in Italy when monody was having its first sensational successes. Elise Jorgens feels that Coperario's threnodies have a monodic quality and that he understood the ethical and rhetorical function of the words.[28]

The monodic connection with Lawes is reinforced by his having been cited by Ben Jonson as having his masque *Lovers Made Men* sung in "stylo Recitativo" in 1617.[29] Lawes's experience with masques as composer and performer is extensive, including Townshend's *Albion's Triumph* and *Tempe Restored*, in which he may have played the part of a man in "skie colored robe" and a "yellow mantle." This may be the same yellow mantle he wore in *The Triumph of Peace*. He may have worn a white mantle in Carew's *Coelum Britannicumaltz*, and definitely wore an iris-colored mantle in Milton's *A Maske*. Mantles played a prominent role in the masques in which Lawes took part.[30]

According to Edward Phillips, when Milton was in Italy he bought music by Orazio Vecchi, Luca Marenzio, Don Carlo Gesualdo, Antonio Cifra, and Claudio Monteverdi. Mortimer Frank points out that they share "apart from the general excellence of their work, one strikingly common trait: each composed vocal music in the new homophonic, harmonic style that (at the time Milton journeyed to Italy) had been flourishing in Italy for many years, but was only beginning to evolve in England."[31]

Today Cifra is one of the least known of these composers, but he is one of the most interesting for several reasons. He was born in Rome in

---

[26] Jorgens, 210. Clay Hunt also claims "Sweet Echo" as a monody and points out that it enchants Comus. Clay Hunt, *"Lycidas" and the Italian Critics* (New Haven: Yale Univ. Press, 1979), 167.

[27] Willa MacClung Evans, *Henry Lawes: Musician and Friend of Poets* (New York: Modern Language Association, 1941), 202.

[28] Jorgens, 182 f.

[29] Jorgens, 273 n. 1. See also Philip Brett, ed., *Consort Songs: Musica Britannica* (1967), 32:273 n. 1; and Clay Hunt, 168.

[30] See Evans, 72–101.

[31] Mortimer H. Frank, "Milton's Knowledge of Music: Some Speculations," in J. Max Patrick and Roger Sundell, eds., *Milton and the Art of Sacred Song* (Madison: Univ. of Wisconsin Press, 1979), 87.

1583/84 and died in Loreto in 1629, where he was choirmaster of the Holy House. He was a prolific composer in many forms, both secular and religious, and "his heart was in the new style," as Alfred Einstein says. "In monodies and duets Cifra is the Ariosto and Tasso composer par excellence."[32]

Cifra is remarkable for his settings of *ottavi* from two of Milton's favorite Italian works, *Orlando Furioso* and *Gerusalemne Liberata*. He is sometimes faulted for having continued to set Ariosto long after *Orlando Furioso* had gone out of fashion. Like sonnets, *ottavi* were favorite texts for monodists, and they especially preferred the first *ottavi* of certain cantos of both works because of their special pathos and their ethical content.

Lycidas: The Dramatic Structure

By comparison with any other poem in *Justa Edovardo King*, *Lycidas* is extraordinary on several counts. First, its deviation from the couplet rhyme pattern sets it apart. Second, its creation of a persona distinct from the author makes it unlike all the English poems. And third, its introduction of speaking "characters" renders it dramatic in a way different from the rest of the volume. Archie Burnett says baldly, " 'Lycidas' is the most dramatic pastoral ever written."[33]

The dramatic quality of *Lycidas* is anticipated in Milton's ascription of monody, whether or not we think of its adaptation from Greek drama in recitativo by the Camerata. However, in light of Milton's recent experience with Lawes, the most likely dramatic tradition out of which *Lycidas* could have risen is that of the masque, with its obvious roots in the Camerata. Elise Jorgens says, "It has been argued that the special performing conditions of the drama, and particularly of the masque, provide the source for the declamatory musical style in England.... Their texts become, in fact, like cantata texts, with the entire dramatic framework worked into the narration, except that ... they are still first-person complaints with all the conventional invocations and rhetorical gestures."[34]

The masque-like qualities of *Lycidas* center on the processional of Phoebus and the mourners, Camus and St. Peter. Their appearance suggests the suddenness and dramatic surprise achieved by the deus ex machina tradition familiar to masque audiences. The gods present

---

[32] Einstein, 866. See also Fortune, 24, 33, and 72 in Appendix 2.
[33] Archie Burnett, *Milton's Style* (London: Longman, 1981), 93.
[34] Jorgens, 173.

themselves usually with the symbols of their "office," stand and make their statement, then retire, much as main figures often did in the Jonsonian masque. Even the frame-setting is masque-like, and certainly the exiting gesture of the swain suggests the masque. Perhaps the most important masque quality of *Lycidas* is apparent in the manner in which the reader becomes part of an audience by the transformation of the point of view from first to third person at the end of the poem. The audience is virtually a participant, since at the end of the poem—and the end of the volume—his only choice is to follow the swain to "fresh woods and pastures new."

In music theory the concept of the *affetti* is much clearer than it was in certain poetry. For example, two contributors to *Justa Edovardo King* were Rhetoric Readers to the university: John Milton and John Cleveland. The contributions of both are rhetorical performances. Milton represents several emotional states and resolves his poem in emotional terms. Cleveland, on the other hand, forces the material of his invention—his wit—to such an extreme that he hoped by analogy it would represent the depth of his feeling. Unfortunately, today lines like "my penne's the spout / Where the rain-water of mine eyes run out" sound preposterous to most ears. But in a context of wit and rhetorical invention, such an extreme performance allegorizes anguish and grief. The conventional rhetorical patterns of the elegy were well understood by the contributors to the volume, and there are very few innovations on the part of anyone but Milton and Cleveland.

The rhetorical function of a monody centers on the transforming therapy of the musical experience. As Peacham expresses the general view: "The Physitians will tell you, that the exercise of Musicke is a great lengthner of the life, by stirring and reuiuing of the Spirits, holding a secret sympathy with them; Besides, the exercise of singing openeth the breast and pipes; it is an enemy to melancholly and deiections of the mind, which S. *Chrysostome* truely calleth, *The Diuels Bath.*"[35] *Lycidas* remedies grief by recreating it in the audience and, in the manner in which Aristotle described when discussing tragedy, acting as a catharsis.

A special rhetorical function of *Lycidas* may be tied to Milton's addition to the 1645 headnote, "And by occasion foretells the ruin of

---

[35] Peacham, 97. This idea is supported by many commentators, including Alsted, who says, "For Musick doeth penetrate the Interiors of the mind, it moveth Affections, promoveth Contemplation, expelleth Sorrow, dissolveth bad Humours, exhilerateth the animal Spirits: and so is beneficial to the Life of Men in general, to the Pious for Devotion, to the Contemplative Life for Science, to the Solitary for Recreation, to the domestick and publick Life for Moderation of mind, to the Healthful for the temperament of their Body, and to the cheerful for Delight ..." (3–4).

our corrupted Clergy then in their height." This is not a vatic claim, but a reminder that the digression in *Lycidas* was a therapy in itself: it helped rid the nation of corruption, just as the musical level of the poem would help relieve the grief of those who knew Edward King. In other words, *Lycidas* may be seen as a lament that raises itself to the level of the Jeremiad, lamenting the state of the nation, rather than limiting itself to the personal, as is common in the *lamenti* of Italian monody. Likewise, Henry Lawes's *Ariadne* has been cited as unusually successful in part because it expressed a lament suitable for the entire nation suffering the grief of civil war—although it does so with no reference whatever to the political situation. "Throughout his poem Milton purposefully maintains the fiction that *Lycidas* is a song with musical accompaniment," and if had been set to music by Lawes, rather than having to wait until William Jackson's 1767 setting, it too might have been a fit expression for a nation's grief.[36] If the rhetorical function of *Lycidas* was to be curative, then he saw an opportunity to be physician to a nation as well as a college.

Forward and Backward Looking Rhymes

Most critics deal with the rhyme in *Lycidas* as John Carey and Alastair Fowler do, by saying that the poem does not have a regular rhyme pattern and that eleven lines (1, 13, 15, 22, 39, 51, 82, 91, 118, and 161) are unrhymed. Joseph Wittreich proposes a radical revision in which we see that certain rhymes are distant and that the only unrhymed lines are 51, 91, and 161: "*Lycidas*," "winds," and "mount." Both Wittreich and F. T. Prince are concerned with what Prince calls a rhetoric of rhyme.[37] Each sees the rhyme as looking both forward and backward, uniting what was with what must be, just as the short lines jolt us into an awareness of grief reinforced by the rhymes. The backward looking rhymes remind us of our loss, while those that look forward make us

---

[36] See Wittreich, 153. Professor Andrew Sabol informs me in correspondence that he has seen a seventeenth-century manuscript setting of *Lycidas*. However, neither he nor I have been able to locate it.

[37] Prince, 85: "The rhetoric of rhyme derived from the *canzone* has thus provided Milton with an invaluable instrument—a type of rhyme which looks both back and forward." And on page 87: "The six-syllable lines, which are also placed so as to give a sense of expectation: they not only rhyme with a previous longer line (thus looking back), but they give the impression of a contracted movement which must be compensated by a full movement in the next line (which is always of full length), and they thus look forward." Wittreich says much the same, but in connection with "Madrigal ... tenaciously repeated rhymes, simultaneously looking forward and backward" (169).

aware of what is yet to be completed. To some extent, those critics who have maintained, along with Woodhouse, that there is an ostensible subject, Edward King, and a real subject, John Milton, are forward looking in their view of the poem: Milton, they feel, is worried about his capacity to complete his future life's work.[38] In 1645 Milton saw how providential the poem was in looking to a time when the corrupt clergy would be routed from their pulpits.

The three unrhymed lines in Wittreich's analysis each perform a rhetorical function. The first, "Lycidas," is backward looking, an uncompleted rhyme that reminds us of the uncompleted potential of Edward King. The second, "felon winds," is forward looking, possibly threatening to Woodhouse's real subject, Milton, or to anyone gifted in the fashion of King. The third, "mount," looks toward Spain, as Todd tells us,[39] guarded to protect England from invasion by the Roman church. This is Michael's Mount, and Michael is asked to look homeward—to turn his gaze from Spain to England itself. The contrast between the lost *Lycidas* and the blind mouths of the clergy should, indeed, touch Michael's emotions. Looking backward in 1645, one could see, too, that the military Michael, "l'homme armée," was the proper lookout. An appropriated future rhyme for "mount," would have been "account," which is what the corrupt clergy were to be brought to. Milton was signaling an alarm in this rhyme—suggesting that the danger did not lie without, but within.

We can consider the three unrhymed lines as either waiting to be completed in a future time, or pointing in directions both past and future as rhymes that are so distant that they are not present in the poem. The lines that do rhyme, 158 according to Wittreich, offer interesting problems. Their irregularity has been accounted for by comparison with the canzone and madrigal, forms which do not demand regularity. Yet, the entire poem's pattern of consolation depends upon a belief in regularity, in a pattern, and a plan.

The musical value of rhyme is to help supply a sense of completeness, a sense of regularity, and a sense of cadence. Rhymed couplets of the kind common in all the other commemorative poems in *Justa Edovardo King* create an overwhelming cadential quality, one that is especially welcome in the older madrigal style, since the varying polyphonic lines of text welcome a cadence that marks the end of one text and the beginning of the next. However, most monodists resisted strong cadences within the texture of their pieces and usually depended on enjambed rhymes to lessen the cadential endings. The rhymes in *Lycidas*

---

[38] Woodhouse, "Milton's Pastoral Monodies," 272.
[39] Todd, 3:340.

act as cadences for verses and for each of the three main sections of the poem, when they are always couplet rhymes. One of the problems with Lawes's *Ariadne* is that its rhythms are hobbled by strong end-stop rhymes. The only relief Cartwright permitted was the occasional combination of long and short lines, interspersing a six-syllable line, usually as an expressive device. Milton's rhymes are used cadentially where necessary.

The incomplete *ottava* that Edward Weismiller and George Nitchie note at line 124 is also a rhetorical gesture with musical implications. It is an imperfect *ottava*, ending part 2, the procession of the mourners.[40] Because the second rhyme, "fed," looks backward to the close rhyme at line 122 (which has no close previous rhyme) and also forward to the next rhyme at line 125, the sense of the *ottava* is destroyed. The lines are not separated in a verse as they are at the end of the poem, and the cadential sense of conclusion and perfection is missing.

This false *ottava* is equivalent to a musical false recapitulation and serves something of the same rhetorical function. It prepares us for an ending, and a patterned conclusion. But the gesture of ending *Lycidas* with an *ottava* is rhetorically rich. The disorder of the earlier parts of the poem, as expressed in rhymes which are in some cases so distant we may need to look outside the poem for their resolution, and in lines of irregular lengths, is resolved perfectly in a heroic form. Using the *ottava* form of Ariosto and Tasso, as is common in the Italian monody, Milton links himself with a heroic epic tradition as well as what, for England, was an avant-garde musical development designed to express emotion and affect an audience in the ancient Greek manner.

The perfection of the final *ottava* is perhaps the poem's most impressive source of consolation. From apparent disorder grows understanding that will reveal order. Alistair Fowler sees the ending as expressing either the "octave of harmony or the eternal life beyond mortality's."[41] Certainly, the number 8 signalled the new beginning, as it still does in the musical scale. And because it is a heroic stanza, the final *ottava* gives Milton the courage to detach himself from the poem, to stand back and frame the singer whom he can view with the same detachment as his audience. In this sense, too, the audience detaches itself from the grief expressed in the poem and can follow the singer off stage.

The headnote tells us that it was the author who bewailed his friend, and it is usually accepted that the swain is the author, as Merrit Hughes's notes say. Gretchen Finney explains that monody demands that "the singer put himself in the place of the person whose emotions

---

[40] See *Variorum*, vol. 2, part 3, p. 1072.
[41] *Variorum*, vol. 2, part 2, p. 636.

were being expressed,"[42] and Milton has performed that fascinating final dramatic and rhetorical flourish by adopting the composer's position and letting his singer step aside from him and with a flourish of his mantle dramatically close the event that his sung poem has become. He stands behind his creation and, if not paring his nails, at least relieved of his grief.

University of Connecticut—Storrs

---

[42] Finney, 218.

R. A. SHOAF

"Our Names are Debts": Messiah's Account of Himself

"Account me man" (3.238)

IN A SERMON DATED 1628, ON STEPHEN PROTOMARTYR, JOHN DONNE argues that

> [o]ur Names are Debts, every man owes the world the signification of his name, and of all his names; every addition of honour, or of office, layes a new Debt, a new Obligation upon him; and his first name, his Christian-Name above all.[1]

Donne's affirmation is a useful introduction to Messiah's crucial response to God, "Account me man." Another argument equally helpful and illuminating, though not a potential source of Milton's line, is the famous saying of Anaximander, which reads in Diels's translation:

But where things have their origin, there too their passing away

---

[1] Cited from *John Donne and the Theology of Language*, ed. P. G. Stanwood and Heather Asals (Columbia: Univ. of Missouri Press, 1986), 214; and see also 225. On the scope and significance of economic imagery in Donne's sermons, see Winfried Schleiner, *The Imagery of John Donne's Sermons* (Providence: Brown Univ. Press, 1970), 122–37. For a particularly vivid example of the currency of Donne's figure, see *As You Like It* 2.5.19–22:
  Jaques: Call you 'em stanzos?
  Amiens: What you will, Monsieur Jaques.
  Jaques: Nay, I care not for their names, they owe me nothing.
Here, Jaques's meaning depends on the fact that "debtors signed their names in the lender's record book" (Anne Barton, ed. *As You Like It*, in *The Riverside Shakespeare*, gen. ed. G. B. Evans [Cambridge, 1974], 379 nn. 21–22). On Shakespeare's economic vocabulary, see also Sandra K. Fischer, *Econolingua: A Glossary of Coins and Economic Language in Renaissance Drama* (Newark, 1985).

occurs according to necessity; for they pay recompense and penalty to one another for their recklessness, according to firmly established time."[2]

In his famous essay, Heidegger translates this fragment as follows:

But that from which things arise also gives rise to their passing away, along the lines of usage: for they let order and thereby also reck belong to one another (in the surmounting) of disorder."[3]

I will return to this curious and controversial but moving translation. Here, I want only to observe how, at the dawn of Western metaphysics, *payment* and *exchange* are inescapable elements of thought and discourse. Being and debt, as Milton also understood, are inseparable.[4]

In Book 3 of *Paradise Lost* God asks one of the poem's most momentous questions:

"and so *losing* all,
To expiate his treason [man] hath *naught left*,
But to destruction sacred and devote,
He with his whole posterity must die,
Die he or Justice must; unless for him
Some other able, and as willing, *pay*
The rigid *satisfaction*, death for death....
Which of ye will be mortal to *redeem*
Man's mortal crime, and just the unjust to save,
Dwells in all Heaven charity so *dear*?"[5]

Alone of all the heavenly host Christ is willing to respond to this

---

[2] Quoted by Martin Heidegger in "Der Spruch des Anaximander" ("The Anaximander Fragment"), trans. David Farrell Krell and Frank A. Capuzzi, in *Early Greek Thinking: The Dawn of Western Philosophy* (New York, 1975), 13. For a modern study of the fragment, see G. S. Kirk, J. E. Raven, and M. Schofield, *The Presocratic Philosophers: A Critical History with a Selection of Texts*, 2nd ed. (Cambridge: Harvard Univ. Press, 1983), 117–21.

[3] Heidegger, 20 and 57. It should be observed, however, that Heidegger's entire essay (13–58) constitutes his attempt at translating the fragment.

[4] We experience this necessity most vividly in natality: each is indebted to the body from which he or she emerged. The most eloquent discussion of this necessity I know of is that by Hannah Arendt in *The Human Condition* (Chicago: Univ. of Chicago Press, 1958), 176–78; Arendt's remarks, however, as she acknowledges, are themselves heavily indebted to St. Augustine, in whom Milton also would have encountered an exquisite sensitivity to the mutual necessity of being and debt.

[5] *Paradise Lost* 3:206–12; 214–16; my emphasis. All citations of *Paradise Lost* are from Fowler's edition (London: Longman, 1971).

question, and he says "'Account me man'," thus assuming the debt of his name, the Mediator (10.60–61):

> on man's behalf
> Patron or Intercessor none appeared,
> Much less that durst upon his own head draw
> The deadly *forfeiture* and *ransom* set....
> [The Son of God] His dearest mediation thus renewed....
> "Atonement for himself or offering meet
> *Indebted* and undone, [man] hath none to bring:
> Behold me then, me for him, life for life
> I offer, on me let thine anger fall;
> *Account* me man."
>
> (3.218–21; 226; 234–8; my emphasis)

The word *account*, to be sure, participates in an entire system of economic discourse which Milton appropriates from Scripture and from the Fathers.[6] But it also, I want to suggest, carries a special valence here, even multi-valence, and this multi-valence is crucial to the economics of Milton's poetics.

---

[6] Studies of this discourse would include, among others, C. A. Patrides, "Milton and the Protestant Theory of the Atonement," *PMLA* 74 (1959): 7–13, and *Milton and the Christian Tradition* (Oxford: Oxford Univ. Press, 1966), 131–42; and W. W. Kerrigan, *The Sacred Complex: On the Psychogenesis of "Paradise Lost"* (Cambridge: Harvard Univ. Press, 1983), 44–46, 190–93, 166–70. For a recent marxist study of such discourse, see Christopher Kendricks, *Milton: A Study in Ideology and Form* (New York, 1986). Milton and Donne, of course, are joined by other Renaissance poets in the use of such discourse—most notably, perhaps, by Herbert, as in the sonnet "Redemption"; see, further, Bernard Knieger, "The Purchase-Sale: Patterns of Business Imagery in the Poetry of George Herbert," *SEL* 6 (1966): 111–24. Studies of economic language in literature more generally include Marc Shell, *The Economy of Literature* (Baltimore: Johns Hopkins Univ. Press, 1978) and *Money, Language, and Thought: Literary and Philosophic Economies from the Medieval to the Modern Era* (Berkeley: Univ. of California Press, 1982); R. A. Shoaf, *Dante, Chaucer, and the Currency of the Word: Money, Images, and Reference in Late Medieval Poetry* (Norman, Okla., 1983); and Eugene Vance, *Mervelous Signals: Poetics and Sign Theory in the Middle Ages* (Lincoln, Neb., 1986), 86–151 and 230–310. In the work in progress from which the present paper is drawn, *Account Me Man: The Economies of Milton's Poetry*, I include comments on several of the numerous occurrences of the word "account" elsewhere in Milton—e.g., *The Reason of Church-Government*, "I have the use, as I may account it, but of my left hand" (*The Complete Prose Works of John Milton*, ed. Don M. Wolfe, 8 vols. [New Haven: Yale Univ. Press, 1953–82], 1:808; all citations of Milton's prose in this paper are from this edition, hereafter *CPW*). I attempt to assess the value of the word "account" generally in Milton's vocabulary; however, I will observe here that I think the occurrence at *Paradise Lost* 3.238 the most important of all the many in Milton's works.

When Christ utters these words, he is, in effect, *opening an account with God*. Not only is he telling God what to do (even as earlier in this same episode he said, "That be from thee far, / That far be from thee, Father"—3.153–54), he is also crediting God with the means to account him man.[7] He is, in short, authoring God—authoring him as accountable for him, Christ—and he thus becomes evidence of and witness to God's solvency: without him God could not redeem mankind, would not have the means to afford this purchase—"Dwells in all Heaven charity so dear?" The redundancy in this line ("charity" and "dear" both look back to Latin *carus*) is instructive. God asks, in effect, if anywhere in heaven charity is charity. He asks, in short, for repetition, for only repetition now can save men and the economy of creation. But repetition bespeaks, therefore, the difference which empowers it as well as necessitates it: Christ possesses charity so dear insofar as he is different from God.[8]

Here, I think, Milton remembers Matthew 16:21 and following, an episode in which Christ enunciates the fundamental economic principle of his ministry: "For whosoever will save his life shall lose it; and whosoever will lose his life for my sake shall find it" (Matt. 16:25).[9] This episode begins with Jesus informing his disciples that "he must go unto Jerusalem ... and be killed, and be raised again the third day" (16:21). Peter immediately "took him, and began to rebuke him, saying, Be it far from thee, Lord: this shall not be unto thee" (16:22). Here, in the Authorized Version's translation of Peter's words, we have one of Milton's possible models for Christ's words to God: "That be from thee far, / That far be from thee, Father"—3.153–54). Christ speaks to God as Peter speaks to Christ. We must not forget, however, what Christ then says to Peter: "Get thee behind me, Satan ... for thou savourest not the things that be of God, but those that be of men" (16:23). If Milton's Christ resembles Peter, he also resembles Satan, standing up to God, standing apart from God—with, of course, a difference. Christ's difference from Satan, in the economy of Milton's poem, is his manhood—

---

[7] See further my study of Christ's dual relation with God, in this and related passages, in *Milton, Poet of Duality: A Study of Semiosis in the Poetry and the Prose* (New Haven: Yale Univ. Press, 1985), 122–25.

[8] "The Word is not of the same essence as God"; see *On Christian Doctrine* 1.5 (*CPW* 6:239).

[9] An excellent study of the response of early Christianity to the economic discourse of the Gospels is Martin Herz, *Sacrum Commercium: Eine begriffsgeschichtliche Studie zur Theologie der Römischen Liturgiesprache*, Münchener Theologische Studien 2. 15 (Munich, 1958). Patrides, *Christian Doctrine*, 131–42, offers a helpful survey of the Protestant response, especially as it pertains to Milton.

paradoxically, but profoundly, he savors the things that are of man in addition to the things that are of God. He stands up to God and apart from God, repeating God, *as man*, not as alternative God—which is what Satan desired to be.[10] Christ as man saves not only man but also God. He saves God from the loss of man.

How can Christ do this? The answer, or at least the beginning of the answer, is actually in the word *account*. *Esteem me, in your estimate, esteem me man*, is what Christ is saying to God.[11] Christ, in other words, is willing to exist in another system of value, wholly determined by God (in his estimate, in his account).[12] He is willing to be counted in a different order (if you will, in a different numerical base). He is willing to assume responsibility for another, man, becoming himself *accountable* for this other.[13] In short, he is willing to be *exchanged* for another, on an occasion when the other is esteemed to be *worth* him, Christ. He will love another so much that he will take that other's place, to die in that place, that he or she may live—he or she is worth his life. This is, in effect, to create or, if you will, re-create, that other—even as God does, by giving of himself.

"Account me man," then, says a good deal more than simply "Let me be man." It says, "Exchange me with man" where *exchange* also and already entails *change*: Christ is willing to be changed into man. This will in Christ implies that man is *worth* the change; Christ, in fact, by this change "assume[s] / [His] merits" (3.318-19). If man is worth Christ, Christ, by the same token, is worth man. His exchange and

---

[10] See *Poet of Duality*, 81–82 and 116–19; cf. Kerrigan, 168–69.

[11] This sense of "account" is well attested in the seventeenth century; see the OED A:65b (branch IV, sense 12), where among the witnesses cited is Psalm 144, verse 3 (Authorized Version): "Or the sonne of man, that thou makest account of him?" I suspect we have in this Psalm verse a distant but still potent inspiration for Christ's words "Account me man."

[12] We could also say, "in his [God's] version of the narrative," recognizing the idiomatic sense of "account" as "narrative" or "story," a sense well attested in the seventeenth century (OED A:65b; branch V, sense 16). In God's account or version of the story of creation as it will now unfold, Christ will take man's part; in effect, he will become the metaphor of God *as* man. Although I believe this sense of "account" is subordinate to its economic sense in the passage, it is still obviously important, and in a longer study, I attempt to investigate its implications.

[13] For the sense of "answering for conduct" (i.e., "being responsible") in "account," see OED A:65a (branch III, sense 8). And cf. the Ghost of Hamlet's father (*Hamlet*, ed. Kermode, in *The Riverside Shakespeare*, 1.5.76-79; my emphasis):
    Cut off even in the blossoms of my sin,
    Unhous'led, disappointed, unanel'd,
    No *reck'ning* made, but sent to my *account*
    With all my imperfections on my head.

change—his love, in a word—are the means by which he becomes *Son of God*, with the power to act as God acts. By "opening an account" with God, Christ becomes Son of God; by going into debt with God, Christ "assume[s] his merits." More: by going into debt with God, "opening an account" with him, Christ becomes who he is. His words, "Account me man," inscribe the origin of being in the confession of debt.

By being in debt with God, Christ credits God (and saves God), and this credit [read also: faith] makes him wealthy, "worthiest" (3.310). By "opening an account" with God ("account me man") Christ credits God with the generosity, love, and grace to make him man and to make men sons of God ("by adoption"—Gal. 4:5-6). And this act redounds to his credit: he becomes full of merit by going into debt. And when Milton, at the end of this scene, exclaims "Thy Name / Shall be the *copious matter* of my song / Henceforth" (3.412-14), his language is beautifully precise: the name of Christ is *copious*—its copiousness is the *copia* of inexhaustible debt.[14]

The name of Christ, we know, is also Logos or Verbum. And if we propose now that the Verbum also commands, "Account me man," we can see how the Word—and also, perhaps more important, words—go into debt, how they open an account with God or with an audience. The Word cannot be understood as, or, say, translated into, man, unless and until "accounted" so by God; the Word must go into debt with God in order to acquire the meaning "man." Similarly, words, human words, cannot be understood as having whatever meaning unless and until they are "accounted" as such by their audience. They must go into debt with the audience if they would be meaningful: in effect, they must borrow on account the understanding they seek; they must presume already to own the understanding the lack of which caused them initially to be uttered.[15] In this way they also save the understanding.

---

[14] Hence it is also the exact opposite of narcissism: "inopem me fecit copia" ("my own plenty makes me poor") cries Narcissus when he realizes what has happened to him (*Metamorphoses* 3.466)—refusing to go into debt by refusing to love and thus be indebted for pleasure and meaning to another, the boy loses the very life he presumes to own, paying the final debt of Being (i.e., death) without ever having himself been paid by someone else's love for him, which would have made him, had he become indebted for it, copious.

[15] Cf. Maurice Merleau-Ponty, *Le Visible et l'invisible* (Paris, 1964), 243, on the operation of *Gestaltung* and *Rückgestaltung* in the process of understanding a discourse: "Ce n'est pas une série d'inductions—C'est *Gestaltung* et *Rückgestaltung*. 'Mouvement rétrograde du vrai'.... Cela veut dire: il y a germination de ce qui va avoir été compris" ("It's not a series of inductions—it's positing of the form and re-positing of the form. 'The retrograde movement of the truth'.... That is to say:

Their origin is in debt to the lexicon of possible meanings (which, in turn, is saved by their debt).

The most convenient illustration of this argument is probably the pun, with its peculiar problematics. No appeal to authorial intentionality in and of itself is adequate to persuade an audience that a pun actually exists; that audience, as a community of hearers, must credit the pun or, inversely, discredit the hearer or hearers who credit the pun and thus deny the pun's existence. Take, for example, the pun in the word "decEiVEd" in Books 9 and 10. In this word, I hear the real effects of Eve's sin:

> Forsake me not thus, Adam, witness heaven
> What love sincere, and reverence in my heart
> I bear thee, and unweeting have offended,
> Unhappily *deceived*; thy suppliant
> I beg, and clasp thy knees; bereave me not,
> Whereon I live, thy gentle looks.
>   10.914–19 (my emphasis)

Indeed, she is "unhappily decEiVEd"; if you will credit me enough to let me spell out the word's dual, she is "dis-Eve'd."[16] She has, obeying

---

there is germination of what is going to have been understood"; my translation). In other words, the structure of understanding is always *anticipatory* (which is to say the obverse of "the movement of the truth is retrograde")—i.e., it *borrows* from across the momentary future the form it anticipates the discourse will have as it moves to interpret the discourse, thus crediting the discourse by its loan. For further commentary, see Jonathan Culler, *Structuralist Poetics: Structuralism, Linguistics and the Study of Literature* (Ithaca: Cornell Univ. Press, 1975), 91–93. Cf. also John Freccero's discussion of confession and Christian allegory in Dante's *Comedy*: "Both confession and Christian allegory have their roots in the mystery of language. As language is unfolded along a syntagmatic axis, governed at each moment of its articulation by a paradigm present in the mind of the speaker and made manifest at the ending of the sentence, so the authorial voice in the text is the paradigm of the entire narrative, of which the evolution of the pilgrim is, as it were, the syntax"— "Medusa: The Letter and the Spirit" in *Dante: The Poetics of Conversion*, ed. Rachel Jacoff (Cambridge: Harvard Univ. Press, 1986), 119–35, esp. 133. Both of these arguments, of course, look back to Saussure and the fundamental distinction he articulates between paradigm and syntagm in the *Course in General Linguistics*.

[16] That Milton may have pronounced "deceived" differently from a modern speaker of English (a rebuttal which attempts to reintroduce authorial intention into the argument) in no way impedes my case: changes in sound, like all other changes in its language, are an inevitable part of the accumulated meaning of a given historical discourse—they cannot be suppressed by any simple fiat of positivism. Moreover, there may have been and probably were many different pronunciations of "deceived" in seventeenth-century England, and this very multiplicity is to the point: different hearers must credit different speakers speaking differently. For a

Satan, lost her identity, no longer the Eve God created, not yet the Eve she will become.

Here let me also request credit for the identical puns in Book 9. First, as Eve prepares to follow the serpent, Milton exclaims:

> O much decEiVEd, much failing, hapless EVE,
> Of thy presumed return! EVEnt pErVErse!
> Thou nEVEr from that hour in Paradise
> Found'st either sweet repast, or sound repose.
>
> 9.404–07 (my emphasis)

Eve is not only now "dis-Eve'd"; she is also, as this passage illustrates, dismembered in a graphic sparagmos, her name scattered across the ensuing lines like fragments of her former self.[17] Next, recall also that, at the moment of Adam's fall, Milton declares:

> [H]e scrupled not to eat
> Against his better knowledge, not decEiVEd,
> But fondly overcome with female charm
>
> 9.997–99 (my emphasis)

where "not deceived" means, by the double negative, precisely "Eve'd" (i.e., not not [dis-] Eve'd)—Adam has been "Eve'd," he has become an Eve, losing his identity, by obeying her instead of God.[18]

Returning to the passage in Book 10, I would request credit on account of the puns in Book 9 for the argument that, like the (visual) pun in "rEVErence" (she is *re-eve*['d] for Adam when she bears reverence in her heart for him), like the pun in "berEaVE" (do not *be-r-eve* Eve [turn Eve into "reave" or "loss"] by removing what Eve lives on), and like the pun in "unWEeting" (she did *un-we* the couple when she

---

philological discussion, see E. J. Dobson, "Milton's Pronunciation," in *Language and Style in Milton: A Symposium in Honor of the Tercentenary of "Paradise Lost,"* ed. Ronald D. Emma and John T. Shawcross (New York: Ungar, 1967), 154–92.

[17] Note how in this particular case Milton's pun is as much visual as aural, if not more so. In a study now in progress, " 'For There Is Figures in All Things': A Theory of Duality in English Poetry from Chaucer to Milton," I attempt to compare Milton and Spenser as two poets who frequently have recourse to visual as well as aural puns, often playing the visual off against the aural, the aural against the visual. Cf. Richard Bradford's recent study, "Milton's Graphic Poetics," in *Re-membering Milton: Essays on the Texts and Traditions*, ed. Mary Nyquist and Margaret W. Ferguson (New York, 1987), 179–96.

[18] Note that Milton reinforces the work of the pun with the careful alternation of alliterating "v's" and "f's": "not deceiVed, / But Fondly oVercome with Female charm"—v / f / v / f. The whole verbal environment of the passage is heavy with the sounds of EVe.

offended against God), the pun in "decEiVEd" demands credit from the lexicon of possible meanings; the puns (and their hearers) ask to be accounted credible (and this request must necessarily bracket authorial intentionality). Without such credit, without an account with the audience, the puns are not valid—they have no value.[19]

Every text brings with it the command, "account me thus and so," though the pun is perhaps the most graphic case. But not every text is the Word of God, able to incarnate what it says (though, arguably, this is the ideal the poetic text always seeks). Nor is every audience divine, though again, arguably, this is the ideal the poet desires. As a result, the texts of men are conflicted, different accounts of them opened all the time. And frequently many of them none too charitable. Obviously, no hearer's account is inexhaustible; none of us can, like God, credit so huge a debt, we cannot afford that words (or sons) mean so differently—God mean man?[20]

Of course, this is another way of saying that none of us is God. None of us has the grace and charity to afford so much meaning. Each of us must protect his account, protect his credibility. Who of men could possibly say,

>   "all Power
> I give thee, reign for ever, and assume
> Thy merits?"   (3.317–19)

But once we concede this, we can also admit, I think, the usefulness of

---

[19] We know that the structure of language can produce meaning only by non-tautology; if we think, then, of a pun as a tautology that is non-tautologous—e.g., "deceived is deceived (dis'Eve'd)", we can appreciate the necessity of the account with the audience—only they will hear who can "afford" to hear, who can "afford" (momentary) non-sense. — Language is meaningful through differentiality, lability, change—ultimately time itself. From this it follows that the structure of language is also entropic (consider the recent phenomenon of "rap," freshly randomizing American English); I take this to be one of the more important implications of such philosophical investigations of language as those of Frege and Wittgenstein. For further reflection along similar lines, see my "The Play of Puns in Late Middle English Poetry: Concerning Juxtology," in *On Puns: The Foundation of Letters*, ed. Jonathan Culler (London, 1988), 44–61.

[20] Here obviously the Renaissance fascination with paradox is relevant to my argument; see Rosalie L. Colie, *Paradoxa Epidemica: The Renaissance Tradition of Paradox* (Princeton: Princeton Univ. Press, 1966), esp. 96–189, and consult *Milton, Poet of Duality*, 10. In my study now in progress, " 'For There Is Figures in All Things' " (n. 17 above), I attempt to demonstrate the relevance also of Cusanus's notion of the "coincidence of opposites" to Milton's poetics and its economics; even though Cusanus is a Catholic writer, he articulates certain Plotinian ideas closely pertinent to the Protestant Milton's understanding of language.

the model we find in Milton's poem. The poet addresses his audience even as Christ addresses God: Account me poet. Consider, for example, the following famous passage from *The Reason of Church-Government*:

> Neither doe I think it shame *to covnant* with any knowing reader, that for some few yeers yet *I may go on trust with him toward the payment of what I am now indebted*, as being a work not to be rays'd from the heat of youth, or the vapours of wine ... but by devout prayer to that eternall Spirit who can *enrich* with all utterance and knowledge ... to this must be added industrious and select reading, steddy observation, insight into all seemly and generous arts and affaires, till which in some measure be compast, at mine own peril and *cost* I refuse not to sustain this *expectation* from as many as are not loath to *hazard* so much *credulity* upon the best *pledges* that I can give them.[21]

Clearly, the *expectation* "from as many as are not loath to hazard so much credulity [where we can also read: credit] upon the best pledges that [he] can give them" is an *account* with them which Milton holds by their grace and charity and good will; he "go[es] on trust with [his reader] toward the payment of what [he is] now indebted" in order to have an *account* in which he is *credited* as a poet—to be in debt as a poet is to become a poet, to "assume his merits."

It is also, and as importantly, to eschew, in a Christ-like manner, the sin of Satan, which is always "others to make such / As I" (9.127–28). Rather than make others such as certainhe, Milton, imitating Christ, attempts to make himself such as others—it may be the English people, who need an author to praise their deeds,[22] or the Church, who needs defense in her hour of peril.[23] But above all Milton is himself, only *as* another. He becomes who he is, repeating another: he is himself only in account with as well as on account of another. Everything he owns he has in account with another:

> certain it is that he who hath obtained in more then the scantest measure to know anything distinctly of God, and of his true worship, and what is infallibly good and happy in the state of mans life, what in it self evil and miserable, though vulgarly not so esteemed, he that hath obtain'd to know this, the only high *valuable* wisdom indeed, remembering also that God even to a

---

[21] Bk. 2, Preface (*CPW* 1:820–21; my emphasis).
[22] Ibid., *CPW* 1:810–12.
[23] Ibid., *CPW* 1:804–6.

> strictnesse requires the improvement of these his *entrusted gifts*, cannot but sustain a sorer burden of mind, and more pressing then any supprotable toil, or waight, which the body can labour under; how and in what manner he shall *dispose* and *employ* those *summes* of knowledge and illumination, which God hath sent him into this world *to trade with*.[24]

But if he has his talent in account *with* God and wishes to spend it on account *of* men, many of them, clearly, are not interested:

> And that which aggravats the burden more, is, that having receiv'd amongst his *allotted parcels* certain *pretious* truths of such an orient lustre as no Diamond can equall, which never the less he *has in charge to put off at any cheap rate*, yea *for nothing* to them that will, the great Merchants of this world fearing that this cours would soon discover, and *disgrace* the fals glitter of their deceitfull wares wherewith they abuse the people, like poor Indians with beads and glasses, practize by all means how they may suppresse the *venting* of such rarities and such a *cheapnes* as would undoe them, and turn their trash upon their hands. Therefore by gratifying the corrupt desires of men in fleshly doctrines, they stirre them up to persecute with hatred and contempt all those that seek to bear themselves uprightly in this *their spiritual factory*: which they foreseeing, though they cannot but testify of Truth and the excellence of that heavenly *traffick* which they bring against what opposition, or danger soever, yet needs must it sit heavily upon their spirits, that being in Gods prime intention and their own, selected heralds of peace, and *dispensers of treasure inestimable without price* to them that have no *pence*, they finde in the discharge of their commission that they are made the greatest variance and offence, a very sword and fire both in house and City over the whole earth.[25]

Many do not wish to *account* Milton poet or apologist or secretary—they would close his "spiritual factory" because they *account* him "a very sword and fire both in house and City." But even in this account, we can readily see, Milton "assumes his merits," for even here, he *is, as* another (or say, he is, *indebtedly*).

Milton always writes in account with as well as on account of another. This way of writing, in fact, is crucial to the economics of his

---

[24] Ibid., *CPW* 1:801 (my emphasis).
[25] Ibid., *CPW* 1:801–2 (my emphasis).

poetics. His poetics embraces also an economics in that he assumes that language in general, any text in particular, has its being in the confession of debt. For Milton, in fact, the structure of language is debt. One man's words are always indebted to another man's account of them: or, as Milton puts it elsewhere, "opinion in good men is but knowledge in the making."[26] This is the source of human community. It is also the source of human tragedy. Even as individual words are indebted for their lexical values to the differences which are forgotten in the assimilative reduction of signification—the differences of individual trees, for example, are forgotten in the word *tree*—so men who use those words in patterns of discourse or arcs of meaning are indebted to the difference from them of other men who forget the differences or at least suspend them for a while in order to credit the speaker.[27] Without such debts, without such accounts, no man is redeemed from the loneliness of his subjectivity, the finitude of his privacy, the possibility of his tragedy.

Each of us, in fact, must say, "account me ... poet, it may be, it may be lover, it may be teacher." To be sure, each of us must also labor to pay the debt, to be worthy of the accounting, to assume his or her merits; but we all, I think we would agree, remember times when we could not pay what was due. And then all we could say was (and is), "account me ... such and such." And here, finally, we have, perhaps, part of the explanation why Milton's Christ has moved so many human beings over the centuries; he not only says, "Account me *man*," he also says, "*Account* me man"—which is a very human thing to say (human perhaps even as Peter is human): let me be indebted to you for my name of man even as I assume responsibility for man.

In fact, so human a thing is it to say that if we listen again to the saying of Anaximander—in Heidegger's translation, this time—we can hear how intently Milton listened to the call of Being, understanding the debt of Being to the being of debt: "But that from which things arise

---

[26] *Areopagitica* (*CPW* 2:554).

[27] Cf. Samuel Weber, "The Debts of Deconstruction and Other, Related Assumptions," in *Taking Chances: Derrida, Psychoanalysis, and Literature*, ed. Joseph H. Smith and William Kerrigan (Baltimore: Johns Hopkins Univ. Press, 1984), 33–65, esp. 45–52, where he discusses Nietzsche's argument that "in the oldest and most primitive personal relationship, that between buyer and seller, creditor and debtor ... one person first confronted another person, one person first *measured itself* against another. Setting prices, measuring values, devising equivalents, exchanging—this preoccupies the earliest thinking of man to such an extent that in a certain sense it *is* thinking itself" (47–48, citing *The Genealogy of Morals*). This *measuring* presupposes the debt of difference which enables men to credit each other.

also gives rise to their passing away, along the lines of usage: for they let order and thereby also reck belong to one another (in the surmounting) of disorder." "Reck," Heidegger says, is Middle High German *ruoche*, meaning "solicitude" or "care." "Care tends to something [he continues] so that it may remain in its essence. [It is a] turning-itself-toward...."[28] When Messiah says "Account me man," it is as if he had also said, "*Reck*on me man": he utters and embodies the care Heidegger so carefully describes, this turning-toward (he pays this "reck" also a reckoning) that enables man to remain in his essence, human.

University of Florida

---

[28] "The Anaximander Fragment," 46–47: "This turning-itself-toward, when thought of what lingers awhile in relation to presencing, is *tísis*, reck. Our word *geruhen* [to deign or respect] is related to reck ... to deign means to esteem something, to let or allow something to be itself. What we observed concerning the word 'consideration,' that it has to do with human relations, is also true of *ruoche*. But we shall take advantage of the obsolescence of the word by adopting it anew in its essential breadth; we will speak of *tísis* as the reck corresponding to *díkē*, order."

LARS ENGLE

Milton, Bakhtin, and the Unit of Analysis

I REMEMBER FROM BOYHOOD A PHOTOGRAPH OF THE GREAT CINCINnati Reds catcher, Johnny Bench, smiling broadly, perhaps lasciviously, surrounded by admiring young women, and holding in one large hand an irregular pyramid of baseballs. The caption, quoted from an admirer, read, "Johnny Bench can hold seventeen baseballs in one hand: think of the possibilities!" In such a charged field of gender oppositions and suggestive shapes, with many women and many baseballs and one centering signal-calling man in apparent control, I could think of many possibilities, but I wasn't at all sure I was thinking of *the* possibilities. That's rather how I feel about "Milton and the possibilities of theory." This paper offers a brief description of Bakhtin's theoretical position, balances bits of *Paradise Lost* on the platform thus created, and hopes to leave you thinking of possibilities.

There are a number of reasons to be surprised that Milton and Bakhtin are not infrequently brought together, and that, more specifically, Bakhtin is not frequently invoked in discussions of *Paradise Lost*. One is the natural expectation that the encyclopedic synthesis of one brilliant, disabled, idiosyncratically Christian polymath writing in disgrace and danger in the disappointing aftermath of revolution should have a bearing on the encyclopedic synthesis of another. Bakhtin, however, as far as I have been able to discover, never mentions Milton, and Miltonists have so far made relatively little of Bakhtin.

Bakhtin's work returns over and over to a distinction which can be crudely introduced as the difference between the one and the many, as it appears in his analysis of discourse. He distinguished epic from novel, poetry from prose, the authoritative word from the word of the people, by reference to the difference between what he calls monologic and what he calls dialogic. It is clear throughout his writings that this is to some extent a distinction also between bad and good, and that, while at times Bakhtin seems to accept nostalgic reifications of "naive poetry" as the expression of a single-voiced heroic culture (following

Lukács and Schiller), he treats nostalgia for naive literature as a mistake, an undervaluation of the achievements of the present. At times in his voluminous and repetitive discussions of this distinction, Bakhtin treats it as an historical evolution: with complexity and stratification in society comes multivoicedness in fictions and the necessity of a variety of ideological positions and discourses.[1] At other times, Bakhtin treats this basic distinction as a generic one, as the division between poetry and the novel.[2] Relatively early in his career he made large claims for Dostoyevsky's originality as a polyphonic writer; at other times, however, he treats dialogic as such a basic feature of discursive representation that it must always already be with us. And in line with this latter position, he finds the origins of the novel in the rise of polyphonic Greek and Latin prose genres and is fascinated by Apuleius and Petronius.[3]

What makes it appropriate to call this distinction a theoretical one rather than simply a useful and widely applicable bit of speculative taxonomy is its intimacy with Bakhtin's general ideas about language, society, and human beings. For Bakhtin proposes that in our analysis of life we take as our unit the *utterance*, with the proviso that all utterance arises as response and seeks reply. As Michael Holquist and Katerina Clark say in their critical biography of him, Bakhtin rewrites the Terentian *homo sum* as "My life is an utterance: therefore nothing in discourse is foreign to me."[4] Building on the assumption that much of our speech is reported speech (all of our words are clearly others' words), Bakhtin's psychology emphasizes that part of consciousness in which we form answers or replies to a circumambient discourse. His critique of Freud, for instance, emphasizes affinities between the structure of consciousness and that of language, while it resists the elevation of the unconscious and, generally speaking, the privileging of any one discursive encounter (such as the analytic) in a description of psychic life. A markedly dialectical form of discourse emerges between analyst and patient.[5] In Bakhtin's view, for all the varied activities of human sub-

---

[1] See, e.g., "Form and Chronotope in the Novel," in *The Dialogic Imagination*, ed. Michael Holquist, trans. Caryl Emerson and Holquist (Austin: Univ. of Texas Press, 1981), 206–15.

[2] See, e.g., "Discourse in the Novel," in *The Dialogic Imagination*, 285–88.

[3] On this see Bakhtin's *Problems of Dostoevsky's Poetics*, ed. and trans. Caryl Emerson (Minneapolis: Univ. of Minnesota Press, 1984), chap. 4, esp. 109–22 on Socratic dialogue and menippean satire.

[4] *Mikhail Bakhtin* (Cambridge: Harvard Univ. Press, 1984), 212. My account of Bakhtin is greatly indebted to Holquist and Clark's.

[5] See "V. N. Volsinov," *Freudianism: A Marxist Critique*, trans. I. R. Titunik, ed. Titunik and Neal H. Bruss (New York: Academic Press, 1976), 78–80; see also the

jects, there are sub-languages within the language the subject speaks, and the analytic encounter is one such activity, with its own identifiable social aspects. By the same token, the behavior of words used as examples by linguists and philosophers constitutes a dialect of language use which should not be taken as a proper synecdoche for the whole.

Bakhtin thus offers an interesting and compelling theoretical alternative to a Derridean language description as well. Derrida takes Saussure to task, for instance, for failure to see the revolutionary implications of the idea of arbitrariness in signification, and (familiarly) for the elevation of speech over writing;[6] Bakhtin, on the other hand, complains that Saussure's opposition of langue and parole ignores the vital and manifold sub-languages whose choice is the main element of any particular utterance: that is, like Derrida, Bakhtin claims that Saussure erects false oppositions and maintains non-existent purities in mapping discourse, but for Bakhtin one needs to move toward pragmatism rather than *differance* to correct Saussure.[7] And Bakhtin argues that in true discourse there is never a sender and a receiver, always a previous message and an idiosyncratic arena of responsiveness. Thus Bakhtin in some ways anticipates and defuses Derrida's critique of self-presence since for Bakhtin the "self" is a dialogic process of interchange in a field of discourses.[8] The metaphysics of presence, for Bakhtin, is always a centralizing *tendency* in language with plenty of ongoing opposition.

If Bakhtin's psychology is linguistic, his linguistics is social: languages are like societies in being full of pockets of resistance to dominant ideas. His map of society grows out of his account of medieval and Renaissance carnival: he opposes the irreverent open marketplace to the solemn enclosures of church (or, later, committee room); in the market square occur the carnival reversals, the ritual uncrownings of authority, and the play of opposed and fluctuating perspectives which have their analogues in the low dialects of language and the low comic and parodic genres of literature. Bakhtin claims that each natural language is in

account in Holquist and Clark, *Mikhail Bakhtin*, 178–83.

[6] *Of Grammatology*, trans. Gayatri Spivak (Baltimore: Johns Hopkins Univ. Press, 1976), 31–73; Jonathan Culler discusses other Derridean comments on Saussure in *Ferdinand de Saussure*, 2nd ed. (Ithaca: Cornell Univ. Press), 140–46.

[7] See "V. N. Volsinov," *Marxism and the Philosophy of Language*, trans. Ladislav Metejka and I. R. Titunik (Cambridge: Harvard Univ. Press, 1986), 70; see also Holquist and Clark, *Mikhail Bakhtin*, 221.

[8] See Don Bialostosky, "Dialogics as an Art of Discourse in Literary Criticism," *PMLA* 101 (1986): 788–97, for a discussion of the consequences for the critic's self-conception of what he considers the foundation of Bakhtin's dialogics, "the inseparability of thesis and person" (789).

a state of heteroglossia, that is, of many-voicedness, at all times, and that any given utterance, spoken or written, can be analyzed according to whether it furthers the diversification of language or its centralization toward some authoritative norm: whether it leads to the expansion of the market square or of the committee room. Here I must ask your indulgence for a fairly lengthy quotation from Bakhtin's essay, "Discourse in the Novel," a quotation which illustrates the sweep of Bakhtin's philology and gives as thrifty and thorough a summary as I have been able to find of his view of the role of language in culture.

> Aristotelian poetics, the poetics of Augustine, the poetics of the medieval church, of "the one language of truth," the Cartesian poetics of neoclassicism, the abstract grammatical universalism of Leibniz (the idea of a "universal grammar"), Humboldt's insistence on the concrete—all these, whatever their differences in nuance, give expression to the same centripetal forces in sociolinguistic and ideological life; they serve one and the same project of centralizing and unifying the European languages. The victory of one reigning language (dialect) over the others, the supplanting of languages, their enslavement, the process of illuminating them with the True Word, the incorporation of barbarians and lower social strata into a unitary language of culture and truth, the canonization of ideological systems, philology with its methods of studying and teaching dead languages, languages that were by that very fact "unities," Indo-European linguistics with its focus of attention, directed away from language plurality to a single proto-language—all this determined the content and power of the category of "unitary language" in linguistic and stylistic thought, and determined its creative, style-shaping role in the majority of the poetic genres that coalesced in the channel formed by those same centripetal forces of verbal-ideological life.[9]

According to Bakhtin, then, the institutions in which all of us have our being are dedicated on the whole to centralization and are thus, often without knowing it, in conflict with centrifugal energies of marketplace heteroglossia. I mean here the institutions of philology and the teaching of standard English and of formal speech, not the creation of the rich evanescent jargons that characterize the successful individuation of professional groups.

Bakhtin's "utterances" are thus subject to several sorts of description, and literary forms may be described in the same ways as other utter-

---

[9] *The Dialogic Imagination*, 271.

ances. This gives his criticism a populist feel, despite his extraordinary menagerie of learned examples. An utterance is always contextualized; if abstracted for formalist discussion, it has been implicitly contextualized into the discourse of a particular critical community, and when written in one time but read in another, it is of course recontextualized by new ideological pressures. But an utterance, especially an ambitious formal written one, can also be described in a more sweeping way, as either participating in or combatting the centripetal movements of its time. Thus in assessing an utterance historically we must possess some sort of map of the dialectal varieties present in its language at the time it was written. Bakhtin, in discussing fictions, tends to divide them according to whether they embrace a variety of distinctive ideological positions and thus speak in a variety of languages or, on the other hand, cleave to a single style and the language of a single social group. He calls forms which allow a paradoxical kind of autonomy to different viewpoints "dialogical," and as I suggest above he associates dialogic literary art with the novel, with Dostoyevsky, and with prose genres as opposed to verse genres. As it turns out, however, Pushkin's *Eugene Onegin* and Heine's lyrics are also dialogic novels, properly understood. But the consistent elevation of epic style, to Bakhtin's mind, reinforces the thematic affinity of epic subjects to centralizing and authoritarian positions.

If Bakhtin *had* mentioned *Paradise Lost*, then, it seems likely enough that he would have presented it as a triumph of monologic utterance, perhaps indeed as a last attempt at a Christian-scientific-classical synthesis of the whole of human activity as the manifestation of a single authoritative Word. Such a description by Bakhtin might, however, be more epitaph than encomium. Here, perhaps, is one reason why Bakhtin has not been juxtaposed with Milton in the past. But it is not a particularly good reason: Bakhtin's interest in dialogic is, implicitly, a brilliant analysis of the nature of monologic and of the psychological, linguistic, and social opposition it faces, thus of the natural difficulties a project like *Paradise Lost* faces. Nonetheless, the poem is not the sort of work Bakhtin chooses to celebrate.

Speculations that Bakhtin might not be enthusiastic about *Paradise Lost* are reinforced, moreover, by local descriptions of the poem's texture. Even the points where *Paradise Lost* approaches the "grotesque realism" of Rabelais, for instance, are moments of containment, rather than explosion. Bakhtin's book on Rabelais celebrates carnival, laughter, and the resistance to official culture marked by what he calls grotesque realism and the representation of the lower bodily stratum. But the most grotesquely comic moments of *Paradise Lost*—when for instance Satan is barked at by his grandsons (who turn out also to be his great-grandsons, so that the iniquity of the father is visited on two generations simultaneously in each dog)—do not produce or aim at the kind of laughter Bakhtin celebrates in *Gargantua*: "a laughter ... of all the people ... directed at all and everyone, including the carnival participants," which shows "the entire world ... in its droll aspect, in its gay relativity."[10] Bakhtin remarks in his 1970-71 "Notes" that "Everything that is truly great must include an element of laughter. Otherwise it becomes threatening, terrible, or pompous; in any case, it is limited. Laughter lifts the barrier and clears the path." He goes on immediately to contrast "The joyful, open, festive laugh" to "the closed, purely negative, satirical laugh" and says of the latter, "This is not a laughing laugh."[11] Just such non-laughing laughter, and only such, appears in *Paradise Lost*: the laughter of authorities directed at manifestations of heteroglossia. Raphael suggests that the varied descriptions of celestial motion offered by Renaissance astronomers in the midst of a paradigm shift will move God's "laughter at their quaint opinions wide" (8.78),[12] and, still more directly, Michael predicts God's vengeance on the tower builders of Babel:

> God ... in derision sets
> Upon their tongues a various spirit to raze
> Quite out their native language....
>   great laughter was in heaven
> And looking down, to see the hubbub strange
> And hear the din; (12.52 ff.)

The devils, moreover, though prone to parody, are deadly serious parodists. They never laugh; at the one moment when Satan asks them to, God turns them into snakes before they have a chance (10.485).[13]

So if we are to see possibilities for an appreciative discussion of *Paradise Lost* in Bakhtin's theories, we will have to cut against some of his habitual distinctions and some of his own apparent generic tastes. This I think we can do. Bakhtin's rigorous opposition of epic and novel as monologic vs. dialogic is a mistake, as Gary Saul Morson suggests in offering Milton's Satan as an exception to Bakhtin's generalizations

---

[10] *Rabelais and His World*, 11.

[11] *Speech Genres & Other Late Essays*, 135.

[12] All quotations from *Paradise Lost* are from Alastair Fowler's edition in *The Poems of Milton*, ed. John Carey and Fowler (London: Longman, 1968). Book and line references are included in the text.

[13] God, however, says his "scornful enemies ... laugh" (10.626), so presumably either Satan's audience laughs on cue or Satan punctuates his own speech with a melodramatic "ha" now and then.

about epic character.[14] Holquist and Clark, indeed, suggest that Bakhtin's description of epic, at least in the essay "Epic and Novel" which begins *The Dialogic Imagination*, is really aimed at the ideological conformity of Soviet socialist realism rather than at a description of even primary epic.[15] This is not to say that the monologic/dialogic distinction fails to show us a central difference between the *Iliad* and *The Idiot*, but the diversity of languages in a poem like *Paradise Lost* entitles it to something like novel status. I want to suggest some general ways in which the description of Bakhtin I have given can illuminate discussions of *Paradise Lost*. The relation of theory to practice in the discussion of literature is, of course, rarely one of simple application; rather, a theory can provide a new descriptive and contextualizing vocabulary and provoke conversation in which different aspects or details of a literary work appear important, worth arguing about. Bakhtin's analytic unit of the utterance, poised among centripetal and centrifugal forces in discourse, offers I think a useful modern secular parallel to Milton's analytic unit of the conscious choice, poised among discursive voices persuading the subject toward and away from God. If Milton was a dialogist, he did not know it: Milton takes pains in *Paradise Lost* to present ideological independence from God as self-contradictory and, from the viewpoint of the subject, ultimately self-denying. God's discourse allows, enables, even demands choice. But to seek to separate one's own discourse from having God as its center or ground (which is what ideological independence would consist of) is closely allied to processes of growth which Milton probes with enormous intelligence, subtlety, and sympathy. One contribution of Bakhtinian theory and example to interpretation of *Paradise Lost* may be, then, that it gives us a descriptive vocabulary for Milton's attempt to unite a variety of discourses under the aegis of obedience. The discourse of individuation—the way Adam asks God for Eve, for instance—offers striking manifestations of dialogical tendencies.

The problem comes, as might be expected, in the crucial area of moral responsibility. Bakhtinian analysis of utterance positions the moral subject as an area of activity in the surrounding fields of discourse. This makes it a rather significant matter, for instance, that conversation with God and angel guests in *Paradise Lost* is the sole prerogative of Adam, that Eve never hears an unmediated divine prohibition of the apple, and that in general the promises of ascent in the poem seem likely to benefit Adam more than Eve since what they promise is more

---

[14] "Who Speaks for Bakhtin?" in *Bakhtin: Essays and Dialogues on His Work* (Chicago: Univ. of Chicago Press, 1986), 14.

[15] *Mikhail Bakhtin*, 273–74.

of the angelic discourse from which she is largely excluded. To go on in this way about the poem would be to suggest that Milton's understanding of various discursive relations to authority, which comes out in the representation of character, is at odds with his commitment both to unfallen perfection in Paradise and to the ultimate uniformity of moral choices.

The same sort of paradox may be hinted at in the dialogic energies released by the elevation of the Son, which creates a conversational partner for God and excites revolutionary energy in Lucifer and, thereby, heroic nonconformist virtue in Abdiel, all under the sign of the unification into a whole in which discursive exchanges may no longer need to take place:

> This day I have begot whom I declare
> My only Son, and on this holy hill
> Him have anointed, whom ye now behold
> At my right hand; your head I him appoint;
> And by my self have sworn to him shall bow
> All knees in heaven, and shall confess him Lord:
> Under his great vicegerent reign abide
> United as one individual soul
> For ever happy: him who disobeys
> Me disobeys, breaks union, and that day
> Cast out from God and blessed vision, falls
> Into utter darkness, deep engulfed, his place
> Ordained without redemption, without end.
>
> (5.603–15)

The moment of discursive provocation—the provocative speech from which the variety of both good and bad discourses in the poem springs—is also the prediction of an ultimate end to discourse in an eternity of undifferentiated and undialogical self-awareness, "one ... soul / For ever happy." Milton's sensitivity to the strain between the ultimate monologic of a successful theodicy and the dialogic attendant on imaginative representation of discourse results in a mystical promise that discourse will eventually be unnecessary.

A more extended and in some ways more subtle instance of God's intervention to contain the dialogic tendencies of conversation occurs, as I suggested above, in the exchange which precedes the creation of Eve. A monologic society or language is not without variation, but varieties occur only as branches of a hierarchically organized whole branching out from a center or source or root. If Eve's relation to Adam is a strictly hierarchical one, the conversation between them is unlikely to be genuinely dialogical; conversely, dialogical conversation will tend to suggest that their relation is not a strictly hierarchical one, not one which reinforces centripetal tendencies in the prelapsarian universe. Adam appreciates the first half of the previous sentence, God the second, and this produces an exchange between God and man long found puzzling. Eve is, of course, made to order, but Adam has to ask for her several times and in two distinct ways before God makes her. Adam first raises the issue after he has, in the presence of the creating God, surveyed and named the animals in their mated pairs, a fine monologic exercise.[16] Adam, who has shown himself precocious in appreciation, now begs leave to ask for more:

>   with hands so liberal
> Thou hast provided all things: but with me
> I see not who partakes. In solitude
> What happiness, who can enjoy alone,
> Or all enjoying, what contentment find?   (8.363–66)

"Thus I presumptuous," Adam tells Raphael, and God's reply seems irritated, couched as it is in the imperative:

> What call'st thou solitude, is not the earth
> With various living creatures, and the air
> Replenished, and all these at thy command...?
>   with these
> Find pastime, and bear rule; thy realm is large.
>   (8.369 ff.)

We might paraphrase God's advice as: "I have given you power: enjoy it." When first introducing Adam to the animals, God emphasizes Adam's dominance over them: "I bring them to receive / From thee their names, and pay thee fealty with low subjection" (8.343). God does, admittedly, imply that the animals are reasonable and says that Adam knows their language and thus can converse with them, but God

---

[16] Because of 7.405–7 and 420, where the Creator refers to Himself as "Who am alone / From all eternity, for none I know / Second to me or like, equal much less," it seems appropriate to refer to the union of forces that makes the world as "God"; from 7.163–64 it is clear that Father, Son, and "spirit" (Milton never calls it "Holy" and avoids reference to the Trinity), act as one in making the world, for though the Father may "uncircumscribed [him] self retire" in 7.170, He sends both his strength and spirit with the Son on this creative venture: "thou my Word, begotten Son, by thee / This I perform, speak thou, and be it done: / My overshadowing spirit and might with thee / I send along." Thus, though the Son appears to be as it were the main agent, and is yet more pointedly so in Book 10, the Father acts through Him. Cf. Milton's discussion of this issue in *On Christian Doctrine*, in *Complete Prose Works of John Milton*, gen. ed. D. M. Wolfe, 8 vols. (New Haven: Yale Univ. Press, 1953–1982), 6:301. I am grateful to Professor R. A. Shoaf for advice on this point.

nonetheless orders Adam to content himself with the joys of power over them and specifically to abjure the possibility of conversation of a dialogic kind.[17] "So spake the universal Lord, and seemed / So ordering" (8.376), says Adam. Given God's special powers as an interlocutor who knows beforehand what others mean to say, He might be taken here as hinting that power relations are all there are and that Adam had better learn to enjoy his position in a monologic hierarchy. Clearly, then, Adam's continued resistance to divine suggestion must spring from deep (though in his condition necessarily recent) conviction. His response to God's seeming order is crucial, so I give it in full.

> Let not my words offend thee, heavenly power,
> My maker, be propitious while I speak.
> Hast thou not made me here thy substitute,
> And these inferiors far beneath me set?
> Among unequals what society
> Can sort, what harmony or true delight?
> Which must be mutual, in proportion due
> Given and received; but in disparity
> The one intense, the other still remiss
> Cannot well suit with either, but soon prove
> Tedious alike: of fellowship I speak
> Such as I seek, fit to participate
> All rational delight, wherein the brute
> Cannot be human consort; they rejoice
> Each with their kind, lion with lioness;
> So fitly them in pairs thou hast combined;
> Much less can bird with beast, or fish with fowl
> So well converse, nor with the ox the ape;
> Worse then can man with beast, and least of all.
>
> (8.379–97)

Adam thus defies a command—what seems a command to him—in order to express his need for a partner who equals him and who will reciprocate his interest. It is a puzzle whether he is asking for a woman here or another man: he mentions animal pairs, and notes lion and lioness specifically, possibly to point out to God that the king of beasts does not have to relish the submission of the rest of the animals without

---

[17] See 8.372–74. Man apparently loses the capacity to understand the animals at the Fall: see Fowler's note. Eve is surprised at 9.563 to find the serpent suddenly "speakable of mute," however, so prelapsarian understanding of animals apparently does not extend to real discourse.

a partner.[18] Certainly at this point Adam does not seem to have a sexual partner in mind. Rather, he is close to demanding someone who will make Eden into a dialogical community.

Though Milton eloquently defends married sexuality as a kind of "rational delight" (or one at any rate not incompatible with rationality) at various points,[19] and though Adam says of animals that "they rejoice / Each with their kind" and may thus hint at sex, his emphasis falls on conversation (itself of course a potentially erotic term), and he seems most to fear having no one to talk with.[20] He insists, at any rate, that he will not be happy with a companion whom he thoroughly dominates, and his intuitive conception of good society is obviously that of equals. He has, of course, already learned that he is in a hierarchically ordered world; he speaks to a superior and is surrounded by inferiors. Yet he seeks a partner whom he will not command, but with whom he will form a musical whole.[21] Although conflictual or parodistic aspects of dialogic have no place in his thinking, he specifically seeks a relation which is not bound by issues of relative power.

God's reply to Adam is puzzling in turn:

> A nice and subtle happiness I see
> Thou to thy self proposest, in the choice
> Of thy associates, Adam, and wilt taste
> No pleasure, though in pleasure, solitary.
> What think'st thou then of me, and this my state,
> Seem I to thee sufficiently possessed
> Of happiness, or not? Who am alone
> From all eternity, for none I know
> Second to me or like, equal much less.

---

[18] Diane Kelsey McColley, in *Milton's Eve* (Urbana: Univ. of Illinois Press, 1983), 87, implies that Adam asked for a male companion or at any rate one more like him than Eve is. "Adam [at 8.520] is still struggling with the problem of having asked for an equal and been given instead someone who is engagingly different." To people, lionesses look more like lions than women do like men—but presumably not to lions. It is perhaps relevant that Adam, in mentioning lions and lionesses, chooses beasts with marked secondary sexual characteristics, since lionesses do not have manes.

[19] See 4.750 ff. and Adam's ardent defense of sexuality to Raphael at 8.596 ff.

[20] See, however, John Halkett, *Milton and the Idea of Matrimony* (New Haven: Yale Univ. Press, 1970), chap. 3 on Milton's extended and enriched sense of "conversation" between husband and wife.

[21] See Fowler 8.384–89n. The terms *proportion, intense,* and *remiss* are all subject to a musical interpretation. Halkett (60) quotes *Tetrachordon* (*Complete Prose* 2:596) illustrating this more circumstantially: "No mortall nature can endure either in the actions of Religion, or study of wisdome, without sometime slackning the cords of intense thought and labour."

> How have I then with whom to hold converse
> Save with the creatures which I made, and those
> To me inferior, infinite descents
> Beneath what other creatures are to thee?   (8.399–411)

Outside heaven, God and the Son are never separate. The narrator always refers to the creating Son as "God." Nevertheless, the bending of separate wills and distinct persons to a single love that we find in the relation between Father and Son as described in the scenes in heaven is often taken as an example for human love and specifically for the love of Adam and Eve.[22] It seems then particularly perverse that, on the occasion of the creation of Eve, God should represent his own singleness to Adam with such disingenuous intensity, denying just that aspect of His nature which Adam and the companion with whom he hopes to form a mutual whole might dimly imitate. Why, at this point, should God (or God-speaking-through-the-Son) insist here on what Fowler calls "the theology of the monad"(8.416–19n)?

Milton's sensitivity to subtle centrifugal tendencies in discourse offers us a Bakhtinian answer to this question, I believe. Adam has, after all, been appealing against the strenuously hierarchical relations within a monologic order to which he is limited, with inferiors below him and (as far as he knows at the point of his own creation) only God high above. God's insistence on His singleness at this point seems intended to warn Adam that no conversational companion will free Adam from this monologic hierarchy: despite Adam's commitment to the formation of a mutually responsive conversational "society" around him, God suggests, he must not forget this primary allegiance. This seems to me a plausible version, at any rate, of the message implied in God's apparently perverse speech: it is a kind of warning. God cannot, after all, be (as He rather ironically or flirtatiously pretends) unaware that He is about to create Eve.[23]

Adam responds to this warning by changing his tack, and in doing this he stumbles on an argument for a companion that sounds less mutual and more sexual than his former description. His request

---

[22] E.g., by McColley (51–57) and G. K. Hunter, *Paradise Lost* (London: Allen and Unwin, 1980), 195–96. See also Stella P. Revard, "Eve and the Doctrine of Responsibility in *Paradise Lost*," *PMLA* 88 (1973): 74, though Revard refers to the loving obedience of heavenly citizens generally rather than the nearly mutual relation of Father and Son.

[23] Though Adam is a bad enough theologian at 8.554–56 to think so: he complains to Raphael of Eve that "Authority and reason on her wait, / As one intended first, not after made / Occasionally." She was, we may presume, intended all along; God is no improviser, properly understood.

changes, however, as much in address as in content. He has learned from God's reply to center his plea not on what he is asking for, but on the power and nature of the person he addresses: Adam is learning to be a courtier, we might say. And he is learning to stress monologic tendencies of his utterance.

> He ceased, I lowly answered. To attain
> The highth and depth of thy eternal ways
> All human thoughts come short, supreme of things;
> Thou in thy self art perfect, and in thee
> Is no deficience found; not so is man,
> But in degree, the cause of his desire
> By conversation with his like to help,
> Or solace his defects. No need that thou
> Shouldst propagate, already infinite;
> And through all numbers absolute, though one;
> But man by number is to manifest
> His single imperfection, and beget
> Like of his like, his image multiplied,
> In unity defective, which requires
> Collateral love, and dearest amity.   (8.412–26)

Adam now couches his request as an acknowledgement of his difference from and dependence on God, and as a probably unintentional (but avoidable) consequence has played down the potentially dialogic independence he has hoped for in his partner. He now needs a companion to fulfill a divine plan. His face is turned upward, even though he has not forgotten his hopes of an equal ("collateral") friend or lover. And in this form Adam's request is granted:

> Thus far to try thee, Adam, I was pleased,
> And find thee knowing not of beasts alone,
> Which thou hast rightly named, but of thy self,
> Expressing well the spirit within thee free,
> My image, not imparted to the brute,
> Whose fellowship therefore unmeet for thee
> Good reason was thou freely shouldst dislike,
> And be so minded still; I, ere thou spakest,
> Knew it not good for man to be alone,
> And no such company as then thou saw'st
> Intended thee, for trial only brought,
> To see how thou couldst judge of fit and meet:
> What next I bring shall please thee, be assured,

> Thy likeness, thy fit help, thy other self,
> Thy wish exactly to thy heart's desire.   (8.437-51)

God, then, has "tried" Adam, and found him able to judge "of fit and meet."

But has the trial been passed when Adam shows himself capable of imagining a mutual free conversational companion for himself, one capable of making Eden a field for dialogical discursive energies? Or has Adam rather passed by responding tactfully to implicit divine criticism of his original request, retailoring it as a compliment to God and a part of the monologic divine intent? God praises Adam's expression of his own freedom and at the same time calls that "free spirit" "My image." He promises to give Adam "Thy wish exactly to thy heart's desire," but Adam expressed two desires in two separate speeches, the first an ardent need for mutual conversational companionship, the second a grateful willingness to fulfill a divine plan for humanity. God's phrase "Thy likeness, thy fit help, thy other self," while promising Adam "collateral love" in that he will get a partner like himself, has none of Adam's earlier emphasis on mutual responsiveness and the capacity to form a self-sufficient social whole. God may feel He has educated Adam out of such dangerous desires. But Adam remains unsure throughout Books 8 and 9 whether the utterly delightful companion he has been given fulfills his first request or his second. Her own sense that she is meant for dialogic relations with Adam is clear in the separation colloquy which begins Book 9.

Bakhtin's discourse analysis, then, illuminates local events in *Paradise Lost* and, more forcibly, suggests that both Milton and Milton's God are poets of dialogic energies and monologic ends. More generally, *Paradise Lost* as a whole may be well described by Bakhtin's map of language and society: the poem is a dynamic system in which strong centralizing voices assert their own centripetal triumph while, in pockets of disengaged conversation, centrifugal energies release tangential utterances and these in turn, at least momentarily, recenter the whole or cast doubt on the entire centripetal enterprise.[24]

University of Tulsa

---

[24] I am grateful to Holly Laird, Dan Kinney, and Michael Holquist for helpful discussions of this paper and to Michael Levenson for introducing me to Bakhtin's work.

RONALD J. CORTHELL

Milton and the Possibilities of Theory

BIBLICAL PARALLELISM, A REDEMPTIVE ECONOMICS OF EXCHANGE, dialogic energies versus monologic ends—binary tropes seem to control the discourse of Mary Ann Radzinowicz, R. A. Shoaf, and Lars Engle. This thematics of the binary is at once a limitation and a strength: a strength because it responds to Milton's two-testament model of intertextuality and his poetics of choice and, therefore, helps to satisfy "the desire to understand," as Shoaf put it in introductory remarks at the session; a limitation because "strong reading," as I understand the term, is also the expression of a desire to resist the text. While I sense some resistance or "misreading" in Shoaf's paradoxes or Engle's contradictions, I expected more wilfulness, more disobedience, from the three readers at the time of "rewriting the Renaissance." To echo a new-historicist refrain, Is subversion of Milton possible?

Or first, Is subversion of Milton something worth pursuing? And what is meant by "Milton"? In updating my response to papers delivered in 1987, I am all too aware that this revision will look dated by the time it reaches print. Since this discussion of "Milton and the Possibilities of Theory" at Binghamton, the profession has become increasingly skeptical of the claims of theory. The "New Pragmatism," the De Man debacle, the sharp critiques of new historicism to be found in H. Aram Veeser's recent collection[1] and elsewhere—all contribute to an ongoing demystification of theory. At this writing I also note that Stanley Fish, perhaps the leading literary New Pragmatist, received the Milton Society's James Holly Hanford Award for Distinguished Article of 1989 and has a book forthcoming.[2] Milton studies have proven to be remarkably

---

[1] *The New Historicism* (London: Routledge, 1989).
[2] "Spectacle and Evidence in *Samson Agonistes*," *Critical Inquiry* 15 (1989): 556–86, and *Milton's Aesthetic of Testimony*. In 1991, he was named Honored Scholar of the Milton Society.

theory-proof over the past two decades, although, as John Peter Rumrich notes in a recent article, "Milton scholarship has become increasingly adventuresome and theoretically varied."³ Contrarians as usual, Miltonists are being energized by the possibilities of theory at precisely the moment that theory itself is being vigorously critiqued.

Indeed, Milton would seem to afford a prime site both for new-historicist critique, the dominant theoretically-nuanced approach to Renaissance literature, and for critique of new historicism. Milton's open hostility to the court culture of the period marks him as a special subject of new-historicist inquiry, a kind of boundary for testing its theories of Renaissance culture. At the same time one might argue along new-historicist lines that Milton's major works enact the decisive imaginary resolution of contradictions in the paradoxical Renaissance project of interrogating and recuperating power, a power "whose quintessential sign," asserts Greenblatt, "is the ability to impose one's fictions upon the world."⁴ This attempted resolution and the related opposition to royalism are in part enabled by an emergent ideology of literary authority: problematizing the subject of power in terms of his own literary project, Milton invites the sort of historicizing critique of poetic authority begun by Thomas Greene, David Quint, and John Guillory, and continued in the work of Christopher Kendrick and Marshall Grossman.⁵ In another important study published since the Binghamton conference, Keith Stavely has offered at once a means of positioning new-historicist reconstructions of Renaissance culture by way of a reading of Milton and an historicist interrogation of *Paradise Lost*; his disclosure of fundamental contradictions of Puritan culture within *Paradise Lost* richly problematizes its ideological content and, in the process, begins to historicize new historicism's privileging of court culture as the ideological node of the period.⁶

But if theory has made inroads, Rumrich is still right, I think, in stating that "recent opinions of Milton and his epic are, historically

---

³ Rumrich, "Uninventing Milton," *Modern Philology* 87 (1990): 249.

⁴ *Renaissance Self-Fashioning: From More to Shakespeare* (Chicago: Univ. of Chicago Press, 1980), 13.

⁵ Greene, *The Light in Troy: Imitation and Discovery in Renaissance Poetry* (New Haven: Yale Univ. Press, 1982); Quint, *Origin and Originality in Renaissance Literature: Versions of the Source* (New Haven: Yale Univ. Press, 1983); Guillory, *Poetic Authority: Spenser, Milton, and Literary History* (New York: Columbia Univ. Press, 1983); Kendrick, *Milton: A Study in Ideology and Form* (New York: Methuen, 1986); Grossman, *"Authors to Themselves": Milton and the Revelation of History* (Cambridge: Cambridge Univ. Press, 1987).

⁶ Keith W. Stavely, *Puritan Legacies:* Paradise Lost *and the New England Tradition* (Ithaca: Cornell Univ. Press, 1987).

speaking, more notable for their harmony than for their discord." Rumrich attributes this concord to "Fish's theoretically sophisticated update of Lewis's orthodox model" in *Surprised by Sin* (249). I suggest another cause—what might be called the "Kerrigan effect." In *The Sacred Complex* Kerrigan brilliantly demonstrated the openness of Milton's texts to Freudian theory on the one hand, and the critical power of Milton's texts to reshape our readings of Freud on the other.[7] Something like this dialectic is likely to inform other theoretical interventions in Milton studies as well. Milton studies is perhaps not so much resistant to theory as it is capable of *absorbing* theory, of discovering always already there in Milton the paradoxes and problems of signification, power, and desire. At this writing the greatest possibilities for "uninventing Milton" would seem to belong to feminism. Two distinct feminist projects seem to be under way and at odds with each other. Joseph Wittreich's *Feminist Milton* opens by "critiquing the feminist critique" of Milton to the end of demonstrating the historical links between feminism and the reading of Milton; drawing upon Hans Robert Jauss's theory of reception, Wittreich proposes that we move away from accounts of the culturally inscribed Miltonic text to "a literary history of Milton's readers, both male and female—a 'reader-response' criticism, to be sure, but one that is de-idealized, truly professionalized, and newly historicized."[8] On the other hand we have feminist work best represented by the outstanding essays of Mary Nyquist. Like Wittreich, Nyquist places her work in contrast to other forms of feminist critique (I suspect Wittreich's would be among these) when she writes of "third-wave feminism as well as 'post-feminist feminism.' "[9] Like Wittreich, Nyquist is also deeply concerned with history and especially the history of reception of Milton. But two radically different Miltons are constructed by these critics—one a Milton Regained in history as an "early sponsor"

---

[7] *The Sacred Complex: On the Psychogenesis of* Paradise Lost (Cambridge: Harvard Univ. Press, 1983).

[8] *Feminist Milton* (Ithaca: Cornell Univ. Press, 1987), 153.

[9] "The Genesis of Gendered Subjectivity in the Divorce Tracts and in *Paradise Lost*," in Nyquist and Margaret W. Ferguson, eds., *Re-membering Milton: Essays on the Texts and Traditions* (New York: Methuen, 1988), 99. See also "Fallen Differences, Phallogocentric Discourses: Losing *Paradise Lost* to History," in *Post-Structuralism and the Question of History*, ed. Derek Attridge, Geoff Bennington, and Robert Young (Cambridge: Cambridge Univ. Press, 1987), 212–43. Julia M. Walker, ed., *Milton and the Idea of Woman* (Urbana: Univ. of Illinois Press, 1988); Richard Halpern, "Puritanism and Maenadism in *A Mask*," and John Guillory, "Dalila's House: *Samson Agonistes* and the Sexual Division of Labor," both in Margaret W. Ferguson, Maureen Quilligan, and Nancy J. Vickers, eds., *Rewriting the Renaissance: The Discourses of Sexual Difference in Early Modern Europe* (Chicago: Univ. of Chicago Press, 1986), 88–105 and 106–22.

of feminism, the other a Milton Lost to history (a happy fall for Nyquist) or if found in history, found as a site of contradiction.[10]

R. A. Shoaf's paper, about another type of losing and finding, combines the interests of his earlier books in monetary semiotics and puns.[11] But I suppose his chief display of strength is yoking by violence what would appear to be the heterogeneous ideas of Heideggerian metaphysics and Matthew 16 in order to suggest a new way of thinking about the Son in *Paradise Lost*. The relationship posited between Matthew 16 and *Paradise Lost* 3.238 depends upon (implicitly) a poetics of biblical "transumption" like that outlined in Mary Ann Radzinowicz's essay. This biblical indebtedness of Milton's text provides the historical ground on which Shoaf plays his serious, Heideggerian game of names and debts. His insistence on the economic vehicle of Matthew's and Milton's language issues in a series of puns that, on the one hand, transumes Scriptural word-play and, on the other, allows Shoaf to surprise us with the paradoxical notion of Christ "saving God"—both in the sense of saving God from the loss of man and in the sense of "saving up" or banking on God. This kind of linguistic and intellectual looping is not uncommon in "metaphysical" wit of the seventeenth century and also seems consonant with other instances of Milton's foregrounding of Latinate roots in *Paradise Lost*. Positioned by these contexts of gospel language and seventeenth-century literary theory and practice, Messiah-Milton's puns look more Donnean than Heideggerian.

The next step in Shoaf's argument, his attempt to relate this heavenly debt structure to a Heideggerian attentiveness to the call of Being on Milton's part, merits further consideration. The thesis seems appropriate in general terms to Book 3, as both Poet and Satan emerge from Hell into the Light. Shoaf's suggestive paradox on Messiah's "crediting" and "saving" of God might be usefully compared to the theological paradoxes that Milton draws on in the invocation to Book 3:

> Hail holy Light, offspring of Heav'n first-born,
> Or of th'Eternal Coeternal beam
> May I express thee unblam'd? since God is Light,
> And never but in unapproached Light
> Dwelt from Eternity, dwelt then in thee,
> Bright effluence of bright essence increate.

I find an interesting parallel here between Milton's use of traditional

---

[10] Wittreich, ix; Nyquist, "Losing *Paradise Lost* to History," 234.
[11] *Dante, Chaucer, and the Currency of the Word* (Norman: Pilgrim Books, 1983) and *Milton, Poet of Duality* (New Haven: Yale Univ. Press, 1985).

theological paradoxes (according to William B. Hunter and others, imagery designed to transcend the Arian controversy) and Shoaf's equivocal notion of "saving" God: saving God from the loss of mankind would correspond to the notion of Milton's muse or the Son (the "holy Light") as "Coeternal beam," whereas the Son's "saving up" of God for man (God as banker, Son as depositor) would imply a secondary status corresponding to the (Arian) idea of the muse or Son as "offspring of Heav'n first-born." This equivocality concerning the status of Milton's muse and the Son, whether treated in terms of theological paradoxes or the (to me) equally mystifying terms of accounting, is at the center of Shoaf's argument about the equivocal relationships of Messiah to God and man. That is, Shoaf has hit upon what might be called the metaphysical conceit that is Christ and that underlies the more conventional theological imagery of the invocation.

This Christ, Shoaf continues, "resembles Satan, standing up to God, standing apart from God," with the profound reservation that Christ repeats God "as man, not as alternative God—which is what Satan desired to be." Here again I find an anticipation of this resemblance in the invocation, where the equivocation on the origins of the "holy Light" encourages a comparison later with Satan's fallacious arguments on his own origins in Book 5. A further complication germane to Shoaf's thesis about authoring and indebtedness is introduced here as well, since the invoker of this paradoxical muse is the poet, the author of *Paradise Lost*—that is, like Shoaf's Christ, the author of God. Putting it this way reminds us of Milton's problematization of origins in *Paradise Lost*, including the origin of the poem: Who is the author of *Paradise Lost*?

But is it only the poet who invokes the Light? There does seem to be a moment of indeterminacy as to the speaker of this invocation. The poet and Satan emerge together from Hell at the end of Book 2. Equivocation, an obsession with God's exacting and mysterious law ("May I express thee unblam'd?"), and a problematizing of origins ("offspring of heaven first-born,/ Or of the eternal co-eternal beam")—all of them operative in the invocation—mark Satan's discourse on his relationship to God throughout the poem. Are we not allowed to hear Satan, if only for a few lines? In wanting, like Christ, to author God, might not Milton also be like Satan?

In any case, Shoaf's account of Messiah in Book 3 is consistent with the paradoxical introduction to the book which fuses traditional theological representations of the Son with problems of authoring. This fusion is, I take it, Shoaf's chief concern. But he could have developed his notion of authoring as indebtedness in another direction. He writes:

The Word cannot be understood as, or, say translated into, man, unless and until "accounted" so by God; the Word must go into debt with God in order to acquire the meaning "man." Similarly, words, human words cannot be understood as having whatever meaning unless and until they are "accounted" as such by their audience community of hearers.... [T]hey must borrow on account the understanding they seek.

Shoaf's analogy—"The poet addresses his audience even as Christ addresses God"—seems asymmetrical, particularly when the poet in question is a self-described prophetic writer. Milton's "crediting," as Shoaf would have it, his faith, is always in the direction of God. This means that Milton's career is directed toward the end of "saving" God in the witty senses proposed by Shoaf's earlier argument. The genesis of his project of authoring God, *Paradise Lost*, is powered by the desire to "justify the ways of God to men"; Milton's oft-noted use of the theologically resonant "justify," a particularly brilliant example of his foregrounding of the ideology that produces him as God's subject, seems to encourage an identification of the poet and Christ even as it denies such an identification in its inversion of the usual understanding of the spiritual mechanics of justification; instead of saving men for God, the poet wants to save God for man. In the earlier sonnet on his career (or, rather, the apparent lack of a career) "When I consider how my light is spent," we find another Miltonic paradox on this strange kind of crediting; as Kerrigan has compellingly argued in *The Sacred Complex*, the spending of that light is paradoxically the means to the saving (read "saving up") of God and the saving (justifying) of Milton.

In brief, I think Shoaf releases some powerful contradictions in his analysis of Christ's "account" of himself, but it may be that he rushes to a resolution. His discussion contributes to the, in my view, still unresolved dialogue on the question of Milton's (and Puritanism's, for that matter) position on the Son.[12] He is right in hearing a Heideggerian "reck" in Book 3: Christ does let man be man. But, in Milton's view of sonship, doesn't He also let Milton be Christ? And this, of course, opens the possibility that in authoring God Milton might also be Satan.[13]

---

[12] For differing views on Arianism and Book 3, see William B. Hunter, C. A. Patrides, and J. H. Adamson, *Bright Essence: Studies in Milton's Theology* (Salt Lake City: Univ. of Utah Press, 1971); and Michael Bauman, *Milton's Arianism* (Frankfurt am Main, 1987).

[13] For a recent discussion of Milton's relationship to the figure of Satan, see Stavely's chapter on Satan in *Puritan Legacies*.

Mary Ann Radzinowicz's paper, while not explicitly theorized, drew upon (perhaps I should write "transumed") recent work on the binary in Milton (including Shoaf's *Poet of Duality*) and a powerful new criticism of the Bible, a criticism that would seem to support the Jesus of *Paradise Regained* in its challenging of a hellenized undervaluing of the literary qualities of Scripture and an overemphasis on textual discontinuity and redundancy by historical scholarship. Her ideas have been set forth in great detail in her book on Milton and the Psalms.[14] Not the least effect of this book, from which her paper was excerpted, will be to turn critics interested in Milton's biblicism toward the current revaluation of scriptural literature which, as I suggested, seems to match in some respects Milton's critical orientation toward the Bible. It should also be noted that the paper she delivered at the conference dealt with *Paradise Regained* and that, as she writes in the preface of her book, Milton's use of Psalms in *Paradise Regained* is simple and "distilled" as compared to "the more variable and complex strategies of *Paradise Lost*."[15] From a theoretical perspective, the paper is most interesting in its combination of this biblical criticism with what theorists (but not Radzinowicz) might call intertextuality; indeed, the argument points toward a specifically scriptural form of intertextuality in Milton's plain style.

Radzinowicz's argument for a psalmic style in *Paradise Regained* is an elegant and convincing one. But more interesting than the stylistic analysis are her discussions of transumptions (echoes) of entire biblical pericopes and themes in *Paradise Regained*, for in those sections of her paper one glimpses not just contrastive parallel structures in the lines of *Paradise Regained* but also something like the structure of the poem's intertextuality. Her treatment of these larger echoes suggests that binary tropes of similitude and dissimilitude control the process of transumption itself.

In these instances of transumption, Milton's text forms itself by standing for or against Scripture as one half of a binary trope; Radzinowicz finds a relationship of similitude and dissimilitude between Psalm 8 and Satan's display of the world in *Paradise Regained* 3.260, or, to pick another example, between the biblical thematics of human self-exile into the wilderness and "that self-made wilderness to which the Son must go." This latter transumption occurs in a passage in Book 4 following the Son's speech on the excellence of Hebrew poetry; Satan asks,

---

[14] *Milton's Epics and the Book of Psalms* (Princeton: Princeton Univ. Press, 1989).

[15] Book 12; interested readers will find a much expanded version of the paper in her "Interchapter," 85–110.

> What dost thou in this World? The wilderness
> For thee is fittest place; I found thee there,
> And thither will return thee.   (4.372–74)

This Hebraic form of transumptive intertextuality is particularly telling since *Paradise Regained* is a poem about the Son, a binary figure if ever there was one. If Radzinowicz's understanding of biblical transumption is correct, then the poetics of *Paradise Regained* matches its subject. It is also a poetics that harmonizes with Shoaf's "account" of Messiah: Shoaf positions the Son in a redemptive economy of exchange which he then relates to the problem of authoring as a kind of indebtedness; Radzinowicz's biblical poetics of transumption seems to me to be a specific, textual form of such indebtedness as Shoaf argues for in more philosophical terms.

Although I have tried to suggest "the possibilites of theory" by examining Radzinowicz's discussion of transumption as a type of intertextuality, it is clear that she does not subscribe to a post-structuralist notion of intertextuality; the first part of her essay is aimed at demonstrating that Milton "recognized parallelism as the basis of psalm poetry" and that "Jesus's praise of Hebrew verse ... signals Milton's intention to imitate psalm poesis." The emphasis here, as in mainstream Milton criticism generally, is on Milton's mastery of technique, conventions, and learning. A hard-line intertextualist approach to psalm poesis in *Paradise Regained* would position Milton's intention here by emphasizing the constructedness of intentionality itself in discourse, and so "Milton" would be less the agent than a subject of imitation here. A less author-centered reading than Radzinowicz's will be more likely to interrogate (as distinct from explicating) the text, and therefore more likely to see its construction as a socio-political or cultural rather than a personal matter.[16] Radzinowicz suggests that the parallelistic schemes of psalm compensate for Milton's blindness, thus providing one answer to a question not explicitly asked in her paper, Why psalm poesis? It seems to be the role of the more aggressively theorized criticism of today to be explicit and even awkward in asking such questions, rudely brushing past the blind bard to pry into, say, the ideological stakes of his poetics. Jesus's (and, if Radzinowicz is right, Milton's) transumption of Psalms in opposition to hellenic tradition is itself a binary trope. To deconstruct that trope would be to de-center hero and bard, to challenge their certainties, their intentions—opposing

---

[16] For a recent attempt to mark out subject positions between agency and subjection, see Paul Smith, *Discerning the Subject* (Minneapolis: Univ. of Minnesota Press, 1988).

Satan, trashing western literature, etc. In letting us hear the Psalms in *Paradise Regained*, Radzinowicz helps us to understand the work; in regarding the intertextuality of *Paradise Regained* as a privileging of one discourse over another, we put that understanding in question. This is not to fall into the Empsonian trap of satanic response to the poem; it is, I think, to struggle with the always unsettling experience of reading Milton, an experience recorded in the history of readers' responses to Milton—from Marvell's sometimes uneasy tribute in 1674 to, say, the heteroglossia of feminist attacks and defenses of the 1980s.

Invoking the name of Bakhtin, Lars Engle most overtly engages the topic of Milton and the possibilities of theory. He recommends caution, arguing, for instance, that to discuss Milton in the context of Bakhtin's work we must "cut against some of Bakhtin's habitual distinctions and . . . generic tastes." Engle provides a delightful example of such a discrepancy in Milton's denial to his devils their due of a good Rabelaisian laugh; Milton prefers quite the reverse—"the laughter of authorities directed at manifestations of heteroglossia." Profoundly true, I think, but I would want to go on to submit my own experience of being taught and of teaching Milton as evidence that the laughter of authorities is not the whole story. Why is teaching Milton so much fun? If Satan and his crew are forbidden a laughing laugh, readers are repeatedly tempted, and repeatedly succumb to the temptation, to carnivalize Milton's text. It may be that Bakhtin offers only a means of resisting Milton, not a means of understanding him. We understand that laughter of the authorities all too well.

But there is another way of thinking about Milton and Bakhtin. In the dialogical spirit of a respondent, I would like to rearrange Engle's figure of this relationship. The binary opposite of Engle's view would be that in order to discuss Bakhtin in the context of Milton we would have to cut against some of Milton's habitual distinctions and generic tastes. Engle's overview of Bakhtin's thinking suggests that my inversion would not state the case, that, in some respects, Milton and Bakhtin subscribe to similar views on literature.

Engle is certainly correct, for instance, to argue that Bakhtin's exclusion of the dialogic from epic is wrong, but I think Engle also indicates that Milton essentially agrees with Bakhtin on this point.[17] The aim of a Bakhtinian analysis of *Paradise Lost*, approached from this perspective,

---

[17] Barbara Lewalski makes a similar objection to Bakhtin's exclusion of the dialogic and multiform, although she also insists that "Multiple genres give Milton's modern epic great complexity, but not the indeterminacy and inconclusiveness Bakhtin identifies as the product of generic multiplicity in the modern novel." *Paradise Lost and the Rhetoric of Literary Forms* (Princeton: Princeton Univ. Press, 1985), 17.

would be the disclosure of what Shoaf calls the "cunning desire" of both Milton and Bakhtin. To put it another way, a strong reading of *Paradise Lost* might begin with an interrogation of the binary system of monological versus dialogical discourse that seems to underlie Bakhtin's theory and Milton's practice of the epic. Such a critical project might lead to discussion of the conflicted discourses so brilliantly "resolved" by Milton's, and Milton scholarship's, ideology of literature. Engle opens such an inquiry with his observation "that Milton's understanding of various discursive relations to authority, which comes out in the representation of character, is at odds with his commitment both to perfection in paradise and to the ultimate uniformity of moral choices." In the context of Shoaf and Radzinowicz, it seems particularly significant that Engle sees this contradiction played out in another form in the elevation of the Son in Book 5 of *Paradise Lost*: Milton's representation of Christ emerges in these papers as one test of the possibilities of theory and Milton. Engle's reading of the passage on the elevation (5.603–15) is either too much or not enough under the influence of Bakhtin:

> Thus the moment of discursive provocation—the provocative speech from which the variety of both good and bad discourses in the poem springs—is also the prediction of an ultimate end to discourse in an eternity of undifferentiated and undialogical self-awareness, "one ... soul / For ever happy."

Engle, it seems to me, puts an end to difference before Milton does. Milton's fallen angels and hell do seem to remain after the apocalypse, stoppered by the "crammed and gorged" Sin and Death (10.632–37). Heteroglossia seems to survive the fall into utter darkness, but it is non-Bakhtinian, undialogical heteroglossia. Thus we are offered an eternity of "undifferentiated and undialogical self-awareness" and an eternity of difference. Milton seems unable or unwilling to imagine a monological end.

From the divisions in Milton's text as described by Engle we might proceed in a number of directions. Mary Nyquist has presented a Lacanian and poststructuralist approach to the "dialogic energies" released by the Father's exaltation of the Son in Book 3 and Satan's counter-statement to logocentrism in Book 5.[18] Another course might begin with Engle's "natural suspicion" of a connection between these survivors of revolution and with the belief mentioned earlier, that the literary ideologies of Milton and Bakhtin are a match. This isn't to say

---

[18] Mary Nyquist, "The Father's Word / Satan's Wrath," *PMLA* 100 (1985): 187–202.

their literary systems are the same. Bakhtin's inconsistencies and prejudices are being historicized by expositors like Holquist and Clark;[19] Milton's might be similarly positioned by historically-oriented studies like Stavely's, which builds upon the work of Christopher Hill, or neomarxist critique like that of Christopher Kendrick. Beyond Hill's pioneering studies, the fresh, contentious, and voluminous historiography of the English revolution (if it ever occurred—a debated topic still) over the past decade or so could do much to reopen and refocus some debates about Milton. As already suggested above, perhaps one of the less predictable consequences of theory in Milton studies since the Binghamton Renaissance conference has been to lead us back to history.

But which, or whose history? Historical criticism of Milton continues to dominate the field, but the most interesting current work in this vein is dialogically related to poststructuralist theory, one of whose effects has been a raising of the "question of history."[20] I sense good possibilities for "Milton and theory," insofar as this entails opening the question of history, and particularly the history of reception of Milton. I do not think theory will help us to understand Milton better. The move seems to be towards a better understanding of what Shoaf might call our investment in Milton. Tony Bennett's concept of the "reading formation" describes the focus of this type of criticism on "a set of discursive and inter-textual determinations which organise and animate the practice of reading, connecting texts and readers in specific relations to one another in constituting readers as reading subjects of particular types and texts as objects-to-be read in particular ways."[21] The possibilities of theory in Milton studies would seem to be in helping us think dialogically about what has been and is still at stake in reading Milton.

Kent State University

---

[19] Michael Holquist and Katerina Clark, *Mikhail Bakhtin* (Cambridge: Belknap Press, 1984).

[20] I refer to the previously cited collection by Attridge, Bennington, and Young, *Post-structuralism and the Question of History*.

[21] "Texts in History: The Determinations of Readings and Their Texts," in Attridge et al., *Post-Structuralism and the Question of History*, 70.

GORDON CAMPBELL

Popular Traditions of God in the Renaissance

THE GOD WHO CONSTITUTES THE SUBJECT OF THIS ESSAY IS A Christian god and is accordingly a sensitive subject. Were I to write about the gods of the ancient world, the subject would not be provocative; no one any longer believes in those gods, and we are not attached emotionally to them or to their existence. In the case of a Christian god such detachment is not possible. In the Renaissance the existence of this god was uncontroversial, for the long period of deconversion which broke the surface of history in late eighteenth-century France had not yet begun. The process of deconversion is now well advanced, and European culture is now relatively secular, though there is a rump of committed believers. It is of course essential to acknowledge that this process has not yet ended, for a few people still believe, and, perhaps more importantly, many people still feel an obligation to disbelieve. As a result the god of the Renaissance is not someone from whom we can feel wholly detached, as our feelings about him are related to our feelings about Christianity and about religious belief. The rate at which religious belief is disappearing varies between cultures, and in countries such as America and Iran the tide of deconversion has in some measure been reversed; in the case of America this process has sustained an engagement with religion and its literature which in Europe has a large following only in the Celtic fringe. For students of English literature, the main areas of activity are Britain and America, and the religious cultures of those countries are markedly different. We have recently been assured by an American Miltonist that at her university (admittedly in the deep South) "sin, redemption, and the complexities of church government are live issues ... [her] students still recognize Milton's world";[1] this could not be said of my secular

---

[1] Anna K. Nardo, "Their Faith Is Strong, But Their Prose Is Weak: Teaching *Paradise Lost* at Louisiana State University," in *Approaches to Teaching Milton's "Paradise Lost,"* ed. Galbraith M. Crump (New York: MLA, 1986), 48.

British students. British undergraduates show a marked resistance to religious poetry, and we need to develop secular approaches to this literature if it is not to become the preserve of critics who think that it can only be elucidated by reference to the truths of the faith. My central contention is that the study of Christian literature is stifled by piety, and that an historical approach to the faith which informs that literature can enliven the study of both the religion and the literature. This essay is not a scholarly exploration of its subject, but is rather an attempt to demonstrate a tone and line of approach which might make Christian literature more attractive to secular students.

My interest is in popular traditions, or at least a subspecies of popular tradition. I am not going to attempt to supplement the marvelous array of popular heretics whom Christopher Hill has collected, or to emulate Peter Burke's wide-ranging work on European popular cultures. My interest is specifically in ideas which have biblical roots, and in the manifestations of those ideas in literature. Nor do I propose to set the ideas which I am going to outline against a mainstream Christian tradition, partly because I am suspicious of the idea of such a tradition, and partly because I have no vested interest in the notion of orthodoxy, which seems to me more closely related to political power than to truth. I shall treat *god* as an idea related to a period. Like other ideas, the idea of god has a history. Or perhaps more precisely, theology has a history; it is not a collection of fixed and eternal truths which develop only in expression. Piero Camporesi has recently argued with baroque exuberance that the doctrine of hell, for example, reached its apogee in the seventeenth century and has since suffered a decline which may be terminal.[2] Some doctrines, such as the doctrine of original sin, have not only a history but also an identifiable starting point. Original sin is not, as Tom Lehrer explains in "The Vatican Rag," a sin which one has invented oneself. It is the *peccatum ex origine*, the state of sin which derives from our origins. Orthodox Renaissance theologians, both learned and popular, believed that the doctrine was biblical. Protestant theologians pointed to Romans 5.12, in which Paul explains that "as by one man sin entered the world, and death by sin, so death passed to all men, because all have sinned." My translation of the final clause obscures the doctrine, but mine is not an authorized translation. The origin of the doctrine lies not in the Greek text of the closing phrase of this verse, but rather in a mistranslation of that phrase by Ambrosiaster which was in turn endorsed by Augustine. Both followed an Old

---

[2] Piero Camporesi, *La casa dell'eternità* (Milan: Garzanti, 1987), Parte prima, "L'inferno" (15–166); see also D. P. Walker, *The Decline of Hell: Seventeenth-Century Discussions of Eternal Torment* (London: Routledge & Kegan Paul, 1984).

Latin version in translating ἐφ' ᾧ πάντες ἥμαρτον as *in quo omnes peccaverunt*, and thus accidentally turned "because all have sinned" into "in whom all sinned," and so invented the doctrine of original sin.³ Other biblical texts were then read in the light of this howler, and so the doctrine was consolidated into the Christian tradition. The Pelagians demurred but to no avail.

The lack of a substantial biblical foundation for many Christian doctrines has always kept the theologians busy, but when Protestantism appeared on the theological scene the lid was in some measure lifted off the pot, and large numbers of popular variations of theological doctrines appeared. I should like to illustrate this process by reference to the doctrine of the Trinity, and in the first instance should like to examine John Bunyan's views, which were typical of an important strain in popular English theology. In *The House of the Forest of Lebanon* Bunyan proclaimed:

> The doctrine of the trinity! That is the substance, that is the ground and fundamental of all. For by this doctrine, and by this only, the man is made a Christian; and he that has not this doctrine, his profession is not worth a button.⁴

What are the origins of this fundamental doctrine? There is of course no biblical doctrine of the Trinity. The word *trinitas* was first used by Tertullian, but he had been pipped at the post by Theophilus of Antioch, the second-century theologian who was the first to decide that Jesus must have been born on 25 December. Theophilus discerned a divine triad (τριάς) of God and his word and his wisdom, though his sense of the two latter terms distinguishes his trinity from later versions.⁵ The notion of one god existing in three equal persons was not hardened into dogma until the Council of Constantinople in 381, although various trinitarian theories had been championed in the preceding centuries as monotheistic Judaic Christianity absorbed the trinitarian formulations of

---

³ The point is commonplace, but a convenient account may be found in J. N. D. Kelly, *Early Christian Doctrines*, 5th ed. (London: Adam & Charles Black, 1977), 354.

⁴ *Works*, ed. George Offor, 3 vols. (Glasgow: 1860–1862), 3:520. The material on Bunyan in this essay is drawn from my chapter on "Fishing in Other Men's Waters: Bunyan and the Theologians," in *John Bunyan: Conventicle and Parnassus. Tercentenary Essays*, ed. N. H. Keeble (Oxford: Oxford Univ. Press, 1988), 137–51.

⁵ Kelly, 102. See also *Oxford Dictionary of the Christian Church*, ed. F. L. Cross (London: Oxford Univ. Press, 1957), s.v. "Trinity, Doctrine of the." Theophilus's assertion that Jesus was born on 25 December is cited (in Latin) by the Centuriators of Magdeburg in their *Historia ecclesiae Christi* (Basle, 1559–1574), 1.3.118; the passage may be spurious.

middle Platonism[6] and the tricephalous gods of pagan Europe.[7] The form in which pagan trinitarian thinking evolved into Christian dogma was related to early baptismal formulae. These formulae drew their authority from the exhortation of Jesus, newly risen from the dead, to "teach all nations, baptizing them in the name of the Father, and of the Son, and of the Holy Ghost" (Matt. 28.19). The fact that the phrase "in the name" (εἰς τὸ ὄνομα) is singular rather than plural may have suggested the idea of a "trinal unity" to the Christians of late antiquity. Trinitarianism has always had its detractors; in the early church various champions of subordinationism had to be dealt with, and a radical strain in Reformation theology survived in Bunyan's time in the form of Socinianism and Unitarianism. Christopher Hill has uncovered anti-trinitarianism under many bushes, and one need only remember the Racovian Catechism to realise how important was the rebellion against orthodoxy.[8]

Trinitarianism, Bunyan assures us, was the central doctrine of his faith. It seems odd that only once in his profuse writings did he attempt a theological exposition of this fundamental doctrine. He proved the truth of the doctrine with an unargued reference 1 John 5.7. It is hard to believe that Bunyan did not know that this verse had been widely recognized as a spurious medieval insertion into the text of the Bible. Sometime in the third century, a Christian read the verse which we know as 1 John 5.8: "and there are three that bear witness in earth, the spirit, the water and the blood: and these three agree in one." Thinking that he had found a proof-text for the doctrine of the Trinity, he wrote a gloss in the margin that may have said "Quoniam tres sunt, qui testimonium dant in caelo: Pater, Verbum, et Spiritus sanctus: et hi tres unum sunt." This seemed such a splendid gloss that by the eighth century it had been inserted into Latin translations of the Bible; it entered the Greek manuscript tradition in the twelfth century, and so became part of the Bible, in which it appears today as 1 John 5.7: "for

---

[6] Kelly, 126–28; see also W. B. Hunter, "Milton's Arianism Reconsidered," in *Bright Essence: Studies in Milton's Theology* (Salt Lake City: Univ. of Utah Press, 1971), 34–44.

[7] See R. Pettazzoni, "The Pagan Origins of the Three-Headed Representation of the Trinity," *Journal of the Warburg and Courtauld Institutes* 9 (1946): 135–51, and plates 13–15. Pettazzoni does not consider the possibility that these early three-headed gods may have influenced the doctrine of the Trinity, concentrating instead on their influence on Christian iconography.

[8] *Milton and the English Revolution* (London: Faber, 1977), 285–96. On the Racovian Catechism see the useful account of Renaissance antitrinitarianism by Maurice Kelley in *Complete Prose Works of John Milton*, gen. ed. D. M. Wolfe, 8 vols. (New Haven: Yale Univ. Press, 1953–1982), 6:47–73.

there are three that bear record in heaven, the Father, the Word, and the Holy Ghost: and these three are one."[9] It seems likely that Bunyan was aware of the challenge to the authenticity of this verse, and chose to ignore it because it appeared in his English translation of the Bible. This is a subject to which I shall return. But let us return to Bunyan's exposition of the doctrine. He worries about the terminology:

> Now the godly in former times have called these three, thus in the godhead, persons or subsistances; the which, though I condemn not, yet choose rather to abide by the scripture phrases, knowing, though the other may be good and sound, yet the adversary must needs more shamelessly spurn and reject, when he doth it against the evident text.[10]

The nervous admission that the traditional formulation "may be good and sound" amounts to a confession that Bunyan is out of his depth. He goes on to affirm the version of the Trinity which was then current in the Western church, insisting on the co-equality of the three persons. Bunyan's visual elaboration of the doctrine in his diagrammatic "Mapp of Salvation"[11] shows that he subscribed to a popular (and heretical) variation on the doctrine. The doctrine of the double procession of the Holy Spirit, according to which the Spirit had proceeded conjointly from the Father and the Son, had made the equilateral triangle a popular symbol of God in the Western church; the Eastern church had of course separated over the word *filioque* at the third Council of Toledo in 589, and thereafter advocated a form of inter-trinitarian procession, which in the ninth century, at the hands of Photius, Patriarch of Constantinople, became the modern Eastern doctrine that the Spirit proceeded from the Father alone. As an Englishman Bunyan was naturally an advocate of the Western view, and accordingly placed a triangle at the top of his chart [fig. 1]. Traditionally the three corners of the triangle represented the Father, Son, and Holy Spirit, and the center of the triangle was occupied by an appropriate symbol of godhead, such as an eye or the tetragrammaton. But Bunyan placed "God" at the vertex of his triangle, "Father" on the lower left, and "Spirit" on the lower right. In the center, in defiance of orthodox Christian doctrine, he placed the

---

[9] On the "Johannine Comma," as it is known to New Testament scholars, see for example J. L. Houlden, *A Commentary on the Johannine Epistles* (London: Adam & Charles, 1973), 42.

[10] Bunyan, *Works*, 2:415.

[11] On the background of the "Mapp" see my note on "The Source of Bunyan's *Mapp of Salvation*," *Journal of the Warburg and Courtauld Institutes* 44 (1981): 240–41, and plates 38–39, in which the date of the "Mapp" is misprinted as 1646 instead of 1664.

Fig. 1. Detail from John Bunyan, *The Mapp of Salvation* (c. 1664).

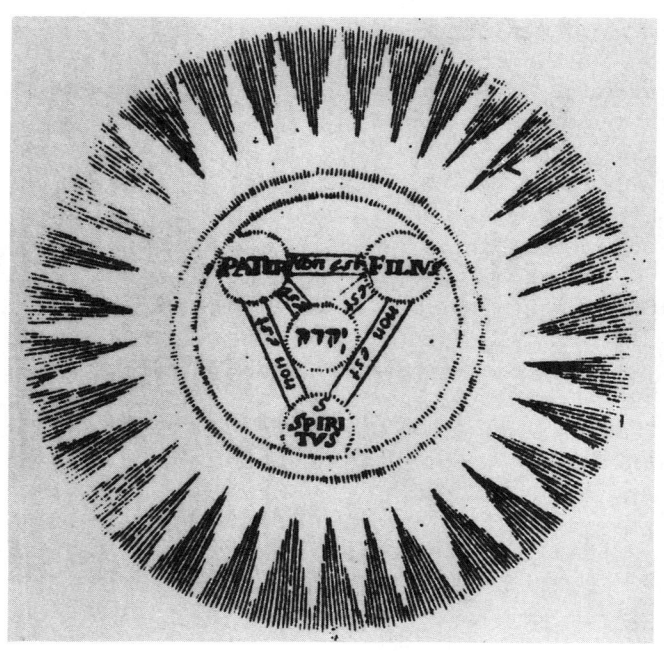

Fig. 2. J. A. Comenius, *Orbis Sensualium Pictus*, trans. Charles Hoole (London, 1659), 6.

"Son," and accentuated his position by printing underneath the name of the Son the phrase "he is Lord of all." This gaffe provides the clearest possible illustration of Bunyan's conviction that the Son is the most important figure in the godhead. In an earlier century he could have been burnt for this aberration, but in the sectarian thought of the seventeenth century (and in its twentieth-century successors) soteriology is so much the central doctrine of the faith that the Son becomes the central figure of the Christian faith. Bunyan thus becomes a sort of popular crypto-heretic, in that the orthodoxy of paternal priority has been displaced by the priority of the Son.

Bunyan is not of course the only crypto-heretic in the garden of the Renaissance. When Charles Hoole adapted the German-Latin version of Comenius's *Orbis sensualiam pictus* (Nuremberg, 1658) to produce an English-Latin version (London, 1659), he replaced the original woodcuts with copper engravings; in most cases he retained the original illustrations, but in the case of the diagram illustrating "God/Deus," he supplied a new diagram of the Trinity [fig. 2]. The three corners are duly labeled *Pater, Filius,* and *Spiritus,* each linked along the sides of the triangle by the words *non est.* In the center of the triangle there is a badly printed tetragrammaton, which is linked to *Pater* and *Filius* by lines labeled *est.* No line links the tetragrammaton to *Spiritus.* The diagram thus affirms the double procession of the Holy Spirit but denies the full divinity of the Spirit. If it is not a misprint, the diagram propounds a heresy which students of English literature associate with Milton.

In his youth Milton was an orthodox trinitarian, but in later life he ceased to believe in the Trinity on the grounds that it is unbiblical. In his Latin theological treatise, *De doctrina Christiana,* Milton expends scores of pages attacking it, and he was enough of a scholar to do quite a good job. He sets up his target by alluding to the central proof text, 1 John 5.7, mildly observing that "the orthodox view of the essential unity of the three persons of the trinity finds its clearest Biblical expression in this verse." He then destroys the authenticity of the verse, explaining that it is not to be found, "in the Syriac or the other two Oriental versions, the Arabic and the Ethiopic, nor in the majority of ancient Greek codices."[12] Indeed, it does not even appear in Milton's usual New Testament, Tremellius's Latin translation of the Syriac version, so he is forced to cite it from Beza's translation.

In *Paradise Lost,* the Trinity is generally notable for its absence. When

---

[12] Milton, *De doctrina Christiana* 1.5, in *Complete Prose Works,* 6:221. Confirmation of the facts which Milton adduces may be found in Brian Walton's *Biblia sacra polyglotta* (1654–57), in which the Syriac and Ethiopic texts omit the verse altogether, and the Arabic text prints an unrelated version.

the baptismal injunction of Jesus is introduced, for example, it appears stripped of its triadic formula ("baptizing them in the name of the Father, and of the Son, and of the Holy Ghost"), which is replaced by a partisan remark about the necessity of running water in baptism. Michael prophesies that Jesus will appear to his disciples, and

> to them shall leave in charge
> To teach all nations what of them they learned
> And his salvation, them who shall believe
> Baptising in the profluent stream, the sign
> Of washing them from guilt of sin to life.[13]

Milton does of course introduce God the Father and God the Son into his poem. The absentee is the Holy Spirit. Indeed, when the Father says to the Son "my overshadowing spirit and might I with thee / I send along" (7.165–66), he seems to be doing little more than sending along his best wishes for every success. Milton seems to have been a latter-day pneumatomachian; the heresy of this fourth-century sect was the denial of the full godhead of the Holy Spirit, and for this error the sect was liquidated under the anti-heretical laws enacted by Theodosius in 383. Milton regarded the spirit as an attribute of God, not one of a trio, and this belief colors his portrayal of the divine council in book 3 of *Paradise Lost*. Earlier literary depictions of the divine council, such as the one in the *Ludus Coventriae* "Parliament of Heaven," include all three members of the Trinity; in book 3 of *Paradise Lost*, only two figures appear—the Father and the Son. Once again one suspects a popular tradition. Menocchio, Carlo Ginzburg's marvelous miller, said to his fellow villagers, "What is this Holy Spirit? This Holy Spirit can't be found."[14]

This does not mean, however, that there is no Trinity in *Paradise Lost*. Milton places a Trinity in the place where he deems it to belong, in Hell, and thus contributes to a tradition of Satanic trinities which has been explored by scholars such as Hoogewerff and Pettazzoni.[15] His allegory of Sin and Death derives from James 1.15: "Then, when lust hath conceived, it bringeth forth sin; and sin, when it is finished, bringeth forth death." The allegory was not original with Milton; it has

---

[13] *Paradise Lost* 12.440–43. In *De doctrina Christiana* Milton argued that believers should be baptized *in profluentem aquam*; see *The Works of John Milton*, gen. ed. F. A. Patterson, 18 vols. (New York: Columbia Univ. Press, 1931–1940), 16:169.

[14] Carlo Ginzburg, *Il formaggio e i vermi: Il cosmo di un mugnaio del '500* (1976), translated by John and Anne Tedeschi as *The Cheese and the Worms: The Cosmos of a Sixteenth-Century Miller* (London: Routledge & Kegan Paul, 1980), 65.

[15] G. J. Hoogewerff, "Vultus trifons: emblema diabolico, immagine improba della Santissima Trinità," *Rendiconti della pontificia accademia romana di archeologia* 19 (1942–1943): 205–45; for Pettazzoni see note 7.

a history stretching back at least as far as Basil the Great in the fourth century.[16] Milton's elegant variation on the traditional use of the allegory was to set it in Hell. In Milton's version of the allegory of Sin and Death, Satan has a daughter called Sin, who had popped out of his head like Athena from the head of Zeus ("a goddess armed / Out of thy head I sprung"), a story which was thought by Christian mythographers such as Conti[17] to adumbrate the father's generation of the Son, who in pre-incarnational days never enjoyed a childhood. Sin is surrounded by hell-hounds "with wide Cerberian mouths full loud"; the three heads of Cerberus are, as Curione explains in his appendix to Valeriano's *Hieroglyphia*, a Satanic reflection of the Trinity.[18] Milton's Satan takes a fancy to his daughter Sin, and their son Death is conceived in due course. This is, I would contend, a savage parody of the Western version of the Trinity, which Milton is denouncing as a kind of Satanic incest. It is usually misread by Christian critics as a Satanic parody of Milton's heavenly trinity. The truth of the matter is that Milton's poem does not contain a heavenly Trinity, and that his Satanic Trinity is not a foil to the Godhead, but rather an attack on a theological doctrine which Milton regards as unsound. The sexual nature of the relationship between Milton's Satan and his Sin suggests that Milton may be aiming at the font of the Western tradition, for in his *De Trinitate* Augustine had articulated the idea (apparently of his own invention) that the Holy Spirit was the embodiment of the mutual love of the Father and the Son.[19]

I should now like to turn to the question of anthropomorphic descriptions of God. God has always been described as if he were human. Old Testament writers speak unabashedly about God's eyes, mouth, lips, and hand. God is portrayed baring his arm (Is. 52.10), walking in the garden of Eden (Gen. 3.8), and wrestling with Jacob (Gen. 32.24–32). Such crude anthropomorphisms are to be expected in descriptions of a tribal god whose local seat was Mount Sinai. The god of Sinai never claims to be the only god; indeed, his first commandment—thou shalt have no other gods before me—acknowledges the existence of other gods, as indeed does the name Elohim, which is now thought of as an

---

[16] On Basil's allegory see John M. Steadman, "Milton and St. Basil: The Genesis of Sin and Death," *Modern Language Notes* 73 (1958): 83–84.

[17] *Paradise Lost* 2.757–58. The *Observationum libellus* attached to Conti's *Mythologiae* is cited by Alastair Fowler in *The Poems of John Milton*, ed. John Carey and Alastair Fowler (London: Longman's, 1968), 544, s.v. "ii.752–61."

[18] Cited by Edgar Wind, *Pagan Mysteries in the Renaissance* rev. ed. (Oxford: Oxford Univ. Press, 1980), in his excellent appendix on "Pagan Vestiges of the Trinity" (241–55), 251 n. 41.

[19] *Oxford Dictionary of the Christian Church*, s.v. "Trinity, Doctrine of the."

intensive plural but probably reflects early polytheism. The household gods of the early Israelites, which were called teraphim, were sufficiently humanoid to be used as a decoy (1 Sam. 29.13). As the religion of the Israelites evolved, such anthropomorphisms became something of an embarrassment, and worship of teraphim came to be regarded as idolatrous. When the Pentateuch was transliterated into Samaritan, many of the Hebrew anthropomorphisms were excised; and later, when the Septuagint was prepared, anthropomorphisms were removed by recourse to paraphrase. If these alternations in the Septuagint were due in part to Hellenic influence, the origins of this influence may perhaps be traced to pre-Socratic philosophers such as Xenophanes of Colophon, the clear-headed sixth-century philosopher who attacked anthropomorphic descriptions of the gods, cannily observing in a fragment of verse preserved by Clement of Alexandria that if horses and cows could draw, they would draw gods who looked like horses and cows:

Ἀλλ' εἴ τοι χεῖρας γ' εἶχον βόες ἠὲ λέοντες,
ὡς γράψαι χείρεσσι καὶ ἔργα τελεῖν ἅπερ ἄνδρες,
ἵπποι μέν θ' ἵπποισι, βόες δέ τε βουσὶν ὁμοίας
καί κε θεῶν ἰδέας ἔγραφον καὶ σώματι ἐποίουν
τοιαῦθ' οἷόν περ καὶ αὐτοὶ δέμας εἶχον ὁμοῖον.[20]

Throughout the centuries of the Christian era, the church moved further and further away from anthropomorphic descriptions of God, and a parallel development can be seen in Jewish exegetical commentary: whereas, for example, the Hebrew text of Genesis 18.8 baldly records of Abraham and the Lord that "they did eat," the recently discovered first-century Palestinian Targum says that "they were seen as if they did eat," and the Midrash Rabba, following in this tradition, says that "they pretended to eat."[21] God only becomes a human figure

---

[20] Xenophanes of Colophon, cited by Clement of Alexander, *Stromateis* 5.14.109.3, in Migne, *Patrologiæ Græcæ* 9.168. The extraneous lions and the absence of horses in the first line point to a corrupted text, which has often been reconstructed; I have printed the version in Alain Le Boulleuc's edition: Clément d'Alexandrie, *Les Stromates: Stromate V* (Paris: Editions du Cerf, 1981), 206.

[21] The Palestinian Targum (Neofiti I) was discovered in the Vatican Library in 1956. I quote the text from R. Le Déaut's edition, *Targum du Pentateuque* (Paris: Editions du Cerf, Paris, 1978), 1:816. For the Midrash see H. Freedman and Maurice Simon, *Midrash Rabba*, 10 vols. (London: Soncino Press, 1939), 1:415. On the history of the manuscript see R. Le Déaut, "Jalons pour une histoire d'un manuscrit du Targum palestinien," in *Biblica* 48 (1967): 509–33; on the relation of this Targum to the New Testament, with which it is contemporary, see Alejandro Diez Macho, "Targum y Nuevo Testamento," in *Mélanges Eugène Tisserant* (Vatican City, 1964), 1:153–85. Of the other early versions, the Syriac of the Peshitta and the Aramaic of the Onkelos Targum say that "they did eat" (Walton, 1:66–67). Milton would have

again with the emergence of the mystery plays of fifteenth-century Europe, in which the character of God is played by a human actor. In Protestant countries God disappeared from the stage with the Reformation, and indeed did not reappear until Marc Connelly's *Green Pastures* was performed in 1930, but he nonetheless remained a distinctly human figure in popular traditions. The Baptists of Kent and Sussex believed that God existed in the shape of a man, and Muggleton famously remarked that God was about six feet tall.[22]

The god of *Paradise Lost* is distinctly anthropomorphic; in book 8, for example, he interviews Adam, and adopts a tone of voice which is distinctly jocular; he lacks utterly the *gravitas* which was traditionally associated with God. One of the most striking features of the god of *Paradise Lost* is that although he is omniscient, he is not very quick-witted. There is good biblical precedent for this defect, for although he is there endowed with supernatural perceptions of man's thoughts, he did not become omniscient until late antiquity; certainly by the time of the Council of Nicea in 325 he had become all-knowing. The problem is that the Bible reflects a theology markedly less sophisticated than that of the early church. There are moments in the Old Testament when the patriarchs must deal with an irascible god, and they are able to cope only because they can outwit their creator.[23] When the god decides to destroy Sodom and Gomorrah (Genesis 18), for example, Abraham asks the god, "Wilt thou also destroy the righteous with the wicked? Peradventure there be fifty righteous within the city: wilt thou also destroy and not spare the place for the fifty righteous that are therein? That be far from thee." The god concedes the point, and Abraham then poses the possibility of forty-five righteous, asking if the god would destroy the city for want of five righteous people. He bargains enthusiastically, and wears his god down from forty-five to forty to thirty to twenty to ten, which is the god's bottom line. Reflecting on this episode in his tract on the *Doctrine and Discipline of Divorce*, Milton observed that "*Abraham* e'en to the face of God himselfe seem'd to doubt of divine

---

had access to the gloss in the Palestinian Targum through one of its descendants, Pseudo-Jonathon (The Jerusalem Targum), the relevant passage of which is printed in Walton, 4:30. Milton's familiarity with the Jerusalem Targum is attested by his mention of it in De doctrina Christiana 1.14, though both Bishop Sumner and Professor Carey failed to recogize the allusion, and so invented a new commentator called "Hierosolymitanus" (*Works of John Milton*, 15:283, and *Complete Prose Works*, 6:429).

[22] Hill, 289, 297.

[23] In this account I am indebted for the examples (though not for the interpretation) to John E. Parish, "Milton and an Anthropomorphic God," *Studies in Philology* 56 (1959): 619–25.

justice."[24] The phrase "face of God," incidentally, suggests that Milton was translating from the Hebrew of Genesis 18.22; the translators of the Authorised Version ignored the anthropomorphism of God's face (*liphne*), saying only that Abraham "stood yet before the Lord," but Milton did not flinch from such phrases. In the divorce tract Milton goes on to cite Abraham's argument in Genesis 18: "*Wilt thou destroy the righteous with the wicked? That be far from thee.*" This reproachful phrase, "that be far from thee," also appears in *Paradise Lost*, but in a startlingly different context. In book 3 Milton's God the Father works himself into a rage at the thought of man's fall: "Whose fault? / Whose but his own? Ingrate, he had of me / All he could have." God the Son tries to calm him down, insisting that it would be foolish of the Father to allow man to be altogether lost. And what are the Son's words? "That be from thee far, that far be from thee, father" (3. 153–54).

The other arrows in the Son's quiver are sharpened by reference to two occasions when Moses had to negotiate with God. The episode of the golden calf (Exodus 32) so annoyed the god with his people that he said to Moses "Let me be [not *alone*, as in the King James Version], that my wrath may wax hot against them, and that I may consume them." Moses responds to this tantrum with a tactful reminder that the god's intended victims are his own people, that he had made promises to Abraham, Isaac, and Jacob, and that he would look silly in the eyes of the Egyptians if he delivered his people only to destroy them. These arguments worked, for the god "repented of the evil which he thought to do unto his people"; this early god, unlike his successor in systematic theology, is capable of both evil and repentance. The second occasion on which Moses must persuade his god to stay his hand occurs when Moses guides his flock to the border of Canaan (Numbers 13–14); Moses sends scouts ahead to reconnoiter the land, and in due course the scouts report that the land is peopled with giants. The reaction of the Israelites is an ill-considered decision to return to Egypt. The Lord appears in his glory, and promptly loses his temper: "How long will this people provoke me? and how long will it be ere they believe me? ... I will smite them with pestilence, and disinherit them." Moses quickly replies "then the Egyptians shall hear it ... and they will tell it to the inhabitants of this land." He develops this argument, and then appeals to the Lord's better qualities: "The Lord is longsuffering, and of great mercy, forgiving iniquity and transgression." The Lord yields to Moses and pardons his people, although he adds with what seems to be spite that those who provoked him would not be permitted to see the promised

---

[24] *Doctrine and Discipline* 2.4, in *Complete Prose Works*, 2:298.

land: in his picturesque phrase, "your carcasses shall fall in this wilderness"; the Hebrew text is even harsher, for *peger* refers not merely to dead animals, but to animals who have died of disease in the wilderness, and are therefore unfit for food.[25]

Milton's Son draws on the experience of Moses to formulate his arguments, pointing out that the destruction of mankind would fulfill the ambitions of Satan, and that the abolition of a creation made for God's glory would sully that glory. If mankind were to be lost, he concludes,

> So should thy goodness and thy greatness both
> Be questioned and blasphemed without defence.
> (3.165–66)

These are not, one should emphasize, orthodox delineations of God's character. But one must remember that one of the most fertile sources of popular characterization of God was, paradoxically, the Bible itself.

One of the most delightful of such popular biblical traditions is the tradition of the *conceptio per aurem*, the conception of the madonna through the ear. This peculiar route enabled Mary to preserve her virginity—the same aim dictated that in a related tradition she give birth to Jesus through the same orifice. This is a popular tradition of remarkable antiquity, and it seems to have its origins in a misreading of the Greek text of Luke 1.28—"and the angel came in onto her and said, 'Hail highly favored, the Lord is with thee.'" New Testament Greek deals in euphemism, and clearly the opening phrase—καὶ εἰσελθὼν ὁ ἄγγελος—was misread in the light of the phrase about "the Lord is with thee"; and εἰσέρχομαι ("enter") is capable of the same ambiguity in Greek as in English.

The *conceptio per aurem* is a commonplace among medieval theologians. Pseudo-Augustine, for example, says "Deus per angelum loquebatur, et virgo auribus impraegnebatur." In the eighth century St. Agobard wrote "Descendit de coelis missus ab arce Patris, introivit per aurem Virginis in regionem nostrum, indutus stola purpurea et exivit per auream portam lux et decus universae fabricae mundi." In the Greek tradition Euthymius Zigabenus, the twelfth-century Byzantine theologian, wrote in his Πανοπλία Δογματική that the Spirit εἰσρυῆναι διὰ τοῦ δεξιοῦ ὠτὸς τῆς Παρθένου.[26] Eventually the theme appeared as

---

[25] On this and other points concerning Hebraic matters I am indebted to the late Leo Miller, who offered salutary corrections of an earlier draft of this paper.

[26] Pseudo-Augustine, *Sermo* 121.3, in Migne, *Patrologiae Latinae* 29.1988; St. Agobard, in Migne, *Patrologiae Latinae* 115.332.; Euthymius, in Migne, *Patrologiae Graecae* 130.1301. Jones (n. 27) cites Pseudo-Augustine (as Augustine) and Agobard, but both

a visual image, common in medieval and Renaissance art, of the dove which represents the Holy Spirit approaching the ear of Mary. The psychoanalyst Ernest Jones, who wrote a well-known essay on the *conceptio per aurem*, prints a stanza from a hymn which the interested reader may care to sing to one of the settings of the *Dies Irae*, the meter of which it imitates:

> Gaude, Virgo, mater Christi,
> Quae per aurem concepisti,
>   Gabriele nuntio.
> Gaude, quia Deo plena
> Peperisti sine pena
>   Cum pudoris lilio.

Jones notes that fear of conception by this unusual route has not entirely disappeared amongst Catholics, as "is shown by the custom with which all nuns still comply of protecting their chastity from assault by keeping their ears constantly covered."[27] He gives many pictorial examples in the art of the Renaissance which the interested reader may consult, but does not give literary examples. One of the most obvious occurs in *Hamlet*, a play on which Jones wrote a famous book, *Hamlet and Oedipus* (1949). In Shakespeare's play the death of Hamlet's father is presented in a dumbshow. The king enters with the queen and lies down upon a bank of flowers. The queen leaves, and the actor who is meant to represent Claudius enters, removes the king's crown and kisses it, and "pours poison in the sleeper's ears." The evocation of the *conceptio per aurem* is surely unmistakable. Shakespeare believed that the killing of the king was not merely murder, but was rather an act of blasphemy. He therefore arranged for death rather than birth to enter through the ear of Claudius. Similarly Lady Macbeth, addressing her absent husband, asks him to come "that I may pour my spirits into thine ear" (1.5.26); and Cleopatra instructs a messenger to "Ram thou thy faithful tidings in my ears, / That long time have been barren" (2.5.24–25). The same tradition appears in *Paradise Lost*, where Adam, who can never resist a pun, says "O Eve, in evil hour thou didst give ear / To that false worm" (9.1067–68). Perhaps the most explicit literary

---

his transcriptions and his references are grossly inaccurate. I am uncertain about what Agobard means when he refers to Jesus having been born "through the golden gate"; in a footnote Migne notes that the usual phrase was "per clausam portam."

[27] Ernest Jones, "The Madonna's Conception through the Ear: A Contribution to the Relation between Aesthetics and Religion," first published in German in *Jahrbuch der Psychoanalyse* 6 (1914) and here quoted in the expanded English version which is printed in Jones's collected *Essays in Applied Psychoanalysis* (London: Hogarth Press, 1951), 2:266–357. On the hymn see 269, and on the nuns, 345.

example of the tradition is Gargantua, who "sortit par l'aureille senestre"; the choice of the left ear suggests a demonic parody, as the usual route (as explained by Euthymius, quoted above) was through the right ear. The context of the passage makes clear that Rabelais is mocking the credulity of those who believe in such miracles.[28]

I have referred on several occasions to the original biblical languages, but it is a truism to say that since the Reformation the Bible has increasingly been read in vernacular versions. One of the problems in Milton studies is that scholars persist in pretending that Milton read an English Bible,[29] when in fact his daily Bible was the Junius-Tremellius Latin version of the Bible. He also read the Hebrew and Greek texts, but few Miltonists follow him along this road. As for the Peshitta and the Septuagint, which we know him to have used, no one bothers to look; in the case of the former our command of Syriac is not what it could be, and in the case of the latter we assume, erroneously in my view, that he always read the Old Testament in Hebrew or in English. In Bunyan we have an interesting seventeenth-century version of the view enshrined in the old joke to the effect that if the King James Version was good enough for the apostle Paul, it is surely sufficient for the modern reader.

Bunyan could read no language other than English, and his Bible had of necessity to be an English Bible. My impression is that in his early works he relied on a sixteenth-century translation, probably the Geneva version; departures from that translation may be due to Bunyan's habit of quoting from memory, or he may have used one of the related translations. Sometimes his quotations from memory contain echoes of the King James Version, which he would have heard read in church, even if, in common with many Puritans and sectaries, he regarded it as an Anglican translation. Puritan distrust of the King James Version was deeply rooted. One manifestation of these misgivings was a bill presented to the Long Parliament in 1653. This bill, which was designed to enable revision of the King James Version, spoke darkly of its inaccuracies and "prelatical language."[30] In his later works, on the

---

[28] *Gargantua*, ed. Ruth Calder and M. A. Screech (Geneva and Paris: Librairie Droz, 1970), chap. 6 ("*Comment Gargantua nasquit en faczon bien estrange*"), 49. Professor Screech's annotations on 50–52 chart the relation of the passage to the tradition of the *conceptio per aurem*.

[29] Philip J. Gallagher, for example, argues (absurdly) that "verbal parallels demonstrate to a moral certainty that Milton's source for the creation is the Bible in the Authorized Version"; see "Creation in Genesis and *Paradise Lost*," *Milton Studies* 20 (1984): 197.

[30] The bill received its first reading on 4 March 1652/53; see *Journals of the House of Commons* 7:245, 264.

other hand, Bunyan seems to have turned to the King James Version; sectarian misgivings about the King James Version were receding, and the new enemy was the Book of Common Prayer.

In common with many sectaries, Bunyan presented his inability to read the Bible in its original languages as a virtue. In a memorable exchange recorded by Bunyan's friend Charles Doe, Bunyan's right to preach was once challenged by a scholar (probably Thomas Smith, professor of Arabic at Cambridge) on the grounds that Bunyan did not have a Bible written in the original languages:

> Then said Mr Bunyan, Have you the original? Yes, said the scholar. Nay, but, said Mr Bunyan, have you the very self-same original copies that were written by the penmen of the scriptures, prophets and apostles? No, said the scholar, but we have true copies of those originals. How do you know that? said Mr Bunyan. How? said the scholar. Why, we believe that what we have is a true copy of the original. Then, said Mr Bunyan, so do I believe our English Bible is a true copy of the original. Then away rid the scholar.[31]

In some book-centered religions, adherents are obliged to study and recite the holy book in its original language, and translations into the vernacular are forbidden. Seventeenth-century sectarians are unusual in their elevation of an English translation to the status of a holy book. Bunyan never felt the need to learn the biblical languages. In his account of his examination before the justices in November 1660, Bunyan records that William Forster, the Bedford lawyer, accused him of ignorance of the Bible in that he knew no Greek. Bunyan replied

> that if that was his opinion, that none could understand the Scriptures, but those that had the original Greek, &c. then but a very few of the poorest sort should be saved, (this is harsh) yet the Scripture sayeth, That God hides his things from the wise and prudent, (that is from the learned of this world) and reveals them to babes and sucklings.[32]

Bunyan saw his religion as the faith of the poor. As the study of Greek was restricted to the wealthy educated classes to whom God denied access to his wisdom, therefore the poor who could not study Greek had a privileged access to the wisdom of the Bible. He championed

---

[31] Bunyan, *Works*, 3:767.
[32] *A Relation of the Imprisonment of Mr John Bunyan*, in John Bunyan, *Grace Abounding to the Chief of Sinners*, ed. Roger Sharrock (Oxford: Oxford Univ. Press, 1962), 111.

those who "cannot, with Pontius Pilate, speak Hebrew, Greek and Latin."[33] In viewing competence in the biblical languages not merely with suspicion, but with contempt, Bunyan was aligning himself with those radicals who saw all knowledge as an impediment to salvation.[34] And in his elevation of the poor Bunyan was touching on a much debated question of poverty and property in the church. "You will never," as one earlier theologian commented, "be able to establish on the basis of the gospels whether, and to what extent, Christ considered as his property the tunic which he wore"; the theologian in question is of course William of Baskerville.[35]

It is clear that in this case Bunyan's theology was shaped by his hatred of the opposition. Such hatred was often the source of popular theology, even in the case of Milton: if Papists believed it, it must be wrong. Milton felt, for example, that the doctrine of the incorporeality of angels was misguided and tainted with popery. When Raphael comes to lunch in book 5 of *Paradise Lost*, Eve assumes the role of the world's first topless waitress and serves a cold lunch—"no fear lest dinner cool" (5.396), says the patronizing narrator's voice. Suddenly it occurs to Adam that angels may not eat. To understand what is happening in this passage we must remember that Raphael comes from an apocryphal book, the Book of Tobit, in which Raphael explains to Tobit that as an angel he "did neither eat nor drink, but ye did see a vision" (Tobit 12.19). As Milton was a protestant he would not base doctrine on an apocryphal book, as the detested Catholics did, so he regarded the idea that angels could not eat as mere superstition. He records that

> down they sat
> And to their viands fell, nor seemingly
> The angel, nor in mist, the common gloss
> Of theologians, but with keen despatch
> Of real hunger, and concoctive heat
> To transubstantiate; what redounds, transpires
> Through spirits with ease.   (5.433–39)

---

[33] *The Miscellaneous Works of John Bunyan*, gen. ed. Roger Sharrock, 12 vols., in progress (Oxford: Oxford Univ. Press, 1976–), 1:304.

[34] Bunyan's fellow radical Samuel How, for example, published a book entitled *Sufficency of the Spirit's Teaching without Humane Learning: Or a Treatise tending to Prove Humane Learning to be no help to the Spirituall Understanding of the Word of God* (London, 1639); see Roger Lejosne, "Samuel How: La Religion du Savetier," *Travaux du Centre d'Histoire des Idées des Iles Britanniques* (Université de Paris IV-Sorbonne), 4 (1986).

[35] Umberto Eco, *Il nome della rosa*, translated by William Weaver as *The Name of the Rose* (London: Secker & Warburg, 1983), 345.

Angels do not suffer from constipation; being able to excrete through the pores was clearly part of Milton's vision of heaven. And Milton's abusive use of the word "transubstantiate" shows that the doctrine was not dead for him, but retained its power to offend.

I have described a few of the varieties of belief which are conditioned by various biblical strains in the Christian tradition, and I should like to finish by raising briefly the problem of disbelief. My purpose is not to offer answers to the complex questions which this problem raises, but rather to point out that in the world of English scholarship we have yet to contend with the formidable problems raised by our colleagues whose particular interest is French literature. I refer in particular to the debate on Rabelais. Sixty-five years ago Abel Lefranc argued with great eloquence that the theological conviction which underlay the imaginative genius of Rabelais was atheism.[36] Lefranc assumed that all right-thinking people were rationalists and saw in Rabelais a man ahead of his time who perceived Christianity as a reactionary force in society. We have seen similar books in English, the best example being Sir William Empson's book on *Milton's God* (1961). Empson assumed that his idol Milton was such an intelligent chap that he couldn't have believed in the goodness of the Christian god, and set out to show that what Milton was really doing was subverting Christianity. Empson has never been challenged, except by Christian scholars who want to show that Milton was one of their own faith. C. S. Lewis, for example, tried to turn Milton into an honorary Anglican, and Douglas Bush used Milton's faith as a club with which to berate the secularism of the twentieth century. The only reasonably successful attempt in this vein has been Dennis Danielson's book on *Milton's Good God* (1982), and it works only because of the improbable coincidence of conviction shared by Professor Danielson and Milton on the subject of Arminianism. What we have not had in English scholarship, however, is the equivalent of Lucien Febvre. *Le problème de l'incroyance au seizième siècle: la religion de Rabelais*[37] was published some fifty years ago, and although some of its readings of Rabelais have been persuasively challenged by scholars such as Professor Screech, its basic arguments continue to challenge our casual assumptions.[38] Febvre argues that not only can Rabelais not be shown to

---

[36] Abel Lefranc, "Etude sur *Pantagruel*," which forms the introduction to François Rabelais, *Oeuvres*, ed. Abel Lefranc et al. (Paris, 1922), 3:i–lxx.

[37] First published by Albin Michel (1942) and recently translated by Beatrice Gottlieb as *The Problem of Unbelief in the Sixteenth Century: The Religion of Rabelais* (Cambridge: Harvard Univ. Press, 1982).

[38] See M. A. Screech, *Rabelais* (London: Duckworth, 1979), in which Febvre is never openly confronted, but is often corrected.

be freethinking and atheistical, but that the attempt to construct such a portrayal constitutes an anachronistic reading of the *mentalité* of sixteenth-century Europe. I do not propose to enter into the specific debate about Rabelais, but rather to raise a few analogous questions about English literature. One could discuss Sir Walter Raleigh in this context, but I propose instead to raise the question of Christopher Marlowe. Marlowe is one of the standard examples of the Renaissance atheist. In his plays he creates a series of blaspheming supermen who reject the conventions of Christianity. There is also ample biographical evidence for this view. In the Baines note, which was handed to the authorities two days after Marlowe was killed in a tavern brawl, Marlowe is said to have mocked both the Old and New Testaments. Baines also attributes to Marlowe the view that "the first beginning of Religioun was only to keep men in awe." He testifies that "almost into every Company he Cometh he perswades men to Atheism willing them not to be afeared of bugbeares and hobgoblins, and utterly scorning both God and his ministers." Another informer, one Richard Cholmeley, testified that Marlowe "is able to shew more sounde reasons for Atheisme then any devine in Englande is able to geve to prove devinitie" and that Marlowe read a lecture on atheism to Sir Walter Raleigh and others. Thomas Kyd testified in a similar vein.[39]

Certainly Marlowe's table-talk in the taverns of London was infamous. But what can we conclude from it? When Baines attributes to Marlowe the dictum that "all they that love not tobacco and boys were fools," are we to conclude that Marlowe was a chain-smoking child molester? He did smoke, but so did Milton; he may well have been homosexual, but we can see evidence of the same preferences in the early Milton, and because we have learned to resist the connection between homosexuality and atheism that was so common in the thinking of Renaissance England,[40] we are hardly inclined to charge Milton with atheism. The mystery plays provide plenty of evidence that the Bible could be viewed mirthfully, and yet we don't assume those plays to be secular. What I am suggesting, with some hesitation, is that Marlowe could not have been an atheist because that way of thinking was not available to anyone, however radical and intelligent, until it was developed as a system of thought in the eighteenth century.[41]

---

[39] For Baines see Millar Maclure, ed., *Marlowe: The Critical Heritage* (London and Henley: Routledge & Kegan Paul, 1979), 36–38; for Cholmeley, which Maclure does not print, see John Bakeless, *The Tragicall History of Christopher Marlowe*, 2 vols. (Cambridge: Harvard Univ. Press, 1942), 1:125.

[40] See Alan Bray, *Homosexuality in Renaissance England* (London: Gay Men's Press, 1982).

[41] On the origins and history of atheism see the recent studies by David Berman,

However much Marlowe kicked against the constraints of Christianity, he could not free his mind from the religious tradition which he had inherited. The plays themselves provide evidence to support this view. Barabas and Tamburlaine have some marvelous anti-Christian speeches, but in the end they receive their comeuppance. And Marlowe may present the fall of Doctor Faustus as a deplorable tragedy, but it is a hard fact that Faustus blasphemes and at the end of the play is dragged off to eternal torment. The play may deplore the truth of Christianity, but it acknowledges that truth even as it despises it. In short, Marlowe was not an atheist, and his blasphemy may be accounted for as a protest against the Christian faith the truth of which he acknowledged through gritted teeth. Through his discussion of Rabelais, who in many ways resembles Marlowe, Febvre has demonstrated that we cannot claim Marlowe as one of us; he is irrevocably locked in the mental world of the Renaissance. As students of that period we must acknowledge that it is built on a faith which many moderns find repugnant, but we must resist anachronistic judgements which deny the existence of that faith. In that respect, we are in an intellectual dilemma which is clearly analogous to Marlowe's.

University of Leicester

A History of Atheism in Britain: From Hobbes to Russell (London: Croom Helm, 1987) and Michael J. Buckley, *At the Origins of Modern Atheism* (New Haven: Yale Univ. Press, 1987).

Index

Index

acting, styles 322, 323
actors, and Shakespeare 315–19 passim; — actors' "lines" 319; — boy-actors 332–37 passim. *See also* Armin, Bottom, Burbage, Kempe, theater
Aeneas, and Dido 441, 442; — descent to Underworld 441
Alberti, Leon Battista, *De pictura* 165; — *Self-portrait* 164–68
Alexander, William, *Julius Caesar* 399–402, 405–7
Alleyn, Edward 320–23
Angoulême, Marguerite d', *see* Marguerite de Navarre
Anon., *Caesar and Pompey, or Caesar's Revenge* 399, 402, 403
Anon., "Hymn to Demeter" 182
Anon., *Masque of Queens* 369
anthropomorphism 509–18
Antonello da Messina, *Portrait of a Man* 169
Apostolis, Michael 56, 57
Argyropoulos, John 56, 57
Ariosto, Lodovico, *Orlando furioso* 279–86; — 23.80–81: 280
Aristotle 42, 276
Aristotle and Phyllis 343
Armin, Robert 315
art, and homosexuality 149
artist, and melancholy 152, 157, 159
astrology 11, 69, 70, 87, 88, 125–40 passim; — and spas 10
atheism, in the English Renaissance 501–20 passim

Bakhtin, Mikhail 475–88 passim; — *Dialogic Imagination* 478; — and Milton 475–88 passim

Barbaro, Ermolao, influence on Giorgione 153
Barnes, Barnabe, *Parthenophil and Parthenophe* 308
Barnfield, Richard, *The Affectionate Shepherd* 308
Bellini, Giovanni 151
Bessarion, Cardinal 56, 60
Bible, King James Version 515–17; — languages 504, 509, 510, 515–17; — Genesis 418; — Genesis 18: 510–12; — Exodus 32: 512; — Numbers 13–14: 512, 513; — Tobit 517; — Matthew chap. 16, and Milton 464, 465; Matthew 28: 504; — Romans 5: 502, 503; — James, epistle of 507, 508; — John, first epistle of 504, 505
Blenerhasset, Thomas 310–12
Boccaccio, *Decameron* 253
Bodin, Jean 365, 366
Bonifacio, Giovanni, *L'arte di cenni* 180
Bottom, character of 316–18
Bunyan, John, and conception of God 503–7, 515–18
Burbage, Richard 320–26
Burton, Robert 367

Caesar, Julius, career 400; — English plays on 395–412 passim
Cambrai, Wars of, 125–40 passim
Camerata, Florentine 448, 449, 451, 455
Caravaggio 149, 160; — *David with Head of Goliath* 160
Cariteo, *see* Chariteo
Caron, Antoine 246, 247, 251, 254
Castagno, Andrea del, *Portrait of a Man* 169, 170
Castiglione, Baldassare, *Book of the Courtier*, Bk. 3: 253

Catiline 198
Catullus, and George Herbert 436, 437
Chapman, George, *Caesar and Pompey* 395–412 passim
Chariteo 103–7; — *Endimione, canzone* 105–7; — *Endimione* sonnets 103–5
Cholmeley, Richard 519
Churchyard, Thomas 302–4
Cicero 35–39 passim; — Ciceronianism 215–27 passim
Cifra, Antonio 452, 454, 455
Ciriaco d'Ancona 54, 55
classical allusion, in George Herbert's Latin poetry 429–45 passim
Claudian, *Laus Serenae* 182
Cleveland, John 456
Colleoni, Bartolomeo 19
Colonna, Francesco, *Hypnerotomachia Polifili* 253
conceptio per aurem 513, 514
Council of Ferrara-Florence, *see* Ferrara-Florence
cultural materialism, *see* new historicism

daemon, Socrates' 64, 65, 67, 68
daemons, daemonology, in Ficino 63–88
Dante, *Purgatorio* 114, 115; — *Vita nuova* 112; — and Julius Caesar 401
Danvers, Lady, *see* Herbert, Magdalen
Davison, Francis 306, 307
deconstruction, and feminist criticism 390–92; — and Milton 462, 473, 474
del Piombo, Sebastiano, *Portrait of a Man in Armor* 149
delle Opere, Francesco, gem engraver (d. 1496) 171
Derrida, Jacques 477
desire, in Marguerite de Navarre, *Heptaméron* 230–35, 241–44
dialogic discourse, and Milton 475–88 passim
Divine Right 358, 369, 371–80 passim
Dolet, Etienne 215–27; — and printing 215, 216, 226, 227; — influenced by Cicero, 215–27 passim; — *Erasmianus sive Ciceronianus* 215; — *Orationes duae in Tholosam* 215–27 passim
Dolfo, Floriano 26, 27
Donne, John, concept of self, 413–27 passim; — concept of soul, 413–27 passim; — *Divine Poems* 424–26; — *Sermons* 426, 427, 430, 431, 461; — *Songs and Sonnets* 415–17, 420–24
drama, in England 315–26 passim; —

historical, in England 395–412 passim; — Neo-Latin 39, 40; — Renaissance humanist 395–412 passim

economic imagery, in Milton, *Paradise Lost* Bk. 3: 463–73
effeminacy 339–54 passim. *See also* female, feminine writing, feminism, women
Elizabeth I 362, 363
England, Polydore Vergil's history of 191–214
Engle, Lars, as critic of Milton 497–99
epic 109, 121, 271–86 passim
epistolography 38
Erasmus, Desiderius 33, 215–27; — *Education of a Christian Prince* 344
Este, Alfonso d', Duke 279
Este, Isabella d' 279
Estienne, Charles 248

Falco, Pietro 16, 17
female rule, and Catherine de' Medici 245–55
feminine writing, and Marguerite de Navarre 229–44
femininity, and tyranny 339–54 passim
feminism, and Milton 491, 492
feminist criticism, and deconstruction 390–92; — and new historicism 385–90; — of Shakespeare 381–93 passim
Ferrara-Florence, Council of 51, 52, 54, 59
Ficino, Marsilio 46, 52, 63–88 passim, 152; — and daemonology, 63–88 passim; — and seances 85–87; — and visual arts 152; — *De stella magorum* 70, 71; — *Plotini Enneades*, transl. and commentary, 66–73, 79–81, 84–88
Florentine Platonism 63–88 passim
Freud, Sigmund 109, 123
fumigation, and Orphic hymns 79–81, 84; — in cult practices 79–81

Gabriel, Archangel 70, 71
Galilei, Vincenzo 449, 451
gardens 247–49, 251–55
Gareth, Benedetto, *see* Chariteo
Garnier, Robert, *Cornelie* 399
Gemistus Pletho, George, *see* Pletho
gender, and Shakespeare 327–38 passim
Gentile da Foligno 6, 8
George of Trebizond 59–61
Ghiberti, Lorenzo, self-portraits 161, 164
Giorgione, inventions 141–76 passim; —

and Ermolao Barbaro 153; — "turning portrait" 143; — *Judith* 161; — *Portrait of Girolamo Marcello* 143, 146, 147; — *Portrait of Giustiniani* 171, 174, 175; — *Self-portrait as David* 149–51, 161; — *Tempest* 125–40
God, conceptions of, in the English Renaissance 501–20 passim; — in Bunyan 503–7, 515–18; — in Milton 507–9, 511–18. See also anthropomorphism, Trinity
Góngora, Luis de, *Dorotea* 186, 187; — *Polifemo* 188
Gonzaga, Alessandro 12, 13
Gonzaga, Federico II, Marquis of Mantua 26
Gonzaga, Ludovico, Marquis of Mantua 10–12
Googe, Barnaby 311
Greek, study of 35
Greenblatt, Stephen 328, 329, 336, 337
Guarino Veronese 30
Guicciardini, Francesco 139
Gutenberg, Johann 33

Harvey, Gabriel 311, 312
Heidegger, Martin, "Anaximander Fragment" 462, 472, 473
Heliodorus, *Ethiopica*, source for Tasso 282
Henry V (of England) 207
Henry VII (of England) 208
Herbert, George 429–45 passim; — and Catullus 436; — *Memoriae Matris Sacrum* 429–45 passim; — *The Temple* 430
Herbert, Magdalen 429–45 passim
Hesiod, *Theogony* 182
historians, classical, and Polydore Vergil 191–214 passim
Homer, *Iliad* 14 182
homosexuality, and art 149; — in Shakespeare 334–39
honor, in Marguerite de Navarre, *Heptaméron* 232, 233, 236, 240–44
Hoole, Charles 506
Horace 39
Houel, Nicholas, and Catherine de' Medici 245–55
Humanism, Italian 29–43; — defined 29
Hutton, Henry, *Follie's Anatomie* 343

Iamblichus 71, 72, 83
idleness, in Montaigne's early essays 257–69 passim

imagination, in Montaigne's early essays 257–69 passim
inscriptions, at spas 9, 20, 22
introspection, in Montaigne's early essays 257–69 passim
Italy, northern, spas in 3–20, 22–27

James I 357, 358, 361, 365, 369, 371; — *Basilikon Doron* 371–80 passim
Jugurtha 198
Juvenal (15th-century Byzantine) 59

Kavakes, Demetrius Raoul 57, 58, 60
Kempe, Will 315–19
King, Edward 455–60
Knox, John 341–43, 362; — *Against the Monstrous Regiment of Women* 341–43
Kyd, Thomas, *Cornelia or Pompey the Great* 399, 400

La Perriere, *Mirrour of Policie* 343, 344
La Primaudaye, Peter de, *French Academie* 339
Latin poetry, sound in 89–108
Lawes, Henry 449, 450, 453, 454, 457
Leonardo, influence on Giorgione 146, 147, 175, 176; — *Ginevra de' Benci* 174, 175
letters 38
Livy 192
Lombardo, Tullio 148, 151; — *Vendramin Warrior* 151
Loredan, Leonardo, Doge 139
Lucretius, *De rerum natura* 182

Machiavelli, Niccolò 9, 31; — *Mandragola* 9
Mancini, Dominic, on Richard III 201, 209
Mannerism 177, 178, 180–89
Mantegna, Andrea 153, 157, 158
manuscript and print 301–13 passim
manuscripts, discovery of 34
Margaret of Bavaria 13
Marguerite de Navarre 229–44 passim; — *Heptaméron* 229–44; — Novella 2: 236–38; — Novella 4: 234–36; — Novella 10: 238–44; — *Heptaméron*, desire in 230–35, 241–44; — *Heptaméron*, honor in 232, 233, 236, 240–44; — *Heptaméron*, rape in 232–44
Marino, Giambattista, *Adone* 187, 188
Marlowe, Christopher, and atheism 519, 520; — *Dr. Faustus* 72, 73

marriage 330–35 passim, 371, 374, 375, 379, 380
Marston, John 309, 310
Marxist criticism 381, 382, 387
Massinger, Philip, *The Roman Actor* 346, 347
medical treatises, about spas 5–9, 14, 15, 20, 22
Medici, Catherine de' 245–55
melancholy, and the artist 152, 157, 159
Mercury 82
Middle Platonists 64, 69
Milton, John, *De doctrina Christiana* 506; — *Lycidas*, 455–60; — *Paradise Lost* Bk. 2: 508, 509; — Bk. 3: 461–73 passim, 492–94, 507, 512, 513; — Bk. 5: 481, 482, 517, 518; — Bk. 8: 187, 482–88; — Bk. 9: 468, 470, 514; — Bk. 10: 467–69; — Bk. 12: 480, 507; — *Paradise Regained* 495–97; — *Reason of Church-Government* 470, 471; — and conception of God 507–9, 511–18; — and feminism 491, 492; — and Bakhtin 475–88 passim; — and modern theory 489–99 passim; — and music 447–60 passim; — and Psalms 495–97; — modern criticism of 475–88 passim
Milton, John, Sr. 450
monody, musical 447–60 passim
Montaigne, Michel de 3, 9, 27; — "De l'oisivité" ("On Idleness," *Essais* 1.8) 258–69; — "De la solitude" ("On Solitude," *Essais* 1.39) 260, 263–67, 269; — early essays, imagination in 257–69; — idleness in 257–69; — introspection in 257–69
Monteverdi 449, 451–53
motherhood 355–69 passim 355
music, and poetry 447–60 passim; — and Milton's poetry 447–60 passim

Napier, Richard 324, 325
Naples 109–23
Navarre, Marguerite de, *see* Marguerite de Navarre
Neo-Latin poetry 39, 89–108, 429; — of George Herbert 429–45 passim; — sound in 89–108
Neo-Platonism 63–88 passim
new historicism and feminist criticism 385–90
Niccolò Niccoli 32

Odysseus 441, 443; — and Antikleia 441;
— descent to Underworld 441
oratory, civic function of 215–27
original sin 502
Orpheus 73–88
Orphic Hymns 73–88
Ovid, *Fasti* 118; — *Metamorphoses* 120, 282; — source for Ariosto 282

Padua 125–40
paganism, fifteenth-century 45–61
paradise 187, 252, 461, 463, 467–70, 480–88, 492–97, 507–9, 512–14, 517, 518
Parmigianino, *Madonna of the Long Neck* 177, 178, 180–89
pastoral poetry 109–23
patriarchy 371–80 passim
Peacham, Henry 451, 456
pelican 363
Percy, William 311, 312
Perugino, Pietro, *Portrait of Francesco delle Opere* 171, 174, 176
Petrarch, Francis 29, 31, 32, 37, 177, 178, 180–89; — *Canzoniere* 105, 181, 183–85; — *Triumphus Famae* 183; — "bel piede" topos 177, 178, 180–89
Petrarchism 177, 178, 180–89
philosophy, Italian Renaissance, 29–43
Pico della Mirandola, *Oration on the Dignity of Man* 418, 419
Pius II, Pope 22–25
Plato 63–88 passim
Platonism, Florentine 63–88 passim; — Platonism, Middle 64, 69
Pletho, George Gemistus 45–61
Pliny the Elder, *Natural History* 6
Plotinus 63–88 passim
Plutarch, and Elizabethan ideology 400; — and Julius Caesar 401, 404, 405
poetry, and print 301–13 passim; — Latin 89–108 passim; — love lyrics, 287–300 passim; — Neo-Latin 39, 89–108 passim, 429–45 passim; — pastoral 109–23 passim
Poliziano, *Stanze per la giostra* 185, 186
Polydore Vergil, *Anglica historia* 191–214; — and classical historians 191–214 passim
Pontano, Giovanni Gioviano 97–103, 112, 115; — *Eridanus* 2.1: 97, 100–103; — *Parthenopei [liber]* 1.18: 97–100
Porphyry 85; — *Vita Plotini* 63–65
portraiture, in Italian Renaissance 141, 143, 146–53, 157–61, 164–71, 174–76; — and self-portraiture 142

power 371-80 passim
Pozzuoli, spas near 3, 4
Preston, Thomas, *Cambyses* 345, 346, 349
print, and manuscript 301-13 passim; — and poetry 301-13 passim 301; — stigma of, 301-13 passim
printing, early 34
Propertius, Sextus 89-108; — 1.1: 94-97; — 1.3: 92, 93; — Propertius, 1.7: 93; — 2.1: 104; — 2.30a: 105; — 3.3: 97, 98
Psalms, and John Milton 495-97
pseudonyms 307, 309
publication, anonymous 306-10; — pirate 310-12
Pythagoras 65, 66

Quintilian, *Institutio oratoria* 180, 181

Rabelais 225, 479, 480, 515, 518, 520; — *Gargantua* 225, 515; — and atheism 520
Radzinowicz, Mary Ann, as critic of Milton 495-97
rape, in Marguerite de Navarre, *Heptaméron* 232-44
Ravenna, Battle of 279
religion, and spas 14-17
revenants 441
rhetoric 37; — rhetoric, humanist, and Etienne Dolet, 215-27
rhymes, in Milton's *Lycidas* 457-59
Richard III 198, 201, 203-6, 209, 210, 351; — and Catiline 198; — and Jugurtha 198; — portrayed by Polydore Vergil 198, 203-6, 210
Richard of York 206
Rizzo, Antonio, *Mars* 152
Rowlands, Samuel 308-10

Salic Law 246
Sallust, influence on Polydore Vergil 191-214
Salutati, Coluccio 29
Sannazaro, Jacopo 109-23; — *Arcadia* 109-23
Saussure, Ferdinand de 477
Savonarola, Michele 7, 8, 20
Scholarius, George 47, 49, 50, 56, 59
seances, Ficino and 85-87
self, and portraiture, in Italian Renaissance art 142
self, Donne's concept of 413-27 passim
sexual differences 327-38 passim
sexuality, feminine 371-80 passim; — feminine, in Shakespeare 327-38 passim; — masculine 371-80 passim; — masculine, in Shakespeare 327-38 passim
Shakespeare, William 381-93 passim; — *Antony and Cleopatra* 385, 514; — *Hamlet* 514; — *Julius Caesar* 395-412 passim; — *Macbeth* 347-51, 355-69 passim, 514; — *Measure for Measure* 371-80 passim; — *Richard III* 351-54; — *Tempest* 384, 409; — *Twelfth Night* 327-38 passim; — actors 315-26 passim; — and contemporaries 395-412 passim; — bardolatry 395-97; — feminist criticism of 381-93 passim; — and gender 327-38 passim; — and homosexuality 334-39 passim; — and theater 315-26 passim
Shoaf, R. A., as critic of Milton 492-94
Sidney, Sir Philip, *Arcadia* 186
Skelton, John 303
Socrates 64, 65, 67, 68
soliloquies 323, 324
soul, Donne's concept of 413-27 passim
spas, and astrology 10; — buildings at 23, 24; — civic governments and 17-20; — entertainment at 24-27; — in northern Italy 3-20, 22-27; — inscriptions at 9, 20, 22; — medical treatises about 5-9, 14, 15, 20, 22; — religion and 14-17; — treatments at 10-14, 22, 23, 26, 27
Spenser, Edmund 312; — *Mutabilitie Cantos* 187
Statius, *Thebaid*, source for Ariosto 284
Suetonius, and Elizabethan ideology 400; — and Julius Caesar 401, 404; — influence on Polydore Vergil 191-214

Tacitus, and Elizabethan ideology 400; — influence on Polydore Vergil 191-214
Tasso, Torquato, *Discorsi del poema eroico* 271; — *Discorsi dell'arte poetica* 271-86; — *Gerusalemme liberata* 186, 271-86; — 1.52: 277; — 4.96: 273; — *Rinaldo* 271
theater, England, acting 315-26 passim; — and Shakespeare, 315-26 passim. *See also* actors
theory, modern, and Milton 489-99
Titian 147, 148, 159; — *Il Bravo* 147, 148
Toulouse, and Etienne Dolet, 215-27
tragedy, Shakespearean, 319-26
Trebizond, *see* George of Trebizond
Trinity, doctrine of, 502-9; — and Milton 508
"turning portrait," of Giorgione 143

Tyndale, William, *Obedience of a Christian Man* 340, 341
tyranny, and femininity 339–54 passim

Ugolino da Montecatini 6, 8, 11, 14, 18–20
universities 29–43

Valla, Lorenzo 37, 56
van Eyck, Jan 166–69; — *Man in a Red Turban (Self-portrait)* 166–69
Vasari, Giorgio 159, 177
Venice 125–40
Vergil 39, 111, 121–23, 182, 183, 191–214, 284, 285, 307, 308; — career of, as model 307, 308; — *Bucolic* 4 182, 183; — *Georgics* 111, 121; — *Aeneid* 111, 122, 123, 284, 285; — Bk. 5: 111, 122; — *Aeneid*, and Ariosto 284, 285
Vergil, Polydore, *see* Polydore Vergil
vernacular 227

Verrocchio, Andrea, *Bartolommeo Colleoni* 152
Vespasiano da Bisticci 32
Virgil, *see* Vergil
Vittorino da Feltre 30

witchcraft 355–69 passim
women, and power 355–69 passim; — John Knox on 341–43, 362; — Tyndale on 340, 341; — in early modern Europe 339–54 passim. *See also* effeminacy, female, femininity, feminism, marriage, sexuality
Wyatt, Sir Thomas, love lyrics 287–300; — "In eternum" 288–93; — "They fle from me" 296–300; — "To rayle or geste" 294, 295

Xenophanes of Colophon 510
Xenophon, *Apology* 64; — *Cyropaedia* 252

Zeno, Iacopo 52, 53

Reconsidering the Renaissance ranges over art, music, literature, philosophy, and history, approaching the problems, texts, and themes of contemporary Renaissance studies from divergent points of view. The thirty-one papers, selected from those presented at the Twenty-First CEMERS conference, bring to bear a challenging array of approaches and assumptions which echo some of the rich diversity in the debate about Renaissance studies today. Among these approaches are social history and linguistic analysis of poetry, feminism and politics, self-fashioning and history of ideas, humanism and new historicism.

Individual papers make forays into such subjects as astrology, historiography, acting, spas, early publishing, monody in music and literature, witchcraft, gardens, popular conceptions of God, neopaganism and Neoplatonism, homosexuality, and classical allusion. The contributors include Michael Allen, Lee Jacobus, Paul Kristeller, David Chambers, Sheila ffolliott, Linda Carroll, Gordon Campbell, Dympna Callaghan, James Mirollo, Jane Tylus, Donald Friedman, Rebecca Bushnell, Wendy Stedman Sheard, R. A. Shoaf, and John Monfasani.

Mario A. Di Cesare is Distinguished Professor of English and Comparative Literature at State University of New York at Binghamton, and the founder and director of MRTS. He has published more than a dozen books, including *Vida's Christiad and Vergilian Epic* (Columbia Univ. Press, 1964) and a full critical bibliography of Vida (Florence: Sansoni, 1974); *The Altar and the City: A Reading of Vergil's Aeneid* (Columbia, 1974), and a Norton Critical Edition of George Herbert's poetry. With Rigo Mignani he has published a concordance to Herbert (Cornell), a translation of Juan Ruiz, *Libro de buen amor*, and a concordance to that poem (SUNY Press). He has held fellowships from the Fels Fund, the Guggenheim Foundation, and the National Endowment for the Humanities. Forthcoming is his diplomatic edition of the Bodleian manuscript of Herbert's poetry.

mRts

medieval & Renaissance texts & studies
is the publishing program of the
Center for Medieval and Early Renaissance Studies
at the State University of New York at Binghamton.

mRts emphasizes books that are needed —
texts, translations, and major research tools.

mRts aims to publish the highest quality scholarship
in attractive and durable format at modest cost.